THE
Entrepreneur
Magazine

SMALL BUSINESS ADVISOR

THE
Entrepreneur
Magazine
SMALL BUSINESS ADVISOR

John Wiley & Sons, Inc.
New York • Chichester • Brisbane • Toronto • Singapore

The checklists on pages 8, 9, and 30 are reprinted with permission of Princeton Creative Research.
The figures on pages 126 and 156 were created by Jacque Imri.
The figures on pages 171 and 565 were created by Lorraine Choy.
The figure on page 562 was created by Michael Taylor.

This text is printed on acid-free paper.

Copyright © 1995 by Entrepreneur Media, Inc.
Published by John Wiley & Sons, Inc.

All rights reserved. Published simultaneously in Canada.

Reproduction or translation of any part of this work beyond
that permitted by Section 107 or 108 of the 1976 United
States Copyright Act without the permission of the copyright
owner is unlawful. Requests for permission or further
information should be addressed to the Permissions Department,
John Wiley & Sons, Inc.

This publication is designed to provide accurate and authoritative
information in regard to the subject matter covered. It is sold
with the understanding that the publisher is not engaged in
rendering legal, accounting, or other professional services. If
legal advice or other expert assistance is required, the services
of a competent professional person should be sought.

Library of Congress Cataloging-in-Publication Data:

The Entrepreneur small business advisor / the
    Entrepreneur Magazine Group.
        p.   cm.
    ISBN 0-471-10988-6. — ISBN 0-471-10989-4 (pbk.)
    1. Small business—Handbooks, manuals, etc.   2. Entrepreneurship—
Handbooks, manuals, etc.   I. Entrepreneur Group.   II. Title: Small
business advisor and desk reference.
HD62.7.E568   1995
658.02'2—dc20   94-40079
                                                     CIP

Printed in the United States of America

10 9 8 7 6 5 4 3 2 1

To the millions of entrepreneurs
who have dreamed and fulfilled their visions;
and to the millions more
whose dreams will inspire the future.

Acknowledgments

ENTREPRENEUR MAGAZINE GROUP

Editor	Charles Fuller
Assistant Editor	Ken Ohlson
Copy Editors	Heather Page
	Laura Read
	David Pomije
Contributing Editors	Maura Hudson
	Anne Callot
	Imran Husain
	Lauren Fischbein
	Barbara Frantz, Esq.
	David Juedes, CPA
Illustrative Artwork	Michael Taylor
	Lorraine Choy
	Jacque Imri
	Brian Ayuso
	Joel Kilian
Editorial Assistants	Kimberly Hoelscher
	Meredith Kaplan
	Glen Webber
	Stephanie Casat

We would also like to thank the following individuals for their support and efforts in the production of this manuscript: Rieva Lesonsky, Maria Anton, Maria Valdez, Erika Kotite, Frances Huffman, Janean Huber, Debra Phillips, Cynthia Griffin, Karen Sulkis and Ruth Mills, our editor, at John Wiley & Sons.

In addition we would also like to thank the Small Business Administration, Department of Commerce, Department of Labor, U.S. Bureau of the Census, Link Resources, TRW Information Systems and Services, Apple Computer, Lillian Vernon, Ira Fischbein, Subway Sandwiches & Salads, Inc., Herschell Gordon Lewis, National Textbook Company, Janet Lynn House, Lake Forest Limousines, Princeton Creative Research.

Preface

Do you really *know* what it takes to succeed in a small business? If you answered yes, congratulations, you're way ahead of the game. But, if you are like most entrepreneurs and those interested in starting their own business, you grapple with this question on a daily basis.

For many, the answer is as elusive as the mythical fountain of youth, and like the Spanish explorer, Ponce de León, these entrepreneurs are always searching. Most often, however, they find schemes that are initially profitable but not really successful. Nevertheless, what makes a successful business is not that mysterious at all. True success stems from *knowledge*.

This is really not an earth-shattering observation. John Naisbitt, the author of *Megatrends* and *Megatrends 2000* (William Morrow & Co., Inc., New York), points out that we have entered the age of the information society. Information—and access to it—is shaping the way we conduct business because with information comes knowledge and the ability to succeed.

This is the key to a profitable business. Sure you have to have a good product, sufficient capital to effectively promote that product, and support to keep customers satisfied. All of these are an integral part of a successful business, but ultimately they are offspring of knowledge. Therefore, the more you build your base of knowledge, the better your chances of successfully starting, managing, and expanding a business.

That's why the editors at Entrepreneur Magazine Group have put together this book. We want to help you build that base of knowledge by providing the information you need to start, manage, and expand your business.

Each and every month for close to 20 years now, *Entrepreneur* magazine has reported on the world of small business. During this period, we've seen phenomenal successes that have spawned modern-day heroes like Lillian Vernon, Ben Cohen and Jerry Greenfield, Steve Jobs and Steve Wozniak, and Bill Gates. We've also seen the failure of ideas that have eventually faded into memory.

We've explored new ideas and opportunities, and more than anything else, we've tried to educate—to provide the knowledge that is so critical to business success.

Through it all, we've witnessed the transformation of small business from an image associated with small "mom-and-pop" stores at local shopping centers, to one of the major driving forces behind the growth and vitality of the U.S. economy. According to the U.S. Bureau of the Census, small business (defined as companies with fewer than 100 employees) accounts for over 97 percent of all business in the United States, with an annual payroll above $1 trillion. To put this into perspective, the total payroll of federal, state, and local governments is approximately $494.8 billion according to the *Public Employment* report published by the U.S. Bureau of the Census.

Small business today still includes the mom-and-pop stores, but it is much more. The truth is that small business embraces a wide array of opportunities from home-based companies to growing, multiple-unit businesses. They are run by sole proprietors, partners, and corporate boards made up of directors and officers, whose business is retailing, manufacturing, wholesaling, brokering goods, providing a service, and more. The boundaries of small business are far-flung, encompassing every venture that can be conceived and crossing virtually every socioeconomic, racial, religious, and sexual barrier.

Small business has become the American dream, and many articles in *Entrepreneur* magazine have celebrated the culmination of this dream. Still, millions of dreamers haven't taken the next step toward starting their own business because they lack the information they need to do so. And millions of others are following the path their dreams have set them on only to reach hurdles that can sometimes spell failure, all because they don't have the necessary knowledge to overcome these difficulties.

During the years *Entrepreneur* magazine has been published, we've studied areas of importance to entrepreneurs in developing a business. The *Entrepreneur Small Business Advisor and Desk Reference* is the product of these observations. This is not just another book that rehashes concepts and techniques that are hammered into middle managers and executives of large, multinational corporations. The *Small Business Advisor and Desk Reference* has been written with the entrepreneur in mind. Its goal is to provide entrepreneurs of all types who are planning to start—or who have started—their own business with the information they need to build the base of knowledge necessary for success.

To make the *Small Business Advisor* as easy to use as possible, the chapters in this book have been arranged within the three major areas of small business development: Part I—"Starting Your Business"; Part II—"Managing Your Own Business"; and Part III—"Growing Your Business."

You will find the material is presented in a practical manner that emphasizes not only why a particular topic is useful to the entrepreneur, but how you can use it to your best advantage. To help you further research each topic, every chapter contains a Resources section for *quick reference.* These listings include information about trade associations, trade periodicals, on-line services, software, government agencies, and more. Therefore, the book is not only a valuable educational tool, but a complete resource kit as well.

The *Small Business Advisor and Desk Reference* also includes an extensive Glossary at the end of the book with definitions of key business terms. This means you will not have to go searching through a whole chapter to look up a term someone has used in a conversation or meeting. It will be right there in front of you.

As you read through the *Small Business Advisor and Desk Reference* you will encounter many terms and subjects in more than one chapter. This is not an error; it simply indicates the vast amount of material covered, as well as the overlap in many business activities.

For readers interested in starting their own business, or for those individuals already in business, owning the *Small Business Advisor and Desk Reference* is like having a consultant at your fingertips. No longer do you have to shake your head with knowledgeable conviction when asked if you know a specific concept, only to run down to the local library and scour through myriad books to find the answer. No longer do you have to call up one of your friends who just happens to be an accountant to ask questions that deal with basic tax concepts.

In this respect, think of the *Small Business Advisor and Desk Reference* as a tool that provides you with a competitive advantage. That's important because you'll be competing against businesses, both large and small. Link Resources reports that there are approximately 24.9 million full-time and part-time home-based businesses in the United States. To this number, add another 6.2 million businesses that have employees, from the smallest store to Fortune 500 corporations. The more information you have at your disposal, and the faster you can access this information, the more competitive you will be.

Ultimately, this is the goal of the *Entrepreneur Small Business Advisor and Desk Reference*. We hope that it will help you decide what course of action is best for you—that through knowledge you will be armed for success.

Contents

PART III   GROWING YOUR BUSINESS

I

Starting Your Business

Businesses are born from dreams. For some, those dreams are of economic freedom and the goal of financial security. These individuals aren't so much interested in developing a new idea as they are in finding the opportunity that will provide them with the greatest chance for fulfilling their dream of financial independence. For others, those dreams lie within the passion of their idea and the gradual genesis of that idea into a business entity. Whatever the dream, starting the business and forging it into an organization that meets the entrepreneur's goals takes a great deal of hard work and dedication.

This portion of the *Small Business Advisor* provides the necessary information to take those first steps that will lead you from your dreams into a brave new world wrought with new challenges. In this portion of the *Small Business Advisor* you will find the following chapters:

Chapter 1 Personal Evaluation. Taking an inventory of personal and professional skills, goals, and objectives prior to starting a business is important. This chapter contains information on risk assessment and how to determine the amount of personal capital available to commit to a new business.

Chapter 2 Ideas and Trends. The advantages and disadvantages of starting a business using your own ideas, as well as where to find information that could form the foundation of a new venture. There will also be a discussion regarding how to evaluate business ideas and perform test marketing.

Chapter 3 Market Research. The importance of market research, the different types of information that need to be gathered, methods used to acquire market data, and what's involved in building an information network.

Chapter 4 Legal Forms. The different legal forms under which a business can operate as well as a discussion regarding the advantages and disadvantages of each type.

Chapter 5 Licensing. The various factors involved in applying for a business license as well as other special permits your business may require. County and state licenses will also be discussed along with the circumstances under which you'll need them. Finally, federal requirements will be covered.

Chapter 6 Location. The importance of location to a business and the factors that will need to be considered such as selling zones. Also the location requirements for retail, service, wholesale, and manufacturing operations will be covered.

Chapter 7 Leasing. The advantages of leasing over other financing options. The different types of real estate and equipment leases. How to choose a leasing company.

Chapter 8 Developing a Business Plan. The importance of a business plan, not only from a financing standpoint but also for strategic purposes. The components you need to include in an effective business plan as well as a standard structure that can be used. Complete sample business plans.

Chapter 9 Sample Business Plan.

Chapter 10 Buying a Business. How to evaluate a business you are considering buying, including methods used to value a specific business. What is involved in the investigation of a business for sale as well as common mistakes made by buyers.

Chapter 11 Franchise Opportunities. Why franchising has exploded in popularity and the benefits it has to offer. Requirements of franchisers under the FTC Rule including elements that need to be disclosed in the UFOC. The importance of a thorough investigation of any franchise being considered and the type of information you should acquire, as well as important questions you need to ask.

Chapter 12 Business Opportunities. The difference between a business opportunity offering and a franchise opportunity. How the FTC defines a business opportunity. What is involved in evaluating a potential business opportunity.

Chapter 13 Start-Up Financing. Evaluating your personal financial condition to determine your financing requirements. The items lenders and investors will consider when evaluating your business. Plus debt and equity financing sources.

Chapter 14 Small Business Administration Loans. Prerequisites required by the SBA before an application will be considered. Guidelines used for guaranteed loans. The different types of lenders the SBA uses in its loan guarantee program. How to apply for an SBA loan.

Personal Evaluation

1

Why do you want to be in business for yourself? This is a valid question, whether or not you've already entered the entrepreneurial world. Surprisingly, money may not be the primary motivating factor for many people. Freedom is often ranked first. Whatever your purpose, you will want to review your reasons so you can best determine what type of business you want to enter.

Before embarking on your own business, you must take the following factors into consideration:

- Your primary reason for being in business for yourself.
- Amount of risk capital available.
- Amount of credit available to you.
- Your skills.
- Your likes and dislikes.
- Amount of effort you are willing to expend.
- Your financial goals.
- Whether you can begin full- or part-time.
- Inventory of business management experience and knowledge.
- Capacity for meeting new challenges and following through on commitments.

PERSONAL PLANNING

An old proverb states, "Businesses don't fail, people do." Sure, businesses are affected by strategies employed by competitors, market saturation, and so forth, but planning and adjusting to market conditions are all functions of the people running the business. A business is merely an extension of the people managing it and mirrors their abilities. If the individuals running the business are strong in one area and weak in another, the business will reflect this. This correlation is even more apparent in small businesses.

As an entrepreneur, you have to know your strengths and weaknesses so you can compensate in some way for the areas where you will not be proficient. You can determine your strengths and weaknesses by evaluating the major accomplishments in your personal and professional life and the skills required to complete these tasks. To perform this evaluation, you should do the following:

1. **Create a personal résumé.** Start by listing your professional experience. For each job you've held, write short descriptions of the various duties you were responsible for and the degree of success you experienced. Next, list your educational background and any extracurricular activities you participated in during your scholastic career. Finally, write down your hobbies.

2. **List your personal attributes.** Are you personable? Do you feel comfortable around other people? Are you self-motivated? Are you a hard worker? Do you possess common sense? Are you good with numbers? Do you have effective verbal and written communications skills? Are you well organized?

3. **Detail your professional attributes.** Write down the various management roles and tasks within a business such as sales, marketing, financial planning, accounting, advertising, administrative, personnel management, and research. Beside each function, write down your competency level—excellent, good, or poor.

By putting together a résumé and quickly listing your attributes, you will have a fairly good idea of your likes and dislikes as well as your strengths and weaknesses. Once you identify these characteristics, you will have a good idea of the qualities you will bring to the business and the areas that may require training or assistance.

If you don't think that knowledge is important, think again. Not only do areas of expertise and track records of yourself and any partners play an important part in assessing your strengths and weaknesses as they apply to business in general and specifically any opportunity you are researching, but they are also determining factors when approaching lenders and investors. In fact, Gerald Benjamin, president of International Capital Resources, a venture capital firm in San Francisco, says that angels, or private investors, invest in people as much as they do the business concept, and if you don't have the type of expertise you need to effectively start and operate the business, you should definitely recruit that help.

Setting Objectives

Many people go into business to meet personal goals they've established for themselves. For some people, it's as simple as having the freedom to do what they want, when they want, without anyone telling them otherwise. For other people, achieving financial security is a major personal goal. Whatever your goals, setting specific personal objectives is an integral part in the selection of a business that is going to be right for you. The sample Entrepreneurial Evaluation Checklist will help you identify your entrepreneurial potential.

When you form goals, whether personal or business-related, they will work best when you break them down as follows:

1. **Specific and detailed.** Whether your goal is to start a business, raise capital, or lose weight, you must be very specific (size, shape, color, location, and time).

2. **Positive and present tense.** A financial goal is not to pay bills or get by, but to be financially secure. This is set with a specific minimum of at least X amount of dollars in a given period.

3. **Realistic and attainable.** If you set a goal to earn $100,000 a month and you've never earned that in a year, this goal is not very realistic. Some people may not be able to conceive complete financial security, whatever that may mean to them. You should begin with a "first step"; a percentage increase you feel comfortable with that represents the realm of reality. Once you meet your first goal, you can project larger ones.

4. **Short term and long term.** Short-term goals should include the preceding characteristics and be attainable in a period of weeks, months, or one year. The long term can be much greater but it should still be realistic. The only one who can set these parameters is you. You must decide what is a realistic time frame and what is not.

After establishing parameters, you have to decide what exactly you want to achieve by going into business for yourself. Most people set objectives according to specific areas in their life that are crucial for survival and self-satisfaction. These areas usually include:

- **Be your own boss.** One of the foremost reasons people go into business for themselves is that they have what they think is a great idea and are tired of working for someone else. Because they've built up certain areas of expertise, they want to "call the shots." Generally, this area centers around control issues. If you are the type of person who likes to have complete and total control over the direction of the business, you need to consider this issue when determining management responsibilities, especially if you are dealing with partners.

- **Income.** Many entrepreneurs go into business to obtain financial security, not only for themselves, but for their families as well. When setting financial goals, consider what you would like to make during the first year of operation and each year thereafter, up to five years.

- **Lifestyle.** This encompasses several areas related to your personal assets and life including travel, physical labor, work hours, investment of personal assets, and location. When setting lifestyle goals, you need to consider whether or not you want to do a lot of traveling, whether physical labor is a priority or even something you can do, what type of hours you

PRINCETON ENTREPRENEURIAL INNOVATION CHECKLIST

Read each statement carefully, then respond by marking the answer that most accurately describes your behavior, feeling, or attitude as it actually is, not as you would like it to be, or think it should be. Try to mark your first reaction. (Created by Eugene Raudsepp, Princeton Creative Research)

	Agree	Disagree
1. My parents encouraged me to take an interest in discovering things for myself.	☐	☐
2. At least one of my close relatives is an entrepreneur.	☐	☐
3. Throughout my education, I had many part-time jobs.	☐	☐
4. One or both of my parents had many unorthodox or unconventional ideas.	☐	☐
5. If I were stranded in an unfamiliar city without friends or money, I would cope quite well.	☐	☐
6. I am curious about more things than most people are.	☐	☐
7. I enjoy ventures in which I must constantly keep trying new approaches and possibilities.	☐	☐
8. I always seek challenging problems to solve.	☐	☐
9. I am not too painstaking in my work.	☐	☐
10. I am able to work for extended periods of time, frequently to the point of exhaustion.	☐	☐
11. When faced with a problem, I usually investigate a wide variety of options.	☐	☐
12. While working on one project, I often think of the next one I want to tackle.	☐	☐
13. Before taking on an important project, I learn all I can about it.	☐	☐
14. When confronted with a difficult problem, I try solutions others would not think of.	☐	☐
15. Once I undertake a new venture, I'm determined to see it through.	☐	☐
16. I concentrate harder on projects I'm working on than most people do.	☐	☐
17. I cannot get excited about ideas that may never lead to anything.	☐	☐
18. When brainstorming with a group of people, I think up more ideas quicker than others.	☐	☐
19. I have broader interests and am more widely informed than most people.	☐	☐
20. When the chips are down, I display more personal strength than most people do.	☐	☐
21. I need social interaction and am very interested in interpersonal relationships.	☐	☐
22. I find it easy to identify flaws in others' ideas.	☐	☐
23. I regard myself as a "specialist," not a "generalist."	☐	☐
24. When evaluating information, I believe the source is more important than the content.	☐	☐
25. I am easily frustrated by uncertainty and unpredictability.	☐	☐
26. I can easily give up immediate gain or comfort to reach long-term goals.	☐	☐
27. I have great tenacity of purpose.	☐	☐
28. Things that are obvious to others are not so obvious to me.	☐	☐

	Always	Often	Some-times	Rarely	Never
29. I get a kick out of breaking the rules.	☐	☐	☐	☐	☐
30. I become upset if I cannot immediately come to a decision.	☐	☐	☐	☐	☐
31. Ideas run through my head at night to the point that I can't sleep.	☐	☐	☐	☐	☐
32. I get into trouble because I'm too curious or inquisitive.	☐	☐	☐	☐	☐
33. I am able to win other people over to my point of view.	☐	☐	☐	☐	☐
34. I tolerate frustration more than the average person does.	☐	☐	☐	☐	☐
35. I rely on intuition when trying to solve a problem.	☐	☐	☐	☐	☐
36. I can stick with difficult problems for extended periods of time.	☐	☐	☐	☐	☐
37. My problem-solving abilities are stronger than my social abilities.	☐	☐	☐	☐	☐
38. A logical step-by-step method is best for solving problems.	☐	☐	☐	☐	☐
39. I can readily allay other people's suspicions.	☐	☐	☐	☐	☐

40. Below is a list of adjectives and descriptive terms. Indicate with a check mark 12 words that best describe you:

ENERGETIC	☐	PREDICTABLE	☐	OPEN-MINDED	☐	PERSUASIVE	☐	SELF-CONFIDENT	☐
TACTFUL	☐	OBSERVANT	☐	INFORMAL	☐	INHIBITED	☐	FASHIONABLE	☐
DEDICATED	☐	ENTHUSIASTIC	☐	FORMAL	☐	ORIGINAL	☐	INNOVATIVE	☐
PERSEVERING	☐	QUICK	☐	POISED	☐	CURIOUS	☐	GOOD-NATURED	☐
ACQUISITIVE	☐	CAUTIOUS	☐	HELPFUL	☐	PRACTICAL	☐	HABIT-BOUND	☐
PERCEPTIVE	☐	ALERT	☐	RESOURCEFUL	☐	COURAGEOUS	☐	FORWARD-LOOKING	☐
EGOTISTICAL	☐	STERN	☐	ORGANIZED	☐	INDEPENDENT	☐	CLEAR-THINKING	
UNEMOTIONAL	☐	EFFICIENT	☐	FACTUAL	☐	THOROUGH	☐	UNDERSTANDING	
DYNAMIC	☐	MODEST	☐	POLISHED	☐	REALISTIC	☐	SELF-DEMANDING	
INVOLVED	☐	ABSENT-MINDED	☐	FLEXIBLE	☐	SOCIABLE	☐	WELL-LIKED	☐

Scoring Instructions

To score the test, circle and add up the values for your answers.

	Agree	Disagree		Agree	Disagree		Always	Often	Sometimes	Rarely	Never
1.	4	1	15.	4	1	29.	2	3	5	1	0
2.	3	1	16.	4	1	30.	0	2	3	5	1
3.	4	1	17.	1	4	31.	2	4	5	3	0
4.	3	1	18.	4	1	32.	3	4	5	1	0
5.	4	1	19.	4	1	33.	3	4	5	1	0
6.	4	1	20.	4	1	34.	3	4	5	1	0
7.	4	1	21.	1	4	35.	5	4	3	1	0
8.	3	1	22.	3	1	36.	4	5	3	1	0
9.	0	4	23.	1	4	37.	4	5	3	1	0
10.	4	1	24.	1	4	38.	1	2	5	3	0
11.	4	1	25.	1	4	39.	3	4	5	1	0
12.	3	1	26.	4	1						
13.	4	1	27.	4	1						
14.	4	1	28.	4	1						

40. The following characteristics score 2 points each:

energetic, observant, persevering, resourceful, independent, dedicated, original, perceptive, enthusiastic, innovative, curious, involved, flexible.

The following score 1 point each:

self-confident, forward-looking, informal, courageous, thorough, open-minded, alert, dynamic, self-demanding, absent-minded.

Interpreting Your Score

125–186. If you scored in this range, you are probably a highly innovative person. Ideas come readily to you and you have a keen awareness of and concern for unsolved problems. On the whole, you take an innovative approach to solving problems. You also discern possibilities and opportunities in areas where others find little potential. You are original and individualistic, and you have no problem resisting pressures to conform. You have the courage to pit yourself against uncertain circumstances and you have the innovation to come out ahead.

77–124. A score in this range indicates that you are moderately innovative. While you lack some of the autonomy, self-sufficiency, and self-confidence of the highly innovative entrepreneur, you compensate with your predilection for method, precision and exactness. You also have faith in the successful outcome of your present and future entrepreneurial efforts.

While entrepreneurs with an innovative flair may succeed in a variety of enterprises, they are sometimes surpassed by other less creative entrepreneurs who possess keener abilities in marketing, deal-making, negotiations, finance and human relations. So although you may need to beef up on innovation, your abilities in other areas will still help you succeed.

27–76. If you scored in this range, you may be more successful operating a franchise or working for someone else than you would be starting your own business. However, remember: Innovative abilities can be developed and cultivated, either through self-training, or by attending workshops or seminars. So if you're determined to own your own business, don't give up!

want to work, the amount of personal assets available for investment into the business, such as your house or car, and how close to the business you want to be located.

- **Type of work.** It's no secret that the more you like your work, the greater satisfaction you will derive from your efforts and the more successful you'll be. When setting goals for type of work, you need to determine whether you like working outdoors, in an office environment, with computers, on the phone, with a great number of people, and so on.
- **Ego gratification.** Let's face it, many people go into business to satisfy their egos as well as their bank accounts. Owning a business can be very ego gratifying because of the perception other people have of you. Owning a so-called glamour business such as a software development firm can be even more ego gratifying. You need to decide how important ego gratification is to you and what industries will fill that need.

Once you've set your personal goals, you can prioritize them according to the importance you place on each. This will help you examine your entrepreneurial desire and how it relates to other important aspects of your life.

Risk Assessment

Every business venture, regardless of timing, products, personnel, and capitalization has some inherent risks. The first task you should complete is assessing those risks; then you can begin taking steps to diminish them.

Here are some techniques for assessing risks:

- **Research similar businesses.** Look at their locations, advertising, staff requirements, and equipment. These will be your competition, so you will want to know what you will be up against.
- **Research the current market trends.** What seemed like a hot idea over the past few months may have been a fad. Find last year's phone book and call several of these businesses. Are they still around? (If you live in a small community or want to expand your research, your local telephone company may have a library of phone books from other cities.)
- **Know your strengths and preferences.** Does this type of business fit you? Is it too physical? Not physical enough? Does your staff have experience to handle the areas that you have little or no expertise in?
- **Create a family budget.** How long can you live without a paycheck in case you need to put it all back in the business? What other income can you reasonably expect while you're in the start-up phase? Make sure your family understands what you are doing and engage their support. Since they are also sharing in the risk, they will be more willing to assist you if they understand exactly what you are doing.
- **Know how changes in the economy will affect your business.** Is this the type of business that could be damaged if inflation rose by two points? What's its history during various economic waves?

- **The business plan.** Once you are serious about starting, this will be your blueprint. It can be simple or complex, depending on the type of business, number of investors, and so on that you may be dealing with. But it is necessary if you want to increase your entrepreneurial odds of success. See Chapter 8 for a detailed description of forming a business plan.

THE IMPORTANCE OF PLANNING

When you are starting a business, proper planning and research are absolutely necessary. There is no way of getting around these tasks. Many people get into business, put up the money, and then fail without ever really knowing why. So they say to themselves, "I know what I did wrong. I'm going to change A, B, and C, and go back and try it again." So they go back and try it again. And the same thing happens.

It is almost predictable. If you don't take the time to analyze the prospective business concept, you'll probably find yourself confronted by one of the following situations:

- Insufficient capital requirements.
- Optimistic market opportunities resulting in an overestimation of projected sales.
- Saturation of the market by the competition.
- Poor access to markets due to a bad location.
- Inadequate equipment projections.

Don't let this happen to you. Do the required market research as detailed in Chapter 3 and form the necessary plans.

On a personal scale, however, your first research and planning step is to assess your start-up requirements so you will know how much income you are going to need to get your business off the ground.

How Much Money Will You Need to Start?

There are a great many philosophies regarding the actual start-up costs associated with a business. We've talked with many entrepreneurs who have begun successful operations on a minimal budget, often using bootstrap financing techniques, as discussed in Chapter 21. There is nothing wrong with this approach if you're willing to sacrifice yourself and invest a great amount of time and energy into making the business work. But it is also true that undercapitalization is one of the primary reasons for business failure. For instance, if it is going to cost you $500,000 to cover all your start-up costs, and you only spend $100,000, chances are you are going to fail. It is less a question of "How much?" than of "Is it enough?"

To make this determination, you must account for all your start-up costs—not just opening expenses, but initial operating expenses as well. Although different businesses have different costs associated with them, the main start-up costs include the following:

- **Rent.** Under many lease agreements, you will be expected to provide the first month's rent plus a security deposit. Many lessors also require the final month's rent.
- **Phone and utilities.** Some telephone and utility companies require deposits, while others do not. A deposit may not be required if you own real estate or have a previously established payment record with the company. Telephone deposits are determined by the number of phones and the type of service required. Unless you need a large number of phones and lines, the deposit is likely to range from $50 to $350. Deposits for gas and electricity (when required) will vary according to your projected usage. It is possible to lower them by not overestimating your initial consumption of these utilities.
- **Equipment.** Equipment costs will vary from operation to operation depending on how equipment intensive they are. At a minimum, most businesses need office equipment, signage, and security systems. To determine your costs, list all of the equipment you must have to operate your business efficiently. Next, price those items by obtaining quotes or bids from several vendors. Three quotes would be a good minimum to start with. Use the quotes you receive to estimate your start-up equipment costs.
- **Fixtures.** The broad category of "fixtures" includes such items as partitions, paneling, signage, storage shelves and/or cabinets, lighting, checkout counter(s), and all shelves, tables, stands, wall systems, showcases, and related hardware for product display. The cost of fixtures depends on a number of variables including the store's location, its size and present condition, the type of merchandise to be sold, what kind of image you want it to project, and whether you are purchasing new or used fixtures.
- **Inventory.** Like equipment, inventory requirements change from business to business. Some businesses, such as retail stores, are inventory-intensive whereas others, such as personal shopping services, don't require any inventory at all except office supplies.
- **Leasehold improvements.** These nonremovable installations, either original or the result of remodeling, include carpeting and other floorings, insulation, electrical wiring and plumbing, bathrooms, lighting, wall partitions, windows, ceiling tiles, sprinkler system, security systems, some elements of interior design, and sometimes heating and/or air-conditioning systems. Because the cost of improvements can vary tremendously (from $5 per square foot to over $50 per square foot), you must investigate this carefully.
- **Licenses and tax deposits.** Most cities and counties require business operators to obtain various licenses or permits to show compliance with local regulations. Licensing costs will vary from business to business in conjunction with the particular start-up requirements. In addition to these fees, you'll also need start-up capital for tax deposits. Many states

require a deposit against future taxes to be collected. For example, in California, if you project $10,000 in taxable sales for the first three months of operation, you must deposit 7.25 percent ($725) with the state tax bureau when applying for your sales tax permit number.

- **Marketing budgets.** Most businesses require a strong grand opening push to get their ventures off the ground and build a customer foundation. Most companies determine their first year's advertising budget as a percentage of projected gross sales. Many businesses peg their ad budgets at 2 to 5 percent of their projected gross sales.
- **Professional services.** During your preopening phase, you'll need the help of a good lawyer and accountant to make sure you meet your legal requirements. Their fees will range according to expertise and region.
- **Pre-opening payroll.** If your business will be a full-time function for yourself, then you'll have to set aside a pre-opening salary of at least one month for yourself in addition to a three-month reserve. This rule of thumb will also apply to any employees you might hire during this phase of business start-up.
- **Insurance.** Plan on allocating the first quarter's cost of insurance to get your business rolling.

A word of caution when estimating these costs: If there is ever a time for conservative realism, exercise it when planning these costs. To assure your company's success, a cushion of excess money that can support start-up costs is better than the dilemma of insufficient capital.

How Much Income Will You Need?

To determine just how much money you have to invest in a business, you must evaluate your finances on the credit and debit sides using the *personal balance sheet* (see Figure 1.1). Begin by listing all your assets and their value in the top portion of the form: house, car, jewelry, and so on. Next list all your debts in the bottom portion: credit cards, mortgage, bank notes, personal debts, auto loans, and so on. Now compute the ratio between total assets and total liabilities to determine your net worth or degree of indebtedness. This ratio is assets:liabilities, or line A:line B. The ratio will look something like 2:1, or if you are like most people nowadays, 1:2. This is generally referred to as the *acid-test ratio* or *quick ratio*. If your assets exceed liabilities, you should be able to keep the creditors from knocking on your door.

Evaluating the Business

The final phase of evaluating yourself for business is to determine just what type of business would be most suitable for you given all the variables such as the amount needed to start the business and the income available to support it. To evaluate a business, you must first develop a list of possibilities. In Chapter 2, we discuss how to find suitable ideas for businesses.

Figure 1.1 Personal Balance Sheet

STATEMENT OF FINANCIAL CONDITION AS OF_____ 19,____

ASSETS   TOTALS

Cash, checking, & savings		
Marketable securities		
Non-marketable securities		
Real estate owned/home		
Partial interest in real estate equities		
Automobiles		
Personal property		
Personal loans		
Cash value—Life Insurance		
Other Assets—Itemize		
TOTAL ASSETS	**A**	

LIABILITIES   TOTALS

Secured loans		
Unsecured loans		
Charge account bills		
Personal debts		
Monthly bills		
Real estate mortgages		
Unpaid income tax		
Other unpaid taxes and interest		
Other debts—Itemize		
TOTAL LIABILITIES	**B**	
NET WORTH (A minus B=C)	**C**	
TOTAL LIABILITIES & NET WORTH	**D**	

DEGREE OF INDEBTEDNESS

Note:
If total liabilities exceed total assets,
subtract assets from liabilities to determine
degree of indebtedness (B minus A=E)

TOTAL LIABILITIES	**B**	
TOTAL ASSETS	**A**	
DEGREE OF INDEBTEDNESS	**E**	

Once you have a list of businesses to choose from, you should audit them to determine which one would be the best for you. This test simply determines whether or not you feel comfortable with a particular business as you read down the list. The goal is to narrow down your list of opportunities to three or four that elicit the most excitement based on your audit. Then you need to screen this small group of opportunities according to your personal objectives, experience, and lifestyle. This procedure is described in detail in Chapter 2.

Failure Factors

Much has been written about business failures. Every year, thousands of businesses fail—small, medium-size, and big. While business failures know no size boundaries, for years the statistic that four out of five small businesses fail during their first five years has been accepted unquestioningly. But no one is sure where that figure came from—and some think the truth is far more promising.

Bruce Kirchhoff, professor of entrepreneurship at the New Jersey Institute of Technology in Newark, studied small-business activity from 1978 to 1986. His numbers, based on Dun & Bradstreet data, indicate that only 18 percent of small businesses started during those years failed (closed with losses to creditors), while 28 percent were voluntary terminations. That means a whopping 54 percent were still in business after eight years.

Although those numbers are encouraging for entrepreneurs, the fact is that the majority of business failures are classified as small businesses. According to data from the Administrative Office of the U.S. Courts, more than 98 percent of businesses filing for bankruptcy since 1980 were small firms. Most small business surveys show that the primary reasons for failure lie in the following areas:

1. Inefficient control over costs and quality of product.
2. Bad stock control.
3. Underpricing of goods sold.
4. Bad customer relations.
5. Failure to promote and maintain a favorable public image.
6. Bad relations with suppliers.
7. Inability of management to reach decisions and act on them.
8. Failure to keep pace with management system.
9. Illness of key personnel.
10. Reluctance to seek professional assistance.
11. Failure to minimize taxation through tax planning.
12. Inadequate insurance.
13. Loss of impetus in sales.
14. Bad personnel relations.
15. Loss of key personnel.
16. Lack of staff training.
17. Lack of knowledge of merchandise.

18. Inability to cope adequately with competition.
19. Competition disregarded due to complacency.
20. Failure to anticipate market trends.
21. Loose control of liquid assets.
22. Insufficient working capital or incorrect gearing of capital borrowings.
23. Growth without adequate capitalization.
24. Bad budgeting.
25. Ignoring of data on the company's financial position.
26. Inadequate financial records.
27. Extension of too much credit.
28. Bad credit control.
29. Overborrowing; use of too much credit.
30. Bad control over receivables.
31. Loss of control through creditors' demands.

The last quarter of the twentieth century has witnessed the twin phenomena of more new businesses being started and more failing, year by year. This suggests that while business owners may display a good deal of confidence and enthusiasm in opening their businesses, they also experience a high mortality rate. A careful examination of the preceding list reveals that a lack of planning is the principal or underlying cause of business difficulty. All of these problems, including money-related reasons for failure, are indicators of poor planning. Other things being equal, planning can make the difference between success and failure in business, and that starts with choosing the right business.

RESOURCES

Associations

Association of Small Business Development Centers, 1050 17th Street NW, Suite 810, Washington, DC 20036, 202-887-5599

Center for Entrepreneurial Management, Inc., 180 Varick Street, New York, NY 10014, 212-633-0060

Small Business Service Bureau, 554 Main Street, Worcester, MA 01601, 508-756-3513

Small Business Network, 10451 Millrun Circle, Suite 400, Owensville, MD 21117, 410-581-1373

Magazines and Newspapers

Barron's National Business & Financial Weekly, 200 Liberty Street, New York, NY 10281, 212-416-2700

The Business Journal, 101 Southeast 2nd Place, Suite 202, P.O. Box 2879, Gainesville, FL 32601-6592, 904-371-9228

Business Opportunities Journal, 1050 Rosecrans Street, Suite 8, P.O. Box 60762, San Diego, CA 92166-0762, 619-223-5661

The Business Owner, Thomas Publishing, Inc., 383 South Broadway, Hicksville, NY 11801, 516-681-2111

In Business, 2718 Dryden Drive, Madison, WI 53704, 608-246-3580

Journal of Small Business Management, West Virginia University, College of Business Economics, Bureau of Business Research, P.O. Box 6025, Morgan-town, WV 26506-6025, 304-293-5837

Kiplinger's Personal Finance Magazine (formerly *Changing Times*), 1729 H Street, Northwest, Washington, DC 20006-3904, 202-887-6400

Marketing News, 250 South Wacker Drive, Suite 200, Chicago, IL 60606-5819, 312-993-9517

Nation's Business, 1615 H Street NW, Washington, DC 20062, 202-463-5650

Opportunity, 73 Spring Street, Suite 303, New York, NY 10012, 212-925-3180

Small Business Reports, 135 West 50th Street, New York, NY 10020, 212-903-8160

The Wall Street Journal, Subscription Distribution Customer Service, 800-568-7625. This number can connect the caller to any of the following editions of *The Wall Street Journal:*

> *The Wall Street Journal*—Eastern Edition, 200 Liberty Street, New York, NY 10281, 212-416-2000

> *The Wall Street Journal*—Midwest Edition, 1 South Wacker Drive, Suite 2100, Chicago, IL 60606-3388, 312-750-4100

> *The Wall Street Journal*—Southwest Edition, 1233 Regal Row, Dallas, TX 75247-3613, 214-631-7250

> *The Wall Street Journal*—Western Edition, 201 California Street, Suite 1350, San Francisco, CA 94111-5002, 415-986-6886

2

Ideas and Trends

Really successful entrepreneurs are innovators; they explore new markets long before the rest of the world knows about the idea. They are perceptive enough to spot or discover a new trend or market. They see openings and needs long before they are publicized or noticed by other businesspeople. They get in on the ground floor of their industry.

There is really nothing better or more fulfilling than starting a business from your own idea. The idea may be building a better mousetrap or developing something completely original. The main point is that the idea for the business is yours, and yours alone. You are completely at the mercy of your own imagination and ambitions. If the business succeeds, it is your success. You are the one who will receive the accolades and the rewards, not someone else. If the business fails, it is your failure. Even franchises are not failure-proof.

The many advantages to starting a business must be weighed against the disadvantages. The advantages are:

- You do not have to pay someone royalties for the use of their idea.
- You aren't required to follow strict guidelines of operations and profit reporting.
- You aren't hampered by a previous image, someone else's problems, old technology, wasteful inventory, or the wrong supplies.
- You can choose a location, name, and logo that will create a strong marketable presence, and relationships with suppliers and lenders are fresh so there are no credit problems.
- You have the opportunity to evaluate new suppliers and order new equipment, supplies, and inventory based on exact requirements and specifications.
- You can exploit new markets and explore different directions that can't be reached through any other means.
- Finally, there is the satisfaction of seeing your dreams come true.

The disadvantages are:

- There is greater risk associated with starting a business from your own idea.
- Everything has to be created from the bottom up; this may result in costly trial and error.
- Lack of a proven track record may make it difficult to obtain capital and credit.
- Recruiting employees may be difficult at first.
- Starting a business and building volume until you are finally operating in the black often can be time energy-consuming, not to mention frustrating.

However, even with the disadvantages, starting a business from scratch is the most popular choice of entrepreneurs. A start-up from a new idea is unique. It places you on the cutting edge of a new trend or market. You become the leader, not the follower.

Keep in mind though, that it is much harder to develop a business from an original idea than from one that has already been used. Everything has to be developed from scratch. This involves a lot of research and conceptualization beginning with the analysis of trends and ideas.

FINDING NEW BUSINESS IDEAS

Searching for new ideas and concepts for a business opportunity can be a formidable task. To create an opportunity evaluation checklist for each opportunity see Opportunity Evaluation Checklist. Along the left-hand side of the form are pertinent factors. For each factor, rate the potential of the opportunity on a scale of zero to three, with a rating of three being the best. Once you've scored all the potential businesses, total the ratings for both opportunity and marketability. The one with the highest rating will most likely conform to your goals and lifestyle.

Because the world market has become so interdependent, you routinely see cookies from Australia, cars from Korea, beer from Kenya, and electronics from Asia—all for sale in the American market. Once you start thinking about it, you will be able to identify many more examples of this trend. New products and new product ideas or concepts are being introduced daily, from virtually everywhere in the world. So, when you begin searching for sources from which to draw a new product, you have the whole world to consider.

No one has the time, money, or the inclination to journey from one corner of the planet to another to locate the perfect, million-dollar idea. So, to help you organize your personal new business search, we've broken down "the world" into the major groups of sources, which we will discuss in the following sections. How many sources of new business ideas and products should you investigate before deciding which one you believe is right for you? Try to look into as many sources as physically possible. Of course, the type of product you are interested

OPPORTUNITY EVALUATION CHECKLIST

This evaluation form will help you determine how successful you will be if you enter a given business and sell a given product. Fill out the entire form for each business and product you consider. In the column on the right side of the form, indicate how well a given opportunity or product meets a given requirement for success (3–Excellent, 2–Good, 1–Fair, 0–Poor). The opportunity and product with the highest total points are your strongest candidates for success.

OPPORTUNITY

	3	2	1	0
Relevance of your previous experience to opportunity				
Familiarity with the daily operations of this type of business				
Compatibility of business with your investment goals				
Compatibility of business with your income goals				
Likely profitability of business				
Likelihood of business to meet your desire for personal fulfillment				
Projected growth for the industry				
Acceptability of risk level				
Acceptability of hours you will need to work				

MARKETABILITY OF PRODUCT

Probability of use by target market				
Compatibility with image desired				
Competitiveness of price				
Number and strength of promotable features				
Probability that product will enhance sales of current line				
Projected stability of demand				
Ability to overcome seasonal or cyclical resistance				
Uniqueness of product				
Ability of business to obtain needed equipment				
Likely acceptance potential				
Ability of business to afford the development and production of product				
TOTAL				

in will have a direct bearing on how many sources of new ideas and products are actually available to you.

What About You?

Start at home, with yourself. What kind of work do you do (have you done)? Whether you are a welder or clerical worker, you have probably spent several years within the working environment and have developed a set of finely honed skills to do your job. Many times, the best ideas come from people who are already in a certain type of business and decide to spin off and start one in some other segment of the same market.

Taking a self-assessment test could lead you in the right direction. Ask:

1. What skills do I have?
2. What industries do I know about?
3. What do I like to do?
4. What hobbies do I have?
5. Do I want to run a business from home or would I rather be around other people?
6. Am I service oriented or would I like to sell a product?
7. Does retail appeal to me or am I better suited to a mail-order operation?

For a more thorough self-evaluation, see Chapter 1.

There is a wealth of wisdom in the adage, "Do not reinvent the wheel [or mousetrap]." Far too many entrepreneurs waste time and money in a vain attempt to invent the better mousetrap. It's been done! A far better strategy is to look for a successful concept that you can emulate. Although you have to be careful not to infringe on any patent, trademark, copyright, or other form of legal protection, countless shrewd entrepreneurs have made significant money by emulating a currently successful product. Next time you're in the supermarket, stop by the freezer section and count the number of brands of designer or upscale ice cream. You can do the same thing with chocolate-chip cookies, beer, running shoes, teddy bears, computers, and so on.

The key element in selecting a successful concept to emulate is market share. Has the original product captured and capitalized on a significant share of the available market, or is a sizable portion of the market as yet untapped? If a market is far from saturated, it contains future profits that you can tap into. If an original product has already captured the significant share of the market, you'd have to enter into head-to-head competition with that product, to become successful, and, at best, that can be an uphill battle leading to a hollow victory. So if you run across a new product that interests you and appears to have good profit-making potential, see if there's room for another player in that market. If there is, your road is clear.

Inventor and Trade Shows

Trade and inventor shows, as well as conventions and civic groups, are also important. They can yield a wealth of information within one day. Many trade shows and conventions are sponsored by trade associations for specific industries. There are thousands of associations and just as many trade shows. To find an appropriate association for the industry you are interested in researching, look through the *Encyclopedia of Associations* published by Gale Research. You may also want to check magazines and newsletters such as *Tradeshow Week* or go through the *Tradeshow Week Data Book*. All these publications should be available at your local library.

A classic source of new products and ideas is the inventors show. For someone like you, searching for a business idea or new product, these shows are like a smorgasbord. At any one show, you can preview a staggering number of new products—some of which may just end up being another Hula Hoop or Frisbee success story. Whatever sources you decide to investigate, this is one that you should not miss. The sheer numbers of new products displayed at any one show simply improve your odds of finding a winner.

To find out when the next trade or inventor show will occur in your area, contact your local convention facility. The space for shows of such size must be reserved well in advance, and if there's one planned during the next year, the facility manager's office will be able to give you the dates. Another information source is your local chamber of commerce, which usually sponsors inventor shows because they are a forum for interaction between inventors and manufacturers. Check with your local chamber of commerce for the next show.

Also, do not forget to check for any local inventors' organizations. Inventors in most areas meet regularly to socialize, talk shop, and receive mutual support for their efforts. Not only will such a group know exactly where and when the upcoming inventor shows will occur, you may be able to tap into a great find *before* the next show, and get a head start on all your potential competitors.

Foreign Products

Foreign products are desirable to many because they are, by definition, different. Every country produces fine products that are wonderful examples of innovation, practicality, and profitability. Another factor you should recognize when considering overseas sources for products is the American fascination with all things foreign. Our language is a mixture of many tongues, just as our population is a melting pot. Therefore, foreign products possess an exotic, sometimes almost irresistible appeal. That's one reason products like Irish lace, Swiss watches, Colombian coffee, and Limoges china are perennial favorites.

There's another factor involved in obtaining new products from foreign sources that you should consider. No matter how old a product might be in its country of origin, in a new market, it's a new product. Many of the finest products in the world are limited to specific countries because international distribution systems for them do not exist. If you can develop a distribution system for a foreign product, then you will be able to capitalize on the uniqueness of the product in the American market.

The world market is a cornucopia of products that would make excellent imports into the United States or other international markets. These products are just waiting to be discovered by clever entrepreneurs and introduced into new markets. To investigate how and where you can obtain such profitable finds, contact the foreign consulate in your area, or the Department of Commerce in Washington, DC. Many foreign countries that have products available for export also publish trade magazines, which you should be able to find either at your library or through a specific consulate.

The Media

Stop and think for just a second—pretend you are that inventor who has just perfected a terrific new product. What is your next step? In a word: *Publicity.* The greatest invention in the world will not sell if no one knows about it. To overcome that hurdle, inventors and new product manufacturers are constantly seeking media coverage to educate the public about one or another fantastic new innovation that everyone must have. As the first step in creating demand, inventors must raise the profile of their new product to firmly implant it in the mind of the public. That's why your search for new product ideas and leads should not overlook the media—both newspapers and magazines that focus on business.

There are four dailies you should scan regularly that cover the major markets where new trends and ideas are regularly developed. They are the *The Wall Street Journal, New York Times, Los Angeles Times,* and the *London Times* (or any other daily that reports on the Western European market).

While newspapers are an important source to tap, do not neglect trade magazines and journals. Obviously, you cannot subscribe to every trade magazine or journal in the world, but try to read some of the more important and relevant ones. In this area, *Entrepreneur Magazine* and *Business Start-Ups* are also excellent sources. If you already have a good idea of the type of industry that you would like to concentrate your efforts around, then subscribing to a good trade publication in that area would be very helpful.

Usually, both dailies and trade journals will have classified ads in the back pages of the publication. Look through these ads. You may find a product or concept that would be worth pursuing. Also, do not forget television. A quick glance at your local cable listings will reveal a wide range of business programming that is designed to inform and educate the public about new products and new ideas. If you do not have the time to catch each of these shows, program your VCR to tape them. You can quickly review the tapes at a later time, scanning them just as you would skim through a textbook for pertinent information.

Much of your new product search is just a matter of processing existing information. The media have discovered that business information is a very fertile market segment—that's why you see so much of it in every medium. Take the few minutes required to access these sources of information, and they will make your search for the right product much easier. A checklist of sources of information about new business trends follows.

Manufacturers

You would be remiss in your new product investigation if you failed to contact original equipment manufacturers (OEMs). Just as a very old foreign product can be brand-new in an untapped market, a product that a manufacturer has decided to take out of production can also be a great seller. Many manufacturers begin the production process on a product and then, for a variety of reasons, decide not to commit to full-scale manufacturing or distribution. This does not always imply that the product is faulty or that a market for it doesn't exist.

By contacting manufacturers, you will significantly advance your education in the marketplace. You will learn which products are being introduced and which concepts are being capitalized heavily, as well as which projects manufacturers have decided not to fund. You could easily discover a new product for which a manufacturer is seeking distributors. A large operation may opt to discontinue a product because it no longer generates big sales figures in the nationwide market. It may, however, still possess plenty of salability in a regional, state, or local market. When you contact a manufacturer and learn that the company has decided to discontinue Product X, chances are you will also learn the basis for the decision. This means the large company's extensive and expensive market research may easily become available to you. Not only can you learn what products might fit your needs, you can also obtain valuable information on what products *will not* sell.

The Government

The U.S. government publishes mountains of useful information that most of us ignore. To get acquainted with this unending flow of data, locate a U.S. government directory of publications. The amount of material available—much of it at not cost whatsoever—will quite literally stagger your imagination. Just to give you a quick example, let's take a look at the space program. Many critics have said that the space program fails to provide us with material benefits, yet nothing could be farther from the truth. What about Teflon? It is a direct result of our efforts to adapt to the environment of space, and has myriad uses in everyday life. Such by-products of our NASA programs are routinely written up in publications such as the *National Aeronautics and Space Administration* (NASA) *Tech Briefs*, which can be ordered by writing the National Technical Information Service (see Resources).

NASA innovations can also be found at Regional Technology Transfer Centers (RTTC), which were formed in 1991 to help federal agencies make technology developed in government labs available to American companies, thereby making them more competitive, especially in international markets. There are six technology transfer centers throughout the country. They will perform searches through federal technology databases, engineering reports and other sources to find information consistent with what you require. RTTCs can also help put together a feasibility study of the new technology showing how it

TRACKING SMALL BUSINESS TRENDS CHECKLIST

To track emerging trends that can affect small businesses in general and your business in particular, you need to stay informed. To do so, do the following:

☐ Read a major metropolitan newspaper, as well as one or two papers serving your local community. This way, you can say informed of current events on both a local and a global scale.

☐ Join associations that serve your industry. These are an excellent source of current news geared specifically to businesses like yours. To find an appropriate association, consult the Encyclopedia of Associations, published by Gale Research, Inc. You can find this publication in larger libraries.

☐ Keep track of the kinds of nonfiction books that sell well. Although these books may not always apply directly to your business, they may indicate trends that you can exploit.

☐ Contact government agencies or consult government publications for specific questions. The Departments of Commerce and Labor and the Census Bureau, for instance, may have data indicating various trends. You might also consult large libraries, particularly those in large public universities, for information gathered by the government. Such libraries often have sections devoted to government publications.

☐ Contact manufacturers, wholesalers, and distributors serving your industry. They can furnish information not only on the products they provide, but also on market research they may have done.

☐ If you have access to an on-line information service or to electronic bulletin boards, you might be able to find a source of the latest information on your industry.

☐ Subscribe to relevant trade periodicals and newsletters. Many trade associations publish periodicals that report on your industry. These publications are usually filled with valuable management tips, industry trends, buying guides, etc.

☐ Attend industry conventions and inventor trade shows. These venues offer an exciting array of information regarding specific industries as well as new product ideas.

☐ Read journals and magazines on a local as well as national level that deal with small business or business in general. Publications like the *Wall Street Journal* and *Entrepreneur* are valuable sources of trends that are developing on a national scale as well as detailed information on specific business opportunities. Just as important are local business journals that cover key developments in your own community so you can track new ideas and trends that appeal to that geographic market.

might best be applied in your business, and they will help you conduct in-depth value-added studies on different ways to utilize a specific technology.

In addition, RTTCs can also refer you to university researchers, federal laboratories, or private companies that might be interested in working with you. They may even be able to recommend you to venture capital sources interested in funding the commercial application of new technology.

Of course, NASA is just one segment of the government. Another fertile source of information is the *Patent Abstracts Bibliography,* published twice a year by the National Technical Information Service. It details all new patents and applications for new patents. It is a perfect information source for those entrepreneurs interested in new products to license.

For more immediate information, you may also wish to obtain *The Official Gazette of the U.S. Patent Office.* This publication, generated weekly, lists patents that have been granted, as opposed to those merely applied for. You can subscribe to this information source, just like a newspaper or magazine, by contacting the Superintendent of Documents at the Government Printing Office in Washington, DC. Other relevant publications you may want to receive are the *Atomic Energy Commission Tech Briefs, Topical Announcements,* and *FAST Announcement Service on Selected Scientific and Technical Reports.* All these publications can be ordered through the National Technical Information Service. Get a list of public domain patents from the U.S. Patent Office. After a 17-year period, patents are no longer valid and can be developed without any licensing requirements or royalties to the original patent holder. Remember, however, that just because a patent has expired does not mean the product will cease to exist. A perfect example of this is the single-element typewriter patented by IBM. Once the period of protection ended at the time the patent expired, many manufacturers produced their versions of this product—most of which sold quite well.

The Small Business Administration (SBA), specifically its Small Business Investment Companies (SBICs), is also a fine source of information. The SBA licenses SBICs for the sole purpose of funding new companies—a great many of which have new products for sale. It is only logical that a new company would welcome inquiries from potential marketers, distributors, wholesalers, or retailers for its products. The need of each party for the other party's success creates the foundation for a business relationship in which everybody profits. Thus, contacting an SBIC can be a direct route to your success. Contact the SBA for a list of currently active SBICs.

Another good program to look into is the Small Business Technology Transfer (STTR) program. Not only is STTR a good program to help small businesses deliver promising technology to the marketplace, it also provides up to $100,000 for the first phase of work, provided the companies applying for the funds conduct at least 40 percent of the work themselves.

The Department of Energy (DOE), which manages the largest collection of federal laboratories in the nation, is spearheading the effort to implement the STTR program. Contact the Office of Technology Utilization at DOE headquarters (see Resources). This is the starting point for all small businesses. For more information regarding technology transfer, subscribe to *Newslink,* a free monthly newsletter about technology transfer activities published by the Federal Laboratory Consortium (FLC). Also, purchase the *1994 CRADA (Cooperative Research and Development Agreement) Handbook,* published by Technology Publishing Group. This handbook provides information about current agreements between private companies and the federal government. CRADAs are the result of the Federal Technology Transfer Act of 1989, which enabled federal laboratories to enter into cooperative arrangements with private partners. Under this type of program, laboratories and businesses share personnel, services, facilities, and equipment to conduct specified research and development. According to the DOE, about 25 percent of the nearly 400 CRADAs are involved with small-business partners.

Research and Development

With the evolution of business and the increasingly technical nature of the products being invented, large corporations have come to play a dominant role in research and development (R&D). If a major corporation is large enough to operate a research and development division or department, then it's a near certainty that some of the products and ideas developed are not brought into production. Some of these "rejects" from large national firms may be perfect for your smaller operation. Also, you can investigate products springing from R&D efforts that are available to license. On a word processor or computer develop a form letter that you can send to Fortune 500 companies. Your letter should concentrate on obtaining information from their R&D efforts and might read something like this: "We are a small company specializing in the marketing and distribution of new products. We would be interested in obtaining information regarding products that have recently been developed or are currently in development, that are available to license." Some firms may not respond, but you will be surprised how many of these giants are happy to correspond with you.

New products must be manufactured, marketed, distributed, and sold. At each of these points along the chain of distribution, niches occur that can mean opportunities for you. While you may not be able to become involved in dealing with a new car, new 35mm camera, or new copying machine, many new products on the market are within your grasp. Just think for a second how many millions of Bic pens have been sold in this country. As sure as you are reading this, the disposable ballpoint pen introduced by Bic will not be the last story of a huge entrepreneurial success. With some intelligent investigation, you may be a part of the next big product success and build a business around it. All you have to do is ask.

The Licensing Broker

Just as you are searching for products to license, manufacturers who have those products available are searching for you. The method many of them use to discover potential licensees is the licensing broker. These consultants have many contacts, not to mention years of experience in the manufacturing field. Their profits stem from matching manufacturers to licensees, so this is a natural source for you to investigate. Many of these professionals can also help you finalize the actual licensing agreement you will need to get underway.

How can you find them? You can call the International Licensing Industry Merchandisers' Association (ILIMA). Their membership comprises agents and property owners who are involved in licensed properties. Find out if they can recommend a broker in your area (see Resources for contact information). Look in the business-to-business yellow pages under "Brokers—Merchandise." Many of these companies deal in licensed property. Finally, ask your attorney to recommend a qualified licensing broker. The great aspect of working with licensing brokers is that they are in business to make money for you and the manufacturer, because that's how they profit as well.

The Ultimate Scavenger Hunt

When you look at the situation correctly, choosing the right business is a lot like a scavenger hunt. The difference here is that you are digging for the *information* that will lead you to the pot of gold. The more sources you investigate, the more knowledge you will amass, and the more qualified you will be to make the best choice for your particular goals and needs. Question people and pursue information aggressively. As an entrepreneur in search of the right business, you simply cannot ask too many questions. That's the best way to discover what *not* to do—and that only improves your chances of selecting a winner.

EVALUATING YOUR IDEA

How good is your idea? Quite often, entrepreneurs—particularly first-time business owners—don't know what to do with their ideas. This is usually because they do not know how to evaluate their ideas correctly before investing time, money, and/or energy. Many flawed ideas fail in the marketplace, when sadly enough, a detailed and systematic evaluation could have corrected these defects, or at the very least, prevented the entrepreneur from committing capital and efforts to a lost cause. If you plan to enter the marketplace with a new concept, performing a strenuous evaluation of your idea beforehand will significantly improve your chances for success. Conduct your product analysis as rigorously as possible; in the long term, such detailed analysis and evaluation will be repaid many times over.

Effective evaluation of your ideas not only will screen out those with less than a strong chance for success, but will also help you determine what kind of idea you've developed. Your idea should fall into one of the following categories:

- **Simple.** Ideas that you could implement now without a great deal of expense or delay.
- **Moderate.** Ideas that could probably be realized in six months, with a reasonable outlay of capital.
- **Difficult.** Ideas that would take a year or more to actualize, perhaps including laboratory research or a great deal of coordination among different departments, divisions, or company functions.

Product Life Cycle

Traditional theory suggests that every product, idea, or concept has a five-stage life cycle that can be charted with the following criteria:

1. **Introduction.** The product debuts in the market; sales are being built from a low level even though prices are usually high.
2. **Growth.** Sales increase rapidly while price begins to decline.
3. **Maturity.** Sales level off and competition increases, placing more pressure on pricing.
4. **Saturation.** An overabundance of competition has entered the market, leading to very low profit margins.
5. **Decline.** Sales begin to fall, prices can no longer be sustained, and profits are almost nonexistent.

To avoid entering a saturated or declining market, your first order of business after developing an idea is to think it through. This occurs in three stages:

1. Thinking about the problem, plan, or project.
2. Thinking into the problem, plan, or project.
3. Thinking through the problem, plan, or project.

The preceding three-step process involves using your best judgment in every phase and feature of bringing your idea to fruition. In its most basic sense, this means facing realities, assessing the possibilities of failure, planning your approach, and organizing as carefully as possible by considering every detail. Essentially, you want to constantly ask "What if" with your idea, to determine whether your idea is too complex, inherently unworkable, or simply not profitable. See Chapter 3 for more information on conducting a feasibility study.

Additional Factors for Consideration

Several factors can—and in all probability will—directly affect your company, your product, and your staff once you begin to bring your idea to life. The Princeton Checklist for Evaluating Ideas will help you evaluate the feasibility of your idea. Your objective in considering these factors is to determine whether or not any external or internal changes in the status quo will threaten your success. To prevent any unforeseen elements or circumstances from harming your efforts, you must consider:

1. **Stability.** How durable is the market for your new idea? Is there significant foreign competition within the market? Is it a fad market? Can your product be used nationwide and be exported to foreign markets? Do you have a captive market? Is your product difficult to protect or easy for other manufacturers to copy? How would the market react to a recession?
2. **Growth.** Is your product or idea truly unique? Will demand for it grow? Can it survive a major technological surge, or will it become obsolete? Can

PRINCETON CHECKLIST FOR EVALUATING IDEAS

Princeton Creative Research has developed an excellent criteria checklist for evaluating ideas that is particularly well-suited to the entrepreneur. Ask yourself the following questions when evaluating an idea for a business or a product.

☐ 1. Have you considered all the advantages or benefits of the idea? Is there a real need for it?

☐ 2. Have you pinpointed the exact problems or difficulties your idea is expected to solve?

☐ 3. Is your idea an original, new concept, or is it a new combination or adaptation?

☐ 4. What immediate or short-range gains or results can be anticipated? Are the projected returns adequate? Are the risk factors acceptable?

☐ 5. What long-range benefits can be anticipated? Will they support the company's objectives?

☐ 6. Have you checked the operational soundness of the idea? Can it be produced by the company? Are the company's engineering, production, sales, and distributions facilities adequate for implementation?

☐ 7. Have you checked the idea for faults or limitations?

☐ 8. Are there any problems the idea might create? What are the changes involved?

☐ 9. Have you considered the economic factors of its implementation? What development time, capital investment, marketing costs, etc. does it entail? What personnel will be involved? Who else is needed to perform the job? What other divisions or departments of the comapny will be affected?

☐ 10. How simple or complex will execution or implementation be?

☐ 11. How well does it fit into the current operation of the organization?

☐ 12. Could you work out several variations of the idea? Could you offer alternative ideas?

☐ 13. Does it have a natural sales appeal? Is the market ready for it? Can customers afford it? Will they buy it? Is there a timing factor?

☐ 14. What, if anything, is your competition doing in this area? Can your company be competitive?

☐ 15. Have you considered the possibility of user resistance or difficulties?

☐ 16. Does your idea fill a real need, or does the need have to be created through promotional and advertising efforts?

☐ 17. Is it compatible with other procedures or products of the company and its overall objectives?

☐ 18. Is it a good idea or a good product area for the organization to pursue?

☐ 19. Are there any specific circumstances in your organization that might make the acceptance of the idea difficult?

☐ 20. How soon could it be put into operation?

As you can see by the preceding examples, there are many methods available for evaluating your idea. You should pick and choose the criteria that best suit your needs, depending on the type of company and/or the type of product you seek to evaluate.

you multiply growth through exporting? If the idea or product involves new technology, will consumers willingly learn the necessary skills to use it, or will you encounter significant consumer resistance?

3. **Marketability.** What type of sales structure will you require to market the product? How well has your competition been doing in this market? Will you be targeting a market niche where you will be able to generate a large volume to just a few customers?

4. **Research and development.** Can you develop your new product idea with your current knowledge? Will you need additional R&D staff to complete the project? Will you be able to utilize existing lab and/or pilot plant equipment and facilities? Does sufficient lead time exist for your R&D efforts to be satisfactorily completed before your competitors enter the market? Will the new product idea require extensive product improvement work after its introduction to the market? Can you incorporate any improvements into the production process smoothly without seriously disrupting the production schedule?

5. **Engineering.** Do you have all the required production knowledge or are there unknowns that may add to costs and/or delay production? Can you use standardized equipment to produce the product? If not, will you have to commit extensive capital to obtain the right equipment? Can your present engineering staff handle the load?

6. **Production.** Does the manufacturer of the new product employ familiar production techniques? Will it require substantial investment for utilities, such as power, gas, water? Is production of the new product free from hazards? Does it create difficult maintenance problems? Waste disposal problems? Will you have to conduct training prior to beginning full-scale production?

Based on these structured self-questioning approaches, you can construct a method that will be useful in evaluating almost any type of business problem. For example, if the problem involves training, the factors would be an analysis of your company's objectives, present performance of personnel, areas of deficiencies, and the overall quality of the human resources available to you and under consideration for use in the idea's development.

Sound evaluation techniques can mean the difference between the bankruptcy of your small business and huge profits. As your business expands and you gain experience, you will develop methods individually geared to your ideas. But when you're just starting out, it's wise to have a solid, proven set of parameters with which to gauge your ideas so you'll make fewer mistakes along the way—especially since every mistake costs you money. Following is a list of parameters for product development:

1. Choose your products on your past experience in business and life. Sell what you know.
2. Look for products that require small capital investment.
3. Get a proprietary position (patent, trademark, copyright) on your product as soon as possible.

4. Aim for products with low unit manufacturing costs and high markup potential.
5. In general, because of red tape and high cost, avoid high-energy or heavily government-regulated industries.
6. Look for products that can be shipped easily.
7. Look for products with built-in obsolescence.
8. Do not rely on a single product. Develop similar products in addition to your first one so that you do not put all your eggs in one basket.
9. Find a sales agent or manufacturer's rep to help get your product into the marketplace. Also check out channels of distribution other than manufacturer's reps.
10. Do not rest on your laurels once you get that first product on the market. Continually test-market your products and ideas for pricing, distribution, and technical improvements.

MARKET TESTING

Introducing a new product without first testing the market is like jumping off a cliff into the sea blindfolded. You do not know how high you are, how far you have to fall, or how deep the water might be. Many new ideas and products are successful because their creators identified an unmet need in the market and verified the viability of that concept through market testing. Although accurately determining the demand or consumer reaction to a new product in advance may be tough, you need as much information as you can get to guide your entry into the market. Every dollar and every hour you spend researching will be time and money well invested in the long term. Through correct and vigorous marketing research, you will uncover the following vital information:

- Total demand for a product or service. With that information in hand, you can also determine the regional or geographic demand for the product.
- Total sales figures within a market for a particular product or service.
- Customer demographics, or profiles of the individuals who will use your product or service.
- Customer opinions on your product and/or your competitor's product so you know why they would buy your competitor's model rather than yours, or vice versa. This information is extremely valuable to you if you seriously intend to capture and maintain a significant share of the market.
- The most effective distribution or marketing channels so you know where customers will most likely purchase your product or service.
- Pricing structure so you can determine not only what a competitive price is but what price point will provide you with a suitable profit.
- Characteristics of the competition. You need to be aware of products and services that compete with you both directly and indirectly.

- The best way to position your product or service so that you take advantage of your *unique selling proposition.*
- The governmental regulations your product or service will be subject to on a local, state, and federal level.
- The most effective sales, advertising, display, and promotion method(s).

One way to begin your research is to go to the library and look up names of relevant trade publications in the business publications volume of the *Standard Rate and Data Service Directory* (SRDS), or *Bacon's Publicity Checker.* Find all the trade publications that you can on the particular industry that you are interested in, and subscribe to as many of them as you can afford. After all, trade publications are in the business of providing market information on their respective industries. They will make you aware of new products and trends in the field where you are planning to launch your product.

Another good resource is the *Encyclopedia of Associations* published by Gale Research. There are well over 15,000 trade associations in the country, and almost all of them produce trade publications. Be sure to subscribe to those that relate to the specific field you are investigating. If you cannot afford to subscribe to all of them, see which ones your library receives. You can gather information from the library's copies at no cost to yourself, and subscribe to those others you might need to cover the field completely.

You will not become an expert in the field simply by reading trade magazines. Reading is no match for experience. But you will obtain vital information, and finding out as much as you can about your proposed field is key to entering the market with confidence. Knowledge is power, and you must be able to speak as though you were an authority. Adopting the persona of an authority in business is very helpful in launching any kind of new product or idea. For more information on market research and gathering information, see Chapter 3.

Idea Protection

Before you begin marketing an idea or even show it to anyone, make sure that you can protect your interest in it. You can get a patent, which may cost you $3,000 to $5,000 or so in legal fees. But you don't need to do the patenting before you begin to test the idea. There is no need to invest all that money up front. The government has now made it simpler for the average person to protect an idea. You can file a disclosure statement with the federal government documenting your claim that you were the first person with your idea.

A disclosure is not a patent, and it does not provide you with complete protection; however, it will protect your claim to the idea for two years, and for one year after the first public exposure of the product. So if you have a brand-new product that you want to bring into the market, it makes sense for you to file a disclosure document. You have one year from the point of first public exposure to actually file the patent. If you do this, you can find out whether the idea is going to work and whether or not you have a big winner on your hands before you invest all the money needed to get through the patent process. Make sure you enclose a disclosure document with any mailings you do on the product to manufacturers, reps, and the like. You need to be careful because you can easily lose an idea to copiers who may have more capital and distribution channels available than you do; they can take your idea and run with it before you have a chance to protect it yourself.

Idea Insurance

While idea protection vehicles such as a copyright, trademark, or patent provide you with some protection, they should be viewed as the first line of defense. In reality, much abuse of copyrights, trademarks, and patents takes place. Although these instruments are available for protection, it is up to you to prove any type of infringement of your intellectual property as well as the extent of the damages. This costs time and money. In fact, the Intellectual Property Law Association reports that the median cost of enforcing a patent is $396,000 and rising. So what do inventors in small businesses do to protect themselves beyond the scope of the patent? They can take out *patent abatement insurance*. While still rare with most insurers, patent abatement insurance provides patent holders with a safety net if they do have to challenge an infringement of their intellectual property. There is an annual premium for the policy, and if a claim is filed, there is a copayment, usually 25 percent of the total claim.

Breadboards, Models, and Prototypes

Once you have taken the initial steps to protect your idea, the next step is to determine whether or not the invention will work. To do this, you will need to first make a breadboard of the invention, then a model, and finally a prototype.

Jacquelyn Denalli, in her "Inventor's Circle" column for *Business Start-Ups*[1] magazine, offers the following definitions of a breadboard, model, and prototype:

- A *breadboard* is a rough construction of your invention that proves the idea works. The breadboard doesn't have to look good or even work well; it simply proves your idea can be reduced to practice. It may take several breadboards, each improving on the earlier one, before you are ready to build a model.
- A *model* is a representation of the product as it will be manufactured. The model demonstrates what your invention will do, but it is not always a precise duplicate of the finished product. In building your model, consider these issues: the item's sale price, materials, manufacturing costs, marketing details, safety factors, how it will be sold and distributed, and the profit margin. If you plan to license your invention to a manufacturer, you can often do so with a model.

[1] Jacquelyn Denalli, "Inventor's Circle—Terms of Invention," *Business Start-Ups* (November 1993), Entrepreneur Magazine Group.

- A *prototype* is an exact replica of the product as it will be manufactured, down to details such as color, graphics, packaging, and instructions. The cost for making a prototype or sample is usually much greater than the actual unit cost once the item is in full production. For example, a prototype might cost $500, though the product itself might retail for only $2 to $10 in the marketplace. But it's well worth the investment. First of all, you can make drawings or photographs of the sample to use in brochures, mailings, pamphlets, advertising, and so on. You can also use the prototype to show to potential buyers, whether manufacturers or buyers for department stores.

When you are ready to put together your prototype, get several bids from various manufacturing companies. Get prices for producing 1, 1,000, and 5,000 units. Make sure the bid you get includes tooling costs and specifies the terms the manufacturer will provide. At the same time, make sure you know what the delivery turnaround time will be, so that you can speak authoritatively with buyers. This will help you determine what your initial pricing structure is going to have to be and what kinds of quality discounts will be available.

When people hear the word prototype, they tend to assume that its purpose is to test the effectiveness of manufacturing or production methods. Although this is one motive for making a prototype, employing it in your marketing research is just as important to the ultimate success of your product. Nothing can replace the data obtained through the use of a prototype. Whether a product is as complex as a computer or as simple as a welding torch, market testing with a prototype will tell you how your potential buyers—and those are the folks who actually have to use what you sell—will react to your product.

Competition Analysis

Compare your product with similar competitive products on the market already. The most effective way to do this is to make a competition grid. Down the left side of a piece of paper, write the names of four or five products you think will be your competition. If the consumer did not buy your product, what product would he or she buy?

Across the top of the paper, list the main features and characteristics of each product including price, size, color, shape, and utility. Your matrix will make your analysis visually clear. Check off the competing products that have the features you have listed and include your own product as well. A glance at the competition grid puts everything into a logical, organized picture and will help you see where your product fits into the overall market.

Reevaluate Your Idea

Using your prototype, price estimates, and preliminary test-market data, test the market by selling a limited number of your products in a couple of stores or whatever other principal channel of distribution you have chosen. Make sure the stores don't give your new product any unusual treatment or attention, so that it will be a fair test of your product against competitors or as an entirely new development. Based on its success or failure in this experiment, modify your product to make it better and more attractive to the consumer. Do not give up if your invention does not do as well as you expected; it may simply need some solid advertising to increase its sales.

Consult the Experts

Another important consideration in developing your test marketing program is the industry expert. There are two sides to this coin. For example, if you're about to introduce a new welding torch for sale in the auto aftermarket, it is a very good idea to have welders try the product out. They will give you feedback about how well the product works—how well it fulfills the needs for a properly operational torch that you just can't get from any other source.

In addition to the actual end user, you should also consider whether you need the services of a marketing expert or firm. The average rate for market research provided by such a firm is built around an hourly rate for personnel, plus a 50 to 60 percent override or surcharge for the company. You will also be billed for travel and expenses. The rate and override can vary, depending on the competition and whether you are in a small town or a large metro area. Contact the Marketing Research Association for referrals on market research firms in your area (see Resources for contact information).

If you do not want to absorb the expense of retaining either a consultant or a market-research firm, another viable alternative is to contact the marketing department of your local college or university, preferably one with a strong program on small business or entrepreneurship, or one that houses a Small Business Development Center. Visit the dean of the business school and investigate the possibility of having the business school's students do your testing—for a nominal to reasonable cost, (or perhaps even without charge if they do it for course credit). This type of real-world work would be especially interesting for students involved in an entrepreneurship program. For instance, the students may be able to perform on-site survey work. They (or you with their help) can tabulate the results and perform any computations or analyses you deem necessary.

You may also want to consult with invention marketing companies. Not only will such companies help with the initial test marketing if they feel the product or service has potential, will also help with the actual marketing activities once the business is an ongoing concern. Most invention marketing firms operate on either a flat-fee or a fee-plus-commission basis. If at all possible, negotiate for a flat-fee basis. Be careful when considering an invention marketing company. You should research it as you would any prospective business relationship. A good idea is to contact the Inventors Awareness Group (IAG) in West Springfield, Massachusetts. The IAG can provide you with free materials such as the pamphlet *Invention . . . Truth or Consequences* that explains how to verify an invention marketing company's credibility. In addition, the Federal Trade Commission (FTC), in response to hundreds of complaints about invention promotion firms, has published the brochure *Facts for Consumers: Invention Promotion Firms.*

In addition to using the preceding resources, you should do the following:

- Ask early about the total cost of the services, and be cautious if it is a percentage of royalties.
- Ask for a list of products the company has placed on the market to determine its success rate—how many people have made more money than they have paid. If the business says this information is confidential, consider this a red flag.
- Get the rejection rate. Legitimate companies tend to reject 90 out of every 100 ideas that come their way.
- When you meet with a company representative, bring an objective listener with you, who isn't necessarily sold on your idea.
- Determine the expertise of the people providing the services.
- Talk with other inventors the broker has helped.
- Check to see whether the company has a registered patent attorney on its staff and whether this attorney is going to file you patent.
- Find out if any lawsuits have been filed against them.
- Comparison shop.
- Check your local consumer protection agency and invention trade groups to see if any complaints have been made against the company.

A good alternative to an idea marketing firm is a business incubator. There are approximately 500 business incubators nationwide according to the National Business Incubation Association. The goal of most business incubators is to help a business grow from an idea to a fully functioning and competitive firm. Business incubation programs are often sponsored by private companies and public institutions such as colleges and universities.

Incubators give business owners numerous benefits. They often provide office and manufacturing space at well below market rates, and the incubator staff is on hand for advice and much-needed expertise in developing business and marketing plans as well as helping to meet financing requirements to fund fledgling businesses. Companies typically spend an average of two years in a business incubator, during which time they often share telephone, secretarial, office and production equipment expenses with other start-up companies to cut their overhead and operational costs.

Be careful. Not all business incubators are alike, so if you have a specialized idea for a business, try to find the incubator that best suits your individual requirements. For instance, there are two unique incubators in Richmond, Virginia, one tailored for biomedical firms and another targeted toward accounting and consulting companies.

If you are interesting in finding an incubator, contact your nearest SBA office. You may also want to call your area economic development agency. Also, as mentioned earlier, educational institutions often sponsor incubators. Call the information offices of local community colleges and universities and find out if they have such a program.

Should you wish to enter an incubation program, be prepared to submit a well-thought-out business plan. The plan will be reviewed by a screening committee to determine whether or not you meet the criteria for admission. Incubators screen potential businesses because their space, equipment, and finances are limited; therefore, they want to commit those resources to businesses with the best possible chance for success.

RESOURCES

Entrepreneurs who want an objective eye to give their ideas or products the once-over can find plenty of help in the private sector and academic arena. The following resources can assist you with everything from developing and protecting your idea to securing financing and finding manufacturers.

Center for Business Innovation, 4747 Troost Avenue, Kansas City, MO 64110, 816-561-8567

Innovation Center, 5233 MacArthur Boulevard NW, Washington, DC 20016, 202-636-4332

Minnesota Inventors Congress, 1030 East Bridge Street, Redwood Falls, MN 56283, 507-673-2344

National Project Innovation, 5047 29th Avenue South, Minneapolis, MN 55417, 612-721-4247

Southern California Technology Executives Network, 17772 East 17th Street, Suite 200, Tustin, CA 92680, 714-573-7800

Government Agencies

National Technical Information Service, United States Department of Commerce, Springfield, Virginia 22151, 703-487-4600

Office of Technology Utilization, Department of Energy, 1000 Independence Avenue SW, Washington, DC 20585, 202-586-5388

United States Patent and Trademark Office, 2011 Crystal Drive, Arlington, VA 22202, 703-305-8341; Fax 703-308-5258 Public Affairs Office)

United States Printing Office, Dept. 33, Washington, DC 20402, 202-783-3238 (Superintendent of Documents)

United States Small Business Administration, 1441 L Street NW, Washington, DC 20416, 202-653-6565; SBA Answer Deck 800-827-5722 (see also On-Line Services)

Associations

American Association of Inventors, 2309 State, Sagimaw, MI 48602, 517-799-8208

American Association for Public Opinion Research, 19 Chamber Street, Post Office Box 17, Princeton, NJ 08542, 609-924-8670

American Marketing Association, 250 South Wacker Drive, Suite 200, Chicago, IL 60606, 312-648-0536

American Society of Inventors, 1 Meridan Plaza, Suite 900, Philadelphia, PA 19102, 215-546-6601

International Internet Association (IIA), 2020 Pennsylvania Avenue NW, Suite 852, Washington, DC 20006, 202-387-5445

International Licensing Industry Merchandiser's Association, 350 Fifth Avenue, Suite 6210, New York, NY 10118, 212-244-1944

Invention Marketing Institute, 345 West Cypress Street, Glendale, CA 91204, 818-246-6540

Inventor's Awareness Group, 171 Interstate Drive, Suite 6, West Springfield, MA 01089-4533, 413-739-3938.

Marketing Research Association, 2189 Silas Deane Highway, Rocky Hill, CT 06067, 203-257-4008

Marketing Science Institute, 1000 Massachusetts Avenue, Cambridge, MA 02138, 617-491-2060

National Business Incubation Association, One President Street, Athens, OH 45701, 614-593-4331

National Congress of Inventor Organizations, 727 North 600 West, Logan, Utah 84321, 801-753-0888

National Inventors Foundation, 345 West Cypress Street, Glendale, CA 91204, 818-246-6540

On-Line Services

CD Plus Technologies (formerly BRS Information Technologies), 333 Seventh Avenue, 4th Floor, New York, NY 10001, 800-955-0906

CompuServe, 5000 Arlington Centre Boulevard, Columbus, OH 43220, 614-457-8600; 800-336-3330; 800-848-8199; 800-848-8990

Delphi, General Videotex Corp., 1030 Massachusetts Avenue, Cambridge, MA 02138, 800-544-4005

DIALOG Information Services, Inc., Marketing Dept., 3450 Hillview Avenue, Palo Alto, CA 94304, 415-858-3785; 800-334-2564

Dow Jones News/Retrieval Service, P.O. Box 300, Princeton, NJ 08543-0300, 609-452-1511

GEnie, General Electric Information Services, P.O. Box 6403, 401 North Washington Street, Rockville, MD 20850, 800-638-9636

NewsNet, 945 Haverford Road, Bryn Mawr, PA 19010, 610-527-8030; 800-345-1301

NEXIS, Mead Data Central, P.O. Box 933, Dayton, OH 45401, 800-543-6862

SBA Online (United States Small Business Administration Electronic On-Line Service-202-205-6400 (e-phone Assistance and General Information); 202-401-9600 (Direct Dial Access); 800-697-4636 (800-Number Access); 900-463-4636 (900 Service Access)

The Source, 5000 Arlington Center Boulevard, Columbus, OH 43220, 614-457-8600; 800-336-3330; 800-848-8199; 800-848-8990

VU/TEXT Information Services, Inc., 325 Chestnut Street, Suite 1300, Philadelphia, PA 19106, 215-574-4400; 800-258-8080

CD-ROM Databases

DIALOG Information Services, Inc., 3450 Hillview Avenue, Palo Alto, CA 94304, 415-858-3785; 800-334-2564

Grolier Electronic Publishing, Inc., Old Sherman Turnpike, Danbury, CT 06816, 800-955-9877; 203-797-3500

H.W. Wilson Company, 950 University Avenue, Bronx, NY 10452, 800-367-6770; in New York, 800-462-6060

Lotus Information Services, Lotus Development Corporation, 55 Cambridge Parkway, Cambridge, MA 02142, 617-577-8500

OCLC, Incorporated, 6565 Frantz Road, Dublin, OH 43017, 614-764-6000

PsycINFO, American Psychological Association, 1400 North Uhle Street, Arlington, VA 22201, 703-247-7829; 800-336-4980

Document Delivery Services

FIND/SVP, 625 Sixth Avenue, New York, NY 10011, 212-645-4500

Information on Demand, Inc., 2030 Addison Street, Suite 400, Berkeley, CA 94704, 415-841-1145

The Information Store, 140 Second Street, Third Floor, San Francisco, CA 94105, 415-543-4636

NASA Industrial Application Center (NIAC), 3716 South Hope Street, Suite 200, Los Angeles, CA 90007, 213-743-6132

Magazines and Newspapers

Business Opportunities Journal, 1050 Rosecrans Street, P.O. Box 60762, San Diego, CA 92106-3053, 619-223-5661

Kiplinger's Personal Finance Magazine, 1729 H Street NW, Washington, DC 20006-3904, 202-887-6400

Los Angeles Times, Times Mirror Square, Los Angeles, CA 90053, 213-237-5000

Newslink, Federal Laboratory Consortium Administrator, DelaBarre & Associates Inc., P.O. Box 545, Sequim, WA 98382, 206-683-1828

New York Times, 229 West 43rd Street, New York, NY 10036-3959, 212-556-1234

Opportunity, 73 Spring Street, Suite 303, New York, NY 10012, 212-925-3180

Tradeshow Week, 12233 W. Olympic Boulevard, Suite 236, Los Angeles, CA 90403-9956, 310-826-5696

The Wall Street Journal—Eastern Edition, 200 Liberty Street, New York, NY 10281, 212-416-2000

The Wall Street Journal—Midwest Edition, 1 South Wacker Drive, Suite 2100, Chicago, IL 60606-3388, 312-750-4100

The Wall Street Journal—Southwest Edition, 1233 Regal Row, Dallas, TX 75247-3613, 214-631-7250

The Wall Street Journal—Western Edition, 201 California Street, Suite 1350, San Francisco, CA 94111, 415-986-6886

Directories

Bacon's Publicity Checker, Bacon's Information, Inc., 332 S. Michigan Avenue, Chicago, IL 60604, 800-972-9252

Encyclopedia of Associations, Gale Research, Inc., 835 Penobscot Bldg., Detroit, MI 48226, 313-961-2242

The *1994 CRADA Handbook,* Technology Publishing Group, P.O. Box 5692, Washington, DC 20016-5692, 202-966-9610

The *Standard Rate and Data Service Directory,* 3004 Glenview Road, Wilemette, IL 60091, 800-851-7737

Tradeshow Week Data Book, 12233 W. Olympic Boulevard, Suite 236, Los Angeles, CA 90403-9956, 310-826-5696

Regional Technology Transfer Centers

Far West (WA, OR, CA, AL, HI, NV, AZ and ID), 3716 S. Hope Street, Suite 200, Los Angeles, CA 90007, 213-743-6132

Mid-Atlantic (PA, WV, VA, DE, MD and Washington, DC), University of Pittsburgh, 823 William Pitt Union, Pittsburgh, PA 15260, 412-648-7000

Mid-Continental (MT, ND, SD, WY, NE, CO, UT, NM, TX, KS, OK, MO, AK and IA), State Headquarters Building, 301 Tarrow, College Station, TX 77843-8000, 409-845-8762

Midwest (OH, IN, IL, WI, MI and MN) Great Lakes Industrial Center, 25000 Great Northern Corporate Center, Suite 450, Cleveland, OH 44070, 216-734-0094

Northeast (NY, NJ and New England states), 100 N. Drive, Westborough, MA 01581, 508-870-0042

Southeast (KY, TN, NC, SC, GA, AL, MS, FL and LA), University of Florida College of Engineering, Progress Center, Box 24, Alachue, FL 32615; in FL, 800-354-4832; outside FL, 800-225-0308

3

Market Research

I t's often been said that "research is the cornerstone of any successful business venture," and for good reason. Thorough market research provides an array of information about potential and existing customers, competition, and the industry in general. It allows the entrepreneur to determine the overall feasibility of a business before committing a substantial investment in the venture. Failure to conduct market research is like driving a car with a dirty window. You may not see what is ahead of you until it is too late.

The purpose of market research is to provide relevant data that will help solve marketing problems a business will encounter. This is absolutely necessary in the start-up phase. Conducting thorough market surveys is the foundation of any successful business. In fact, strategies such as market segmentation (identifying specific segments within a market) and product differentiation (creating an identity for your product or service that separates it from your competitors') would be impossible to develop without market research.

According to William A. Cohen in his book, *The Entrepreneur and Small Business Problem Solver*,[1] the marketing research process can be broken down into specific stages:

1. Determine the problems that must be solved.
2. Do those problems require research in order to solve them?
3. List the goals and objectives you will achieve through market research.
4. Identify the type of data that you need to gather to meet those goals.
5. Plan the method that you will use to acquire the desired information.
6. Define the sample audience that will best provide you with the data required.
7. Conduct your market research and gather the information.

[1] William A. Cohen, *The Entrepreneur and Small Business Problem Solver*, 2nd ed. (New York: John Wiley & Sons, 1990).

8. Analyze the data. Market research information is usually analyzed on a percentage basis so that you can further segment markets according to viability.
9. Finally, develop conclusions based on the information gathered and determine a course of action.

GATHERING INFORMATION

There are four methods generally used to gather market research: the *historical* method, the *observational* method, the *experimental* method, and the *survey* method. Under the historical method, past data are studied to define current market conditions. With the observational method, current market data are studied to predict future conditions. Using appropriately controlled tests, the experimental method seeks to discover if specific marketing activities will be effective. With the survey method, information is gathered concerning the defined market to determine the feasibility of business entry. The survey method is by far the most popular method.

Whether you are conducting market research using the historical, experimental, observational, or survey method, you'll be gathering two types of data.

1. Primary information. Research that you will compile yourself or hire someone to gather for you.
2. Secondary information. Research that is already compiled and organized for you. Examples of secondary information are reports and studies by government agencies, trade associations, or other businesses within your industry. Most of the research you gather will be secondary.

Primary Research

When conducting primary research, you can gather two basic types of information: *exploratory* and *specific*. Exploratory research is open-ended in nature, helps you define a specific problem, and usually involves detailed, unstructured interviews in which lengthy answers are solicited from a small group of respondents. Specific research, on the other hand, is precise in scope and is used to solve a problem that exploratory research has identified. Interviews are structured and formal in approach. Of the two, specific research is the more expensive. Figure 3.1 shows a sample cost analysis form for different research methods.

When conducting primary research using your own resources, you must first decide how you will question your target group of individuals. There are three avenues you can take: direct mail, telemarketing, or personal interviews.

If you choose a direct-mail questionnaire, the following guidelines will increase your response rate:

• Make sure your questions are short and to the point.
• Make sure questionnaires are addressed to specific individuals and are of interest to the respondent.

Figure 3.1   Cost Analysis of Primary Research Methods

MAIL SURVEYS   COST

Printing questionnaires		
Envelopes		
Postage for mailing questionnaire and return postage		
Incentives for questionnaire response		
Staff time and cost for analysis and presentation of results		
Independent researcher cost, if any		
Other costs—Itemize		
TOTAL MAIL SURVEY COSTS		

PHONE SURVEYS   COST

Preparation of the questionnaire		
Interviewer's fee		
Phone charges		
Staff time and cost for analysis and presentation of results		
Independent researcher cost, if any		
Other costs—Itemize		
TOTAL PHONE SURVEY COSTS		

PERSONAL INTERVIEWS   COST

Printing of questionnaires and prompt cards		
Interviewer's fee and expenses		
Incentives for questionnaire response		
Staff time and cost for analysis and presentation of results		
Independent researcher cost, if any		
Other costs—Itemize		
TOTAL PERSONAL INTERVIEWS COSTS		

GROUP DISCUSSIONS   COST

Interviewer's fee and expenses in recruiting and assembling the groups		
Renting the conference room or other facility and cost of recording media such as tapes, if used		
Incentives for group participation		
Staff time and cost for analysis and presentation of results		
Independent researcher cost, if any		
Other costs—Itemize		
TOTAL GROUP DISCUSSION COSTS		

- Limit the questionnaire's length to two pages.
- Enclose a professionally prepared cover letter that adequately explains what you need.
- Send a reminder about two weeks after the initial mailing. Include a postage-paid self-addressed envelope. Postage-paid envelopes are available through the post office and use a special-reply permit indicia.

Unfortunately, even with the preceding tactics, mail response is always low, sometimes less than 5 percent.

Phone surveys are generally the most cost-effective. Following are some phone survey guidelines:

- At the beginning of the conversation, your interviewer should confirm the name of the respondent if calling a home, or give the appropriate name to the switchboard operator if calling a business.
- Avoid pauses, as respondent interest can quickly drop.
- Make sure that a follow-up call is possible if you require additional information.
- Make sure that interviewers do not divulge details about the poll until they reach the respondent.

As mentioned, phone interviews are cost-effective, but speed is another big advantage. Some of the more experienced interviewers can get through up to 10 interviews an hour (however, speed for speed's sake is not the goal of any of these surveys). A rate of five to six interviews per hour is more typical. Phone interviews also can cover a wide geographic range relatively inexpensively. Phone costs can be reduced by taking advantage of cheaper rates during certain hours.

One of the most effective forms of marketing research is the face-to-face or personal interview. There are two main types of personal interviews:

1. **The group survey.** Used mostly by big business, group interviews can be useful brainstorming tools for product modification, new product ideas, buying preferences, and purchasing decisions among certain populations.

2. **The depth interview.** In these one-on-one interviews, the interviewer is guided by a small checklist and basic common sense. Depth interviews are either focused or nondirective. Nondirective interviews encourage respondents to address certain topics with minimal questioning. The respondent, in essence, leads the interview. The focused interview, on the other hand, is based on a preset checklist. From this, however, the choice and timing of questions are left to the interviewer, depending on how the interview goes.

When considering which type of survey to use, keep the following cost factors in mind:

- **Mail.** Costs here include the printing of questionnaires, envelopes, postage, the cover letter, time taken in the analysis and presentation, the cost of researcher time, and any incentives used.

- **Telephone.** The main costs are the interviewer's fee, phone charges, preparation of the questionnaire, cost of researcher time, in addition to the analysis and presentation.
- **Personal interviews.** Costs include the printing of questionnaires and prompt cards if needed, the incentives used, the interviewer's fee and expenses, cost of researcher time, and analysis and presentation.
- **Group discussions.** Your main costs are the interviewer's fee and expenses in recruiting and assembling the groups, renting the conference room or other facility, researcher time, any incentives used, analysis and presentation, and the cost of recording media such as tapes, if used.

Secondary Research

Secondary research uses outside information assembled by government agencies, industry and trade associations, labor unions, media sources, chambers of commerce, and so on; it is usually published in pamphlets, newsletters, trade and other magazines, and newspapers. It's termed secondary data because the information has been gathered by another, or secondary, source. The benefits of this are obvious—time and money are saved because you don't have to develop survey methods or do the interviewing.

Secondary sources are divided into three main categories:

1. **Public.** Public sources are the most economical, as they're usually free, and can offer a lot of good information. These sources are typically governmental departments, business departments of public libraries, and so on.
2. **Commercial.** Commercial sources are equally valuable, but usually involve cost factors such as subscription and association fees. Commercial sources typically consist of research and trade associations such as Dun & Bradstreet and Robert Morris & Associates, banks and other financial institutions, and publicly traded corporations.
3. **Educational.** Educational institutions are frequently overlooked as viable information sources, and yet more research is conducted in colleges, universities, and polytechnic institutes than virtually any sector of the business community.

Government statistics are among the most plentiful and wide-ranging public sources. An excellent resource is the Census Bureau's helpful *Hidden Treasures—Census Bureau Data and Where to Find It!* This book includes information on where to find federal and state information compiled by the Census Bureau. Other helpful government publications include:

- **State and Metropolitan Area Data Book.** Statistical snapshots of metropolitan areas, central cities, and counties.
- **Statistical Abstract of the United States.** Over 1,000 pages of statistical information from both government and private sources.

- **Case Studies in Using Data for Better Business Decisions.** Income and age statistics for the United States by region.
- **U.S. Industrial Outlook.** Growth statistics of 200 industries and five-year forecasts for each.

Do not neglect to contact specific government agencies such as the Small Business Administration (SBA). They sponsor several helpful programs like SCORE (Service Corps of Retired Executives) and Small Business Development Centers (SBDCs). Call your local SBA field office to find out how to contact the local SCORE chapter and where the nearest SBDCs are to you. The counselors at SCORE can provide you with free consultation on what type of research you need to gather and where you can go to obtain the information. They may also be able to suggest other means of gathering the information from primary sources. Most SBDCs are located at local colleges. They have counselors on hand to help you and usually maintain an extensive business library containing a great deal of secondary sources for you to review.

Another good government source is the Department of Commerce. They not only publish helpful books like the *U.S. Industrial Outlook,* but also produce an array of products with information about domestic industries as well as statistical information on foreign markets through its International Trade Administration (ITA) branch.

One of the best public sources is the business section of your public library. The services provided vary from city to city but usually include a wide range of government and market statistics; a large collection of directories with information on domestic and foreign businesses; and a wide selection of magazines, newspapers, and newsletters.

Almost every county government publishes population density and distribution figures in accessible *census tracts.* These will show you the number of people living in specific areas, such as precincts, water districts, or even 10-block neighborhoods. Some counties publish reports that show the population 10 years ago, 5 years ago, and currently, thus indicating population trends.

Other public sources include city chambers of commerce or business development departments, which encourage new businesses in their communities. They will supply you (usually for free) with information on population trends, community income characteristics, payrolls, industrial development, and so on.

Banks are also an important public source of information. Most major banks offer advisory services to businesspeople on finance-related problems. Bank-generated research is also sometimes available. Services are usually free to existing customers.

Among the best commercial sources of information are research and trade associations. Information gathered by trade associations is usually confined to a certain industry and available only to association members, with a membership fee frequently required. However, the research gathered by the larger associations is usually thorough, accurate, and worth the cost of membership. Two excellent resources to help you locate a trade association that reports on the business you are researching include:

- *Encyclopedia of Associations* published by Gale Research.
- *Business Information Sources* by Lorna M. Daniels and published by the University of California Press.

Local newspapers, journals, magazines, and radio and television stations are among the most useful of all commercial information outlets. Not only do they maintain profiles of their audiences outlining key characteristics such as income, age, amount of disposable income, and types of products and services purchased, but many also have information about economic trends in the local area that would be significant to your business. Contact the sales departments of these businesses and let them know you are putting together a marketing plan for a new product and need information regarding rates and audience demographics. This information will help you determine the financial situation of your potential customers and allow you to start piecing together your advertising strategy.

One of the best media sources is *The Wall Street Journal,* whose parent company offers additional information services such as Dow Jones News/Retrieval. As the nation's leading economic monitor, *The Wall Street Journal* offers broadbased domestic information that may impact your business such as new tax developments, overviews of specific industries, trends in technology, and new marketing strategies. *The Wall Street Journal* also has a section specifically devoted to international trade.

Dun & Bradstreet is another commercial source of market research that offers an abundance of information including:

- **State Sales Guides.** A state-by-state compilation that lists the estimated financial conditional and D&B credit rating of companies within a particular state.
- **D&B's Regional Business Directories.** A listing of company profiles by region. Company profiles include a company description, telephone number, address, when the company was started, sales volume, number of employees, parent company, and whether or not it is a public company.
- **D&B's Census of American Business.** This directory lets you track the locations of specific businesses and the impact of their payroll on a specific region.

On-line services are another commercial source for many of the preceding resources. Several consumer on-line services can be subscribed to for a modest fee of under $20 a month offering access to many business databases. For instance, CompuServe provides access to several databases that contain government statistics as well as Dun & Bradstreet research. Other popular on-line services include Prodigy, America Online, Dialog, and GEnie.

Educational institutions are prolific sources of research. Educational institutions conduct research in various ways, ranging from faculty-based projects often published under professors' bylines, to student projects, theses, and assignments. You may also be able to enlist of the aid of students involved in business classes, especially if they are enrolled in an entrepreneurship program. This can be an excellent way of generating research at little or no cost, utilizing students who welcome the professional experience either as interns or for special credit. Contact the university administration departments and marketing/management-studies departments for further information. University libraries are additional sources of research.

CUSTOMER RESEARCH

Now that you have a good idea of the type of research tools available, you need to start focusing on specific areas. When performing market research, you must first concentrate on defining your customer base. By determining the characteristics of the customer base, you will narrow your scope of research when analyzing the competition as well as the industry in general.

A thorough customer analysis is usually broken down into areas: *segmentation* and *customer requirements*. Through identifying profitable customer segments and analyzing their requirements, you'll be able to uncover specific information about the customer base of the product or service you are marketing.

Segmentation

First, you must define the market segment(s) you intend to target. You can choose among numerous segmentation factors, but the most common denominators used by professional planners are *customer attributes, geographic zones,* and *product factors.*

Customer attributes refer to market segments associated with the composition of the product or service's user base. These segmentation factors often include:

- Lifestyle.
- Social class.
- Sex.
- Age.
- Income level.
- Business organization.
- Company size.
- Annual sales.

Customer attributes focus on demographics such as lifestyle, social class, sex, age, and income level to define any specific segments of the market that are sizable but might be overlooked. For instance, cosmetics is traditionally a female dominated market, but many such companies actively target the male segment to boost sales.

You can also use customer attributes to divide the market by factors such as business organization segments, which are more concerned with specific operations, their size, and amount of sales. This segmentation strategy is especially useful for companies that primarily target business through their marketing strategies.

Geographic segments would divide the market into regions as:

- International markets.
- National reach.
- Regional zones.
- Community districts.

Product factors, on the other hand, concentrate on the product itself and will include the following segmentation factors:

- **Usage.** Revolves around the frequency of product use. For example, airlines actively target frequent flyers by providing them with incentives such as free trips and discounts on rates, if they log enough air miles with a particular airline.
- **Type of benefits.** Concentrates on the needs that are fulfilled through the purchase of the product or services. The benefits derived from the product or service are the primary factors that motivate a customer to buy. For instance, a benefit may be the speed of a specific personal computer or the promise of weight loss.
- **Pricing sensitivity.** Centers on product price as the main purchasing criterion. For instance, economy hotels and motels appeal to a more price-conscious market than do luxury hotels.
- **Major competitors.** Defines market segments by competitor. In the personal computer market, customers can be segmented by whether they have purchased an Apple Macintosh or a product of any one of the IBM-compatible manufacturers such as AST, ALR, Dell, or Gateway.
- **Utilization.** Focuses on what the customer uses the product or service for. Car buyers can be segmented by usage. There are buyers of commuter vehicles, off-road vehicles, luxury vehicles, and so on.
- **Brand loyalty.** Identifies the number of users committed to a particular product. Many customers are very loyal to a specific brand of product and brand loyalty segment factors detail these users. For instance, there are customers that prefer Levi's over all other types of jeans.

When developing a marketing strategy, you will have to decide what market segments you will use to define the scope of your market and that they all work together toward a common goal of determining the total potential market of your product or service. For instance, if you decide to use a combination of specific customer attributes and geographic zones to define the market, your segmentation factors might focus on individuals who meet a specific age, income level, and lifestyle in a particular geographic zone (e.g., the San Francisco bay area).

You can continue to use additional segmentation factors to further define your marketing strategy. The more specific you are regarding the market you wish to reach, the more targeted your market strategy and message will be.

Customer Requirements

Once you have identified customer segments, the next step in gathering customer research is to determine the customer requirements for a particular product or service. To find out what motivates people to buy a particular product, use your own past experience to guide you if you have ever purchased the particular product you are researching. You should also prepare a questionnaire that you can mail to consumers, ask over the phone, or complete through a personal interview. The questionnaire should deal with the attributes of your product and how they would affect the purchase decision. You can also include tradeoff questions that ask customers if they would give up one benefit to gain another. This way you can determine just which factors are more important than others.

When creating a questionnaire for products that may be unique or unfamiliar, you may have to use an existing similar item or a well-known product as a model. This way, you can determine the factors motivating sales for that particular product and apply that information to your new product. For instance, you may be developing an electric car. Since there are very few electric cars on the market, most consumers won't have any experience purchasing these vehicles, yet you still need to know what would motivate them to buy the electric car. In this instance, you could use the traditional internal-combustion automobile as the basis for your questionnaire. By understanding what motivates customers to buy a traditional car, you can then apply that knowledge toward creating a more marketable electric car.

You can also use your motivation questionnaire to determine features of the product or service the customer feels would aid in the purchase decision. This can be done by listing all the potential problems of the product and asking your survey audience to rate them according to level of importance they attach to each problem. Or you can turn that scenario around by conducting a benefit structure analysis instead. In the questionnaire, you would ask the users to point out the benefits of the product and rate them in terms of importance.

RESEARCHING THE COMPETITION

Researching your competition will provide you with a clear picture of potential threats, opportunities, and strategic questions developed from your competitors' current strategies, weaknesses, and strengths.

The first step in researching your competitors is to identify them. There are two basic ways to identify competitors:

1. **Customer groupings.** Competitors are grouped by how strongly they contend for the buyer's dollar.
2. **Strategic groupings.** Competitors are grouped based on their competitive strategy.

Customer Groups

Using the customer grouping method of identifying competitors, you would group competitors according to how intensely they compete with you for a share of the customer's dollar. The most common method is to divide competitors into three core groups:

- **Direct competitors.** Those businesses that have similar assets and skills and are the most aggressive in their competition for a share of the customer's dollar. For example, McDonald's competes directly against other fast-food chains such as Burger King, and Wendy's.
- **Secondary competitors.** Those businesses that share some common assets and skills but do not compete as aggressively for a share of the customer's dollar. In the case of McDonald's, secondary competitors might consist of sit-down gourmet hamburger restaurants.
- **Indirect competitors.** Those businesses that are not in the direct sphere of competition for a share of the customer's dollar but are still applicable. Again, using McDonald's as an example, indirect competition might be any other food-service establishment that competes on the same price scale as McDonald's. This would refer to cafes, pizzerias, and so on.

Usually, the most in-depth research should be focused on your direct competition for the buyer's dollar. Businesses that produce very little competition should receive less scrutiny.

To determine the intensity of competition within the industry, you can send out a questionnaire to customers of the product you are proposing to market. For instance, if you are compiling research for a lingerie boutique, you would want to send a questionnaire to a suitable sampling of previous purchasers of lingerie within the targeted geographic area. You can rent a list of prospects from a list broker (names of list brokers can be found in the business-to-business yellow pages under "Mailing Lists").

In the questionnaire, ask a series of *brand loyalty questions* such as which brand the consumer currently buys. Has the person tried other brands? If so, which brands? Ask respondents to rank the different brands of products according to preference. The idea behind this type of questionnaire is to help measure the competition from a customer's point of view. By doing so, you can identify groupings from a conceptual as well as practical angle.

Strategic Groups

Grouping competitors by strategies is far different from grouping them by customer attitude. The strategic group concept relies heavily on classifying

competitors by similar strategies that are pursued over time, uniform characteristics, or similar assets and skills. Similar strategies include:

- The type of advertising and promotion pursued and the size of the budget allocated.
- The type of sales tactics such as direct response or personal sales.
- The type of distribution channels utilized.
- The type of pricing strategy.

Typical uniform characteristics are:

- Size of business or number of employees.
- Amount of sales.
- Amount of market share.

Similar assets and skills would refer to:

- Strategic partnerships with key suppliers.
- A strong customer service program.
- Ownership of intellectual property.
- Goodwill among customers.

The Information Stage

Whether you are using customer groups or strategic groups, you will have to
gather information on your competition. Many companies communicate extensively with their suppliers, customers, distributors, government legislators
and regulators, and security analysts and stockholders if they are selling stock.
Some of this information will be on public record, but other data (e.g. information about suppliers) won't be. While your competitors' suppliers will most
likely not reveal contract terms or any other confidential facts, you can find
out their pricing structure and the type of equipment or supplies your competitors may use. Some of the best information you can gather, however, will
come directly from your competitors. Contact your competitors directly and
ask them if they'll spend a few minutes over the phone to talk about their business. Although not every competitor will talk to you, those who do often provide a great deal of input.

When talking to operators already in business, start by asking general questions about their company—when they started, how much capital they started
with, their growth over the years. Once you have broken the ice with these casual background inquiries, move toward more precise questions such as the
suppliers they use, the type of customers they target, the pricing strategy they
utilize, gross sales, and so on. The idea is to gather as much information as possible directly from your competitors. You may have to conduct these interviews
in several short sessions to maintain the goodwill of the respondent business
owner.

Contacting any one of these sources may provide you with valuable data
about your competitors' proposed objectives. You should also subscribe to all

relevant magazines to evaluate your competitor's ads, which usually indicate company objectives through their body copy. Trade shows are another good source of information. Many of your competitors will be displaying their products and may discuss their objectives in the industry.

RESEARCHING THE INDUSTRY

Make sure your research of the industry is focused and purposeful. You do not need to tear apart the entire industry to obtain the facts you need. As previously mentioned, by following the steps for conducting market research, you can pinpoint specific areas you need to concentrate on to achieve your goals and objectives.

Investigating the industry supplies additional data for determining its attractiveness and profit potential. In addition, it will help you identify the industry's key success factors, trends, threats, and opportunities along with their associated assets and skills.

Before you can begin researching the industry, you first need to define its boundaries, which can be formed from your customer and competition research. You can either confine your boundaries to the most relevant competitors and their products or extend them to include competitors and products that compete less intensely against you. The decision on boundaries is usually dictated by the complexion of the industry and the amount of competition from secondary competitor groups. For instance, if you were researching the frozen yogurt industry, the boundaries could include total frozen yogurt sales, or it could be broadened to include indirect competitors such as ice cream stores that sell yogurt.

In addition to researching the industry as a whole, you should also research critical market segments. When researching the industry, whether as a whole or as a segment, David A. Aaker, in his book *Developing Business Strategies*[2] identifies the following topics where you will generally need to compile information.

- Actual and potential size of the industry.
- Industry growth prospects.
- Structure of the industry.
- Cost patterns.
- Distribution channels.
- Trends and developments within the industry.
- Key industry assets and skills.

[2] David A. Aaker, *Developing Business Strategies,* 2nd ed. (New York: John Wiley & Sons, 1988).

Actual and Potential Size

The actual and potential size of the industry is important not only to help evaluate investment decisions but also to give you an overview of the market share of each of your competitors.

Actual industry size can be determined by referring to secondary research sources such as the Census Bureau and Department of Commerce, as well as trade associations involved in that particular industry. These sources often provide market information, charting sales by product line, growth, geographic markets, and major players in the industry.

To gauge the potential size of the industry, you will have to look closely at gaps within the industry. Such gaps may be in the product line, distribution, usage, competitiveness or any number of areas. Through your research of your customers, competitors, and the industry, you are going to have to spot those gaps.

Forecasting Growth

To forecast industry growth, it is helpful to set up several growth models and examine what has to happen for each to occur. Most projections involve a minimum of two models. You can set up your models by writing down two different scenarios, then listing the events that would have to take place for that scenario to develop. The model with the most realistic past, present, and future variables would be the most attractive in terms of growth.

As an example, using a historical analysis of industry activity, you project that the industry will grow 15 percent during the upcoming year. Using that 15 percent as a benchmark, you come up with two projections for your business— one is a conservative projection of 3 percent and the other is slightly more aggressive at 6 percent. Based on these projections, you can determine the strategies you will need to implement in generating this growth. Will you need to increase your advertising budget? Will you need to hire additional sales personnel? Will you increase your direct response marketing efforts? You need to map out just what you will need to do as a business to accomplish the growth you've projected.

The idea behind the growth models is to develop an idea of when the turning points in growth will occur and what will cause them to happen. Gathering data on leading indicators will provide gauges that you can use to chart growth. This will most likely be industry sales, industry segment sales, demographic data, and historical precedence.

Forecasts for new industries can be developed from examples provided by analogous industries. For instance, Digital Audio Tape (DAT) technology might be able to use cassette tape technology as an example for sales forecasts. If you were concentrating on the actual players, you could chart the product life cycle of cassette tape players and develop industry growth forecasts based on that example.

Industry Structure

A study of the industry structure will reveal just how attractive the industry is for a return on long-term investment. The evaluation of the industry structure is built around five components:

1. **Competition between current firms.** Determine the number of competitors in the industry, their comparative size, product lines, strategies, fixed costs, and commitment to the industry. Much of this information can be gathered during your research on the competition.
2. **Threat of competition from potential entrants.** Ascertain the size and characteristics of the industry's entry barriers. For instance, if the cost to establish shelf space through retail distribution avenues is too costly, that barrier would prevent many small food product manufacturers from gaining even a small foothold in that industry. If the entry barriers are too formidable, many potentially competitive companies may consider investment into the industry undesirable in light of the projected return on their money.
3. **Threat of competition from alternate products and technology.** Define the products or services whose presence affects the sales growth of the industry. This data can usually be gathered by analyzing secondary competitor groups and contacting associations that keep tabs on those products.
4. **The buying power of customers.** Determine the buying power of customers by gauging the amount of competition and charting prices. If a business is discounting price because of customer pressures and is not producing a sustainable profit, investment in the industry may be unwise.
5. **The negotiating power of suppliers.** To determine supplier power within the industry, find out who the major suppliers are and the extent of their product line. You can do this by looking through trade periodicals and contacting associations.

Cost Structure

When researching the cost structure of an industry, the first thing you will have to do is identify the stages where value is added to a product or service. According to the Management Analysis Center,[3] in most instances, you will have the following stages:

- Procurement.
- Processing.
- Fabrication.
- Assembly.
- Distribution.
- Marketing.

Each stage provides additional value to the final product or service.

[3] Management Analysis Center, *Strategy Formulation*, (Cambridge, MA: Author, 1992).

Most trade associations have percentages on the cost of producing and marketing a product based on surveys of their members. If you cannot gain these cost percentages from the association, you will have to conduct your own survey of competitors or suppliers for the required information.

Distribution Systems

When researching the industry, you need to identify the various distribution channels currently in use and the companies that are deemed the channel commanders. In addition to defining current distribution channels, you also must identify emerging channels that could provide additional opportunities.

Many large industrial companies use their own sales force to sell directly to their customer base. Other, smaller firms, might sell directly to retailers or reach their customers through wholesale distributors, jobbers, or brokers. Generally, companies that sell more directly to the end user have more control over their marketing efforts but experience a greater margin of risk.

If a distribution channel is dominated by a few companies, you may need to consider alternative distribution channels. To determine the alternate distribution systems within the industry, you need to look closely at the strategies employed by both your primary and secondary competitors.

There may also be alternate distribution channels in the development of new trends with the industry. For instance, as discount stores, catalog discount houses, convenience food stores, and specialty kiosks open up, they may create new distribution opportunities. You have to note and analyze the possible impact such trends will have on the industry.

Industry Trends

Spotting industry trends is a function of asking yourself several questions concerning your customers, competitors, and the industry in general. Questions you need to ask include:

- What is important to customers?
- What needs are not being met?
- What new strategies are your competitors starting to employ?
- What are the new trends in distribution?

You need to sit down and take a close look at your market analysis up to this point to recognize the most significant trends in the industry that will affect your future strategy.

Key Success Factors

Perhaps the most important result of your industry analysis will be to identify the key success factors for your strategic groups of competitors. Key success factors are assets and skills that a company requires to be successful within a

✔ MARKET PLANNING CHECKLIST

Before you launch a marketing campaign, answer the following questions about your business and your product or service.

☐ Have you analyzed the total market for your product or service? Do you know which features of your product or service will appeal to different market segments?

☐ In forming your marketing message, have you described how your product or service will benefit your clients?

☐ Have you prepared a pricing schedule? What kinds of discounts do you offer, and to whom do you offer them?

☐ Have you prepared a sales forecast?

☐ Which media will you use in your marketing campaign?

☐ Have you planned any sales promotions?

☐ Have you planned a publicity campaign?

☐ Do your marketing materials mention any optional accessories or added services that consumers might want to purchase?

☐ If you offer a product, have you prepared clear operating and assembly instructions, if required? What kind of warranty do you provide? What type of customer service or support do you offer after the sale?

☐ Do you have product liability insurance?

☐ Is your packaging likely to appeal to your target market?

☐ If your product is one you can patent, have you done so?

☐ How will you distribute your product?

☐ Have you prepared job descriptions for all of the employees needed to carry out your marketing plans?

particular industry; they include name recognition, distribution channel power, financial resources, product loyalty, purchasing procedures, or access to raw material. Whatever the key success factors happen to be in your industry, the completed analysis of the industry should define those and provide you with enough information to make an educated guess about future success factors. This may lie in the development of new technology, new distribution channels, or the exploitation of usage gaps. Failure to forecast the key success factors of an industry may result in a slip within the market or a business collapse altogether. The Marketing Planning Checklist will help you determine whether your research has uncovered adequate information about the business under consideration.

INFORMATION NETWORKS

An information network should provide information from two types of sources: (1) published sources and (2) the field.

Sources for business information are most commonly identified with published sources of information: newspapers, business magazines, trade journals, and Wall Street reports. There are thousands of such sources and several good guides to them. Some of the more common sources of published information include:

1. **Business periodicals.** Business magazines provide recent gossip and intelligence, as well as analysis. Some offer compilations of corporate data. They are also a prime source for broad-issue scanning.
2. **Trade press.** Trade literature is probably the best published source read and used by the executives. It includes such information as personnel changes, background on people in the industry, meetings, new products, and appointments of agents.
3. **Speeches and announcements.** These reveal management philosophies and intentions. *The Wall Street Transcript* contains a compilation of speeches by company officials to security analysts.
4. **Annual reports.** The reports reveal priorities, investment strategy, plans for growth, goals, even inconsistencies in policies. Footnotes to financial statements reveal problems to those who know how to read them. The need to appear optimistic in public makes some of the reports less useful, but tracking and comparing reports of several years may reveal trends in management thinking.
5. **Testimony, lawsuits, antitrust information.** Court records that can be inspected include transcripts, evidence, testimony, and judgments in civil and criminal cases. These records of bankruptcies, customer complaints, and disputes with creditors can be quite interesting and may offer useful insights.

In addition to published sources, there are field or human sources. The following field sources are very important to a business's intelligence system:

1. **Customers.** Customers can provide information about competitor products, plans to introduce a new product, pricing, service, personnel and personnel changes, planned plant location, and strategic changes. According to several studies, customers are the primary source for market and competitive intelligence. In tapping this source, you should note that purchasing agents of corporate customers have a lower reliability as a source than top management and engineers.

2. **Suppliers.** Second only to customers as sources of competitive and market intelligence, suppliers can provide a wide range of data about competitors. You should recognize that suppliers comprise more than just sellers of materials to the company. They also include suppliers of services such as banks, advertising agencies, and public relations firms. Most suppliers will have an incentive to provide data to you if they believe you may be a good prospect for future business. However, while suppliers will generally provide you with a great deal of information about their pricing, product specifications, and delivery terms, all of which would be applicable to your competitors as well, depending on their relationship with your competitors, most worthwhile suppliers will not impart highly sensitive information.

3. **Trade associations.** The main usefulness of contacts at the trade association is in providing general industry data. The officers of the association know that to keep the lines of communication open they need the confidence of their members; therefore, they usually give out only general industry information.

4. **Chambers of commerce.** Especially in locations where your competitor has its business, the local chamber of commerce can provide data about employment, size of the competitor's facility, interest of companies in relocating, consumer complaints against local businesses, and more.

5. **Journalists.** They are excellent sources, particularly those who work in local press and trade journals. Journalists can only touch on a company in an article. Although often busy and hard to contact, they are open to sharing information, especially if you reciprocate.

6. **Former employees.** New employees with relevant backgrounds can be very helpful to a company's intelligence efforts. To make use of the information available from new employees, the human resources department of your company should regularly report to the intelligence area about new professional employees and managers hired and forward their résumés for review. A debriefing should be conducted by the head of the employee's department with an intelligence person present. The employee should be assured of the right not to answer any questions.

Internal Networks

Almost every business collects and stores important information about their competitors. Following is a list of the many resources each department has to offer:

1. **Customer service.** The customer service department, because of its daily contact with the company's clients, is often the first to hear of a competitor's special promotions, price changes, and new product features. Too frequently, companies fail to make the most of this untapped resource. The customer service department may be among the first in a company to hear of significant changes in competitors' distribution networks.

2. **Distribution.** The distribution department often collects information on freight charges, warehouse costs, and warehouse availability. You may discover that distribution is also knowledgeable about competitors' shipping costs. Your company's distribution experts may also be able to help you map out competitors' distribution networks and utilization of warehouse space.

3. **Purchasing.** Many of your company's vendors also sell to your competitors. The purchasing department, which deals with these vendors on a daily basis, may hear these vendors talk about the competition. For example, a vendor's salesperson may complain that he cannot meet your company's delivery date because a competitor has just come through with a big order that backlogged his company. A salesperson may also brag about her sales to a competitor, revealing previously unknown information about that competitor.

RESOURCES

Associations

Marketing Research Association, 2189 Silas Deane Highway, Suite 5, Rocky Hill, CT 06067, 203-257-4008

On-Line Services

America Online Incorporated, 8619 Westwood Center Drive, Vienna, VA 22182, 703-448-8700 or 800-827-6364

CD Plus Technologies, 333 Seventh Avenue, 4th Floor, New York, NY 10001, 800-955-0906

CompuServe, 5000 Arlington Centre Boulevard, Columbus, OH 43220, 800-336-3330

Delphi, General Videotex Corp., 1030 Massachusetts Avenue, Cambridge, MA 02138, 800-544-4005

DIALOG Information Services, Inc., Marketing Dept., 3460 Hillview Avenue, Palo Alto, CA 94304, 415-858-3785; 800-334-2564

Dow Jones News/Retrieval Service, P.O. Box 300, Princeton, NJ 08543-0300, 609-452-1511

GEnie, General Electric Information Services, 401 North Washington Street, Rockville, MD 20850, 800-638-9636; Fax 301-251-6421

NewsNet, 945 Haverford Road, Bryn Mawr, PA 19010, 610-527-8030; 800-345-1301

NEXIS, Mead Data Central, P.O. Box 933, Dayton, OH 45401, 513-859-5398; 800-543-6862

Prodigy Services Company, 445 Hamilton Avenue, White Plains, NY 10601, 800-776-0845 [1-800-PRODIGY]

The Source, 5000 Arlington Center Boulevard, Columbus, OH 43220, 800-336-3330

CD-ROM Databases

DIALOG Information Services, Inc., 3460 Hillview Avenue, Palo Alto, CA 94304, 415-858-3785; 800-334-2564

Grolier Electronic Publishing, Inc., Sherman Turnpike, Danbury, CT 06816, 203-797-3500

H.W. Wilson Co., 950 University Avenue, Bronx, NY 10452, 800-367-6770

Lotus Information Services, Lotus Development Corp., 55 Cambridge Parkway, Cambridge, MA 02142, 617-577-8500

OCLC, Inc., 6565 Frantz Road, Dublin, OH 43017, 614-764-6000

Document Delivery Services

FIND/SVP, 625 Sixth Avenue, New York, NY 10011, 212-645-4500

NASA Industrial Application Center (NIAC), 3716 South Hope Street, Suite 200, Los Angeles, CA 90007, 213-743-6132

Magazines

Barron's National Business and Financial Weekly, 200 Liberty Street, New York, NY 10281, 212-416-2700

Business Marketing, 740 North Rush Street, Chicago, IL 60611, 312-649-5260

The Business Owner, Thomas Publishing, Inc., 383 South Broadway, Hicksville, NY 11801, 516-681-2111

In Business, 2718 Dryden Drive, Madison, WI 53704, 608-246-3580

Journal of Small Business Management, West Virginia University, College of Business Economics, Bureau of Business Research, P.O. Box 6025, Morgantown, WV 26506-6025, 304-293-5837

Journal of Marketing Research, 250 South Wacker Drive, Suite 200, Chicago, IL 60606-5819, 312-648-0536

Marketing News, 250 South Wacker Drive, Suite 200, Chicago, IL 60606-5819, 312-648-0536

Marketing Research: Management and Applications, 250 South Wacker Drive, Suite 200, Chicago, IL 60606-5819, 312-648-0536

Nation's Business, 1615 H Street NW, Washington, DC 20062, 202-463-5650

Quirk's Marketing Research Review, 6607 18th Avenue South, P.O. Box 23536, Minneapolis, MN 55423-2784, 612-861-8051

Publications

Business Information Sources by Lorna M. Daniels, University of California Press, 2120 Berkeley Way, Berkeley, CA 94720, 510-642-4247

Dun & Bradstreet publications (*State Sales Guides, Regional Business Directories,* and *Census of American Business*): Reference Services, c/o Dun & Bradstreet, 430 Mountain Avenue, New Providence, NJ 07054, 908-771-7635

Hidden Treasures—Census Bureau Data and Where to Find It!, Bureau of the Census, Attn: Customer Service, Washington, DC 20233, 202-763-4100

The Wall Street Transcript, 100 Wall Street, Ninth Floor, New York, NY 10005, 212-747-9500

U.S. Industrial Outlook, U.S. Government Printing Office, P.O. Box 371954, Pittsburgh, PA 15250, 202-512-1800

4

Legal Forms

When you start a business, one of your most important decisions will be the legal form under which your business will operate. Which form is most correct for you will depend on the potential liability involved in the business you are entering and on the tax consequences you desire to achieve. Your business can be a sole proprietorship, general partnership, limited partnership, corporation, or a subchapter S corporation, and in some states a limited liability company (LLC). Each type of entity has its advantages and disadvantages, which are discussed in the following sections (see Table 4.1). It is wise to discuss your choices with a knowledgeable attorney and tax expert who can help you make the right choice.

All too often, people automatically incorporate if they intend to start a new business. Many times, incorporation will not accomplish the financial and legal goals you desire. Also, it is often encouraged by attorneys since incorporations are a profitable and relatively easy service for them to perform.

You should consider all the possible alternatives and the cost versus benefits of each choice.

SOLE PROPRIETORSHIP

The simplest and most common business form is the sole proprietorship. In fact, if you are the sole owner of your business, you automatically end up as a sole proprietor if you do not establish yourself in another structure. In terms of taxes, as a sole proprietor there are no separate income tax returns, unlike other forms of business, and FICA (Federal Insurance Contributions Act) taxes for the owner are less than other legal forms of operations such as partnerships and corporations.

To establish a sole proprietorship, you will need to secure a business license, if required, from the city or county where your business will be headquartered.

Table 4.1 Legal Forms for Businesses

CONTROL	LIABILITY	TAX	CONTINUITY
SOLE PROPRIETORSHIP			
Owner maintains complete control over the business.	Owner is solely liable. His or her personal assets are open to attack in any legal case.	Owner reports all income and expenses on personal tax return.	Business terminates on owner's death or withdrawal. Owner can sell the business, but will no longer remain the proprietor.
GENERAL PARTNERSHIP			
Each partner has the authority to enter contracts and make other business decisions, unless the partnership agreement stipulates otherwise.	Each partner is liable for all business debts.	Each partner reports partnership income on individual tax return. The business does not pay any taxes as its own entity.	Unless the partnership agreement makes other provisions, a partnership dissolves on death or withdrawal of a partner.
LIMITED PARTNERSHIP			
General partners control the business.	General partners are personally responsible for partnership liabilities. Limited partners are liable for the amount of their investment.	Partnership files annual taxes. Limited and general partners report their share of partnership income or loss on their individual returns.	Death of limited partner does not dissolve business, but death of general partner might, unless the partnership agreement makes other provisions.
LIMITED LIABILITY COMPANY			
Owner or partners have authority.	Partners are not liable for business debts.	Partners report income and income tax on their individual tax returns.	Different states have different laws regarding the continuity of LLCs. In some states, LLCs dissolve on death or withdrawal of an owner.
CORPORATION			
Shareholders appoint board of directors, which appoints officers, who hold the highest authority.	Shareholders generally are responsible for the amount of their investment in corporate stock.	Corporation pays its own taxes. Shareholders pay tax on their dividends.	The corporation is its own legal entity, and can survive the deaths of owners, partners, and shareholders.
SUBCHAPTER S			
Shareholders appoint the board of directors, which appoints officers, who hold the highest authority.	Shareholders generally are responsible for the amount of their investment in corporate stock.	Shareholders report their shares of corporate profit or loss in their individual tax returns.	The corporation is its own legal entity and can survive the death of owners, partners, and shareholders.

If you open additional locations in a different city or county, you will have to obtain a business license from each jurisdiction that requires one. Even if you don't maintain a physical location in another city or county but do business within that jurisdiction, you may still be responsible for obtaining a business license for that area to legally conduct your business. Call the licensing division of each city where you plan to conduct business as well as the county registrar to determine the licensing requirements.

In addition to a business license, you will also need to obtain a federal and state payroll I.D. number if you plan to hire employees or if the entities you plan to do business with require one. (The federal employer identification number is secured by filing a form SS-4 with the Internal Revenue Service.) If you operate using any name other than your own, you will have to file a fictitious business name statement to put the public on notice that you are the owner of that business operating under a fictitious name.

To file taxes as a sole proprietor, you report all your income and expenses on Schedule C or C-EZ of IRS Form 1040. You must also pay self-employment tax on your tax return since there will be no withholding from your earnings. Schedule C—the long form for sole proprietors—must be filled out if you have gross receipts above $25,000 and expenses greater than $2,000.

Schedule C-EZ is a simplified version of Schedule C with just three lines reporting:

1. Gross receipts.
2. Total expenses.
3. Net profit (line 1 minus line 2).

To qualify to use Schedule C-EZ, you must have gross receipts of $25,000 or less, report expenses of $2,000 or less, use the cash method of accounting (discussed in Chapter 17), not have had any inventory during the year, own only one business as a sole proprietor, and not have a net loss from that business.

As a sole proprietor, all of your personal assets are subject to any legal liabilities you might encounter while operating the business. Therefore, to guard against potential lawsuits from your customers, you should secure liability insurance. General liability insurance will cover you against slips and falls, and so on. If you manufacture or sell products, you may wish to secure product liability insurance. It is a good idea to get insurance since you may be sued even if you are not at fault. Insurance will usually cover the high cost of the attorneys who will still have to defend you even in an unfounded lawsuit.

PARTNERSHIP

General Partnership

If you will own your business with one or more individuals, you may operate as a partnership. Choosing a partner is one of the most important steps you'll take in your venture, so proceed with caution. To ensure a picture-perfect relationship, consider these factors:

- **Divvying up.** Do not assume it's clear who will do what; explicitly state your responsibilities to prevent any misunderstandings.
- **Buyer's remorse.** In case one partner decides to sell out later on, talk about a buy-sell agreement early on.
- **Life insurance.** If you or your partner dies, a "key man" insurance policy ensures the surviving partner is able to buy the deceased partner's share from his or her heirs.
- **Consulting outsiders.** Just because you have split responsibilities doesn't mean you've covered all the bases. Make sure to consult an attorney, accountant, or other business expert for matters outside your expertise.

Partnerships may be oral or in writing. A written agreement governing the relationships and operations between partners will avoid any possible conflict or future problems in the event the partners find they do not work well together. A lawyer's charge for forming a partnership contract is about the same as for a corporation. Partnership agreement forms can be purchased at just about any stationery store or you can purchase software such as *Nolo's Partnership Maker* for DOS.

A good general partnership agreement is complex, since it should cover all possible business situations the partners may encounter and resolve any conflicts that result between them. Like marriages, it seems that after one to three years, over half of all business partnerships break up due to disputes between partners. Some of the many items that should be covered in a partnership agreement include:

1. Capital contribution of partners.
2. Profit and loss sharing of partners.
3. Voting rights of partners.
4. Delegation of management authority to partners.
5. Disposition of a partner's interest on death of that person.
6. Methods to resolve possible tie votes between partners on crucial partnership decisions.
7. Admission of new partners.
8. Signature authority and number of signatures on partnership bank accounts.
9. Option to purchase a selling partner's interest and a method to determine the purchase price of that interest.

A general partnership under most state laws automatically dissolves on the death of a partner or if more than 50 percent of the partnership interests change hands. Partnership law is complex. Therefore, ask an attorney to review your agreement even if you write it yourself. The attorney can give you valuable suggestions that will save future problems that could cost many times the attorney's legal fees. Figure 4.1 shows a standard partnership agreement.

Figure 4.1 Partnership Agreement Form

DATE _____

COMMENCES_____

EXPIRES _____

LOCATION_____

THIS PARTNERSHIP AGREEMENT is made on
this _____ day of _____ , 19 ____ ,
between the individuals listed below:

_____

_____

_____

The partners listed above hereby agree that they shall be considered partners in business upon the commencement date of this PARTERNSHIP AGREEMENT for the following purpose:

_____

_____

The terms and conditions of this partnership are as follows:

1. The **NAME** of the partnership shall be: _____

2. The **PRINCIPAL PLACE OF BUSINESS** of the partnership shall be: _____

3. The **CAPITAL CONTRIBUTION** of each partner to the partnership shall consist of the following property, services, or cash to which each partner agrees to contribute:

Name of Partner	Capital Contribution	Agreed Upon Cash Value	% Share

Furthermore, the **PROFITS AND LOSSES** of the partnership shall be divided by the partners according to a mutually agreeable schedule and at the end of each calendar year according to the proportions listed above.

4. Each partner shall have equal rights to **MANAGE AND CONTROL** the partnership and its business. Should there be differences between the partners concerning ordinary business matters, a decision shall be made by unanimous vote. It is understood that the partners may elect one of the partners to conduct day-to-day business of the partnership; however, no partner shall be able to bind the partnership by act or contract to any liability exceeding $_____ without the prior written consent of each partner.

5. In the event a partner **WITHDRAWS** from the partnership for any reason, including death, the remaining partners may continue to operate the partnership using the same name. The withdrawing partner shall be obligated to sell their interest in the partnership. No partner shall **TRANSFER** interest in the partnership to any other party without the written consent of each partner.

6. Should the partnership be **TERMINATED** by unanimous vote, the assets and cash of the partnership shall be used to pay all creditors with the remaining amounts to be distributed to the partners according to their proportionate share.

9. Any **DISPUTES** arising between the partners as a result of this agreement shall be settled by voluntary mediation. Should mediation fail to resolve the dispute, it shall be settled by binding arbitration.

In witness whereof, this **PARTNERSHIP AGREEMENT** has been signed by the partners on the day and year listed above.

_____   _____
PARTNER   PARTNER

                                                      _____
                                                          PARTNER

In a general partnership, absent of any restrictions in the agreement, any partner may legally bind the partnership to a contract, and each partner is liable for any and all partnership debts. In any legal or creditor action, each partner will be sued personally, with the property and bank accounts of each attached. If one partner skips town, the other is left holding the bag. Also, when an individual contributes assets to a partnership, he or she does not retain a claim to those specific properties, but merely acquires an equity in all assets of the firm. The partner with the most to lose usually is hit the hardest.

As in a sole proprietorship, due to the unlimited liability, it is wise to secure good liability insurance for the partnership and partners. If the partnership operates under a fictitious name, it will have to file a fictitious business name statement. You should secure a business license or licenses if you have physical locations in more than one jurisdiction, and apply for a Federal Employee Identification number from the Internal Revenue Service using Form SS-4.

Generally, all partnerships must now operate using a calendar year and file a Form 1065 with the IRS reporting partnership incomes and expenses. That form includes Form H-1 that reports each partner's share of the income or loss. Each partner will report his or her share of their partnership income each year on their Form 1040 using Schedule K-1. The partnership itself does not pay any taxes with its tax return.

Limited Partnership

A limited partnership is in most respects similar to a general partnership, except that it has two classes of partners. The *general partner(s)* have full management and control of the partnership business but also accept full personal liability for partnership liabilities. *Limited partners* have no personal liability beyond their investment in the partnership interest. Limited partners cannot participate in the general management and daily operations of the partnership business without being in danger of becoming general partners in the eyes of the law.

The general partner can be either a sole proprietor or a corporation. In the classic "silent partner" situation, one or more limited partners put up money and the general partners run the business. A limited partnership in this case protects the assets of wealthier silent partners and acts as a conduit to pass current operating profits or losses to them as well as to preserve the special tax character of certain items.

Limited partnership agreements are required by most jurisdictions to be in writing and, for the most part, contain the same provisions as those in a general partnership agreement—with some complex additions. Legal costs of forming a limited partnership can be even higher than for a corporation because in some states they are governed by securities laws.

Another aspect of limited partnerships is that in some lines of business, the limited partner (also called the passive investor) may be subject to special tax liabilities that can offset tax shelter advantages. The IRS tends to look at these facts on a case-by-case basis.

Limited partnerships file a Form 1065 once a year. Individual limited and general partners include their allocable share of partnership income or loss on their individual income tax return and pay taxes on that share based on their tax bracket. Partners cannot deduct losses greater than their basis in the partnership, which includes their investment plus any funds loaned to the partnership (except for real estate limited partnerships that are governed by a special rule).

The 1986 Tax Reform Act now limits the amount of losses a limited partner can deduct on a personal tax return. If the partnership is expected to generate tax losses in its early years, you should consult your accountant to determine whether those losses will benefit you.

CORPORATIONS

A corporate structure is perhaps the most advantageous way to start a business because the corporation exists as a separate entity. In general, a corporation has all the legal rights of individuals except for the right to vote and certain other limitations. They are given the right to exist by the state that issues their charter. If you incorporate in one state to take advantage of liberal corporate laws (such as Delaware and Nevada) but do business in another state, you will have to file for "qualification" in the state in which you wish to operate the business. There is usually a fee that must be paid to qualify to do business in a state.

You can incorporate your business by filing articles of incorporation with the appropriate agency in your state. Usually only one corporation can have any given name in each state. After incorporation, stock is issued to the company's shareholders in exchange for the cash or other assets they transfer to it in return for that stock. Once a year, the shareholders elect the board of directors, who meet to discuss and guide corporate affairs anywhere from once a month to once a year.

Each year, the directors elect officers such as a president, secretary, and treasurer to conduct the day-to-day affairs of the corporate business. There also may be additional officers such as vice presidents, if the directors so decide. Along with the articles of incorporation, the directors and shareholders usually adopt the bylaws of the corporation that govern the powers and authority of the directors, officers, and shareholders.

Even small, private, professional corporations such as a legal or dental practice, need to adhere to the principles that govern a corporation. For instance, on incorporation, common stock needs to be distributed to the shareholders and a board of directors needs to be elected. If there is only one person forming the corporation, that person is the sole shareholder of stock in the corporation and can elect himself or herself to the board of directors as well as any other individuals that person deems appropriate.

Corporations, if properly formed, capitalized, and conducted (including the proper annual meetings of shareholders and directors) limit the liability of their shareholders. Even if the corporation is not successful or is held liable for damages in a lawsuit, the most that a shareholder can lose is his or her investment in the stock. The shareholder's personal assets are not on the line for corporate liabilities.

Corporations file a Form 1120 with the IRS and pay their own taxes. Salaries paid to shareholders who are employees of the corporation are deductible; however, dividends paid to shareholders are not, and therefore, do not reduce the corporation's tax liability. A corporation must end its tax year at the same time as the calendar year if it derives its income primarily from personal services (such as dental care, legal counseling, business consulting, etc.) of its shareholders.

If the corporation is small, the shareholders should prepare and sign a shareholders buy-sell agreement. This contract provides that if a shareholder dies or desires to sell his or her stock, it must first be offered to the surviving shareholders. It also may provide for a method to determine the fair price that should be paid for those shares. Such agreements are usually funded with life insurance to purchase the stock of deceased shareholders.

If a corporation is large and will sell its shares to many individuals, it may have to register with the Securities and Exchange Commission (SEC) or state regulatory bodies. More common is the corporation with only a few shareholders, which can issue its shares without any such registration under private offering exemptions. For a small corporation, responsibilities of the shareholders can be defined in the corporate minutes, and a shareholder who wants to leave can be accommodated without much legal difficulty. Also, until your small corporation has operated successfully for many years, you will most likely still have to accept personal liability for any corporate loans made by banks or other financial institutions.

The corporate form of doing business is also popular since many feel it gives a business a better image. Another advantage of a corporation is that it, as a separate legal entity, goes on forever, and does not terminate on the death of an owner or partner.

The only disadvantage is potential double taxation because the corporation must pay taxes on its net income, and you must also pay taxes on any dividends you may receive from the corporation. As of January 1, 1993, corporate tax rates were as follows:

- 15 percent on the first $50,000 of income.
- 25 percent on the next $25,000.
- 34 percent on all taxable income over $75,000.

If a corporation has taxable income over $100,000, but less than $335,000, then the tax as determined under the preceding rates is increased by 5 percent of the excess over $100,000 or $11,750, whichever is less. If your income is $335,000 or more, then it is a flat 35 percent.

Business owners often increase their own salaries to reduce or wipe out corporate profits and thereby lower the possibility of having those profits taxed twice (once to the corporation and again to the shareholders on receipt of dividends from the corporation).

Subchapter S Corporations

The disadvantage of potential double federal taxation is completely negated by filing a Subchapter S election with the IRS. (Many states do not recognize a Subchapter S election for state tax purposes and will tax the corporation as a regular corporation.) Qualifications for electing Subchapter S were changed well over a decade ago. The Subchapter S Revisions Act of 1982 liberalized many of the old rules, and the new flexibility of these corporations makes them popular with small and medium-size businesses. Subchapter S allows profits or losses to travel directly through the corporation to you and other shareholders. If you earn other income during the first year and the corporation has a loss, you can deduct against the other income, possibly wiping out your tax liability completely, provided you have materially participated in the operations of the business on a regular, continuous, and substantial basis. If you did not materially participate in the operations of the business, then the losses incurred from the S corporation would be termed passive and would be deductible only against passive income.

Subchapter S corporations elect not to be taxed as corporations. Instead, the shareholders of a Subchapter S corporation include their proportionate shares of the corporate profits and losses in their individual gross incomes. For small businesses, Subchapter S corporations are excellent devices to avoid double taxation. If your company does produce a substantial profit, forming a Subchapter S corporation would be wise, because the profits will be added to your personal income and taxed at an individual rate which, when compared with the top tax brackets for a C corporation may be lower than the regular corporate rate on that income.

To qualify under Subchapter S, the corporation must meet the following standards:

- It must be incorporated within the United States.
- It can't be part of an affiliated group that can file a consolidated tax return.
- It can't have more than 35 shareholders.
- Shareholders of the corporation must all be either individuals or estates and citizens or resident aliens of the United States.
- It must not have more than one class of outstanding stock.

For more information on the rules that apply to a Subchapter S corporation, call your local IRS office.

FORMING A CORPORATION

Before you form a corporation, you should first understand how one is structured. Corporations have three-tiers consisting of the following:

1. **Shareholders.** Individuals who hold stock in the company. The shareholders generally have very few powers in regard to the day-to-day operations of the corporation but are responsible for electing the board of directors and removing them from office. In smaller corporations, the shareholders can give themselves more operational powers by including provisions in the articles and bylaws of the corporation.
2. **Board of Directors.** Responsible for the corporate management of the corporation. The board of directors' legal authority over the corporation extends to all decisions of policy, personnel, compensation, delegation of authority, declaration of dividends, and the general supervision over all corporate activities.
3. **Officers.** Selected by the board of directors to carry out the day-to-day operations of the business. Officers can be directors as well, as is the case in small corporations. Officers—typically with titles of president, vice-president, secretary, and treasurer—are frequently the most powerful group in the corporation.

With this structure in mind, the individuals organizing a corporation should make some vital preincorporation decisions before actually filing with the state in which they wish to incorporate.

Preincorporation Decisions

Before attempting to form a corporation, the organizers of the business should decide on a number of things and enter into a preincorporation agreement so all participants know the roles they will play in the corporation. A sample form for such an agreement is shown in Figure 4.2. These preincorporation agreements will generally cover the following:

- Who will serve of the first board of directors.
- Who will purchase the different types of stock in the corporation, in what amounts, and for how much.
- Any documents already drafted by the individuals organizing the corporation that will be adopted once the first board of directors is formed. Documents that have already been drafted prior to incorporation include lease agreements, equipment rental, inventory purchases, and so on.

Preincorporation agreements with third parties are usually made between the organizers and the third party. Therefore, the organizers of the business are usually liable for provisions in the contract, unless otherwise stipulated through a written contract signed on behalf of the prospective corporation. A contract of this nature usually includes items includes the following items:

- Scope of potential liability.
- Rights and obligations under the contract for both the organizers of the corporation as well as the corporation itself once it is formed.
- Provisions should the corporation never be formed.

Figure 4.2   Preincorporation Agreement Form

AGREEMENT made this _____ day of _____, 19_____,
between _____, _____, and _____.

WHEREAS the parties hereto wish to organize a corporation upon the terms and conditions hereinafter set forth; and

WHEREAS the parties wish to establish their mutual rights and responsibilities in relation to their organizational activities;

NOW, THEREFORE, in consideration of the premises and mutual covenants contained herein, it is agreed by and between the parties as follows:

FIRST: The parties will forthwith cause a corporation to be formed and organized under the laws of _____.

SECOND: The proposed Articles of Incorporation shall be attached hereto as Exhibit A.

THIRD: Within seven days after the issuance of the corporation's certificate of incorporation, the parties agree that the corporation's authorized stock shall be distributed, and consideration paid, as follows:

1 . _____ shares of _____ (insert *common* or *preferred*) stock shall be issued to _____ in consideration of his/her payment to the corporation of $ _____ cash.

2. _____ shares of stock shall be issued to _____ in consideration of his/her transfer to the corporation of _____ (list property, real or personal, to be transferred).

3. _____ shares of stock shall be isssued to _____ in consideration of his transfer to the corporation of _____.

4. ...etc...

FOURTH: The corporation shall employ _____ as its manager for a term of _____ years and at a salary of $ _____ per annum, such employment not to be terminated without cause and such salary not to be increased or decreased without the approval of _____% of the directors.

FIFTH: The parties agree not to transfer, sell, assign, pledge, or otherwise dispose of their shares until they have first offered them for sale to the corporation, and then, should the corporation refuse such offer, to the other shareholders on a pro rata basis. The shares shall be offered at their book value to the corporation, and in the event the corporation refuses, the other shareholders shall have thirty (30) days to purchase the shares. If the corporation or other shareholders do not purchase all the offered shares, the remaining shares may be freely transferred by their owner without price restrictions.

SIXTH: The parties to this agreement promise to use their best efforts to incorporate the organization and to commence its business.

_____

_____

_____

- Provisions for declining the contract once the corporation is formed.
- A statement declaring the corporation does not exist at the time of the agreement.
- A disclaimer of any implied agreements.

When forming such a contract, it is best to see your lawyer.

Incorporation

Any corporation that is not formed as a bank or insurance company can be incorporated under Section 3 of the Model Business Corporation Act. This statute allows businesses to file for incorporation under a vast array of activities so long as they file under an appropriate name with their accompanying articles of incorporation.

When incorporating your business, choose your name carefully—it cannot resemble the name of an existing corporation in the same jurisdiction, nor can it inaccurately describe what the corporation does. Many corporate names are fairly nebulous in nature, but one thing you have to avoid is a name that implies something which the corporation doesn't do.

In addition, the name of the corporation must include the one of the following terms:

- Corporation.
- Company.
- Incorporated.
- Limited.

One of the preceding terms is required so that people who are unfamiliar with the corporation are put on notice that the business they are dealing with is a legal entity under the law and, therefore, the firm, not the officers managing it, is responsible for all its debts and actions.

If you've chosen a name for your corporation but are not yet ready to incorporate and want to reserve the name, or if you want to check on the validity of the name, you can file an application for reservation of corporate name with the state where you wish to incorporate. This state will then notify you as to whether the name is available. If it is, it will be held for 120 days.

The next document you need to file with the state is the articles of incorporation. The articles need to be signed by one of the individuals forming the corporation and sent in duplicate along with the filing fee to the secretary of state or any other designated official.

To determine the filing fee for the articles of incorporation, check your state's statute or write the secretary of state. In addition to the filing fee, most states also impose a fee for each authorized share of stock that is issued.

Once the state receives the articles of incorporation, processing them will generally take several weeks. Once the articles of incorporation have been accepted, the state will issue you a certificate of incorporation to signify the birth of the new corporation.

LIMITED LIABILITY COMPANY

A new business form called the limited liability company (LLC) has sprung up in 38 states. The LLC arose from the desire of business owners to adopt a business structure permitting them to operate like a traditional partnership. This distributes the income and income tax to the partners (reported on their individual income tax returns) but also protects them from personal liability for the business's debts, as with the corporate business form. In general, unless the entrepreneur establishes a separate corporation, the owner and partners (if any) assume complete liability for all debts of the business. Under the LLC concept, on the other hand, an individual is not responsible for the firm's debt.

The LLC offers a number of advantages over S corporations. For example, while S corporations can issue only one class of company stock, LLCs can offer several different classes with different rights. In addition, S corporations are limited to a maximum of 35 individual shareholders (who must be U.S. residents), whereas an unlimited number of individuals, corporations, and partnerships may participate in an LLC.

The LLC also carries significant tax advantages over the limited partnership. For instance, unless the partner in a limited partnership assumes an active role, his or her losses are considered "passive" losses and are ineligible for use as tax deductions against active income. But if the partner does take an active role in the firm's management, he or she becomes liable for the firm's debt. It's a Catch-22 situation. The owners of an LLC, on the other hand, do not assume liability for the business's debt, and any losses can be used as tax deductions against active income.

In exchange for these two considerable benefits, however, the owners of LLCs must meet the "transferability restriction test," which means the ownership interests in the LLC must not be transferable without some restrictions. It's this restriction that makes the LLC structure unworkable for major corporations. For corporations to attract large sums of capital, their corporate stock must be easily transferable in the stock exchanges. However, this restriction should not prove to be detrimental to the typical entrepreneurial business in which ownership transfers take place relatively infrequently.

A number of quirks in current state LLC legislation require tricky maneuvering and plenty of advance planning. For example, LLC legislation in Colorado and Wyoming does not allow for continuity of the business. In those states, the business is dissolved on the death, retirement, resignation, or expulsion of an owner. While the same is true for both individual proprietorships and partnerships, you must still plan accordingly.

In Florida, the state's 5.5 percent corporate tax also applies to LLCs. And with state shortfalls in tax revenues and strained budgets, other states may look to LLCs for additional tax revenues, even though similar businesses such as S corporations are typically exempt from state and federal income taxes.

Also, since the LLC is a relatively new legal form for businesses, federal and state governments are still looking at ways to tighten the regulations surrounding this business tool. This comes from a concern that some investment promoters are using LLCs to evade securities laws. Although most LLCs are legitimate, the Securities and Exchange Commission (SEC) is moving quickly to tighten control of those firms engaged in irregular activity.

If this form of business sounds as if it would fit your needs, explore new and pending legislation concerning LLCs in your area.

FICTITIOUS NAME

Sole proprietorships and partnerships have the option of choosing distinct names for their businesses. If you want to operate your business under a name different from your personal name (e.g., John Doe doing business as [d/b/a] "The Pantry"), you may be required by the county, city, or state to register your fictitious name.

Procedures vary. In many states, you need only go to the county offices, fill out a fictitious business name statement and pay a registration fee to the county clerk. Other states require placing a fictitious name ad in a local newspaper. In some cases, the newspaper that prints the legal notice for your business name will file the necessary papers with the county for a small fee.

The cost of filing a fictitious name notice ranges from $10 to $100. The easiest way to determine the procedure for your area is to call your bank and ask if it requires a fictitious name registry or certificate to open a business account. If so, inquire where you should go to obtain one.

Fictitious name filings do not apply to corporations in most states unless the corporation is doing business under a name other than its own. Documents of incorporation have the same effect for the corporate business as fictitious name filings have for sole proprietorships and partnerships.

Whatever entity you choose to operate your business under, you must pay careful attention to the documents and written agreements to make certain they protect you from any eventual problems or the potential failure of the business and outside lawsuits. Also, annual tax returns and other state filing requirements must be complied with carefully.

RESOURCES

Associations

American Bar Association, 750 North Lake Shore Drive, Chicago, IL 60611, 312-988-5000

Magazines

Barron's National Business & Financial Weekly, 200 Liberty Street, New York, NY 10281, 212-416-2700

The Business Owner, Thomas Publishing, Inc., 383 South Broadway, Hicksville, NY 11801, 516-681-2111

Business Review, One Kwik Kopy Lane, P.O.Box 777, Cypress, TX 77429-2164, 713-373-3535

D&B Reports, 299 Park Avenue, New York, NY 10171-0102, 212-593-6723

Entrepreneurial Manager, Center for Entrepreneurial Management, 180 Varick Street, New York, NY 10014, 212-633-0060

Entrepreneurial Manager's Newsletter, 180 Varick Street, 17th Floor, New York, NY 10014-4692, 212-633-0060

In Business, 2718 Dryden Drive, Madison, WI 53704, 608-246-3580

Journal of Small Business Management, West Virginia University, College of Business Economics, Bureau of Business Research, P.O. Box 6025, Morgantown, WV 26506-6025, 304-293-5837; Fax, 304-293-7061

Nation's Business, 1615 H Street, NW, Washington, DC 20062, 202-463-5650

Software

Nolo's Partnership Maker for DOS, Nolo Press, 950 Parker Street, Berkeley, CA 94701, 510-549-1976

5

Licensing

Although most businesspeople tend to think of the process of licensing and obtaining necessary permits as a tax collecting act by the cities, counties, state and federal governments that implement these regulations, most of these programs are created with the intent to protect the general public. The whole act of licensing, with its increased paperwork, fees, and interaction with government officials is designed to show compliance with local regulations based on the type of business you are conducting. In big cities, license bureaus are also set up to control business locations—to keep people from operating an auto-repair business next door to a home and to keep people from operating a business from the home at all.

Failure to comply with the licensing and permit requirements for the type of business you plan to start in the jurisdiction(s) you intend to locate could expose you to additional fees in the aspect of penalty payments as well as restriction of operation until conditions specified by the regulating authority have been met.

So, no matter what you think of the licensing process, don't neglect it. The following chapter describes the types of licenses and permits you may be subject to and how to find out the specific requirements for your business.

BUSINESS LICENSING

Many entrepreneurs starting their own small business will require only a local business license, which allows the business to operate within the city and county where it is located. This business license will either be a municipal license if your business is located within a city, or a county license if you are located in an unincorporated area of the county. If you intend to open multiple locations or conduct business in different cities and counties, you will also need to apply for a license in those jurisdictions.

Operating some specialized businesses may require state as well as federal licensing. These are usually businesses that operate across state lines or are involved in specific occupations.

Business License

Licensing requirements vary from city to city and county to county. Some cities and counties do not require a business to obtain a license, while others collect a business licensing fee on an annual basis. For cities that require a business license, the departments mandated for collection of the licensing fee generally operate as tax-collecting bureaus and do not perform any public service. You simply pay a fee to operate your business in that city. In addition to the license fee, some cities receive a percentage of your gross sales as well as sales taxes if your business is required to collect them.

Before spending your time visiting city hall or the county administrative building, call the licensing bureau of the city you plan to operate in or the county registrar's or recorder's office to find out their licensing requirements and application procedure. This will save you time because you can have all the necessary materials ready prior to applying for the license.

Your application will probably be processed through the planning or zoning department, which will check to make sure the zone covering your property allows the proposed use and that there are enough parking places to meet the code. You should not encounter many problems if you are opening your business in an existing structure that previously housed a similar business.

You will not be allowed to operate in an area not zoned for your business unless you first have a variance or conditional-use permit (explained under "Zoning Ordinances" later in this chapter). But before you knock yourself out to obtain this authorization, see how far up through the bureaucracy you can go. Remember that many bureaucrats may not be genuinely familiar with the laws they administer. Ask the same question of three license clerks, and you may receive three different answers.

County Licenses

Most county licensing requirements apply to enterprises located outside a municipality in an unincorporated area of the county. As mentioned, if you plan to locate in an unincorporated area of the county where you will be conducting business, you will need to obtain a county business license instead of a municipal license. In addition to a county business license, sole proprietors and partnerships that choose to operate under a fictitious name will usually be required to file a fictitious business name statement (see Chapter 4 for more information on fictitious business name statements).

Educate yourself about county ordinances that apply to your business if you locate outside a city or town's jurisdiction. County regulations are often less strict than those of adjoining cities.

State Licenses

Many states require a license or occupational permit for persons engaged in certain occupations. Often, these persons must pass state examinations before they can conduct business. Licensing is commonly required for auto mechanics, plumbers, electricians, building contractors, collection agents, insurance agents, real-estate brokers, repossessors, and workers providing services to the human body (barbers, cosmetologists, doctors, nurses, etc.). Your state government can provide a complete list of occupations that require licensing in your state.

Federal Licenses

A few types of businesses/businesspeople require federal licensing such as meat processors, delivery people, radio and television stations, and investment advisory services. The Federal Trade Commission can tell you if your business will require a federal license.

BUSINESS PERMITS

Along with licenses, you may need to obtain several permits, at both the local and state level to show compliance with local and state laws regulating structural appearances and safety as well as the sale of products.

The Seller's Permit

In many states, wholesalers or manufacturers will not sell to you at wholesale prices unless you can show them your sales tax permit or number, also called a seller's permit. You will usually have to sign a tax card for their files.

Where and how do you get such a permit? Agencies issuing permits vary with each state; generally the Equalization Board, the State Sales Tax Commission, or the Franchise Tax Board has this responsibility. Contact the entity that governs taxes in your state and apply for your resale tax or wholesale permit. You will have to provide documentation that proves you are a retailer. Usually your business permit is acceptable.

Your resale permit allows you to avoid putting out money for sales tax on merchandise at the time you purchase it from suppliers. This does not mean you will not be remitting taxes on the merchandise; it means you will defer them until you sell the merchandise. The sales taxes will then be added (where applicable) to customers' purchases. You then remit it to the appropriate agency, using the forms designed for that purpose.

When conducting business across state lines, you are not required to collect taxes for any other state except those in which you maintain offices or stores.

Health Department Permit

Purveying and distributing food requires a county health department permit. The health department will want to inspect your facilities before issuing the permit. The fee for such a permit will range from about $25 up, depending on the size of the operation and the quantity of equipment.

Liquor, Wine, and Beer Licenses

In most states, one type of license is required to serve wine and beer and another to serve hard liquor. A liquor license is more difficult to obtain. In some areas, no new liquor licenses are being issued at all; you can obtain one only by buying it from the present license holder. Although the original license may have cost less than $100, competition has probably forced the going price to anywhere from $2,000 to $10,000 or more, depending on the location.

An advantage of buying out a restaurant that has served liquor is the possibility of acquiring the existing license as part of the deal. Typically, the rules will require filing an application with the state beverage control board, then posting notice on the premises of your intent to dispense liquor.

In some states, the beverage control board requires holders of liquor licenses to keep all purchase records for a specified number of years, during which time they are subject to inspection by the control board and/or the Internal Revenue Service.

Under most circumstances, a license to serve wine and beer with meals will be much easier to obtain than a hard-liquor license. Beer-and-wine licenses are usually issued for an annual period and are easily renewable if you haven't committed any offenses, such as selling to minors. The white pages of your phone directory will have the number for the nearest beverage-control agency, which can supply you with the information you need.

Fire Department Permit

Many fire departments require your business to obtain a permit if it uses any flammable materials or if your premises will be occupied by customers or the public at large. In some cities, you must secure a permit before you open for business. Other jurisdictions do not require a permit; instead, they conduct periodic inspections of the premise for compliance. If you have infractions, they will issue a citation.

Theaters, restaurants, clubs, bars, retirement homes, day-care centers, and schools are examples of uses that will be subject to especially close and frequent scrutiny by the fire department.

Air and Water Pollution Control Permit

Many cities now have departments that supervise the control of air and water pollution. If you burn any material, discharge anything into the sewers or waterways, or use gas-producing products (such as paint sprayers), you may be required to obtain a special permit from this department of your city or county.

Environmental-protection regulations may require you to obtain approval before construction or operation. Check with your state agency regarding federal or state regulations that may apply to your business.

Sign Permit

Many cities and suburbs have instituted sign ordinances that restrict the size, location, and sometimes the lighting and type of sign used. Landlords may also impose their own restrictions; these are likely to be most stringent in a mall. To avoid costly mistakes, be sure to check regulations and secure the written approval of your landlord before you invest in a sign.

ZONING ORDINANCES

If you want to run your business from your home—and do it legitimately—you will have to find out the zoning ordinances for your area. The first rule is, Don't go to the zoning officer for advice. Go to the township clerk's office and ask for a copy of any ordinances concerning home-based business. Then find out—if you do not already know—exactly how your residence is zoned.

Once you know how your area is zoned, you can get a good idea of whether your planned business is permitted or prohibited. Whatever your conclusion is, consult an attorney who will be able to interpret the fine points of the ordinance. There is often a substantial difference between what an ordinance says and the way it is enforced.

If you locate your business in a structure previously used for commercial purposes, zoning regulations in most cases will not be a problem. However, if you are constructing a new facility, acquiring an existing building for a different purpose than its original use, or undertaking extensive remodeling, you should carefully check local building and zoning codes. If zoning regulations do not allow operation of the type of business you wish to open, you may file for a zoning variance, a conditional-use permit, or a zone change.

A variance or conditional-use permit grants you the privilege (conditionally) of operating a business on land not zoned for that purpose. The filing fee may be as high as $1,200, and it may take 90 days or more before you get a decision. A zone change, on the other hand, amounts to a permanent change in the way a particular area is zoned, and therefore in the way it will be used long into the future. It involves a lengthy procedure—six months or more—of filing a petition with the city planning commission, issuing notice, presenting your case at public hearings, and finally getting the city council or other governing body to make a decision.

In some cases, any change in land use, whether permanent (by zone change) or temporary (by variance or conditional-use permit), will require environmental clearance. Local planning or zoning departments can tell you whether your project is exempt from the law or whether you should seek a negative de-claration from its regulations. If your project will displace residents, generate a lot of traffic, or impact natural habitat, some municipalities will require you to prepare an environmental-impact report. This can be a costly and time-consuming procedure for which you will need expert help.

If your request for a zoning variance or change is approved, many restrictions still apply. In addition to meeting local building codes, you will probably be required to observe minimum setbacks at the front, side, and rear of the structure; maximum floor space in relation to land area; maximum heights; minimum provisions for parking; and other factors. We cannot generalize on this subject, since each government entity has its own specific policies.

Essentially, zoning ensures that the community's land uses are properly located in relation to each other, that adequate space is available for each type of development, that the density of development in each area is in proper proportion to the development of streets, schools, recreational areas, and utility systems, and that the development is sufficiently open to permit light, air, and privacy for persons living and working within the area.

OTHER REGULATIONS

In addition to licenses and permits, other regulations may apply to your business. Federal and state laws designed to encourage competition prohibit practices such as contracts, combinations, and conspiracies in restraint of trade; they prohibit discrimination in price between different purchasers of commodities similar in grade and quality that may injure competition; and they make unlawful "unfair methods of competition" and "unfair or deceptive practices."

The term "deceptive practices" refers to false advertising, misrepresentation, simulation of competitive products, and bad-mouthing competitors. Even on violations by a manufacturer or distributor, a retailer may be considered equally guilty if he or she knowingly accepts an illegal concession offered by the vendor.

Any firm conducting business across state lines is subject to federal regulations—usually those of the Federal Trade Commission (FTC). Any business that advertises in more than one state is subject to FTC regulations. Even the smallest mail-order business comes under FTC jurisdiction.

A fairly common statute forbids the sale of any article at less than the seller's cost if the intent is to injure competitors. Other laws deal with "bait-and-switch" selling, withholding appropriate refunds on deposits made by customers, misrepresenting warranties and guarantees, and quality requirements for certain products.

In November 1988, the Reagan administration lifted a 46-year-old ban on at-home work in five apparel-related industries. The new regulation, which went into effect in January 1989, means that people will no longer be prohibited from manufacturing various apparel items at home, including gloves, buttons, handkerchiefs, and some types of jewelry. This new ruling should allow more individuals to make a living as home-based business owners. However, because of the complexities of these regulations and the penalties imposed for violations, it is essential that you consult a lawyer if your business may be subject to them.

RESOURCES

Associations

American Management Association, 135 West 50th Street, New York, NY 10020, 212-586-8100

Center for Entrepreneurial Management, Inc., 180 Varick Street, 17th Floor, New York, NY 10014, 212-633-0060

Small Business Network, 10451 Mill Run Circle, Suite 400, Baltimore, MD 21270, 410-581-1373

Small Business Service Bureau, 554 Main Street, Worcester, MA 01601, 508-756-3513

Magazines

Barron's National Business and Financial Weekly, 200 Liberty Street, New York, NY 10281, 212-416-2700

The Business Owner, Thomas Publishing Inc., 383 South Broadway, Hicksville, NY 11801, 516-681-2111

Business Review, One Kwik Kopy Lane, P.O. Box 777, Cypress, TX 77429-2164, 713-373-3535

D&B Reports, 299 Park Avenue, New York, NY 10171-0102, 212-593-6723

Entrepreneurial Manager, Center for Entrepreneurial Management, 180 Varick Street, New York, NY 10014, 212-633-0060

Entrepreneurial Manager's Newsletter, 180 Varick Street, 17th Floor, New York, NY 10014-4692, 212-633-0060

In Business, 2718 Dryden Drive, Madison, WI 53704, 608-246-3580

Journal of Small Business Management, West Virginia University, College of Business Economics, Bureau of Business Research, P.O. Box 6025, Morgantown, WV 26506-6025, 304-293,5837; Fax, 304-293-7061

Nation's Business, 1615 H Street NW, Washington, DC 20062, 202-463-5650

6

Location

One of the first things you need to consider in structuring your business is the appropriate location and a suitable physical plant or office that will allow for an efficient operation and future expansion. Location is the most important factor in real estate. A good location will do more for you than even the most ambitious advertising campaign.

While location is a vital concern for retailers because they rely a great deal on visibility and exposure to their target markets, location is equally important in the planning of service and manufacturing ventures.

Service businesses may not have the foot traffic and high visibility requirements of retailers, but that doesn't mean they can locate miles from their customer base either. It doesn't make sense for you or your clients to be out on the road for a tremendous length of time. You will run the risk of alienating those clients, and eventually they will find someone closer to service their needs.

Manufacturers also have to take location into consideration. They need to keep operating costs down, and that means locating near key suppliers in an area that will be cost efficient and zoned for manufacturing.

The two major aspects in locating your business are (1) deciding on the particular community and (2) choosing a site within that community. This type of research is typically referred to as a *trade area analysis*.

TARGETING THE RIGHT COMMUNITY

The community or trade area where you will operate your business is generally that geographic domain from which you will draw the major portion of the customers needed to support your business on a continuing basis. According to

Hal Pickle and Royce Abrahamson in their book, *Small Business Management*,[1] the trade area can usually be divided into three district zones of influence:

1. **The primary trading area.** The geographic area within the community where you will be able to exert the most influence. It usually accounts for 75 percent of sales.
2. **The secondary trading area.** The geographic area immediately beyond the primary trading zone. The secondary trading area usually accounts for 15 to 20 percent of sales.
3. **The tertiary trading area.** Business generated from customers who do not reside in the area but still patronize your business. The tertiary trading area usually accounts for 5 percent or more of sales.

To conduct an analysis of the community you will consider many factors. The important concerns are:

- Is the population base large enough to support your business?
- Does the community have a stable economic base that will promote a healthy environment for your business?
- Are demographic characteristics compatible with the market you wish to serve?
- What are the community attitudes or outlook?

Weigh these considerations according to your business needs and goals.

Population Requirements

Each year, the United States Bureau of the Census publishes Economic Censuses that are comprehensive studies on the number of firms in different spheres of business and the populations of the communities where they are located. For more information, write to Customer Services, Bureau of the Census, Washington, DC 20233.

An area as small as a county would be ideal for a start-up investigation. The first thing you want to do is isolate a Standard Metropolitan Statistical Area (SMSA) in which to locate your business. These areas contain the largest cities and their surrounding communities. Then you can extrapolate the information you need, such as population.

Economic Base

A community's economic base determines your opportunities. The wealth produced in or near the community greatly affects local employment, income, and population growth.

---

[1] Hal B. Pickle & Royce L. Abrahamson, *Small Business Management*, 5th ed. (New York: John Wiley & Sons, 1990).

People move from one community to another for better employment opportunities and higher income prospects. The occupational makeup of a community depends on the types of jobs its resources and location will support, while its population density depends on the number of such jobs available. The nature and number of jobs largely determine the size and distribution of incomes earned by the community's residents.

To evaluate a community's economic base, obtain the following information:

1. The percentage of people employed full-time and the trend in employment.
2. The average family income.
3. Per capita total annual sales for your goods.

You can find these statistics by studying census data and other business statistics. You can also learn a great deal about your prospective community by looking and listening. Some danger signals include the following:

1. The necessity for high school and college graduates to leave town to find suitable employment.
2. The inability of other residents to find local jobs.
3. Declining retail sales and industrial production.
4. An apathetic attitude on the part of local business owners, educational administrators, and other residents.

Favorable signs are:

1. The opening of chain- or department-store branches.
2. Branch plants of large industrial firms locating in the community.
3. A progressive chamber of commerce and other civic organizations.
4. Good schools and public services.
5. Well-maintained business and residential premises.
6. Good transportation facilities to other parts of the country.
7. Construction activity accompanied by a minimal number of vacant buildings and unoccupied houses for sale.

Demographic Profile

You must know the demographic profile of your potential customers to properly evaluate a community for location. (Figure 6.1 provides a sample Demographic Comparison form.) To see if the community you are considering offers a population with the demographic traits necessary to support your business, look at the following:

1. **Purchasing power.** Find out degree of disposable income within a community.
2. **Residences.** Determine whether they are rented or owned, houses, condos, or apartments.
3. **Places and kinds of work.** These factors will suggest the social affinity of the population within the area.

Figure 6.1   Demographic Comparison

To see if the community you are considering offers a population with the demographic traits you need for your business, fill out the following form.

Population	Market A	Market B	Market C
Within one mile of your business			
Within five miles of your business			
Within 25 miles of your business			

Predominant Income	Market A	Market B	Market C
Under $15,000			
$15,000-$25,000			
$25,000-$35,000			
$35,000-$50,000			
$50,000 +			

Age	Market A	Market B	Market C
Preteen			
Teens			
20-29			
30-39			
40-49			
50-59			
60-69			
70 +			

Density	Market A	Market B	Market C
Homeowners			
Renters			
Urban			

4. **Means of transportation.** Do potential customers in the area own a vehicle, ride the bus, ride a bicycle, and so on?
5. **Age ranges.** Does the community consist primarily of young people still approaching their prime earning years or are most residents retired people?
6. **Family status.** Are there a lot of families in the area or mostly singles?
7. **Leisure activities.** What type of hobbies and recreational activities do people within the area participate in?

Detailed demographic information should be available from established businesses within your industry or from a trade association. There are a few national headquarters for trade associations, many of them located in Washington, DC. These are, by and large, lobbying organizations whose stated aim is to protect the interests of business in relation to the government.

There is at least one trade association serving virtually every industry in the world. Become familiar with Gale's *Encyclopedia of Associations,* available in most libraries. It contains the national headquarters for most associations. Many associations also have local or regional chapters that serve members in a variety of ways, with everything from market newsletters to lobbying actions.

In addition, the Bureau of Labor Statistics publishes the Consumer Expenditure Survey (CES). The CES annually samples 5,000 households to learn how families and individuals spend their money. Unlike other surveys that might ask only how much people are spending on household or home appliances, the CES questions participants about nearly every expense category—from alcoholic beverages and take-out food to pensions and life insurance. Bureau of Labor Statistics analysts then sort the information and group consumers by income, household size, race, and other factors.

Once you're established in a location, you must remain aware of the community's demographic characteristics. As communities and the people within them change, business owners must either change their locations or redefine the markets they wish to serve. Failure to follow one of these courses can mean reduced revenue or even business collapse.

When you are satisfied that the community you plan to serve has the qualities to support your business, you must choose your site.

Community Attitudes

The way the community feels about itself and its future outlook plays an important part in the success or failure of a small business. If the people in a community are apathetic and don't care about the future of the area, then they will generally adhere to the status quo, and the community's economic vitality will eventually decline.

A community where people are actively involved in the promotion of its attributes can stimulate the local economy with programs designed to build existing business as well as attract new business. Look for signs of positive community attitudes by checking for any special tax breaks from the local government and low-interest loans for business start-up or renovation of existing sites.

SITE LOCATION

Site location is a critical factor in determining success, not only for a retail business but for wholesaling, service, and manufacturing as well. According to studies conducted by the SBA, poor location is among the chief causes of all business failures.

In determining a site for a retailing operation, you must be willing to pay for a good location. The cost of the location often reflects the volume and/or quality of the business you will generate. Never select a site location merely because the facility is open and available. Base your selection of site on the market information you've obtained and the potential in that area. The sample Location Checklist will be helpful in choosing a location.

There are many types of service-oriented businesses, and just as many parameters are used in choosing an appropriate site. The most important considerations for a service site location are the type of customers you will attract and how you will service them. Service businesses like nail salons, travel agencies, and dry cleaners do not need to locate in high-rent districts, but they do need to be close to traffic generators such as malls so that they are readily visible to their resident customers. On the other hand, service businesses like TV repair shops and pest control operators are rarely visited by their customers and don't need to locate near traffic generators of any sort. Nevertheless, even if you don't require high visibility, you should locate in an area near your target markets to reduce travel time.

Manufacturers will usually be restricted to industrial areas by the zoning laws of most cities. Your main criteria in these sites will be the suitability of shipping and loading facilities, the distance to key suppliers of raw materials and markets, the availability of cheap fuel, and the skill of the support staff in the local area. The ideal location for most manufacturers is a site central to its total market and key vendors. The only exception to this rule is a manufacturer that deals with perishable materials or produces waste in the processing of its product.

Like manufacturers, wholesalers are restricted by zoning laws within most cities. The main criterion for wholesalers is to be in a site with excellent shipping and receiving facilities near main transportation arteries. A secondary consideration for most wholesalers is the nearness of their local markets. You don't want to locate so far away from your local markets that delivering orders takes an undue amount of time. In addition, the farther you are from your markets, the more money it will cost to deliver the product. You must either absorb that cost or pass it along to the customer. If you pass it along, your price may then become noncompetitive.

✔ LOCATION CHECKLIST

Answer the following questions by indicating whether it is a strength (**S**) or weakness (**W**) of the potential site as it relates to your business. Once you have completed the checklist for each prospective location, compare their relative strengths and weaknesses to determine the value of each to the strategic success of your business.

SITE QUESTIONNAIRE

	S	W
Is the facility large enough for your business?	☐	☐
Does it meet your layout requirements well?	☐	☐
Does the building need any repairs?	☐	☐
Will you have to make any leasehold improvements?	☐	☐
Do the existing utilities meet your needs, or will you have to do any rewiring or plumbing work? Is ventilation adequate?	☐	☐
Is the facility easily accessible to your potential clients or customers?	☐	☐
Can you find a number of qualified employees in the area in which the facility is located?	☐	☐
Is the facility consistent with the image you would like to maintain?	☐	☐
Is the facility located in a safe neighborhood with a low crime rate?	☐	☐
Are neighboring businesses likely to attract customers who will also patronize your business?	☐	☐
Are there any competitors located close to the facility? If so, can you compete with them successfully?	☐	☐
Can suppliers make deliveries conveniently at this location?	☐	☐
If your business expands in the future, will the facility be able to accommodate this growth?	☐	☐
Are the lease terms and rent favorable?	☐	☐
Is the facility located in an area zoned for your type of business?	☐	☐

SITE SELECTION FACTORS

Among the factors to consider when pinpointing an exact location for your business are:

- **Anticipated sales volume.** For many lines of business, only one medium- or large-volume operation offering a particular range of goods or services can successfully locate in a small shopping center or shopping district. You must consider the presence (or, in the case of a new mall or shopping center, the potential presence) of other businesses that will be in direct competition with you. If the foot traffic is high and/or you sell a broad range of goods or services, there might be enough business to divide.
- **Accessibility to potential customers.** When determining accessibility, it is helpful to spot main thoroughfares and major arteries on a map; then measure the distance to your location. Next, spend several days analyzing the site. Sit in your car and judge traffic (foot and auto) patterns at different times of the day. See if the traffic pattern fits the time when you would want to do business. Revisit the prospective site on several different days to observe any changes in the pattern.
- **The rent-paying capacity of the business.** If you have done a sales-and-profit projection for your first year of operation, you will know how much sales you can expect your business to generate. To judge your rental expenses (leased space plus any "add-on" costs), you can express the total amount you expect to pay, on a monthly or annual basis, as a percentage of projected net sales (gross sales minus returns and discounts) and compare that percentage with those of similar businesses.
- **Restrictive ordinances.** You may encounter unusually restrictive ordinances that detract from an otherwise ideal site, such as limitations on the hours of the day when trucks are permitted to load or unload. Cities and towns are composed of areas—from a few blocks to many acres in size—zoned for only commercial, industrial, or residential development. Within each zone are often further restrictions. A commercial zone may permit one type of business but not another, so check the zoning codes of any potential location before pursuing a specific site or spending a lot of time and money on a market survey.
- **Traffic density.** For retail and service businesses that depend on a great amount of traffic, either auto or foot, you must be sure there is a sufficient volume of both. Modern site analysis distinguishes between automobile and pedestrian traffic. If only auto traffic were considered, most businesses would be located near highways or main roads. With careful examination of foot traffic, you can determine the approximate sales potential of each pedestrian passing a given location. To make a pedestrian-traffic count, select a few half-hour periods during the busy hours of the day. Only possible customers for your particular business should be counted. Interview those passing by the site you are considering. Do they

feel a need for this type of business at this location? Would they patronize it? What kinds of goods or services would they be interested in buying? Where do they now shop for these goods and services?

- **Customer parking facilities.** Does the particular site provide easy, adequate parking and access for customers? Is it well lit? Is there sufficient security? What is the condition of the parking area? (Will it need expansion, resurfacing, or striping—possibly at additional cost?) Keep in mind that even large shopping centers and business parks sometimes do not have adequate parking for all their customers. If you plan to locate in a mall, strip center, or business park, evaluate the parking conditions over a period of days at different times and judge whether or not they are acceptable.
- **Proximity to other businesses.** Your business neighbors may influence your volume of business. Their presence can work for you as well as against you, particularly if you locate next to businesses in the same affinity class.
- **Side of the street.** Marketing research has demonstrated that the going-home side of the street is usually preferable to the going-to-work side. People are more likely to stop at stores on the way home than when they are in a hurry to get to work on time. Also, the sunny side of the street is generally less desirable for retail operations than the shady side, especially in warm climates. Research shows that rents are higher on the shady side in high-priced shopping areas.
- **History of the site.** You should learn at least the recent history of each site under consideration before you make a final selection. These are sites—in malls and big shopping centers, as well as independent locations—that have been occupied by a succession of business failures. However, the reason for one or several businesses failing in a given site may be completely unrelated to the success potential of your business.
- **Terms of the lease.** Leasing considerations can sometimes be the deciding factor in your choice of a site. Occasionally, an otherwise ideal site may have unacceptable leasing terms. The time to negotiate leasing terms is before you sign the lease.
- **The rent-advertising relationship.** The amount you plan to spend on advertising may be closely related to your choice of site and the proposed rent. If you locate in a shopping center or mall supported by huge ad budgets as well as the presence of large, popular chain and department stores, you will most likely generate revenue from the first day you open your doors—with no individual advertising at all. Of course, your rental expenses will be proportionately higher than those for an independent location.

FACILITY CHOICES

In choosing a site, a major consideration is the type of facility you prefer. Depending on where you decide to start your business, you will probably have a number of choices. Smaller towns may be limited in the sites and structures available, but larger towns and cities will offer you a wide array of options.

Shopping Centers

For retailers and service businesses that rely on a great deal of walk-in traffic, a shopping center may offer the best exposure. These commercial centers house many different small businesses as well as one or more well-known chain stores that act as anchors and traffic generators. Shopping centers are generally managed by the developer or a professional organization hired by the developer, and most of them require their business tenants to join the center's merchant association. Since the association is responsible for funding the marketing and maintenance of the center's common area, each tenant is expected to pay an additional fee beyond the rent in the lease. In fact, triple-net leases (see Chapter 7) are very popular among many shopping center developers, as are percentage leases.

Shopping centers cover a wide variety of structures that vary in size and scope of the areas served. They are defined, according to the Urban Land Institute, by the type of tenants or major tenants, as follows:

- **Regional shopping center.** Caters primarily to communities that generally fall within a 15-mile radius. It is usually anchored by at least four well-known chain stores at different wings of the structure. In addition to the prominent chain stores, there will also be an array of specialty retail shops, restaurants, and services.
- **Community shopping center.** Usually targets a specific vicinity within a 10-mile radius. It can be anchored by well-known regional chain store, supermarket, or discount store. In addition to these establishments, there are restaurants, specialty retail shops, and personal services.
- **Neighborhood shopping center.** Attracts customers from local residential districts. Main traffic generators include supermarkets and/or drug stores. Other tenants usually include convenience-related shops such as video stores, fast-food restaurants, banks, and hair salons.
- **Convenience shopping centers.** Also relies heavily on customers from local residential districts. The difference between convenience and neighborhood shopping centers is size and the anchor of the establishment. Convenience shopping centers are usually anchored by convenience stores with maybe five other businesses such as fast-food restaurants, gas stations, and laundromat.

Within these geographic definitions of shopping centers, there are many different types of establishments such as malls, factory outlet centers, and strip centers or minimalls.

Of all the shopping centers, malls are probably the most expensive in terms of the rent, ranging between $4 and $5 per square foot a month, but they are also popular places for shopping among consumers. Malls can be either totally enclosed, multilevel buildings or open-air facilities. If you start your business from a mall location, the chances of generating a profit from day one will be a lot greater than starting in any other type of facility.

Factory outlet centers have been a recent phenomenon that tend to be regional in basis. If you are a manufacturer of retail goods, a factory outlet center offers an opportunity to open a distribution channel where you deal directly with the end-user of your product(s). The main attraction of a factory outlet center for the end-user is better prices, usually 30 to 40 percent less than retailers. Rent can be high, however, ranging anywhere from $3 to $5 per square foot a month.

A strip center or minimall is another kind of popular shopping center. Most are open-air facilities that feature a row of stores stretching from one end of the structure to the other. A strip center usually includes a major chain store and a supermarket as its anchor. Compared with malls, strip centers are a bargain in terms of rent. Depending on proximity to major traffic generators like regional malls, rents for strip centers can range anywhere from $1.50 to $4 per square foot a month.

The main complaints from shopping center tenants relate to the exorbitant marketing and maintenance fees stipulated in the leases. For some small businesses, these expenses can literally eat up any potential net profit. As mentioned already, you should determine the sales volume your business can reasonably hope to attain and decide whether or not you can afford the rent at a heavy-traffic shopping center.

Business Parks and Office Buildings

Professional and service businesses that deal with many business clients may want to consider an office within a business park or office building. Business parks are usually one or more office buildings located on the same lot and managed by the developer or a professional management company hired by the developer. Office space is commonly leased out on a triple-net basis with the tenants sharing in the maintenance costs of the building. Many times, this maintenance cost will include service to your own office as well as security.

The advantage of leasing office space within a business park is the professional image it provides for your company, which is designed to build professional relationships with your client base. This is especially important when dealing with the corporate sector. Most managers in corporations prefer to deal with professional organizations. To compete with other companies vying for the same business, you must portray your business as one that is just as competent and professional. This takes on greater significance if your clients will be coming to your office on a regular basis.

Executive Suites

Another office option for professional and business service entrepreneurs is an executive suite. Executive suites lease office space and provide secretarial services to a number of small—often one-person—businesses like yours.

According to the Executive Suite Network, the average executive suite occupies about 14,500 square feet and houses 50 offices. The average office is about

180 square feet. Monthly rent, running about $500 to $1,200 per month, varies by the market, size of the office, and location of the office within the building.

Executive suites provide tenants with short-term leases, generally six months to one year. Suites usually include a telephone, use of common areas (lobby, conference room, kitchen, etc.), a receptionist, and incoming mail reception. Office utilities are also usually included in the tenant's monthly rent and a professional office manager runs the group of suites.

Executive suites offer a range of support services to their clients, including faxing, photocopying, and word processing. Tenants only use these services as needed and pay for them as used, which minimizes operating costs.

To find executive suite facilities in your area, look in the business-to-business telephone directory under "Executive Suites."

Freestanding Buildings

Freestanding locations can be beneficial for both retailers, service-oriented companies, and restaurants. They traditionally offer a lower fixed rent, usually based on square footage, less extensive rules and regulations governing the operations of the business, and no extra advertising or common-area fees that must be paid to a merchant's association. Also, dealing with an eager lessor may give you more freedom to negotiate favorable lease terms. What the freestanding businessowner loses, however, are the shared (and thus lower) expenses for utilities, pest control, security, trash service, maintenance, and advertising.

LEASING CONSIDERATIONS

Leasing considerations can sometimes be the major determining factor in your choice of a site. Occasionally, a site that is otherwise ideal may have to be ruled out because the leasing terms are not right for your business. Remember that terms are negotiable, and the time to negotiate is before you sign the lease. For more information on leasing, see Chapter 7.

PHYSICAL PLANT REQUIREMENTS

The physical plant requirements are directly related to location. You may have found the perfect location, but what if the present structure or lack of structure is incompatible with your requirements? You'll have to either find a different site, expand the present facility, or build one from the ground up. Don't choose a site that is too small or that will conflict with the image you want to project.

Physical plant requirements will vary from business to business based on a number of factors:

- Size of staff.
- Storage requirements.

- Sales floor or production area space.
- Office space.
- Parking requirements.
- Projected growth.
- Image.

While each of the preceding factors is important to every business when evaluating physical plant requirements, a different amount of emphasis is placed on each depending on the type of business.

Retailers

Most operations are designed to do one thing—sell merchandise. The interior and exterior of the building are set up around that one theme. Retailers place their emphasis on the sales floor space, adequate parking for customers, and an overall image that draws in auto and foot traffic. Secondary to many retail operations is office space and storage requirements, since most inventory is on the sales floor.

Available space in a retail operation is usually subdivided into retail display space and storage space. Depending on the original floor plan and individual design, retail space can take up well over 90 percent of the total. Obviously, the more retail space you have, the more merchandise you can promote. However, storage and office space are also important parts of the floor plan for a retail operation—to handle shipping and receiving and related chores, to take care of paperwork, and to store extra inventory. Those shops with a fair number of cabinets and shelves require less back-room storage space. Generally, office/storage space should take up 10 to 25 percent of your total floor area.

Service Firms

The physical plant requirements for service firms will vary according to the type of business. There are really no common factors that can be applied to each service firm except that the physical plant should be consistent with the volume and type of business conducted. For instance, nail salons need a facility with an attractive waiting area and with a sufficient number of workstations where technicians will perform their service. The facility should be large enough to allow for a growth in volume and have sufficient parking for the clientele who will be utilizing the service. Storage is also another consideration that nail salon operators have to take into account. A sufficient amount of product has to be available not only to service the client but to offer for resale as well.

However, while nail salons require a physical plant built around the service of their customers, other businesses like pool cleaning and repair businesses need only limited office space for sales and clerical work, and storage for chemicals and equipment. Services like pool cleaning are mobile. The service operator visits the home or complex, cleans the pool, and is paid. After completing the route of jobs for the day, the service operator returns to the main facility, stores the chemicals and equipment, performs any paperwork in the office, and that's the extent of the physical plant.

Since service firms vary so much from business to business, the main thing to keep in mind is current volume and projected growth of business. You don't want to locate in such a large facility that it dwarfs your staffing, storage, and service requirements. On the other hand, you don't want to settle in a facility that will be obsolete for your needs within a month.

Manufacturers

The physical plant requirements for manufacturers depend largely on the type of product and the processing it requires. But the main goal of every manufacturer is to prevent the unproductive movement of work and materials through the manufacturing process. Therefore, a lot of emphasis is placed on the production area and the layout of that space.

Different products require different types of layouts. Some of the principles of plant layout are as follows:

1. Plan the shortest route from entrance to exit for materials and semifinished product.
2. Minimize handling by having as many operations as possible performed at each stop.
3. Eliminate bottlenecks in the production process caused by slowdowns of processes at strategic locations. Although this depends in part on the adequacy and care of machinery, the location of the machinery is a vital factor.
4. Recognize that the misuse of space is as important as the misuse of machinery and human resources.
5. Eliminate backtracking, overlapping of work, and unnecessary inspection by constantly considering possibilities for new sequences and combinations of steps in processing or fabricating.

Management consultants may solve the more complicated problems of factory planning, but you can do a lot for yourself. First, prepare a route sheet for each standardized part or product you manufacture and/or for each job order you process, indicating the proper sequence of factory operations. By arranging production equipment according to the sequence of operations, you eliminate backtracking, reduce materials handling, and streamline the flow of work. The Manufacturer's Site Planning Checklist will help you complete this task.

By planning your layout beforehand, you'll be able to determine your physical plant requirements. In addition to production layout, however, you'll have to take into consideration storage facilities for raw materials and finished products, staffing requirements, office space for employees not on the production line, and any future expansion of operations.

MANUFACTURER'S SITE PLANNING CHECKLIST

When planning the layout of your manufacturing site, you want to be able to move raw material into the plant and process it through the manufacturing routine as efficiently as possible. With this in mind, ask yourself the following questions.

☐ Does your receiving area provide easy access to large trucks?

☐ Is suitable equipment on hand in the receiving area to unload incoming shipments efficiently?

☐ Do you have enough space to adequately warehouse your raw materials inventory?

☐ Are your raw materials properly labeled in the warehouse area for easy retrieval?

☐ Is your warehouse space for raw material near the first station used in the manufacturing process?

☐ Have you planned out the steps in the manufacturing process—accounted for space on the manufacturing floor for the necessary equipment in appropriate areas so the product can be processed through each step without having to backtrack to other stations on the floor?

☐ Have you analyzed each station in the manufacturing process to assure equipment is arranged in the most efficient manner?

☐ Are you maximizing the potential of each station for performing as many tasks as possible in that area without creating a bottleneck?

☐ Is your finished product warehouse area located near the last station in the manufacturing process?

☐ Are there proper storage materials and equipment such as floor racks, slip sheets, and pallets to handle the finished product?

☐ Is there appropriate materials handling equipment to move the finished product into storage and out once it is ready to ship?

☐ Is your shipping area in proximity to the warehouse area for the finished product?

☐ Is your shipping area easily accessible to large trucks?

Wholesalers

Most wholesalers design their facilities around the idea of filling orders with speed and efficiency. Most of their physical requirements center around two main items: storage, where merchandise is warehoused and orders are fulfilled; and offices, where orders are received and processed.

Over 60 percent of a wholesaler's operation will be devoted to storage. This area houses all the products the wholesaler sells in an easily accessible and ordered layout that expedites the handling of orders.

The offices of a wholesaler have to be large enough to comfortably allow for all inside sales personnel. Many times this will only be from 30 to 40 percent of the entire facility. The main consideration is to create an efficient office area for placing and processing the order entries to be fulfilled in the warehouse.

For wholesalers, image plays an important part but is based primarily on the speed of order fulfillment. Therefore, while the interior and exterior of the wholesaler's facility should be clean and presentable, there doesn't have to be that sense of merchandising that is associated with a retail operation.

Leasing and Leasehold Improvements

Generally speaking, it will be easier to build from the ground up to meet your physical plant requirements, but it is also the most expensive way to tackle your needs in this area. For the small business concern, it may be better to lease a facility and alter the interior and exterior to meet your requirements. This will reduce your start-up costs and free up cash for other things.

Leases are usually strong contracts. If you sign a lease for $1,000 per month for a period of one year, you are agreeing, in essence, to pay $12,000, regardless of what happens to your business. Therefore, some operators recommend starting out with the shortest lease term possible until you can see where you are going.

A one- or two-year lease with an option on renewal for five years at an agreed upon rental is a desirable target for most beginning retailers. The option to renew protects you from losing your lease at a good location and having to build your business from scratch at a new one.

It may not always be possible to rent premises on a year-to-year basis or on a short, multiyear lease, but you should never feel pressured to accept what's offered to you; there will always be another site opening up elsewhere—perhaps one even better suited for your business.

A good lease from your point of view is one that can easily be assigned to another tenant in the event your business fails or you need another facility. Therefore, make certain it contains a provision for assignment or subletting. Such a clause will allow you to close or move your business while permitting you to get another tenant to pay your rental obligation for the balance of the lease term. It will also allow you to sell your business to a new owner who can assume your lease under the same good terms you have.

Improvements to the interior of the facility are often referred to as leasehold improvements. These are nonremovable installations that are either original or the result of remodeling. Depending on the condition of the physical plant and your requirements, leasehold improvements can represent a substantial portion of your capital investment, or they can amount to a few minor repairs. Either way, improving an existing facility will be less expensive than building from the ground up.

Finishing work on the "shell" left by builders can include such things as carpeting and other flooring; insulation; electrical wiring and plumbing; bathroom installations; lighting; wall partitions; windows; ceiling tiles; painting; a sprinkler system; security systems; some elements of interior design; and sometimes heating and/or air-conditioning systems.

The type of facility you have, where it is (mall/shopping strip center/freestanding; regional/nonregional), and whether it is "raw" or established will primarily determine how much you spend. Because the cost of improvements can vary tremendously (from $5/sq. ft. to over $50/sq. ft.), you must investigate this carefully. Because the cost can run very high, some developers will partially finance lease improvements—but usually only for "promising" lessees with previous success records.

Improvements on a freestanding location will be far less expensive than on a shopping-center shell. You might need to add to or change some elements of the "HVAC" (heating, ventilation, air conditioning) and make some design changes (including lighting), but the basic structure, with insulation, plumbing, wiring, etc. is provided. Another way to save on leasehold improvements is to find and buy a business that is already designed and set up to fit the image of your venture.

PURCHASING

Many small retail and services businesses find it impractical and financially unfeasible to purchase a site. If you do your homework in scouting a good location and negotiate the best and most appropriate lease for your needs, leasing will scale down your financial obligations while providing you with the best possible location. There are businesses—among them quick-lube centers, tennis/racquetball clubs, health clubs, car washes, bed-and-breakfast inns—where it's frequently advantageous to buy property. But even in these businesses some operators prefer to lease.

So why purchase? There are a number of advantages you should consider in any decision regarding whether or not you will purchase or lease your facility. The advantages to purchasing are:

- **Increased tax benefits.** The substantial interest payments accompanying the purchase of a property are tax-deductible as are property taxes.

- **No forfeiture of asset at end of term.** Since lessees do not own their property, they won't obtain the value of the asset when the lease is up unless they purchase the property.
- **Increased net worth.** Both you and your business benefit from the appreciation of your land and building(s).
- **Ability to liquidate.** You can sell your property when the need arises, in the process benefiting from the accrued appreciation. Lessors, on the other hand, sometimes face noncancelable clauses in a lease contract or are charged a severe penalty for early termination.

The following problems are among the disadvantages that drive the owners of businesses to lease a facility instead of purchasing:

- Frequently, purchasing represents a higher monthly financial outlay than a lease, absorbing capital that could best be put to other uses.
- Frequently, there is a hefty downpayment, anywhere from 10 to 30 percent of the purchase price.
- In the event of bankruptcy, creditors can claim your property as an asset.
- Maintenance is not provided. You're solely responsible for the maintenance of your property; some leases include maintenance costs.
- In a depressed or tight real estate market, you might have a difficult time selling, perhaps taking a loss.
- If you've made major alterations to the property that are unique to your business, you may have difficulty selling to merchants in other industries, or may have to reduce the selling price to compensate for necessary buyer renovations.

If yours is a business in which the purchase of property clearly could be an advantage, consider the following methods of purchasing.

Methods of Purchasing

Whether to lease or buy will depend on several factors, your start-up capital chief among them. If operating a business that requires a large facility built from the ground up, one method is to negotiate a triple-net lease with a developer, who either buys the land and leases it back to you or buys the land and bankrolls the construction of the building, leasing the entire property back to you at a prearranged annual interest rate and in some cases taking a percentage of the gross. In this case, the developer becomes a silent partner.

This arrangement reduces otherwise hefty front-end costs to a first-and-last-month payment but also reduces your autonomy. Some operators have taken this plan a step further, negotiating a lease-purchase, with a balloon buyback at a specified time; this assures eventual sole ownership while reducing front-end costs.

Seller- or bank-financed purchases are more common, requiring up to 30 percent down and in some cases involving balloon payments. A typical bank-financed arrangement is 20 percent down, with the balance paid over a 15-year period. The cost of land and construction will vary by region and according to your needs.

They are many ways to structure the purchase of property. They include:

- **Adjustable rate mortgage (ARM).** Adjustable rate mortgages come in many forms, but they all have interest rates that move with the prevailing interest rates. The adjustments are limited by a floor and ceiling cap, setting the parameters to avoid extreme fluctuations. Without an overall cap rate, you run the danger of not ever paying on the principal. This is called negative amortization, which occurs at the point where your payments are less than what it takes to pay off the principal. Set up the worst-case scenario, in which interest rates skyrocket the day after you sign the loan. Are the payments still within the realm of your budget?

- **Fixed rate mortgage.** Payments remain constant for the term of the loan. With a fixed-rate conventional mortgage, you are paying for an inherent form of insurance. The bank will absorb the risk of the rise and fall of the prime lending rate.

- **Growing equity mortgages (GEMs).** These are fixed-rate mortgages in which the monthly payments increase each year by a fixed increment, usually 3 percent. The mortgage is paid off faster, because the additional payments go directly toward reduction of the principal.

- **Graduated payment mortgages (GPMs).** These are one of the more popular flexible loans from a lender's point of view. They operate on the basis of negative amortization; instead of your principal decreasing, it actually increases during the early years of the loan. The GPM is a fixed-rate loan with lower monthly payments during the first few years, usually 5 or 10 years. Throughout the graduation period, the monthly payments will increase slowly from year to year based on a schedule agreed on by the lender and borrower.

In short, if you're expecting to sell the property or business within three to five years and interest rates are trending downward, we recommend an adjustable-rate mortgage. If you're expecting to hold onto the property/business for more than five years and interest rates are hard to predict (they usually are), a fixed rate is generally preferable.

Pitfalls

Consider the following when buying a property:

- You buy a property in an area that seems economically healthy but is actually in decline; business is moving out for any number of reasons, all of which you slowly find out as you search for your customer base well after escrow has closed. Make sure the area is economically sound and conducive to the business you plan to operate—now and in the foreseeable future.

- You purchase a property near a vacant, corner gas station. That property is subsequently purchased by a minimall developer, who leases to a franchising competitor with wider name recognition than yours. Thoroughly scout the area before buying; you can't prevent competitors from moving in, but by doing your homework and establishing worst-case scenarios, you can eliminate—or at lease be prepared for—surprises.
- You buy a property from a developer and develop a thriving business. The developer then buys a property down the street and establishes a competing business. If you buy from anyone who conceivably could compete with you in your area, make sure you include a no-competition clause in the agreement that covers silent-partner involvement.

RESOURCES

Associations

Industrial Development Research Council, 40 Technology Park/Atlanta, Suite 200, Norcross, GA 30092, 404-446-6996

International Institute of Site Planning, 715 G Street SE, Washington DC 20003, 202-546-2322

Magazines

Site Selection and Industrial Development, 40 Technology Park/Atlanta, Norcross, GA 30092-2906, 404-446-6996

Publication

Encyclopedia of Associations, Gale Research, Inc., 835 Penobscot Building, Detroit, MI 48226-4094, 313-961-2242

7

Leasing

A small business just getting underway will most likely need all the operating capital it can lay its hands on. Therefore, investing most of its equity into equipment or a building could drain much of the capital that could be used toward product development, services that could be marketed, or the all-important advertising/promotional package. Also, a large debt could restrict the possibilities of other financing options.

Leasing allows you to obtain the needed equipment or facility without a large capital outlay. You should always investigate the option of leasing versus purchasing. Leasing companies will lease everything from computers to farm machinery, sometimes with the option to purchase the item at the end of the lease term. Lenders, including manufacturers, may offer leasing plans for longer terms and lower monthly payments than if you purchased the item and made loan payments. The tax benefits granted to the owner are usually worth more to the lessor, who will be in a higher tax bracket than the entrepreneur in the start-up phase of his or her business.

A lease is a contract between an owner and a user of property. With respect to the new business owner, this agreement will allow the rental of equipment, land, buildings, or any other assets. The difference between renting and leasing usually depends on the length of the contract. Whereas renting constitutes a short-term contract (a day, month, or year), leasing normally implies a stronger contract; a three- to five-year lease is common.

Unlike purchasing loans, which require heavy down payments, leasing offers 100 percent financing. This is where your company saves money initially. In the long run, leasing costs more money, but it might be the most efficient route to follow at this point in your new business. You, the small business owner, are considered the *lessee*, and the owner of the property is the *lessor*.

The lessor benefits from this relationship by covering the cost of the leased equipment or property, receiving tax benefits, and at the same time making a profit. The lessee benefits by making smaller payments, retaining the ability to walk away from the equipment or property at the end of the lease term, and perhaps having the lessor pay for the costs of maintenance.

LEASING CONSIDERATIONS

When making a decision between leasing and purchasing, you should understand the advantages and disadvantages of leasing. Let's look at the advantages first:

- **Minimum cash outlay.** Through leasing you acquire the use of an asset without a large initial capital outlay. In fact, leases are often 100 percent financed.
- **Less stringent financial requirements.** Lessees usually find it easier to obtain financing to lease an asset than to obtain credit to purchase it.
- **No equipment obsolescence.** You can use new or updated equipment by negotiating a short-term lease and exchanging the equipment at the end of the lease term.
- **Built-in maintenance.** Depending on the terms of the lease, maintenance of the equipment can be included in the lease, thereby reducing your working capital expenses.
- **Tax advantages.** The primary benefit is the deductibility of the lease as an operating expense.
- **Greater payment flexibility.** Not only can leases be spread over a longer period than a loan, thus reducing the monthly payments, they can also be structured to account for variations in cash flow, especially for companies that experience major seasonal sales.
- **Expert advice available from lessor.** This is especially true if the lessor is the manufacturer.

The disadvantages of leasing include:

- **No ownership of the asset.** Since lessees do not own their property, they not only lose the tax benefits associated with ownership (e.g., depreciation, investment tax credit), they do not build any equity in the property unless a lease-to-purchase option agreement is added to the lease.
- **Higher long-term cost.** While leases generally offer lower monthly payments, since they do not offer significant tax benefits and provide no equity in the leased property, the ultimate cost at the end of the lease could be higher than if you purchased the asset.
- **Noncancelable lease contract.** Some leases have noncancelable clauses in the contract or else charge a severe penalty for early termination.

REAL ESTATE LEASES

Real estate leases are typically broken down into the following categories, though occasionally you may see a creative combination of more than one type.

- **Flat lease.** As the term implies, the flat lease is a set price for a set period of time. This lease, which is the oldest and the simplest, is becoming hard to find but is naturally the best deal for the lessee. The danger here is not to be tempted if the term is too short. A series of short-term leases could cost you more in the long run. For instance, suppose your business has been successful in your present location, but your lease is up. To keep the same location, you might have to pay the landlord's high rent increases. If your rent term is short, this could happen over and over again.
- **Step lease.** The step lease recognizes the inevitable increases in the landlord's expenses over time. Taxes will go up, insurance premiums will increase, and the cost of repairs certainly will pace wage inflation. The step lease attempts to second-guess what these expenses will be in the future. It compensates the landlord by annually increasing the monthly rental rate. Therefore, the lease rate may make stepped increases like these over the term of the agreement: 1st year, $450/month; 2nd year, $480/month; 3rd year, $510/month; 4th year, $540/month; 5th year, $570/month.
- **Net lease.** A net lease takes the guesswork out of the step lease problem. You pay the base rent, and when the taxes go up, you pay the dollar increase or your share if more than one tenant is housed within the same facility. Where proportionate sharing occurs, yours is based on the square footage you occupy versus the total size of the facility. If store A has 1,450 square feet, store B has 2,400 square feet, and store C has 850 square feet, then the building has a total of 4,700 square feet. Let's say taxes on the building property go up $880, or 18.7 cents per square foot. So store A's increase is 1,450 × 18.7 cents or $271.15 per year. Store B's increase is 2,400 × 18.7 cents or $448.80 per year, and store C's increase is 850 × 18.7 cents or $158.95 per year. This method ensures that everyone pays a fair share.
- **Double-net lease.** There are net-net (or double-net) versions of the net lease that pick up added insurance premiums as well as tax increases, singularly or on a proportionate basis. Keep in mind that if you do something within your particular business that raises insurance premiums, you alone will pick up the tab.
- **Triple-net lease.** The most popular version of the net lease, it includes similar sharing by tenants of costs for repairs to the building or parking area as well as taxes and insurance. However, remember this is not your building that you are agreeing to maintain. If you pay taxes, insurance, and maintenance costs, the lessor might have little interest in keeping these expenses to a minimum because most of the reimbursement will be coming out of the pockets of the tenants.

- **Cost-of-living lease.** This lease ignores specific expense items, ties everything together, and attaches itself to the *Cost of Living Index*. In short, it takes into account general inflation. At the end of the year, the government's cost of living figures are evaluated. If the inflation has been, for example, 6.8 percent, your rent is increased by a like amount.
- **Percentage lease.** The percentage lease is a favorite among landlords. It allows them to "share the wealth" of a tenant's prospering business. It sets a minimum or base rent to be paid and/or a percentage of the business's gross, whichever is the largest number. Such percentages commonly run from 3 to 12 percent, depending on area, type of business, and desirability of location. They are usually paid on a quarterly, semiannual, or annual basis and adjusted backward, though many shopping centers require a monthly accounting and payment. The percentage lease is usually most applicable to properties in prime retail areas. Within those prime areas, specific locations (e.g., corner locations) may be subject to a higher percentage rate. If you have a percentage lease, the lessor will probably require you to furnish proof of gross sales periodically. This is done by examination of your books, sales tax records, or in some cases by copy of the appropriate attachment to your IRS Form 1040.

Other Terms

A real estate lease usually covers other important matters, such as any remodeling to be done, who is to pay for it, liabilities and duties assumed by each party, and permission for the tenant to erect external signs, engage in additional lines of business, or make future alterations if needed. A lease is an important legal document, and as a small-business owner you should always seek competent legal counsel before signing one.

You can negotiate the lease prepared by the lessor. It is not engraved in stone but is extended to you for your consideration. If you accept it without discussion, you have met the lessor's conditions entirely. By simply asking, though, you may be able to negotiate much better terms, particularly for the length of the lease. If the lessor's answer is no, you have lost nothing. You can always look elsewhere and come back to the first location if you don't find a better offer.

Any of the real estate leases can be good or bad depending on your kind of business, its exact situation, and above all its realistic growth potential. A good rule of thumb is to revert back to hard numbers. Consider not only the present price per square foot, but even more the price at the end of the leasing term. Remember, it's easy to view things at face value and put aside other considerations. This is why financial projections are so important.

Leasehold Improvements

As mentioned, a lease will usually cover any type of remodeling to the physical structure that needs to be done and specifies who will pay for it. Some of this remodeling will fall into the realm of what is known as *leasehold improvements.*

These can include carpeting and other flooring, insulation, electrical wiring and plumbing, bathroom installations, lighting, wall partitions, windows, ceiling tiles, painting, a sprinkler system, security systems, some elements of interior design, and sometimes heating and/or air conditioning systems.

Leasehold improvements in new shopping centers or malls are by far the most extensive. Prospective operators often discover to their amazement that the shopping center provides only concrete walls and flooring. The finishing work often comes out of the retailer's pocket; however, you can negotiate a *construction allowance* of anywhere from $5 to $25 per square foot to help offset the cost of some leasehold improvements.

Helpful Hints

If you are concerned about the length of your lease and want to protect your location indefinitely, get a "right of refusal" clause into the agreement. Lessors usually won't object as they aren't giving up anything.

Simply stated, this clause provides that before selling the real estate, the lessor must first offer you the chance to buy it at the same price as the offer that has been received. If you really have your heart set on the property, but can't afford it, nail the price down with an option. This will cost you the up-front option money should you finally decide not to buy, but it can be far less than the appreciated price next year or the year after.

The time to ask for that new coat of paint outside or inside is immediately, before you sign the lease. Get it in writing, if not in the lease itself then by a "letter of addendum" that automatically becomes part of the lease. Make sure the lease specifies the landlord is responsible for damages such as roof leaks, faulty plumbing, or wiring. You'll have enough worries in the start-up phase of your business without worrying about your building falling in on you.

Don't hassle your landlord with petty maintenance problems. You should be covered if your lease is written correctly. Save your negotiations for the big problems.

If you need to modify the premises, don't be shy about asking the landlord to cut appreciably or to forgo the first month's rent. You might not get it, but on the other hand, you might be pleasantly surprised. Always point out that you are going to increase the value of the property with your operation and with improvements you will make to the facility from time to time.

Some leases include charges for common area expenses such as maintenance of walkways, landscaping, parking lots, and security. Though charging for these services is acceptable, some lessors try to turn common area charges into profit centers, adding on charges such as administration expenses. Also, beware of leases that give landlords the right to remodel at the tenants' expense without their prior approval (see Business-Lease Checklist).

BUSINESS-LEASE CHECKLIST

After you have chosen a particular site, check the following points before you sign the lease:

- ☐ Is there sufficient electrical power?
- ☐ Are there enough electrical outlets?
- ☐ Is there enough parking space for customers and employees?
- ☐ Is there sufficient lighting? Heating? Air conditioning?
- ☐ Do you know how large a sign and what type you can erect at your facility?
- ☐ Will your city's building and zoning departments allow your business to operate in the facility?
- ☐ Will the landlord allow the alterations that you deem necessary for your business?
- ☐ Must you pay for returning the building to its original condition when you move?
- ☐ Is there any indication of roof leaks? (A heavy rain could damage stored goods.)
- ☐ Is the cost of burglary insurance high in the area? (This varies tremendously.)
- ☐ Can you secure the building at a low cost against the threat of burglary?
- ☐ Will the health department approve your business at this location?
- ☐ Will the fire department approve the operation of your business at this location?
- ☐ Have you included a written description of the real property?
- ☐ Have you attached drawings of the property to the lease document?
- ☐ Do you have written guidelines for renewal terms?
- ☐ Do you know when your lease payment begins?
- ☐ Have you bargained for one to three months free rent?
- ☐ Do you know your date of possession?
- ☐ Have you listed the owner's responsibility for improvements?
- ☐ Do you pay the taxes?
- ☐ Do you pay the insurance?
- ☐ Do you pay the maintenance fees?
- ☐ Do you pay the utilities?
- ☐ Do you pay the sewer fees?
- ☐ Have you asked your landlord for a cap of 5 percent on your rent increases?
- ☐ Have you included penalty clauses in case the project is late and you're denied occupancy?
- ☐ Have you retained the right to obtain your own bids for signage?
- ☐ Can you escape if the center is never more than 70 percent leased?
- ☐ Has a real estate attorney reviewed your contract?

EQUIPMENT LEASES

Equipment leases differ from real estate leases in that equipment leases usually specify an option to buy or not to buy. In addition, these leases must consider several variables: depreciation, selling price, residual values, equipment maintenance, and tax benefits. The following sections explore these factors.

Conditional Sales Contract

The conditional sales agreement specifies that the purchaser does not receive title to the equipment until it is paid in full. In this type of agreement, the lessee is bound to purchase the equipment at the end of the lease term. However, a conditional sales agreement can be structured differently for different situations. One lease option specifies a minimum and maximum purchase price that can be put on the equipment at the end of the lease term. This protects the interests of both the lessee and the lessor and leaves room for negotiations on a fair price. The lessee is protected from paying a price for the equipment higher than the market price and the lessor is protected from coming out on the wrong end of the deal because of rapid depreciation.

Another lease structure in the conditional sales contract recognizes the lessee as the *owner* of the equipment from the beginning of the lease term. This structure grants the tax benefits to the lessee. At the end of the term, the lessee is bound to buy the equipment at a predetermined price that is documented in the contract. This price has been agreed on beforehand by both parties and takes into consideration the lessee's monthly payments and the residual value of the equipment. The residual value is the estimated selling price of the equipment at the end of the lease. It is usually expressed as a percentage of the original selling price.

Net Lease and Gross Lease

The net lease and gross lease both recognize that the ownership of the equipment will return to the lessor at the end of the term. The lessee must make all payments for the entire term, as these contracts are irrevocable. The difference in the two leases is that in the net lease contract the lessee is responsible for all maintenance, taxes and insurance during the term, and in the gross lease the lessor is liable.

True Lease

A true lease states that the lessor is the owner during the entire term and leases out the equipment during a specified period of time for periodic payments by the lessee. This lease is similar to renting equipment as no equity is built up by the lessee, and if he/she wishes to purchase the equipment at the end of the term, the selling price will not take into account any previous payments.

Other Equipment Leases

In addition to the preceding equipment leases, other common ones include:

- **The nonpayout lease.** For equipment with a good resale value history, the lessor might choose to offer a *nonpayout lease* where the equipment is leased for less and the costs aren't completely recovered. At the end of the term, the lessor will either sell the equipment or lease it out again.
- **The payout lease.** The *payout lease* simply distinguishes that the lessor will charge a payment schedule that will recover the cost of the equipment.
- **The sale and leaseback lease.** This lease offers an option for the small business owner to free up some capital in the assets he or she already owns. In this case, the owner sells the asset and leases it back for a specific term. The lessee is bound to a long-term contract, usually with renewal options, at an annual rental computed as a percentage of the selling price. This annual return for the purchaser will fully amortize his or her investment over the original term of the lease.
- **The operating lease.** Under the terms of this lease, the lessor is responsible for maintenance of the equipment, and the lessee can usually be released from the contract before the term is over. This clause must be documented in the contract.

Deciding on an Equipment Lease

You should answer the question of which lease approach to take when leasing equipment only after carefully evaluating your economic situation. The first question you should ask yourself is whether you would like the option to buy the equipment when the leasing term is up. To decide, estimate the residual value of the equipment to determine whether it will be to your advantage to purchase the equipment after the term is expired. Will the equipment have depreciated so rapidly that it will no longer be a profitable asset for your business? If you determine you would like to purchase the equipment, your best bet would be to go with the conditional sales contract. A lessor who knows there is a guaranteed buyer at the end of the term is likely to give you a better leasing contract.

You must also decide whether or not you want to act as owner and receive the tax benefits available to you as the owner. Or if the lessor remains the owner and retains all benefits, will he or she be willing to give you reduced payment charges?

TO LEASE OR BUY?

After looking at the advantages and disadvantages of leasing you'll want to compare the facts between leasing and purchasing. To decide which method is best for you, consider the importance of cash flow when you're starting a new business. An analysis of money figured over a determined period of time will show you what will be the most advantageous in your situation. The Leasing versus Purchasing Equipment Checklist shown will aid in this analysis. Look at a number of variables and write down all the information you can on each. For example, you'll want to consider the following:

- Cost of equipment.
- Economic life of equipment.
- Lease terms.
- Loan terms (for purchase).
- Lease rate.
- Interest rate on loan.
- Tax benefits.
- Payment schedule (which plan fits better into your cash availability).
- Any other factors that will affect your decision, such as the length of time you will need the property.

Another factor worth considering is the depreciation rate of equipment. Depreciation is an expense that can be claimed on your tax statement. It is generally a recapture expense that is calculated over a specific period that represents the equipment's useful life. Depreciation can be calculated using a straight-line method or a declining-balance method (see Chapter 19 for more information on depreciation).

You should also take into account maintenance costs if paid by the lessor; such costs can be taken as a cash savings since there will be no inclusion for these costs under operating expenses.

Also, tax laws allow the following deductions in the lease situation:

- **Owner-lessor.** The net income from the operation of real estate or equipment is taxable. The rate of taxation depends on the type of ownership such as personal or corporate. Net Income is the total income less allowable expenses. Allowable expenses include depreciation, mortgage interest, real estate taxes (if paid by owner), cost of operation and maintenance (if paid by owner).
- **Lessee.** The lessee may deduct the following as business expenses: Rentals paid under the lease, real estate taxes (if paid by lessee), cost of operation and maintenance (if paid by lessee), depreciation on leasehold improvements (if improvements are paid for by the lessee).

Choosing a Leasing Company

Veterans advise you to never put all your eggs in one basket; rather, negotiate two or three proposals. This gives you bargaining power in the final negotiations and increases your chances of obtaining a good, fair lease. Carefully evaluate what each company has to offer you in terms of the lease rate and the lessor's reputation. You can check with both the Better Business Bureau and the

LEASING VERSUS PURCHASING EQUIPMENT CHECKLIST

Answer the following questions to help determine whether it is better to lease (**L**) or purchase (**P**) equipment for your business in terms of cost, cash availability, tax benefits, and obsolescence.

COST

	L	P
What is the required down payment for the lease or loan?	☐	☐
What is the length of the lease or loan?	☐	☐
What is the monthly payment of the lease or loan?	☐	☐
Are there balloon payments associated with the lease or loan?	☐	☐
What is the amount of the balloon payment?	☐	☐
What is the cost of an extended warranty, if purchasing one?	☐	☐
What is the total cost of the lease or loan (including maintenance and warranties) over its lifetime?	☐	☐

CASH AVAILABILITY

	L	P
Is there sufficient cash flow to handle the monthly lease or loan payments (answer Yes or No)?	☐	☐
Are maintenance costs included in the lease or loan (answer Yes or No)?	☐	☐
What maintenance costs are associated with the item?	☐	☐
What insurance costs are included in the lease or loan, if any?	☐	☐
What are the estimated insurance costs associated with the item?	☐	☐
If business is seasonal, does the lease or the loan fit periods of sufficient cash flow better?	☐	☐

TAX BENEFITS

	L	P
Can the item be depreciated for tax purposes in a lease or loan?	☐	☐
What is the depreciable life of the item?	☐	☐
What is the estimated depreciable expense of the item over its depreciable life?	☐	☐
What is the amount of other tax benefits associated with this item?	☐	☐

OBSOLESCENCE

	L	P
What is the operable lifetime of the item?	☐	☐
What is the total cost of the item spread over this lifetime (divide cost by lifetime)?	☐	☐
What is the technological lifetime of the item?	☐	☐
Will the item need to be replaced due to technological advancement?	☐	☐
What is the total cost of the item spread over the technological lifetime (divide cost by lifetime)?	☐	☐

company's present and former customers to find out any complaints or comments. If you employ a lease broker, he or she should research this information for you.

The lease rate is probably where you will find the greatest variance in lease companies. Their rate will be based on several factors, including:

- The party who receives the tax credit. Lessors might give a better rate if they retain this benefit.
- The length of the lease term.
- What kind of equipment the lessee wants to lease.
- Credit history of the lessee.

Be sure you ask a lot of questions. Never assume anything. Look at the leasing language. Are there some terms you don't understand? When leasing different kinds of equipment or property, lessors might use a different term to describe something you're familiar with. Automobile lessors, for example, distinguish their loans as either open or closed. Most open leases bind the lessee to either provide a buyer or pay for at least some determined amount of the car's residual value. Closed leases give the lessee an option to buy the car; however, the lessee is not obligated to provide a buyer or pay part of the residual value.

In addition, a car company lessor might lease directly or indirectly. "Directly" implies that the company carries its own financing. "Indirectly" means that the company uses another source for its financing, such as a bank or other lending institution. Most companies that finance indirectly work with several lending institutions. Ask to see the comparative rates.

The interest charged on a lease isn't called "interest" and no part of it is tax deductible; however, it is there and you should be aware of its amount. It will be included in your monthly payment and might be called a "money factor" or "cost of money" by some leasing companies. Money factors are expressed in a range. Ask for the money factor in terms of annual percentage rate. This will be more useful to you in your decision making.

NEGOTIATING A LEASE

The negotiation of a lease usually begins with an informal discussion between lessee and lessor. If all goes well, they will make a verbal agreement. The next step requires the lessor to draw up written documentation of the proposal and send it to the lessee for approval. Remember, we advise you to negotiate for more than one proposal to get the best deal.

Further negotiations might occur at this point, and assuming the lessee's credit has been approved, both parties will come to a final agreement. Again, the lessor (or the lessor's lawyer) will prepare a final proposal and submit it to the lessee for signing. If you can avoid it, wait until this time to consult with an attorney. Lawyers can be very costly, but in this final stage of the contract agreement, they are indispensable. Unlike yourself, lawyers are trained to look for terms that might not have your best interest in mind.

After you are comfortable with the terms in your lease, sign the contract, make a copy for your records, and return the original to the lessor.

Terms of a Lease

William A. Cohen in his book, *The Entrepreneur and Small Business Problem Solver,*[1] lists the following as major terms of a lease.

1. **The period or term of the lease.** Usually expressed in months or years.
2. **The rate or lease payment.** The determined payments derived from the total equipment cost paid and length of term.
3. **Specific financial terms.** Usually requested by the lessor, includes items such as the day of the month payment is due and additional charges for late payment.
4. **Residual values and purchase options.** Terms that take effect at the expiration of the contract dictate whether or not the lessee is legally bound to purchase and at what price.
5. **Financial terms.** Terms that spell out the market value of the property for insurance in the event of damage or loss of equipment.
6. **Tax responsibility.** Designates a party responsible for taxes, insurance, and maintenance costs as well as the investment tax credit.
7. **Modern equipment substitution provision.** Provides for updating the equipment or exchanging it for later models during the lease term.
8. **Renewal options.** States whether or not the lessee can renew the lease.
9. **Cancellation clause.** Specifies any penalty for early cancellation.
10. **Miscellaneous options.** Any other specific terms or stipulations such as security deposits, warranties, or extra fees.

Standard Clauses

There are many standard clauses common to all commercial business leases. A standard opening clause identifying the names of the parties to the lease might be written like the following example:

> This indenture made the _____ day of _____ between _____ party of the first part, hereinafter called the "lessor" and the _____ Company, a duly organized and existing corporation, having an office and place of business at City of _____ State of _____ , party of the second part, hereinafter called the "lessee" . . . .

---

[1] William A. Cohen, *The Entrepreneur and Small Business Problem Solver,* 2nd ed. (New York: John Wiley & Sons, 1990).

Subjects covered using standard clauses range from "Insurance Hazard" to "Destruction of Premises" and "Entry by Owner." You should examine certain standard clauses carefully and make sure that a clear understanding exists between you and the owner. One of these is the "Repairs and Maintenance" section. The interior of the building is yours to repair and maintain in "good and sanitary" condition. If you, the tenant, fail to maintain the property as is required by the lease, the landlord may make the repairs and charge labor and parts to you.

The section usually titled "Acceptance of Premises As Is" can be tricky. Remember the up-front paint job you may have requested? This section does not relieve the owner of normal maintenance responsibilities, but it can be used as a loophole to override such verbal agreements.

Alterations

Alterations usually can be made only after receiving the landlord's consent. If the alterations constitute an addition to the structure, this becomes the property of the landlord. At the end of the lease term, the landlord may require the removal of any modifications and the restoration of the property to its original condition. "Broom clean" is a common term used in a lease to describe the condition the landlord expects the property to be in.

Liability Insurance Key

This clause spells out the amount and kind of insurance the lessee must carry, to relieve the lessor of liability and/or damage. The lessor is worried mostly about personal liability if someone gets hurt.

Whatever the type of business, insurers will have an acceptable package deal for you and the owner. But you must definitely shop for the best price among several insurance companies. Ideally, you should work with a business broker who handles a number of different labels of business insurance coverage.

You will usually need upper limits of $300,000 on personal liability, product liability, and "unowned auto" or similar coverage (employee in a company car or his or her own vehicle takes a business-related trip where an accident occurs). Two patrons who collide in your parking area may also blame you for their problem.

The lessor must carry fire insurance but may require you to carry "fire legal," which protects the lessor if you start the fire. You should also plan to carry contents damage insurance with a minimum of $5,000 of protection. Loss coverage of $1,000 for valuable papers (e.g., accounts receivable) is a good idea as well.

Many insurance packages contain provisions for "loss of income" protection in the event of fire, disaster, and so on. Set a percentage of, say, 40 percent of your normal income for a period of 90 days. And make sure a clause in your lease states that you are released from the obligation of rent if the landlord can't repair in that time.

Assignment or Sublet Clause

From your point of view, a good lease is one that can easily be assigned to another tenant if you want to sell or relocate your business. Therefore, be certain it contains a provision for assignment or subletting. This clause will only be made available in a short-term lease, if at all. Such a clause will allow you to close or move your business while permitting you to get another tenant to pay your rental obligation for the balance of the lease term. It will also allow you to sell your business to a new owner who can assume your lease under the same good terms you have. Make sure the lease contains words to the effect that "lessor cannot withhold such permission providing sublessee meets original requirements of lease."

In the sale of your business, you may want to effect a sublease rather than an outright transfer of ownership. You are still responsible for the rent if the sublessee doesn't pay it. But if for any reason the new owner fails and you want to take the business back, you still have a facility to keep it in.

Bailout Clause

A bailout clause in your contract could save you in the event of extremely damaging circumstances to your business performance. Usually, this clause makes the contract void in such cases as war, riots, labor strikes, and acts of God, when it will be impossible to continue your lease agreement.

Another clause to be aware of is the "right of successors" clause. It gives heirs the right to continue the lease under all present terms and conditions in the event of your death. While it's never comfortable to consider your mortality, why let the business you've worked so hard for be taken away from your family after you are gone?

Recapture Clauses

If you enter into a percentage lease agreement, the landlord might include a *recapture* or cancellation clause. This clause, which could be potentially dangerous to you and your business, states that if your company is not doing the business necessary for the landlord to receive the minimum rent set for the premises, this will be considered a breach of contract and you could be evicted.

In this situation, your only recourse would be to pay an excess amount over the percentage actually produced by the business to bring the amount up to the minimum amount required by the landlord (predetermined in the lease). Then you would do one of two things, either build your business volume up to the amount necessary to meet the percentage requirement, or give up the lease and vacate.

Cotenancy Clause

A cotenancy clause allows you to break the lease if an anchor store closes or moves. If, for example, you signed your lease knowing Wal-Mart would generate a lot of foot traffic, you can break the lease if Wal-Mart closes or moves.

Hidden Costs

Read your contract carefully before signing it. A few common hidden costs to look for and recognize include *lease term jargon,* such as "three plus three," or "five, five, and five." As you might suspect, this means "years" and "options" in the term of the lease. What it doesn't cover is whether your option is defined (three years plus a three-year option to renew). Are the second three years at the same cost? Or are costs left dangling, without definition, to be negotiated with the lessor at that time? Often they are. This is yet another way to hedge inflation for the lessor.

If your location is in a shopping area, are there added costs for maintenance of common areas? What are these costs? Are they fixed or variable? What kind and amount of insurance does the landlord require you to have? Are you paying for coverage that should be the landlord's responsibility? If you're in a small complex, are you being charged for more than your share? Are there city-imposed merchant assessments for common customer parking?

RESOURCES

Associations

American Automotive Leasing Association, 1001 Connecticut Avenue, NW, Suite 1201, Washington, DC 20036, 202-223-2600

Equipment Leasing Association of America, 1300 North 17th Street, Suite 1010, Arlington, VA 22209, 703-527-8655

National Vehicle Leasing Association, P.O. Box 281230, San Francisco, CA 94128-1230, 415-548-9135

Magazines

Corporate Cashflow, 6151 Powers Ferry Road, NW, Atlanta, GA 30339-2941, 404-955-2500

Corporate Financing Week, 488 Madison Avenue, 12th Floor, New York, NY 10022-5751, 212-303-3300

Journal of Cash Management, 7315 Wisconsin Avenue, No. 1250 West, Bethesda, MD 20814, 301-907-2862

Modern Purchasing, 777 Bay Street, Toronto, Ontario M5W 1A7, Canada, 416-596-5706

Purchasing Magazine, 275 Washington Street, Newton, MA 02158-1611, 617-964-3030

8

Developing a Business Plan

A strong business plan holds few surprises for its audience. It conforms to generally accepted guidelines to form and content. Each section should include specific elements that will clarify your business goals.

Your plan should address all the relevant questions that will be asked by individuals who review it, mainly, investors. If your business plan is not structured to provide the appropriate information in a concise and logical progression, then your chances of satisfying the key questions concerning development and operations will decrease.

Generally, a business plan has seven major components:

1. Executive summary.
2. Business description.
3. Market strategies.
4. Competitive analysis.
5. Design and development plans.
6. Operations and management plans.
7. Financial components.

An optional component is a section for Small Business Administration (SBA) materials, which should be included only if the purpose of developing your business plan is to obtain financing from this source. Documents required by the SBA may be useful to you in setting up your business.

TITLE PAGE AND TABLE OF CONTENTS

While the business plan can be divided into seven segments, a few elements don't fall within these broad classifications but are, nevertheless, critical to the plan's success. These elements are a *cover,* a *title page* and a *table of contents.*

A business plan should have a cover. There is no reason to have your work bound in leather; what is required is a neat cover of adequate size to hold your material. Buy a blue, black, or brown cover at a stationery store. A lender is more likely to think well of you if you are conservative in presentation than if you spend money on unnecessary show. Subtle factors like this reflect your business acumen. In some respects, the way a person reads your business plan will affect his or her judgment of your management ability.

Include a title page in your business plan. On this page, put the name of the business, the name(s) of the principals who own it, as well as the business address and phone number. If you have a professional logo, you can use it to dress up your title page. On some plans, the first page has the name of the packager or the person who assisted the business owner in preparing the plan. We believe this is a mistake. A business plan should be represented as a personal document by the principals themselves. There is a place in the plan where you can show professional assistance, but the business and the plan itself are yours.

You'll also need a table of contents that should follow the *executive summary* or *statement of purpose*, which we'll discuss later. Although the table of contents is included toward the beginning of the book, you will naturally prepare this last. Be aware, however, that this item is essential. Readers of the plan should be able to quickly find desired information, financial data, market information, and the like.

THE BUSINESS DEFINITION

The first component of the business plan should describe the nature of the business through the *executive summary*, or *statement of purpose*, and the *business description*. These two elements define the business, the type of product it will offer, and its role within the context of the overall industry.

Executive Summary

Within the overall outline of the business plan, the executive summary will follow the title page. The summary should tell the reader what you want. This is very important. All too often, what the business owner desires is buried on page eight. Clearly state what you are asking for in the summary.

The statement should be kept short and businesslike, probably no more than half a page. It could be longer, depending on how complicated the use of funds may be, but the summary of a business plan, like the summary of a loan application, is generally no more than one page. Within that space, you'll need to provide a synopsis of the entire business plan. You should include the following key elements:

1. **Business concept.** Describes the business, its product, and the market it will serve. It should point out just exactly what will be sold, to whom, and why the business will hold a competitive advantage.

2. **Financial features.** Highlights the important financial points of the business including sales, profits, cash flows, and return on investment.

3. **Financial requirements.** Clearly states the capital needed to start the business and to expand. It should detail how the capital will be used, and the equity, if any, that will be provided for funding. If the loan for initial capital will be based on security instead of equity within the company, you should also specify the source of collateral.

4. **Current business position.** Furnishes relevant information about the company, its legal form of operation, when it was formed, the principal owners, and key personnel.

5. **Major achievements.** Details any developments within the company that are essential to its success. Major achievements include patents, prototypes, location of a facility, any crucial contracts that need to be in place for product development, or results from any test marketing that has been conducted.

When writing your executive summary, don't waste words. If the executive summary fills eight pages, nobody's going to read it because it will be very clear that the business, no matter what its merits, will be a bad investment because the principals are indecisive and don't really know what they want. Make it easy for the reader to identify at first glance both your needs and capabilities.

The Business Description

The business description usually begins with a short description of the industry. When describing the industry, discuss the present outlook as well as future possibilities. You should also provide information on all the various markets within the industry, including any new products or developments that will benefit or adversely affect your business. Base all your observations on reliable data to be sure to footnote sources of information as appropriate. This is important if you're seeking funding; the investor will want to know just how dependable your information is, and won't risk money on assumptions or conjecture.

When describing your business, the first thing you need to concentrate on is its structure. By structure we mean the type of operation (wholesale, retail, food service, manufacturing, or service-oriented). State this right away in the description, along with whether the business is new or already established.

In addition to structure, legal form should be reiterated once again. Detail whether the business is a sole proprietorship, partnership, or corporation, list its principals, and state what they will bring to the business.

You should also mention who you will sell to, how the product will be distributed, and the business's support systems. Support may come in the form of advertising, promotions, and customer service.

Once you've described the business, you need to describe the products or services you intend to market. The product description statement should be complete enough so the reader has a clear idea of your intentions. This might mean a discussion on the application and the end uses. You may want to emphasize any unique features or variations from concepts that can be typically found in the industry.

In fact, the investor will be looking for any proprietary information that will set your concept apart from the crowd. Most investors call this the "USP" or "Unique Selling Proposition." Almost every business has one. It can be a patented product or a trade secret like Kentucky Fried Chicken's recipe.

Be specific in showing how you will give your business a competitive edge. For example, your business will be better because you will supply a full line of products; competitor A doesn't have a full line. You're going to provide service after the sale; competitor B doesn't support anything he sells. Your merchandise will be of higher quality. You'll give a money-back guarantee. You'll provide parts and labor for up to 90 days after the sale. Competitor C has the reputation for selling the best french fries in town; you're going to sell the best Thousand Island dressing.

Now you must be a classic capitalist and ask yourself, "How can I turn a buck? And why do I think I can make a profit that way?" Answer that question for yourself, and then convey that answer to others in the business description section. You don't have to write 25 pages on why your business will be profitable. Just explain the factors you think will make it successful (e.g., it's a well-organized business, it will have state-of-the-art equipment, its location is exceptional, the market is ready for it, it's a dynamite product at a fair price).

If you're using your business plan as a document for financial purposes, explain why the added equity or debt money is going to make your business more profitable. Show how you will expand your business or be able to create something by using that money. How will the money help your business?

Show why your business is going to be profitable. A potential lender is going to want to know how successful you're going to be in this particular business. Factors that support your claims can be broad-brushed here; they will be detailed later. Give the reader an idea of the experience of the other key people in the business. They will want to know what suppliers or experts you've spoken to about your business and their response to your idea. They may even ask you to clarify your choice of location or reasons for selling this particular product.

The business description can be a few paragraphs in length to a few pages depending on the complexity of your plan. If your plan is not too complicated, keep your business description short, describing the industry in one paragraph, the product in another, and the business and its success factors in three or four paragraphs that will end the statement. While you may need to have a lengthy business description in some cases, a short statement may convey the required information in a much more effective manner. It doesn't attempt to hold the reader's attention for an extended period, and this is important since the investor needs to read other plans as well. If the business description is long and drawn out, you will lose the reader's attention, and possibly any chance of receiving the necessary funding for your project.

MARKET STRATEGIES

Market strategies are the result of a meticulous market analysis, which is covered in greater detail in Chapter 3. A market analysis forces the entrepreneur to become familiar with all aspects of the market so that the target market can be defined and the company can be positioned to garner its share of sales. A market analysis also enables the entrepreneur to establish pricing, distribution, and promotional strategies that will allow the company to become profitable within a competitive environment. In addition, it indicates the growth potential within the industry, and this will allow you to develop estimates for the future of your own business.

Defining the Market

Begin your market analysis by defining the market in terms of size, structure, growth prospects, trends, and sales potential.

The total aggregate sales of your competitors will provide you with a fairly accurate estimate of the *total potential market*. For instance, within the beer brewing industry, the total market potential would be the total sales of malt beverages in the United States, which is $35 billion.

Once you have determined the size of the market, the next step is to define the target market. The target market narrows down the total market by concentrating on segmentation factors that will determine the total addressable market—the total number of users within the sphere of the business's influence. As detailed in Chapter 3, the segmentation factors can be geographic, customer attributes, or product oriented.

For instance, if the distribution of your product is confined to a specific geographic area, then you would want to further define the target market to reflect the number of users or sales of that product within that geographic segment.

Determining Market Share

After detailing the target market, you need to further define it to determine the total feasible market. You can do this in several ways, but most professional planners will delineate the feasible market by concentrating on product segmentation factors that may produce gaps within the market.

In the case of a microbrewery that plans to brew a premium lager beer, the total feasible market could be defined by determining how many drinkers of premium pilsner beers there are in the target market.

It is important to understand that the total feasible market is the portion of the market that can be captured provided every condition within the environment is perfect and there is very little competition. In most industries this is simply not the case. Other factors will affect the *share* of the feasible market a business can reasonably obtain. These factors are usually tied to the structure

Figure 8.1   Market Equation Graphic

of the industry, the impact of competition, strategies for market penetration and continued growth, and the amount of capital the business can spend to increase its market share.

Arriving at a projection for the *market share* for a business plan is very much a subjective estimate. It is based not only on an analysis of the market but on highly targeted and competitive distribution, pricing, and promotional strategies. For instance, even though a sizable number of premium pilsner drinkers may form the total feasible market, you need to be able to reach them through your distribution at a competitive price point and then you have to let them know it is available and where they can buy it. How effectively you can achieve your distribution, pricing, and promotional goals is the extent to which you will be able to garner market share. Figure 8.1 charts the progression used for defining market share in a given industry.

For a business plan, you must be able to estimate market share for the time period the plan will cover. To project market share over the time frame of the business plan, you will need to consider two factors:

1. **Industry growth that will increase the total number of users.** This is determined by growth models, as described in Chapter 3. Most projections utilize a minimum of two growth models by defining different industry sales scenarios. The industry sales scenarios should be based on leading indicators of industry sales, which will most likely be industry segment sales, demographic data, and historical precedence.
2. **Conversion of users from the total feasible market.** This is based on a sales cycle similar to the five distinct stages of a product life cycle: early pioneer users, early users, early majority users, late majority users, and late users. Figure 8.2 shows a typical conversion rate curve. Using conversion rates, market growth will continue to increase your market share during the

Figure 8.2 Conversion Rate of Users from Total Feasible Market

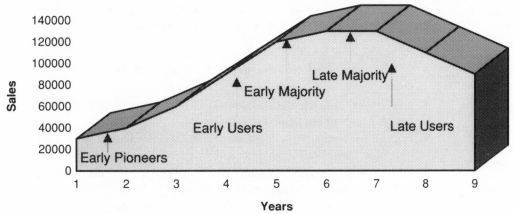

period from early pioneers to early majority users, level off through late majority users, and decline with late users.

Defining the market is but one step in your analysis. With the information you've gained through market research, you need to develop strategies that will allow you to fulfill your objectives.

Positioning Strategy

When discussing market strategy, positioning inevitably will be brought up. Positioning a product in the market is essential in establishing its identity within the eyes of the purchaser. A company's positioning strategy is affected by a number of variables that are closely tied to the motivations and requirements of customers within the target market as well as the actions of primary competitors.

The strategy used to position a product is usually a result of an analysis of your customers and competition. Before a product can be positioned, you need to answer several strategic questions such as:

1. How are your competitors positioning themselves?
2. What specific attributes does your product have that your competitors' don't?
3. What customer needs does your product fulfill?
4. Is there anything unique about the place of origin?

Once you've answered your strategic questions based on research of the market, you can then begin to develop your positioning strategy and illustrate that in your business plan. A positioning statement for a business plan doesn't have to be long or elaborate. It should merely point out just how you will want your product perceived by both customers and the competition.

Pricing Strategy

How you price your product is important because it will have a direct effect on the success of your business. Though pricing strategy and computations can be complex, the basic rules of pricing are straightforward:

1. All prices must cover costs.
2. The best and most effective way of lowering your sales prices is to lower costs.
3. Your prices must reflect the dynamics of cost, demand, changes in the market, and response to your competition.
4. Prices must be established to assure sales. Do not price against a competitive operation alone. Rather, price to sell.
5. Product utility, longevity, maintenance, and end use must be judged continually, and target prices adjusted accordingly.
6. Prices must be set to preserve order in the marketplace.

Many methods of establishing prices are available to you:

- **Cost-plus pricing.** Used mainly by manufacturers to assure that all costs, both fixed and variable, are covered and the desired profit percentage is attained.
- **Demand pricing.** Used by companies that sell their products through a variety of sources at differing prices based on demand.
- **Competitive pricing.** Used by companies that are entering a market where there is already an established price and it is difficult to differentiate one product from another.
- **Markup pricing.** Used mainly by retailers, markup pricing is calculated by adding your desired profit to the cost of the product.

Each method has its strengths and weaknesses (see Chapter 18).

Distribution Strategy

Distribution includes the entire process of moving the product from the factory to the end user. The type of distribution network you choose will depend on the industry and the size of the market. It is helpful to analyze the distribution channels of your competitors before deciding whether to use the same type of channel or an alternative that may provide you with a strategic advantage.

Some of the more common distribution channels include:

- **Direct sales.** This is the most effective distribution channel if the basic plan is to sell directly to the end user.
- **OEM (Original Equipment Manufacturer) sales.** When your product is sold to the OEM, it is incorporated into the manufacturer's finished product and distributed to the end user.
- **Manufacturer's representatives.** Manufacturer reps, as they are known, are salespeople who operate out of agencies that handle an assortment of complimentary products and divide their selling time between them. This is one of the best ways to distribute a product.
- **Wholesaler distributors.** Using this channel, a manufacturer sells to a wholesaler, who in turn sells it to a retailer or other agent for further distribution through the channel until it reaches the end user.
- **Brokers.** These third-party distributors often buy directly from the distributor or wholesaler and sell to retailers or end users.
- **Retail distributors.** Distributing a product through this channel is important if the end user of your product is the general consuming public.
- **Direct mail.** In this approach, you sell to the end user using a direct-mail campaign.

As mentioned earlier, the distribution strategy you choose for your product will be based on several factors including the channels being used by your competition, your pricing strategy, and your own internal resources.

Promotion Strategy

With a distribution strategy formed, a promotion plan must be developed. The promotion strategy in its most basic form is the controlled distribution of communication designed to sell your product or service. To accomplish this, the promotion strategy encompasses every marketing tool utilized in the communication effort:

- **Advertising.** Includes the advertising budget, creative message(s), and at least the first quarter's media schedule.
- **Packaging.** Provides a description of the packaging strategy. If available, mockups of any labels, trademarks, or service marks should be included.
- **Public relations.** A complete account of the publicity strategy including a list of media that will be approached as well as a schedule of planned events.
- **Sales promotions.** Establishes the strategies used to support the sales message. This includes a description of collateral marketing material as well as a schedule of planned promotional activities such as special sales, couponing, contests, and premium awards.
- **Personal sales.** An outline of the sales strategy including pricing procedures, returns and adjustment rules, sales presentation methods, lead generation, customer service policies, salesperson compensation, and salesperson market responsibilities.

Once the market has been researched and analyzed, conclusions need to be developed that will supply a quantitative outlook concerning the potential of the business. The first financial projection within the business plan must be formed utilizing the information drawn from defining the market, positioning the product, pricing, distribution, and promotional strategies. The sales or revenue model charts the potential for the product, as well as the business, over a set time period. Most business plans will project revenue for up to three years, although five-year projections are becoming increasingly popular among lenders.

When developing the revenue model for the business plan, the equation used to project sales is fairly simple: It consists of the total number of customers and average revenue from each customer. In the equation, T = total number of people, A = average revenue per customer, and S = sales projection. The equation for projection sales is:

$$T \times A = S$$

Using this equation, the annual sales for each year projected within the business plan can be developed. Of course, you'll need to evaluate other factors from the revenue model. Since the revenue model is a table illustrating the sources for all income, every segment of the targeted market that is treated differently must be accounted for. To determine any differences, the various

Table 8.1 Revenue Model for Backbay Brewing Company

REVENUE SUMMARY

	1995	1996	1997
Product One—Six-Packs			
No. of customers	13,778	14,742	16,510
Units/customer	24	24	24
Total units	330,672	353,808	396,240
New customers	13,778	964	1,768
Price/unit	$3.85	$3.85	$3.85
Revenue	$1,273,087	$1,362,161	$1,525,524
Product Two—22-Ounce Bottles			
No. of customers	11,273	12,062	13,508
Units/customer	48	48	48
Total units	541,104	578,976	648,384
New customers	11,273	789	1,446
Prince/unit	$1.20	$1.20	$1.20
Revenue	$649,325	$694,771	$778,061
Product Three—15-Gallon Kegs			
No. of customers	172	178	199
Units/customer	12	12	12
Total units	2,064	2,136	2,388
New customers	172	6	21
Price/unit	$105	$105	$105
Revenue	$216,720	$224,280	$250,740
Total revenue	$2,139,132	$2,281,212	$2,554,325

strategies utilized to sell the product—distribution, pricing, and promotion—must be considered. Table 8.1 shows a sample revenue model.[1]

COMPETITIVE ANALYSIS

The competitive analysis is a statement of the business strategy and how it re-lates to the competition. The purpose of the competitive analysis is to deter-mine the strengths and weaknesses of the competitors within your market, strategies that will provide you with a distinct advantage, the barriers that can be developed to prevent competition from entering your market, and any weaknesses that can be exploited within the product development cycle.

The first step in a competitor analysis is to identify the current and potential competition. Essentially, there are two ways you can identify competitors. The

[1] The sample tables in this chapter are taken from the sample business plan presented in Chap-ter 9 of this book. Readers are urged to review the tables in the context of that business plan.

first is to look at the market from the customer's viewpoint and group all your competitors by the degree to which they contend for the buyer's dollar. The second method is to group competitors according to their various competitive strategies so you understand what motivates them (see Chapter 3).

Once you have grouped your competitors, you can start to analyze their strategies and identify vulnerable areas by examining their weaknesses and strengths. These strengths and weaknesses are usually based on the presence and absence of key assets and skills needed to be competitive in the market.

To determine just what constitutes a key asset or skill within an industry, David Aaker in his book *Developing Business Strategies*[2] suggests concentrating your efforts in four areas:

1. Reasons behind successful as well as unsuccessful firms.
2. Prime customer motivators.
3. Major component costs.
4. Industry mobility barriers.

According to theory, the performance of a company within a market is directly related to the possession of key assets and skills. Therefore, an analysis of strong performers should reveal the causes behind such a successful track record. This analysis, in conjunction with an examination of unsuccessful companies and the reasons behind their failure, should provide a good idea of just what key assets and skills are needed for success within a given industry and market segment.

For instance, in the personal computer operating system software market, Microsoft reigns supreme with DOS and Windows. It has established dominance in this industry because of superior marketing and research as well as strategic partnerships with a large majority of the hardware vendors that produce personal computers. This has allowed DOS and Windows to become the operating environment, maybe not of choice, but of necessity for the majority of personal computers on the market.

Microsoft's primary competitors, Apple and IBM, both have competing operating systems with a great deal of marketing to accompany them; however, both suffer from weaknesses that Microsoft has been able to exploit. Apple's operating system for its Macintosh line of computers, while superior in many ways to DOS and Windows, is limited to the Macintosh personal computers; therefore, it doesn't run many of the popular business applications that are readily available to DOS and Windows. To an extent, IBM's OS/2 operating system suffers from the same problem. Although it will run on all the personal computers DOS and Windows can run on and even handle Windows applications, the programs produced for OS/2 in its native environment are very small. This is the type of detailed analysis you need to make when evaluating an industry.

Through your competitor analysis, you will also have to create a marketing strategy that will generate an asset or skill competitors do not have, which will

---

[2] David A. Aaker, *Developing Business Strategies*, 2nd ed. (New York: John Wiley & Sons, 1988).

provide you with a distinct and enduring competitive advantage. Since competitive advantages are developed from key assets and skills, you should sit down and put together a competitive strength grid. This scale lists all your major competitors or strategic groups based on their applicable assets and skills and shows how your own company fits on this scale.

To put together a competitive strength grid, list all the key assets and skills down the left margin of a piece of paper. Along the top, write down two column headers: "Weakness" and "Strength." In each asset or skill category, place all the competitors that have weaknesses in that particular category under the Weakness column, and all those that have strengths in that specific category in the Strength column. After you've finished, you'll be able to determine just where you stand in relation to the other firms competing in your industry.

After you have established the key assets and skills necessary for success in the business you are researching and have defined your distinct competitive advantage, you need to communicate this information in a strategic form that will attract market share as well as defend it. Competitive strategies usually fall into five areas:

1. Product.
2. Distribution.
3. Pricing.
4. Promotion.
5. Advertising.

Many of the factors leading to the formation of a strategy should already have been highlighted in previous sections, specifically in marketing strategies. These strategies primarily revolve around establishing the point of entry in the product life cycle and an endurable competitive advantage by defining the elements that will set your product or service apart from your competitors or strategic groups. You need to clearly establish this competitive advantage so the reader understands not only how you will accomplish your goals, but why your strategy will work.

DESIGN AND DEVELOPMENT PLANS

The purpose of the design and development plan section is to provide investors with a description of the product's design, chart its development within the context of production, marketing, and the company itself, and create a development budget that will enable the company to reach its goals.

Generally, you will cover three areas in the development plan section:

1. Product development.
2. Market development.
3. Organizational development.

Each of these elements needs to be examined from the funding of the plan to the point where the business begins to experience a continuous income. Although these elements will differ in content, each will be based on structure and goals.

The first step in the development process is setting goals for the overall development plan. From your analysis of the market and competition, most of the product, market, and organizational development goals will be readily apparent. Each goal you define should have certain characteristics within it. Your goals should be quantifiable to set up time lines, directed so they relate to the success of the business, consequential so they have impact on the company, and feasible so that they aren't beyond the bounds of actual completion.

Goals for product development should center around the *technical* as well as the *marketing* aspects of the product so that the development team can work from a focused outline. For example, a goal for product development of a microbrewed beer might be "Produce recipe for premium lager beer" or "Create packaging for premium lager beer." In terms of market development, a goal might be "Develop collateral marketing material." Organizational goals would center around acquiring expertise to attain your product and market development goals. This expertise usually needs to be present in areas of key assets that provide a competitive advantage. Without the necessary expertise, the chances of bringing a product successfully to market diminishes.

With your goals set and expertise in place, a set of procedural tasks or work assignments needs to be formed for each area of the development plan. Procedures will have to be developed for product development, market development, and organization development. In some cases, product and organization can be combined if the list of procedures is short enough.

Procedures should include how resources will be allocated, who is in charge of accomplishing each goal, and how everything will interact. For example, to produce a recipe for a premium lager beer, you would need to do the following:

- Gather ingredients.
- Determine optimum malting process.
- Gauge mashing temperature.
- Boil wort and evaluate which hops provide the best flavor.
- Determine yeast amounts and fermentation period.
- Determine aging period.
- Carbonate the beer.
- Decide whether or not to pasteurize the beer.

The development of procedures provides a list of work assignments that need to be accomplished, but it doesn't provide the stages of development that coordinate the work assignments within the overall development plan. To do this, you first need to amend the work assignments created in the procedures section so that all the individual work elements (detailed breakdown of the work assignments) are accounted for in the development plan. The next stage involves setting deliverable dates for components as well as the finished product for

Table 8.2 Development Expenses

ITEM	BUDGETED AMOUNT
Materials	$ 129,000
Direct labor	21,840
Overhead	376,790
General and administrative	14,560
Equipment	485,000
Miscellaneous	2,000
Total	**$1,029,190**

testing purposes. Terence McGarty's book, *Business Plans That Win Venture Capital*,[3] states that there are primarily three steps involved in the delivery and testing stage before the product is ready for final delivery:

1. **Preliminary product review.** All the product's features and specifications are checked.
2. **Critical product review.** All the key elements of the product are checked and gauged against the development schedule to make sure everything is going according to plan.
3. **Final product review.** All elements of the product are checked against goals to assure the integrity of the prototype.

Scheduling, which is one of the most important elements in the development plan, includes all the key work elements as well as the stages the product must pass through before customer delivery. It should also be tied to the *development budget* so that expenses can be tracked. But its main purpose is to establish time frames for completion of all work assignments and juxtapose those within the stages the product must pass. When producing the schedule, provide a column for each procedural task name, duration of time, start date, and stop date. If you want to provide a number system for each task include a column in the schedule for the task number.

When forming your development budget, you need to take into account not only all the expenses required to design the product but also expenses to take it from prototype to production. Table 8.2 is a sample table of development expenses.

The following costs should be included in the development budget:

- **Material.** All raw materials used in the development of the product.
- **Direct labor.** All labor costs associated with the development of the product.
- **Overhead.** All overhead expenses required to operate the business during the development phase such as taxes, rent, phone, utilities, office supplies.

[3] Terence P. McCarty, *Business Plans That Win Venture Capital* (New York: John Wiley & Sons, 1988).

- **General and administrative (G&A) costs.** The salaries of executive and administrative personnel along with any other office support functions.
- **Marketing and sales.** The salaries of marketing personnel required to develop prepromotional materials and plan the marketing campaign that should begin prior to delivery of the product.
- **Professional services.** Those costs associated with consultation of outside experts such as accountants, lawyers, and business consultants.
- **Miscellaneous costs.** Costs that are related to product development.
- **Capital equipment.** To determine the capital requirements for the development budget, you first have to establish what type of equipment you will need, decide whether to acquire the equipment or use outside contractors, and finally, if you decide to acquire the equipment, whether or not you will lease or purchase it.

To succeed, the company has to have the proper expertise in key areas; however, not every company will start a business with the required expertise in every key area. Therefore, the proper personnel must be recruited, integrated into the development process, and managed to create a team focused on the achievement of the development goals.

Before you begin recruiting, however, you should review those goals to determine which areas within the development process will require additional personnel. After you have identified the positions that need to be filled, you should produce a *job description* and *job specification.*

Once you've hired the proper personnel, you need to integrate them into the development process by assigning tasks from the work assignments you've developed. Finally, each member of the team needs to know his or her role within the company and how that role interrelates with every other position within the development team. To do this, you should develop an organizational chart for your development team.

Finally, you should assess the risks involved in developing the product and present a plan to address each one. These risks will usually center around technical development of the product, marketing, personnel requirements, or financial problems. By identifying and addressing each of the perceived risks, you will eliminate not only some of your own major fears concerning the project but those of investors as well.

OPERATIONS AND MANAGEMENT

The operations and management plan is designed to describe just how the business functions on a continuing basis. The operations plan will highlight the logistics of the organization such as the various responsibilities of the management team, the tasks assigned to each division within the company, and capital and expense requirements related to the operations of the business. In fact, the set of financial tables that you develop within the operations plan will form the foundation for the "Financial Components" section. These tables include:

- The operating expense table.
- The capital requirements table.
- The cost of goods table.

The factors that will affect these financial tables are directly attributable to the operations of the business. They should cover a time frame corresponding to the scope of your plan's overall projections.

Operating Expenses

Two areas need to be accounted for when planning the operations of your company: (1) the organizational structure of the company, and (2) the expense and capital requirements associated with its operation.

The organizational structure of the company is an essential element of the business plan because it provides a basis from which to project operating expenses. This projection is critical in formulating financial statements, which are heavily scrutinized by investors; therefore, the organizational structure has to be well defined and based within a realistic framework that reflects the parameters of the business.

Although every company will differ in its organizational structure, most can be divided into several broad areas:

- Marketing and sales (includes customer relations and service).
- Production (including quality assurance).
- Research and development.
- Administration.

These are broad classifications, and it is important to keep in mind that not every business can be divided this way. In fact, every business is different, and each one must be structured according to its own requirements and goals. Table 8.3 shows a sample table of operating expenses.

Terence McGarty in his book, *Business Plans That Win Venture Capital,*[4] lists four stages for organizing a business:

1. Establish a list of the tasks using the broadest classifications possible.
2. Organize these tasks into departments that produce an efficient line of communication between staff and management.
3. Determine the type of personnel required to perform each task.
4. Establish the function of each task and how it will relate to the generation of revenue within the company.

[4] McCarty, *Business Plans That Win Venture Capital.*

Table 8.3 Operating Expenses

	1995	1996	1997
Marketing expenses	$ 85,000	$ 90,950	$101,864
Sales expenses	80,000	85,600	95,872
Brewery operations expenses	70,000	74,900	83,888
Administrative expenses	35,000	37,450	41,944
Overhead	410,224	438,940	491,613
Total expenses	**$680,224**	**$727,840**	**$815,181**

Once you have structured your business, however, you need to consider your overall goals and the amount of personnel required to reach those goals.

To determine the number of employees you'll need to meet the goals you've set for your business, you'll need to apply the following equation to each department listed in your organizational structure:

$$C \div S = P$$

In this equation C = the total number of customers, S = the total number of customers that can be served by each employee, and P = the personnel requirements. For instance, if the number of customers for first year sales is projected at 10,110 and one marketing employee is required for every 200 customers, you would need 51 employees within the marketing department.

$$10,110 \div 200 = 51$$

Once you calculate the number of employees that you'll need for your organization, you'll need to determine the labor expense. The factors that need to be considered when calculating labor expense (LE) are the personnel requirements (P) for each department multiplied by the employee salary level (SL). Therefore, the equation would be:

$$P \times SL = LE$$

Using the preceding marketing example, the labor expense for that department would be:

$$51 \times \$40,000 = \$2,040,000$$

After you have planned the organization's operations and labor expenses, you can develop the expenses associated with the operation of the business. These are usually referred to as overhead. Overhead refers to all nonlabor expenses required to operate the business. Expenses can be divided into *fixed*—those expenses that must be paid, usually at the same rate, regardless of the volume of business—and *variable* (or semivariable)—those that change according to the amount of business.

Overhead usually includes the following expenses:

- Travel.
- Maintenance and repair.
- Equipment leases.
- Rent.
- Advertising & promotion.
- Supplies.
- Utilities.
- Packaging and shipping.
- Payroll taxes and benefits.
- Uncollectible receivables.
- Professional services.
- Insurance.
- Loan payments.
- Depreciation.

To develop the overhead expenses for the expense table used in this portion of the business plan, the number of employees needs to be multiplied by the expense of each employee. Therefore, if *NE* represents the number of employees and *EE* is the expense per employee, the following equation can be used to calculate the sum of each overhead (*OH*) expense:

$$OH = NE \times EE$$

Capital Requirements

In addition to the operating expense table, you'll need to develop a capital requirements table depicting the amount of money necessary to purchase equipment that will establish and continue operations (see Table 8.4). It also illustrates the amount of depreciation your company will incur based on all equipment elements purchased with a lifetime beyond one year.

To generate the capital requirements table, you first have to establish the various elements within the business that will require capital investment. For service businesses, capital is usually tied to the various equipment used to service customers. For instance, a janitorial service would need a vehicle, cleaning equipment, and cleaning supplies.

Capital for manufacturing companies, on the other hand, is based on the equipment required to produce the product. Manufacturing equipment usually falls into three categories: testing equipment, assembly equipment, and packaging equipment.

With these capital elements in mind, you then need to determine the number of units or customers, in terms of sales, that can be adequately handled by each equipment factor. This is important because capital requirements are a

Table 8.4   Capital Requirements

	1995	1996	1997
Initial capital	$0	$0	$0
Net capital	$0	$370,476	$358,395
Malting equipment (ME)			
No. barrels	10,000	10,700	11,984
ME/barrel	3,500	3,500	3,500
ME capital	$11,500	$11,500	$11,500
ME capital requirement	$32,857	$35,157	$39,376
New ME capital	$32,857	$2,300	$4,219
Mashing/Brewing Equipment (MBE)			
No. barrels	10,000	10,700	11,984
MBE/barrels	1,700	1,700	1,700
MBE capital	$15,500	$15,500	$15,500
MBE capital requirement	$91,176	$97,559	$109,266
New MBE capital	$91,176	$6,383	$11,707
Fermentation/Aging Equipment (FAE)			
No. barrels	10,000	10,700	11,984
FAE/barrel	840	840	840
FAE capital	$10,500	$10,500	$10,500
FAE capital requirement	$125,000	$133,750	$149,800
New FAE capital	$125,000	$8,750	$16,050
Finishing Equipment (FE)			
No. barrels	10,000	10,700	11,984
FE/barrel	3,500	3,500	3,500
FE capital	$22,000	$22,000	$22,000
FE capital requirement	$62,857	$67,257	$75,328
New FE capital	$62,857	$4,400	$8,071
Packaging Equipment (PE)			
No. barrels	10,000	10,700	11,984
PE/barrel	7,500	7,500	7,500
PE capital	$75,000	$75,000	$75,000
PE capital requirement	$99,750	$107,000	$119,840
New PE capital	$99,750	$7,250	$12,840
Total new capital	$411,640	$29,083	$52,887
Total capital	$411,640	$399,559	$408,374
Depreciation	$41,164	$44,072	$49,361

product of income, which is produced through unit sales. To meet the demand of sales, a business usually must invest money for increasing production or supplying better service. In the business plan, capital requirements are tied to projected sales discussed earlier in this chapter.

For instance, if the capital equipment required can handle the needs of 10,000 customers at an average sale of $10 each, that would be $100,000 in sales; should the company grow beyond this point, additional capital will be required to purchase more equipment. This leads us to another factor within the capital requirements equation—equipment cost. If you multiply the cost of equipment by the number of customers it can support in terms of sales, it would result in the capital requirements for that particular equipment element. Therefore, you can use an equation where capital requirements (CR), equals sales (S) divided by number of customers (NC) supported by each equipment element multiplied by average sale (AS), which is then multiplied by the capital cost (CC) of the equipment element. With these variables, your equation would look like the following:

$$CR = [(S \div NC) \times AS] \times CC$$

The capital requirements table is formed by adding together all your equipment elements to generate the *total new capital* for that year. During the first year, total new capital is also the *total capital* required. For each successive year thereafter, total capital (TC) required is the sum of total new capital (NC) plus total capital (PC) from the previous year, less depreciation (D), once again, from the previous year. Therefore, your equation to arrive at total capital for each year portrayed in the capital requirements model would be:

$$TC = NC + PC - D$$

Keep in mind that depreciation is an expense that shows the decrease in value of the equipment throughout its effective lifetime. For many businesses, depreciation is based on schedules tied to the lifetime of the equipment. Be careful when choosing the schedule that most fits your business. Depreciation is also the basis for a tax deduction as well as the flow of money for new capital. You may need to consult with an expert in this area.

Cost of Goods

The last table that needs to be generated in the operations and management section of your business plan is the cost of goods table (see Table 8.5). This table is used only for businesses that place their product into inventory. For a retail or wholesale business, *cost of goods sold,* or *cost of sales,* refers to the purchase of products for resale—the inventory. The products that are sold are logged into cost of goods as an expense of the sale, while those that aren't sold remain in inventory.

For a manufacturing firm, *cost of goods* is the cost incurred by the company to manufacture its product. This usually includes three elements:

1. Material.
2. Labor.
3. Overhead.

Like retail, the merchandise that is sold is expensed as a cost of goods, while merchandise that isn't sold is placed in inventory. Cost of goods has to be accounted for in the operations of a business. It is an important yardstick for

Table 8.5 Cost of Goods—Barrels

	1995	1996	1997
Barrels sold	10,000	10,700	11,984
Begin FB	0	4,500	4,815
FB% sales (barrels)	45	45	45
End FB	4,500	4,815	5,393
Inventory/FB	4,500	315	578
Begin PB	0	3,500	3,745
PB% sales (barrels)	35	35	35
End PB	3,500	3,745	4,194
Inventory/PB	3,500	245	449
Begin I	0	2,000	2,140
I% sales (barrels)	20	20	20
End I	2,000	2,140	2,397
Inventory/I	2,000	140	257
Barrels sold	10,000	10,700	11,984
Barrels FBI	4,500	315	578
Barrels PBI	3,500	245	449
Barrels II	2,000	140	257
Total barrels inventory	20,000	11,400	13,268
Ingredients/barrel ($)	32	32	32
Ingredient costs ($)	640,000	364,800	424,576
Barrels sold	10,000	10,700	11,984
Barrels FBI	4,500	315	578
Barrels PBI	3,500	245	449
Total L&OH barrels	18,000	11,260	13,011
Labor/PA% (barrels)	50	50	50
Labor/barrel ($)	39	39	39
OH/barrel ($)	18	18	18
Labor costs ($)	633,750	434,363	498,674
OH costs ($)	292,500	200,475	230,157
Total L&OH ($)	926,250	634,838	728,831
Inventory/I ($)	64,000	4,480	8,224
Production costs ($)	1,502,250	995,158	1,145,183
Inventory/PB ($)	211,750	14,823	27,165
COG production ($)	1,290,500	980,334	1,118,018
Inventory/FB ($)	400,500	28,035	51,442
COG sold ($)	890,000	952,299	1,066,576
COGS/barrel ($)	89	89	89
Begin II ($)	0	64,000	68,480
Change II ($)	64,000	4,480	8,224
End II ($)	64,000	68,480	76,704
Begin PBI ($)	0	211,750	226,573
Change PBI ($)	211,750	14,823	27,165
End PBI ($)	211,750	226,573	253,738
Begin FBI ($)	0	400,500	428,535
Change FBI ($)	400,500	28,035	51,442
End FBI ($)	400,500	428,535	479,977
Begin inventory ($)	0	676,250	723,588
Change inventory ($)	676,250	47,338	86,831
End inventory ($)	676,250	723,588	810,419
Revenue/barrel ($)	213.91	213.19	213.14
Revenue ($)	2,139,132	2,281,212	2,554,325
Inventory turn	3.16	3.15	3.15

Abbreviations: I = Ingredients; PB = Partially brewed; FB = Fully brewed.

measuring the firm's profitability for the cash flow statement and income statement.

In the income statement, the last stage of the manufacturing process is the item expensed as cost of goods, but it is important to document the inventory still in various stages of the manufacturing process because it represents assets to the company. This is not important not only from a cash flow point of view but also in the production of the balance sheet.

That is what the cost of goods table does. It is one of the most complicated tables you'll have to develop for your business plan, but it is an integral part of portraying the flow of inventory through your operations, the placement of assets within the company, and the rate at which your inventory turns.

To generate the cost of goods table, you need a little more information in addition to the cost per unit for labor and material. You also need to know the total number of units sold for the year, the percentage that will be fully assembled, the percentage that will be partially assembled, and the percentage that will be in unassembled inventory. Much of this information is dependent on the capacity of your equipment as well as the inventory control system you develop.

Along with these factors, you also need to know at what stage the majority of labor is performed.

FINANCIAL COMPONENTS

After defining the product, market, and operations, you need to address the real backbone of the business plan—the financial statements including the *income statement,* the *cash flow statement,* and the *balance sheet.*

The Income Statement

The income statement is a simple and straightforward report on the proposed business's cash-generating ability. It is a scorecard on the financial performance of your business that reflects when sales are made and when expenses are incurred. It draws information from the various financial models developed earlier such as revenue, expenses, capital (in the form of depreciation), and cost of goods. By combining these elements, the income statement illustrates just how much your company makes or loses during the year by subtracting cost of goods and expenses from revenue to arrive at a net result—which is either a profit or loss. It differs from a cash flow statement because the income statement doesn't show when revenue is collected or when expenses are paid. It does, however show the projected profitability of the business over the time frame covered by the plan. Table 8.6 shows a sample income statement.

For a business plan, the income statement should be generated on a monthly basis during the first year, quarterly for the second, and annually for each year thereafter. It is formed by listing your financial projections in the following manner:

1. **Income.** Includes all the income generated by the business and its sources.
2. **Cost of goods.** Includes all the costs related to the sale of products in inventory.
3. **Gross profit margin.** The difference between revenue and cost of goods. Gross profit margin can be expressed in dollars, as a percentage, or both. As a percentage, the GP margin is always stated as a percentage of revenue.
4. **Operating expenses.** Includes all overhead and labor expenses associated with the operations of the business.
5. **Total expenses.** The sum of all overhead and labor expenses required to operate the business.
6. **Net profit.** The difference between gross profit margin and total expenses. The net income depicts the business's debt and capital capabilities.
7. **Depreciation.** Reflects the decrease in value of capital assets used to generate income. It is also used as the basis for a tax deduction and an indicator of the flow of money into new capital.
8. **Net profit before interest.** The difference between net profit and depreciation.
9. **Interest.** Includes all interest derived from debts, both short-term and long-term. Interest is determined by the amount of investment within the company.
10. **Net profit before taxes.** The difference between net profit before interest and interest.
11. **Taxes.** Includes all taxes on the business.
12. **Profit after taxes.** The difference between net profit before taxes and the taxes accrued. Profit after taxes is the bottom line for any company.

In addition to the income statement, you should include a note analyzing the results. The analysis should be very short, emphasizing the key points of the income statement.

Table 8.6 Income Statement

	JANUARY	FEBRUARY	MARCH	APRIL	MAY	JUNE	JULY	AUGUST
Income	42,783	64,174	85,565	128,348	149,739	171,131	181,826	203,218
Cost of goods	17,800	26,700	35,600	53,400	62,300	71,200	75,650	84,550
Gross profit	24,983	37,474	49,965	74,948	87,439	99,931	106,176	118,668
Margin %	58%	58%	58%	58%	58%	58%	58%	58%
Expenses	34,011	40,813	47,616	47,616	49,656	52,377	55,778	63,261
Net profit	−9,029	−3,339	2,350	27,332	37,783	47,553	50,398	55,407
Margin %	−21%	−5%	3%	21%	25%	28%	28%	27%
Depreciation	3,430	3,430	3,430	3,430	3,430	3,430	3,430	3,430
Net profit before interest	−12,459	−6,770	−1,081	23,902	34,353	44,123	46,968	51,976
Margin %	−29%	−11%	−1%	19%	23%	26%	26%	26%
Interest	13,350	13,200	13,050	12,900	12,750	12,600	12,450	12,300
Net profit before taxes	−25,809	−19,970	−14,131	11,002	21,603	31,523	34,518	39,676

Cash Flow Statement

The cash flow statement is one of the most critical information tools for your business, showing how much cash you will need to meet obligations, when you will require it, and from where it will come. It shows a schedule of the money coming into the business and expenses that need to be paid. The result is the profit or loss at the end of the month or year. In a cash flow statement, both profits and losses are carried over to the next column to show the cumulative amount. If you run a loss on your cash flow statement, it is a strong indicator that you will need additional cash to meet expenses.

Like the income statement, the cash flow statement takes advantage of previous financial tables developed in creating the business plan. The cash flow statement begins with cash on hand and the revenue sources. The next item it lists is expenses, including those accumulated during the manufacture of a product. The capital requirements are then logged as a negative after expenses. The cash flow statement ends with the net cash flow.

The cash flow statement should cover the same amount of time as the business plan. Unlike the income statement, the cash flow statement doesn't show whether the business will be profitable, but it does show the cash position of the business at any given point in time by measuring incoming revenue against outgoing cash (see Table 8.7 for a sample cash flow statement).

The cash flow statement should be prepared on a monthly basis during the first year, on a quarterly basis during the second year, and on an annual basis thereafter. The following items that you will need to include in the cash flow statement are listed in the order they should appear:

1. **Cash sales.** Income derived from sales paid for by cash.
2. **Receivables.** Income derived from the collection of receivables.
3. **Other income.** Income derived from investments, interest on loans that have been extended, and the liquidation of any assets.

Table 8.6   (continued)

SEPTEMBER	OCTOBER	NOVEMBER	DECEMBER	1995	1ST QTR	2ND QTR	3RD QTR	4TH QTR	1996	1997
213,913	246,000	310,174	342,261	2,139,132	410,618	501,867	638,739	729,988	2,281,212	2,554,325
89,000	102,350	129,050	142,400	890,000	171,414	209,506	266,644	304,736	952,299	1,066,576
124,913	143,650	181,124	199,861	1,249,132	239,204	292,361	372,096	425,252	1,328,913	1,487,749
58%	58%	58%	58%	58%	58%	58%	58%	58%	58%	58%
71,424	71,424	72,104	74,144	680,224	160,125	167,403	196,517	203,795	727,840	815,181
53,490	72,227	109,020	125,717	568,908	79,080	124,958	175,579	221,457	601,073	672,568
25%	29%	35%	37%	27%	19%	25%	27%	30%	26%	26%
3,430	3,430	3,430	3,430	41,164	11,018	11,018	11,018	11,018	44,072	49,361
50,059	68,796	105,590	122,286	527,744	68,062	113,940	164,561	210,439	557,001	623,207
23%	28%	34%	36%	25%	17%	23%	26%	29%	24%	24%
12,150	12,000	11,850	11,400	150,000	36,135	34,903	33,671	32,166	136,875	127,716
37,909	56,796	93,740	110,886	377,744	31,927	79,037	130,890	178,273	420,126	495,491

Table 8.7 Cash Flow Statement

	JANUARY	FEBRUARY	MARCH	APRIL	MAY	JUNE	JULY	AUGUST
Cash sales	17,113	25,670	34,226	51,339	59,896	68,452	72,730	81,287
Receivables	0	0	25,670	38,504	51,339	77,009	89,844	102,678
Other income	0	0	0	0	0	0	0	0
Total income	17,113	25,670	59,896	89,843	111,235	145,461	162,574	183,965
Material	0	0	0	0	0	0	0	0
Direct labor	7,800	11,700	15,600	23,400	27,300	31,200	33,150	37,050
Overhead	0	0	0	0	0	0	0	0
Marketing and sales	8,250	9,900	11,550	11,550	12,045	12,705	13,530	15,345
Brewery operations/R&D	3,500	4,200	4,900	4,900	5,110	5,390	5,740	6,510
General and administrative	1,750	2,100	2,450	2,450	2,555	2,695	2,870	3,255
Taxes	0	0	40,528	0	0	40,528	0	0
Capital	3,430	3,430	3,430	3,430	3,430	3,430	3,430	3,430
Loans	25,000	25,000	25,000	25,000	25,000	25,001	25,000	25,000
Total expenses	49,730	56,330	103,458	70,730	75,440	120,950	83,720	90,590
Cash flow	−32,617	−30,660	−43,562	19,113	35,795	24,511	78,854	93,375
Cumulative cash flow	−32,617	−63,277	−106,840	−87,727	−51,932	−27,421	51,433	144,808

4. **Total income.** The sum of total ca0sh, cash sales, receivables, and other income.
5. **Material/merchandise.** The raw material used in the manufacture of a product (for manufacturing operations only), the cash outlay for merchandise inventory (for merchandisers such as wholesalers and retailers), or the supplies used in the performance of a service.
6. **Direct labor.** The labor required to manufacture a product (for manufacturing operations only) or perform a service.
7. **Overhead.** All fixed and variable expenses required for the production of the product and the operations of the business.
8. **Marketing/sales.** All salaries, commissions, and other direct costs associated with the marketing and sales departments.
9. **R&D.** All the labor expenses required to support the research and development operations of the business.
10. **G&A.** All the labor expenses required to support the administrative functions of the business.
11. **Taxes.** All taxes, except payroll, paid to the appropriate government institutions.
12. **Capital.** The capital requirements to obtain any equipment elements that are needed for the generation of income.
13. **Loan payments.** The total of all payments made to reduce any long-term debts.
14. **Total expenses.** The sum of material, direct labor, overhead expenses, marketing, sales, G&A, taxes, capital, and loan payments.
15. **Cash flow.** The difference between total income and total expenses. This amount is carried over to the next period as beginning cash.

Table 8.7 (continued)

SEPTEMBER	OCTOBER	NOVEMBER	DECEMBER	1995	1ST QTR	2ND QTR	3RD QTR	4TH QTR	1996	1997
85,565	98,400	124,070	136,904	855,652	164,247	200,747	255,496	291,995	912,485	1,021,730
109,096	121,931	128,348	147,600	892,019	458,720	261,317	323,540	398,190	1,441,767	1,552,160
0	0	0	0		0	0	0	0	0	0
194,661	220,331	252,418	284,504	1,747,671	622,967	462,064	579,036	690,185	2,354,252	2,573,890
0	0	0	0		0	0	0	0	0	0
39,000	44,850	56,550	62,400	390,000	91,806	95,979	112,671	116,844	417,300	467,376
0	0	0	0		0	0	0	0	0	0
17,325	17,325	17,490	17,985	165,000	38,841	40,607	47,669	49,434	176,550	197,736
7,350	7,350	7,420	7,630	70,000	16,478	17,227	20,223	20,972	74,900	83,888
3,675	3,675	3,710	3,815	35,000	8,239	8,614	10,112	10,486	37,450	41,944
40,528	0	0	40,528	162,113	41,538	41,538	41,538	41,538	166,150	186,451
3,430	3,430	3,430	3,430	41,164	11,018	11,018	11,018	11,018	44,072	49,361
25,000	25,000	25,000	25,000	300,000	75,000	75,000	75,000	75,000	300,000	300,000
136,308	101,630	113,600	160,789	1,163,277	282,920	289,982	318,230	325,292	1,216,422	1,326,756
58,353	118,701	138,818	123,715	584,394	340,048	172,083	260,807	364,894	1,137,830	1,247,134
203,160	321,861	460,679	584,394	584,394	924,442	1,096,524	1,357,331	1,722,224	1,722,224	2,969,358

16. Cumulative cash flow. The difference between current cash flow and cash flow from the previous period.

As with the income statement, you will need to analyze the cash flow statement for a short summary in the business plan. Once again, the analysis doesn't have to be long and should cover only key points derived from the cash flow statement.

The Balance Sheet

The last financial statement you'll need to develop is the balance sheet. Like the income and cash flow statements, the balance sheet utilizes information from all the financial models developed in earlier sections of the business plan; however, unlike the previous statements, the balance sheet is generated solely on an annual basis for the business plan and is, more or less, a summary of all the preceding financial information broken down into three areas:

1. Assets.
2. Liabilities.
3. Equity.

Balance sheets are used to calculate the net worth of a business or individual by measuring assets against liabilities. If your business plan is for an existing business, the balance sheet from your last reporting period should be included. If the business plan is for a new business, try to project what your assets and liabilities will be over the course of the business plan to determine what equity you may have accumulated in the business. More importantly, to

Table 8.8   Balance Sheet

	1995	1996	1997
Assets			
Current assets			
Cash	855,653	912,485	1,021,730
Accounts receivable	892,018	1,441,768	1,552,160
Inventory	676,250	723,588	810,419
Total current assets	2,423,921	3,077,840	3,384,309
Fixed assets			
Capital/plant	370,476	399,559	408,374
Investment	41,164	44,072	49,361
Miscellaneous assets	0	0	0
Total fixed assets	411,640	443,631	457,735
Total assets	2,835,561	3,521,471	3,842,044
Liabilities			
Current liabilities			
Accounts payable	717,303	1,034,785	1,075,601
Accrued liabilities	660,000	706,200	790,944
Taxes	162,113	166,150	186,451
Total current liabilities	1,539,416	1,907,135	2,052,996
Long-term liabilities			
Bonds payable	0	0	0
Notes payable	300,000	300,000	300,000
Total long-term liabilities	300,000	300,000	300,000
Total liabilities			
Owner's equity	996,145	1,314,337	1,489,047
Total liability/equity	2,835,561	3,521,471	3,842,044

obtain financing for a new business, you'll need to include a personal financial statement or balance sheet instead of one that encompasses the business. A personal balance sheet is generated in the same manner as one for a business. Refer to the balance sheet in this chapter (Table 8.8) as well as the personal balance sheet in Chapter 1.

As mentioned, the balance sheet is divided into three sections. The top portion lists your company's assets classifying them as current assets and long-term, or fixed, assets. Current assets are assets that will be converted to cash or will be used by the business in a year or less. Current assets include:

- **Cash.** The cash on hand at the time books are closed at the end of the fiscal year. This refers to all cash in checking, savings, and short-term investment accounts.
- **Accounts receivable.** The income derived from credit accounts. For the balance sheet, it is the total amount of income to be received that is logged into the books at the close of the fiscal year.
- **Inventory.** This is derived from the cost of goods table. It is the inventory of material used to manufacture a product not yet sold.

- **Total current assets.** The sum of cash, accounts receivable, inventory, and supplies.

Other assets that appear in the balance sheet are called long-term or fixed assets. They are called long-term because they are durable and will last more than one year. Examples of this type of asset include:

- **Capital and plant.** The book value of all capital equipment and property (if you own the land and building), less depreciation.
- **Investment.** All investments by the company that cannot be converted to cash in less than one year. For the most part, companies just starting out have not accumulated long-term investments.
- **Miscellaneous assets.** All other long-term assets that are not "capital and plant" or "investment."
- **Total long-term assets.** The sum of capital and plant, investments, and miscellaneous assets.
- **Total assets.** The sum of total current assets and total long-term assets.

After listing the assets, you need to account for the liabilities of your business. Like assets, liabilities are classified as current or long-term. Debts that are due in one year or less are classified as current liabilities. If they are due in more than one year, they are long-term liabilities. Examples of current liabilities are as follows:

- **Accounts payable.** All expenses incurred by the business that are purchased from regular creditors on an open account and are due and payable.
- **Accrued liabilities.** All expenses incurred by the business that are required for operation but have not yet been paid at the time the books are closed. These expenses are usually the company's overhead and salaries.
- **Taxes.** These are taxes that are still due and payable at the time the books are closed.
- **Total current liabilities.** The sum of accounts payable, accrued liabilities, and taxes.

Long-term liabilities include:

- **Bonds payable.** The total of all bonds at the end of the year that are due and payable over a period exceeding one year.
- **Mortgage payable.** Loans taken out for the purchase of real property that are repaid over a long-term period. The mortgage payable is that amount still due at the close of books for the year.
- **Notes payable.** The amount still owed on any long-term debts that will not be repaid during the current fiscal year.
- **Total long-term liabilities.** The sum of bonds payable, mortgage payable, and notes payable.
- **Total liabilities.** The sum of total current and long-term liabilities.

Once the liabilities have been listed, the final portion of the balance sheet needs to be calculated. This portion is owner's equity. The amount attributed to owner's equity is the difference between total assets and total liabilities. The amount of equity the owner has in the business is an important yardstick used by investors to evaluate the company. Many times, it determines the amount of capital they feel they can safely invest in the business.

In the business plan, you'll need to create an analysis for the balance sheet just as you need to do for the income and cash flow statements. The analysis of the balance sheet should be kept short and cover key points about the company.

RESOURCES

Associations

Center for Entrepreneurial Management, Inc., 180 Varick Street, New York, NY 10014, 212-633-0060

Small Business Service Bureau, 554 Main Street, P.O. Box 1441, Worcester, MA 01601, 508-756-3513

Magazines

The Business Owner, Thomas Publishing, Inc., 383 South Broadway, Hicksville, NY 11801, 516-681-2111

Entrepreneurial Manager, 180 Varick Street, Penthouse Suite, New York, NY 10014-4692, 212-633-0060

Entrepreneurial Manager's Newsletter, 180 Varick Street, Penthouse Suite, New York, NY 10014-4692, 212-633-0060

Journal of Small Business Management, West Virginia University, College of Business Economics, Bureau of Business Research, P.O. Box 6025, Morgantown, WV 26506-6025, 304-293-5837

9

Sample Business Plan

Backbay Brewing Company, Inc.

A Brewing Company Incorporated Under the Laws
of the State of California

Company Headquarters: 13732 Main Street,
Irvine, CA 92614 (714) 332-8789

A Proposal/Business Plan

Owner: Will Gillette

EXECUTIVE SUMMARY

Backbay Brewing Company is a small microbrewery incorporated in 1993 in
the state of California. It was formed with the intent to provide beer drinkers of
discerning taste with a premium lager beer called "Diamond Tap," which will
feature a robust flavor while still maintaining the high effervescence lagers are
known for. The company's CEO, president, and vice president have over 30
years of combined experience in the beer brewing industry.

Backbay Brewing Company will target beer drinkers in California who
have an affinity for quality beer—drinkers of microbrewed beers as well as

mass-produced domestic premium beers and imports. These beer drinkers are typically classified as "good" beer drinkers and are generally more inclined to give microbrewed beer a try. To reach this market, Backbay Brewing Company will sell through wholesalers to bars, taverns, and other drinking establishments as well as to liquor stores, convenience stores, and major supermarkets. With projected net sales of $2.5 million in its third year, the business will generate pretax net profits of 27 percent. Given this return, investment within the company is very attractive. Backbay Brewing Company will require a total of $1.5 million over two stages to start the business.

1. The first stage of financing will require $1.1 million for product, market, and operational development.

2. The second stage of financing will consist of $400,000 for implementation and working capital until break-even is reached.

First-stage capital will be used to purchase needed equipment and materials to develop the product and market it initially. Second-stage financing will be required for the implementation of the company's marketing strategies. To obtain its capital requirements, the company is willing to relinquish 25 percent equity to first- and second-stage investors.

The company has registered its recipe for Diamond Tap as a *trade secret* with its patent attorney, Robert Pack of Newport Beach, California. Lease agreements are also in place for a 15,000-square-foot facility in a light industrial area of Irvine, as well as major equipment needed to begin production. Currently, the company is being funded by $250,000 from the three principals, with purchase orders for 30,200 six packs, 49,480 22 oz. bottles, and 45 kegs already in hand.

THE BUSINESS DESCRIPTION

In the mid-1980s, the American consciousness was tapped by a startling realization: Beer is supposed to have flavor. Europeans have been savoring ale, porter, pilsner, and stout for centuries. But in the United States, such news was a revelation. Small breweries sprouted tentatively here and there. One by one, American beer drinkers sat down with unfamiliar brews from unknown sources—Anchor Steam, Redhook, Sierra Nevada, Bigfoot Ale. As they sipped, they were quietly converted. American "microbrews" became the beer aficionado's small stash of secret joy.

Ten years later, it's a beer bath. In 1992, specialty brews accounted for more than 1 million barrels of beer, according to the Institute for Brewing Studies, a division of the Association of Brewers, with the industry growing at an annual clip of 40 percent. That's really not surprising. The beer industry is a $35-billion-a-year business with Americans consuming an average of 22.7 gallons of beer annually. California is one of the top regional markets in terms of beer consumption with approximately 11 percent of total malt beverage sales.

While major brewers still account for most of the beer production in the United States, small microbreweries (production plants that turn out 15,000 barrels or less per year for the wholesale market) are where most of the growth is occurring. In fact, microbreweries are at the forefront of the beer revolution. Recognizing the tremendous growth opportunities in this industry and the continued demand for good-quality beer, Backbay Brewing Company was formed in 1993 to develop a premium lager beer that would appeal to beer drinkers who enjoy a full-bodied beer (such as current drinkers of micro-brewed beer and those of mass-produced premium domestic and import beer) and are willing to pay extra to get a superior tasting product. Backbay Brewing Company has perfected a recipe for its premium lager beer called "Diamond Tap" and is ready to proceed with the next step, which is development of a finished product in sufficient quantity to meet projected market demand.

Priced competitively with other premium microbrewed beers, Diamond Tap will be sold through wholesalers for distribution to bars, taverns, liquor stores, convenience stores, and supermarkets in the state of California, which meets the state's regulatory requirements of three-tiered distribution. The pricing structure for Diamond Tap will provide for a retail price of $6.99 per six-pack of 12-ounce bottles, $2.20 per 22-ounce bottle, and $195 per keg, the three products Backbay Brewing plans to use for packaging Diamond Tap.

During the first three years of operation that this plan covers, Backbay Brewing Company projects that it will be able to obtain 2.8 percent of the micro-brewed beer market in California by adhering to the following strategies:

- The first year of business, our goal will be to concentrate on marketing and distribution to raise awareness among consumers and retailers alike. Projected sales goals for the first year, at an average wholesale cost of $3.85 for a six-pack, $1.20 for a 22-ounce bottle, and $105 for a keg, at $2.1 million from 10,000 bbl. (barrels) is a 2.4 percent market share.
- The second year, our goals will be to reinvest profits to increase our marketing and production staff. With these elements in place, our goal is to increase sales from the first year by 7 percent, resulting in $2.3 million in sales and a 2.5 percent market share.
- The third year, our goals are to increase our marketing and production staff in order to handle an increase in sales by 12 percent to $2.5 million, which will enable us to reach our objective of a 2.8 percent market share.

MARKET STRATEGIES

Current drinkers of microbrewed beers as well as mass-produced domestic premiums and imports are the largest markets for Diamond Tap premium lager. However, segments within this primary group of customers are targeted by each group of competitors Diamond Tap will be marketed against. Positioned as a premium microbrewed lager for beer drinkers of discerning taste,

Diamond will compete directly with other microbreweries producing a premium lager beer and with significant distribution in California such as Alpine Village Hofbrau Lager from Alpine Village Hofbrau, Cable Car Lager from Thousand Oaks Brewing Company, Calistoga Lager from the Napa Valley Brewing Company, Cherokee Choice Lager from the Okie Girl Brewery, Eureka Lager from the Los Angeles Brewing Company, Loggers Lager from Boulder Creek Brewing Company, Nevada City Brew (dark & gold) from Nevada City Brewing Company, and Truckee Lager from the Truckee Brewing Company.

Market Definition

Americans love their beer! In fact, beer is a $35 billion industry in the United States with over 85 million beer drinkers consuming an average of 22.7 gallons of beer (per capita) annually according to *Modern Brewery Age.* Overall industry sales, however, have remained flat over the past few years with 31-gallon barrels production rising from 184,478,000 in 1990 to 188,985,000 currently, a growth of 2.7 percent. While the industry has remained flat, sales of micro-brewed beers have skyrocketed with shipments of 31-gallon barrels rising from 300,000 in 1990 to 1 million currently, a growth of 233 percent.

That increase illustrates the strength of the microbrewery market; however, it isn't the extent of the target market. Drinkers of import beers will also be a key market Backbay Brewing plans to target in its marketing efforts. According to *Modern Brewery*, sales of import beer have decreased since 1990 when this segment accounted for 8,783,000 31-gallon barrels. Currently, imports account for 8,322,884 31-gallon barrels, a 5.2 percent decrease. While this segment has decreased, it is critical to show the total target market for Diamond Tap Premium Lager, which is 9,322,884 31-gallon barrels. California accounts for 12 percent of the total market according to the *Brewers Almanac.* Using this number as a barometer, the total microbrew and import market in the state of California would be 1,118,746 31 gallon barrels. Industry sales breakdowns are shown in Figure 9.1. The growth of microbrewed beer sales is shown in Figure 9.2.

The increase in the microbrewery market as opposed to the decrease in the import market reflects several trends in the beer brewery business:

1. Beer drinkers are tiring of bland, mass-produced beers and want a quality beer with a distinct, full-bodied taste.
2. Many beer drinkers are pursuing a healthier lifestyle and prefer micro-brewed beers because they are typically brewed without preservatives and unnatural additives.
3. Beer drinkers are searching for beer that is fresh, and microbrewed beers aren't pasteurized.

Beyond these factors lies the enormous impact of the baby boomer generation. Many have reached or are reaching their peak earning potentials, and they are changing their attitudes and spending patterns to reflect their affluence. This

Figure 9.1 U.S. Beer Industry Sales Breakdown (31-Gallon Barrels)

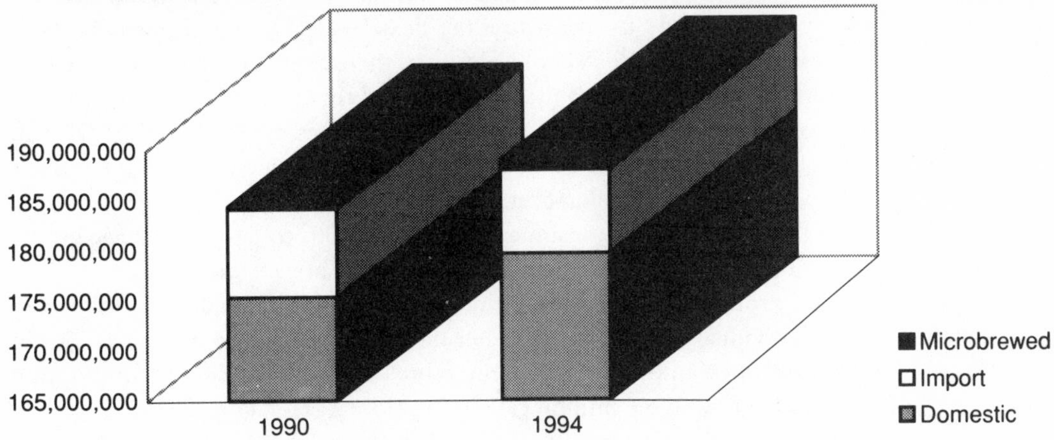

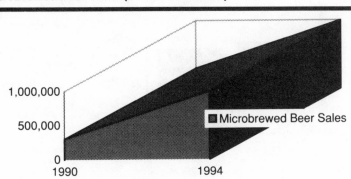

not only has led to a boom in microbrewed beers as the majority of baby boomers seek out high-quality gourmet products, but has also fueled the growth of premium wines, gourmet coffees, bread, and so on.

From the total U.S. population of 252.7 million, 40.6 percent, or 102.7 million, are considered baby boomers, those individuals between the ages of 30 and 49, according to the U.S. Bureau of the Census. In the state of California, there are 12.3 million baby boomers, and of that, it is estimated that 33.6 percent, or 4.1 million, are beer drinkers who consume an average of 23.7 gallons of beer (per capita) annually in California. Therefore, baby boomers in the state of California drink approximately 97.2 million gallons of beer annually, or 14 percent of the total 688.5 million gallons consumed.

Much of this consumption is of microbrewed and import beer. It is estimated that baby boomers make up 60.2 percent of the market for total microbrewed and import beer consumption in the state of California. All totaled, this would account for 673,485 31-gallon barrels, or 20.9 million gallons.

Figure 9.2 Microbrewed Beer Sales (31-Gallon Barrels)

In addition to the baby boomer market, the post baby boomers who can legally consume alcohol in the state of California—those individuals between the ages of 21 and 30—constitute the next largest market segment Backbay Brewing will tap. In the state of California, there are 4.3 million individuals in this age group, according to the U.S. Bureau of the Census. Of that, 1.4 million are beer drinkers who consume 33.2 million gallons of beer annually. Of that, microbrewed and import beer consumption in this age group is 7.2 million gallons or 231,580 31-gallon barrels.

The third significant consumer market is the 50- to-64-year-old age group. According to the U.S. Bureau of the Census, there are 3.9 million individuals in this age group residing in the state of California. Approximately 1.3 million of these individuals drink beer. Together they account for 30.8 million gallons of beer consumed annually. Of that, microbrewed and import beer consumption in this age group is 6.6 million gallons, or 213,680 31-gallon barrels.

Altogether, the total market for Backbay Brewing's Diamond Tap Premium Lager would be the total of these three highlighted segments which is 1.1 million 31-gallon barrels, or 34.7 million gallons. Figure 9.3 shows a complete breakdown of the target market for Backbay Brewing.

With the introduction of Diamond Tap Premium Lager, Backbay Brewing Company will compete directly against other microbrewed beers for a share of the defined market. Aside from being a premium microbrewed beer, the main attraction for Diamond Tap Premium Lager beer for this target group will be

Figure 9.3   California Market Breakdown

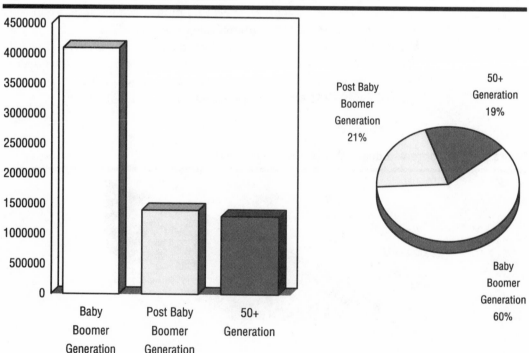

its lager heritage. Lager beers are the most popular type of beer brewed in North America. In fact, according to *Beverage Industry* magazine, all styles of lagers account for 89.6 percent of the total market, with premium lager beer at 37.3 percent. Using 37.3 percent as a barometer, the total feasible market for Diamond Tap Premium Lager would be 417,292 31-gallon barrels of beer. Of the total feasible market, it is estimated that Diamond Tap Premium Lager can capture 2.4 percent for total production of 10,000 31-gallon barrels during its first year for total sales of $2.1 million.

Distribution Strategies

Diamond Tap Premium Lager will be packaged in three different containers: a six-pack of 12-ounce bottles, 22-ounce bottles, and 15-gallon kegs. While all three products will be available through retail channels, the 15-gallon kegs will be marketed mainly toward bars and other drinking establishments with a reputation for serving quality beer.

To effectively reach our customers, Backbay Brewing Company will use a four-tiered channel of distribution through which Diamond Tap Premium Lager will be sold to a wholesale distributor that will in turn sell the product to retail distributors for sale to consumers. See Figure 9.4 for an illustration of our distribution channels.

Through these distribution channels, Backbay Brewing will target mainly liquor stores as well as drinking establishments. In addition, Backbay Brewing will also target upscale convenience stores, supermarkets, and membership warehouses. Figure 9.5 has a complete breakdown of distribution channels Backbay Brewing Company will be using.

Pricing Strategies

Since Backbay Brewing Company is positioning Diamond Tap as a premium lager, pricing will not only be based on a markup strategy to cover our costs, but will also be geared competitively to produce an aggressive pricing strategy. The costs to produce a 31-gallon barrel of Diamond Tap Premium Lager are as follows:

Full-grain malt, yeast, hops, water, bottles, kegs, caps, labels, beer boards, printed boxes, direct labor, and brewing overhead	$75.50
Operating expenses	$68
State excise tax	$ 6.50
Federal tax	$ 7

Given the four-tiered distribution channel Backbay Brewing Company will be using, Diamond Tap Premium Lager will be sold to a wholesale distributor at the following prices:

- Six-pack of 12-oz. bottles, $3.85
- 22-oz. bottles, $1.20
- 15-gal. keg, $105

Figure 9.4 Distribution Channels

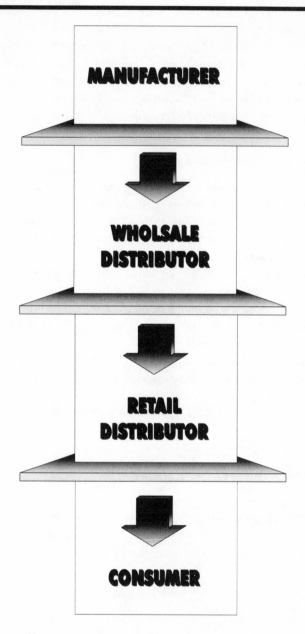

The preceding pricing structure will allow Diamond Tap Premium Lager to be sold on a retail basis at very competitive suggested prices of:

- Six-pack of 12-oz. bottles, $6.99
- 22-oz. bottles, $2.20
- 15-gal. keg, $195

Figure 9.5 Geographic Distribution Channel Chart

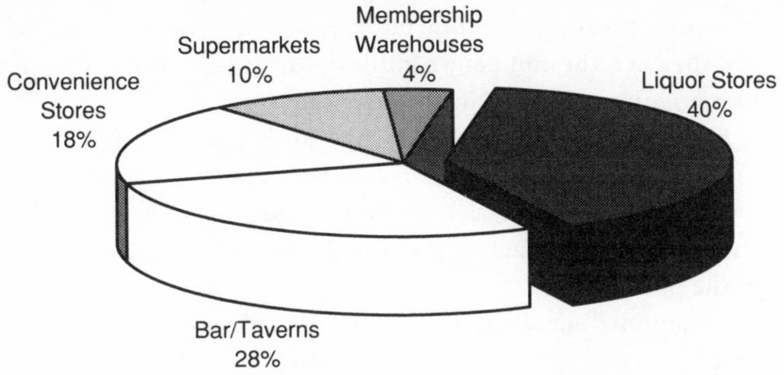

This pricing structure compares favorably with other premium brand lagers, which sell on an average between $5.99 at the low end and $8.99 at the high end for a six-pack of 12-ounce bottles, $1.99–$3.99 for a 22-ounce bottle, and $150–$225 for a 15-gallon keg.

Promotional Strategies

The main goals of the promotional strategy for Diamond Tap Premium Lager are to develop relationships with a core group of regional distributors with strong access to liquor stores, bars, convenience food stores, supermarkets, and membership warehouses, to support the wholesale distributors in their sales efforts to the retailer, and finally, to educate the consumer market.

The first step Backbay Brewing will adopt in its promotional efforts is to identify a group of wholesale distributors with sufficient clout in the distribution channels we have defined for Diamond Tap Premium Lager and enter into exclusive relationships with those distributors. Backbay Brewing will define exclusive areas for distribution of Diamond Tap Premium Lager by geographic area. Those areas will include:

- **Southern California.** Ventura down to San Diego and up through Palm Springs and Indio.
- **Central Valley.** Santa Barbara up to San Luis Obispo and over to the Mammoth Mountain area.
- **Central California.** Monterey up through the San Francisco Bay area over to Lake Tahoe.
- **Northern California.** From Ukiah up to the Oregon border and over to the Nevada border.

To enter into these relationships and service them afterward, Backbay Brewing will hire a sales manager prior to Diamond Tap Premium Lager's launch date.

We will also develop (not only for our inside sales force, but also for our distributors) collateral marketing material: a pricing sheet illustrating the various price breaks for volume purchases, and a brochure highlighting the brewery, the beer, the company's philosophy, and our commitment to brewing the best premium lager in North America.

Backbay Brewing's goal is to line up Southern California during development and the Central Valley area no later than the first quarter after the launch of the product. Thereafter, we hope to add the Central California area by the end of the second quarter, and finally the Northern California area by the end of the third quarter.

To support our distributors, Backbay Brewing will make available product samples as well as point-of-purchase displays and materials that draw attention to the product in the retail environment. These materials will include cardboard displays, flyers, bar mirrors, etc.

The final phase of our promotional strategy will consist of consumer education. The main objective in this phase is to stimulate initial purchases of the product and maintain those customers through repurchases. To accomplish this goal, Backbay Brewing will utilize a combination of advertising and sales promotion events. The following promotional strategies will be aimed at the consumer market:

1. Obtain in-store display and price feature support from retailers by implementing a merchandising allowance program where we will make contractual payments of $15 per day for a 20 six-pack in-store display at liquor stores, convenience food stores, and supermarkets. We will also institute a merchandising allowance program with bars to distribute counter and tabletop cards advertising Diamond Tap Premium Lager. We will also provide initial discounts of 15 percent to our distributors that they will pass along to bars on purchases of 15-gallon kegs to initiate draft sales through this distribution.

2. A coupon program will be instituted through advertisements in local newspapers, direct mail, and local green sheets, as well as in conjunction with liquor stores and supermarkets for inclusion in their sales flyers, for which we will make coop money available. The coupons will offer a discount of $1 off the regular price. One million coupons will be distributed through newspapers, magazines, and the mail.

3. Along with the coupon program, we will also participate in major beer-tasting events and shows that will serve to promote Diamond Tap Premium Lager; we not only will compete but will have sampling booths as well.

During the first year of sales, 10 percent of projected sales will be set aside for promotional purposes. This will total $210,000. Of this, 30 percent will be budgeted for advertising, 65 percent to sales promotion, and the remaining 5 percent will be held in a contingency fund. Figure 9.6 provides an example of the cost breakdown and schedule for the promotional strategy of Diamond Tap Premium Lager.

Figure 9.6 Promotional Schedule

PROMOTIONAL SCHEDULE FOR 1995	COST	JANUARY	FEBRUARY	MARCH	APRIL	MAY	JUNE	JULY	AUGUST	SEPTEMBER	OCTOBER	NOVEMBER	DECEMBER
Sales Promotion													
Counter Tabletop Cards	$20,000	▓			▓	▓			▓			▓	▓
Beer Tasting Events/Shows	33,500	▓			▓	▓			▓			▓	▓
Marketing Materials	16,500	▓			▓	▓			▓			▓	▓
Cardboard Displays & Flyers	22,000	▓			▓	▓			▓			▓	▓
Merchandising Allowance Program–Bars	22,000	▓			▓	▓			▓			▓	▓
Merchandising Allowance Program–Stores	21,000	▓			▓	▓			▓			▓	▓
Sales Promotion Total:	**$136,500**												
Advertising													
Coupon Program	$30,000	▓		▓	▓		▓	▓			▓	▓	
Radio Advertising	20,000	▓		▓	▓		▓	▓			▓	▓	
Other Advertising Expenses	13,000	▓		▓	▓		▓	▓			▓	▓	
Advertising Total:	**$63,000**												
Contingency Fund Total:	**$10,500**												
Total Promotional Budget:	**$210,000**												

Sales Potential

The sales potential for Diamond Tap Premium Lager is based on the following factors:

- Number of beer drinkers who *will* purchase a premium microbrewed beer.
- Number of units per customer.
- Average price per unit—Backbay Brewing.
- Average price after discounts/commissions.

Table 9.1 illustrates the revenue projections for Backbay Brewing Company for its first three years of operation. For example, during its first year, the projections would be based on the following:

- The target market is 1,118,746 31-gallon barrels.
- The feasible market is 37.3 percent of target, or 417,292 31-gallon barrels.
- A conversion rate of 2.4 percent is projected during the first year of operation for a market share of 10,000 31-gallon barrels.
- Revenue is projected at $2.1 million.
- The total revenue potential after three years is $2.5 million.

COMPETITIVE ANALYSIS

The business outlined in this plan relies on reaching the consumer market on a mass basis in an effective manner. To do this, the business will have to develop

Table 9.1 Revenue Model for Backbay Brewing Company

REVENUE SUMMARY

	1995	1996	1997
Product One—Six-Packs			
No. of customers	13,778	14,742	16,510
Units/customer	24	24	24
Total units	330,672	353,808	396,240
New customers	13,778	964	1,768
Price/unit	$3.85	$3.85	$3.85
Revenue	$1,273,087	$1,362,161	$1,525,524
Product Two—22-Ounce Bottles			
No. of customers	11,273	12,062	13,508
Units/customer	48	48	48
Total units	541,104	578,976	648,384
New customers	11,273	789	1,446
Price/unit	$1.20	$1.20	$1.20
Revenue	$ 649,325	$ 694,771	$ 778,061
Product Three—15-Gallon Kegs			
No. of customers	172	178	199
Units/customer	12	12	12
Total units	2,064	2,136	2,388
New customers	172	6	21
Price/unit	$105	$105	$105
Revenue	$216,720	$224,280	$250,740
Total Revenue	$2,139,132	$2,281,212	$2,554,325

key assets and a distinct presence that will allow it to compete effectively within the retail market.

The Competition

The market for microbrewed premium lager beer can be divided into several strategic groups starting with the primary competitors that will compete directly against Backbay Brewing Company for a share of the market. These primary competitors include beers such as Alpine Village Hofbrau Lager from Alpine Village Hofbrau, Cable Car Lager from Thousand Oaks Brewing Company, Calistoga Lager from the Napa Valley Brewing Company, Cherokee Choice Lager from the Okie Girl Brewery, Eureka Lager from the Los Angeles Brewing Company, Loggers Lager from Boulder Creek Brewing Company, Nevada City Brew (dark & gold) from Nevada City Brewing Company, and Truckee Lager from the Truckee Brewing Company. In California, these companies control 14 percent of the target market.

The second strategic group is made up of secondary competitors including domestic and import brewers of mass-produced premium lager beer such as Michelob and Budweiser from Anheuser-Busch, Lowenbrau and Miller from

Miller Brewing Company, Coors from Coors Brewing Company, Moosehead from Moosehead Breweries, and Henry Weinhard's from Blitz-Weinhard Brewing Company. This group of strategic competitors account for the largest part of the target market at roughly 83.6 percent.

Brewpubs represent the last group of competitors. While these competitors are not a major competitive force since they do not distribute their product through the same channels as Backbay Brewing, they do, nonetheless, account for 2.4 percent of the market and are a significant factor in areas of California where they exert some influence. Refer to Figure 9.7 for a complete breakdown of the microbrew and premium beer industry in California.

Key Assets and Skills

The success of Backbay Brewing Company will be contingent on establishing key assets and skills in two primary areas: marketing and production. The following major factors need to be present within the realm of marketing:

- The formation of key alliances with several established wholesale distributors in California that will lead to the development of a statewide distribution network.
- The implementation of a statewide marketing campaign designed to support distributors as well as educate consumers about Diamond Tap Premium Lager by promoting quality, taste, and freshness of the beer compared with its competitors. This marketing campaign will feature print advertising, coupons, and direct mail, as well as collateral material such as flyers, counter cards, and other point-of-purchase displays.

Production will require the following assets and skills:

- Brewing experience, especially at the microbrew level.
- Establishment of strategic partnership with key suppliers of high-quality ingredients to produce Diamond Tap Premium Lager.

Figure 9.7 California Competition: Where's It Coming From?

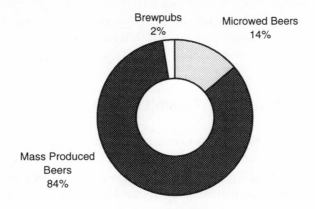

Brewpubs
2%

Microwed Beers
14%

Mass Produced
Beers
84%

- Experience in package design for mass-marketed products, premium lager brewery production, physical distribution, and inventory.

Distinct Competitive Advantages

Diamond Tap will compete against a number of competitors for a share of the consumer's dollar. Almost all the microbreweries defined as primary competitors produce and distribute a premium lager beer that boasts superior taste and quality as well as freshness. Many of these competitors do in fact produce a very good beer. The main differences that will set Diamond Tap Premium Lager apart from its competitors are better and more targeted marketing as well as a more effective distribution system. Pricing is another area where Diamond Tap will hold a competitive advantage. The suggested retail price for Diamond Tap will be $6.99 per six-pack, $2.20 for a 22-ounce bottle, and $195 for a 15-gallon keg. That is almost 10 percent less than 80 percent of our primary competitors. Quality coupled with aggressive pricing will provide us with a distinct competitive advantage over our primary competitors, as well as our larger base of secondary competitors. Diamond Tap's main competitive advantage is the quality of the product. Without a doubt, mass-marketed beers will hold an advantage in price, distribution, and promotional efforts. One area where they will not be able to compete against Backbay Brewing is in the quality department. Diamond Tap Premium Lager not only will have a more robust yet smooth taste but will also be fresher. The premium quality of Diamond Tap as opposed to the mass-produced beers has proven to be a stronger selling point than price to the audience Backbay Brewing is targeting.

Competitive Strategies

Backbay Brewing Company will seek to establish a solid distribution network throughout the state of California thus creating a forceful presence in liquor stores, bars, convenience food stores, and supermarkets. We will undertake this goal by capitalizing on several key assets such as the quality of the product, a growing interest in premium microbrewed beer, and a very competitive price point. We will promote these key strengths in marketing efforts designed to support wholesale distribution efforts as well as our target audience of mostly upper-income beer drinkers who enjoy a quality brew.

DESIGN AND DEVELOPMENT PLANS

Backbay Brewing needs to consider several areas of development to begin marketing Diamond Tap Premium Lager. Those areas include the development of Diamond Tap Premium Lager to perfect the brewing process so that the product meets our marketing goals; establishment and beginning implementation of a premarket campaign to recruit wholesale distributors and build a solid base of customers; and acquisition of the necessary expertise at all levels of the company.

It is important to recognize that in terms of product development, Backbay Brewing has already formulated and registered its recipe for Diamond Tap as a *trade secret* with our patent attorney, Robert Pack of Newport Beach, California. We intend to use this recipe to perfect the final brewed version of Diamond Tap Premium Lager.

Outline for Product/Market Development

1. Gather ingredients
  1.1 Choose type of barley malt
      1.1.1 Select suppliers of barley malt
      1.1.2 Test barley malt to determine which suppliers provide the best flavor, body, head, and color
  1.2 Choose type of hops
      1.2.1 Select suppliers of hops
      1.2.2 Test hops to determine which suppliers provide the best flavor
  1.3 Choose suppliers of dried lager yeast
      1.3.1 Test lager yeasts to determine which suppliers have the best fermentation agent
  1.4 Test Diamond Tap recipe with final selections for malt, hops, and yeast
2. Brewing process
  2.1 Determine optimum malting process
  2.2 Gauge mashing temperature
  2.3 Boil wort and add hops
  2.4 Determine yeast amounts and fermentation period
  2.5 Determine aging period
  2.6 Carbonate the beer
  2.7 Conduct taste tests
3. Container development
  3.1 Select bottle and keg style
  3.2 Select bottle color
  3.3 Test appeal of bottle with beer integrated
  3.4 Deliver bottles and kegs
4. Label and package development
  4.1 Create label and package design, which will require recruiting free-lance graphic designer
  4.2 Integrate label with container
  4.3 Develop prototype for six-pack product and 22-oz. bottle
5. Test market prototypes
  5.1 Enter into relationship with regional distributor of Southern California market
  5.2 Deliver prototype units

5.3 Gauge reactions

5.4 Make modifications as a result of test marketing

6. Production

6.1 Make preproduction run

6.2 Conduct cost-reduction check to achieve goal of $155 in costs per barrel

6.3 Begin brewing

7. Final delivery

7.1 Develop distribution, which will include the recruiting of a sales manager and account representatives to obtain purchase orders from targeted state distributors that service liquor stores, bars, convenience food stores, and supermarkets in the market areas defined in distribution strategies

7.2 Deliver initial orders for distributors and retailers

7.3 Implement sales promotion campaign, which is budgeted at $210,000 during the first year of operation and is geared toward supporting wholesale distributors and raising consumer awareness at the retail level

Figure 9.8 illustrates the development program throughout the first year. The major benchmarks include:

- Selections of ingredients and suppliers for Diamond Tap Premium Lager.
- Perfection of brewing process.
- Label and package design.
- Test marketing to Southern California market.
- Retail and distributor price points of $3.85 and $6.99 for a six-pack, $1.20 and $2.20 for a 22-ounce bottle, and $105 and $195 for a 15-gallon keg.
- Establishment of relationships with Southern California and Central Valley distributors and obtaining of purchase orders.
- Initiation of a merchandising allowance program among liquor stores, bars, convenience food stores, and supermarkets.

Organizational Development

To properly develop Diamond Tap Premium Lager, it will be necessary to recruit a sales manager. This position will provide Backbay Brewing with the expertise to establish the distribution channels and promotional campaign necessary for Diamond Tap's success.

With the addition of this key position, company management will consist of the following:

- **Chief Executive Officer—Will Gillette.** Responsible for company operations as well as market development. An accomplished businessperson with 15 years' experience in the malt brewing industry, Mr. Gillette has extensive contacts at all phases of product development as well as marketing.
- **President—John Melrose.** Reporting directly to the CEO, responsibilities include brewery operations, quality control, and package design.

Figure 9.8 Development Schedule

DEVELOPMENT SCHEDULE FOR BACKBAY BREWING COMPANY—1994-1995

Task	May	June	July	August	September	October	November	December	January	February	March	April
1.1	■											
1.1.1	■											
1.1.2	■											
1.2	■											
1.2.1	■											
1.2.2	■											
1.3	■											
1.3.1	■											
1.4		■										
2.1		■										
2.2		■										
2.3		■										
2.4			■									
2.5				■								
2.6					■							
2.7					■							
3.1				■								
3.2				■								
3.3					■							
3.4					■							
4.1					■							
4.2					■							
4.3												
5.1						■						
5.2						■						
5.3						■						
5.4												
6.1							■					
6.2							■					
6.3							■					
7.1								■				
7.2									■			
7.3									■			

Mr. Melrose has 10 years' experience managing brewing operations and developing product.

- **Vice President of Operations—William Barney.** Reporting directly to the President, responsibilities include the management of all purchasing and inventory control operations. Mr. Barney has a tremendous amount of contacts among raw material suppliers as well as knowledge of modern inventory control systems.

- **Sales Manager.** A position that will be responsible for establishment of wholesale distribution accounts, product presentation, and customer service. Will work in conjunction with the CEO to develop a statewide distribution network. This executive will need a successful track record in alcoholic beverage sales.

Risks

The development of Diamond Tap Premium Lager has several associated risks:

- **Creating an efficient network of statewide distributors.** Backbay Brewing Company must quickly build relationships with key distributors throughout the state to sufficiently penetrate the markets it has defined. We will begin with the recruitment of a Southern California distributor, then provide for a phased introduction of distributors over the first year of the product's introduction, making this risk minimal and controllable.

- **Obtaining sufficient shelf space and promotion at the retail end.** This is crucial to deliver the type of sales we have projected. It is the main reason we will implement an aggressive merchandising allowance program with retailers as well as bars, greatly reducing this risk.

- **Product acceptance by consumers.** Product quality will be a major factor in overcoming this risk. That is why Backbay Brewing will launch a coupon program to introduce consumers to the product. We want them to try the product. If they do, we feel we will have high repeat sales. Backbay Brewing will also participate in major taste-testing contests and promote the success we experience at these events. In addition, through advertising and POP displays, we will create visibility at the retail level to provide consumers with an incentive to try the product. Through these programs, we feel the risk associated with product acceptance will be very small.

- **Product delays.** Backbay Brewing has already developed what we feel is an award-winning recipe for Diamond Tap Premium Lager. We also have the expertise in place to perfect the brewing process, making this risk acceptable.

- **Increased competition from major competitors.** There is little doubt that large breweries are beginning to create premium beers to compete against microbrewed products; however, their attempts, while good in terms of mass-produced products, do not have the same richness of flavor or freshness. They cannot compete against a good microbrewed product in quality.

Table 9.2   Development Expenses

ITEM	BUDGETED AMOUNT
Materials	$ 129,000
Direct labor	21,840
Overhead	376,790
G&A	14,560
Equipment	485,000
Miscellaneous	2,000
Total	$1,029,190

Financials

Table 9.2 depicts the major development expenses.

OPERATIONS AND MANAGEMENT

Backbay Brewing Company will be organized as a microbrewery of high-quality beers, starting with Diamond Tap Premium Lager beer. The headquarters for Backbay Brewing will be located in Newport Beach, California, a coastal community located in Orange County, just 50 miles south of Los Angeles and 80 miles north of San Diego. Backbay Brewing has already concluded a lease agreement for a 15,000-square-foot facility in Newport Beach.

In the following section, the business operations and management requirements of Backbay Brewing Company will be detailed along with projections for operational expenses, capital requirements, and cost of goods.

Operations

Following is the organizational structure for Backbay Brewing Company.

Marketing

Managed by the CEO, Will Gillette, this department's scope of responsibilities will revolve around sales promotional support at the wholesale and retail level. The marketing department will define the markets, outline the prospective customers within those markets, plan the various sales and promotional campaigns, measure response, and analyze the market to produce competitive strategies that will generate sales leads, and coordinate with brewery operations to meet the needs of the customer base.

Sales

As a microbrewer, Backbay Brewing Company will have sales at three different stages: brewer to distributor; distributor to retailer; and retailer to consumer. At the brewer-to-distributor level, a sales manager will be hired during the development phase to set up initial distributors for the Southern California and

Central Valley areas. During the year, we will add one other account representative. This sales force will be responsible for all statewide sales to wholesale distributors in the following four key areas: Southern California, Central Valley, Central California, and Northern California.

In addition to initiating sales, the two salespeople will also be responsible for handling problems originating at the brewer-to-distributor level. This includes making sure distributors receive their shipments and that the billing and payment schedules are consistent with the agreements signed between both parties. They will also handle returns and other issues arising at the retail level.

As sales grow, it is expected that an assistant will be needed to help with customer service.

Brewery Operations

Handled directly by the President, John Melrose, the function of brewery operations is to coordinate the actual brewing of Diamond Tap Premium Lager. The brewing process for Diamond Tap Premium Lager is as follows:

1. Purchasing of ingredients and inventory control.
2. Malting of the barley.
3. Mashing of the malted barley to produce the wort.
4. Boiling of the wort and addition of hops.
5. Addition of yeast to promote fermentation of the wort.
6. Removal of carbon dioxide.
7. Sterilization of the wort.
8. Addition of yeast to promote the second round of fermentation.
9. Carbonation of the beer using previously removed carbon dioxide for natural carbonation (krausened).
10. Filtration of the wort.
11. Aging of the beer.
12. Chilling of the beer and filtration to remove any remaining yeast.
13. Packaging of the beer for shipping.

At each step of the brewing process, the staff will be required to perform exact checks of measurements of ingredients, temperatures of the kilns, brew kettles, bright beer tanks, and the levels in storage barrels, fermenter tanks, and so on. The goal behind these measurements and checks is to ensure the quality of the finished beer product. Each batch of beer, once it reaches the bright brewing tanks and prior to packaging, will be taste tested to ensure the highest quality of beer. See Figure 9.9 for a depiction of our beer-brewing process.

The costs associated with the brewery operations of Backbay Brewing are detailed in Table 9.3. The cost-of-goods breakout is based on two elements: ingredients and labor. During the brewing process, the product may be in any one of four stages:

1. Ingredients (I).
2. Partially brewed (PB).

Figure 9.9   Diamond Tap Beer Brewing Process

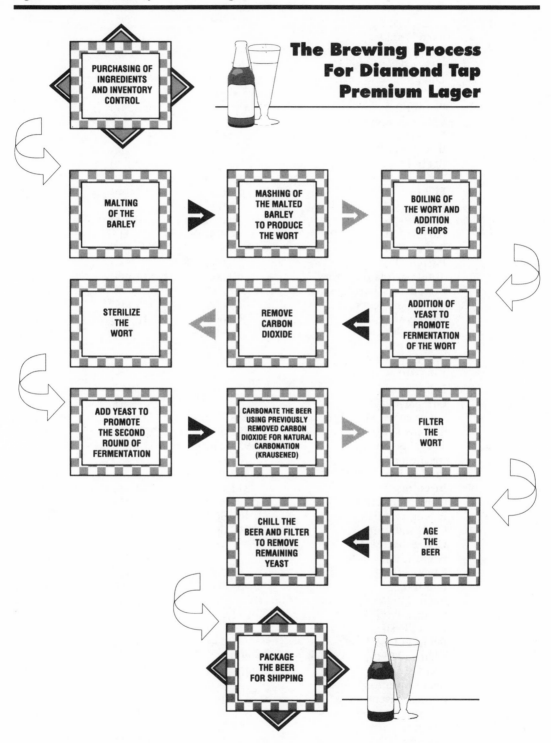

Table 9.3   Cost of Goods—Barrels

	1995	1996	1997
Barrels sold	10,000	10,700	11,984
Begin FB	0	4,500	4,815
FB% sales (barrels)	45	45	45
End FB	4,500	4,815	5,393
Inventory/FB	4,500	315	578
Begin PB	0	3,500	3,745
PB% sales (barrels)	35	35	35
End PB	3,500	3,745	4,194
Inventory/PB	3,500	245	449
Begin I	0	2,000	2,140
1% sales (barrels)	20	20	20
End I	2,000	2,140	2,397
Inventory/I	2,000	140	257
Barrels sold	10,000	10,700	11,984
Barrels FBI	4,500	315	578
Barrels PBI	3,500	245	449
Barrels II	2,000	140	257
Total barrels inventory	20,000	11,400	13,268
Ingredients/barrel ($)	32	32	32
Ingredient costs ($)	640,000	364,800	424,576
Barrels sold	10,000	10,700	11,984
Barrels FBI	4,500	315	578
Barrels PBI	3,500	245	449
Total L&OH barrels	18,000	11,260	13,011
Labor/PA% (barrels)	50	50	50
Labor/barrel ($)	39	39	39
OH/barrel ($)	18	18	18
Labor costs ($)	633,750	434,363	498,674
OH costs ($)	292,500	200,475	230,157
Total L&OH ($)	926,250	634,838	728,831
Inventory/I ($)	64,000	4,480	8,224
Production costs ($)	1,502,250	995,158	1,145,183
Inventory/PB ($)	211,750	14,823	27,165
COG production ($)	1,290,500	980,334	1,118,018
Inventory/FB ($)	400,500	28,035	51,442
COG sold ($)	890,000	952,299	1,066,576
COGS/barrel ($)	89	89	89
Begin II ($)	0	64,000	68,480
Change II ($)	64,000	4,480	8,224
End II ($)	64,000	68,480	76,704
Begin PBI ($)	0	211,750	226,573
Change PBI ($)	211,750	14,823	27,165
End PBI ($)	211,750	226,573	253,738
Begin FBI ($)	0	400,500	428,535
Change FBI ($)	400,500	28,035	51,442
End FBI ($)	400,500	428,535	479,977
Begin inventory ($)	0	676,250	723,588
Change inventory ($)	676,250	47,338	86,831
End inventory ($)	676,250	723,588	810,419
Revenue/barrel ($)	213.91	213.19	213.14
Revenue ($)	2,139,132	2,281,212	2,554,325
Inventory turn	3.16	3.15	3.15

3. Fully brewed (FB).
4. Sold (S).

Product that is sold is expensed as a cost of good, while product that isn't sold is placed in inventory. To assure the finest quality beer during the production process, Backbay Brewing will utilize state-of-the-art equipment from the initial malting process all the way through finishing and packaging. In addition, as we've mentioned, the President of the company will oversee production and there will be a total of three skilled brewers during the first year to control every aspect of beer production. The investment costs for the brewing equipment are depicted in Table 9.4.

Table 9.4   Capital Summary

	1995	1996	1997
Initial capital	$0	$0	$0
Net capital	$0	$370,476	$358,395
Malting Equipment			
No. barrels	10,000	10,700	11,984
ME/barrel	3,500	3,500	3,500
ME capital	$11,500	$11,500	$11,500
ME capital requirement	$32,857	$35,157	$39,376
New ME capital	$32,857	$2,300	$4,219
Mashing/Brewing Equipment			
No. barrels	10,000	10,700	11,984
MBE/barrels	1,700	1,700	1,700
MBE capital	$15,500	$15,500	$15,500
MBE capital requirement	$91,176	$97,559	$109,266
New MBE capital	$91,176	$6,383	$11,707
Fermentation/Aging Equiment			
No. barrels	10,000	10,700	11,984
FAE/barrel	840	840	840
FAE capital	$10,500	$10,500	$10,500
FAE capital requirement	$125,000	$133,750	$149,800
New FAE capital	$125,000	$8,750	$16,050
Finishing Equipment			
No. barrels	10,000	10,700	11,984
FE/barrel	3,500	3,500	3,500
FE capital	$22,000	$22,000	$22,000
FE capital requirement	$62,857	$67,257	$75,328
New FE capital	$62,857	$4,400	$8,071
Packaging Equipment			
No. barrels	10,000	10,700	11,984
PE/barrel	7,500	7,500	7,500
PE capital	$75,000	$75,000	$75,000
PE capital requirement	$99,750	$107,000	$119,840
New PE capital	$99,750	$7,250	$12,840
Total new capital	$411,640	$29,083	$52,887
Total capital	$411,640	$399,559	$408,374
Depreciation	$41,164	$44,072	$49,361

Administration

Administration is in charge of those overhead functions that support operations such as accounting, legal, human resources, and other functions related directly to internal operations.

The expenses for Backbay Brewing Company are illustrated in Table 9.5. They are divided according to the functional lines detailed earlier.

Management

As mentioned in the "Design and Development" phase of the business plan, four key management positions will be strategic to the growth of the Backbay Brewing Company. Those key positions and the accompanying responsibilities are described in the following sections.

Chief Executive Officer

This position will be held by William Gillette. Mr. Gillette has been active in the brewing industry for the past 15 years, serving as a marketing director for a brewer of mass-produced beer. In the capacity of CEO for Backbay Brewing Company, Mr. Gillette will handle the marketing of Diamond Tap Premium Lager. His duties will include the compilation of market information as well as the formation of market strategies and materials. Mr. Gillette will also head Backbay Brewing's new product research and development. In addition, Mr. Gillette will provide direction in conjunction with Backbay Brewing's President and Vice President of Operations concerning the management and overall operations of the business.

President

This position will be held by John Melrose. Mr. Melrose has over 10 years' experience managing brewery operations for a brewer of mass-produced beer. As the President of Backbay Brewing, Mr. Melrose will be responsible for all brewery operations. This includes not only the actual brewing process but also purchasing and inventory control as well as packaging and delivery to wholesale

Table 9.5 Operating Expenses

	1995	1996	1997
Marketing expenses	$ 85,000	$ 90,950	$101,864
Sales expenses	80,000	85,600	95,872
Brewery operations expenses	70,000	74,900	83,888
Administrative expenses	35,000	37,450	41,944
Overhead	410,224	438,940	491,613
Total expenses	$680,224	$727,840	$815,181

distributors. In addition, Mr. Melrose will provide direction in conjunction with Backbay Brewing's CEO and Vice President of Operations concerning the management and overall operations of the business.

Vice President of Operations

This position will be held by William Barney. Mr. Barney has developed many contacts among suppliers of ingredients for the malt brewing industry as a purchasing director for a brewer of mass-produced beer. As the Vice President of Operations, Mr. Barney will handle all the purchasing and inventory control functions of Backbay Brewing. He will report directly to the President in coordinating brewing operations with those of purchasing. In addition, Mr. Barney will provide direction in conjunction with Backbay Brewing's CEO and President concerning the management and overall operations of the business.

Sales Manager

The responsibilities of this position will include the management of all inside sales operations. This will include recruiting reputable wholesale distributors and maintaining those relations by acting as the liaison between Backbay Brewing and its network of wholesale distributors. This will involve taking orders, making sure they are fulfilled according to the terms set forth in the distributor agreements, providing support for the distributors so they have appropriate marketing materials, and handling any problems that may occur at the wholesale level or that are passed along through the distribution channel from the retail level.

FINANCIAL COMPONENTS

The following section outlines the financial specifications for this business venture.

Income Statement

As detailed in Table 9.6, the net profit of Backbay Brewing Company is a healthy 27 percent during the first year of operation, indicating a strong product concept in a highly competitive market. With continued growth in the acquisition of market share, the net profit will continue to increase, thereby supporting the expansion plans of the company during the second and third years.

Cash Flow Statement

Table 9.7 shows the cash flow for the first three years of operation for Backbay Brewing Company. As detailed, the cumulative cash flow after the first year shows a positive that will be used in the second year for reinvestment into

Table 9.6   Income Statement

	JANUARY	FEBRUARY	MARCH	APRIL	MAY	JUNE	JULY	AUGUST
Income	42,783	64,174	85,565	128,348	149,739	171,131	181,826	203,218
Cost of goods	17,800	26,700	35,600	53,400	62,300	71,200	75,650	84,550
Gross profit	24,983	37,474	49,965	74,948	87,439	99,931	106,176	118,668
Margin %	58%	58%	58%	58%	58%	58%	58%	58%
Expenses	34,011	40,813	47,616	47,616	49,656	52,377	55,778	63,261
Net profit	−9,029	−3,339	2,350	27,332	37,783	47,553	50,398	55,407
Margin %	−21%	−5%	3%	21%	25%	28%	28%	27%
Depreciation	3,430	3,430	3,430	3,430	3,430	3,430	3,430	3,430
Net profit before interest	−12,459	−6,770	−1,081	23,902	34,353	44,123	46,968	51,976
Margin %	−29%	−11%	−1%	19%	23%	26%	26%	26%
Interest	13,350	13,200	13,050	12,900	12,750	12,600	12,450	12,300
Net profit before taxes	−25,809	−19,970	−14,131	11,002	21,603	31,523	34,518	39,676

Table 9.7   Cash Flow Statement

	JANUARY	FEBRUARY	MARCH	APRIL	MAY	JUNE	JULY	AUGUST
Cash sales	17,113	25,670	34,226	51,339	59,896	68,452	72,730	81,287
Receivables	0	0	25,670	38,504	51,339	77,009	89,844	102,678
Other income	0	0	0	0	0	0	0	0
Total income	17,113	25,670	59,896	89,843	111,235	145,461	162,574	183,965
Material	0	0	0	0	0	0	0	0
Direct labor	7,800	11,700	15,600	23,400	27,300	31,200	33,150	37,050
Overhead	0	0	0	0	0	0	0	0
Marketing and sales	8,250	9,900	11,550	11,550	12,045	12,705	13,530	15,345
Brewery operations/R&D	3,500	4,200	4,900	4,900	5,110	5,390	5,740	6,510
General and administrative	1,750	2,100	2,450	2,450	2,555	2,695	2,870	3,255
Taxes	0	0	40,528	0	0	40,528	0	0
Capital	3,430	3,430	3,430	3,430	3,430	3,430	3,430	3,430
Loans	25,000	25,000	25,000	25,000	25,000	25,001	25,000	25,000
Total expenses	49,730	56,330	103,458	70,730	75,440	120,950	83,720	90,590
Cash flow	−32,617	−30,660	−43,562	19,113	35,795	24,511	78,854	93,375
Cumulative cash flow	−32,617	−63,277	−106,840	−87,727	−51,932	−27,421	51,433	144,808

Table 9.6   (continued)

SEPTEMBER	OCTOBER	NOVEMBER	DECEMBER	1995	1ST QTR	2ND QTR	3RD QTR	4TH QTR	1996	1997
213,913	246,000	310,174	342,261	2,139,132	410,618	501,867	638,739	729,988	2,281,212	2,554,325
89,000	102,350	129,050	142,400	890,000	171,414	209,506	266,644	304,736	952,299	1,066,576
124,913	143,650	181,124	199,861	1,249,132	239,204	292,361	372,096	425,252	1,328,913	1,487,749
58%	58%	58%	58%	58%	58%	58%	58%	58%	58%	58%
71,424	71,424	72,104	74,144	680,224	160,125	167,403	196,517	203,795	727,840	815,181
53,490	72,227	109,020	125,717	568,908	79,080	124,958	175,579	221,457	601,073	672,568
25%	29%	35%	37%	27%	19%	25%	27%	30%	26%	26%
3,430	3,430	3,430	3,430	41,164	11,018	11,018	11,018	11,018	44,072	49,361
50,059	68,796	105,590	122,286	527,744	68,062	113,940	164,561	210,439	557,001	623,207
23%	28%	34%	36%	25%	17%	23%	26%	29%	24%	24%
12,150	12,000	11,850	11,400	150,000	36,135	34,903	33,671	32,166	136,875	127,716
37,909	56,796	93,740	110,886	377,744	31,927	79,037	130,890	178,273	420,126	495,491

Table 9.7   (continued)

SEPTEMBER	OCTOBER	NOVEMBER	DECEMBER	1995	1ST QTR	2ND QTR	3RD QTR	4TH QTR	1996	1997
85,565	98,400	124,070	136,904	855,652	164,247	200,747	255,496	291,995	912,485	1,021,730
109,096	121,931	128,348	147,600	892,019	458,720	261,317	323,540	398,190	1,441,767	1,552,160
0	0	0	0		0	0	0	0	0	0
194,661	220,331	252,418	284,504	1,747,671	622,967	462,064	579,036	690,185	2,354,252	2,573,890
0	0	0	0	0	0	0	0	0	0	0
39,000	44,850	56,550	62,400	390,000	91,806	95,979	112,671	116,844	417,300	467,376
0	0	0	0	0	0	0	0	0	0	0
17,325	17,325	17,490	17,985	165,000	38,841	40,607	47,669	49,434	176,550	197,736
7,350	7,350	7,420	7,630	70,000	16,478	17,227	20,223	20,972	74,900	83,888
3,675	3,675	3,710	3,815	35,000	8,239	8,614	10,112	10,486	37,450	41,944
40,528	0	0	40,528	162,113	41,538	41,538	41,538	41,538	166,150	186,451
3,430	3,430	3,430	3,430	41,164	11,018	11,018	11,018	11,018	44,072	49,361
25,000	25,000	25,000	25,000	300,000	75,000	75,000	75,000	75,000	300,000	300,000
136,308	101,630	113,600	160,789	1,163,277	282,920	289,982	318,230	325,292	1,216,422	1,326,756
58,353	118,701	138,818	123,715	584,394	340,048	172,083	260,807	364,894	1,137,830	1,247,134
203,160	321,861	460,679	584,394	584,394	924,442	1,096,524	1,357,331	1,722,224	1,722,224	2,969,358

capital equipment and expansion of brewery operations. It also indicates a very attractive break-even point and ROI that will allow us to attract additional investment for expansion.

Balance Sheet

The balance sheet in Table 9.8 assumes that all cash generated by the business is reinvested back into the company. Since the accounts receivable and payable are kept short and are controlled, they will not lead to large working capital requirements.

Table 9.8   Balance Sheet

	1995	1996	1997
Assets			
Current assets			
Cash	855,653	912,485	1,021,730
Accounts receivable	892,018	1,441,768	1,552,160
Inventory	676,250	723,588	810,419
Total current assets	2,423,921	3,077,840	3,384,309
Fixed assets			
Capital/plant	370,476	399,559	408,374
Investment	41,164	44,072	49,361
Miscellaneous assets	0	0	0
Total fixed assets	411,640	443,631	457,735
Total assets	2,835,561	3,521,471	3,842,044
Liabilities			
Current liabilities			
Accounts payable	717,303	1,034,785	1,075,601
Accrued liabilities	660,000	706,200	790,944
Taxes	162,113	166,150	186,451
Total current liabilities	1,539,416	1,907,135	2,052,996
Long-term liabilities			
Bonds payable	0	0	0
Notes payable	300,000	300,000	300,000
Total long-term liabilities	300,000	300,000	300,000
Total liabilities			
Owner's equity	996,145	1,314,337	1,489,047
Total liability/equity	2,835,561	3,521,471	3,842,044

10

Buying a Business

hile building a business from scratch is probably the quintessential mark of the true entrepreneur, it can be a very risky venture. In fact, starting a business from scratch is the most difficult way to get into business. One alternative to starting a business from scratch is to *buy* one. Buying a business certainly can save time and avoid many of the errors that you might make in developing your own business from the ground up. Everything is in place from customers to a credit line at the bank. Buying an existing business has many advantages, and as you will see later, it also has a number of pitfalls. The *advantages* include:

- You don't have to wait to build up the business to enjoy success. Since the business already has a proven track record, you should experience immediate profit if the business has been successful, creating a quick return on your investment and reducing the chance of failure.
- You are buying a proven concept with an established customer/client foundation, supplier base, and trained employees.
- Investment requirements will be mainly for the purchase of the business since most of the equipment and fixtures will already be present.
- Financing is easier because an existing business has established credit, and growth can be financed through traditional sources like banks. Financing is always available to help someone buy a profitable business.
- You will have the experience of the previous owner to fall back on for consultation as well as existing records to help you formulate a strategic business plan.
- Buying a business is almost like buying a franchise, without paying a franchise fee or royalty.

Disadvantages of buying include:

- The business could suffer from a poor image due to equipment obsolescence, poor marketing material, a poor location, or inadequate customer relations, requiring a greater investment from both a time and cash standpoint.

- You may experience culture clash as current employees resist changes you institute in the operation.
- Any loans incurred from the purchase of the business as well as insufficient financial control and credit management policies of the previous owner may place pressure on cash flow and profitability.
- The appraised value of the business may be too high due to misrepresentation and result in an inordinately high purchase price.
- You may be unaware of new competition entering the marketplace.

When buying an existing business, be sure that all the elements of a potentially successful operation are present. All businesses go through cycles. All services and products have cycles of demand. Business locations even have cycles. (Sometimes there are indications of a location's failure, but many times there are not.)

In some businesses, the new owner will have to compete with the reputation already established by the old owner. Frequently you'll see signs on buildings reading, "Under New Management." These announcements bring in customers who might have been dissatisfied with the previous management, but will give the business another chance. Indeed, it sometimes pays to change the name of the business for that particular reason. In cases where previous management was strong and had a good rapport with the public, however, it's not a good idea to change the name or put up an "Under New Management" sign. This invites comparisons with the previous owner that may be unfavorable to you. You have to analyze whether the business's reputation is valuable or detrimental.

As the new owner of a business, you could be saddled with the result of bad buying habits by the previous owner. For example, the previous owner might have overstocked a certain inventory that can't be moved, or the company could have been overloaded with long-term debts that would make it difficult for the business to produce a sufficient profit. In addition to your research before buying a business, make sure your suppliers don't saddle you with inventory or services just because that's the way the previous management worked.

Another point you should keep in mind is that many businesses for sale have a problem. It will be up to you to discover the real problem, whether it is financial or personal. Whatever the problem is, you will most likely have to be a better business operator than the present owner. By using the suggested evaluation procedures in this chapter, you can learn exactly why the business is being sold before you make your first offer.

HOW TO INVESTIGATE BEFORE BUYING

The scope of your investigation will be in direct proportion to the size and scope of an existing business, but every investigation should be thorough.

Business Failures

One of the primary reasons for selling a business is that it has failed or is about to fail. The symptoms of failure are important to recognize so you can isolate the problems and either overcome them if you buy the business, or refrain from buying it at all.

Some businesses try to expand without proper capitalization or credit, and in doing so, they ruin their credit. Suddenly they're on a COD or cash-only basis and have limited cash flow. The business might be very productive and profitable if it could be expanded to the next level, where it would operate economically and with sufficient cash flow. Business sellers who are undercapitalized usually aren't going to admit it to you, so be wary. However, there is always the chance you could get a good buy if the seller is up front with you.

A healthy business operating at the proper economic level shouldn't have any financial problems if it was properly capitalized to begin with. Usually you can determine whether overexpansion has happened by looking at the aging of payables and observing whether the company has been slow to pay its bills or has any suits, judgments, or liens against it.

To determine the aging of payables, look at the invoice dates and see when the bills are paid. If typically, bills in the industry are paid in 30 to 60 days, and these invoices were paid in 90 days, you have an indication that the seller was short of capital.

Another way you can gauge cash flow and determine whether the business is properly capitalized is to look at its bank statements. You can also run a credit check on the company through the local credit bureau; if you are not a member of the credit bureau in your area you may be able to have your lawyer or your banker do this for you. Sometimes businesses have poor collection procedures with their receivables, which creates a cash flow problem. Or they can be careless about the way they grant credit.

A bad cash flow alone need not deter you from buying a business. Many financial problems can be remedied through the implementation of proper credit procedures and strong financial controls.

Next to undercapitalization, poor management is the most common reason businesses fail. A business may have everything going for it, but the owners don't know how to, or are reluctant to delegate.

People often go into business with optimistic, even grandiose, ideas of what they're going to do and what kind of money they're going to make, but they are not very realistic. While optimism is useful for a business owner, reality is also important. Unless businesses expand to include a sufficient number of employees to take care of the business, they may show low profits, requiring a lot of time and hours on the part of the owner. Their businesses may fail because they do not know how to manage their workload.

Many people are big spenders and can't control their overhead. They may have elaborate offices, big cars, and take big vacations, spending money lavishly just because they own their own businesses and have complete control over the finances. It is quite true that business owners can deduct and be reimbursed for many business-related expenses. But they have to exercise some judgment when incurring expenses. The business may be losing money because the owner is milking it. This is important to analyze when you are examining the operating data.

While thoroughness pays off, you will frequently feel pressured for a variety of reasons:

- Another buyer in the wings (real or otherwise).
- Rising interest rates.
- A lack of time.
- Anxiety to get started.
- "It just looks so good."

Where to Look for a Business

Once you've decided on a business you can be comfortable with, it's time to start looking for an existing operation that is for sale. Where do you find these businesses? There are many sources to tap in your search for the right business.

First, check the classified sections in newspapers and trade magazines. The Sunday editions of newspapers usually have numerous listings in the classified section, especially in large metropolitan newspapers like the New York Times. The Wall Street Journal *also lists businesses for sale under "Business Opportunities." In addition, trade magazines usually have classified sections in the back pages offering businesses for sale.*

Realtors are also another good source. Many brokers not only deal in residential and commercial properties, but also offer a number of other services. One of them is selling businesses.

You may want to inform people you see frequently (friends, neighbors, business associates) that you're in the market for a business. This could lead you to a company with an immediate reference that can be advantageous in your initial dealings with the seller.

Business brokers will be one of your best routes for finding an existing company. They deal in nothing but brokering of businesses that are for sale. You should be careful when dealing with brokers, however, because some will list businesses on an exclusive basis only; thereby limiting your exposure to other firms that may be for sale in your area.

The local chamber of commerce can also be an invaluable resource. Many maintain files of businesses for sale within the area as well as interested buyers. Most chambers of commerce will not only be able to bring together a buyer and a seller, but will also supply information about business conditions within the area.

Additional avenues to find existing businesses for sale might require more research on your part but could end up paying off with the right business for you. These sources include suppliers, distributors, manufacturers, and trade associations that deal in the type of business you're interested in starting. They may be able to tell you whether such a business is for sale in your area.

Also, check with attorneys, accountants, and bankers that deal with small businesses. They usually know what is happening in the business community or can guide you in the right direction. Bankers can be extremely helpful. They usually maintain files on companies that are indebted to them or are up for sale.

As a last resort, you might question business owners within the area. You'll find that most people with small businesses are very helpful toward one another. They also are knowledgeable about business conditions within their market areas and can tell you whether or not a business is for sale. You might even get lucky and run into an owner who is getting ready to sell a business.

While many people do not take adequate time to investigate, there are others who never get started because they never finish investigating. You are the only person who can decide whether or not you've investigated the business thoroughly enough. Just remember, this is a decision you may be living with for many years to come.

Buying a business—like the purchase of a home—is a highly emotional transaction. For you to make the best decision and achieve the most favorable terms, you must be aware of your emotional state at all times. Always ask yourself, "Am I making this decision based on emotion, data, or a combination?" Neither raw data or raw emotion should be the sole basis for your decision. As you will see later in this chapter, we will provide a number of checklists for you to review before finalizing any deal. Your emotions will come in handy when you ask yourself if this is a business you feel some passion for, either because of what it may mean to you and your family, or because of what being in that business means to you personally.

Preliminary Evaluation

Before making a major investigation, do some preliminary work to evaluate the business. This will help you decide if you want to pursue this further. Use the sample Business Evaluation Checklist in this chapter to perform your own evaluations of prospective businesses. Make a separate copy of the form for each business you evaluate.

To conduct your preliminary investigation, make an outline of items to research that will be readily apparent without having to involve the seller. These items include:

- **Location.** How important is location to this particular business? Is the location ideal? Is the area undergoing any major changes such as high-rise office buildings, shopping centers, apartment complexes? Are there any other changes in the neighborhood that could eventually alter the location's present status either positively or negatively? How dependent is the company on walk-in business?
- **Management.** Does the owner or management have good relationships with the customers and employees? How will a change in ownership affect the clientele and employees?
- **Goodwill.** Has the management supported local or industry events either through membership or participation? If so, to what extent? What is the procedure for handling customer complaints? Check the written and stated policies. How long has the business been in that location?
- **Environment.** How well is the physical location maintained? Is it clean and well organized?
- **First impressions.** What is your first reaction to the business, including the preceding points? Compare your feelings about the business now and later after completing the other checklists.

✔

BUSINESS EVALUATION CHECKLIST

If you find a business that you would like to buy, you will need to consider a number of points before you decide whether to purchase it. Take a good, close look at the business and answer the following questions. They will help you determine whether it is a sound investment.

☐ Why does the current owner want to sell the business?

☐ Does the business have a high potential for future growth, or will its sales decline?

☐ If the business is in decline, will you be able to save it and make it successful?

☐ Is the business in sound financial condition? Have you seen audited year-end financial satements for the business? Have you reviewed the most recent statements? Have you reviewed the business's tax returns for the past five years?

☐ Have you seen copies of all of the business's current contracts?

☐ Is the business now, or has it ever been, under investigation by any governmental agency? If so, what is the status of any current investigation? What were the results of any past investigation?

☐ Is the business currently involved in a lawsuit, or has it ever been involved in one? If so, what is the status or result?

☐ Does the business have any debts or liens against it? If so, what are they for, and in what amounts?

☐ What percentage of the business's accounts are past due? How much does the business write off each year for bad debts?

☐ How many customers does the business serve on a regular basis?

☐ Who makes up the market for this business? Where are your customers located? (Do they all come from your community or from across the state, or are they spread across the globe?)

☐ Does the business vary with the seasons?

☐ Does any single customer account for a large portion of the sales volume? If so, would the business be able to survive without this customer? (The larger your customer base is, the more easily you will be able to survive the loss of any customers. If, on the other hand, you exist mainly to serve a single client, the loss of that client could finish your business.)

☐ How does the business market its products or services? Does its competition use the same methods? If not, what methods does the competition use? How successful are they?

☐ Does the business have exclusive rights to market any particular products or services? If so, how has it obtained this exclusivity? Is it making the best possible use of this exclusivity? Do you have written proof that the current business owner can transfer this exclusivity to you?

BUSINESS EVALUATON CHECKLIST *(Continued)*

☐ Does the business hold patents for any of its products? Which ones? What percentage of gross sales do they represent? Would the sale of the business include the sale of any patents?

☐ Are the business's supplies, merchandise, and other materials available from several suppliers, or are there only a handful who can meet your needs? If you lost the business's current supplier, what impact would that loss have on your business? Would you be able to find substitute goods of the appropriate quality and price?

☐ Are any of the business's products in danger of becoming obsolete or of going out of style? Is this a "fad" business?

☐ What is the business's market share?

☐ What competition does the business face? How can the business compete successfully? Have the business's competitors changed recently? Have any of them gone out of business, for instance?

☐ Does the business have all of the equipment you think is necessary? Will you need to add or update any equipment?

☐ What is the business's current inventory worth? Will you be able to use any of this inventory, or is it inconsistent with your intended product line?

☐ How many employees does the business have? What positions do they hold?

☐ Does the business pay its employees high wages, or are the wages average or low?

☐ Does the business experience high employee turnover? If so, why?

☐ What benefits does the business offer its employees?

☐ How long have the company's top managers been with the company?

☐ Will the change of ownership cause any changes in personnel?

☐ What employees are the most important to the company?

☐ Do any of the business's employees belong to any unions? If so, have they ever held any strikes? How long did the strikes last?

Establish a Relationship with the Seller

If after your preliminary investigation you decide to pursue the purchase of a business, begin to establish a positive relationship with the owner and if possible, with anyone else in management. Too often, people feel they must create an adversarial relationship in a negotiation. The atmosphere may be adversarial, but the relationships needn't be; you will gain a great deal, both before and after the sale, if you maintain a pleasant attitude.

Make arrangements to meet the seller at a neutral location—a restaurant is a good location. Give a sincere compliment to the seller on what he or she has done with the business. Then ask questions that will help you get to know the person without causing offense. Don't begin asking about the business right away; ease into it. The seller won't just fork over the business because you're on friendly terms, but you may be able to reason more effectively and negotiate more successfully if you know the person better.

You may want to start out by providing the seller with a résumé of your background and qualifications to indicate whether you can operate that particular kind of business. Also, include a financial statement, so the seller can verify your ability to deal in good faith. A CPA can prepare an audited financial statement, or you can have an unaudited one prepared by a bank. The key is to provide the seller with some references. And, now that you have presented all the information about yourself, you can then ask the seller all about the business for sale.

Here are some suggested questions to ask the seller, possibly at the first meeting but not later than the second meeting. Remember, be casual (feel free to take notes but try not to refer to them when asking the questions) while trying to obtain the following information:

- What do you like best about this business?
- Would you be available for consultation for a period of time?
- How quickly do you want to sell?
- How did you get started in this business?
- If you were the new owner, knowing what you know about this business, where would you spend additional capital?
- Do the employees know the business is being sold? How do they feel about it? (Ask permission to chat with any upper or midlevel management, just to get the feel of the business.)

In-Depth Evaluation

After you have met with the seller and you are satisfied with the answers to your questions, you should take the next step in the evaluation process—conducting an in-depth investigation. Some small business sellers may complain about providing the data you are requesting, if only because they may not have analyzed their business very closely. Your response should be that without that kind of information you cannot consider buying the business. If the business is being sold through a broker or you enlist the services of one, a good broker will usually stress the importance of providing financial data to ensure the deal goes through.

You will probably have to assure the owner that you will not contact anyone without prior approval, including suppliers or employees, for additional information about the business. But, it makes sense for you to ask to see relevant documentation of the operation of the business up for sale. There are variations in the kinds of information that will be needed, along with industry variations. You may have to vary your checklist to fit the particular business you are considering. Some major corporations have checklists several pages long. Typically, however, the checklist of required data will be a one- or two-page document.

You should evaluate the following 25 items to verify the value of a business before making a decision to buy.

1. **Inventory.** Refers to all products and materials inventoried for resale or use to service a client. Important note: You or a qualified representative should be present during any inventory proceedings. You should know the status of inventory, what's on hand at present, and what was on hand at the end of the last fiscal year and the one preceding that. You should also have the inventory appraised. After all, this is a hard asset and you need to know what dollar value to associate with it. Also, check the inventory for salability. How old is it? What is its quality? What condition is it in? Keep in mind, you do not have to accept the value of this inventory, it is subject to negotiation. If you feel it is not in line with what you would like to sell, or if it is not compatible with the target market, then by all means bring those points up in negotiation.

2. **Furniture, fixtures, equipment, and building.** This includes all products, office equipment, and assets of the business. Get a list from the seller that includes the name and model number for each piece of equipment. Then determine its present condition, market value when purchased versus present market value, and whether the equipment was purchased or leased. Find out how much the seller has invested in leasehold improvements and maintenance to keep the facility in good condition. Determine what modifications you'll have to make to the building or layout for it to suit your needs.

3. **Copies of all contracts and legal documents.** This would include all lease and purchase agreements, distribution agreements, subcontractor agreements, sales contracts, union contracts, business employee agreements and any other instruments used to legally bind the business. Also, evaluate all other legal documents such as fictitious business name statements, articles of incorporation, registered trademarks, copyrights, and patents. If you're considering a business with valuable intellectual property such as a trade name, patent, or trade secret, have an intellectual property attorney evaluate it. In terms of a real estate lease, you need to find out whether it is transferable, how long it runs, the terms, and whether the landlord's permission is necessary for the assignment of the lease.

4. **Incorporation.** If the company is a corporation, check to see what state it is registered in and whether it is operating as a foreign corporation within its own state.

5. **Tax returns for the past five years.** Many small business owners make use of the business for personal needs. They may buy products they personally use and charge them to the business or take vacations through the company, go to trade shows with their spouses, and so on. You have to use your

analytical skills and those of your accountant to determine the actual financial net worth of the company.

6. **Financial statements for the past five years.** Evaluate these through the past five years to match the tax returns, including all books and financial records. This is especially important for determining the earning power of the business. The sales and operating ratios should be examined with the help of an accountant familiar with the type of business under consideration. The operating ratios should also be compared against industry ratios, which can be found in annual reports produced by Robert Morris & Associates as well as Dun & Bradstreet. We will discuss financial statements later in this chapter.

7. **Sales records.** Although sales will be logged in the financial statements, you should evaluate the monthly sales records as well for the past 36 months or longer. Break sales down by product categories if several products are involved, as well as by cash and credit sales. This is a valuable indicator of current business activity and provides you with some understanding of cycles that the business may go through. Compare the industry norms of seasonal patterns with what you see in the business. Also, obtain the sales figures of the 10 largest accounts for the past 12 months. If the seller doesn't want to release his or her largest accounts by name, it will be perfectly acceptable to do them by code. Again, you are only interested in the pattern of sales.

8. **Complete list of liabilities.** Consult an independent attorney and accountant to examine the list of liabilities to determine the potential costs involved and legal ramifications. These may be items like lawsuits, liens by creditors against assets, or the use of assets such as capital equipment or account receivables as collateral to secure short-term loans. Your accountant should also be on the lookout for unrecorded liabilities such as employee benefit claims, and out-of-court settlements being paid off.

9. **All accounts receivable.** Break these down by 30, 60, 90 days and beyond. Checking the age of receivables is important because the longer the period they are outstanding, the lower the value of the account. You should also make a list of the top 10 accounts and check their creditworthiness. If the clientele is creditworthy and the majority of the accounts are outstanding beyond 60 days, a stricter credit collections policy may speed up the collection of receivables.

10. **All accounts payable.** Like accounts receivable, accounts payable should be broken down by 30, 60, and 90 days. This is important in determining how well cash flows through the company; also on payables beyond 90 days, you should check to see if any creditors have placed a lien on the company's assets.

11. **Debt disclosure.** This includes all outstanding notes, loans, and any other debt to which the business has agreed. See, too, whether there are any business investments in the books that may have taken place outside of the normal area. Look at the level of loans to customers as well.

12. **Merchandise returns.** Does the business have a high rate of return? Has it gone up in the past year? If so, can you isolate the reasons for returns and correct the problem(s)?

13. **Customer patterns.** If this is the type of business that can track customers, you will want to know specific characteristics concerning current customers: How many are first time buyers? How many customers were lost over the past year? When are the peak buying seasons for current customers? What are low median price points? Average median price points? High median price points? What type of merchandise is the most popular?

14. **Marketing strategies.** How does the owner obtain customers? Does he or she offer discounts or conduct public-relations campaigns? Is there aggressive advertising? You should get copies of all sales literature to see the kind of image that is being projected. When you look at the literature, pretend that you are a customer being solicited by the company. How does it make you feel? This can give you some idea of how the company is perceived by its market.

15. **Advertising costs.** Analyze advertising costs. Many times it pays for a business at year end to postpone that profit until the next year by spending a lot of money on advertising during the last month of the fiscal year.

16. **Price checks.** Evaluate current price lists and discount schedules of all products, the date of the last price increases, and the percentage of increase. You might even go back and look at a second price increase to see what percentage it was and determine when you are likely to be able to raise prices. Here again, compare what you see in the business you are looking at with standards in the industry.

17. **Industry and market history.** As discussed in Chapter 3, you should analyze the industry as well as the specific market segments the business targets. You need to find out if sales in the industry, as well as the market segment, have been growing, declining, or remained stagnant. This is very important to determine future profit potential.

18. **Location and market area.** Evaluate the location of the business and the market area surrounding it. This is especially important to retailers who draw the majority of their business from the primary trading area. As detailed in Chapter 6, conduct a thorough analysis of the business's location and the trading areas surrounding the location including economic outlook, demographics, and competition. For more service-oriented businesses, get a map of the area covered by the business. Find out, based on the locations of various accounts, if there are any special quality requirements for delivering the product or any special transportation difficulties encountered by the business in getting the product to the market.

19. **Reputation of the business.** The perceived image of the business by customers as well as suppliers is extremely important and can be an asset or a liability. Interview customers, suppliers, the bank, and owners of other businesses in the area to determine the reputation of the business.

20. **Seller-customer ties.** You *must* find out if any customers are related or
    have any special ties to the present owner. How long has any such account
    been with the company? What percentage of the company's business is ac-
    counted for by this particular customer or set of customers? Will this cus-
    tomer continue to purchase from the company if the ownership is changed?
21. **Inflated salaries.** Some salaries may be inflated. The owner may have a
    relative on staff who isn't working for the company. All of the possibilities
    should be analyzed.
22. **List of current employees and organizational chart.** Current employees
    can be a valuable asset, especially key personnel. Evaluate the organiza-
    tional chart to understand who is responsible to whom. You must look at
    the management practices of the company. You have to know the wages of
    all employees and their length of employment. Examine any management-
    employee contracts that exist aside from a union agreement, as well as de-
    tails of employee benefit plans, profit-sharing, health, life, and accident
    insurance, vacation policies, and any employee-related lawsuits against the
    company.
23. **Occupational Safety and Health Administration (OSHA) requirements.** If
    a manufacturing plant is involved, find out whether the plant has been in-
    spected and meets all occupational safety and health requirements. If you
    feel the seller is hedging and that some things on the premises may be un-
    safe, as a prospective buyer of a business that may come under OSHA
    scrutiny you can ask the agency to help you with a check. Some sellers may
    perceive your asking for OSHA's help as a dirty trick. But you must realize
    that as a prospective, serious buyer, you need to protect your position.
24. **Insurance.** Establish what type of insurance coverage is held for the opera-
    tion of the business and all of its properties, the underwriter and local
    company representative, and the cost of the premiums. Some businesses
    are underinsured and operating under potentially disastrous situations in
    case of fire or other catastrophe. If you come into an underinsured opera-
    tion, you could be wiped out by an insurance-related incident.
25. **Product liability.** Product liability insurance is of particular interest if you
    are coming into a manufacturing company. Certain insurance coverages
    dramatically change from year to year, and this can markedly affect the
    company's cash flow.

Financial Documents and Review

Some of the following information may be repetitive; however, incomplete financial reviews are key reasons for new owner failures. The income statement
is the initial document you will want to analyze. When reviewing the income
statement, concentrate on hard-core facts that will impact the profitability of
the business. This is important because in many income statements, there will
be "waste" that can be eliminated. You need to decipher that waste as well as the
hard fixed and variable costs associated with the business.

Following are areas of the income statement you need to evaluate and some key concerns when doing so:

- **Monthly gross sales.** As mentioned, try to obtain a minimum of three years' data with as much detail as possible, including product category, and sales personnel. This information is invaluable for future sales projections. In addition to checking sales data in the income statement, you may want to check sales tax reports and IRS statements. Be sure to cross-check any single source against a second to verify the validity of these numbers. If you are dealing with a service business in which no sales tax is collected, only the federal income tax statement will provide sufficient information.

- **Cost of product or sales.** This can be based on comparisons with national averages or from reviewing the invoices paid to the existing suppliers. For retailers, wholesalers, and manufacturers, a cost-of-goods statement might have been kept. If so, ask to look at this statement as well. This information will help determine an accurate profit margin for the business in question. When dealing with multi-unit operations, be sure to check invoices from the other units as well. Sometimes owners will inflate the cost of goods or products to create a lower profit margin.

- **Rent.** In specific, evaluate terms and conditions of the lease. You can also find this data in the lease agreement. Cross-check the lessee's numbers and agreements with that of the lessor's.

- **Salaries.** Review the company's payroll records and 1099 statements and use this information to cross-check the numbers on the income statement. It may also be a good idea to ask the seller for permission to review payroll statements submitted to the IRS as another safety measure.

- **Advertising and sales expenses.** For most companies, advertising and sales are crucial to producing revenue. These expenses are usually padded with a great deal of waste. Check the business records as they relate to sales commissions, creative expenses for advertising, and media schedules and costs, as well as any sponsorships the company may be involved in. Cross-check this information with 1099 statements issued to salespeople, invoices from designers and copywriters, and representatives at the advertising agencies used.

- **Utilities, insurance, miscellaneous expenses.** These can be estimated if you observe carefully and have an idea of business ratios in the industry. To cross-check, look through the company checks and year-end tax statements, as well as insurance records.

- **Profitability.** This can be determined by subtracting the cost of goods from monthly gross sales to arrive at a gross profit. Next, add together all the operating expenses and then subtract those from the gross profit, and your result will be the net profitability of the firm. Be careful, however, when dealing with sole proprietorships and partnerships. They do not actually produce a definable net profit. They produce an income for the owner. This won't be listed in the income statement. To determine profitability in these instances, you need to check the owner's income. If the owner is serious about selling the business, there should be no problem in the disclosure of this information.

To illustrate how to evaluate an income statement, refer to Figure 10.1, Example 1, which is the sample income statement of a restaurant earning $100,000 annually. After deducting food costs, operating costs, and debt service, the restaurant's net profit is $6,300. If the asking price is $30,000 and you make a down payment of $15,000 discharging the remaining debt (10% note amortized 3 years) out of business earnings, $6,300 profit is actually a 21 percent return on investment. Not bad. That's three times what you could get in most banks.

But hold on. You only put up $15,000 as a down payment. A $6,300 return on $15,000 is really 42 percent! A good deal? You bet. And if you had put up even less down payment through the techniques of leveraged buyout, you could have had an even better return.

In the income statement, however, you are evaluating the current operating figures. What about potential? Suppose you are really hot about the restaurant and decide to stay open an additional day each week and serve breakfast in addition to lunch and dinner. You might be able to increase business by 25 or 30 percent. Your fixed and variable costs will increase a little, but so will your profit margin.

Now, suppose you can persuade the seller to take a five-year note instead of a three-year note. At 10 percent interest, that reduces your debt discharge from $5,500 to $3,300. While this means the ultimate cost of money will be higher, it also means that short-term cash flow is markedly strengthened.

Example 2 of Figure 10.1 reviews the same restaurant with these revised conditions. Your return has just increased from $6,300 to $19,100. That's an increase of over 200 percent, improving your return on investment to 64 percent.

To see the subtle, but important, differences between the first and second examples is an aspect of logically analyzing the position of an existing business versus its potential. This approach can be applied to virtually any business opportunity you may encounter. Although there will be added factors to consider in various industries, particularly where technical processes are concerned, the financial implications of such factors should fall into place if you bring some industry knowledge to your consideration of highly specialized businesses.

Additionally, you have an advantage over the person who runs the business now. To some degree, he or she is tired or bored or has succumbed to the old adage, "Familiarity breeds contempt." You're fresh, full of ideas, and still thinking like a customer, putting yourself in your future customers' shoes. You know what you want and how you'd like to receive it if you were buying the product or service for sale. This degree of innovation, applied to your analysis, can greatly assist you in bringing about the positive changes in direction you envision for your new business.

Several programs on the market can help you analyze and write a report on the business you plan to purchase. One is called *Buy-Out Plan* by MoneySoft,

Figure 10.1 Sample Income Statements

EXAMPLE 1		TOTALS
Gross Annual Sales	$ 100,000	
Food Cost (40%)	$ 40,000	
GROSS PROFIT		$ 60,000
Rent	$ 7,200	
Salaries	$ 16,000	
Utilities, Insurance, Overhead	$ 5,000	
Owner Salary	$ 20,000	
OPERATING COSTS		$ 48,200
(10% Note Amortized 3 years)	$ 5,500	
TOTAL		$ 54,000
NET PROFIT		$ 6,300

EXAMPLE 2		TOTALS
Gross Annual Sales	$ 125,000	
Food Cost (40%)	$ 45,000	
GROSS PROFIT		$ 80,000
Rent	$ 7,200	
Salaries	$ 23,000	
Utilities, Insurance, Overhead	$ 7,400	
Owner Salary	$ 20,000	
OPERATING COSTS		$ 57,600
(10% Note Amortized 5 years)	$ 3,300	
TOTAL		$ 60,900
NET PROFIT		$ 19,100

Inc., located in Phoenix, Arizona. Available in DOS only, *Buy-Out Plan* walks the user through the acquisition, evaluation, and planning process, then assembles that information in an easy-to-read narrative format.

THE RIGHT PRICE

Nothing is more emotionally charged than deciding on a price for an existing business. The owner has one idea of how much the business is worth, while the buyer will typically have another viewpoint. Each party is working from a different perspective, and usually the one who is best prepared will have the most leverage when the process enters the negotiating stage.

Keep in mind that most sellers determine the price for their business arbitrarily or through a special formula that may apply to that industry only. Either way, there usually isn't very much solid fact to back up their decisions.

Price is a very hard element to pin down and, therefore, hard for the buyer to assess. There are a few factors that will influence price, including economic conditions. Usually, businesses sell for a higher price when the economy is expanding, while they will sell for a much lower price during recessions. Motivation also plays an important part. How badly does the seller want out? If the seller has serious personal financial problems, you may be able to buy the business at a discount rate by playing a waiting game. On the other hand, don't ever let the seller know how badly you want to buy the business. This can adversely affect the price you pay.

Beyond these factors, determining the value of a business can be performed using several different methods discussed in the following pages.

Multipliers

Simply put, some owners gauge the value of their business by using a multiplier of either the monthly gross sales, monthly gross sales plus inventory, or after-tax profits. While the multiplier formula may seem complex and quite accurate to begin with, if you delve a little deeper and look at the components used to arrive at the stated value, there is actually very little to substantiate any claim.

Most of the multipliers aren't based on fact. For example, individuals within a specific industry may claim that certain businesses sell at three times their annual gross sales, or two times their annual gross sales plus inventory. Depending on which formula the owner uses, the gross sales are multiplied by the appropriate number, and voila! a price is generated.

For instance, if the business was earning $100,000 a year and the seller was using a formula where the multiple of gross sales was 30% based on industry averages, then the price would be generated using the following equation:

$$\$100,000 \times .30 = \$30,000$$

You can check the monthly sales figure by looking at the income statement, but is the multiplier an accurate number? After all, it has been determined arbitrarily. Seldom is a formal survey performed and verified by an outside source to arrive at these multipliers.

In addition, even if the multiplier was accurate, there is such a large spread between the low and high ends of the range that it really just pins down a ballpark figure. This is true whether a sales or profit multiplier is used. In the case of a profit multiplier, the figure generated becomes even more skewed because businesses rarely show a profit due to tax reasons. Therefore, the resulting value of the business is either very small or the owner has to use a different profit factor to arrive at a higher price.

Don't place too much faith in multipliers. If you run across a seller using the multiplier method, use the price only as an estimate and nothing more.

Book Values

This is a fairly accurate way to determine the price of a business, but you have to exercise caution using this method. To arrive at a price based on the book value, all you have to do is find out the difference between the assets and liabilities of a company; this is its net worth. This has usually been done already on the balance sheet. The net worth is then multiplied by one or two to arrive at the book value. This might seem simple enough. To check the quoted price, all you have to do is list the company's assets and liabilities. Determine their value, arrive at the net worth, and then multiply that by the appropriate number. Assets usually include any unsold inventory, leasehold improvements, fixtures, equipment, real estate, accounts receivable, and supplies. Liabilities can be unpaid debts, uncollected taxes, liens, judgments, lawsuits, bad investments—anything that will create a cash drain on the business.

Now here is where it gets tricky. In the balance sheet, fixed assets are usually listed by their depreciated value, not replacement value. Therefore, there really isn't a true cost associated with the fixed assets. That can create very inconsistent values. If the assets have been depreciated over the years to a level of zero, there isn't anything to base a book value on.

Return on Investment (ROI)

The most common means of judging any business is by its return on investment, or the amount of money the buyer will realize from the business in profit after debt service and taxes. However, don't confuse return on investment with profit. They are not the same thing. Return on investment is the amount of money the buyer puts into the business measured against the performance of the business. Profit is a yardstick by which the performance of the business is measured.

In an example of return on investment, the business is selling for $80,000. The buyer plans to offer $40,000 down and finance the rest through a five-year note at 12 percent. Gross sales for the business is $200,000 annually with a net profit after taxes of $20,000, which results in a return on investment of 25 percent. Typically, a small business should return anywhere between 15 and 30 percent on investment. This is the average net in after-tax dollars. Depreciation, which is a device of tax planning and cash flow, should not be counted in the net because it should be set aside to replace equipment. Many novice business owners will look at a financial statement and say, "There's $5,000 we can take off for depreciation." Well, there's a reason for a depreciation schedule. Eventually, equipment does wear out and must be replaced, and it sometimes has to be replaced much sooner than you expect. This is especially true when considering a business with older equipment.

The wisdom of buying a business lies in its potential to earn money on the money you put into it. You determine the value of that business by evaluating how much money you are going to earn on your investment. The business should have the ability to pay for itself. If it can do this and give you a return on your cash investment of 15 percent or more, than you have a good business. This is what determines the price. If the seller is financing the purchase of the business, your operating statement should have a payment schedule that can be taken out of the income of the business to pay for it.

Does a 15 percent net for a business seem high? Everybody wants to know if a business makes two, three, or 10 times profit. They hear price-earnings ratios tossed around and forget that such ratios commonly refer to stock-exchange listed companies. In small businesses, such ratios have limited value. A big business can earn 10 percent on its investment and be extremely healthy. Big supermarkets net 2 or 3 percent on their sales, but this small percentage represents enormous volume.

Small businesses are different. The small business should typically earn a bigger return because the risk of the enterprise is higher. The important thing for you, as a buyer of a small business, is to realize that regardless of industry practices for big business, it is the ROI that you need to worry about most. Is it realistic? If the price is realistic for the amount of money you have to invest, then you can consider it a viable business.

Capitalized Earnings

Valuing a business based on capitalized earnings is similar to the return-on-investment method of assessment, except normal earnings are used to estimate projected earnings. This figure is then divided by a standard capitalization rate. So what is a standard capitalization rate?

The capitalization rate is determined by learning what the risk of investment in the business would be compared with other investments such as government bonds or stock in other companies. For instance, if the rate of return on investment in government bonds is 18 percent, then the business should return 18 percent or better on the investment into it. To determine the value of a business based on capitalized earnings, use the following formula:

$$Projected\ Earnings \div Capitalization\ Rate = Price$$

So, after analyzing the market, the competition, the demand for the product, and the organization of the business, you determine that projected earnings could increase to $25,000 per year for the next three years. If your capitalization rate is 18 percent, then the value of the business would be:

$$\$25,000 \div .18 = \$138,888$$

Generally, a good capitalization rate for buyouts will range between 20 and 40 percent. If the seller is asking much more than what you've determined the capitalized earnings to be, then you will have to try and negotiate a lower price.

Intangible Value

Some business owners try to sell goodwill as an asset. Normally, in everyday accounting procedures, most companies put down perhaps a dollar as the value of goodwill. There is no doubt that goodwill has value, particularly if the business has built up a regular trade and a strong base of accounts. But it is the financial value of the accounts, not their psychological value, that should be placed on any financial statements. Goodwill as such is not an asset. You as a buyer should assess the business based on the return on investment.

Certain rules of the game may change when you jump into the fields of acquisition and merger. Suppose you buy out your competition, merge all your facilities, and double your volume. Now the labor and overhead factors are much lower. Thus, even if the seller was losing perhaps 5 percent a year, if you bring the business into your company, which is making 15 percent a year, it might allow you to increase sales and end up making 20 percent.

NEGOTIATION

Rarely does a business sell for the price listed when it first goes on the market. The process is no different from the maneuvering involved in buying a home or a car. Very seldom will you pay the first price advertised. Sellers get worried when their businesses don't sell really fast. Prospective buyers, brokers, or associates may say that the price is too high and will not consider looking into the business. The owner gets scared and drops the price. This is why you should find out how long the business has been on the market. You must first realize that people who have started a business from scratch are psychologically attached to the company. The owner has pride in the business and has put a lot of hard work into developing a successful operation. Because of this, the initial price of the business may be too high.

What is your position in all of this? In negotiation, the smartest approach is to be nice, friendly, and a good salesperson. Many people don't realize that an important part of negotiation is the personal sales angle. You have to sell yourself and your ideas, and people have to like you. That is why being friendly and cordial is the way to make the best deals.

Many individuals perceive a successful negotiator as a hard-headed person who's really rough on people. This is simply not true. Rarely do such people make the best negotiators or the best deals. Indeed, they run a risk of being conned because they fail to learn from their mistakes or from the signals that the opposite party may be sending. If the initial price set by the seller is too high, you need to handle your objection and the seller's perceptions in the correct way. Many times the seller will not understand your objection if you simply say that the price is too high. Point out that the asking price will not allow you to make a decent return, and that consequently the business is of no value to you. This is the approach of an intelligent buyer: It either does or does not make sense for you to buy the business, and the test of that decision is the return on investment you can expect.

When negotiating alone with the seller, you must confirm in writing the terms on which you have agreed at every step of the way. Do this immediately—either that night or that day. This does not mean that you have to write a formal contract. Rather, make a memorandum of your points of agreement, and get it in the mail right away, requesting immediate corrections of anything that may have been misunderstood. You should word it something like this: "This will confirm our understanding of . . ." The reason for this should be obvious. Many times, an owner who says, "Yes, I'll do X and Y," will suddenly develop a case of amnesia when writing a contract and say, "Oh, I never said that. I never promised to do that." Making a memorandum in the form of a letter will save you headaches in later negotiations. And for sellers who play games, this will limit their moves. Confirming everything in writing will make your negotiations easier at the time of the contract. Unfortunately, a lot of contracts fail after coming out of escrow. (See Chapter 22 for information on the practice termed "papering the file.")

Also, keep in mind that in negotiation, no one gets everything his or her own way. Every transaction involves some compromises whether you're buying or selling. A lot of sellers are not willing to compromise at all. They are rigid, and have their mind set in a particular way. If you establish proper criteria for buying a business and this conflicts with the seller's perception of its value, don't buy. You don't have to have any particular business and don't have to make an emotional commitment to one operation. Those emotions can get you into big financial trouble.

Dealing with Sellers

Sellers sometimes do things that will restrict a sale. Certain such actions can be surmountable, but others cannot. In any event, you need to be aware of potential difficulties in this area. Such problems can sometimes serve as a "red flag," an indication of negatives in the business that may be concealed for one reason or another. Following are some problems you may encounter while dealing with a seller:

- **Price that is too high.** The owner may decide not to sell unless a specific price can be attained and may even take the business off the market. The seller may demand too high a down payment for the buyer to handle; this is often the case where the business has had problems and is in a real cash bind. The seller thinks the business is going to fail, so he or she tries to get as much money up front as possible.

- **Failure or refusal to provide records.** You will need this data to properly evaluate a business. A seller who doesn't provide crucial documents may be afraid you'll find the problem that will kill the sale and so tries to get around that danger by refusing to give you information. Yet, how else can a business be evaluated except after close examination of its financial data? If you encounter a secretive or adamant seller, your beset bet is probably to look elsewhere for a business to buy, or to start your own in competition with this one.

- **A hard-line seller.** Many sellers are often one-sided and have no interest in the buyer's standpoint. They don't try to understand that the buyer needs to make a certain amount of money on the investment. They may not look at their business that way (this may be the chief reason the business is up for sale). This is the most uninformed type of business owner you are likely to encounter. Such a seller may want to strip the business of its quick assets.

- **Some sellers want too much security.** They may ask for financial security to guarantee the business if they are financing the sale, even as they maintain that their business is a good buy for the buyer. If you run across a seller who wants security in addition to the business, you are probably dealing with a rather naive individual where negotiation leverage is concerned. After all, a good business that is being purchased is its own security. The seller may argue that you may not be the fine manager he or she is and that you might run the business down the drain. Do not accept that argument; at some point you have to stand behind your own integrity and business ability. In a worst-case scenario, the seller can always recoup the business. Don't put up any other security to buy a business apart from the business itself.

Common Tricks

Now let's look at some of the ways a business seller can "put one over" on the buyer. There are 10,000 variations on these themes, but we will hit the most common ploys so that you can make a judgment in a sale about whether you are being fooled.

- **Claiming additional income.** If a seller says, "The income shown is for tax purposes. I actually take a little bit more out," look at that statement carefully: The owner is admitting to felony tax evasion by not reporting income for tax purposes. But has the seller really committed a felony? This may just be a dodge to make you believe there is much more money and potential in the business than the financial records indicate. There are ways to verify the volume of the business. If the seller insists the reported profit to the IRS is not the actual profit, pursue the issue and ask for an explanation of how the money has been isolated, or how it's been hidden from any audits that might have been performed. Sometimes the seller will tell you. But veterans of business sales also know that just as often the seller will be unable to tell you. This should warn you that the business may not be in a strong revenue position at all.

- **Business relationship cover-ups.** Suppose a business is sold, and it has one primary customer whose trade accounts for 30 to 40 percent of the volume. After researching the business and determining who this major account is you find out that it is the brother-in-law of the seller of the business; as soon as you buy the business, the brother-in-law disappears along with almost half of your volume. Hiding business relationships is fairly easy since the emphasis of most research isn't placed in this area. So be very careful when evaluating the vendors of the business you want to buy. Determine as fully as possible the major customers of the business, and their relationships with the business owner.

- **"Round-robin" invoices.** A round-robin invoice is one that shows money coming in, but the money on the invoice never goes into the bank. The invoice may be for material or services that were never rendered. They are stamped PAID and indicate that the account is up to date. Yet the company never really purchased what the invoice indicates. In extreme cases, the customer company never existed! If you have your CPA conduct a proper audit, you should be able to detect any discrepancies between what the statements show and the actual financial condition of the business.

- **Cash-float accounts.** A seller with a lot of money aside from that generated by the business, may float this money through the operation to make it look like sales. This increases the apparent value of the business and, with it, the purchase price. Cash-floating is easy to conceal if a seller has two different businesses. Money will be floated from one business (so there are no taxes paid on the operation of that business) to the one being sold so that taxes are paid on that operation only. This is done in several ways:

  Floating cash through the bank account makes it appear as if the second business is taking in money. It can have great impact on the sale price of certain retail businesses, where a lot of cash changes hands. This is particularly true if the retail business is one with relatively low ticket prices.

  Invoices will come in for one company but be paid by the other, or sellers will funnel receivables from a more profitable business into the less profitable business that might be for sale, thus making a business that doesn't do much volume look good on paper.

In labor-intensive businesses, a seller will take a low salary from one business or put some of the employees from one company on the payroll of the other; therefore, the payroll expense implicit in the business for sale is not reflected in the P&L. The seemingly low labor costs in a labor-intensive business can make it extremely attractive to an unwary buyer. Yet high labor costs may be the very reason that the business is being sold. The message to you as a buyer is to find out whether the seller of the business you want to buy owns any other businesses, and then what kind of businesses they are. Let the seller realize that you know the facts of the cash-float scam. It can have the effect of keeping the seller honest. In any case, you need to be careful of the tactics of floating cash. When the seller you are dealing with owns more than one business, make sure you can isolate what he or she is doing with each of them.

- **Juggling dates.** Instead of showing a nine-month-old invoice, an owner will redate the invoice and show it in the books as current from a client company. From time to time, you may find that a substantial amount has been updated (retyped). The new date on the invoice doesn't offend the company that owes the money. On the contrary, client companies that are the cause of badly aging receivables are only too happy to be given a new lease on life. Suddenly they are not behind in their payments. Why should they care?
- **Inflated inventory value.** A common deception is inflating the value of inventory that the seller hasn't been able to move. The inventory may be showing on the books. If you're not wise to standards and practices in the industry you are about to enter (how various products sell, what doesn't sell), you may be buying old or outdated material. An apparel or gift retailer may have too much inventory, or inventory that is going out of style.
- **Inflated equipment value.** In recent years, microcomputers have decreased in cost while increasing in capability. Multiuser processors supporting as many as 10 users can be purchased for as little as $3,000 today, though 10 years ago it would have cost $50,000 for the same system. Suppose the seller has one of these multiuser computers and shows it on the books as being worth $50,000, less the depreciation for several years' use. It is possible you could buy the same or better equipment for a fraction of the cost and five times the capability of the equipment being sold to you. You may have to get an appraisal on equipment from an independent source rather than accepting without question what the owner or the statement of book value says the equipment is worth.
- **Hiding maintenance costs.** To increase the value of equipment included in the purchase price, the owner may try to bury the maintenance costs or

fail to provide you with information. This is more likely if the equipment is old and reaching the end of its serviceable life. Accordingly, it is a good idea to find out the life expectancy of the equipment and how long it can operate effectively between maintenance calls.

Common Mistakes

Don't be too anxious when you're looking to buy a business. As we've mentioned already, if you're too anxious, this can affect the price. Tremendous mistakes are made by people who are anxious. Business consultants called in by anxious buyers can sometimes salvage the situation, but oftentimes consultants are not called in until a deal has been closed. And once your signature goes on that dotted line, you're stuck with the purchase. So keep in mind that anxiety or impatience is not going to help you buy a business. Take your time. Recognize that there is always time to reflect on the business that's for sale. No matter what a business broker, a business seller, or any other person may tell you, there is always time. Nine times out of 10, the business that is up for sale is going to be around for awhile. And if it is not, then it is the seller who is going to be the anxious one; and the seller's anxiety is something that can be manipulated to your advantage as buyer.

The following are some of the more common mistakes:

- **Buying on price.** Buyers don't take into account ROI. If you're going to invest $20,000 in a business that returns a 5 percent net, you're better off putting your money in stocks and commodities, the local S&L, or municipal bonds. Any type of intangible security is going to produce more than 5 percent.
- **Cash shortage.** Some buyers use all their cash for the down payment on the business, though cash management in the start-up phase of any business, new or existing, is fundamental to short-term success. They fail to predict future cash flow and possible contingencies that might require more capital. Further, some revenue has to be set aside for building the business through marketing and PR efforts. So, if you have $20,000 to invest, make sure you don't invest the entire amount. Keep some of the capital. Though figures vary from industry to industry, a common contingency is 10 percent. Additionally, you may want to set aside a sum that you regard as your working capital, which in a number of businesses is enough to cover about three months' worth of expenses.
- **Buying all the receivables.** It generally makes good sense to buy the receivables, except when they are 90 or 120 days old, or older. Too often, buyers take on all the receivables, even those beyond 90 days. This can be very risky because the older the account, the more difficult it will be to collect against. You can protect yourself by having the seller warrant the receivables; what is not collectible can be charged back against the

purchase price of the business. Give receivables beyond 90 days to the owner for collection.

- **Failure to verify all data.** Most business buyers accept all the information and data given them by the seller at face value without the verification of their own accountant (preferably a CPA, who can audit financial statements). Most sellers want to get their cash out of the business as soon as possible, and buyers frequently allow them to take all the quick assets such as receivables, cash, and equipment inventories. The buyer then has to go out and bring in operating capital, more inventories, and sometimes equipment. The seller talks the buyer into virtually anything, knowing that the buyer wants the business badly.

- **Heavy payment schedules.** Novice business owners often overestimate their revenue during the first year and take on unduly large payments to finance the buyout. Revenue, however, rarely pans out. During the first year of any operation, the owner experiences numerous nonrecurring costs such as equipment failures and employee turnover. For this reason, it makes sense to have a payment schedule that is fairly light at first, then gets progressively heavier. This is something that can be negotiated with a seller and should not be difficult to arrange.

- **Treating the seller unfairly.** People sometimes think that because they are buying a business the seller is at their mercy. All too often, the buyer will be cold, rigid, and hard-headed. Sellers with savvy will throw such people out and tell them not to come back. Just because you as the buyer have some money and may be interested in purchasing the business, it does not mean that you can be exempt from the process of give and take.

BUSINESS BROKERS

You will often see ads that say, "Business for Sale by Owner." That's supposed to make the business attractive. Actually, it does not always accomplish that goal. People who do a lot of buying and selling of big properties know the value of a go-between—a professional business broker. This person, who is a veteran negotiator, can be valuable to both buyer and seller for a number of reasons. According to Bob Coleman,[1] vice president of the San Diego business brokerage Jack Coleman Company, a business broker can help a buyer in several ways:

- **Preselect businesses for you.** A good brokerage firm turns down roughly half the businesses it is asked to sell, either because they're overpriced or because the sellers won't provide complete financial records.

[1] Bob Coleman, "Good Buying," *Guide to Business Start-Ups* (Entrepreneur Magazine Group) (1993).

- **Focus your interests.** A good broker first learns about your needs and abilities, then helps you choose the size and kind of business that's right for you. A business you've never even considered may prove to be your perfect match.
- **Smooth the negotiating process.** This is where brokers really earn their money—in keeping tempers even and all parties focused on the goal: a transaction that's good for both sides.
- **Simplify paperwork and eliminate risks.** From licenses and permits to financing and escrow, good brokers know the most efficient channels to use. Sometimes they can shave months off the purchasing process.

When dealing with a seller who is using a broker, never go directly to the property you see advertised. Call first, and try to discover what kind of broker you are dealing with. If this is chiefly a real estate broker who happens to have a business brokerage license and sells an occasional business, he or she may not be effective in selling the business. A business sale is a whole different ballgame from a real estate sale. There are many things that business brokers have to know and deal with that they wouldn't normally encounter in selling a house or apartment building.

To evaluate the broker, it may be useful for you to have an associate or friend call the listed number and find out something about the broker's business, as well as the business or businesses for sale. If the broker is not a business broker, chances are that the business will be around in 30 to 60 days. The broker will lose the exclusive right to peddle the business, at which time the owner will try to take on another broker or try and sell the business personally. An inexperienced business broker may not be much help in the finer points of the negotiation. The principal value of the broker is to act as a buffer between you and the seller.

A broker can say certain things to you, and can say certain things to the business owner that you or the owner cannot get away with and still have a productive discussion. The broker can tell the owner the price is too high, relay what has to be done to make a deal—very openly and candidly—and can discuss how the differences in viewpoint can be ironed out effectively.

You can tell the broker what is holding up the deal. You can tell the broker, "Try this price and see how the seller reacts to it." Many of these things you could not discuss face to face, where the negotiation situation becomes quite delicate. Meanwhile, the owner will be concerned about the broker fee. Fees range anywhere from 5 to 10 percent, depending on negotiations with the broker, state laws, and other factors. In this regard, any seller who does not use a broker or a lawyer as a professional advisor runs a tremendous risk. Industry observers agree that it is foolish for a seller not to be represented in the sale of the business. Although the seller will pay a fee to a broker to handle traffic on the sale, the broker can normally get much more money for the business, smooth the sale, and handle a lot of clerical and other details—even make a sale possible—whereas an individual business seller cannot. The fact that there will be certain add-ons in the price of the business to cover the broker's fee should not concern you unduly, as long as you remember that you are going to be buying on the basis of return on investment.

If no broker is involved initially, it would be smart for you to set up your own go-between. You might hire the broker to do the job for you on a consulting basis; he or she may be able to extract the fee from the owner in line with the custom of having a seller pay such costs. Alternatively, if the owner does not want to handle the entire fee, you can negotiate the fee with the broker or negotiate with the seller to jointly pay the broker. And keep in mind that broker's fees in this kind of sale are negotiable, whether the broker says the fee is 10 percent, 6 percent, or 2 percent.

The point is, it makes sense for you to use a go-between in tricky negotiations. Hire a friend, a CPA, or a lawyer. Have the go-between arrange negotiations in the capacity of consultant. The seller will not have to pay any fee but should agree to work with the middleman. The ultimate effect, insofar as the go-between arranges negotiating sessions and logistic details, is that someone will be working for you both. Usually, there will be no problem as long as the seller won't have to absorb any of the charge.

Though regulations vary from state to state, most persons operating in this capacity are considered consultants in negotiation. The regulations come into play when it comes time to collect a fee, which cannot be figured as a percentage of the sale. Nor can someone who is not a licensed broker close a sale. However, a broker can smooth the rough edges of negotiation and be paid a fee for this effort.

In certain instances, you may have to deal with the seller without the intervention of a broker. If this becomes necessary, you need to prepare yourself well for the encounter, realizing that the negotiation process can take a relatively long time. You cannot expect to close most deals within 48 hours, and seldom will both you and seller walk away from the deal completely satisfied.

Typically, in a business sale, the seller is less prepared than the buyer for negotiation. Businesses that are offered for sale often have some degree of anxiety surrounding them, usually from the seller's insecurity about keeping the business on one hand, or getting rid of it on the other. As a result, the average seller is not going to learn all he or she wants to know about you, and will not be sure how the deal is closing.

A seller who is an unsophisticated business operator has probably never sold a business before, and may not be aware of the process of negotiation, lacking experience in it altogether. If you have some understanding of what is about to happen, you will be better prepared to meet objections and/or inexperience with the knowledge that certain conditions must be met before you will sign on the dotted line.

METHODS OF BUYING

Once you have determined the type of business you want to buy and have evaluated it and are negotiating price, you will need to start thinking about how to finance the deal. Following are some ways to do just that.

Leveraged Buyouts (LBOs)

In its simplest terms, a leveraged buyout is the purchase of a company by an investor group using largely borrowed funds. In a typical deal, an investment banker or other deal organizer assembles a group of investors, almost always including the management of the organization to be bought and usually one or more important financial institutions. These investors acquire the stock or assets of the company, contributing a relatively small amount of equity and arranging a relatively large amount of debt financing. The investment banker packaging the buyout also purchases an interest in the equity, on the assumption that the leveraging will net the investors as much as $20 or $25 for every dollar risked. You can readily see that not every type of business is going to be a candidate for such a transaction.

The leveraged form of purchase has been an accepted investment or merchant banking technique for years and has parallel application in traditional real estate financing. It is not unlike taking a second mortgage on your house, only here it's the people who own the company take something like a "second mortgage" on the company itself.

LBOs are not for everyone. The companies for which they are best suited are stable, mature ones that generate excess cash. Their product lines are well established, they have relatively little debt, and assets have been accumulated that have meaningful additional life. For a leveraged transaction to work, you need to be able to sell investors on the merits of the transaction, ascertain the risks and constraints of debt, adjust the "corporate culture" to the realities of a leveraged independent company, and prepare for the day when the investor group will want to be paid off.

When evaluating businesses for a potential leveraged buyout, you have to look at the capabilities of the current management team, their commitment to forming a new company, and their understanding of the needs the new company will have. Many experts also believe that the existing management team should have some kind of equity in the new company.

The greatest risk to the LBO is that the company won't earn enough to satisfy the investment made by participants in the deal. This might be due to a number of factors, such as a poorly structured transaction that overburdens the company or unanticipated prolonged recessions in the company's markets. Or it could happen if the management isn't given enough financial or investment incentives to make strong business decisions. This is why most experts seem to think that outsiders should make up the majority on the board of the new company. The investment firm sponsoring the transaction should also be active in monitoring the company's activities. This will help the managers of the company make difficult decisions even while treating the investors fairly.

Management of the company in question will need new strategies for operating the business. Growth probably is not going to be an option because of capital constraints, at least in the early years of the buyout. Further, competitors will probably test the product in the market knowing that the newly leveraged company needs to generate cash to service debt and will be reluctant to cut its prices. There may also be problems with suppliers and customers. Suppliers must be assured that the new, debt-heavy capital structure will not jeopardize their payments. Customers must be assured that the quality of the product will be maintained and competitive service levels will continue to be met.

Debt reduction will be the top priority in the early years of the LBO. The business will need to make do with a minimum of working capital and few, if any, corporate amenities necessary for marketing and sales. LBOs often begin with a decrease in working capital and cost reduction along with debt reduction, reflecting the owner's understanding of the needs of the new operating environment.

After the initial cutbacks, a leveraged corporation needs to look toward the future and develop strategies to implement once debt service returns to normal. While bringing the company to this level may take several years, goals should be in place at the very beginning.

As mentioned, you should also prepare for the time when the investors want to get their money back. The timing can be a source of conflict because company personnel may want different things out of the business than the investors' desire for a good return on investment. Solutions are available in the form of a public offering, the repurchase of investor shares by a healthy company, or through a merger of some kind. This is a matter of negotiation, which should be relatively uncomplicated if good management techniques have been employed. The leveraged buyout can offer new life to a business and can be mutually beneficial to both the investors and the current managers if both parties communicate and cooperate. It offers financial gain and flexibility to corporations and the prospect of healthy return on investment (ROI) for those who have invested in them.

Real Estate Leveraging

It is also possible to use real property that is already providing you with a little money to gain ownership of a business that is heavy in debt and not producing enough profit to manage the payments properly. The first step is to analyze the financial profit-making potential of the business in question on a realistic basis. Insufficient capitalization, overbuying on inventory, and poor management policies are among the most frequent causes of business failure. The wise application of capital and/or management might save the business. If you determine that you can save this business and at the same time become its new owner, you're ready to proceed.

Find out to whom the business owner owes money—bank, savings and loan, or insurance company—and approach the institution. Tell the lending institution that you would like to buy the loan on the business, and offer your income-producing real estate as security for a new loan to you. One portion of this loan should be used to buy the debt of the present owner. Another portion of it should be in cash, or working start-up capital.

Doing this, you put yourself in a good financial position (providing you can get the business going) for two reasons:

1. You retain the rental income from your original real estate. You have only used it to secure a loan, not sold it outright to the bank.
2. You have bought yourself the profit potential of the business itself.

The lending institution also realizes substantial benefits from this method:

1. The potential bad debt on a nonproductive and mismanaged business is eliminated.
2. The real-estate collateral you offer on the new loan is worth twice the business itself.

Moreover, if you make a go of the business you are taking over, the new loan will be paid off—probably ahead of schedule. Banks, insurance companies, and savings and loans are not used to looking at this kind of proposal. But it has all the elements of a fairy tale in which you are the hero and there are no losers. The original owner gets out of a bankruptcy situation. The bank has the opportunity to continue receiving an interest on the loan. You as the new owner lock into a business that you have analyzed and think can be profitable. If the business is successful, you will reap the greatest benefit over the long term.

Using the Seller's Assets

Many times, you can raise the capital for the purchase of a business simply by arranging financing based on the company's assets. After all, as soon as you buy the business, you own the assets.

Using the seller's own assets to buy the business out from under the seller is an accepted technique in the financial community. There are several tangible assets you can use to raise capital. They include items like real estate, equipment, accounts receivable, purchase orders, and inventory.

"Real-estate paper" is one way of using the seller's assets. Suppose you want to buy a business but have only 50 percent of the cash needed to complete the deal. You can use real estate to finance the other 50 percent of the business-buying package. If you have some capital, it's possible to obtain second mortgages at a discount rate of 50 percent. With these, you can then purchase the business for sale at the full price. How is this possible? Why will the seller of the business agree to this? There are several reasons. First, when you offer the business owner the discounted mortgages, you're offering something of real, long-term value aside from the monetary value of the sale. The owner is buying relief from day-to-day business operations. Second, the seller of the business receives the tax breaks that go with periodic payments on real estate. Third, the seller receives income on those mortgages—cash-in-hand on a regular and long-term basis.

In businesses that are particularly equipment intensive, you can use this capital asset as a tool to gain control of the business. The first step in this process is to find out the amount of money the business owner could get by selling the business to another party or piece by piece—in this case the major pieces of equipment needed for a viable business operation—whether on consignment or at a business-equipment auction. Sometimes the business is located at a rented site, in which case the equipment is considered by itself. At other times, the building and the real estate are also considered by the party needing to sell. If this is the case, the advantage of using the equipment as capital carries with it the possible benefit of gaining control of a piece of property and a building as well.

It is important to get realistic projections on the amount of money the business owner can receive for the equipment on the open market. If you can come up with a correct figure that meets the realities of the owner's needs versus the market value of the equipment, 9 times out of 10 you'll be able to complete a deal.

After you have determined that you want to buy and the seller wants to sell the business equipment, the next step is to determine how title will pass from party to party. Some sellers prefer to keep title themselves until they receive the cash for their business equipment. If you encounter such a situation, there's a reasonable answer to this that can keep your cash where it belongs—with you. Simply tell the seller that you need ownership of the equipment to complete the sale. If you don't own the equipment you are buying, you won't be able to use it as collateral for a bank loan. No collateral means no loan. If you have no loan, you can't very well buy the owner's equipment in the first place. And unless you have the equipment and the capital to undertake the business, there's no sense in taking the risk. What you can offer the seller is a fair deal of monthly payments for the equipment, backed by a bank loan that capitalizes the business itself.

Usually, a business owner who depends on equipment and who has not been able to make a go of it for one reason or another will be in dire need of cash and will readily agree to these conditions. Your next move is to go to the bank. Bring with you an itemized list of the equipment. If you have technical specifications that explain the equipment's capabilities in lay terms, it's much better. That way, the bank will be able to see that there is intrinsic value in the equipment itself. If the bank determines that there is sufficient value in the equipment, it will most likely grant you a loan. If you can get enough cash for a down payment on the equipment to the seller, plus some "seed" money with which to start up the business itself, then you are in a great position to assume control of the business.

If you are buying land along with the equipment, then you can obtain your cash by assuming a mortgage and refinancing it. With the money from the second mortgage that you obtain, you make the payment to the business seller and you are ready to get the business going again.

Purchase orders are another asset that can be used to raise money to buy the business. Some investors and institutions such as commercial banks will lend money on purchase orders. To obtain financing this way, try to obtain copies of the actual purchase orders from the seller to present either to an investor or finance company.

Accounts receivable offer another financing avenue. Finance companies and banks will lend money based on the receivables of the company. Most lenders will only finance 80 percent of your receivables but will raise that to 100 percent if you include the inventory as collateral. A spin-off of receivables financing is to ask the seller to keep the receivables. A seller who does this in effect is accepting the receivables as part of the payment for the business, thereby reducing the amount of cash you have to pay for it.

Co-Op Buying

Another financing option, especially if you are short on funds but the business is a good prospect, is to enter into a partnership with another buyer who is interested in the business. By combining your liquid assets, you can raise enough money for the purchase.

To find a co-op buyer, ask the business seller for a list of people who wanted to buy the business but couldn't come up with enough cash. Contact these people and see if they're interested in a partnership. Be sure your partnership agreement allows one partner to buy out the other, if necessary (see Chapter 22).

Employee Stock Ownership Plans (ESOP)

A new trend in financing the purchase of a small business is to utilize an ESOP. With this financing method, you raise sufficient capital to purchase the business by selling stock in the company to its employees. To structure an effective ESOP for the purchase of the business, you should divide stock into voting and nonvoting shares. You then sell only the nonvoting shares to the employees so that you still maintain control of the company even though the employees own a percentage of it.

In addition to being a good tool for raising capital to buy the business, ESOPs are attractive to banks. Many banks will lend money more readily to a business with an ESOP in place because they obtain 50 percent of their interest tax free.

Leasing the Business

That's right. If you don't have enough money to buy, some sellers will allow you to lease their businesses with an option to buy. All you need to do is come up with the down payment. If you have the down payment, approach the seller and let him or her know that you are extremely interested in buying the business but don't have enough money at the time. Offer the seller the down payment on the purchase price so that you become a minority stockholder. Then, operate the business as if it were your own, eventually paying off the seller by getting another partner or by using your profits from the business.

Debt Consolidation Loans

It is sometimes possible to take over a business and consolidate its debts. With a debt-consolidation loan, you can work with a bank and perhaps arrange for the creditors to accept 40 or 50 percent on the dollar. In extreme cases, you may want to acquire a Chapter 11 bankruptcy filing, which allows you to obtain protection for the company from its creditors. Again, the creditors may eventually be induced to accept 40 cents on the dollar.

In the past few years, however, the improper use of the Bankruptcy Code's Chapter 11 provisions by larger corporations has put companies in similar situations under strict scrutiny. This method of obtaining some gain from a business that you have bought requires the advice of a competent bankruptcy attorney. Additionally, you should plan on taking from two to four years to complete the judicial cycle of Chapter 11 proceedings.

Do not forget that you can rarely buy a profitable business for very little money. Someone with a profitable company probably has a pretty good head for business.

RESOURCES

Associations

Association of Small Business Development Centers, 1050 17th Street NW, Suite 810, 202-887-5599

National Small Business United, 1155 15th Street NW, Suite 710, Washington, DC 20005, 202-293-8830

Center for Entrepreneurial Management, Inc., 180 Varick Street, New York, NY 10014, 212-633-0060

MoneySoft, Inc., One E. Camelback Road, Suite 550, Phoenix, AZ 85012, 602-226-7719

Small Business Network, P.O. Box 30149, Baltimore, MD 21270, 301-466-8070

Small Business Service Bureau, 554 Main Street, Worcester, MA 01601, 508-756-3513

Small Business Support Center Association, 8300 Bissonnet, Suite 570, Houston, TX 77074, 713-271-4232

Magazines

Business and Acquisition Newsletter, 2600 South Gessner Road, Houston, TX 77063-3214, 713-783-0100

The Business Owner, Thomas Publishing, Inc., 383 South Broadway, Hicksville, NY 11801, 516-681-2111

Entrepreneurial Manager's Newsletter, 180 Varick Street, Penthouse Suite, New York, NY 10014-4692, 212-633-0060

Journal of Small Business Management, West Virginia University, College of Business Economics, Bureau of Business Research, P.O. Box 6025, Morgantown, WV 26506-6025, 304-293-5837

11

Franchise Opportunities

According to industry statistics, a new franchise opens somewhere in the United States every 17 minutes. As John Naisbitt, author of *Megatrends,* says, "Franchising is the single most successful marketing concept ever."

While product and trade name franchises are still extremely prevalent in today's business environment, business format franchises that define a complete business concept, rather than the distribution of a particular product, have been integral to the tremendous explosion in franchising in the United States. On a dollar-volume basis, franchising has exploded in the past few years. According to the Department of Commerce, franchises account for an estimated $266 billion in sales annually, and that number is climbing. About one-third of all retail sales in the United States are made in franchised outlets, and in a study commissioned by the International Franchise Association (IFA), Naisbitt has predicted that fully one-half of all retail sales will be made through franchised outlets by the year 2000.

That's a staggering prediction for potential growth in this lucrative area of business opportunities that employs more than 8 million people in more than 60 major industries. But just what is a franchise? Essentially, a franchise is a written agreement that allows a business owner to expand his or her business by granting franchisees the right to offer, sell, or distribute goods or services under the franchisor's trademark, and utilize a proven marketing plan or system. It is a highly regulated system that can benefit both franchisors and franchisees.

For anyone who's ever wanted to achieve the "American Dream" of financial independence through business ownership, the franchising method of doing business provides a perfect environment. In some ways, franchising is the most supportive business structure for entrepreneurs because it provides something for everyone. For men and women who want to own their own business and seek the freedom of being their own bosses, there's a place for them in franchising. There are now more than 60 different lines of business that are franchised, and the number of categories available continues to expand.

As franchising has grown, it has taken on many different faces. Primarily, franchising fills the gap between two business parties. Under a contractual relation, neither party has to do business with the other or watch out for the other's interests; an agency relation establishes a legal framework allowing one party to act as an agent for the other. Franchising permits both parties to maintain a relation where each has an interest in the other's business without being any type of agent. The extent of the rights and interests of both parties is determined in a written contract that defines the type of franchise.

We will discuss franchise laws later in this section. However, to understand what a franchise is, you first have to learn about the different types of franchises:

- **Product and trade-name franchises.** Product and trade-name franchises are primarily used to set up distribution networks for the franchisor through dealer companies. By franchising out the distribution of its products, the franchisor is able to control the way the dealer company operates by restricting the sale of competitive products or the type of marketing that can be done. In turn, the dealer, or franchisee, receives the recognition that accompanies a well-known firm such as Exxon or Firestone. They may also receive financial, marketing, and managerial support from the franchisor.

- **Business format franchises.** This has become the most popular type of franchise, and the one with which most of us are familiar. The franchisee is granted the name, the use of the products, the marketing techniques, the systems, internal controls, and operations procedures. The franchisee is simply managing an established business—a total business concept—that in some cases is a turnkey package. There are variations of the business format franchise. Sometimes a technical definition of a franchise is determined by the state in which a company is franchising. Various states have various interpretations and requirements. The individual franchise is probably the most common type of business format franchise. Under the individual franchise, the franchisee is granted the right to operate a single unit in a single area using the total concept of the franchisor.

- **Affiliate or conversion franchises.** Affiliate or conversion franchises are primarily used by a group of independent entrepreneurs within a very fragmented industry in order to produce more visibility by combining their resources. They do this by having each business affiliate with all the others under one name to create a franchise network. Under this system, the companies are able to pool their purchasing power, advertising clout, and marketing abilities to capture a greater share of the market. The affiliate companies are not legally bound to use the banner name of the franchise, which doesn't have to be a trademark or brand name. Many affiliates will, in fact, use the franchise name as well as their own, as is the case with Century 21.

The variety and the scope of franchising today are such that anyone planning on opening a business dominated by franchising or characterized by aggressive franchisor advertising would do well to consider joining them rather than beating them. Unless you bring to the business table a good deal of knowledge, expertise, and marketing judgment, you may be getting yourself into trouble by trying to compete with the big guns.

PROS AND CONS

There are a number of advantages and disadvantages to buying a franchise.

Advantages

A franchise offers the following advantages to the buyer:

- **Reduction of risk of failure.** You're buying a business concept where most of the problems have already been worked out by someone else. According to a survey by Arthur Andersen,* almost 97 percent of units owned by franchisees are still in business after five years.
- **Turnkey operation.** In many cases, these operations are absolutely turnkey. You have a trademark that has been registered, patents that have already been filed, and certain design concepts. These are all part of the total package, which includes many other things, such as a proven system of operation and identity (people will recognize the name of your business because they've seen it somewhere else before). The turnkey business is a big advantage for people who don't know what equipment to buy, how much of it to buy, how much space they need to get started in the business, how much inventory they should have, and what kind of items sell in a given area.
- **Standardized products and systems.** There is already an established product line and predeveloped system that, for the most part, take the guesswork out of ordering and administrative procedures.
- **Financial and accounting systems.** Some of these benefits are inventory control forms; hourly cash register readings; profit and loss statement forms and formats. In addition, there are regular reviews of financial and accounting statements on a monthly basis. You are using a standardized system and franchisors can monitor what you are doing even from thousands of miles away.
- **Collective buying power.** This is an increasingly greater advantage because today you have to compete with national chains, conglomerates, buying consortiums, and other large franchises. The small-business person who purchases in small quantities can't compete with their buying

* *1991 Franchisee Owners Survey* (Arthur Andersen, 1991).

power. When you become a franchisee, you have the collective buying power of the entire franchise system.

- **Supervision and consulting.** Most franchisors will offer you ongoing advice, provide updated training, and in many cases be available for emergency problem solving. This means that when you open the doors initially, there'll be someone there to help you open your unit, hire your initial workforce, train those people, and help on a regular basis as problems develop.

- **National and local advertising programs.** You've seen what the big franchisors, like McDonald's, Kentucky Fried Chicken, and the large automotive companies, have been able to accomplish through their advertising. The type of advertising will vary depending on the franchisor and its size and agreement with the franchisee. The franchisee will often have an advertising percentage of gross in addition to the royalty agreement.

- **Point-of-sale advertising.** Things like mobiles hanging from the ceiling, posters, and so on are quite expensive to develop, but they are very helpful in creating that extra point-of-sale impetus for buyers. Sophisticated advertising materials, provided for you by the franchisor, give you a much better image and identity.

- **Uniform packaging.** The franchisor has worked out the best size and type of package. For instance, a food product may need special treatment to resist moisture or to retain heat. As a franchisee, you can take advantage of the protective packaging already developed by the franchisor.

- **Ongoing research and development.** Most franchisors are constantly working on new products, new variations on current products, new ideas, and new systems. They're experimenting. They're doing things that, as an independent businessperson, you can't afford to do yourself. They experiment in their own research and development laboratories, and you are the recipient of their work.

- **Financial assistance.** In some cases, the franchisor will actually finance part of your initial franchise, whether it is equipment, leasehold improvements, or land. At the very least, most franchisors provide some sort of assistance so that you can get in with as little cash as possible. They know that one of the keys to getting good franchisees is to provide some form of financing.

- **Site selection.** What makes a good site for a service station may not make a good site for a restaurant, or for a retail store. Certain kinds of businesses belong in shopping centers, but it's difficult to get into an established shopping mall unless you have the credibility of a successful franchise. The franchisor has already addressed these problems and knows exactly what kind of site is most appropriate for the business. A franchisor can help select a suitable location that will increase your likelihood of success.

- **Operations manual.** You will refer to the operating manual during your own training and when training employees. Since one of the biggest challenges in business is hiring and training people, and one of the major weaknesses is breakdown in training, the operating manual will be a very handy tool.

- **Sales and marketing assistance.** The franchisor will show you the techniques that have made the business successful and that you will utilize in developing your own business. There is a certain way to present a product to the customer. Franchisors will help you by sharing their sales techniques.
- **Planning and forecasting.** It's very important to know what to expect in terms of sales, activity, stock, personnel, and training. Also, it's important to forecast income so that you can determine cash needs in advance.
- **Less capital.** There's no guesswork about the equipment you need. You don't buy any more than you need, or any less. You'll also get better prices on the equipment in most cases because the franchisor, through its buying power, is able to get you equipment for less money. And the franchisor's financing may enable you to buy equipment by amortizing it on a long-term basis rather than by using your initial capital.

Drawbacks

Even with all these advantages, however, there are drawbacks to buying a franchise:

- **Loss of control.** It isn't your name or concept that you'll be promoting through your business. You're subject to guidelines set forth by the franchisor, so in essence you are more of a manager than your own boss.
- **High cost.** Franchises are expensive to purchase, and usually you must pay the franchisor ongoing royalty fees, often 2 to 6 percent a month. Generally, while it will cost less in upfront capital to start a franchise, in the long run the total purchase price will usually be much higher than for an independent operation. The royalty fee, combined with debt service on any financing, may put a drain on the cash flow of the business.
- **A binding contract.** You must sign an agreement with the franchisor that binds you to detailed guidelines on how the franchise will be operated, what types of fees you'll pay, and so on. These agreements tend to be quite restrictive, and if you encounter any problems with the franchisor, remember that you are legally bound by your contract to adhere to its operational guidelines.
- **The franchisor's problems are also your problems.** If the franchisor hits hard times, you'll most likely feel them as well. You are inevitably tied to the franchisor, not only by contract, but by concept, name, product, and services sold.

Franchisee Obligations

In terms of capital investment, your franchise fee will be determined by the profitability of the business. Most companies have a scale of franchise fees ranging anywhere from $4,000 to $20,000 and, in some cases, up to $50,000. In addition to this front-end franchise fee—the one-time charge that a franchisor assesses you for the privilege of using the business concept, attending the training program, and learning the entire business—there will also be a royalty fee.

Some of the other costs associated with a franchise include:

- **Facility/location.** In some cases, you may also have to buy land or a building, or you may have to rent a building. If you rent a building, you will be responsible for not only the monthly lease but the one-time security deposit as well. In addition, you will have to pay for leasehold improvements. In some cases, the owner of the building will put these in and factor it into your rental, giving you an additional charge of $50 to $100. The franchisor might provide you with an allowance for leasehold improvements that runs in the neighborhood of $5,000 to $30,000 for your average franchise. Most franchisors will tell you what their estimated leasehold improvements will be.
- **Equipment.** Different types of businesses will have their own minimum equipment requirements. Long-term payments will be available for most equipment purchases. Banks generally are willing to provide loans for equipment because it also acts as collateral.
- **Signs.** Outside signs can be very expensive for the owner of a small business. Most franchisors have developed a sign package that the franchisee is obligated to purchase.
- **Opening inventory.** This will usually involve at least a two-week supply, unless you're in a business that requires a much more complicated inventory. Most franchisors will tell you what their opening inventory requirements are.
- **Working capital.** For rent, you may be required to deposit funds to cover the first month and last month as well as security. You'll also have to pay a deposit to the electric, gas, and telephone companies prior to receiving service. You'll need some working capital and money in the cash drawer to make change. You'll need money to pay your employees. You'll need money just to operate until there is a cash flow. If you're buying a franchise that relies on charge accounts, then you're going to have to allow yourself some additional capital before the bills are paid by the customers and returned to you.
- **Advertising fees.** There is usually a fee for advertising on either a regional or national basis. Most larger franchisors require their franchisees to pay a certain amount into a national fund used to advance the concept. For example, McDonald's advertising fund approaches $100 million a year, paid by the franchisor and individual franchisees. The benefits are quite substantial in terms of the visibility that you get with this type of advertising.

Usually, you can't negotiate the franchise agreement. It will impose certain conditions, restrictions, and standards on you that you will have to follow. You may not agree with its standards, but under the franchise agreement you will have to operate that way. In most cases, a franchise agreement describes a step-by-step operations procedure and gives the franchisor the option to make changes as desired.

If you have a lot of initiative and like to do a lot of things on your own, you may find that the agreement restricts you. In your own independent business, you might have alternatives that aren't available in a franchised business.

FRANCHISING LAWS

Since the early 1960s, when franchising first took off in the marketplace, there have been ample opportunities for the unwary to be misled. It is important to note that the vast majority of franchisors are legitimate and sincerely want their franchisees to succeed. But as in any situation involving big money, con artists are attracted to the franchising and business opportunity field—in large part because of the gullibility of buyers who lack business experience and are easy targets.

Although in the minority, these unscrupulous people do exist. In response, federal and state authorities have passed a body of disclosure regulations and laws designed to protect the would-be entrepreneur from financial disaster and provide recourse in the legal system. The Federal Trade Commission's (FTC) Franchising and Business Opportunity Ventures Trade Regulation Rules and Subsequent Guidelines operate nationally. In fact, toward the end of 1993, the FTC unanimously voted to approve new Uniform Franchise Offering Circular (UFOC) guidelines proposed by the North American Securities Administrators Association (NASAA). In addition, at the time of this writing, at least 15 states are considered registration states and have disclosure laws. There are also 19 states debating laws regulating the relationship between franchisors and franchisees.

It is vital that potential buyers be aware of the consumer protection afforded by these disclosure laws and regulations when evaluating a franchisor's information the claims of a salesperson or broker and the rights available to a buyer who believes he or she has been ripped off.

The FTC Rule

An important protection for the person planning to buy a franchise is the FTC's franchise rule, put into effect October 21, 1979. The rule requires covered franchisors to supply a full disclosure of information a prospective franchisee needs to make a rational decision about whether or not to invest. This disclosure must take place at the first personal contact where the subject of buying a franchise is discussed. This means a franchisor, franchise broker, or anyone else representing franchises for sale has to present a disclosure document, similar to a prospectus for stock offerings, containing extensive information about the franchise.

This material must be provided at least 10 business days *prior* to signing any contract with the franchisor or paying it consideration. This is a "cooling-off" period so you don't jump in feet first without carefully reviewing and considering what you are doing.

Furthermore, you must be provided with completed contracts covering all material points at least 5 days prior to the actual date of execution of the documents. This provides another cooling-off period and the chance to have an attorney review the contracts prior to execution.

If a franchisor does not provide a disclosure document containing accurate information, or if a salesperson makes outlandish claims that are inconsistent with that document, the franchisor could be liable for a $10,000 fine per violation plus damages, if any.

The same applies if a franchisor does not provide you with contracts at the proper time or fails to refund deposits, such as a down payment that is defined as refundable in the disclosure document. An FTC disclosure rule covers the first meeting with a franchisor. FTC Rule 436.1 states that, ". . . it is an unfair or deceptive act or practice within the meaning of Section 5 of (the FTC Act) for any franchisor or franchise broker: (a) to fail to furnish any prospective franchisee with the following information accurately, clearly, and concisely stated in a legibly written document at the earlier of the "time for making of disclosures" or the first "personal meeting." These are unfair and deceptive trade practices under the Federal Trade Commission Act, Section 5.

State Franchising Laws

The FTC does not require franchisors to register with it or any other government agency. However, as mentioned, several states do have registration rules requiring franchise sellers to register as you would register a security offering as an investment.

Some of these state laws, which are not done away with by the new FTC rules, are tougher than others, but most have adopted the UFOC guidelines for their disclosure requirements. As mentioned, the FTC recently approved new UFOC guidelines to be phased in starting January 1, 1994. Under these new UFOC guidelines, the franchisor will have to disclose more information regarding the history of the parent company and any affiliates. The guidelines will also specify that a franchisor disclose more information regarding markups on products supplied to franchisees as well as any legal settlements involving displeased franchisees. At the time of this writing, the majority of the 15 registration states had adopted the new UFOC guidelines. The FTC says that six months after the last state approves the guidelines, the new UFOC will [become mandatory].

It would be a mistake, however, to assume that simply because a franchise is registered with a state or provides some type of full disclosure document that you as a consumer are going to be protected from the possibility of failure or rip-off. The only thing that a state reviewing agency can do is assure that the franchisor has responded and filed the necessary documents. In fact, state and federal authorities don't have the time or personnel to check information included in the documents. The only time they can act is if a consumer comes to them with information showing that the offering was dishonest. That's why an independent investigation by the would-be entrepreneur is so vital.

If You've Been "Had"

We cannot stress enough the value of a thorough investigation without pressure from the franchisor or business opportunity seller, prior to investing in any venture of this type. The disclosure documents outlined here are a starting point. But what happens if you still get taken?

The most important thing you can do is to react. Almost invariably, authorities cannot get people to admit openly that they have been taken. This ties the hands of consumer protection agencies and law enforcement authorities who need evidence to bring perpetrators to justice. This is particularly true of business opportunity sellers peddling such opportunities as worm farming and "work-at-home" schemes. But there have been instances of fraudulent franchise schemes, too.

If you have reason to believe that acts of misrepresentation or fraud have taken place surrounding a franchise or business opportunity seller, seek the help of the FTC, consumer protection agencies, your district attorney, or state attorney general—if only to prevent the same thing from happening to another person somewhere else in the country.

SELECTING A FRANCHISE

Where do you begin your search for a franchise that will be right for you? Franchising has become a huge business, not only in the United States but internationally as well, and there are many different franchises from which to choose. For almost every business concept, there is a franchise out there waiting for you. In recent years, there has been a proliferation of low-investment franchises that appeal to the budget-minded entrepreneur. These types of franchises usually have start-up investments of anywhere between $5,000 and $20,000 and include opportunities from auto checkup services and direct-mail advertising to house-sitting services and video photography.

In fact, the hardest part of buying a franchise may be selecting one. Once you've gathered some research, it's a fairly simple task to analyze a franchise and make a decision. But selecting one that will be of interest to you and meet all your criteria is a hard task. First of all, you need to know yourself. Refer to Chapter 1 and thoroughly evaluate yourself to identify your strengths and weaknesses on both a personal and a professional level so you can determine what type of business you would be happy owning. After you've listed all your goals and objectives, the next thing you have to do is investigate your options. What type of franchise on the market will help you fulfill those objectives? Which franchise concepts and categories are currently growing at a healthy rate?

In analyzing your options, you want to determine what's hot and what's not. You can accomplish this by keeping an eye on the economy and subscribing to several annuals and periodicals that will help you pinpoint franchising areas that are currently growing. *Entrepreneur Magazine* publishes two annual issues that will be invaluable resources in your search. One is the annual "Franchise 500" issue that hits the newsstand every January. The "Franchise 500" ranks over 500 franchises, providing contact addresses, capitalization requirements, franchise fees, experience requirements, strength of the franchise in number of units, and any royalties. The second is the "Franchise Yearbook," which is a compilation of all existing franchises. It lists contact names and addresses, unit strength, capitalization requirements, franchise fees, experience requirements, and any royalties, and is published in the fall. In addition to these two resources, the IFA is another good source of information.

Analyzing the Franchise

Once you've selected a franchise, the next step is to analyze it thoroughly to determine whether it is really worth buying. Much of the information you'll need to gather in order to analyze a franchise will be acquired through the following:

- Interviews with the franchisor.
- Interviews with existing franchisees.
- Examination of the Uniform Franchise Offering Circular (UFOC).
- Examination of the franchise agreement.
- Examination of the audited financial statements.
- An earnings-claim statement or sample unit income (profit and loss) statement.
- Trade-area surveys.
- Organizational chart.
- List of current franchisees.
- Newspaper or magazine articles about the franchise.
- A list of the current assets and liabilities.

Through this research, you want to find out the following:

1. **Are both the franchisor and the current franchisees profitable?** What is the ability of the franchisor to stay in business? After all, if the franchisor is not making a profit, there probably won't be any help later on down the line when you have problems.
2. **How well-organized is the franchise?** You don't have to know anything specific about the business to know whether or not a franchise is well

organized. If you go into a franchise outlet or the franchisor's company stores and see that they aren't well organized and don't seem to know what they're doing, then the business is not worth buying.

3. **Does it have national adaptability?** You want a franchise that will grow nationally so that it will increase your business locally.

4. **Does it have good public acceptance?** While it's good to have a certain amount of uniqueness, you don't want to be in a business that's so radical you must risk your entire life savings on whether or not people will accept that idea or concept. Many times, you can feel that you are on the crest of a wave of a new concept, and you see that it's taking hold everywhere. But if the concept is not tried and proven, be very cautious.

5. **What is its point of difference or unique selling proposition?** You won't have much success if you try to open just another version of many existing businesses. There has to be something different about the franchise. A franchisor who has some point of difference over other businesses is a much better buy, because that point will set you off from other people.

6. **How good are the financial controls of the business?** You want the franchise to be backed by a franchisor with strong financial management ability so you can determine exactly what the financial health of the franchise is at both the corporate and unit level.

7. **Is the franchise credible?** The franchise should have a good track record. That doesn't mean it has to have been in business for 10 years, but there should be enough of an operating history to show that this is a viable concept. This includes a good credit rating. If the franchise is in financial trouble, it will show in the credit rating.

8. **What kind of exposure has the franchise received and what has been the public's reaction?** Find out if the business has had any write-ups in papers, and determine what the public's opinion of it is. You can find this out in trade journals.

9. **Are the cash requirements reasonable?** If you're getting into a business that promises a $20,000-a-year return to you as the owner/operator, it shouldn't have a $200,000 investment requirement. The investment should be in proportion to the kind of return that you will get as the owner/operator.

10. **Does the franchisor show integrity and commitment?** This is very important. If the franchisor is willing to take your money without checking you out, that's a sign of trouble. The more particular a franchisor is, the more confident you can feel that the other people in the system are going to be good people as well.

11. **Does the franchisor have a monitoring system?** This will allow you to know what your problems are and how you're doing so you deal with them more effectively.

12. **Which goods are proprietary and must be purchased from the franchisor?** Keep in mind that the franchisor generates profit by the sale of proprietary stock at a markup from the wholesale or manufactured cost.

Determine which items are proprietary and must be purchased through the franchisor, and which ones aren't and can be acquired through outside vendors at a lower cost.

13. **What is the success ratio in the industry?** If eight out of every 10 businesses started in this industry fail, that's not a very high success ratio. Although franchises have a considerably low failure rate, they're not immune to bankruptcy.

Don't be shy about asking for the required materials from the franchisor. After all, the company will be checking you out just as completely. If they aren't, that should sound a warning bell inside you. Another warning sign is a request by the franchisor for you to sign a disclaimer stating you haven't relied on any representations not contained in the written agreement. Such a requirement could indicate the franchisor doesn't want to be held responsible for claims made by the company's sales representatives. The franchisor could also be in bad financial trouble and willing to sell a franchise to anyone who comes along to produce a better cash flow. Or the company may not be very well managed, and this could lead to problems in the future. Either way, a complete analysis will reveal any and all problems.

THE UNIFORM FRANCHISE OFFERING CIRCULAR (UFOC)

After you've contacted the franchisor and filled out all its personal and financial questionnaires to determine whether you fit the profile of "their kind" of franchisee, you'll receive two documents in the mail. One will be the UFOC and the other will be the franchise agreement. State and federal laws require that the franchisor give you these documents at least 10 days before taking your deposit and signing you on as a franchisee. This UFOC contains 23 items of information about the franchise. Keep in mind, however, that the UFOC is a starting point. To protect yourself, thoroughly investigate the information in the UFOC. Before ever sitting down with the franchisor or any current franchisees, you should examine the information in these documents carefully, preferably with legal and financial counseling. Don't allow yourself a false sense of comfort because the documents appear to comply with the Federal Trade Commission rules and/or various state filing requirements. Most of those regulations only require the franchisor to make complete and full disclosure of various categories of information the law requires in the document. So long as the disclosure is made in the proper manner, the franchisor can draft the terms and conditions of its franchise and its obligations to you as a franchisee in almost any manner it wishes.

Too many franchisees thumb through the UFOC and franchise agreement, read parts, sign it, and return it to the franchisor. This is the mark of a very naive businessperson. They accept whatever the franchisor hands them, and if they run into problems later on in points of the franchise agreement they either didn't understand or didn't know were present, they have only themselves to blame. Read the UFOC and franchise agreements carefully, then check and double-check these disclosures.

The first section you'll encounter in the UFOC is a brief history of the franchise. The history should document who founded the company, when it legally began doing business, incorporation dates if any, and when it first started franchising. This data lets you know what kind of expertise and experience the franchisor has to offer. A franchisor who has only been in business for a few years and began franchising a year after start-up doesn't have a lot of experience in the business.

The next section you'll come across discusses franchise fees and royalties. The front-end franchise fee and royalties are fully disclosed. The continual royalty (usually monthly) may run up to 15 percent, and an additional advertising royalty may be 5 percent or more. The front-end franchise fee may be $1,000 to $300,000 or more. It usually does not include the costs involved in actually starting the business, such as inventory, equipment, facility, and leases. These costs are going to become burdensome if the business does not do as well as projected. And how will you feel about paying them three or four years down the line when you have learned the business and believe you no longer need the franchise?

Look carefully to determine if another fee is payable when the franchise is sold or when the initial period expires and you exercise your option for an additional period (if such an option exists). Some franchisors require that at the end of the initial period you have to execute a new franchise agreement containing all the then-current charges, including any changes in the royalty fee.

Next, you'll come across a section that contains a brief summary of the officers, directors, and other active executives. You may find that their experience is outstanding or lacking. You may also find that some have present or past ties with suppliers or vendors from whom you will have to purchase your supplies or inventory. Such tie-ins may indicate that those individuals are making additional profits from the franchisee beyond those secured from royalties and fees.

The UFOC will also include a brief description of any major civil, criminal, or bankruptcy actions that the officers and executives have been involved in or that the franchise company is a party to. Lawsuits are common today, and the fact that someone has been sued or has filed suit does not necessarily indicate problems. However, if the lawsuits involve problems with franchisees or vendors, or if they are numerous, you should investigate further to determine the stability and integrity of the franchisor.

One UFOC showed that in the past several years there had been five lawsuits between the franchisor and its franchisees concerning various matters. And there were only 40 franchisees. If you find such a high incidence of poor franchisor-franchisee relations, you should hesitate before becoming involved.

The terms of the franchise agreement are also outlined in the UFOC. This is one of the most crucial parts of the UFOC, and too often it is overlooked.

Many franchisors offer initial terms of 5 to 10 years with options to renew for additional periods. However, it is not uncommon to encounter agreements for 5- to 10-year terms with no option for renewal. That means that when the initial term expires, the franchisor may terminate the franchise and open his own company store, or charge the franchisee a large fee to continue. If the franchise agreement does not give you an option to renew, you have no protection and could lose all the goodwill you built up during the period you operated the business.

Franchisors are also required to list an approximation of the initial costs of starting the franchise in addition to the franchise fees. Those costs usually include equipment, inventory, operating capital, and insurance. These costs are estimates and may actually be over- or understated. In fact, many franchise litigation specialists point out that franchisors show zero working capital or an unrealistically low figure. If there is a working capital figure located in Item 7 of the UFOC, ask if it includes operating expenses for the business until it is fully self-supporting, including an owner's draw or salary, as well as living expenses. When interviewing other franchisees, you should ask them what they consider sufficient working capital for the first year of operation. Most importantly, have your own accountant help you put together your own estimates.

Although some franchisors will supply you with projections of the sales and expenses of a new franchise location, most won't. This area is heavily regulated by the FTC to prevent franchisors from making "unfounded claims." As mentioned, some franchisors will provide projections, and more are beginning to provide them. This shift in philosophy is due to regulatory changes in the late 1980s, which provided guidelines for franchisors on how to present earnings information.

Because financial projections for a new franchise location are generally not provided, ask existing franchisees about the financial performance of their business. This is an essential step that we'll talk about later in this chapter. You may also want to consider purchasing an existing and operating franchise. Although the price may be higher, you have the security of knowing the historical sales and expenses of that business.

There is always a large section of the UFOC that lists the many reasons a franchisor may terminate a franchise before its normal term expires. Also, the UFOC often states that the franchisee cannot terminate the franchise for any reason. Some of the reasons franchisors usually provide for terminating a franchise include poor condition of the location, failure to pay royalties in a timely manner, failure to supply an account, and excess customer complaints.

If you are a good and profitable franchisee, the franchisor will not use these clauses to end its relationship with you. However, if the franchisor thinks it can operate the location better than you can, or has a more desirable applicant for the location, it may use one of those reasons to attempt to terminate you. Therefore, you must be careful to comply with all conditions that, if not met, permit termination.

Regardless of the UFOC provisions permitting termination, some states (California is one) have strong laws that can make it difficult for the franchisor to terminate a franchise early. Much of the litigation between franchisors and franchisees involves attempts on the part of franchisors to terminate franchisees' licenses prematurely.

A well-known example is the case of General Aviation, a franchisee of Cessna Aircraft Company. General Aviation was one of the top two best-selling Cessna dealers in the world and had never received a customer complaint. Yet, when General Aviation's contract expired in 1984, it was not approved for renewal. They were in effect, terminated. General Aviation filed suit against Cessna and in 1993, the Sixth Circuit Court of Appeals held that "a franchisor cannot discriminate between franchisees—renewing one while refusing to renew another who has a similar record or performance."

Never assume that purchasing a franchise will give you an exclusive, protected territory. That is not necessarily true of all franchises. Many UFOCs state that you do not receive an exclusive territory but that it is the "policy of the franchisor" not to locate another franchise within three miles. Of course, "policies" do change! The UFOC may also say that if the franchisor decides to open another location in your area, you have the right of first refusal to purchase the new location. Another common provision allows you exclusivity in an area only if your sales are maintained at a certain predetermined level. See the "Franchising" chapter for a sample UFOC outline.

If you are purchasing a retail-product or food franchise, often the agreement will provide that you must purchase your goods from approved suppliers and that you can only carry goods that are previously approved by the franchisor. One clothing store franchisor requires that all goods sold by their franchisees contain the label of the franchisor. Such a policy greatly restricts the lines you can carry and the sources from which you can purchase your inventory, reducing the effectiveness of controlling costs through competitive sourcing.

Read carefully the sections outlining the franchisor's responsibilities to you. Usually those obligations include providing you with a training manual, picking a suitable location, training you and/or an employee, helping or attending the grand opening, and offering some sort of continuing assistance with advertising and managing the store. In addition, you usually have the right to use certain trademarked symbols and names for the term of the franchise.

The UFOC usually includes only a general description of the duties the franchisor has to the franchisee. Therefore, before signing on the line, ask to see the manual, learn more about the training, and meet the franchisor's personnel who are going to assist you. That investigation may prove to be of substantially more value than reading the dry text of the UFOC.

The Financial Statements

One of the UFOC's strengths is that it delivers three years of audited financial information about the franchisor. In Item 21 of the offering circular, it states that the franchisor should include the balance sheet for the most recent fiscal year and an income statement (as well as changes in financial position for the most recent three years). These financial statements are audited reports prepared by a certified public accountant. Subsidiaries are allowed to use a parent's financial information, but only if the parent corporation will guarantee the obligations of the subsidiary franchisor.

The sample pro forma operating statement provides a forecast of projected sales and expenses that might be incurred by a franchisee in the geographic zone where the unit might be located. Very few franchisors provide this information or make any earnings claim. In part, this is because, according to the Federal Trade Commission, such claims must be substantiated by back-up data.

Any earnings claimed by the franchisor must satisfy rigid FTC criteria. They must now be based on fact, not mere hype, and the franchisor must have substantiating material on file. The claim must also be geographically relevant to your area.

Earnings claims must represent what the average franchisee can achieve, not what one unit made in the program. They can never guarantee that any franchise will achieve a stated level of performance. "Geographically relevant" means that data from nearby franchisees can be used—or data from franchisees in an area similar to yours from a demographic, socioeconomic, or location standpoint.

The sample pro forma will be accompanied by the following caution label required by the FTC:

> These figures are only estimates of what we think you may earn. There is no assurance you'll do as well. If you rely on our figures, you must accept the risk of not doing as well.

Although many franchisors are reluctant to provide earnings projections, insist on seeing one. You'll need a realistic forecast that states what your income and expenses might be. Take caution to heart also. Don't simply rely on these figures as an accurate basis for projected income and expenses. Cross-check the data as much as possible. When interviewing other franchisees, ask them what their income and expenses are. In addition, talk to industry associations and independents involved in the type of business you will be purchasing.

The Franchisee List

Along with the UFOC and financial statement, you'll also receive a list of current franchise operations. This list can be an invaluable resource. Plan to contact as many of those locations as possible and talk with the owners. Some will not want to tell you much, but others will pour their hearts out—telling you more than you ever wanted to know about their businesses. In addition, just visiting those stores will give you a clear picture of how successful and well received they have been. Some franchisees may even reveal their income and expenses, which will allow you to verify your projections.

THE FRANCHISE AGREEMENT

The franchise agreement is the foundation on which your franchise is built. The agreement gives both parties a clear understanding of the basis on which they are going to continue to operate. It should ensure uniformity to protect the franchisee as well as the franchisor. Remember, your business is only as good as that same business down the street or in the next town. If people have a bad experience with your company somewhere else, the odds are they're not going to want to do business with you either.

Uniformity, which is ensured by the franchise agreement, is one of the standards of operation. If you do not operate your business with uniformity, you are going to be a detriment to the system. And uniformity is one of the things you're paying for the ability to have a franchise just like everybody else's. There's an obligation on your part to sustain this uniformity. It establishes standards of operation, including what quality products you are going to use and what quality services you must provide. It eliminates future problems and has a deterrent value. A lot of problems can be avoided by knowing that a certain activity would be a violation of the franchise agreement. The company won't try to take a particular action against you if it knows that it's a violation of the agreement. By the same token, you will not try to do something that you know is a violation.

The franchise agreement provides for remedies in the event of defaults. It outlines what will happen if you do something wrong, including the steps and notices the company must give you. After the company gives you this notice, how much time do you have and why? If you don't agree with the demands, what recourse do you have? The franchise agreement provides for all of this.

What should the franchise agreement include? It states that you are a part of this franchise and have a certain fixed fee to pay as part of the consideration. It has location provisions. The company will have the right to approve sites. If the company desires, it will have the right to go on a direct lease. In some instances, your franchise agreement might even be tied to a lease directly. The company would dictate the plans and specifications of the general location and would make sure that your equipment conforms to company specifications.

By the same token, the company has the responsibility to assist you in site and equipment selection and in the general layout of your business, so that you can have every opportunity to succeed. That's part of the franchisor's obligation and is so stated in most franchise agreements. The agreement will have a section covering the use of the proprietary market, and the use of the franchise name. Franchisors will provide that you may not contest their right to the use of that name. The agreement will also provide that you must notify the franchisor if somebody else is using the name of the franchisor in that area. The agreement will provide that you conform to the operating manual and use the products, systems, and supplies specified by the company.

Here we get into an area of trust. For example, a company cannot require you to buy a product that is available at a better price somewhere else. That is in violation of antitrust laws. These laws have become a great concern to franchisors, since some have gone out of business because of violating those laws. They have been sued by franchisees through the Federal Trade Commission regulations. Basically, a company can require you to use certain secret formulas that it feels are the essence of its product or concept. Franchisors can specify certain standards of quality. But they cannot force you to pay a higher price for something, or charge more than it's worth in the marketplace.

Franchisors can specify a certain product if they don't make a profit on it. For example, they can specify that you use a certain ingredient in the formulation of your product. If they require you to buy breading from them, for example, it must have a secret and legitimate ingredient to qualify under the antitrust laws.

Sign requirements are generally outlined in the franchise agreement in the proprietary market section, including what your use of the sign must be, may be, and may not be. There is usually a section that talks about what training and assistance you're going to get. The agreement will indicate that you must complete a training program, and that the company must give you assistance in starting out and in training you. Franchisors will indicate that they will provide you with an ongoing advisory service and promotional materials, bulletins, and marketing development products and techniques.

There will also be a section on advertising. Generally, franchisors will want to approve all advertising copy, materials, and packaging and promotional materials that you use to ensure that they are consistent with the concept. Companies may establish a national advertising fund to which you will have to contribute and of which you will be a beneficiary during any national advertising campaign. They may require you to spend a certain amount of your gross income on local advertising. All of this will be spelled out in the franchise agreement.

Franchisors will provide that you follow the operating manual, that it be kept confidential, that it is a property of the franchisor, and that you must adopt revisions to the manual. These will be made by the franchisor on an ongoing basis; companies are very concerned about this operating manual because it tells everything about their businesses. There will be sections on maintenance and repairs. They will want you to maintain the interior and exterior of the location. They will want to be able to force you to repair your unit 5 or 10 years from now so that you do not allow it to get run down. In some cases, franchisor provisions require the franchisee to construct additional buildings if the franchisor feels they are necessary to accommodate the business. Generally, these provisions have not been accepted very well by most states.

There will be accounting and records provisions in the agreement requiring you to keep certain records such as weekly sales reports, semimonthly sales reports, and monthly profit and loss sales reports. Franchisors will want to be able to inspect your records through their area supervisors or representatives to ascertain that you are correctly reporting the activity of your business, making sure that you are not understating your sales and thereby cheating them out of royalties. There will also be a section providing that you give them annual, audited statements by a certified public accountant with interim statements. There will be a section dealing with standards and quality that will establish uniformity. It will provide for purchases that conform to their specifications. In some cases, these sections are quite extensive, depending on the franchisor.

The more labor-intensive your operation, the more franchisors will insist on certain procedures. If you're handling a franchise that simply dispenses a premade product, there isn't as great a concern on the part of the franchisor, but in cases where a product is made on the premises, whether it be food or manufactured items, the quality control provisions will generally be substantial. This is for your benefit as a franchisee as much as it is for the franchisor.

The agreement will have a section that deals with modification of the system. Specifically, it will establish the right of the franchisor to modify the concept, but it will also prohibit you as a franchisee from any unauthorized modification of that system. In other words, franchisors want the system to be uniform, and don't want you to change anything without their approval. When they want a change, they want the power to say you must change the procedure. Pricing is a situation that gets back into the antitrust area. In that regard, the franchisor in some cases cannot dictate to you what prices you must charge.

The continuing services and royalty fee is a significant part of the franchise agreement. This establishes that you will be paying a royalty—an ongoing fee of a percentage of sales, or a fixed monthly or annual amount that will be remunerated to the franchisor for the continued use of the franchised concept. The franchisor will determine what kind of program is necessary, as well as what kind of support will be provided on an ongoing basis. The direct and indirect costs associated with those services are projected, and a percentage is established to cover those expenses.

The method in which the franchisor collects and assesses these fees is provided for in the franchise agreement. There will be insurance provisions to protect both you and the franchisor. The franchisor knows what kind of insurance and liability protection you need, as well as the requirements for the protection of the corporation. The agreement will generally establish the amount that will be required for protection, including workers' compensation, general liability, product liability, bodily injury, and property damage in accordance with established limits set by the franchisor.

There will be a section dealing with the terms. How long will your franchise agreement be in effect, and what are the options beyond that period of time? One of the most important bills regarding franchise agreements and the terms for which they are awarded is the Nikva bill, which deals with the renewal and termination of franchise agreements. It was created primarily to overcome abuses by franchisors. A franchisee would build a business, find that the term had expired, and the franchisor would not renew it without imposing unfair restrictions. These abuses by franchisors have been few and far between, but they do happen.

The term clauses are generally coordinated with the lease so that if you have a lease for 15 years, you will have a 15-year agreement. A long-term agreement assures the royalty to the franchisor for a longer period of time, and it gives the franchisee more security. The shorter term gives the franchisor the ability to adjust the royalty upward more quickly, and it eliminates undesirable franchisees. When their term expires, they simply are not renewed.

For a franchisee, the short term can also be an advantage. With the short term, you can get out of the agreement and not pay a royalty. On the other hand, you may want to hold the franchisor to the agreement for a longer period. This is something that you'll have to assess according to your interest in working for the particular franchisor.

There are generally covenant sections restricting a franchisee from copying or diverting business, hiring employees, or divulging secrets. These restrictive covenants are subject to state or antitrust laws. Some states will not allow restrictive covenant sections, while others will. Some antitrust laws prohibit certain restrictions of a person's ability to earn a living. Franchisors will indicate that you as a franchisee cannot simply open an identical business, using all the franchisor's systems and know-how and marketing tools and so on, without using the franchise name and paying a royalty.

A section in the franchise agreement will deal with termination and defaults—in other words, what constitutes the right of the franchisor to terminate you or to say that you're in default. If you become bankrupt, for example, that is usually a condition for terminating the franchise agreement. If the franchisor gives you notice to cure a certain defect, you will have a limited amount of time to comply.

The length of the notice will vary from state to state. In some states it's 10 days, in others it's 30 days. The federal law that is being proposed right now by the Federal Trade Commission will require considerably more time than that— 60 days and longer. The company must notify you that you are doing something wrong and that unless you cure that deficiency, it will not allow you to operate and your franchise will be terminated. For example, if your place is not clean and the company has notified you to clean it up but you do not, you could be terminated. You could be terminated for the following reasons:

1. You don't pay the royalties or the fees to the company.
2. You don't submit the reports or the financial data called for in the franchise agreement.
3. You vacate your premises or abandon your business.
4. You fail to comply with the franchise agreement in general.

According to the Nikva bill, both parties have certain rights and duties on expiration or termination, and they will be spelled out in a special section of your franchise agreement. Usually it will provide that on expiration or termination you must pay all the sums you owe the franchisor, cease using their name, and in some cases, give the franchisor the right to purchase the physical assets. There is often a provision that deals with the operation of the franchise if you are disabled or die. The franchisor then has the right to operate the business.

Usually there's a clause dealing with taxes and permits that requires the payment of any tax assessments, liens, equipment, or previous accounts. It will usually require that you be in full compliance with all federal, state, and local laws. This protects the franchisor as well as you. It will require that you obtain all permits, certificates, and licenses necessary to do business at that particular location. The agreement will provide that you are an independent contractor, that you're not an agent, partner, or employee of the franchisor, that you can't incur any liability for the franchisor, and that you bear the cost of defense of any claims. Generally, this section clarifies that any debts you incur are your own and not the franchisor's.

There is usually a nonwaiver provision that says if the franchisor does not enforce a certain clause in the franchise, that doesn't mean it isn't enforceable at a later date. There is usually a provision on receipt of payments on the same basis. If franchisors don't accept the payment from you, that doesn't mean that they don't have the right to come back and collect it later. There is also a notice provision that dictates the manner of notice, how much notice they have to give you, how it should be served, to whom, and where. Provisions for liability for breach, which involves payment or costs for attorneys' fees by the party in default are sometimes put into an agreement.

There's often a clause that says that each section of the agreement is severable or separate. If, for example, you go to court and the court finds that one section is not enforceable, the rest of the agreement is still in effect. However, there is usually a provision that the agreement can terminate if the parts found unenforceable affect the basic consideration of the agreement. Franchisors will usually retain the right to terminate the agreement. The agreement usually will say in what states the law is applicable, and franchisors will try to make it enforceable in their own state so that the contract that was originally developed is valid.

Franchise agreements have arbitration clauses wherever applicable. Some states won't allow this and won't recognize them, but they do provide a basis for settling disputes without having to go to litigation. These clauses sometimes provide for binding arbitration. Both the franchisor and franchisee provide an arbitrator; then these two pick a third arbitrator. The third arbitrator may do the arbitration, or maybe all three of them will. They listen to the issues, the company's side, and your side. With binding arbitration, whatever the arbitrators decide will dictate the final agreement.

The agreement will also define the term "franchisee" to include not only you, but any successors. There will be a caveat, which is a disclaimer, to any claims made. It indicates that you agree you are assuming certain risks, that the success of the business isn't guaranteed, and that the success of this business depends on your ability as a franchisee.

This section has covered the basic considerations that you'll find in most franchise agreements. Again, we cannot stress enough that you should have legal counsel examine all documents closely. Most franchises are very capital-intensive, and you want to protect that interest as much as you can.

INTERVIEWS: FRANCHISORS AND FRANCHISEES

Once you've received all the documents from the franchisor, you will enter a preliminary negotiation stage before you sign. This is the most critical period in your dealings with the franchisor. At this point in time, you'll meet a representative of the franchisor and conduct interviews with as many franchisees as possible to evaluate the franchise package. This provides an opportunity for both you and the franchisor to gain first impressions and determine whether negotiations will proceed any further.

The representative of the franchisor may be one of three people: the franchise owner/company president, an in-house salesperson, or a franchise broker (an outside salesperson retained by the franchisor to act as a representative). No matter which one of these people you meet, he or she will want to know more specific information about you.

The franchisor is going to want to know about your financial status, your experience, and your general background. As we've already mentioned, if the franchisor doesn't ask these questions or show any interest in your previous background, that should be a danger signal to you. When company representatives ask you questions about these topics, however, don't feel they are prying into your personal life. They aren't. They are just protecting their interests.

On the flip side of the coin, be prepared with questions of your own about the company. You might even want to have your attorney present or have an attorney highlight areas of the franchise agreement and UFOC that should be questioned. Don't leave until you've received all the information that you need. This could take anywhere from a few hours to all day. The primary goal here is to satisfy all your doubts so that you feel comfortable with the data supplied by the franchisor.

Through your meeting with the franchisor, you'll be discussing specific subjects that will affect your decision to purchase a franchise. Those subjects will be covered in a verbal and written form. Take notes and after the meeting, date those notes, detailing whom you received the information from, the person's title, and so on. Do this with any phone conversations you have with the franchisor as well. This will help you in the future should any problems develop.

During your interview, you really want to concentrate on the following key areas that will help you determine the strength of the franchise:

- Ask what the pretax net profits of existing operations are and compare this against the earnings statement or pro forma that the franchisor has already supplied you with.
- Find out specifically what is included in the training program, field assistance, store design, facility construction, site selection, and feasibility studies.

- How will the initial franchise fees and investment be segmented?
- Will any additional working capital be required after the initial fee and investment, and if so, how much?
- How will the franchisor arrange for the supply of product to the business? Ask to see a current price sheet.
- Ask the franchisor to detail exactly what the territorial restrictions and protections are.
- Find out how many franchises have been sold to investors in the state you will be operating in during the past 12 months, and how many have opened a franchised business in that time.
- Ask if the company has any plans for further expansion in the state. Has it identified any locations it plans to develop?
- If purchasing a current franchise, ask to see the operating books and records of the business for the past two years.
- What type of support will the franchisor provide once your franchise has opened its doors?
- Find out if any franchisees have been terminated. If some have, have the franchisor detail the reasons. Have any franchisees failed or gone bankrupt?
- What kind of financing is available from the franchisor, if any?
- Find out if any current lawsuits are pending against the franchisor. Have them elaborate on any past judgments.
- Find out how disputes between the franchisor and franchisees are settled.
- Will the franchisor assist in site selection? This assistance can be enormously helpful. Regardless of whether it does or does not, do your own demographic study so you are familiar with the profile of the audience within the market area.

Don't be afraid to ask questions. And don't be afraid that you'll appear foolish because, frankly, very few people understand the franchise agreement or the UFOC in full. Primarily, you're trying to pinpoint any problems that may exist in a franchise situation. Don't just settle on any franchise. That's an easy way out and very risky in terms of the capital you'll be investing. If for any reason you run across a franchisor that is reluctant to pass along a list of current franchisees, makes promises of earning a fortune on a limited amount of money invested, insists on deposits for holding a franchise unit, tries to convince you to sign before someone else does, or is full of empty rhetoric when answering your questions, then start heading for the door. These are franchisors who are probably trying to pull a fast one to get your money.

That's why you have to cross-check all the information supplied. Are the franchisor's claims backed by performance? Are the advertising claims applicable at the store level? Are the profitability claims justified? You can check this information by contacting as many franchisees as possible. As we've mentioned, some franchisees will be very supportive. After all, they were once in your shoes. However, some may not. Some people are just that way. They don't feel their business is any of yours. This could also be a danger signal. If a franchisee doesn't want to talk to you, that might be an indication that the franchise isn't doing nearly as well as expected.

Do all you can to convince franchisees to talk to you. Stress that the conversation will be kept confidential and be as candid as possible to establish a good rapport. Remember, franchisees aren't required to provide any information. The more amiable and upfront you are with them, the better your chances of obtaining information. However, if a franchisee continues to be uncooperative, just move on to the next person on your list. Someone else will surely talk to you.

You want to ask the franchisees questions that will let you know whether or not the franchisor has been upfront with you. These questions may include:

- Find out if the franchisees are happy with their investment, the support from the franchisor, and entry into the business.
- Ask franchisees if they would purchase a second franchise if it became available in their market area.
- Ask if they feel they were well-trained for the challenges of the business.
- Ask them what their income and expenses are and compare those against the sample pro forma provided by the franchisor. Find out if they have any cash-flow problems.
- What are sales patterns like? Are they seasonal? Ask them to describe the busy season.
- Find out what type of ongoing assistance they have received from the franchisor.
- Are their advertising fees reflected in the marketing support (for example, co-op advertising) received?
- Are the franchise and royalty fees fair and competitive with other franchises in the same industry?
- Is local market penetration in line with national figures?
- Were equipment, signage, logos, and so on, provided without charge or at an additional cost?
- What hidden costs, if any, have been incurred by franchisees?
- What degree of autonomy are franchisees allowed? How tightly regulated are they by the franchisor?
- Ask whether there is a franchise owner's association. Are there any disputes that are the subject of discussion among franchisees?
- What are the actual costs of the products, and are they competitive in the marketplace?
- Have they had any problems with product supply?
- Do they have any complaints about the franchisor?
- What were their initial start-up costs? What major hurdles did they experience during the first few months of start-up? How did they finance the business?
- Find out how long they've been a franchisee and if they will renew.
- Ask franchisees whether they have encountered clauses in the franchise agreement that have caused them problems.
- Find out how long their workdays are and whether they take vacations.

You'll gain a lot of invaluable information from the franchisees, but don't stop there. You should also check out all the bank references supplied by the franchisor to determine the solidity of its financial situation. Run a credit check on the company. Check out any references supplied by the franchisor. Call the Better Business Bureau to find out whether any complaints have been lodged against the company. Have Dun & Bradstreet deliver a status report on the firm through its subscriber service.

After you've completed a thorough evaluation of the franchisor, then you can make a truly informed decision and enter serious negotiations. Remember that you can negotiate items within the franchise agreement. That's why you've gone through a complete analysis of the company. When negotiating with the franchisor, make sure your attorney is present.

FINANCIAL REQUIREMENTS

The financing requirements are quite substantial in some businesses. As a franchisee, you will be pursuing different types of financing. For example, in a general business loan, you go to the bank and borrow money to get into business. The bank will want to know what collateral you have to offer in terms of your personal assets, and what assets of the business could be attached.

There are many sources of investment capital—loans, mortgages, equity conversions, venture capitalists, and even franchisors. Before approaching any lender, you need to determine your net worth. To do this, use a personal balance sheet to list both your assets (what you own) and liabilities (what you owe). Under assets, list all your holdings—cash on hand, checking accounts, savings accounts, real estate (current market value), automobiles (whether paid off or not), bonds, securities, insurance cash values, and other assets—then total them up. The second part of the balance sheet is liabilities. Follow the same steps. List your current bills, all your charges, your home mortgage, auto loans, finance company loans, and so on. Subtract your liabilities from your assets. See the personal balance sheet in the "Personal Evaluation" chapter.

Once you have worked up this sheet, take a good look at your credit rating. All potential lenders look for three common ingredients in a credit rating: stability, income, and track record.

Most lenders are interested in how long you've been at a certain job or lived in the same location, and whether you have a record of finishing what you start. If your past record doesn't show a history of stability, then be prepared with good explanations.

Not only is the amount of income you earn important, but so is your ability to live within that income. Some people earn $100,000 a year and still can't pay their debts, while others budget nicely on $20,000 a year. Most lending institutions look at your income and the way you live within that income for one very good reason. If you can't manage personal finances, the odds against managing business finances are good.

The third element lenders look for is your track record—how successful you've been in paying off past obligations. If you have a record of delinquent payments, repossessions, and so on, then you should get these squared away before asking for a loan. Incidentally, cleaning up these obligations is good training for running your own business since it takes discipline to be successful.

Most lenders will contact a credit bureau to look at your credit file. See the sample credit report in the "Credit Management" chapter. We suggest that you do the same thing before you try to borrow. Under the law, credit bureaus are required to give all the information they have on file about your credit history. Once you have this tool, you should correct any wrong information, or at least make sure your side of the story is on record. For instance, a 90-day delinquency would look bad. But if that 90-day delinquency was caused by being laid off or by illness, then that is taken into consideration. After you've determined your net worth and your credit rating, the final step to take before approaching lenders is putting together your business plan.

A well-thought out business plan will make the difference between having your loan application accepted or rejected. A complete business plan should always include an intimate, technical study of the business you plan to go into; accurate pro formas, projections, and cost analyses; estimates of working capital; an indication of your people skills; and a suitable marketing plan.

It should also include certified statements of your net worth and several credit references. One general rule of thumb is that the more sophisticated the people you're borrowing from, the more detailed your plan should be. Some pros even believe that the plan should have one page for every $1,000 you are seeking. A thorough discussion on forming your own business plan is included in Chapter 8.

When you're borrowing money, two types of sources are available to you: debt and equity. Debt loans simply mean that you pay the loan back over an agreed period of time, whereas equity loans mean that you're giving up a piece of your ownership instead of paying back the loan. The best advice we uncovered from the most successful operators in this field is not to give up equity in the business if at all possible. You're giving up a certain amount of proprietorship by running a franchise, so why give up any more?

The good news about debt financing for a franchise is that even though there are tighter banking regulations and the savings and loan debacle have made financing for start-up businesses more difficult, the odds of obtaining financing for a franchise are much greater than for an independent business, thanks largely to the franchisor's established track record. In fact, the Small Business Administration (SBA) often leans toward franchisees when considering loan applicants because their success rate is generally higher than that of independent small businesses.

Traditionally, the first place franchisees turn for financing is the franchisor. Almost all franchisors in the country provide debt financing only. Some carry the entire loan or a fraction thereof through their own finance company. We found fractions of 15 percent, 20 percent, 25 percent, all the way up to 75 percent of total debt burden. The franchisors we talked to emphasized that these figures are simply guidelines and not hard and fast rules.

In addition, the loans made by the franchisor can be structured a number of ways. Some offer loans based on simple interest, no principal, and a balloon payment five or 10 years down the road. Others offer loans with no payment due until after the first year. Instead of financing the entire start-up cost, franchisors may have financing plans for portions of the entire cost such as for equipment, the franchise fee, operational costs, or any combination thereof.

In addition to financing a portion of the start-up cost, the franchisor usually has arrangements with leasing companies to lease the franchisee the necessary equipment. This can be a significant area for financing since equipment often makes up between 25 and 75 percent of a franchise's total start-up costs.

If the franchise you're considering doesn't offer equipment leasing, look into nonfranchise, nonbank companies that specialize in equipment leasing for franchises. These types of financing companies will often provide asset-based lending to finance franchisees' furniture, equipment, signs and fixtures, and allow franchisees to purchase the equipment at the end of the lease. Keep in mind that you may lose some tax advantages under the current law if you lease that equipment. Remember that a business is franchised for two reasons: to expand the business and to raise capital. So if you have a reasonably good credit record and pass all the financial requirements, most franchisors will bend over backward to get you on their team.

Franchisors usually provide assistance with business plans, application help, and introduction to lending sources; in many cases, franchisors serve as guarantor of the loan.

After you have determined the extent of financing available from the franchisor, make a working list of all available sources of capital. Most sharp operators use the following sequence of contacts: friends and relatives, home mortgages, veterans' loans, bank loans, SBA loans, and finance companies. A complete discussion of finance sources can be found in Chapters 13 and 27.

Often, banks that aren't willing to work with you based on your financial profile become more amenable if you suggest working with an SBA loan guarantee, which protects loans up to 90 percent. Small businesses simply submit a loan application to the lender for initial review, and if the lender finds the application acceptable, it forwards the application and its credit analysis to the nearest SBA office. After SBA approval, the lender closes the loan and disburses the funds; the borrower makes loan payments to the lender. For more information on SBA loans, see Chapter 14.

Franchisors have also reported being approached by financial brokers—historically more interested in big deals—to put together large pools of money using SBA and private funds. These funds would be available to franchisees through the franchisors like a trust fund. Groups of small banks with funds to invest would contribute to the fund from all over the country.

Other options would be to take out a home equity line of credit or a second mortgage on your home. Be careful when utilizing this type of financing, however. The home equity line of credit and a second mortgage are secured by your home. If you can't repay the amount you finance using this source, you risk losing your home.

You can also use assets such as stocks, bonds, and mutual funds to secure a loan so long as they are not part of a qualified plan like an IRA profit-sharing plan. If you are over 59 and have a lot of money tied up in an IRA, however, you could use it for part of your financing requirements. Although you will have to pay taxes on the amount used, not to mention the loss of income from interest, it can be a good financing tool.

If you are under the age of 59 and your IRA is one of your largest assets, you still may be able to take advantage of this avenue without accruing the 10 percent penalty associated with early withdrawal. By taking Substantial Equal Periodic Payments spread over a minimum of five years, based on your life expectancy and a set of annuity tables published by the IRS, you can eliminate the 10 percent penalty, although the money is still taxable.

There are nearly infinite sources of financing available to help you launch the franchise of your dreams. However, operating a franchise without reserves and blinding yourself to the possibility of unexpected financial business problems can lead you to disaster. A good rule to remember: Never invest more than 75 percent of your cash reserves. If you have $10,000, invest $7,500. If you have $25,000, invest $18,750.

Most important, remember that the price of a franchise does not always reflect the actual cost of the business itself. Additional costs can include down payments on the land, building, equipment, fixtures, and signs, and can cover inventory, leasehold improvements, training, opening promotional costs, administrative costs, and even sales commissions.

Be sure you understand the requirements of your cash investment. You will need a "pillow" of working capital to properly guide the business through its ups and downs. If you do your homework thoroughly, and remember that financing a business is the most important sale you will ever make, then you will be head and shoulders above the competition.

RESOURCES

Associations

Franchise Consultants International Association, 5147 South Angela Road, Memphis, TN 38117, 901-761-3085

International Franchise Association, 1350 New York Avenue NW, Suite 900, Washington, DC 20005, 202-628-8000

Magazines

Continental Franchise Review, 9250 East Costilla Avenue, Suite 620, Englewood, CO 80112, 303-649-9910

Franchising World, 1350 New York Avenue NW, Suite 900, Washington, DC 20005-4700, 202-628-8000

Info Franchise Newsletter, 728 Center Street, P.O. Box 550, Lewiston, NY 14092-0550, 716-754-4669

Opportunity, 73 Spring Street, Suite 303, New York, NY 10012, 212-925-3180

Directories

Entrepreneur Magazine's Annual Business Opportunity 500 Survey Issue, P.O. Box 57050, Irvine, CA 92619-7050, 714-261-2325

Government Agencies

Federal Trade Commission Office, U.S. Federal Trade Commission, Sixth and Pennsylvania Avenue NW, Washington, DC 20580, 202-326-2222

12

Business Opportunities

Just what is a business opportunity? That question has plagued a great many people trying to decide whether to buy a current independent business, a franchise, or what we'll refer to in this text as a business opportunity. To allay the confusion, we'll offer a simple analogy. Think back to elementary school when your teacher was explaining the difference between a rectangle and a square. A square is also a rectangle, but a rectangle isn't necessarily a square. The same relationship exists between business opportunities, independent businesses for sale, and franchises. All franchises and independent businesses for sale are business opportunities, but not all business opportunities meet the requirements of being a franchise nor are they in the strictest sense of the word independent businesses for sale.

Business opportunities are difficult to define because the term means different things to different people. In California, for example, small businesses for sale—whether they're a liquor store, delicatessen, dry-cleaning operation, and so on—are all termed business opportunities, and individuals handling their purchase and sale must hold real estate licenses. If common shares are the interest being purchased in the business instead of assets and good will, then the agent selling the firm must also hold a securities license.

Making matters even more confusing, approximately 24 states have passed laws defining business opportunities and regulating their sales. Often these statutes are drafted so comprehensively that they include franchises as well. Not every state with a business opportunity law defines the term in the same manner. However, most of them use the following general criteria:

- A business opportunity involves the sale or lease of any product, service, equipment, and so on that will enable the purchaser-licensee to begin a business.

- The licenser or seller of a business opportunity declares that it will secure or assist the buyer in finding a suitable location or provide the product to the purchaser-licensee.
- The licenser-seller guarantees an income greater than or equal to the price the licensee-buyer pays for the product when it is resold and that there is a market present for the product or service.
- The initial fee paid to the seller to start the business opportunity must range between $300 and $1,000.
- The licenser-seller promises to buy back any product purchased by the licensee-buyer in the event it cannot be sold to the prospective customers of the business.
- Any products or services developed by the seller-licenser will be purchased by the licensee-buyer.
- The licenser-seller of the business opportunity will supply a sales or marketing program for the licensee-buyer that many times will include the use of a trade name or trademark.

The laws covering business opportunity ventures usually exclude the sale of an independent business by its owner. Rather, they are meant to cover the multiple sales of distributorships or businesses that do not meet the requirements of a franchise under the Federal Trade Commission (FTC) rule passed in October 1979. This act defines business-offerings in three formats:

1. Package franchises.
2. Product franchises.
3. Business opportunity ventures.

To be a business opportunity venture under the FTC rule, four elements must be present:

1. The individual who buys a business opportunity venture, often referred to as a licensee or franchisee, must distribute or sell goods or services supplied by the licenser or franchiser.
2. The licenser or franchiser must help secure a retail outlet or accounts for the goods and services the licensee is distributing or selling.
3. There must be a cash transaction between the two parties of at least $500 prior to or within six months after starting the business venture.
4. All terms and conditions of the relationship between the licenser and the licensee must be stated in writing.

You can readily see that business opportunities as defined by the FTC rule are quite different from the sale of an independent business by a real estate agent. When you're dealing with the sale of an independent business, there are no obligations of the buyer to the seller. Once the sales transaction is completed, the buyer can subscribe to any business operations system he or she prefers. No continued relationship is required by the seller.

Business opportunity ventures, like franchises, are businesses where the seller makes a commitment of continuing involvement with the buyer. The FTC describes the most common types of business opportunity ventures:

- **Distributorship.** Refers to an independent agent who has entered into an agreement to offer and sell the product of another but is not entitled to use the manufacturer's trade name as part of the agent's trade name. Depending on the agreement, the distributor may be limited to selling only that company's goods or may have the freedom to market several different product lines or services from various firms.

- **Rack jobber.** Involves the selling of another company's products through a distribution system of racks in a variety of stores that are serviced by the rack jobber. In a typical rack-jobbing business opportunity, the agent or buyer enters an agreement with the parent company to market their goods to various stores by means of strategically located store racks. Under the agreement, the parent company obtains a number of locations in which it places racks on a consignment basis. It is up to the agent to maintain the inventory, move the merchandise around to attract the customer, and do the bookkeeping. The agent presents the store manager with a copy of the inventory control sheet, which indicates how much merchandise was sold, and then the distributor is paid by the store or location that has the rack—less the store's commission.

- **Vending machine routes.** Very similar to rack jobbing. The investment is usually greater for this type of business opportunity venture since the businessperson must buy the machines as well as the merchandise being vended, but here the situation is reversed in terms of the pay procedure. The vending machine operator must pay the location owner a percentage based on sales. The big secret to any route deal is to get locations in high-foot-traffic areas and as close to one another as possible. If your locations are spread far apart, you waste time and traveling expense servicing them—and such expense can be the difference between profit and loss.

In addition to these three types of business opportunities, there are four other categories you should be aware of:

1. **Dealer.** Similar to a distributor, but whereas a distributor may sell to a number of dealers, a dealer will usually only sell to a retailer or the consumer.

2. **Trademark/product licensees.** Under this arrangement, the licensee obtains the right to use the seller's trade name as well as specific methods, equipment, technology, or products. Use of the trade name is purely optional.

3. **Network marketing.** A generic term that covers the realm of direct sales and multilevel marketing. As a network marketing agent, you sell products through your own network of friends, neighbors, coworkers, and so on. In some instances, you may gain additional commissions by recruiting other agents.

4. **Cooperatives.** Similar to a licensee arrangement in which an existing business, such as a hotel or hardware store, can affiliate with a larger network of similar businesses, often for the sole purpose of advertising and promoting through a common identity.

Any business offering falling under the FTC definition of a business opportunity venture must meet all franchise disclosure regulations. That means the seller has to supply the buyer with a prospectus or circular, and a copy of the agreement outlining the terms and conditions of the offering.

Some business opportunity ventures are exempt altogether. A common way for a business opportunity venture to exempt itself from the FTC rule is to take advantage of the *minimal investment* rule. For instance, many business opportunity ventures set their initial fee at less than $500, which technically places them outside the FTC restriction (although if consumer fraud is involved, the FTC will take action).

Other exemptions include *fractional franchises* in which an established distributor adds a franchised product line to its existing line of goods; *leased departments* where a retailer sells its goods from space rented from a larger retailer; *oral agreements; employer-employee and general partnership arrangements;* and *agricultural cooperatives* and *retailer-owned cooperatives.*

So what's the difference between a franchise and a business opportunity venture? As a general rule of thumb, a franchise receives more support from the parent company, gets to use its trademarked name, and is more stringently controlled by the franchiser. Business opportunities, on the other hand, don't receive as much support from the parent company, generally aren't offered the use of a trademarked name, and are independent of the parent company's operational guidelines.

There are numerous forms of business opportunity ventures. Some are even turnkey operations similar to a lot of package format franchises. These business opportunities provide everything you could possibly need to start a business. They help select site location, provide training, offer support for the licensee's marketing efforts, and supply a complete start-up inventory. Unlike a package format franchise, however, these types of business opportunity ventures aren't trademarked outlets for the parent company. The company's name, logo, and how it is legally operated is left solely to the licensee. Many times, the only binding requirement between the seller and buyer is that inventory be purchased solely through the parent company. All these stipulations are outlined in the disclosure statement and contract.

THE ADVANTAGES OF A BUSINESS OPPORTUNITY VENTURE

The days of exploitation are about over. As mentioned, the federal government passed disclosure laws regulating the sale of business opportunity ventures in 1979. A number of states quickly followed suit. In at least 24 states, a business opportunity has been defined by statute and is closely regulated by state agencies, often in a manner very similar to franchises. These laws are meant to protect unsophisticated purchasers from investing their funds in an opportunity after reading a puffed-up advertisement or listening to a slick sales pitch, without knowing all the facts about the business and the background of the seller. If you live in a state that regulates business opportunities and are buying one, you will have strong remedies in the event you don't get what you paid for. These strict laws have helped regulate an industry where some offerings were created only to exploit the buyer. Under these disclosure requirements, the buyer knows exactly what the offering covers and what the relationship will be with the parent company.

This protection has proven to be quite an advantage to the buyer. Other advantages of buying a business opportunity include:

- **A lower initial fee than that required for a franchise.** Although the number of low-investment franchises has increased, the fee to get into a business opportunity is still considerably less. The FTC requires a $500 minimum investment to be considered a business opportunity, but there are many that fall under this set fee, with most averaging around $2,000 to $3,000.

- **A proven system of operation or product.** Existing systems serve to maximize efficiency and returns and minimize problems. It is simply a matter of passing on experience, still the best teacher. Most people, whether they admit it or not, like having their hands held once in a while. During crises, the parent company can help the licensee over the bumps. Many people like this idea of safety in numbers.

- **Intensive training programs.** Any new business consumes a lot of time and money during the trial-and-error period. A good business opportunity venture can eliminate the majority of ineffective moves through an intensive training program.

- **Better financing options.** Many times, the parent company offering the business opportunity, because of its financial size, credit line, and contractual agreements, can arrange better financing than that which could be obtained by the individual. Financial leverage is an important consideration in any investment situation.

- **Professional advertising and promotion.** Most small independent businesspeople don't spend sufficient money on advertising. When they do, their efforts are often poorly conceived and inconsistent. Many business opportunity ventures supply the buyer with print advertising slicks, radio ads, and television storyboards to provide a better marketing effort. Some business opportunity ventures will even have a cooperative advertising agreement splitting the cost of print, radio, or television advertisements. This marketing help is very beneficial in large metropolitan areas where the cost of media is prohibitive to the one-shop owner.

- **Ongoing counseling.** Most business opportunity ventures offer support not only through training but also through counseling from a staff of experts who offer assistance that no independent could afford. Legal advice is available to a certain degree. The most efficient accounting systems—perfect for that particular business—have been designed by experts in the field. Some licensers offer free computer analysis of records, and through comparison with other units can pinpoint areas of inefficiency or loss as well as profitable aspects of the business that are being neglected.

- **Site selection assistance.** Experts in site selection and marketing choose locations using all the scientific tools available, rather than the hunch-and-guess method employed by most independents. Professional negotiators arrange leases and contracts to the best advantage, using the power of a large organization to influence landlords and other important figures.

- **Purchasing power.** Many times, the parent company's tremendous buying power and special buying techniques can bring products, equipment and outside services to the licensee at a cost much lower than an independent could ever get.

- **No ongoing royalties.** In a business opportunity venture, there are no ongoing royalties to the seller. The profits are all yours. You're not making money and putting it in someone else's pockets.

However, while there are a lot of advantages to buying a business opportunity, there are also disadvantages.

THE DISADVANTAGES OF BUSINESS OPPORTUNITIES

Keep in mind that most companies sell business opportunities because it is a way to expand their distribution channels without using additional capital. There are hundreds of variations of business opportunity contracts; consequently, not all the negative points mentioned will apply to every situation. Under ideal conditions, business opportunities are a good, low-investment way to get into business with minimum risk and a good chance for success. But nothing in this world is perfect, so here are some potential problems:

- **Poor site selection.** The majority of business opportunity ventures are consumer-oriented retail operations that rely on good location, visibility, and easy access to the establishment. Most buyers of business opportunity ventures casually accept the location chosen for them. *Don't!* Look it over thoroughly yourself. You might even hire an outside marketing consultant to evaluate and possibly argue with their choice. It could literally mean millions of dollars in profit over 20 years.

- **Deficient lease/contract agreements.** If not done effectively, lease/contract negotiations could mean higher operating expenses. For instance, a real estate broker might raise the leasing cost in a deal with a large company, or hold it higher knowing the company won't waste expensive time in negotiation. This price-raising concept also applies to start-up costs. The way you rate an investment is a ratio between dollars invested and dollars returned. Business opportunity companies must keep their costs in line. They can't afford to have an employee spend a week wandering around a city looking for bargains. They must have a prearranged source to eliminate any expenses in these areas.

- **Lack of ongoing support.** There is usually no requirement for the business opportunity seller to offer ongoing support of any kind. If the seller decides not to supply information or guidelines that could help you once you are in operation, you may not have much recourse available.
- **Exclusivity clauses.** Are you restricted to selling only the manufacturer's merchandise? If this is the case and you deviate for any reason whatsoever, you run the risk of the licenser canceling the agreement. If you do buy from other sources, it will be very hard to hide. Most parent companies will require that you open your books for examination at predesignated periods. Any irregularities will be spotted at that time. Most smart buyers of business opportunities will negotiate the point in the agreement stipulating sources of supply in case product quality is inconsistent or the service becomes bad.
- **Parent company bankruptcy.** Another pitfall is the possibility of the parent company becoming overextended and going bankrupt. While this is not as serious in a business opportunity as it would be in a franchise, you still run the risk of losing the business because your property contracts may have been financed through the parent company.

You should carefully check any business opportunity venture you are considering. Get a list of operators from the parent company and call them. Have a lawyer look over any agreement drafted by the parent company. Make sure you receive a disclosure statement. Then carefully evaluate the licenser. Don't let anyone hurry you. Make sure the business opportunity is backed by a responsible company.

CHOOSING THE BUSINESS OPPORTUNITY

If you are considering purchasing a business opportunity, first make sure it complies with all business opportunity statutes—which vary from state to state—and is registered in states where registration is required. Next, find out if the business opportunity you're interested in provides an offering prospectus to buyers. If they are a business opportunity that falls under the FTC rule, then they are required to disclose specific information to you. When choosing a business opportunity, keep in mind that established concepts, with a sizable number of outlets and at least three years in business, are more expensive than many new enterprises. New offers should be studied for the parent company's history to evaluate its success and longevity in its particular field of operation. The newer offers will not have developed sophistication and service requirements to the same degree as the older firms, but their fees will increase as they become more proficient.

If you were to ask a business consultant how to evaluate the "right" business opportunity, you would probably receive guidelines:

1. Make an honest evaluation of yourself and your abilities. If you've been behind a desk for many years, will you be happy calling on businesspeople and selling them an intangible service? If you've been a field salesperson for years, will you be satisfied to sell snack foods behind a counter?

2. The business you operate must be run enthusiastically. Will you be happy introducing a new product or an unusual service that the public knows nothing about? Can you generate excitement for an item not nationally advertised?

3. You must have complete knowledge of the product or service with which you are involved. If the parent company gives you little or no training in technical or management know-how, be wary. If the licenser-seller has organized all the operating knowledge gained through years of experience in the business into a standard operating manual, look with favor on this business opportunity.

4. Make a market evaluation of the product or service to be offered. Is the time right to introduce it to the public? Is there a need for this type of item, and what is its potential in relation to competition?

5. What is the trend of the particular business opportunity? When Medicare was introduced, the time was ripe for medical and dental assistant schools, doctors' collection services, and so on. With federal subsidies available for low-income families, the time is excellent to go into day-care centers. Automation and labor-saving devices are creating computerized gas stations, automated mini-theaters, and so on. Campgrounds are also a good opportunity today.

6. Find out how many buyers have been in business successfully for a respectable period. A legitimate business opportunity will even provide you with phone numbers of other buyers over the past several years, so you can verify that they're generally satisfied with the opportunity and that the seller is capable of fulfilling his or her promises.

7. Check the training and experience required to run the business properly. Is there a suitable curriculum of training? What and how sincere is the scope of training? Does it demand mathematical data? Does your background fit its requirements?

8. What is its profit ratio to sales; to time and service requirements; to the financial leverage requirements? Can you make more in another type of business?

9. Do you have to expend more hours to earn as much as you do now? Can you invest the same amount in the particular business opportunity yet operate a larger operation and get a better return on your investment?

10. Check with current operators to see how they are making out. Are they happy with their business? What problems do they have, if any, that are common to all units sold?

11. Determine the history of the offering company's operation: Is it a new firm with little expertise and experience? Is it an older firm whose regular products have satisfied customers for years? Are the franchises all offshoots of their regular business?

12. Is the service personnel of the parent company newly recruited, or are they professionals in the business?

13. Is there financial strength and strong credit behind the business opportunity? Can the licenser-seller give you an escrow agreement to deliver a building, equipment, leasehold improvements, inventory, and so on, as the unit is made ready for your use? Check out the bank references given by the licenser-seller; discuss the company's financial strength with the appropriate manager(s).

14. Evaluate the policies and plans of the company with the associations and business groups in which the parent company or seller is involved.

15. The Better Business Bureau will give you a report if others have lodged previous complaints.

16. Dun & Bradstreet will deliver a status report on the firm through the service of their subscriber network.

17. An in-depth study of the subject firm through an attorney, accountant or business consultant may be your best course along with the other points previously mentioned.

18. To complete your evaluation, visit the home office of the licenser-seller at your earliest convenience. Talk to the personnel and the training director. Visit the prototype of the business being sold. Evaluate other outlets. Expose yourself to the other outlets' products and services to determine the quality dispensed.

Unless you have sufficient funds or can finance the business opportunity, you don't want to extend yourself beyond your limits. Operating a business with no reserves and ignoring the possibility of unexpected financial business reversals—which do happen—is a mistake. You won't be able to operate your business effectively. This is a good rule to remember: Invest no more than 75 percent of your cash reserves. If you have $10,000, invest $7,500. If you have $25,000, invest $18,750.

Be sure you know how business opportunities are financed before you sign the application form. When you buy a business opportunity, you actually buy three incomes. First, you are seeking a salary from the business. Second, you must receive a return on your investment that is better than your existing investments in stocks, bonds, real estate, insurance, land, and so on. Third, your market value if/when you sell the business must bring you at least a 2 × earning factor.

The price of the business opportunity does not always reflect the actual cost of the business itself. You must consider the cost of the down payment and scheduled payments to be made in installments, whether financed by the franchiser or a bank or lending institution. You will need a "pillow" of working capital to guide the business through its ups and downs of activity. Furthermore, there must be security on the lease of any items utilized in the operation of the business.

PERFORMING THE ANALYSIS

In the preceding section on choosing a business opportunity, we outlined several things you should do to assure yourself that you are choosing a venture that will be personally appropriate and will also be a sound investment. It is important to cover all your bases before signing a contract with the seller of the business opportunity. The following strategies will help you protect yourself and ensure a successful path into the business opportunity world:

- **Have legal representation.** Your attorney should be present when you are negotiating with the licenser-seller. At the very least, your attorney should go over the contract to purchase the business opportunity and advise you whether to sign it in its present condition. He or she should explain what each aspect of the contract means so that you understand what you're signing. It's critical to consult your attorney before you sign anything.
- **Have financial representation.** Your accountant should look over the financial statements of the licenser-seller. In addition, your accountant should also be able to check out the financial strength of the company and understand whether or not the business is a viable financial investment.
- **Make your own independent survey of other owners of business opportunities sold by the parent company.** Are they happy with the company? Did the company do everything it promised? Is the company good to work with? Does it give its distributors help? Does it send out advertising materials? If they had it to do over again, would these licensees buy another unit? Would they advise you to buy a unit? What do they feel are the strengths?
- **Contact competitors.** This will verify the status of that company in the industry. A competing company will tell you in a hurry what the weaknesses are. You'll also get an opportunity to see whether or not the business opportunity compares favorably in terms of pricing and so on.
- **Check the credit of the seller.** Your accountant or the person auditing the business opportunity can help you in that area.
- **Be sure you understand everything.** Read the disclosure statement, the purchase agreement, and the advertising bulletins carefully.

- **Check the credibility of the parent company.** The parent company doesn't have to be big in terms of dollars to be credible. Use your common sense and advice from people you trust to determine whether or not a company is credible. In many cases, small companies are a great investment for a buyer because you're dealing with the president or the top people in the company. They are going to be training you and working with you. This is a tremendous advantage, as opposed to working with somebody five or six rungs down the ladder who may be just doing a job. Are the seller's people truly interested in you? Do they seem to be sincere? Did they check you out thoroughly? Are they concerned with the kind of buyers carrying their banner? This is very important. If they're just interested in taking your money, you're in trouble.
- **Check the performance of the parent company.** Are the seller's claims backed by performance? Do the claims that the seller makes when advertising products, for example, stand up at the store level? Are the profit claims that the seller makes confirmed by the current operators you've talked to?
- **In the case of the celebrity business opportunity, is the celebrity actually connected to the company?** If the use of that celebrity is going to contribute to your financial success, fine. If it's an important part of the concept, fine. If it isn't, take another look. In the past, buyers have had some bad experiences with celebrities who have lent their names to business offerings, finding out too late that the celebrities were not connected with the companies at all.
- **Check the company's management.** It's not enough that they've got a good idea. Do they have the strength in management to be able to train you, help you, and keep the company running for another 20 years?
- **Know all the costs and obligations, both yours and the seller's.** What costs are you going to have to incur? What are your obligations on an ongoing basis? What kind of training and supervision will be involved?
- **Is the company going to train you?** Is training at your own expense? In most cases you have to pay your own expenses to the training site. How long will it last? Do you have enough staying power, enough income to sustain you while you're in training and before your business starts earning money? What kind of ongoing supervision will the company be giving you?
- **Determine what type of advertising program is available from the licenser, on both a local and national level, if that applies.** Will that advertising program work for you? Check your local market. For instance, if you are buying a business opportunity where you will be selling bathtub liners, will advertising in a trade magazine really help? Also, what are their ads like? Is the copy good? What about visual art? Don't ignore the possibility that their advertising program will hurt you more than it will help. Just because you're dealing with a company that has experience in the field doesn't necessarily mean that their marketing campaigns are going to be successful.

- **Are you getting value for your initial purchase price?** Examine the list of equipment, fixtures, inventory, and operating supplies, and call a few suppliers dealing in these items. Compare the prices those suppliers quote you against the business opportunity's price. You may be able to purchase everything, including the inventory, for less money than you could by affiliating with the licenser.

Remember that even though some federal and state laws may protect you, no one is going to hold your hand and watch over your shoulder to prevent you from buying a business opportunity that might not be right for you. To avoid problems, the best technique is to conduct your own careful and thorough investigation before committing your time and money.

What the Disclosure Statement Tells You

A disclosure statement is a document that contains everything there is to know about the business opportunity and seller's company. It includes the promoter's financial strength, how many operating units there are, and exactly what you're going to be required to pay in total so that there are no hidden fees. The purpose of the disclosure statement is to protect the licensee as well as the licenser and to eliminate some unscrupulous licensers.

As already mentioned, some 21 states have legal requirements for disclosure statements and registration. In most of these states, a licenser can't even offer a business opportunity for sale or send any literature unless the company registers with the state and files a copy of the disclosure statement, pays a fee, and posts a bond. The state will approve or disapprove the offer based on whether the business opportunity appears to be legitimate and whether the seller has the financial strength or the operational capabilities to be beneficial to licensees.

In addition to the states that require disclosure statements, there are also business opportunity laws on the federal level. The most significant is the FTC rule requiring full disclosure of the business opportunity in all states where the licenser is offering the opportunity. The rule doesn't require a registration, but does require a disclosure that follows a specific format. The penalties for violation of state and federal laws, where applicable, are quite substantial. The rules are designed to deter someone from misrepresenting a business opportunity offering. Basically, the disclosure states:

- **Who the licenser is.** The history of the parent company needs to be detailed. It should include the identity and business experience of any persons affiliated with the licenser, whether the company has had any litigation, whether it has been bankrupt or any of the officials in the company have ever been bankrupt, the initial fee that a licensee would have to pay, any other initial payment or any payment in total, and any other fees. There are no hidden costs.
- **Obligations of the licensee.** If there are any financing arrangements, they have to be stated in the disclosure statement. If the buyer is going to

be required to buy from any supplier, it should be stated up front. The disclosure statement also states the obligations of the licenser. It describes what the parent company will have to provide in terms of equipment, training, ongoing services, and a training manual.

- **What the licenser promises to deliver.** The disclosure statement should indicate whether you are getting an exclusive area or a territory as a licensee. Any trademarks, service marks, trade names, logo types, and commercial symbols that you are going to be privileged to use, and are a part of what you are buying, need to be identified in here, as well as any patents or copyrights that you can use.

- **Obligation of the licensee.** This is how you will participate in the actual operation of the business opportunity. If this is an absentee business, it must be stated. If the licenser indicates that you must personally operate the business, that should also be stated. Restrictions on goods and services offered by the licensee are covered. It has some provisions for renewal and termination, repurchase or modification. It also has to list the current licensees and their addresses so you have the opportunity to contact these people.

- **Public figure relationships.** If this is a business opportunity that is identified with a given person, such as Joe Namath Hair Salon or the Roy Rogers Restaurant, it should indicate what arrangements have been made with that person. Is that person active in the business, or receiving a royalty out of the proceeds?

- **Financial statement of the company.** This is required in almost every state. It is an audited financial statement prepared by a CPA. There is usually a letter from the accountant indicating that the books have been audited and are available for people to study. The financial statements will give you a good idea of the financial strength of the seller. Any estimates or projections of earnings would have to be part of the disclosure statement.

Most states that have disclosure requirements parallel the federal standards of information that must be supplied to the buyer. In addition, the disclosure statements required by states often include information stating that the buyer has three to seven days after executing the purchase documents to rescind the agreement. This cooling-off period allows the purchaser/investor to reconsider the subject after being bombarded with slick sales pitches.

Information on the bond posted by the seller is also included in many state disclosure statements. Generally, these bonds are posted with the state to ensure that the purchaser/investor can recover any damages suffered due to violation by the seller of the business opportunity laws. There will be a statement as well that primarily declares the state does not endorse the business opportunity in any way. If a seller fails to comply with a federal or state business opportunity law, he will be subject to criminal and civil penalties. In addition, an injunction may be obtained that will stop any further sales offerings.

A purchaser of a business opportunity who, after operating for a while, learns that there has been misrepresentation by the seller, may file a lawsuit against the parent company to recover damages. In some states, the regulating agency will also initiate proceedings against the seller. Though business opportunity laws are meant to protect you, the best technique to avoid problems is to conduct your own careful and thorough investigation before committing your time and money. View all the seller's promotional material and statements by sales personnel with reservation. The federal and state laws are designed to promote full disclosure, but they in no way promise or imply that any state investigation has been made concerning the value and success potential of the business opportunity.

BUSINESS OPPORTUNITIES AND THE FTC RULE

The FTC Rule has been in effect since the latter part of 1979 and has had a broad-ranging impact on the franchise and business opportunity industry as well as would-be franchisees or licensees. But the most noticeable effect to date has been on the nearly 2,000 franchisers and business opportunity sellers who have been required to undertake the expense of compiling and updating disclosure documents (similar to a stock prospectus) to give each prospective buyer.

The rule is designed to assure all prospective buyers, of either a franchise or business opportunity, that they'll receive a full disclosure of the background information needed to make an informed investment decision. To the extent that franchisers and licensers are complying with the rule, and we have every reason to believe that they are, today's franchise and business opportunity buyers should be the most educated in history; however, many business opportunity sellers are either unaccustomed to disclosure requirements or else have convinced themselves and their unwitting buyers that they are exempt. Caveat emptor ("Let the buyer beware") is the attitude every business opportunity buyer should adopt. In spite of the FTC's rule and aggressive action at the state level, there are sellers who seek every possible means to escape regulation. Neither the FTC rule nor state regulations guarantee success of freedom from fraud. That's why you should pay especially close attention to the FTC disclosure statement that is presented to you.

Every prospective buyer of a business opportunity must receive the FTC disclosure statement at least 10 business days before signing a binding contract or paying money (or other consideration) to the seller. The 10-business-day requirement is minimal. If you meet face to face with the licenser or a representative to discuss proposed sale or purchase of the business opportunity, and if the conversation results in a serious sales presentation, the licenser must provide you with a disclosure document at that time.

Whenever you receive the documents, which should include a copy of the standard purchase agreement, the seller should request that you sign an "acknowledgment-of-receipt" form. If you haven't received an FTC disclosure document, don't sign anything or pay out any money, even if the seller claims that it is "refundable."

If the seller doesn't give you a disclosure document, it is a violation of federal law and may also violate state law. If the salesperson claims that the offering is exempt from the FTC requirements, demand to see an opinion letter from counsel before any further dealings with the company. Also, ask the salesperson for the telephone number of the local state agency or FTC office that has advised the company that it is exempt.

Very few business opportunity offerings are exempt. The only major exceptions are those where the total initial payment within the first six months is under $500, or where payment made is only for initial inventory sold at a bona fide wholesale price.

FINANCES: YOURS AND THEIRS

The financing requirements are quite substantial in some businesses. There are different types of financing that you as a licensee will be pursuing. For example, in a general business loan, you go to the bank and borrow money to get into business. The bank will want to know what collateral you have to offer from your personal assets, and from your prospective business.

Venture capital is another type of financing. It isn't readily available to a buyer of a business opportunity unless you know an individual who wants to loan some capital to you. Usually it's unsecured by collateral of any type. It is highly speculative on the part of the investor, and it's usually an arrangement in which an investor will either want to take a position in your business, or receive an extremely high rate of interest or return based on the profitability. If you are in a business that is going to have a lot of money on the books from people making payments, then you can pledge receivables as collateral for a loan.

The most common type of financing you will be dealing with is equipment financing—this is the most readily available source of money for a licensee. To enable you to get maximum financing, most licensers try to put as much as possible into the equipment package.

Equipment financing is usually based on what the banks assess as the useful life of the equipment. For example, in the restaurant industry, banks usually figure a seven-year amortization period on equipment. You would get a seven-year loan on equipment at about an 8 percent add-on. Eight percent a year times seven years is 56 percent. They'll add 56 percent to the equipment price, divide it by the number of months in seven years, and assess that much of a payment per month, as opposed to simple interest which is based on a declining balance. This is an expensive, but accepted, procedure with equipment financing and is usually readily available. The licenser usually has a source of financing and so can help you.

Profit and loss statements are part of the financing scene. In business offerings, these are usually statements audited by a CPA. When you look at a licenser, you will want to see an audited statement of what that company is doing. You'll know you're getting a legitimate financial statement because CPAs will not write their signatures or stamp a statement that hasn't been properly audited and certified.

You should have an accountant look at the financial statement to interpret for you exactly what the statement represents. You should compare at least two years of statements to see the direction of the company: Is it on an upswing or a downswing? Is it becoming more profitable? More efficient? And so on? The balance sheet, which shows the company's assets and liabilities, is another yardstick in determining the strength of a company. The profit and loss statement tells you how much money the company is making or losing. The balance sheet tells you what the company is worth in terms of what it owns and what it owes. These are both important guidelines in assessing a company's strength.

Companies may give you pro forma projections to show what you can expect to earn in this particular business opportunity. A pro forma is a projected financial statement that takes what the typical costs are for a unit doing, say, $200,000, $300,000 or $400,000 a year and shows you approximately what you can expect to earn at each of those sales levels. The purpose of a pro forma is to give you an idea of what to expect. Some states have outlawed the use of pro forma statements except for currently operating units. In terms of their reliability, they do not always accurately reflect earning potential. We recommend examining actual audited operating statements to get a good feel for what a company is doing.

Larger companies will be able to provide you with these statements. The smaller companies usually can't, and that is where a gamble is involved. This is where you have to use your own personal accounting and legal assistance to thoroughly check out a company. The smaller the company, the more you have to be concerned about credibility. Most companies tend to overstate the income and understate the expenses in a pro forma.

The operating manual furnished by most companies will provide you with the know-how you need to operate that business. It's a good reference book for a licensee because you can refer to it later for many kinds of information. It establishes the rules, standards, and specifications for accomplishing tasks or presenting a certain product or service. Some states require licensers to furnish an operating manual to licensees. It is certainly a valuable guide for training employees. Some companies do an outstanding job on an operating manual. As a licensee, you are forced by the manual to organize. It defines a specific job responsibility and tasks that you have to perform. It's always good to know what's expected of you or specifically how to do something. The manual gives professional assistance anytime you need it.

RESOURCES

Associations

Franchise Consultants International Association, 5147 South Angela Road, Memphis, TN 38117, 901-761-3085

International Franchise Association, 1350 New York Avenue NW, Suite 900, Washington, DC 20005, 202-628-8000

Magazines

Continental Franchise Review, 9250 East Costilla Avenue, Suite 620, Englewood, CO 80112, 303-649-9910

Franchising World, 1350 New York Avenue NW, Suite 900, Washington, DC 20005-4700, 202-628-8000

Info Franchise Newsletter, P.O. Box 550, Lewiston, NY 14092-0550, 716-754-4669

Opportunity, 73 Spring Street, Suite 303, New York, NY 10012, 212-925-3180

Directories

Entrepreneur Magazine's Annual Business Opportunity 500 Survey Issue, P.O. Box 57050, Irvine, CA 92619-7050, 714-227-1200

Government Agencies

Federal Trade Commission Office, U.S. Federal Trade Commission, Sixth and Pennsylvania Avenue NW, Washington, DC 20580, 202-326-2222

13 Start-Up Financing

F or entrepreneurs, the old adage rings true: "It takes money to make money." Or, as Shakespeare put it, "Nothing comes of nothing." If you're just starting out, you need money. Those already in business need financial resources to market new products, pay vendors, or meet payrolls and buy equipment. Capital requirements for new businesses depend on a number of factors. If you've performed all research properly and have formed a thorough business plan, then you should have a clear idea of the amount of money needed to begin your venture and the most likely sources for acquiring those finances.

Traditionally, however, it has been hard for small entrepreneurial ventures to obtain capital, especially the start-up phase, and this difficulty has been magnified by the increasing cost of money in the financial markets. That's why we've stressed the importance of planning. If you're prepared to obtain financing, whether it's for a start-up or for an existing business, you'll reduce the skepticism lenders typically express when the buyer of a small business comes knocking on their door.

The uses of money are the most basic questions in a lender's mind. Bankers, for instance, will not want to make a loan that puts them in the position of investing in your business. They want to stay liquid, to reduce their risk. As a small-business person, you must always have a clear understanding of what you need in terms of capital and how it will be used. By doing this, you'll be able to determine the best source for raising money to finance your business.

EVALUATING YOUR FINANCIAL SITUATION

Frequently, first-time entrepreneurs use their personal funds to get their business going. Yet, this does not mean that once you are in business you won't need additional capital. Indeed, business owners use many techniques for obtaining personal loans for business financing. You can borrow from individuals

259

or from institutions, using a secured loan involving collateral or an unsecured loan made on the basis of your name. The latter is the most advantageous to you as a borrower because you don't risk losing anything tangible. Your promise to pay is made on the basis of your past performance in paying debts.

If you are already loaded with debt, you may not be able to get the long-term financing you want, and it won't be at a favorable rate. In this case, you'll then have to look at equity financing as an option. The difference between equity financing and a regular loan is that you're giving up a piece of your business, profits, and possibly some control. And you may find it more difficult to find someone to buy part of your business, either as a partner, limited partner, or perhaps as a shareholder of your corporation. But with equity money you will be able to move ahead. You can use it to take you through a growth period when you are expanding a facility, buying a new van or piece of equipment, or perhaps going into a new product line with heavy development costs. Any long-term situation that will bring profits in over a period of years can qualify for long-term debt, with lower monthly payments and perhaps lower interest rates.

To plan your financial needs, begin by answering a few basic questions:

1. When are you going to repay the money? (Different situations will also determine what type of money you need—whether equity or individual loans.)
2. How much do you need? (The use and scheduling of the financing will depend on the amount that you need.)
3. Can you afford the cost of the money? (Lenders charge a fee to use their money.)

A lender's fee is added to the principal of the loan in the form of interest. When interest rates rise to a point where borrowers can no longer afford to pay this fee and still make a profit, demand usually dries up. A good example of a sharp decrease in borrowing occurred during the recession of the early 1980s. It's essential that you make an accurate profit-and-loss projection, covering at least three years, and add in the cost of the interest on the money you're borrowing.

Be aware in the beginning that although you make a good profit-and-loss projection with strong estimates and forecasted profits, you can still get into trouble if you don't show a good cash-flow projection. A cash-flow projection will indicate whether or not you can truly afford the loan. This subtracts the actual money you pay out from the money you take in. When the prime rate hit 20 percent, there were a lot of quiet desks and empty chairs in escrow offices and lending departments at banks, and not a lot of action going on. Businesses were forced to curtail their expansion because the costs were so obviously high.

However, it's not always so obvious, and many businesspeople never make cash-flow projections on a regular basis. They might make a profit-and-loss projection, or a balance sheet, or have them prepared by their bookkeeper or accountant every three months or so to see where they stand, but they often lack a cash-flow projection. It's going to be required when you raise money, however, and though it is important, it's not terribly difficult to compose. It's also a handy tool to have any time during the year.

The interest you pay will show on your profit-and-loss statement, but the principal payments will show on your cash-flow statement. This is usually a large item, and sometimes overlooked when people first make their plans. You can make simple projections yourself or give them to an expert such as an accountant or a financial consultant. It helps to identify these needs if, every six or 12 months, you prepare a written summary of projections.

Your banker is going to be looking at these projections to make sure that you can repay the loan from the profits of the business. And the banker is going to check the cash-flow projection to see that you have enough to cover your own draw for your living expenses, unless you have a separate income.

Keep in mind that during the first year of business, it typically takes 12 months before you can break even, so that income and expenses match up. Some businesses may get into a very heavy foot-traffic location (e.g., in a mall) and begin to generate a positive cash flow immediately. But for your own business, with the advice of suppliers and people in the business, you'll want to plan how soon you can realistically expect sales to come in and what expenses are going to be involved so you can estimate when you will hit break-even and start bringing in a positive cash flow.

You'll want to add in some extra money when you're making an application for a loan. A good rule of thumb is to take your first 12 months of expenses and add 20 percent to that amount.

One more financial sheet should be developed—the balance sheet. The balance sheet simply shows the total assets and total liabilities that you have, and subtracts the two to get your total net worth.

The experienced businessperson, however, knows that financial statements are really only part of the package. The rest of presenting your business and business description involves your creative skills in giving an impression that you have a profitable and stable business. Bankers, investors, and suppliers are all going to be looking to see what kind of person you are. Have you repaid your debts? Do you have a reputation of stability? If you've had trouble along these lines, it doesn't necessarily mean that you can't go into business. But wherever you have a problem—if, for example, you have a ratio out of line in your financial statement—you should have an answer and explanation for it.

When you raise money, you become a salesperson. And just as in any selling situation, you want to take care of objections as they arise so that you don't have to handle the objections at the end when you're making the close. If you have a problem area, then footnote or comment on it in your plan so that you handle the objection before it becomes a question in the person's mind.

When you're evaluating your financial situation, take a look at your assets, both personal and business. If you're tight on cash, ask yourself how you can sell those assets to free up the cash. It doesn't matter whether they are of a personal or business nature; they're all assets. So make a careful inventory of everything valuable you have. Analyze the situation to see what you might be able to sell.

Go through and spot the problems in your personal expenditures, especially where you might be spending more than you should. Pick out places where you might be able to cut back because you're going to show a personal statement to the banker, and the banker is going to want to make sure that you can live within the income that you generate. Table 13.1 shows a sample Income Statement that you can use in evaluating the financial status of your business.

What Investors Are Looking For

Let's look at some of the ingredients that investors commonly look for when they deal with loan applicants. Whether it's a small loan, a personal loan, or your first bank business loan, the lender will be looking at it as if it were a personal loan. Your ability to attract money thus depends as much on their perception of your character as on the effectiveness of your paperwork. Some items they look at are:

- **Stability.** They're going to check to see how long you've worked at a particular job, how long you've lived at a particular residence, or how long you've lived in a certain neighborhood. None of these items by itself would keep you from getting a loan. They look at the overall picture. But try to make everything as positive as you can. If there is little evidence of stability, then you want to be prepared to answer any objection that may arise. If you've been moving for one reason or another, or you've changed jobs for better opportunities, come up with a short answer to that particular question.

- **Income.** How well do you live within yours? Some people make a lot of money, yet don't have discipline. They haven't learned to manage money effectively so that they can live within the income. Although lenders may look at the total amount of money that you've been making, they're also going to see how well you managed your money. Obviously, they're thinking that if a person can't manage his or her personal finances effectively, it's going to be difficult for that person to manage the assets of a growing business.

- **Debt management.** Lenders will look at how well you've been able to pay off your debts. What's your track record? If you have a charge account, have you paid it on time? Do you have a lot of late-payment penalties? Did you pay your car loan on time? House payments? Ever late with your rent check? How well will you be able to demonstrate that you pay off your past debts? If you've had some problems in this area, prepare a ready explanation to satisfy these people.

You are probably aware that a lender can check your credit record on a computer immediately. So you should get a copy of your credit record from the major credit company serving your area. You can identify this company by calling a local department store credit office and asking which credit bureau it

Table 13.1 Income Statement

INCOME STATEMENT	JANUARY	FEBRUARY	MARCH	APRIL	MAY	JUNE	JULY	AUGUST	SEPTEMBER	OCTOBER	NOVEMBER	DECEMBER	TOTALS
Income													
Cost of goods													
Gross profit													
Margin %													
Expenses													
Net profit													
Margin %													
Depreciation													
Net profit before interest													
Margin %													
Interest													
Net profit before taxes													
Margin %													

uses, or look in the yellow pages. The most frequently used credit-reporting agencies are TRW (Texas), TransUnion (Ohio), and Equifax (Georgia). For a few dollars, or for free in some cases, the company will give you a complete printout of the same record that the bank gets. Look at it and check it for errors, in anticipation of any potential question a lender might raise.

More than one credit-reporting agency may serve your area. Most credit checks are made by two or three firms. Find out about as many as you can. Why is this important? The lender that you go to may not use the largest credit firm for some reason. Or maybe they'll get two credit reports, one from Firm A and one from Firm B. And you'll be amazed how different the two credit reports look. Check out more than one, get your reports, and clean them up *before* you apply for your loan. The one thing that lenders dislike in any loan-proposal process is a surprise. Handle surprises by eliminating the possibility that they will occur, in advance of making your loan presentation. Prevailing law requires credit bureaus to provide debtors with a copy of their record. Furthermore, they have to allow people the chance to clean it up and clear any mistakes.

Sometimes the reports are a little confusing. If this is so, you can make an appointment with the credit company and have someone explain to you the unfavorable items. They may not like the idea of having to do this, but the law is very clear on this point. You may be able to go directly into, say, a department store credit office and ask them to help you with a problem you may have with your store account. Let's say it was a late payment on a department store account. Go to the department store and explain that you've paid the money off, and you'd like to have them remove that late-payment comment from your record. Have them send a note to the credit bureau and say that it's clean.

A couple of former creditors may not cooperate. Let's say you had a dispute with a plumber: The plumber did a job for you, but it wasn't right, so you didn't pay him the $100 you owed him right away. Finally, after two or three months of haggling, you settle the dispute and pay the plumber. In the meantime, the plumber has reported you as a bad credit risk. It's still on your record. And now, let's say, the plumber holds a grudge and is not going to send a note. You have the right to put a statement in your credit file up to 100 words explaining that there was a misunderstanding. You can clean up your credit record nicely that way.

SOURCES OF MONEY

To understand where you can go to acquire the necessary capital to start or expand your venture, you must first become acquainted with the various types of money, how it's generated, and in what forms you'll be able to obtain it.

There are two forms to choose from when generating capital: *internal* and *external*. Internal funding is the most inexpensive way to generate capital because you are relying on a variety of methods from your own operation to raise the necessary money. External capital is just what it implies: capital generated outside the realm of the company. Sources for external funding include banks, suppliers, commercial finance companies, and investment bankers.

When planning to raise money, you should consider all your internal options before searching for an external lender. Even if you can't generate all your capital requirements internally, at least you'll offset the amount of money required so that only a portion has to be raised through external sources.

There's another plus to using internal funding. Lenders are more apt to take a risk on you and your company if they know that there is an internal commitment to the venture. They will also have more confidence in your management ability if you show you can make the most out of internal resources.

Internal funding involves the danger that you may end up investing a considerable portion of your assets into the business, making yourself unattractive to external funding. Generally speaking, however, entrepreneurs who utilize internal funding before external will experience greater long-term success.

That doesn't mean you shouldn't consider external funding. At some point in time, whether during start-up or business expansion, you will need to raise capital through external sources. As you evaluate these sources, you should realize that there are a few types of capital that can be generated through external funding. Keep in mind that many entrepreneurs use a combination of these external sources of funding to raise capital.

Owner Financing

In most cases, starting a business using your own money is the only way to get the venture off the ground. Many lenders and investors frown on risking any money for a proposed business unless the principal owner or owners have a vested interest in the venture. This is especially true on the small business level, and if you are unwilling to accept that you will have to commit some or all of the funds to start your business out of your own money, then perhaps you should rethink the idea of entrepreneurship.

You'll find many experts and books that say, "Why risk your own money when you can use someone else's?" This is an enticing thought, but in the world of small business, it's very unlikely. Why? Because you simply won't find anyone else to fund 100 percent of the business. And if you do, ask yourself what you'll be giving up. To take that much risk, a lender or investor is going to ask for a substantial return. Either the cost of the money (interest) is going to be extremely high, or you are going to relinquish the majority of equity within the company. Sure, you won't risk your money, but what you are risking is the future of your business.

By utilizing your own money, you risk your own finances but you will not relinquish control of your company. You will reduce your debt service, and you will look more attractive to external sources because of the confidence in the business you've exhibited by investing your own funds.

To determine just how much money you have to invest in a business, you must evaluate your finances on the credit and debit sides using the personal balance sheet in Chapter 1. Begin by listing all your assets and their value in the top portion of the form, including house, car(s), and jewelry. Now list all your debts in the bottom portion, including credit cards, mortgage, bank notes, personal debts, and any auto loans. Now compute the ratio between total assets and total liabilities to determine your net worth or degree of indebtedness. Once you do that, you are ready to realistically evaluate the needs of the business you are planning to run.

Set up this computation so that you have an assets-to-liabilities ratio— Asset:Liabilities (Line A:Line B). The ratio will look something like 2:1, or, if you are like many people nowadays, 1:2. This is generally referred to as the *acid- test ratio* or *quick ratio*. The acid-test ratio is exactly where you are if you run into some bad luck and you don't do anything to correct your financial position. If your assets exceed liabilities, you should be able to keep the creditors from knocking on your door. The Personal Financial Statement shown in Figure 13.1 is another way of presenting your assets and liabilities.

To assist you in obtaining or regaining control of your personal finances, consider the cash-flow statement (see Figure 13.2). Many cash-flow statements are computed by the month. First, enter your variable and fixed expenses. Add these expenses to obtain total monthly expenses. Now write in your gross income, which should include monthly salary, your spouse's salary, and any extra money you earn (e.g., income from an apartment house, stocks, or bonds). Subtract any payroll deductions or other deductions on income checks to arrive at take-home pay. Next, subtract take-home pay from gross income to get your net income. Finally, subtract appropriate living expenses from net income. On the bottom line, enter what you are left with. This is your disposable or discretionary income. Disposable income is money that works for you. Use it for anything from enjoying leisure activities to building a savings or money-market account.

By creating a cash-flow statement, you are charting your leverage. When the standard monthly expenses are deducted every month, what is left shows you how much more debt you can incur. If you incur any more than that, you are forced to borrow. That is why you must understand cash flow. Your knowledge of it can keep you out of trouble, both before and after you start your business.

Debt Financing

Debt financing offers the widest choice of possibilities for raising money. This form of external funding is based on receiving a loan from an outside source that is repayable over a specified period of time at a preset user's fee that is usually competitive with the market for the cost of money.

Debt-financing sources use both secured and unsecured loans. Security is simply offering some form of collateral as an assurance that the loan will be repaid. If the debtor defaults on the loan, that collateral is forfeited to satisfy the

Figure 13.1   Personal Financial Statement

STATEMENT OF FINANCIAL CONDITION AS OF_____ 19,____

INDIVIDUAL INFORMATION

Name	
Home Address	
City, State & Zip	
Name of Employer	
Title/Position	
No. of Years with Employer	
Employer Address	
City, State & Zip	
Home Phone	Business Phone

CO-APPLICANT INFORMATION

Name	
Home Address	
City, State & Zip	
Name of Employer	
Title/Position	
No. of Years with Employer	
Employer Address	
City, State & Zip	
Home Phone	Business Phone

SOURCE OF INCOME	TOTALS	CONTINGENT LIABILITIES	TOTALS
Salary (applicant)		If guarantor, co-maker, or endorser	
Salary (co-applicant)		If you have any legal claims	
Bonuses & Commissions (applicant)		If you have liability for a lease or contract	
Bonuses & Commissions (co-applicant)		If you have outstanding letters of credit	
Income From Rental Property		If you have outstanding surety bonds	
Investment Income		If you have any contested tax liens	
Other Income *		If you listed an amount for any of the above, give details:	
TOTAL INCOME			

*Income from alimony, child support, or separate maintenance income need not be revealed if you do not wish to have it considered as a basis for repaying this obligation

ASSETS	TOTALS	LIABILITIES	TOTALS
Cash, checking, & savings		Secured loans	
Marketable securities		Unsecured loans	
Non-marketable securities		Charge account bills	
Real estate owned/home		Personal debts	
Partial interest in real estate equities		Monthly bills	
Automobiles		Real estate mortgages	
Personal property		Unpaid income tax	
Personal loans		Other unpaid taxes and interest	
Cash value—Life Insurance		Other debts—Itemize	
Other Assets—Itemize			
		TOTAL LIABILITIES	
		NET WORTH	
TOTAL ASSETS		TOTAL LIABILITIES & NET WORTH	

Figure 13.2   Cash Flow Statement

STATEMENT OF FINANCIAL CONDITION AS OF_____ 19,_____

MONTHLY VARIABLE EXPENSES

	TOTALS	
Grocery Purchases: Food, Beverages, Sundries		
Automobile: Gasoline, Repairs, Servicing		
Utility Bills: Electricity, Water, Phone, Etc.		
Clothing		
Medical, Dental, Prescription, Drugs		
Entertainment		
Contingency Food		
Other Monthly Variable Expenses—Itemize		
TOTAL VARIABLE EXPENSES **A**		

MONTHLY FIXED EXPENSES

	TOTALS	
Rent or Mortgage Payment		
Auto Loan: Car 1		
Auto Loan: Car 2		
Credit Card Payment 1		
Credit Card Payment 2		
Credit Card Payment 3		
Credit Card Payment 4		
Major Store Accounts		
Donations		
Insurance Payments		
Home Improvement Loans—Itemize		
TOTAL FIXED EXPENSES **B**		
Total Monthly Expenses (A+B=C) **C**		

MONTHLY INCOME

Gross Income	**D**		
Payroll Deductions	**E**		
Net Income (D-E)	**F**		
Disposable Income (F-C)	**G**		

payment of the debt. Most lenders will ask for security of some sort on a loan. Very few will lend you money based on your name or idea alone.

What type of security can you offer a lender when seeking a loan from an outside source? Here are the more common types of loan security:

- **Guarantor.** A guarantor signs an agreement with a bank that states they will guarantee the payment of the loan.
- **Endorser.** An endorser is the same as a guarantor except for being required, in some cases to post some sort of collateral.
- **Comaker.** This person acts as a principal in the loan.
- **Accounts receivable.** The bank will usually advance 65 to 80 percent of the value of the receivables just as soon as the goods are shipped.
- **Equipment.** Lenders will usually accept 60 to 65 percent of the value of capital equipment as collateral for a loan.
- **Securities.** If your company is publicly held, you can offer stocks and bonds within the company as security for the repayment of a loan.
- **Real estate.** Most lenders will lend up to 90 percent of the assessed value of the real estate, either commercial or private.
- **Savings account.** If you have a savings account or certificate of deposit, you can use it to secure a loan.
- **Chattel mortgage.** Using equipment as collateral, the lender makes a loan based on something less than the equipment's present value and holds a mortgage on it until the loan is repaid.
- **Insurance policies.** Usually loans can be made up to 95 percent of the policy's cash value.
- **Warehouse inventory.** Lenders will usually advance up to only 50 percent of the value of inventory.
- **Display merchandise.** Similar to warehouse inventory, display merchandise such as furniture, cars, and home electronic equipment can be used to secure loans through a method known as "floor planning."
- **Leases.** If the lender you're approaching for a loan holds the mortgage on property that you are trying to lease, you can simply assign the lease payments to the lender.

You can also attempt to acquire debt financing through an unsecured loan. In this type of loan, your credit reputation is the only security the lender will be accepting. You may either receive a *signature* or *personal* loan for several thousand dollars; even more if you have a good relationship with the bank. But these are usually short-term loans with very high interest rates.

Most outside lenders are very conservative and are unlikely to provide an unsecured loan unless you've done a tremendous amount of business with them in the past and have performed above expectations. Even if you do have this type of relationship with a lender, you may still ask to post collateral on a loan due to economic conditions or your present financial condition.

In addition to secured or unsecured loans, most debt will be subject to a repayment period. As discussed in Dan Steinhoff and John Burgess's *Small*

Business Management Fundamentals,[1] there are three primary types of repayment terms:

1. **Short-term loan.** Short-term loans are for short-term uses, typically paid back within 6 to 18 months.
2. **Intermediate-term loan.** Loans are paid back within roughly three years' time.
3. **Long-term loan.** These loans are paid back from the cash flow of the business in less than five years.

Perhaps the best source of debt financing isn't a commercial institution, but your family and friends. Most experienced business operators frown on this source of financing for new start-ups or business expansion, but regardless of the lack of sophistication involved in raising money through these sources, it remains one of the most popular avenues to launch a business. According to the Small Business Administration, over 11 percent of businesses in the United States were started using money borrowed from family and friends. In fact, many new entrepreneurs don't actively seek this money. It is offered by encouraging parents, relatives, or friends.

When borrowing money from your parents, relatives, or friends, have your attorney draw up legal papers dictating the terms of the loan. Why? Too many entrepreneurs borrow money from their family and friends on a very informal basis. The terms of the loan have been dictated verbally and there is no written contract. People, even family and friends, are very touchy about their money. If they don't feel you are running your business correctly, they will step in and interfere with your operational plans. In some cases, you can't prevent this even with a written contract. Many state laws guarantee voting rights to an individual who has invested money in a business. This can, and has, created a lot of hard feelings.

One of the most overlooked avenues of obtaining start-up capital is your credit cards. Most charge extremely high interest rates, but it is a way to get several thousand dollars quickly without the hassle of dealing with paperwork, as long as you don't go above your specified credit amount.

If you have three credit cards with a credit line on each card of $3,000 and you want to start a small business that you think will require approximately $8,000, you could cash in each card for the full amount and start that business. Within six months you could probably build up a very good business and approach your local bank for a $10,000 loan at about 10 percent interest; then you would use this money to pay off your credit-card balances (which most likely have 20-percent annual rates). After another six months, you could pay off the bank loan of $10,000.

The largest source of funds is the bank itself, and banks are definitely conservative lenders. They're a poor place to go usually for the businessperson looking

---

[1] Dan Steinhoff & John F. Burgess, *Small Business Management Fundamentals,* 4th ed. (New York: McGraw-Hill, 1986).

for start-up capital unless it's for a government-guaranteed loan. But banks are the best source for you after you get started.

Banks will require financial statements on you and on the business. They will want character references, a complete business plan outlining what you hope to do, how you're going to do it, and how much money you plan to make. They need a plan on how the loan is going to be used in the business. Above all, they're going to be looking at you as an individual because they're investing in you.

Unless you're unusually well capitalized, you are going to have to cut your living costs down to the bone when you first start in business. You're going to want to show that you have a good cash flow in your personal situation. Banks want to be assured that the money that comes out of the business will be enough to cover your living expenses so that you're not going further into debt. They're looking at you and your business as one entity as far as use of money is concerned.

A small-business loan usually costs a little more than a loan at the regular prime rates, which is the rate that banks charge their most favored customers. Small business usually pays 1 to 3 percent above that prime rate. Most of the time, if you are like most small businesses starting up, you will be more concerned with finding a loan, than with the current interest rate. Shop around.

For most small business owners, commercial lenders are the only game in town. Banks tend to shy away from small companies experiencing rapid sales growth, a temporary decline, or a seasonal slump; in addition, firms that are already highly leveraged (a high debt-to-equity ratio) will usually have a hard time getting more bank funding. Yet business lenders will often step in where banks fear to tread because they are set up to handle just those situations and because they know they can get most, if not all, of their defaulted loan back by selling off the collateral pledged against it. Not that liquidation is a desired goal by any means—most business lenders dislike it almost as much as do banks and try to avoid it wherever possible.

Small and medium-size operations are the usual recipients of such loans, although business lenders are generally reluctant to get involved with high-tech companies (the field's too volatile) or services, which obviously don't have the type of assets (except for receivables) suitable for use as collateral. For similar reasons, start-up loans are rare, and lenders won't loan money on assets that don't exist.

There are two types of SBA loans. One is a direct loan, by which the SBA loans funds appropriated by Congress. The other type, the SBA-guaranteed loan, doesn't use government money; the bank or another financial institution loans the money, but it is guaranteed by the SBA for up to 75 percent of the face value of the loan.

An important point to keep in mind: the Small Business Administration rarely makes direct loans. Rather, it guarantees loans through a participation program set up with a bank and makes direct loans only to persons with disabilities, disabled veterans, or Vietnam-era veterans. Other direct loans funded through the SBA go for disaster relief to businesses experiencing natural catastrophes. Even those who qualify cannot solicit a loan from the SBA if they can legitimately obtain a loan from a bank or private source. Therefore, you must first apply to a bank or alternate lending source and if you live in a city with a population over 200,000 you must have been turned down by two financial institutions before seeking SBA funds. For more information on SBA financing, refer to Chapter 14.

The SBA is, without doubt, the largest single source of federally assisted financing for small business. According to Jack Zwick, author of *A Handbook of Small Business Finance*,[2] five major programs are generally available from year to year:

1. **Farmers Home Administration (FmHA) of the U.S. Department of Agriculture.** Applicants must be residents of cities or areas with a population of 50,000 or less outside major metropolitan areas. FmHA loans are guaranteed long-term loans backed 90 percent by the FmHA. They can be used as a source of start-up or working capital, new equipment purchases, refinancing, or expansion (including purchase of real estate). Loans for real estate and major construction are available for up to 30 years. Equipment and machinery can be financed for up to 15 years or their depreciable life, if shorter. Capital funds can be obtained for 6-year terms. There is no limit on the amount you can borrow. Approval depends solely on need and the way you plan to use the money.

2. **Economic Development Administration (EDA) of the Department of Commerce.** EDA makes loans and guarantees to new and existing businesses in depressed areas (regions with high unemployment and low-to-average income levels). Loans may not be granted to cover working capital or to purchase fixed assets. Working capital loans extend up to 7 years, while loans for fixed assets may extend up to 25 years. The loan applicant is expected to provide 15 percent of the required funding. Interest rates will vary according to the prime rate prevailing at the time the loan is granted.

3. **Department of Energy (DOE).** This loan program is geared toward firms developing methods to increase domestic energy efficiency through conservation, alternate energy sources, or new methods of energy utilization. Funding from the DOE does have to be repaid, and guarantees can run as high as $30 million. For companies operating in geothermal zones, loans can be guaranteed up to $200 million.

4. **Department of Housing and Urban Development (HUD).** HUD has several programs consisting of grants and loans for the construction of commercial and residential building to rehabilitate needy areas in targeted cities. Funds are channeled through local officials in cities and towns. They in turn make

---

[2] Jack Zwick, *A Handbook of Small-Business Finance,* (Washington, DC: U.S. Small Business Administration, 1981).

loans or grants to entrepreneurs to develop properties. In the recent past, over $3 billion in loans and grants were disbursed through HUD for these programs.

5. **Department of the Interior (DOI).** The DOI has a historic preservation-grants program through which it makes grants for the restoration of run-down properties that have been declared historic sites by a state agency. Reports indicate that there are some 2,000 properties listed as historic places in the United States, and the list grows each year.

In addition to the five federal programs listed here, you should consider a few other important financing sources when seeking capital to start a new venture or expand a present one:

- **State Business and Industrial Development Corporations (SBIDCs).** Corporations in these programs are capitalized through state governments. They are usually long-term loans (from 5 to 20 years) for either the expansion of an existing small business or for the purchase of capital equipment. Lender requirements and interests will vary from state to state. Some SBIDCs will commit funds to very high-risk ventures, whereas others will look for minimal risk.
- **Local Development Companies (LDCs).** These companies are capitalized through local investment groups. These agencies differ from community to community in their priorities and interests, but in general will solicit funds from the SBA and bank sources to supply money to local business for the construction or expansion of facilities. The LDC will usually receive a loan guarantee from the SBA—up to $1 million with additional unlimited funds originating from banks. All moneys are directed to the LDC as the loan recipient, not the business applying for the financing. The only drawback to LDCs is that they will only finance up to 10 percent of the project.
- **Export Revolving Line of Credit Program.** This program guarantees up to 90 percent of a bank line of credit to a small business exporter who is eligible according to SBA criteria.
- **Export-Import Bank (EXIMBANK).** Working capital for smaller companies to finance preshipment and foreign marketing operations is available from this program.
- **Small Business Innovation Research Program (SBIR).** An exciting opportunity for small businesses to benefit from over $1 billion in federal grants. The SBIR Program (a result of the 1982 Small Business Innovation Development Act) is intended to stir innovative activities among small companies. Eligibility for receipt of SBIR funding is extended to any small company capable of demonstrating science or high-tech expertise. The program categorizes small businesses as independently owned companies with 500 or fewer employees. Average recipient companies have had fewer than 35 employees, and 45 percent of Phase I awards have gone to companies with 10 employees or less.

Equity Financing

With equity financing you are actually selling off a portion of your business to investors who may or may not actively participate in the management of the company. The main concern with equity financing is how much control to give up. During your start-up phase, you will probably have to give up as much as 50 percent of the equity in the company. If you have capital to invest in the company, you can receive the same proportion of equity for your funds. However, while the 50-50 rule is fairly common, the market is also seeing a trend toward a 51-49 split. Equity investors are beginning to provide capital for a minority share in the business. You can also offset the 50-50 rule by placing an equity value on proprietary knowledge such as patents or specific operating information. You can negotiate a value for this knowledge and receive equity for that contribution.

Keep in mind that how you legally form your business will also have a direct bearing on raising equity capital. A sole proprietorship is the form of business you start and run by yourself. There's one owner, one equity investor—you—and you alone are responsible for the business.

If you form a partnership, you may have a general partner. Then you each own the business equally. You're both responsible for running the business. You're both responsible for the liabilities and responsibilities of that business. If it goes bankrupt, you share that equally.

In a limited partnership arrangement, your goal is to recruit investors to become partners in your company on a limited basis. Sometimes referred to as syndications, limited partnerships consist of a general partner who manages the money raised to actively operate the business, while the investors are limited partners. Should the venture meet with misfortune, the partners' liability is "limited" to what they have invested. They can lose their original investment in the event of collapse, but they can't be assessed everything as they could if they came into a business as a general partner.

As the general partner, you assume the obligation of running the venture on a day-to-day basis. Limited partners, by their legally constituted role, serve as passive investors rather than active managers. There are advantages for the limited partners. They invest the money while someone else produces the profits. These profits, other than the amounts needed for business operation and possible plowback into the business for expansion, must be divided among the partners. If a business succeeds, they can reap profit distribution far in excess of anything they are likely to get as conventional stockholders. Along the same lines, by taking advantage of the limited partnership structure, you don't have to give up the equity in the business permanently to proceed with a specific project venture.

Rules governing limited partnership capitalization vary from state to state and must be strictly observed. In many states, you cannot advertise or offer limited partnership participations publicly without formal "registration" as a securities offering. Where this is the case, you are suddenly facing on a state level many of the same rules, filing procedures, and disclosure headaches that companies going public encounter at the federal (SEC) level. This is expensive and time-consuming and is the sort of activity that you'll undertake with a securities lawyer.

In many states, you can secure exemption from registration if the offering is limited to a preset number of investors and is not trumpeted to the public. For instance, you could hold a cocktail party at which you approach the potential limited partners of your venture, but you couldn't advertise in the local newspaper for limited partners to join your venture. Find out what the rules are in your state with respect to forming limited partnerships, and don't try to exaggerate them.

You can also form a corporation to raise equity financing. Partners forming a corporation can divide ownership into shares, selling this private stock to equity investors; responsibilities can be defined in the corporate minutes, and a partner who wants to leave can be accommodated without much legal hassle or dissolution of the business. Stock can be used as collateral (in a partnership it cannot); death of one shareholder doesn't stop the business (in a partnership it sometimes does). And, you can enjoy many executive privileges that are difficult to justify in a sole proprietorship or partnership.

Banks are more amenable to loaning to a corporation, profits can be delayed, capital can be accumulated without taxation, and the corporation can loan money to you personally. To raise additional capital or even start-up capital, the corporation may elect to offer company stock to the investing public. In this manner, the company has gone from being a privately held corporation to being a publicly held corporation.

The only disadvantage is possible double taxation because the corporation must pay taxes on its net income, and you must also pay taxes on any dividends you may receive from the corporation.

Taking the corporation one step further and infusing elements of the sole proprietorship and partnerships is the Subchapter S corporation. This form of operation allows you to take on passive investors who will contribute money to your business for stock within the corporation. Like a limited partnership, a Subchapter S corporation gives you full operational responsibilities while taking on investors within the company.

Unlike limited partnerships, however, a Subchapter S corporation is still a corporation with all the privileges except one: They elect not to be taxed as corporations. Instead, the shareholders of a Subchapter S corporation include in their individual gross incomes their proportionate shares of the corporate profits and losses. Subchapter S corporations are excellent devices for allowing small businesses to avoid double taxation. If your company produces a substantial profit, forming a Subchapter S corporation would be wise because the profits will be added to your personal income and taxed at an individual rate that may be lower than the regular corporate rate on that income.

To qualify under Subchapter S, the corporation must be a domestic corporation, must not be a member of an affiliated group, must not have more than 35 shareholders (all of whom are either individuals or estates), must not have a nonresident alien as a shareholder, and can only have one class of outstanding stock. Under the new rules, it can now have an unlimited amount of passive income from rents, royalties, and interest.

A passive activity is one in which a taxpayer does not materially participate. Material participation requires involvement in operations on a regular, continuous, substantial basis. Under the 1986 Tax Reform Act, losses and credits from a "passive" business activity can only be deducted against passive income. Passive losses and credits will not be usable against nonpassive income, which includes a compensation and portfolio income; however, rental losses and credits can be used against up to $25,000 of nonpassive income.

Professional investors, such as *venture capitalists,* can be good sources of funds. They have capital available for new and relatively risky enterprises. Many venture capital firms are controlled by banks, but they operate on completely different rules.

Venture capitalists expect two things from the companies they finance—high returns and a method of exit. Since venture capitalists hit the jackpot with only a small percentage of the companies they back, they must go into each deal with the possibility of a return of 5 to 10 times their investment in three to five years if the company is successful. This may mean that they will own anywhere from 25 to 70 percent or more of your company. Each situation is different, and the amount of equity the venture capitalist will hold depends on the stage of the company's development at the time of the investment, the risk perceived, the amount of capital required, and the background of the entrepreneur.

What kinds of businesses do venture capitalists invest in? Venture capitalists invest primarily in technology-related industries—not new technology necessarily—but applications of existing technology. The largest areas of investment for venture capitalists are usually computer-related communications, electronics, genetic engineering, and medical/health-related fields. There are, however, a number of investments in service and distribution businesses and even a few in consumer-related companies.

The key to attracting venture capital is the potential growth prospects for the company. If your company does not have the potential to be a $30- to $50-million company in five to seven years, you are going to have a difficult time raising money from most venture capitalists. They do not invest in small businesses; they invest in large businesses that are just getting started. There are some venture firms that may have an interest in financing your venture even if your growth prospects are not that high, but these are difficult to find.

Before approaching venture capitalists, do your homework and find out if your needs match their preferred investment strategy and find out what strengths the venture capitalist possesses that may help you in building your company. There are a number of directories that list the investment preferences of venture capitalists.

When you have narrowed the field to some 10 companies, the best way to contact them is through an introduction from a third party—another entrepreneur, a lawyer, a CPA, a banker, or anyone who knows you and knows the venture capitalist well enough to get his or her attention. The first meeting with the venture capitalist is very important. Your presentation of your business plan, your appearance, your conduct, what you say and how you say it are all critical. Be prepared. You will be asked many questions about your business plan.

If the venture capitalist decides to finance your firm, the actual investment is negotiable and can take one of a variety of forms ranging from a straight common stock purchase to debentures with conversion features to straight loans. Venture capitalists usually use a combination of investment instruments to structure the deal that will be most beneficial to both parties.

Regardless of whether you are a spectacular success or a catastrophic failure, there will come a time when the venture capitalist will want out—or when you will want the investor out. This is the point at which the venture capitalist will realize the appreciated gain (or loss) on his or her investment. This "exit" will have been discussed in some depth at the time you negotiated the original deal. You will either take your company public, repurchase the investor's stock, merge with another firm, or, in some circumstances, liquidate your business.

Another type of professional investor, called a small business investment corporation (SBIC) operates under the auspices of the federal government. These are private investors, but for every dollar they invest they get three to four dollars in SBA-guaranteed loans. The SBIC's criteria, however, are just as stringent as a bank's or any other private investor's, perhaps even more. That is why it's very difficult, in fact almost impossible, for a brand-new business to use a SBIC.

Under the law, SBICs must invest exclusively in small firms with net worth less than $6 million and average after-tax earnings (over the past two years) of less than $2 million. Being licensed and regulated by a government agency distinguishes SBICs from other "private" venture capital firms. The advantage of this arrangement to the SBIC comes in the form of *leverage*. An SBIC that is in compliance with the regulations and that has invested substantially all its initial private capital can borrow additional investment funds, (this is called leveraging) from the Federal Treasury. Beyond that, the operations of an SBIC are not significantly different from those of a private venture firm.

An offshoot of the SBIC is the MESBIC—the *Minority Enterprise Small Business Investment Company*. MESBIC is privately capitalized. Like the SBIC, borrowers have at least $150,000 when they start, and then they're eligible for government-guaranteed loans. If your business has already gotten started but needs more capital, then check into these investors. They will want a company that looks as if it will become very profitable. When they sell in three or four years, they want three to five times return on their money.

Small Business Development Companies (SBDCs) provide yet another avenue for financing. The only difference between these financing entities and SBICs is that their capital comes exclusively from the following private interests:

- Multinational corporations and conglomerates.
- Utilities.
- Firms dealing with infrastructure.
- Private business consortia.

Like SBICs and MESBICs, the SBDCs that operate in this country invest for the long run. Don't approach them if you are trying to finance a short-term equipment purchase or need an overnight loan; that's why banks exist.

Trade Credit

After you're a regular customer, a supplier normally will extend your credit for 30 to 90 days without charging interest. However, when you're first starting your business, suppliers are not going to give you trade credit. They're going to want to make every order COD until you've established that you can pay your bills on time. To raise money during the start-up period, you're going to have to try to negotiate a trade credit basis with suppliers. One of the things you can do that will help you in these negotiations is prepare a financial plan.

When you visit your supplier to set up your order during your start-up period, ask to speak directly to the owner of the business if it's a small company. If it's a larger business, ask to speak to the chief financial officer or any other person who approves credit. Introduce yourself. Show the officer the financial plan that you have prepared. Tell the owner or financial officer about your business and explain that you need to get your first orders on credit in order to launch your venture.

The owner or financial officer may give you half the order on credit with balance due on delivery. Of course, the trick here is to get your goods shipped to you and sell them before you have to pay for them yourself. You could borrow the money to pay for your inventory, but you would have to pay interest on that money. So trade credit is one of the most important ways to reduce the amount of working capital you need. This is especially true in retail operations.

RESOURCES

Government Agencies

Export-Import Bank of the United States, 811 Vermont Avenue NW, Washington, DC 20571, 202-566-2117

U.S. Department of Agriculture, 14th and Independence Avenue SW, Washington, DC 20250, 202-447-2791

U.S. Department of Energy, 1000 Independence Avenue SW, Washington, DC 20585, 202-586-5000

U.S. Department of Interior, 1849 C Street, NW, Washington, DC 20549, 202-208-3100

U.S. Securities and Exchange Commission, 450 Fifth Street NW, Washington, DC 20549, 202-272-2644

U.S. Small Business Administration, 409 Third Street SW, Washington, DC 20416, 800-827-5722

Associations

American Bankers Association, 1120 Connecticut Avenue NW, Washington, DC 20036, 202-663-5000

American League of Financial Institutions, 900 19th Street NW, Washington, DC 20006, 202-628-5624

Independent Bankers Association of America, One Thomas Circle NW, Suite 950, Washington, DC 20005, 202-659-8111

National Association of Development Companies, 444 North Capital Street NW, Suite 630, Washington, DC 20001, 202-624-7806

National Association of Small Business Investment Companies, 1199 North Fairfax Street, Suite 200, Alexandria, VA 22314, 703-683-1601

National Commercial Finance Association, 25 West 34th Street, Suite 1815, New York, NY 10122, 212-594-3490

National Council of Savings Institutions, 900 19th Street NW, Washington, DC 20006, 202-857-3100

National Venture Capital Association, 1655 North Fort Myer Drive, Suite 700, Arlington, VA 22209, 703-351-5269

Pratt's Guide to Venture Capital Sources, Venture Economics, A Division of Securities Data Publishing Co., 40 Q. 57th Street, Suite 1100, New York, NY 10019, 212-765-5311

Vankirk Business Information, 2800 Shirlington Road, Suite 904, Arlington, VA 22206, 703-379-9200

Magazines

American Banker, One State Street Plaza, New York, NY 10004, 212-803-8200

Bankers Digest, 6440 North Central Expressway, Suite 215, Dallas, TX 75206, 214-373-4544

Banking Week, One State Street Plaza, New York, NY 10004, 212-943-2222

Business Credit, 8815 Centre Park Drive, Suite 200, Columbia, MD 21045, 410-740-5560

Corporate Cashflow, 6151 Powers Ferry Road, Atlanta, GA 30339, 404-955-2500

Corporate Financing Week, 488 Madison Avenue, 12th Floor, New York, NY 10022, 212-303-3300

Credit, 919 18th Street NW, Suite 300, Washington, DC 20006, 202-296-5544

Going Public: The IPO Reporter, 2 World Trade Center, 18th Floor, New York, NY 10048, 212-227-1200

The Independent Banker, 1168 South Main, P.O. Box 267, Sauk Centre, MN 56378-1653, 612-352-6546

Journal of Cash Management, 7315 Wisconsin Ave., Suite 1250 W, Bethesda MD 20814, 301-907-2862

Savings and Community Banker, 900 19th Street NW, Suite 400, Washington, DC 20006, 202-857-3100

The Secured Lender, 225 West 34th Street, New York, NY 10122-0008, 212-594-3490

Securities Week, 1221 Avenue of the Americas, New York, NY 10020, 212-512-6148

14 Small Business Administration Loans

Often called the lender of last resort by small business advocates, the Small Business Administration, established in 1953 by the Department of Commerce, helps entrepreneurs secure the required capital to start a business or expand operations. Neither the SBA nor the federal government generally offers grants to help achieve these objectives. However, the SBA is authorized to make loan guarantees through participating banks and other institutions. In some cases, it will extend direct loans to new and existing businesses. The latter is very rare, though.

The SBA is one of the best sources for small business loans. This is not to say that acquiring a loan from the SBA is a simple task, however. There are numerous requirements you must first meet before the SBA will even consider your application. Additionally, once you are eligible, there is still the matter of reporting requirements and other conditions needed to obtain a loan. This chapter will show you what you need to know when applying for an SBA loan.

TYPES OF SBA LOANS

There are three types of SBA loans. One is a direct loan, by which the SBA loans its own funds, appropriated by Congress. Another is the SBA-guaranteed loan, which doesn't use government money; money is loaned by the bank or other financial institution but guaranteed by the SBA for up to 90 percent of the face value of the loan. A third is a fairly new addition to the SBA roster, called the Microloan Program. Funded by the SBA and handled by nonprofit organizations, it provides start-up businesses with small amounts of capital to give them momentum.[1]

---

[1] Erskine Bowles, "Bite-Sized Loans," *Entrepreneur* (December 1993) p. 152.

An important point to keep in mind—the SBA rarely makes direct loans. Rather, they guarantee loans through a participation program set up with a bank and make direct loans up to $150,000 only to the handicapped, disabled veterans, owners working in economically depressed areas, or Vietnam-era veterans. Other direct loans funded through the SBA go for disaster relief to businesses experiencing natural catastrophes. Even those who qualify cannot solicit a loan from the SBA if they can legitimately obtain a loan from a bank or private source. Therefore, you must first apply to a bank or alternate lending source. Additionally, if you live in a city with a population over 200,000, you must have been turned down by two financial institutions before seeking funds. In addition, the financial assistance required cannot be obtainable on reasonable terms through the public offering or private placing of securities, or through the disposal at a fair price of assets not required to conduct business properly or not necessary to potential growth.

If you do apply for an SBA loan, the lead time it takes to process the loan varies depending on the circumstances involved. It will take at least 12 to 18 months before you get approved. However, a properly prepared application for an SBA loan might be processed in as little as 2 months, with the applicant receiving the money within one week after finding a bank willing to participate in a guarantee.

SPECIFIC LOAN PROGRAMS OFFERED

A summary of the major SBA loan programs follows.

7a Guaranteed Loan Program

SBA guaranteed loans are still the most prominent form of receiving financial help from this agency. These are loans made through a private lending institution that are guaranteed by the SBA for between 70 and 90 percent of the principal loan amount, up to a limit of $750,000. The guidelines for SBA-guaranteed loans are similar to those for standard bank loans: You must establish your equity, history, management experience, and so on. In addition, your company must qualify as a small business according to SBA size standards, which vary from industry to industry.[2] Keep in mind that under a loan guarantee, the SBA itself is not making the loan. It is simply protecting the lending institution against default of the loan. In essence, the SBA is a form of security that reduces the risks perceived by lending sources when dealing with small business loans.

The interest rate charged on SBA guaranteed loans is based on the prime rate. The SBA does not set interest rates since they are not the lender. It does, however, regulate the amount of interest that a lender may charge an SBA

---

[2] Elizabeth Wallace, "Bank on It," *Entrepreneur* (May 1993) p. 85.

borrower. If the loan has a term of seven years or more, the SBA allows the lender to charge as much as 2.75 percent above the prevailing prime rate. If the loan has a term of less than seven years, the rate add-on is the base plus as much as 2.25 percent.

As collateral for an SBA guaranteed loan, you can use certain assets as security:

- Land and/or buildings.
- Machinery and/or equipment.
- Real estate and/or chattel mortgages.
- Warehouse receipts for marketable merchandise.
- Personal endorsement of a guarantor (a friend who is able and willing to pay off the loan if you fail).
- Accounts receivable.
- Savings accounts.
- Life insurance policies.
- Stocks and bonds.

In addition, the applicant may need a minimum of 25 percent of the start-up costs of a new business to be in "good faith" with the SBA. The specific percentage depends on the type of business and the lender involved. Some businesses require between 35 and 40 percent; others require even more.

502 Local Development Company Program

The 502 Loan Program targets long-term, fixed asset financing to rural areas, according to the SBA. The loan amounts are administered through certified development companies through commercial lending institutions. If you are in the market for a major piece of land or equipment, this program could be your secret to start-up success. The SBA will guarantee up to $1 million, or 40 percent of the loan amount, with the maximum amount qualified by an owner being $25 million. This program was developed with the help of certified development corporations. Small start-up business owners will probably not qualify for this type of loan because of the high amount involved, but it is beneficial for large-scale owners in the market for real estate for the purchase of large machinery.[3]

8(a) Participant Loan Program

According to the SBA, this program makes financial assistance available to 8(a) certified firms and minority advocacy groups directly from the SBA or through lending institutions under the agency's immediate participation or guaranty programs. Applicants must be a qualifying firm and eligible for contractual assistance. People who qualify for loans can use the finances for working capital,

---

[3] Shannon Hill, "Help Line," *Entrepreneur* (February 1994) p. 164.

their facilities, or equipment. For start-up and small business, you might want to consider applying for a new lending vehicle called the Microloan Program. Established in June 1992, it offers anywhere from a few hundred dollars to $25,000 in start-up capital to businesses that cannot apply to traditional lenders because the amount they need is too small. Also, if you have little or no collateral, this loan program is certainly for you.

The program is currently offered in 44 states and is run by nonprofit organizations that are experienced in helping others monetarily. They take SBA-funded subsidies and distribute them according to need and amount. According to the SBA, the average loan size as of September 1993 neared $10,000, with 37 percent going to minority-owned businesses and 45 percent awarded to women-owned companies.[4] These groups oftentimes have the biggest problems obtaining a loan. At the end of February 1994, the SBA had appropriated $38 million.

Economic Opportunity Loans

The principal purpose of the Economic Opportunity Loan (EOL) program is to make funds available on reasonable terms and maturities to small business concerns owned by, or to be established by, persons with low incomes; and to provide management assistance to such persons.

To be eligible for an EOL, the business must be at least 50 percent owned by a person or persons who either (1) has/have individual annual family income(s) other than welfare not sufficient to satisfy the basic need of each such individual family; or (2) has/have been denied the opportunity to have access to adequate financing on reasonable terms through normal lending channels because of economic or social disadvantage. Businesses located in urban or rural areas with a high proportion of unemployed or low-income individuals may be considered economically disadvantaged. Economic Opportunity Loans for veterans receive the following considerations:

1. In-depth management assistance counseling of first interviews to apprise veterans of SBA's programs and the potential benefits to them.
2. Special workshops and training.
3. Prompt processing of loan applications of any type.
4. Particular attention to giving maximum loan maturity to veterans.
5. Loans will not be declined solely because of the lack of collateral, on the condition that the veteran, dependent, or survivor will provide any worthwhile collateral.
6. On all direct loans, a flexible approach to the standard repayment schedule will be considered.
7. In all district offices there shall be one or more loan specialists designated as veterans' loan officers.

[4] Erskine Bowles, "Bite-Sized Loans," *Entrepreneur* (December 1993) p. 152.

There are two types of handicapped assistance loans: "HAL-1" is a Handicapped Assistance Loan to an organization over 50 percent of whose employees are handicapped; "HAL-2" is a Handicapped Assistance Loan to an individual small business applicant designated by a court or doctor as being "65 percent" handicapped. These loans have the following requirements:

1. Applicants must provide information from a physician, psychiatrist, and/or professional counselor in writing as to the permanent nature of the handicap and the limitations it places on the applicant.
2. Under HAL-2, financial assistance may be used to buy a business by disabled veterans, Vietnam-era veterans, and the handicapped.
3. Interest on direct loans and the SBA share of an immediate-participation loan is 3 percent per annum; nondisabled Vietnam-era veterans pay $9\frac{7}{8}$ percent at this writing.
4. Repayment will be required at the earliest date feasible, giving consideration to the intended use of the funds and the indicated ability to repay, with 25 years as the absolute maximum and real estate offered as collateral. Most loans must be paid within 7 to 10 years.

The SBA also makes other types of loans to help owners of small businesses. Loans are available to help small businesses comply with the federal air-and-water-pollution regulations and with occupational safety and health requirements. They are available to offset problems caused by federal actions such as highway or building construction or the closing of military bases. They can also relieve economic injuries suffered by a small business as a result of energy or material shortages, or temporary economic dislocations.

TYPES OF LENDERS

The SBA uses three primary types of lenders that fund loans:

1. Infrequent participant lenders are just what the name infers. These are bank and nonbank lending institutions that deal with the SBA on a sporadic basis. Most of the lenders that have contact with the SBA fall into this category. An infrequent lender sends the SBA all paperwork involved with any particular loan guarantee situation. The SBA does an independent analysis of the plan and determines whether it will guarantee the loan that the institution is going to give the borrower.
2. Certified lenders are lending institutions that participate with the SBA on a regular basis and have an SBA-involved staff trained and certified by the agency. Under this program, the lender reviews all the paperwork, decides whether the borrower merits a loan, and the SBA has the final word. Only after the lender has approved the loan does the SBA review the documents, and then they have only three days to do so.

LowDoc Loan Program

The Small Business Administration recently adopted a new program that makes applying for a loan somewhat easier. Called the LowDoc Loan Program, it combines a simplified application process with a more rapid response from SBA loan officers (perhaps two or three days), slashing pages of bureaucracy and red tape out of the loan process.

The LowDoc Program was created in response to complaints that the SBA's loan application process for smaller loans was needlessly cumbersome for both borrowers and lenders that participate in the SBA's 7(a) General Business Loan Guarantee Program. The process tended to discourage borrowers from applying and lenders from making loans of less than $100,000.

LowDoc streamlines the loan application process for guaranteed loans under $100,000. The approval process relies heavily on a lender's experience and judgment of a borrower's credit history and character. The primary considerations are the borrower's willingness and ability to repay debts, as shown by their personal and business credit history, and by past or projected cash flow. No predetermined percentage of equity is required and lack of full collateral is not necessarily a determining factor.

The application form for loans under $50,000 consists of a single page. Applications for loans from $50,000 to $100,000 include that short-form application plus the applicant's income tax returns for the previous three years and personal financial statements from all other guarantors and co-owners of the business. Commercial lenders are likely to require additional paperwork to satisfy their own requirements. Other documents required by legislation, regulation, and executive order are dealt with at the loan closing.

Eligibility

Any small business eligible under the regular 7(a) loan program can apply under LowDoc if its average annual sales for the previous three years is $5,000,000 or less and it employs 100 or fewer individuals, including the owner, partners, or principals.

3. Preferred lenders are certified lenders that have graduated to the top of the list based on performance. Under the Preferred Lenders' Program, the SBA designates its "best and most reliable lending partners" as preferred lenders, which may make final decisions regarding loan approval and processing (with final review by the SBA).

Not all banks are eligible for either the Bank Certification Program or Preferred Lenders Program. Indeed, most preferred lenders tend to be the major commercial banks that may have specialized SBA divisions in their organization. Each bank must meet four criteria:

- **Experience.** A minimum of 10 years' SBA lending.
- **Prudence.** A good record with few loans bought back by the SBA.
- **Community lending.** A solid record of loans to local borrowers, especially to minorities and to women.
- **Assistance to small business.** A record of helping local small firms.

Even with eligibility, some certified banks request a regular credit check from the SBA for some of their loans. One reason for this is that if a bank is negligent in approving a loan under the Certified Lending Program, the SBA can deny liability. The bank Certification Program is not geared toward every type of SBA request. Primarily it's designed for stable business with proven track records.

SBA LOAN RESTRICTIONS

To be considered for any loan funded by or through the SBA, whether you are starting a new business or obtaining capital for an existing one, you must first meet certain conditions. First of all, the business requesting SBA financing must be independently owned and operated, not dominant in its field, and must meet employment or sales standards developed by the agency. Loans cannot be made to speculative businesses, media-related businesses, businesses engaged in gambling, lending, or investing, recreational or amusement facilities, or nonprofit enterprises.

Loans also cannot be made to:

- Pay off a creditor who is adequately secured and in a position to sustain loss.
- Provide funds for distribution to the principals of the applicant.
- Replenish funds previously used for such purposes.
- Encourage a monopoly or activity that is inconsistent with the accepted standards of the American system of free competitive enterprise.
- Purchase property that will be held for sale or investment.
- Relocate a business for other than sound business purposes.
- Effect a change of ownership unless it will aid in the sound development of the company or will engage a person hampered or prevented from participating in the free enterprise system because of economic, physical, or social disadvantages.
- Acquire or start another business besides the present one.
- Expand to an additional location.
- Create an absentee-ownership business.
- Refinance debt of any kind.

Be fully prepared to prove to the SBA that your proposed company has the ability to compete and be successful in its particular field. Whether you are seeking a loan for an untried concept or an established one, do not underestimate the importance of the category into which the SBA groups it. The success or failure of your application may rest on the classification assigned by the SBA. Determine which field or area your business can best compete in, state this in your application, and be prepared to back up your statement.

To help you prepare for this question, you should be aware of how the SBA formulates its guidelines. A key publication it relies on is the *Standard Industrial*

Classification (SIC) *Manual,*[5] published by the Bureau of the Budget, Washington, DC. The SBA also uses published information concerning the nature of similar companies, as well as your description of the proposed business. The SBA will not intentionally work against you; therefore, it is up to you to steer the agency in the direction most beneficial to you.

The standards used by the SBA for judging the size of a business for purposes of qualifying for a loan vary from one industry to another, remembering SBA's basic tenet that the business applying for the loan must qualify as small. Generally, the following guidelines apply, according to William Cohen in his book, *The Entrepreneur and Small Business Problem Solver:*[6]

- **Manufacturing and wholesaling.** Firms engaged in manufacturing a product are constrained by their number of employees. Average employment in the preceding four calendar quarters must not exceed 500. If employment exceeded 500 but not 1,500 for a manufacturing company, the SBA bases its determination on a specific size standard for the particular industry.
- **Services.** Annual receipts not exceeding $3.5 million are ideal. Sales of $3.5 million to $14.5 million will be considered, depending on the particular industry.
- **Retailing.** Annual sales not exceeding $3.5 million are ideal. Sales of $3.5 million to $13.5 million will be considered, depending on the industry.
- **Construction.** This refers to general construction. Average annual receipts should not exceed $17 million for the three most recently completed fiscal years, depending on the industry.
- **Agriculture.** Annual receipts should not exceed $100,000 to $3.5 million.

SBA LOAN STRUCTURE

Product classification and size are not the only things the SBA will want to know about your business. Whether you are applying for a loan to finance a new start-up or fund an existing business, the SBA will want to know the following about you and your business:

- A description of the business you plan to establish.
- Your experience and management capabilities.
- How much money you plan to invest in the business and how much you will need to borrow.
- A statement of your present financial position showing all personal assets and liabilities.
- A detailed projection of what your business will earn in its first year of operation.

---

[5] U.S. Bureau of the Budget, *Standard Industrial Classification (SIC) Manual,* 1994.
[6] William Cohen, *The Entrepreneur and Small Business Problem Solver* (New York: John Wiley & Sons, 1990).

- The collateral you can offer as security for the loan, and an estimate of its current market value.

Accuracy is of utmost importance. Keep notes on everything that goes into the loan package as backup in the event you are called on to explain or prove a figure or statement on any of the documents. Table 14.1 lists the documents to prepare for a new or existing business.

The Personal Financial Statement

This form lists all your assets and liabilities and must be prepared for each major stockholder (at least 20 percent ownership), partner, officer, and owner of the business. Your financial statement must be current (not more than 90 days preceding the date of your loan application), and it must accurately portray your financial position. The SBA may reject your application if it finds any misrepresentation with inflated entries. Obtain copies of SBA Form 413 for preparing your personal balance sheet.

The Financial Plan

Every business, large or small, new or old, needs to have a *financial plan* to guide it. Whether you call this an operating plan, a forecast, or a projection, it must show your potential profit or loss and your cash flow during the first 12 months of operation. Preparing these estimates will probably be the most difficult part of preparing your loan package, and you may want to enlist the services of an accountant to do this for you. You can use SBA Form 1099 for preparing a forecast, or you can have your accountant develop one for you. If your projections show that you will gross more than $250,000 during the first

Table 14.1   Documents Needed for SBA Loans

DOCUMENTS TO PREPARE FOR A NEW BUSINESS
Loan request statement, describing loan amount and a detailed account of the type of business you are starting
Your resume and the resumes of key managers you plan to employ
Statement of your investment capabilities
Current financial statement of all personal liabilities and assets
Projection of revenue statement
Collateral list

DOCUMENTS TO PREPARE FOR AN EXISTING BUSINESS
Balance sheet, with all liabilities and assets listed
Income statement of previous and current year-to-date incomes
Personal financial statement, with each owner itemized
Collateral list
Loan request statement, describing loan amount and purpose

year, then a pro forma balance sheet should be made as of the end of the first-year forecast. Figure 14.1 shows a sample financial planning form.

Take the time necessary to prepare a reasonable and realistic projection of your month-to-month sales, expenses, profits, and cash flow. A reasonable and realistic estimate is based on fact; it is an educated guess, not a dream or a hope that cannot be substantiated. The more documented proof you can get to back up your estimates, the better will be your chance of securing the funding you requested. In addition, the exercise of putting all these numbers together will make you more knowledgeable about your business, and this will increase your chances of success.

The first month in your projection should be the month in which your business is fully operational. This could very well be two, three, or more months after you receive you loan funds. Some people prefer to begin by estimating their sales. Others prefer to start by estimating expenses. As long as your numbers are good solid estimates, you should not worry about how you arrive at them. What is important is that you include the following items in your projection:

- **Total sales (net).** Total sales include both "cash" and "on-account" sales; net sales are total sales minus returns and refunds. If your business has separate profit-making departments, estimate sales for each department separately.
- **Cost of sales.** Cost of sales should include the cost of merchandise sold and freight or transportation charges you pay on incoming inventory. If any of your employees will be paid a sales commission, the amount of commissions should be included in your cost of sales.
- **Gross profit.** Gross profit, sometimes called gross margin, is the difference between net sales and cost of sales.

The second half of your operating plan projections deal with expenses. These are costs incurred on a monthly basis in order to operate your company. They are:

- **Salaries.** This is actually your estimated payroll cost and does not include your own salary compensation.
- **Payroll taxes and benefits.** Payroll taxes include all state and federal obligations. In addition, any company paid benefits you provide your employees, such as vacation, sick pay, health insurance, etc. should be included in this entry.
- **Outside services.** These are any services necessary to operate your business on a monthly basis such as janitorial, pest control, etc.
- **Supplies.** All items purchased for office and operating use in the business (not for resale) are included here. This could include cleansers, paper towels, light bulbs, cash register tapes, ashtrays, stationery supplies, business cards, printing of forms, as well as pens, pencils, staplers, typewriter ribbons, etc. Also include postage expenses here.
- **Repairs and maintenance.** This includes all repairs to equipment used in the operation of the business as well as any maintenance contracts or regularly scheduled service work.

Table 14.2 Cash Flow Projection Form

	1st MONTH	2nd MONTH	3rd MONTH	4th MONTH	5th MONTH	6th MONTH	7th MONTH	8th MONTH	9th MONTH	10th MONTH	11th MONTH	12th MONTH	TOTAL
1. Sales													
2. Cost of sales													
3. Gross profit													
EXPENSES													
4. Advertising													
5. Automobile													
6. Bank discounts													
7. Depreciation													
8. Dues & subscriptions													
9. Insurance													
10. Interest													
11. Office supplies													
12. Payroll taxes													
13. Professional services													
14. Rent													
15. Repairs & maintenance													
16. Salaries													
17. Supplies													
18. Taxes/licenses													
19. Utilities/phone													
20. Miscellaneous													
21. TOTAL EXPENSES													
22. PROFIT BEFORE TAXES													

Table 14.2 (continued)

	1st MONTH	2nd MONTH	3rd MONTH	4th MONTH	5th MONTH	6th MONTH	7th MONTH	8th MONTH	9th MONTH	10th MONTH	11th MONTH	12th MONTH	TOTAL
INCOME													
23. Cash sales													
24. Accounts receivable													
25. Other													
26. TOTAL CASH AVAILABLE													
DISBURSEMENTS													
27. Owner's draw													
28. Loan repayment													
29. Cost of sales (line 2)													
30. Total expenses (less line 7)													
31. Capital expenditures													
32. Tax reserve													
33. Other													
34. TOTAL DISBURSEMENTS													
35. MONTHLY CASH FLOW													
36. CUMULATIVE CASH FLOW													

- **Advertising.** This is your budgeted cost for marketing your company, product or service and should include any special promotions or grand opening events.
- **Cars, delivery, and travel.** Include any costs incurred by you or your employees for air fare, meals, lodging, vehicle rental or lease payments, gas, and the mileage allowance set forth by the IRS for private or company-owned vehicles.
- **Accounting/legal.** These are costs generated to maintain your accounting records, prepare year-end financial statements and tax return, consult with an attorney, or subscribe to a security service.
- **Rent.** Monthly rent, lease or mortgage payment on the use of operating facilities.
- **Phone.** Monthly costs incurred for all telecommunications service such as basic phone, FAX machines, cellular phone, etc.
- **Utilities.** These estimates include cost of electricity, gas or oil for heating water, garbage collection, and sewer charges, if applicable.
- **Insurance.** These costs include property, product and liability coverage. Do not forget to include any special coverage needed for your particular business. Do not include life insurance in this category.
- **Taxes and licenses.** These include all applicable taxes and licensing fees such as business licenses, inventory tax, sales tax, excise tax and personal property tax. Do not include income or payroll tax in this category.
- **Interest.** Only business debts should be considered. Do not include the portion of your payment that covers principal repayment of your loan.
- **Depreciation.** For tax purposes, the IRS will allow you to deduct a certain percentage of the cost of various fixed assets.
- **Other.** Include any miscellaneous expenses that do not appear in the preceding categories.
- **Total expenses.** This is the total of all the preceding expenses.
- **Profit before taxes.** This is the difference between the gross profit of your business and the total expenses.

In making your projections, understand that sales, profits, and cash are not the same thing. Obviously they are related, but it is not unusual for a business to encounter periodic shortages of cash *even though sales and profits may be booming.* For this reason, it is necessary to prepare a separate schedule specifically for cash flow. This involves projecting total cash inflow and total cash outflow month by month for a 12-month period. You can do this after you have prepared your projections for sales and expenses.

A *cash flow projection* is necessary to enable you to manage receipts and disbursements so that cash is always available to meet expenses as they become due. Therefore, in your projection you must pay close attention to timing, taking into account the time lag between sales and the collection of receivables and between expenses and the due dates for their payment. You can prepare your own cash flow statement or use SBA Form 1100. Although Form 1100 is more detailed, it is no more difficult to use than preparing your own. Tablee 14.2 shows a sample cash flow form.

In preparing your cash flow projection, you should include the following items:

- **Cash sales.** This is a monthly total of all cash and credit card sales.
- **Accounts receivable.** This is the percentage of sales on credit accounts that can be collected within a given month.
- **Other.** List all other sources of cash inflow including family members, stock offerings, and any other loans except start-up funding.
- **Total cash available.** This is the total money on hand before making any disbursements.
- **Owner's draw.** List the monthly stipend(s) received by the owner(s).
- **Loan principal repayments.** This is principal only and should not include any interest payments.
- **Cost of sales.**
- **Total expenses.**
- **Capital expenditures.** Include all costs associated with the purchase of equipment, fixtures, tools, leasehold improvements, vehicles, and other capital assets in the first month.
- **Reserve for taxes.** This is a reserve fund for future income tax.
- **Other.** Include any miscellaneous disbursements that do not appear in the preceding categories.
- **Total disbursements.**
- **Monthly cash flow.** This is your total available cash after meeting all disbursements.
- **Cumulative cash flow.** This is the yearly total on the monthly cash flow.

Capital Requirements

If you are obtaining the loan to start a new business, you'll need to consider all your start-up costs in launching your business, how much of these costs you can meet from your personal funds, and how much will come from your loan. The following example shows how to summarize the use of funds required for your business:

Capital equipment/building improvements, $1.2 million
Inventory, $3.5 million
Labor, $1.8 million
Overhead, $8.7 million
Marketing, $1.8 million
R&D, $4 million
G&A, $4 million
Miscellaneous, $.6
TOTAL CAPITAL REQUIRED, $18.4 million
Less: Investment by Applicant, $9.9 million
TOTAL LOAN REQUESTED, $8.5 million

Keep all your notes and worksheets to show how you determined each of the figures on this statement. Obtain written price quotations on all items you plan to purchase. Concerning equipment, you should estimate the amount of money you will need for repair and maintenance of all pieces. The cost for building improvements should be based on three bids from reliable contractors. For inventory, you should budget enough money to carry you through your opening period and the first few months. Prepare a list of your major suppliers, and for each one get information on their prices, delivery schedules and terms of payment. The following example shows a typical supplier list:

Sample List of Suppliers (names are fictional)

Adams Specialties
2 Hilltop Pl.
Brisbane, CA 94123
(Cutting and dye equipment)
Terms: 2% 10 days, net 30

Superior Machinery, Inc.
166 Mill Rd.
Los Angeles, CA 90231
(Stamping, imprinting, and folding equipment)
Terms: 2% 10 days, net 30

Silver Distributing Co.
400 University Ave.
Costa Mesa, CA 92345
(Plastics supplier)
Terms: 2% 10 days, net 30

Hi-Test, Inc.
106 Technology Blvd.
San Francisco, CA 94622
(Testing equipment)
Terms: Net 10 days

Associated Wholesalers Inc.
1633 Eastern Ave.
Los Angeles, CA 92122
(High-absorbent padding and tape fasteners)
Terms: 2% 10 days, net 25

Estimate your working capital needs from your cash flow projection. Your goal is to have enough cash ahead at all times to cover three months' expenses and inventory replenishment. It's unlikely that your business will generate enough cash flow to meet this target; the shortage will have to be made up from the loan funds.

The SBA will expect you, as an owner, to make a considerable investment in the business, preferably 20 percent or more. Your investment can be in any form that will benefit the business—cash, furniture, equipment, and so on. The following example shows a typical investment statement:

INVESTMENT STATEMENT

The undersigned applicants, John Smith, Roger Smith, and Steve Smith, hereby declare that they will make an investment of the assets listed below in the proposed business to be known as "Softie Baby Care, Inc."

Capital equipment/building improvements	$1.2 million
Overhead	$8.7 million
TOTAL INVESTMENT	$9.9 million

(Date)

(Signed) John Smith
        Roger Smith
        Steve Smith

You will also need to prepare a brief description of your business. This does not have to be as involved as the one described in "The Financial Plan" section. You merely need to describe your business and include a paragraph outlining the expected benefits you will receive from the loan. A sample follows:

- Softie Baby Care, Inc. will provide ecology-minded consumers with an environmentally safe disposable diaper that will feature all the elements that are popular among users of disposable diapers, but will include an added benefit—biodegradability. The product, which is patent pending, will target current users of disposable diapers who are deeply concerned about the environment as well as those consumers using cloth diapers and diaper services. This product will be distributed to wholesalers who will in turn sell to major supermarkets, specialty stores, department stores and major toy stores.
- The company was incorporated in 1989 in the State of California under the name of Softie Baby Care. The company's CEO, president and vice president have over 30 years of combined experience within the diaper industry.
- The company has applied for a patent on the primary technology that the business is built around, which allows the plastic within a disposable diaper to break down on extended exposure to sunlight. Lease agreements are also in place for a 20,000 square foot facility in a light industrial area of Los Angeles, as well as major equipment needed to begin production. The company is currently being funded by $3 million from the three principals, with purchase orders for 500,000 units already in hand. Capital will be used to purchase needed equipment and materials for development of the product and initial test marketing.

Collateral

Collateral is important and will be one of the criteria by which the SBA judges a loan application. You need to prepare an itemized list and accurately describe the collateral you are prepared to offer. Obtain copies of SBA Form 4, Schedule A to do this. You can get SBA forms from your bank or from the nearest SBA office. We suggest you get three copies of the required forms: one for preparing a draft, one for the final copy, and a spare one in case you need an extra in a hurry.

The Loan Application

The loan application form is the last document you should fill out. Much of the information on that form is a summary of the data just described and listed in the financial plan. If you have prepared this plan correctly, it should contain all the required information about your proposed new or existing business and the start-up financing it needs.

There are two sides to the application form. The front side is divided into six sections and includes full instructions for completing the information requested. The sections are as follows:

1. **Applicant.** Include all relevant information about yourself and your business in this section, such as your full legal name, fictitious name statement if applicable, trade name of borrower, street address, employer's ID number, type of business, date business established, number of employees, and bank of business account.
2. **Management.** List the name and home address of each person who will assume responsibility for managing the business.
3. **Use of proceeds.** This is similar to the "Use of Funds" statement. You should list all expenditures and estimated costs such as land acquisition; new plant or building construction, building expansion, or repair; acquisition or capital equipment, inventory, working capital; all debt services including the SBA, total loan requested, and term of loan.
4. **Summary of collateral.** This is a summary of the assets you wish to use as collateral for your loan. Assets are grouped under six categories (A through F): A, Land and Building; B, Machinery and Equipment; C, Furniture and Fixtures; D, Accounts Receivable; E, Inventory; and F, Other.
5. **Previous government financing.** Describe government loans that you, any principals, or affiliates have requested.
6. **Indebtedness.** This includes all outstanding debts, including installment contracts, personal loans, mortgages payable, and so on.

The back side of the form lists 13 basic items that must be provided for all loans:

1. Personal history statement.
2. Personal balance sheet.
3. Financial statements.
4. Business description.
5. Management team.

6. Cosigners.
7. Equipment list.
8. Description of any bankruptcies or insolvencies.
9. Description of any lawsuits.
10. Any familial relations employed by the SBA.
11. A list of existing or proposed subsidiaries.
12. Statements of any financial interest in any concern you buy from, sell to, or use the services of.
13. A list of franchise agreements if applicable.

An applicant for an SBA business loan may obtain the assistance of any attorney, accountant, appraiser, or other representative to aid in the preparation and presentation of the application. Such representation is not mandatory, but if a loan is approved, the services of an attorney may be necessary for the preparation of closing documents, title abstracts, and so on. The SBA will allow payment of reasonable fees or other compensation for services performed by consultants engaged to assist the applicant.

RESOURCES

Government Agencies

U.S. Small Business Administration, 409 Third Street SW, Washington, DC 20416, 800-U-ASK-SBA (800-827-5722)

Magazines

The Business Owner, Thomas Publishing, Inc., 383 South Broadway, Hicksville, NY 11801, 516-681-2111

Entrepreneurial Manager's Newsletter, 180 Varick Street, Penthouse Suite, New York, NY 10014-4692, 212-633-0060

PART

II

Managing Your Own Business

Once the dream has become a reality and your business is up and running, you need to face the next challenge: *managing* your business. This area in the growth of a business stifles many entrepreneurs, often even those with management backgrounds. Why? Among the many reasons for the failures of entrepreneurial enterprises, the following are most common:

- **Lack of detail.** A lot of entrepreneurs are concept people. They have an idea and enough courage to "grab the brass ring" and start a business, but their greatest strength often becomes their biggest weakness once the business is operational. Because they are concept oriented, they forget about the details of handling day-to-day business operations.
- **Too much control.** Just like a child with a new toy, entrepreneurs often feel no one can do as good a job as they can, so they fail to share or delegate effectively. The entrepreneur may try to do everything or may experience a high employee turnover because of having unrealistic expectations for work performance.
- **Lack of knowledge.** Managing a business is not easy. Far from it. It requires a great deal of work (often from a team of competent individuals),

as well as *knowledge*. Unfortunately, many entrepreneurs manage their businesses by trial and error because they have never learned any other method.

Part II of the *Small Business Advisor and Desk Reference* provides this essential information. The following chapters present the basics of effective small business management. By acquiring this knowledge, you can meet the challenge of managing your business and foster the dream of being an entrepreneur. Part II comprises Chapters 15 through 22, which cover the following subjects:

- **Insurance.** Chapter 15 discusses factors to consider when purchasing insurance; the differences between a direct writer, an agent, and a broker; options for insuring risks; items covered under a comprehensive general liability plan; plus special coverages available to businesses.
- **Financial control.** Chapter 16 looks at managing your financial resources using financial statements, projections, ratios, and profitability measures.
- **Record keeping.** Chapter 17 focuses on why you need to maintain business records; types of records you'll need to maintain, and what is involved in actually recording business transactions; why accountants can be an asset to your business; choosing an accountant.
- **Pricing.** Chapter 18 considers the dynamics of effective pricing; how economic and competitive factors impact price; the various pricing methods and how they're typically used in small business.
- **Taxes.** Chapter 19 is devoted to the dynamics of taxation and how they impact small business; how legal form affects taxes; taxes you will collect as an employer; standard business deductions and tax-planning tips.
- **Credit management.** Chapter 20 reviews factors to consider when extending credit; how to determine an applicant's credit worthiness; forms of retail and trade credit; aging receivables and strategies for collecting overdue accounts.
- **Bootstrap financing.** Chapter 21 describes the various types of bootstrap financing methods used by business; managing internal resources to create financing opportunities.
- **Legal matters.** Chapter 22 explores legal myths and how they affect business; why it is important to put everything in writing; what a contract is and how it can affect your business.

15

Insurance

Properly insuring the risks in your business climate can save your firm from an unforeseen bankruptcy. By placing the economic burden of your company elsewhere, insurance firms free your business to focus on other operational factors. The relatively small premium (in relation to the assumed financial risk) is well worth the price. Also, small business is finally being wooed by big insurance companies.

According to economist Sean F. Mooney, in an article from *Entrepreneur* magazine,[1] "Insurers are realizing [the small-business market] is profitable if they approach it right." Increased automation and establishment of more regional centers make small-business accounts more feasible by enabling agents to service them more easily. So, agents are now offering more package choices at lower costs to small companies.

Still, insurance is actually a very advanced, complex form of gambling. By giving a small portion of your funds as a premium you are guaranteed a quick recovery from any peril. You place the risks with the insurance firm, and the insurance company as the underwriter accepts or rejects those risks, setting the rates and issuing the terms of agreement of the policy.

As an employer, you owe a degree of care to your employees in five areas:

1. To provide a safe place to work.
2. To employ individuals reasonably competent to carry out their tasks, without endangering others.
3. To warn employees of danger.
4. To furnish appropriate and safe tools.
5. To set up and enforce proper rules of conduct of employees as they relate to safe working procedures.

[1] Erika Kotite, "Business Beat-Small Claims," *Entrepreneur* (July 1993) p. 11.

You also owe a degree of care to your customers, clients, and the public. This risk includes not only physical injuries but also damage to the property of others.

RISK MANAGEMENT

Starting any business is a risk. As the entrepreneur, you must be keenly aware of all phases of your business: management, marketing, contractual, personnel, maintenance, and the ramifications of your service or product. Recognizing the risks in all phases is the first step in effective risk management. Perform the following audit:

- Plan for your risks before talking to an insurance representative.
- Evaluate your liability risks from your customers' point of view.
- Chart the customers' path as they come into contact with your shop, step by step: across the sidewalk, through the door, under the ceiling fan, and up to your counter.
- If you enter customers' homes, envision each critical step as you perform your service in a home.

After identifying the risks inherent to your business, you need to estimate the probability of financial loss from the various sources of possible danger. Essentially, you are developing a worst-case scenario: shop damage, employee injuries, and potential consequences of your product or service in relation to the customer.

Next, decide the best and most economical method of handling the risk of loss and protecting yourself, considering the following factors:

- **Assumption.** This means you will assume the prevailing risk and the accompanying financial burdens. Sometimes absorbing a risk is warranted. If you are a one-person operation and have a fairly low-key wallpapering service, chances are that little is going to happen. By taking considerable precautions to clear the room of valuable furniture and antiques, you should be able to avoid any damages to the household. Even for the owner of a 10-employee car wash, the chances of damaging a car are slim. However, if you forgo the expense of getting garage owner's liability insurance, you must pay for any damages that occur to the vehicles in your shop.
- **Avoidance.** Removing the cause of risk is the most obvious process, yet owners often fail to use it. If some caustic material is causing employee hesitation and fear, replace it with a nonhazardous substance. The extra costs will pay off handsomely. If you run a manufacturing business, responding to employee requests for better or more specialized tools is the most simple, yet most effective means of running a safe, hazard-free

business. An organized company safety program that implements suggestions from employees and insurance safety representatives can also help eliminate dangerous elements in your business.

- **Loss reduction.** The ultimate solution is the transfer of the risk to another party altogether—subcontracting. When your own delivery service has problems—late deliveries, damaged goods, mechanical breakdowns, and employee hassles—consider contracting a delivery service to take all the headaches away. Similar circumstances include contracting for maintenance, electrical, plumbing, carpentry, bookkeeping, landscaping, and security. Such actions are a form of insurance because you have shifted the risk and responsibility to another party for a negotiated fee. However, shifting the risk and responsibility does not necessarily shift the liability. When the new landscaping crew improperly installs a sprinkler head causing water damage to the inside of a nearby Jaguar, you can hold the landscaping firm liable, but the man who falls into the cactus plant by the front office and injures himself will still be able to hold you liable for planting it there. Get a written contractual agreement concerning those shared and mutually exclusive areas of liability.

- **Self-insurance.** This method entails setting aside a specified amount of money into a reserve fund each year to cover any losses incurred. The owner holds the cash in this reserve fund, rather than paying premiums to an insurance company. In practice, this plan has met with bad results for one-store companies. A significant loss for a one-store company will usually result in a net loss for the firm because the reserve fund has not yet become large enough to cover the losses. The risk remains and the protection is inadequate unless the reserve fund is sufficiently developed. A growing business with several geographically separated units is more suited for self-insurance. The method is also more common among nonprofit organizations such as school systems. As schools are not usually hit with catastrophic situations, they can cover a small loss with the reserve fund.

The preceding methods offer some avenues from which to plan your needs based on the level of risk involved. All these methods should be used to some extent to offset the amount of risk incurred. Some areas of risk, however, will require yet another avenue—the transfer of risk through insurance—to make sure your business is not overly exposed.

Sound insurance planning requires attention on all fronts. Common brown-paper insurance packages should be complemented by additional special coverages, indigenous to your business. Figure 15.1, at the end of the chapter, shows a sample Business Planning Worksheet for your use. Before attempting to fill it out, however, carefully read all the information provided in this chapter.

Cover your largest loss exposure first: the lives and health of your workers. You and your employees are the most valuable assets of the firm.

Figure 15.1 Business Insurance Planning Worksheet

TYPES OF INSURANCE	REQUIRED (Yes/No)	YEARLY COST	COST PER PAYMENT
1. General liability insurance			
2. Product liability insurance			
3. Errors and omissions liability insurance			
4. Malpractice liability insurance			
5. Automotive liability insurance			
6. Fire and theft insurance			
7. Business interruption insurance			
8. Overhead expense insurance			
9. Personal disability			
10. Key-employee insurance			
11. Shareholders' or partners' insurance			
12. Credit extension insurance			
13. Term life insurance			
14. Health insurance			
15. Group insurance			
16. Workers' compensation insurance			
17. Survivor-income life insurance			
18. Care, custody, and control insurance			
19. Consequential losses insurance			
20. Boiler and machinery insurance			
21. Profit insurance			
22. Money and securities insurance			
23. Glass insurance			
24. Electronic equipment insurance			
25. Power interruption			
26. Rain insurance			
27. Temperature damage insurance			
28. Transportation insurance			
29. Fidelity bonds			
30. Surety bonds			
31. Title insurance			
32. Water damage insurance			
TOTAL ANNUAL COST		$	$

LIFE INSURANCE

Life insurance is the cheapest insurance you can offer your employees. For a small additional fee ($4 per month per employee), health-insurance companies will provide you with life insurance. In fact, many carriers will not give you health insurance unless you also purchase a life insurance plan, either from them or from another company.

Specialized life insurance options include:

- **The survivor-income plan.** This will provide the surviving dependents of a deceased employee with a monthly income payment.
- **Key-employee insurance.** This indemnifies you against losses resulting from the death or total disability of a key employee in your firm, including yourself, other owners, or partners. If your evening manager, head cook, or swing person is irreplaceable, then insure him or her adequately. Naming your firm as the beneficiary may have negative tax consequences. Consider a partner, family member, or yourself as the beneficiary. By taking out an insurance policy on his or her life, you will have ample funds to recruit a successor.

As far as life insurance for yourself goes, insuring yourself, if you are the heart of the business, and naming a family member as beneficiary will provide an effective tax shelter and sound estate planning. Ask an insurance representative about sole-proprietorship plans.

Partnership Plans

A partnership usually dissolves when one partner dies unless the partners provide otherwise. For all practical purposes, the business is finished. The surviving partners become personally liable for any losses incurred should assets not cover losses. The only practical matters that are allowed to continue are the winding down of the firm.

To avoid this confusion, arrange for an adequately financed buy-and-sell agreement. This agreement provides for the purchase at a prearranged price of your deceased partner's interest. This contractual agreement is the first step.

Under a *general partnership arrangement* for two or more persons, a buy/sell agreement should be arranged in the event of death, disability, divorce, or retirement. A *partnership-insurance* plan, with two partners, is straightforward; it involves purchasing a life insurance plan on the other partner. Each partner in return pays the premiums.

Where there are three or more partners, it is common practice to have the firm buy a policy on the life of each partner. The difficulty lies in trying to set up a formula to determine the future value that will be paid by the partners and partners' heirs. The simplest plan sets an arbitrarily agreed on value for each partner's interest in advance. More complex systems are necessary for small business partnerships that are growing.

Other criteria for disbursement of the partnership's assets include an independent appraisal. Sometimes three independent appraisals are performed, and the middle one, or the average, is chosen.

The valuation is sometimes determined by the day of death or the month's end. Some book-value methodology includes the fair market value of the firm's assets and liabilities at the end of the fiscal year, the day of death, or the month's end.

Corporate Plans

Corporate-business life insurance provides a sound answer to the death of a principal stockholder in a closely held corporation. The death of a major stockholder who has funded the existence of your small incorporated firm can cost you in the form of credit impairment, direct loss of business, or damage to your employee morale.

If the deceased had a controlling interest, the administrator of the estate during the period of the settlement could name a new director and take over control of the firm. Thus the importance of a buy/sell agreement cannot be overly stressed. It will determine in advance what will be done on the death of a stockholder and make funds immediately available for accomplishing the objectives of the plan.

The main benefit is the continuity of the management team. This guarantees uninterrupted business; no outsiders can come into the business unless agreed on in advance.

Stock repurchase agreements, the most common cause of family disputes, are ironed out in an equitable manner, usually with a guaranteed minimum price. The insurance benefit is normally a lump sum payout with some extended payments over time. The bereaved family is not burdened with business responsibilities.

The whole issue of estate planning spills into sophisticated insurance and legal ramifications that can best be individually packaged through an insurance expert or an attorney who specializes in this sector. Don't be overwhelmed by the legal "mumbo jumbo." Simply write down exactly what you wish to accomplish in layperson's terms before you ever walk into the insurance office.

As the entrepreneurial leader of the firm, you may want to consider other options. An alternative to group term life is *executive-bonus* insurance, which is an individually owned cash-value policy that gives the executive more benefits for the taxable cost. The cost of the insurance would be taxed as income, but the executives would receive a supplementary retirement benefit that group-term doesn't provide.

Another alternative is the split-dollar life-insurance policy, which splits ownership between employer and employee. The firm cannot deduct its share of the premiums, but you as the executive get a policy with a cash value at a lower cost. Increased regulations imposing strict nondiscrimination tests between executives and employees may generate even more creative insurance packages for group life and health insurance.

HEALTH INSURANCE

Life insurance often comes in economically attractive packages with group health insurance. Many insurance companies are now offering programs or plans specifically geared toward small businesses. Every insurance company has a different definition of a small group. It might be 25 or 15 or less.

Choosing the most suitable and cost-effective selection of medical benefits can be time consuming. A largely married workforce with children will have considerably different needs, such as dental coverage, than groups of single workers. Outdoor workers or workers who spend their day staring into a computer screen may prefer an optical program for eye care, safety glasses, and sunglasses.

Analyzing your workforce entails determining the following:

- How many workers fall into each age group.
- How many head of households exist.
- Where they live.
- Size of the families.
- Other pertinent information.

Health consultants have designed computer models that calculate the future costs of health-care benefits, based on you and your employees' previous year's experience. The results recommend what would be the most cost-effective means of providing health-care coverage for the coming years.

Your medical insurance costs may be determined solely on the basis of your company's experience, such as the aggregate number and dollar value of claims submitted by your employees. In other cases, you will be a part of a larger statistical group that the insurance company or health-care provider uses in calculating your premiums.

You should explore the wide range of options available in health care coverage today. There are the traditional "fee-for-service" plans, "managed care" plans, and plans that combine elements of both. Understanding all your options will help you select the most appropriate coverage for your business. Following is a list of possible choices:

- **Fee-for-service.** This provides the eligible employee with the services of a doctor or hospital with partial or total reimbursement depending on the insurance company. Most insurance companies offer an 80/20 plan; the insurance company pays 80 percent of the bill and the employee pays 20 percent. Also, 70/30 and 90/10 are not uncommon. The employee can go to any doctor he or she chooses. The fee-for-service plan covers any service that is defined as medically necessary and is specified in the plan.

- **Health maintenance organization (HMO).** HMOs are the most familiar form of managed care. HMOs provide a range of benefits to employees at a fixed price with a minimal contribution (or sometimes no contribution) from the employee, as long as employees use doctors or hospitals specified in the plan. Usually, HMOs are set up so that patients go to the managed care plan facilities. Sometimes, however, the plan can be set up though networks of individual practitioners. In these individual practice associations (IPAs), a patient goes to the physicians' private offices. Under either arrangement, if a patient goes to a doctor or hospital outside the plan—except in the case of an extreme emergency or if the individual was traveling outside the plan's service area—no benefits are paid at all. Make sure the HMO has facilities within your employees' driving range, and scrutinize the organization for community reputation.
- **Preferred provider organization (PPO).** This is regarded as a "managed fee-for-service" plan because some restrictions are put in place to control the frequency and cost of health care. Under a PPO, arrangements are made among the providers, hospitals, and doctors to provide service at an alternative price—usually a lower price. Many times there is a copay amount, which means that the employee pays $5 or $10 for each visit to doctors specified in the plan and the insurance company pays the rest. The PPO differs from an HMO in that if an employee goes to a doctor not specified by the insurance company, the plan still partially covers it. There is usually just a higher copay amount or a deductible with varying percentages.

There are also point of service (POS) plans, and exclusive provider organizations (EPS) that combine features of standard fee-for-service plans and HMOs and offer consumers more flexibility.

Most group insurance plans fall under two types of insurance packages: *comprehensive* and *scheduled*. Comprehensive plans lump all reimbursable expenses under one roof with a corridor or deductible for which the employee is responsible. After the deductible is met, the insurance company will pay a percentage of the expenses up to a predetermined amount. After that amount is reached, coverage is usually 100 percent. Scheduled plans identify each covered benefit and the maximum amount of coverage available for that item. Most scheduled plans also come packaged with a major medical provision tied to a deductible and a percentage reimbursement feature.

"Flexible benefits," the generic term referring to a variety of programs that enable employees to choose from different fringe benefits, has recently gained popularity. This cafeteria plan allows tradeoffs between health, dental, and optical plans.

If your workforce is largely white collar, they may appreciate a health program that encompasses an executive fitness program. Other health programs are meeting social problems head-on by offering reimbursement and rehabilitation for alcohol and substance abuse.

Regardless of which plan you choose, the best designed plan in the world will fail you if it is poorly administered. Ask about the plan. Query claims representatives on specific questions for a typical claim, including ambulance service (if any), outpatient services, and rehabilitation.

If you have narrowed it down to two HMOs, ask each to name a private firm you can speak to that is already using their services. Given equal price and medical services, maybe one has a simplified billing practice or a superior consumer affairs division.

Growing enterprises need to be aware of government legislation requiring that you offer continued coverage in health insurance benefits even after an employee has been released. The Consolidated Omnibus Budget Reconciliation Act (COBRA) calls for this privilege to be extended to any worker in a firm with 20 or more full-time employees. Signed into law in April 1986, this law demands compliance in both union and nonunion plans. There are only two groups exempt from compliance with the provisions: churches or church-operated tax-exempt organizations and federal or District of Columbia employees.

You, the employer, need only offer continued coverage. Any ex-employee who elects to continue coverage must pay the full cost of that coverage. This includes both the employer's and employee's share. Employees may elect to remain covered under the firm's plan up to 18 months, and dependents can maintain coverage up to 36 months.

COBRA has imposed additional administrative burdens and potentially higher plan costs on virtually all group insurance plans. Management and monitoring of the COBRA compliance procedures are essential to avoid severe financial penalties involved with noncompliance.

One penalty is loss of the corporation's tax deduction for its group insurance plan. The plan administrator, in a small firm, is subject to a personal fine of $100 per day for failing to notify an employee of his or her COBRA rights at each step of the termination or hiring process. COBRA provisions include advising all new and terminated employees, and all spouses, of their COBRA continuation rights in writing. Be sure that those electing continued coverage are removed from the plan as soon as they become covered under a new plan.

As you might have anticipated, COBRA presents two major problems for small-business managers: complicated administration and the inevitable higher insurance costs. This has spawned a whole new industry with independent administrators and management programs that offer employers relief from the paper logjam.

LIABILITY

Customers, employees, repair people, delivery people, and anyone else who comes in contact with your business property can hold you liable for your failure to take the proper degree of care. This can be as simple as keeping your sidewalk swept or shoveling the snow on your front walk. If someone is injured as a result of your negligence, the court will generally find in favor of the injured party even if your negligence was only slight. Mike Fox, an account executive with Wausau Insurance Companies, states in *Entrepreneur*,[2] "General Liability is the most confused and misunderstood coverage."

Basically, there are two types of liabilities against which you have to insure yourself and your business: liabilities to nonmembers of the firm and liabilities to members of the firm (employees and partners). Most of the liabilities toward outsiders will be covered under a comprehensive general liability (CGL) policy, according to Mark Greene in *Insurance and Risk Management for Small Business*.[3] A CGL policy covers the following four risks:

1. Payments due to accidents and injury that might happen on your premises or by your employees.
2. Any immediate medical expenses necessary at the time of the accident.
3. The attorney fees and expenses for investigation and settlement.
4. The cost of court bonds or other judgments during appeal.

The limits to liability are determined on a per accident and per person basis. Additional limitations may include a total on bodily injury or property damage.

A CGL insurance does *not* protect you against all liabilities, however. Most prominent among these risks are:

1. Liability caused by an employee automobile accident while on the job.
2. Liability related to products manufactured or sold or services offered by your company.
3. Liability insurance covered under workers' compensation laws.

Other liability insurance policies take up where general comprehensive leaves off; they will be covered in more detail later.

While it can be tricky to determine just what general liability coverage you need, in *Entrepreneur* magazine,[4] Sean Mooney, senior vice president and economist for the Insurance Information Institute explains that there are two extremes a business might consider. The first, which he calls the "empty pocket approach," is to buy little or no insurance so you are not a target of lawsuits. "If people know you have a big policy," says Mooney, "they are more likely to go after you." The other extreme would be to buy the most liability insurance you'll ever need—$2 to $3 million. The soundest approach, though, according to Mooney, would be to figure out what you could be sued for. He adds that, depending on the riskiness of your business it's rare to see an award in excess of $1 million.

[2] David R. Evanson, "Take Care," *Entrepreneur* (September 1993) p. 92.
[3] Mark R. Greene, *Insurance and Risk Management for Small Business,* 3rd ed. (Washington, DC: U.S. Small Business Administration, 1981).
[4] Greene, *Insurance and Risk Management.*

Automotive Liability

The same type of policy you purchase for your personal use is necessary for your business. Working out the figures for coverage on collision and comprehensive is dependent on your business budget. Be certain that all your employees with an active driver's license in your state are listed on the policy. And, beware of coverage gaps between owned, nonowned, and hired vehicles.

Most importantly, do *not* cut corners on coverage. Minimal packages of 25/50/25 (per person bodily injury/ total accident coverage/ property damage) are available; however, hitting an expensive sports car can wipe out the insurance company's coverage quickly. Pay the extra few dollars for higher coverage of 100/300/100. Most states have laws concerning uninsured motorists coverage. You should supplement the standard auto policy as the costs are minimal.

As a businessperson, meetings and seminars may take you out of town. The daily price of rental-car insurance has reached astronomical levels. The addition of a relatively inexpensive endorsement to your company auto policy will save headaches on the road. This also gives you the advantage of rate-shopping with the major rental agencies. Without this endorsement, the costs of collision damage waiver (CDW) offered by the major car rental companies can tack on up to $10 per day. Failure to purchase the CDW results in the renter carrying full responsibility for any damage to the car. It is important to ask your insurance carrier if this coverage is automatically included or if there is an extra fee.

Most states have an insurance watchdog agency to oversee the industry as a whole. They release comprehensive studies citing rates for some typical drivers in average cars, driving safely for a set number of miles. It will have information on the premiums your state's insurance firms charge for the same standard. It is an excellent tool for picking up the maximum coverage of liability at the minimum cost.

Product Liability

In manufacturing, and in certain sectors of retail trade, you may have an assumed product liability. You are responsible for knowing if a product is defective. In a service business, product liability may be a factor if you are in the repair business and inadvertently cause an accident or injury.

As a result of strict judicial interpretations, companies have been held accountable for injuries to those using a product 15 or 20 years after its manufacture or sale. The defense of manufacturers or vendors that the product met all known standards of safety at the time of construction or sale has been ruled unacceptable by the courts.

The implications are far reaching. In one case, a man was reaching down in front of a soda machine to grab the soda and somehow the can hit him on the head. He died days later, and the cause of death was found to be the improper design of the vending machine.

Consult an insurance representative who is well versed in this area of specialization, as premiums vary widely. If you manufacture ski-lift parts, your premiums will be considerably higher than the firm that makes the lenses for snow goggles.

Workers' Compensation

Workers' compensation mandates unlimited medical coverage during the course of employment. This covers all job-related injuries on company property or in pursuit of your livelihood. An injured delivery person could receive compensation if he or she were hurt while unloading your goods at another site.

According to the Alliance of American Insurers, approximately 7 states have a mandatory monopolistic state-run workers' compensation fund into which the employer must pay set premiums. About 14 states have a semicompetitive environment in which employers can choose between a state fund, private company funds, or self-insurance (if they are large enough to qualify). The remaining states have no state-run fund; private insurance companies compete for business. Workers' compensation is required by law in all 50 contiguous states. (Note that many employers in small businesses fail to include themselves within the coverage when they should.)

As with any risk, the generalized rates can be modified higher or lower depending on the company's accident record. The safer the workplace and the better the accident record, the cheaper your company's workers' compensation insurance will be. Safety programs and loss reduction systems force employee participation and involvement.

Concentrate on your overall risk management planning. Take note of those risks that you will assume and those where systematic avoidance can heighten the safety standards and performance of your employees.

PROPERTY INSURANCE

As a property owner, you can improve property insurance rates by making physical improvements in concrete fire construction, smoke vents, and sprinklers. Insurers have established a special rate class that is easier and cheaper to insure: the HPR (highly protected risk). If you are in this category or will soon be, ask about this rate break.

HPRs are based on stringent property-protection programs defined by the insurers. To maintain proper standards and keep a regimented HPR rate, the insurer will make routine checks for compliance. The physical plant is inspected prior to acceptance and at routine intervals throughout the term of the coverage.

Comprehensive

Make sure you get a policy written on an *all-risks* basis rather than on a *named peril* basis. While the latter only covers the specific perils named in the policy, an all-risk policy will cover you for virtually anything (except for a few specific enumerated exclusions). The all-risks policy will allow you to:

1. Eliminate duplication and overlap.
2. Avoid gaps in trying to cover your liabilities through a number of specialized policies.
3. Encourage quicker settlements by working with one agent and one attorney.
4. Reduce the expense of having many different policies.

If your local or regional location has a propensity toward a specific calamity, you may consider additional insurance. Among others, you may choose to pay an additional premium to insure against fire, flood, earthquake, nuclear risks (if near a nuclear plant), hail, windstorm, vandalism, or crime.

A professional agent or broker may roll many coverages into a business owner's policy (BOP)—a ready-made program for small business—or a special multiple peril plan.

Replacement Cost Insurance

Also, according to Sean Mooney, in *Entrepreneur,*[5] you should buy replacement cost insurance. This policy will replace your property at current prices, regardless of what you paid for the items, and thus protect you against inflation. Usually there's a provision that your total replacements can't exceed the policy cap, though. For example, if you have a 40,000-square-foot facility that will cost $40 per square foot to replace, the total replacement cost ($1.6 million) may exceed your $1 million policy limit. To protect yourself, Mooney recommends buying replacement insurance with an insurance guard, which would adjust the cap on the policy to allow for inflation. If this isn't possible, simply review your policy limits from time to time to make sure you have adequate coverage.

Coinsurance

With coinsurance, the owners of a building can actually share the potential loss with the insurance company if they are willing to share the premium cost. These terms are crucial if you are on either end of a leasing agreement. A common percentage of market value of buildings used in coinsurance is 80 percent. Thus the owner bears the brunt of paying 20 percent in the event of a complete loss.

SPECIAL COVERAGES

These are specifically named perils covering the gamut of risks that the entrepreneur of a small business may encounter. Your business will require its own

---

[5] Greene, *Insurance and Risk Management.*

set of special coverages for the risks inherent in your industry. Sometimes these can be added as endorsements to your policy or you can buy them separately.

Care, Custody, and Control

This is a must for the service industry, particularly if you have customer goods in your control at any time during the business transaction. Should some unforeseen accident happen, the insurance will reimburse you (and the customer). This especially applies to the service-repair sector for purposes such as framing pictures, furniture repair, bicycle assembly, and dry cleaning.

Basically, if you have the customers' goods within your grasp at any time in the business transaction, you are liable for the full value. Even with the most insignificant handling of the customers' property, you can be held liable. Holding and losing athletic shoes while your customer is roller skating can be an expensive accident.

Consequential Losses

This clause should be inserted into a standard property or fire insurance policy. For an extra premium, you can insure the extra expenses of obtaining temporary quarters, relocation, and incidental expenses.

Business Interruption

This specialized insurance will reimburse the business owner for future profits lost and fixed charges as a result of damages due to perils specifically accounted for in the policy; weather damage is the most common cause. Other causes (e.g., strike or material shortages) will not be applicable. Depending on your geographic location, the inclusions (e.g., tornado, hurricane) and exclusions (e.g., mud slide or tidal wave), may get technical.

To predict the profitability of the firm at a particular point in the future can be a sticky situation. If the firm was operating at a loss, then only the fixed expenses that it incurred may be reimbursed. However, if your firm is operating at a profit, then good records (underscoring the importance of keeping duplicates at another site) will support your case. If all the records have been destroyed in a fire, the previous year's tax records will be of great value.

This coverage is particularly crucial for restaurants, as they risk complete loss of income in the event of fire, while still being obligated to make rental payments or to amortize their debt.

There are even more specialized provisions within this field. Under the terms of an extended period of indemnity, the period of loss is defined as the period necessary to return to normal business operations. Otherwise the payments are only made until the business can physically reopen (even if in a makeshift pattern).

Peak season endorsements, which are even more specialized, cover those service industries that make all their money during a particular season.

Boiler and Machinery

Is your organization in the snow belt? Take heed, operations can be completely shut down in winter by the death of an aged boiler or machine. Even though the price of a new boiler is within your budget, consider the two months' downtime for delivery, removal, and installation of a new power source.

This specialized form of business interruption insurance can provide funds to find alternate energy sources while waiting for the new machine to arrive. Depending on the provisions you insert, the coverage may also take care of the costs of the new machine.

Profit

What, you may ask, is the difference between profit and business interruption insurance? Interruption covers future profits, while profit insurance covers the loss of goods already manufactured, but destroyed before they could be sold. This specialized coverage is aimed at manufacturers, not the service sector.

Credit

While extending credit to another party, person, partnership, or corporation, difficulties may arise from the following:

- Bankruptcy.
- Closure of a financial institution.
- Death or physical disability.
- Destruction of accounting records.
- Political instability in a foreign country.

The two major classifications for credit insurance are:

1. **General coverage.** Applies to those losses incurred during the one-year policy caused from sales made during the prior year to the starting date.
2. **Forward coverage.** Covers the insured for losses resulting from accounts that were created by sales made during the policy term.

General policies account for the lion's share of the credit policies in force. They cover all debtors falling into given classes of credit ratings on a blanket basis. The policy specifies dollar limits on debtors according to classifications set up by Dun & Bradstreet credit ratings. Various levels of blanket coverage can be assigned depending on the size of the firm. Automatic coverage on unrated accounts can also be provided.

Money and Securities

You may need additional insurance to cover those peak cash holding periods during the business day such as closing, after lunch, or payday. Check to see if your policy covers money in transit, money or securities on the premises during business hours and after business hours, and money at home (when you're just too tired to go to the bank).

Glass

Businesses have the option of purchasing a comprehensive policy insuring breakage of plate glass, neon signs and showcases from any source except fire or nuclear reaction. This includes weather, riots, vehicles, or sonic boom. Determine whether this policy, or another, covers damage to stock by broken glass. Some policies include the costs of replacing lettering and other ornamentation.

Electronic Equipment

Electronic equipment can be insured for fire, theft, malicious damage, accidental damage, mechanical breakdown, or electrical breakdown. A separate electronic data-processing (EDP) policy can cover hardware as well as software. Should a fire occur in the computer room, the standard property insurance policy might pay you the price of replacing a blank, black roll of computer tape; an EDP policy could compensate you for the cost of reconstructing the data. These items and coverage would be above and beyond the normal scope of business property insurance unless you had a comprehensive policy.

Power Interruption

A power interruption endorsement is available on a machinery contract to provide coverage for losses from interruption of electricity, gas, heat, or other energy from public utilities. This is critical for those in the perishable food industry or specialized sectors such as an ice warehouse.

Rain

Rain insurance is designed to cover losses at a certain percentage; for example, 60 percent of the gross revenues on the last day not affected by rainfall. Swap meets, carnivals, auctions, and sporting events would consider this coverage.

Temperature Damage

In the same vein, many businesses, such as bakeries, dairies, and greenhouses require the absolute maintenance of a certain temperature to prevent the loss of vital inventory. This may be of particular interest if you are in a cold mountainous region or hot climate.

Transportation

Transportation insurance indemnifies your materials in transit. Common carriers like United Parcel Service are indeed liable for most shipping damages to your goods. They are not liable for unforeseeable "acts of God" such as floods or lightning.

Land shipments most frequently use an inland transit policy. This would include a train derailment, but exclude a labor strike or riot. Also excluded are breakage and leakage; however, the common carrier is generally liable for these damages.

Truck shipments can be covered by a blanket motor-cargo policy. Federal interstate trucking laws require certain minimum coverage that may not offer you full protection.

Fidelity Bonds

Fidelity bonds protect the firm from losses incurred by employee thefts. It is often difficult to establish losses, and only established losses are reimbursed. These bonds have been used to cover cash losses rather than merchandise losses. Naming only the cashier or money-handlers can be a mistake. It is well known that the loss from stolen merchandise far exceeds cash losses. Thus fidelity bonds should be used more widely to cover losses of both cash and merchandise.

Surety Bonds

A surety bond will protect the firm against losses incurred as a result of the failure of others to perform on schedule. If you are familiar with the construction industry, you know the importance of this insurance contract. Surety bonds, otherwise known as performance bonds, guarantee that a person or corporation will perform the service agreed on. The bond guarantees that you have the financial capacity to perform your duties, and it also backs your credit. Because your work is guaranteed, you are able to compete and bid on jobs with firms that are considerably larger than yourself. It may require extensive credit information and collateral; however, it may place you in the big leagues of your industry.

Title Insurance

Title insurance is available for a nominal fee and should always be requested for real estate purchases. In cases in which the title is not conveyed, even though the purchasers thought they had such a title, they are reimbursed.

Water Damage

It is a distinct entity from flood insurance. This covers risks from leaking pipes, sprinkler systems, backed-up toilets, bursting water tanks, and a leaking roof.

FAIR Plan Program

The Fair Access to Insurance Requirements (FAIR) Plan was established by the federal Housing and Urban Development Act as riot insurance. You cannot be refused insurance even if located in a crime-prone, high-violence area. The FAIR Plan provides coverage for looting, fire, vandalism, building, glass, and inventory if damage occurs during a group demonstration. This special government assistance plan resulted from the riots of the 1960s.

Other Specialized Packages

Specialized packages include an "errors and omissions rider clause" for owners and managers who are in the business of giving professional advice. A director's and officer's liability policy is available if you serve on the board of directors of a corporation. This may ring true even if you sit on the board of a local charity or community group. A garage owner's policy covers any damage to vehicles in your care if you are customizing or repairing automobiles. There is also "special-liquor legal liability" insurance for claims that stem from auto accidents caused by patrons who drink too much at a restaurant or tavern. Companies that use or produce chemicals, drugs, or industrial pollutants are wise to carry specific endorsements for these hazards. If you or your employees work or travel overseas, a special worldwide liability policy is available. This may or may not include kidnap and extortion coverage.

Very special circumstances, including nonbusiness risks can be purchased from Lloyd's of London. Almost any type of risk can be insured against, but the question is: How much can you afford to pay in insurance premiums?

BUYING INSURANCE

Regardless of whether you deal with an independent agent, insurance broker, or directly with an insurance company, do some comparison shopping before you sign up.

Just as you cannot always buy your business products from a single supplier, neither can you always expect to one-stop shop with insurance. Not unlike a backpacking trip, your goal is to outfit yourself with adequate provisions and seamless protection—coverage that has no gaps. High-quality insurance provides the best protection. Cutting corners doesn't make sense, as you pay more in the long run. Overlapping insurance policies result from poor planning and will mean that you may spend more money than necessary.

Depending on which type of insurance you are purchasing, various determining factors will affect the price of your insurance premium. For life insurance, your age, sex, health and family health history are all factored in to determine your rates. Regardless of your health, if your family has a history of heart disease your rate may be slightly higher. Do not misrepresent this information, as the entire policy could be invalidated if you have presented anything less than the truth on the application.

Similarly for standard health indemnity insurance, your age, sex, occupation, health, and family health history are all statistically weighed by the insurance firms. This enlightens the advantages of group health insurance policies, in which often no prior medical exams or evidence of insurability is required.

Auto insurance rates are determined by the type of car/truck you drive, your age, your marital status, the number of drivers, length of time in the state, and the number of miles you drive back and forth to work each day.

Property insurance rates will vary based on the location of your building. Figures on the local crime rate, your industry group, climate, and the condition of the building proper are all computed into the final rate you are quoted.

Regardless of the type of insurance you are purchasing, as long as you take the highest deductible you can afford, the premium should be within a manageable budget. Considering that you can usually get coverage for 1 to 2 percent or less of the total liability insured, by all reasoning it is a bargain.

Your application for insurance is evaluated by the firm you have contacted. After processing, a firm price quotation is given. Auto insurance quotes can normally be given on the spot. Life, health, and property insurance rates may take the insurance representative longer to study. Be aware of this lag time if you are considering changing policies.

Insurance firms are somewhat flexible with payments. The norm is every three months. You can pay monthly, but there is a slight surcharge for this arrangement.

Life insurance policies with a cash value often have provisions in which late payments are automatically deducted from the value of the policy. House payments and new car payments sometimes have the insurance premiums automatically added. Direct-deposit arrangements are possible in some circumstances.

Aside from getting the big picture of the insurance industry, educating yourself on the terminology within the policy permits you to have a sound discussion with the insurance representatives.

The Insurance Information Institute of New York offers a handy guide to risk management titled "Sharing the Risk" that makes the typical policy much more readable. The book explains the basic four sections of the insurance policy as follows:

1. **Declarations page.** This names the policyholder, describes the property or liability to be insured, states the coverage, and specifies the maximum the insurer will pay in case of loss.
2. **Insurance agreement.** This describes both sides' mutual responsibilities while the policy is in force. Often this section will tell the policyholder when, how, and why claims should be filed and the insurers alerted.
3. **Conditions of the policy.** This spells out in detail what is covered and what is required of both parties in case of a loss.
4. **Exclusions.** This lists specific perils, property, and losses that are definitely not covered.

A fifth section, *endorsements* and *coverage expansions,* can be added to show coverage allowed, but that is not standard.

Agents, Brokers, and Direct Writers

Direct writers are employed by a specific firm and may have a specific specialty in the field of insurance. Though tied to one firm, the insurance representative can still handle any number of insurance lines: auto, home, health, and life. The commission paid to the salesperson should be somewhat lower as a result of purchasing it "factory direct."

An agent is an independent businessperson who usually deals with a variety of different coverages and handles any number of different insurers. The independent agent may have gathered a greater breadth of knowledge across many different fields of insurance. This interaction with many firms and policies increases the agent's scope and awareness of cost-effective coverage. Though the commission for an independent agent is generally higher, as an entrepreneur and own boss, the agent may strive to give you the best service possible.

Insurance brokers such as Alexander & Alexander, Fred S. James, or Marsh & McLennan make it their business to negotiate with different insurers for different types of policies. The broker represents you the insurance buyer, not the insurance company, in dealing with a variety of insurers. They are particularly adept in business dealings and thus their costs may be more.

Determining which professional to go with can be frustrating. The insurance companies' true area of expertise is underwriting. The direct writer may not be as knowledgeable as the field agent in customizing an individual package for your company within a specialized field. In any case, an experienced, thorough, conscientious broker or insurance agent has the time and the incentive to take a plain-vanilla insurance policy and come up with a creative application.

Finding an insurance representative whom you can trust and one who will keep your business information strictly confidential is the key. You need a concerned insurance representative who is interested in you and your business, who will be with you for the long run, and who will structure deductibles that suit your budgetary situation.

The labels within the insurance industry can be deceiving. The so-called "captive" agents, who work primarily with one big company, may deal with other insurance underwriters when the need arises.

Almost every insurance company has a few specialists within your specific field. If in doubt, call one or two major insurance companies' public relations offices and ask them to give you the name of an all-star.

An advanced agent will certainly have the designation "CLU" after his or her name. This stands for Certified Life Underwriter, and is the industry's oldest and most recognized official sign of excellence. An even more advanced seal of approval, "ChFC" or Chartered Financial Consultant, has been initiated in the field.

A handful of other certification programs are available through other associations and institutions. The insurance representatives who take the time and energy to reach these higher standards are a cut above the crowd and should be sought when looking for an expert.

Evaluating Insurers

The general axiom of insurance is that the lower the premium, the higher the deductible; the higher the premium, the lower the deductible. The difficulty lies in comparing apples with apples. Some firms have better track records in paying dividends and claims. Their reputation in this matter can be difficult to evaluate, though it's important. This reputation generally is acquired through word-of-mouth within the community. Ask your peers, associates, or even trade associations in your state.

Do research on your own. Consider the following questions when selecting an insurer:

1. **Does the insurer have knowledge about my industry?** As Peter Coyle, a principal in the Coyle-Pearl Agency Inc., explains in *Entrepreneur*,[6] "You are looking for [an agency] you can develop a long-term relationship with." He cautions that you will want someone who understands your problems, or will have to spend a lot of time teaching the ins and outs of your industry. For example, say you own fast-food restaurants, it may be necessary to stick with an agent who understands the specific problems associated with these facilities (e.g., food-related concerns, customer access and safety).
2. **Do they offer all the coverages I need?** Does my business require specialized coverages? Can the insurance company provide the endorsements or extra coverages that I need at a reasonable cost, or can they work with another insurer to do so?
3. **What kind of *service* will they provide?** Will the agency go beyond offering you an 800-number to answer claim questions? Peter Coyle in *Entrepreneur*[7] explains, "The agency that gets involved in the claims process and works with the adjuster can have a positive impact on your settlement, while the agency that doesn't get involved tends to minimize your settlement." Also important: loss-control services to help you reduce claims in the long run. Do they offer fire-safety or employee-risk-reduction programs? And find out how often an agent will be keeping in touch with you. Under normal circumstances, an agent should meet with you at least twice a year, and for more complex situations, monthly.
4. **Are they priced competitively? Do they participate in any premium-reducing programs?** Compare deductibles and premiums between the insurers you are considering. Also, don't ignore other options, such as purchasing pools. A year ago, California piloted the first statewide government-backed health insurance purchasing co-op (the California Health Insurance Plan). It covers 2,500 businesses with 44,000 employees and

---

[6] David R. Evanson, "Take Care," *Entrepreneur* (September 1993) p. 92.
[7] Evanson, "Take Care" p. 92.

dependents. Employers voluntarily join the plan, which gives them the bargaining clout of a large business. On average, premiums are being cut by 6.3 percent! Employees at participating businesses can pick among several plans, and employers are required to cover at least half the cost of the cheapest plan; employees are responsible for the remainder, according to Leslie Scism in *The Wall Street Journal*.[8] National health reformers are considering other kinds of purchasing pools based on this model.

5. **What's the financial stability or solvency of the agency?** This growing trend toward consolidation brings to mind the question of who will be doing the buying and who will be bought out. If you have a suspicion that an agency you're considering could be bought out, don't select it. Consider the size of the agency, says David Evanson in an *Entrepreneur*[9] article. Also, is the owner older and not grooming a successor? These are things to look out for.

Deciding on the Deductible

The general rule is to take the highest deductible your budget can afford without overextending your business. Insurance experts are unanimous that businesses should try to hold down premiums by maintaining reasonable deductibles. Researching the average claim in your industry group can give you a thumbnail sketch of what to expect. Be bold, and ask a friendly competitor for a ballpark figure.

Buying first dollar coverage against accidents that may never occur is unreasonable. At a minimum, accepting a moderate deductible to reduce your premium is the way to go. Many insurers tend to charge disproportionately for low-level deductibles, so retain the amount of risk that you can afford or whatever amount you expect to pay out routinely. Setting deductibles too low means that your company simply pays the insurer to process more paper and pay for losses that actually may be routine. For some businesses, that limit might be $5,000; for others it might be $10,000.

Tax Tips

Insurance premiums for fire, casualty, and burglary insurance coverage on business property are all deductible for tax purposes as trade or business expenses. If a business taxpayer has a self-insurance plan, however, all payments into the self-insurance reserve would not be deductible for tax purposes; actual losses incurred by the taxpayer would be the deductions.

Insurance premiums for life-insurance coverage as a fringe benefit are tax deductible. But premiums paid on a life insurance policy covering the life of

---

[8] Leslie Scism, "Small Business Program in California Cuts Health Premiums," *The Wall Street Journal* (March 24, 1994).
[9] Evanson, "Take Care" p. 92.

an officer, employee, or other key person is not deductible if the business is a direct or indirect beneficiary under the policy. Premiums paid on a life insurance policy where the business is a beneficiary are not deductible since life-insurance proceeds would not have to be included in taxable income when received by the company.

Guidelines for Purchasing Insurance

The following list provides some basic guidelines for purchasers of insurance. In addition, Table 15.1 will help you identify the special needs of your business.

Table 15.1   Choosing Small Business Insurance

LIFE INSURANCE	HEALTH INSURANCE	LIABILITY INSURANCE	PROPERTY INSURANCE	SPECIAL COVERAGE
RETAIL SOLE PROPRIETORSHIP				
Owner and all employees are covered under survivor-income and accidental death and dismemberment plans.	Owner, all employees, and dependents have medical, dental, and vision coverage.	Comprehensive general liability, automotive liability, product liability, and workers' compensation.	All-risks, replacement cost insurance.	Consequential losses have been added to the property insurance policy.
SERVICE PARTNERSHIP (CONSULTING SERVICE)				
Owner and all employees are covered under survivor-income and accidental death and dismemberment plans. Partners, in addition, are covered under a partnership insurance plan.	Owner, all employees, and dependents have medical, dental, and vision coverage.	Comprehensive general liability, automotive liability, product liability, and workers' compensation.	All-risks, replacement cost insurance.	Consequential losses; errors and omissions.
FOOD SERVICE BUSINESS (RESTAURANT)				
Owner and all employees are covered under survivor-income and accidental death and dismemberment plans. Head cook is covered under key-employee insurance, as well.	Owner, all employees, and dependents have medical, dental, and vision coverage.	Comprehensive general liability, automotive liability, product liability, and workers' compensation.	All-risks, replacement cost insurance.	Consequential losses, business interruption, money and securities, glass, electronic equipment, power interruption, special liquor legal liability.
MANUFACTURING BUSINESS				
Owner and all employees are covered under survivor-income and accidental death and dismemberment plans.	Owner, all employees, and dependents have medical, dental, and vision coverage.	Comprehensive general liability, automotive liability, product liability, and workers' compensation.	All-risks, replacement cost insurance.	Consequential losses, business interruption, profit, transportation.

- Before speaking with an insurance representative write down a clear statement of what your expectations are.
- Do not withhold any important information from your insurance representative about your business and its exposure to loss. Treat the individual as a professional helper.
- Get at least three competitive bids using brokers, direct agents, and independent agents. Note the interest that the representative takes in loss prevention and suggestions for specialty coverage.
- Avoid duplication and overlap in policies; you will be paying for insurance you do not need.
- Entire insurance packages for small businesses do exist in certain sectors. Ask for a BOP (business opportunity plan).
- Ask whether the insurance firm is an "admitted insurance company"? If so, make sure it has a solvency fund should a catastrophe put the insurance company in danger of going under. An unadmitted carrier has no such solvency fund.
- The small business entrepreneur should not consider any form of self-insurance. The pool of funds necessary to safely insure losses is extraordinarily large.
- Mutual employer trusts are another form of insurance. Though rates may be attractive, check the backing of funds and note the lack of legislation or guarantees in some arenas.
- Get your insurance coverage reassessed on an annual basis. As your firm grows, so do your needs and potential liabilities. Underinsurance ranks as a major problem with expanding firms. Get an independent appraiser to value your property; if it has been over five years since the previous appraisal, you will be surprised.
- Keep complete records of your insurance policies, premiums paid, itemized losses and loss recoveries. This information will help you get better coverage at lower costs in the future.

Insurance Losses

The following is a list of tips regarding insurance losses:

- Virtually all policies require notification of an accident within 24, 48, or 72 hours of the incident. The claim itself does not necessarily have to be filed at this time; however, the loss must be reported. Failure to do so may nullify your right to recovery.
- There must be some proof of loss, though you will have a reasonable period to provide documentation if need be.
- The insurer usually has three options to fulfill the terms of a replacement policy: paying cash, repairing the insured item, or replacing the insured item with one of similar quality. Don't hesitate to ask if you prefer one of the specific reimbursement methods.

- Disputes in the amount of the settlement are put to arbitration. An independent appraiser acts as judge in the conflict. Don't hesitate to utilize this system of resolving differences in claim amounts or processing. If a compromise cannot be reached, then a lawsuit can be initiated.

RESOURCES

Associations

American Association of Insurance Services, 1035 South York Road, Bensenville, IL 60106, 708-595-3225

American Insurance Association, 1130 Connecticut Avenue NW, Suite 1000, Washington, DC 20036, 202-828-7100

Insurance Information Institute, 110 William Street, New York, NY 10038, 212-669-9200

National Association for the Self-Employed, 9151 Precinct Line Road, Hurst, TX 76054, 817-656-6313

National Insurance Association, P.O. Box 158544, Chicago, IL 60615, 313-924-3308

Risk and Insurance Management Society, 205 East 42nd Street, New York, NY 10017, 212-286-9292

Self-Insurance Institute of America, P.O. Box 15466, Santa Ana, CA 92705, 714-261-2553

Society of Risk Management Consultants, 300 Park Avenue, New York, NY 10022, 800-765-SRMC

Magazines

Best's Insurance Management Reports, A.M. Best Co., Ambest Road, Oldwick, NJ 08858, 908-439-2200

Business Insurance, 740 North Rush Street, Chicago, IL 60611, 312-649-5398

The Insurance Journal, 80 South Lake Avenue, Suite 550, Pasadena, CA 91101, 818-793-7717

Insurance Times, 101 Walnut Street, Watertown, MA 02172, 617-924-8161

Insuranceweek, 1001 Fourth Avenue Plaza, Suite 3029, Seattle, WA 98154-1190, 206-624-6965

Merritt Risk Management Review, P.O. Box 955, Santa Monica, CA 90406-0955, 213-450-7234

Risk and Insurance, 747 Dresher Road, Suite 500, Horsham, PA 19044, 215-784-0860

Risk Management, 205 East 42nd Street, New York, NY 10017, 212-286-9364

16

Financial Control

apital must be regarded as a business tool requiring skilled use. The management of your financial assets will often determine the success of your business. Because of the risks incurred in going into business for yourself, this capital should yield a higher rate of return than could be obtained from an investment in government or corporate securities earning a guaranteed rate of interest. But this requires careful management, especially of your current and future assets.

Many owners of small businesses owners neglect this area. Entrepreneurs often get so caught up in their business that they neglect the financial management of their operations. Most leave the entire spectrum of financial matters to their accountants, who diligently prepare the proper financial statements at least once a year; as long as the business is making money, the owner will in all likelihood leave the task of analyzing the financial position of the business with that assurance.

That's a big mistake! In fact, lack of financial planning and control is a main reason why small businesses fail. It's nice to have an accountant prepare financial statements, but if you don't know what they mean and how they will impact you and your company, you're playing Russian roulette with your business.

There is more to effective financial control of a business than just generating financial statements. Financial control starts with a comprehensive record-keeping system that produces thorough accounting records on a day-to-day basis. See Chapter 17 for more information on forming a good accounting and record-keeping system.

Your accounting records will form the basis for the generation of your financial statements. There are three key financial reports that are extremely helpful in financial management:

1. Income statements.
2. Balance sheets.
3. Cash-flow statements.

These three reports are used to track assets, liabilities, the various components of working capital, and equity to evaluate a business's financial performance, which is expressed in terms of dollars and percentages. By tracking the financial performance of a company, past performance as well as current performance can be evaluated using financial ratios and comparing them against industry standards. This type of financial analysis can point out strengths and weaknesses of a business as well as any recurring trends that will help you manage your resources better from a strategic planning viewpoint.

And that is what this chapter is geared toward—the efficient management of your money. Through effective control measures, you will be able to accomplish the following:

1. Avoid an excessive investment in fixed assets.
2. Understand banking relationships better.
3. Maintain receivables and net working capital in proper proportion to sales.
4. Avoid excessive inventories.

There isn't any financial difficulty of a firm, regardless of size, that cannot be traced to violation of one or more of these principles of financial management.

THE FINANCIAL STATEMENTS

An intelligent reading and analysis of timely financial statements can aid a business owner in making decisions that affect the performance of a business. Basically, financial statements are the tools used in business to keep score. That being so, it is important for the business owner to be able to read and score the card.

The Balance Sheet

A balance sheet is a table of assets and liabilities (i.e., summary of credits and debits), as well as equity within a business at a specific point in time. A balance sheet is typically generated when books are closed after a specific period, either monthly, quarterly, or annually. Keep in mind that the balance sheet does not indicate whether or not the business is making a profit or a loss. It is a summary of the company's financial position, providing a snapshot of the assets, liabilities, and net worth of the business at a given point in time. Figure 16.1 shows a sample balance sheet.

In a financial analysis of the company, you would compare the most current balance sheet against past balance sheets that cover the same reporting period to identify changes in the financial condition of the business. These changes

Figure 16.1 Balance Sheet

ASSETS

CURRENT ASSETS

	TOTALS
Cash	
Account Receivables	
Inventory	

TOTAL CURRENT ASSETS	**A**	

FIXED ASSETS

Capital/Plant	
Investment	
Miscellaneous Assets	

TOTAL FIXED ASSETS	**B**	
TOTAL ASSETS (A+B)	**C**	

LIABILITIES

CURRENT LIABILITIES

Account Payables	
Accrued Liabilities	
Taxes	

TOTAL CURRENT LIABILITIES	**D**	

LONG-TERM LIABILITIES

Bonds Payable	
Notes Payable	

TOTAL LONG-TERM LIABILITIES	**E**	
TOTAL LIABILITIES (D+E)	**F**	
OWNER'S EQUITY (C-F)	**G**	
TOTAL LIABILITIES/EQUITY (F+G)	**H**	

would point out any fluctuations within assets, liabilities, working capital, and equity. For instance, if you were to have an excess in cash but an undue amount of capital tied up in loans and other claims against the company, you would have a business with strong liquidity but low debt capacity. Most companies in this type of situation will use their excess cash to pay down debts and improve their debt-to-equity ratio.

A comparative analysis of balance sheets will point out increases in the rate of receivables compared with cash, an overabundance of inventory compared with sales, decreasing book values of capital assets, inconsistency in maintaining long-term investments, increases in current liabilities in proportion to current assets, and declining return on investment compared with rising bonds payable. It will also show whether the equity is increasing in value or declining within the company.

When you form a balance sheet, the top portion lists your company's assets. Assets are any item of wealth, economic utility, or value. Anything that contributes to the total value of your business is an asset. Assets are classified as current assets and long-term or fixed assets. Current assets are assets that will be converted to cash or will be used by the business in a year or less and include:

- **Cash.** This includes all income derived from cash sales as well as those assets that have been converted to cash during the accounting period. It generally refers to all cash in checking, savings, and short-term investment accounts.
- **Accounts receivable.** This is income generated through the extension of credit that has yet to be collected at the end of the accounting period, less an allowance for bad debt.
- **Inventory.** If your business is a wholesale or retail operation, inventory will consist of finished products and supplies. With service businesses, inventory refers to supplies only. For manufacturers, inventory includes raw material, work in progress, finished goods, and supplies. The value of all inventories should be stated less an allowance for inventory loss.
- **Notes receivable.** All promissory notes extended by the company that are due and payable within a year are notes receivable. If a note is payable in full beyond a year, it should be classified as a fixed asset.
- **Marketable securities.** Those include all the company's short-term investments in items like stocks and bonds that can easily be converted into cash in a period of a year or less.

Other assets that appear in the balance sheet are called long-term or fixed assets. They are called long-term because they are durable and will last more than one year. Examples of this type of asset include:

- **Equipment.** The book value of all equipment less depreciation.
- **Buildings.** The appraised value of all buildings the business owns less depreciation.
- **Land.** The appraised value of all land owned by the business.

- **Long-term investments.** All investments by the company that cannot be converted to cash in less than one year. For the most part, companies just starting out will not have accumulated long-term investments.
- **Miscellaneous assets.** All other long-term assets that do not fit into the preceding categories. These might include patents, trade investment, or even goodwill, at least to the extent that it was purchased. Such assets are generally referred to as intangible assets.

The bottom half of the balance sheet lists the liabilities of the business and the amount of equity or capital you have accumulated. Liabilities are the debts of a business. They are the obligations of the business to creditors. Like assets, liabilities may be classified as current or long-term. Debts that are due in one year or less are classified as current liabilities. If they are due in more than one year, they are long-term liabilities.

Current liabilities indicate short-term cash requirements since they must be paid with cash within a year. Examples of current liabilities are as follows:

- **Accounts payable.** Amounts owed to suppliers of goods and services that are due and payable in a year or less.
- **Accrued liabilities.** Expenses such as operating costs, sales commissions, and property tax that will be incurred by the business but haven't been billed at the close of the reporting period.
- **Notes payable.** Refers to all promissory notes taken out by the business that are due and payable within a year. If a note is payable in full beyond a year, it should be classified as a long-term liability.
- **Taxes.** Amounts still owed for business income, taxable sales, real property, and employee withholding.

Long-term liabilities are obligations of the business that will not be due for at least a year. They include the following:

- **Bonds payable.** Publicly held debts that have been offered for sale by the company. All bonds at the end of the year that are due and payable over a period exceeding one year should be listed.
- **Mortgage payable.** The amount owed to a bank or lending institution on real property. The mortgage payable is that amount still due at the close of books for the year.
- **Notes payable.** Refers to all promissory notes taken out by the business that are payable in a year or more.

Capital represents the claim that the business owner has on the assets of the business. This is also referred to as owner's equity. Capital is not money in an accounting sense. Capital is equal to net assets, or the total value of assets minus the liabilities. For example, if a person has a car worth $5,000 (asset), and that person owes the bank $3,000 (debt), then the equity in the car (the capital claim) is $5,000 − $3,000 = $2,000. The $2,000 is not cash money. It is the monetary value of the owner's claim on the car.

The basic structure of a balance sheet is as follows:

$$\text{Assets} = \text{Liabilities} + \text{Capital}$$

We know that assets are anything of value. The liabilities and capital represent the claim on those items of value. The asset side of the equation tells us what we have and what it's worth. The other side tells us how the assets were financed and to whom they belong. For example, if you start a business by investing $10,000, then the business has $10,000 in assets, and you have a capital claim of $10,000. Should you decide to borrow an additional $20,000, the business would have $30,000 in cash (assets) and liabilities of $20,000 with a capital claim of $10,000.

Income Statement

The second financial report we'll discuss is the income statement. Also known as a profit-and-loss (P&L) report and operating statement, the income statement measures the economic performance of a business for a specific period—usually a month, a quarter, or year. Basically, it determines the profitability of an operation by summarizing revenue and expenses to arrive at the net profit of the firm.

Although the basics of an income statement are the same from business to business, there are notable differences between services, merchandisers, and manufacturers when it comes to the accounting of inventory.

For service businesses, the inventory maintained is that of supplies or spare parts. There is no inventory for manufacture or resale to include in the income statement. In fact, this type of inventory is often considered an overhead cost that is included in operating expenses, except in cases where materials are closely associated with the level of sales. In this instance, inventory may be expensed as a cost of sale.

Retailers and wholesalers, on the other hand, need to account for their resale inventory under cost-of-goods-sold, also known as *cost of sales* (see Figure 16.2(a)). This refers to the total price paid for the products sold during the income statement's accounting period. Freight and delivery charges are customarily included in this figure. Accountants segregate cost of goods on an operating statement because it provides a measure of gross profit margin when compared with sales, an important yardstick for measuring the firm's profitability.

For a retailer or wholesaler, cost of goods sold is equal to total inventory at the beginning of the accounting period plus any merchandise purchased, including freight costs, minus the inventory present at the end of the accounting period. This is your total cost of goods sold.

Although manufacturers account for cost of goods sold in the same manner as merchandisers by reporting beginning and ending inventories, as well as any

Figure 16.2   Cost of Goods Sold—Merchandisers

(a) COST OF GOODS SOLD (MERCHANDISERS) FOR PERIOD ENDING DECEMBER 31, 1994

			TOTALS
NET SALES			$ 155,000
Beginning Inventory, January 1, 19____	$	29,367	
Merchandise Purchases	$	74,190	
Freight & Drayage	$	4,637	
COST OF GOODS AVAILABLE FOR SALE			$ 108,194
Less Ending Inventory, December 31, 19____	$	30,913	
COST OF GOODS SOLD			$ 77,281

(b) COST OF GOODS MANUFACTURED FOR PERIOD ENDING DECEMBER 31, 1994

			TOTALS
Work in Process Inventory, January 1, 19 ____	$	2,318	
Inventory, January 1, 19____	$	20,866	
Purchases	$	35,549	
Freight In	$	1,545	
COST OF MATERIALS AVAILABLE FOR USE			$ 57,960
Less Inventory, December 31, 19 ____	$	22,412	
COST OF MATERIALS USED			$ 35,548
DIRECT LABOR			$ 20,093
Indirect Labor	$	3,091	
Factory Utilities	$	12,365	
Factory Supplies Used	$	3,091	
Insurance & Taxes	$	773	
Depreciation	$	4,637	
TOTAL MANUFACTURING OVERHEAD			$ 23,957
TOTAL MANUFACTURING COSTS			$ 79,598
TOTAL WORK IN PROCESS DURING PERIOD			$ 81,916
Less Work-In-Process Inventory, December 31, 19 ____	$	4,635	
COST OF GOODS MANUFACTURED			$ 77,281

purchases made during the accounting period, they are also very different because they have to track inventory through these three phases:

- **Raw material.** Material purchased to create a finished product.
- **Work-in-progress.** Inventory that is partially assembled.
- **Finished product.** Inventory that is fully assembled and available for sale.

Associated with this process are other costs such as direct labor and factory overhead. To account for all of these costs, manufacturers usually report them on a separate statement called the *cost of goods manufactured* (see Figure 16.2(b)). This statement is formed by first listing the work-in-progress inventory at the beginning of the accounting period. The next items that need to be listed include raw material and direct labor. Raw material should be accounted for by first listing the inventory at the beginning of the accounting period, and then adding in new purchases and freight charges. This will total the cost of materials available for use. Subtract the raw material inventory present at the end of the reporting period from the cost of material available for use. This will provide you with the cost of materials used. Add direct labor and manufacturing overhead to this amount. This will result in your total manufacturing costs. Add the work-in-progress beginning inventory to your total manufacturing costs for your total work-in-progress inventory. Now subtract the work-in-progress inventory present at the end of the accounting period. This will supply you with the cost of goods manufactured.

In the income statement for manufacturers, cost of goods manufactured is added to the finished goods inventory present at the beginning of the inventory, resulting in total cost of goods available for sale. The finished goods inventory present at the end of the reporting period is subtracted from this amount to produce the cost of goods sold (see Figure 16.3).

Aside from cost of goods, the rest of the income statement is the same from business to business and is based on the following format (see Figure 16.4):

Figure 16.3   Cost of Goods Sold—Manufacturer

COST OF GOODS SOLD (MANUFACTURER) FOR PERIOD ENDING DECEMBER 31, 1994		TOTALS	
NET SALES		$	155,000
Finished Goods Inventory, January 1, 19____	$ 29,367		
Cost of Goods Manufactured	$ 77,281		
COST OF GOODS AVAILABLE FOR SALE		$	106,648
Less Ending Inventory, December 31, 19____	$ 29,367		
COST OF GOODS SOLD		$	77,281

Figure 16.4 Income Statement (Manufacturer and Merchandiser)

INCOME STATEMENT (MANUFACTURER AND MERCHANDISER) FOR PERIOD ENDING DECEMBER 31, 1994

			TOTALS	
INCOME			$	155,000
Cost of Goods Sold	$	77,281		
Margin %		50%		
GROSS PROFIT			$	77,719
Payroll	$	34,100		
Rent	$	545		
Utilities	$	1,285		
Office Supplies	$	920	$	
Insurance	$	1,770		
Advertising	$	15,272	$	
Professional Services	$	855	$	
Travel	$	4,655		
Maintenance & Repair	$	1,117		
Packaging/Shipping	$	12,328		
Miscellaneous	$	65		
TOTAL EXPENSES			$	72,912
NET PROFIT			$	4,807
Margin %		3%		
Depreciation	$	123		
NET PROFIT BEFORE INTEREST			$	4,684
Margin %		3%		
Interest	$	118		
NET PROFIT BEFORE TAXES			$	4,566
Margin %		3%		

Figure 16.5   Income Statement (Service Business)

INCOME STATEMENT (SERVICE BUSINESS) FOR PERIOD ENDING DECEMBER 31, 1994		TOTALS
INCOME		$ 155,000
Payroll	$ 34,100	
Rent	$ 545	
Utilities	$ 1,285	
Office Supplies	$ 920	
Insurance	$ 1,770	
Advertising	$ 15,272	
Professional Services	$ 855	
Travel	$ 4,655	
Maintenance & Repair	$ 1,117	
Packaging/Shipping	$ 12,328	
Miscellaneous	$ 65	
TOTAL EXPENSES		$ 72,912
NET PROFIT		$ 69,593
Margin %	45%	
Depreciation	$ 123	
NET PROFIT BEFORE INTEREST		$ 69,467
Margin %	45%	
Interest	$ 118	
NET PROFIT BEFORE TAXES		$ 69,349
Margin %	45%	

- **Income.** All revenue generated by the business minus any discounts and returns.
- **Cost of goods.** See preceding text.
- **Gross profit margin.** The difference between revenue and cost of goods. Gross profit margin can be expressed in dollars, as a percentage, or both. As a percentage, the GP margin is always stated as a percentage of revenue.
- **Operating expenses.** All overhead and labor expenses associated with the operations of the business.
- **Net profit.** The difference between gross profit margin and operating expenses; the net profit depicts the business's debt and capital capabilities.
- **Depreciation.** The decrease in value of capital assets used to generate income.
- **Net profit before interest.** The difference between net profit and depreciation.
- **Interest.** All interest accrued from both short-term and long-term debts.
- **Net profit before taxes.** The difference between net profit before interest and interest.
- **Taxes.** All taxes on the business.
- **Profit after taxes.** The difference between net profit before taxes and the taxes paid. Profit after taxes is the ultimate bottom line for any company.

Figure 16.5 shows an example of an income statement for a service business. Notice that there is no cost-of-goods sold. Since many service businesses do not maintain an inventory from which sales are made, there are no cost-of-goods sold which can be expensed.

The income statement is used by companies to evaluate operating performance; it will let you know whether or not you've met some of your financial goals such as to increase sales, decrease the cost of goods sold, or reduce

Table 16.1   Cash Flow Statement

	JANUARY	FEBRUARY	MARCH	APRIL	MAY	JUNE	JULY	AUGUST
Cash sales	17,113	25,670	34,226	51,339	59,896	68,452	72,730	81,287
Receivables	0	0	25,670	38,504	51,339	77,009	89,844	102,678
Other income	0	0	0	0	0	0	0	0
Total income	17,113	25,670	59,896	89,843	111,235	145,461	162,574	183,965
Material	0	0	0	0	0	0	0	0
Direct labor	7,800	11,700	15,600	23,400	27,300	31,200	33,150	37,050
Overhead	0	0	0	0	0	0	0	0
Marketing and sales	8,250	9,900	11,550	11,550	12,045	12,705	13,530	15,345
Brewery operations/R&D	3,500	4,200	4,900	4,900	5,110	5,390	5,740	6,510
General and administrative	1,750	2,100	2,450	2,450	2,555	2,695	2,870	3,255
Taxes	0	0	40,528	0	0	40,528	0	0
Capital	3,430	3,430	3,430	3,430	3,430	3,430	3,430	3,430
Loans	25,000	25,000	25,000	25,000	25,000	25,001	25,000	25,000
Total expenses	49,730	56,330	103,458	70,730	75,440	120,950	83,720	90,590
Cash flow	−32,617	−30,660	−43,562	19,113	35,795	24,511	78,854	93,375
Cumulative cash flow	−32,617	−63,277	−106,840	−87,727	−51,932	−27,421	51,433	144,808

overhead. Whatever those goals might be, they will be reflected in the income statement.

When comparing several income statements over time, you can chart trends in your operating performance. This will help you chart future goals and strategies for sales, inventory, and operating overhead.

Cash Flow Statement

Your financial picture won't be complete unless you can relate all this information to the actual flow of cash through your business. That is shown in the cash flow statement (see Table 16.1).

The cash flow statement summarizes the operating, investing, and financing activities of the business as they relate to the inflow and outflow of cash. This is important in determining positive and negative cash flows, and whether your investment and financing endeavors are earning or draining cash resources. Just like the balance sheet and income statement, the cash flow statement charts a business's performance over a specific accounting period—monthly, quarterly, semiannually, or annually. In fact, most companies will prepare monthly cash flows and summarize them through an annual report for year-end meetings.

The importance of the cash flow statement shouldn't be underestimated: Its information captures the heartbeat of your business. It reveals the sources of money against the uses of that money to indicate whether there is a cash surplus or deficit. By observing trends in the cash flow, you can monitor the influx of cash from operating activities such as cash sales, accounts receivables, and interest from investments against operating expenses to determine the

Table 16.1 (continued)

SEPTEMBER	OCTOBER	NOVEMBER	DECEMBER	1995	1ST QTR	2ND QTR	3RD QTR	4TH QTR	1996	1997
85,565	98,400	124,070	136,904	855,652	164,247	200,747	255,496	291,995	912,485	1,021,730
109,096	121,931	128,348	147,600	892,019	458,720	261,317	323,540	398,190	1,441,767	1,552,160
0	0	0	0		0	0	0	0	0	0
194,661	220,331	252,418	284,504	1,747,671	622,967	462,064	579,036	690,185	2,354,252	2,573,890
0	0	0	0	0	0	0	0	0	0	0
39,000	44,850	56,550	62,400	390,000	91,806	95,979	112,671	116,844	417,300	467,376
0	0	0	0	0	0	0	0	0	0	0
17,325	17,325	17,490	17,985	165,000	38,841	40,607	47,669	49,434	176,550	197,736
7,350	7,350	7,420	7,630	70,000	16,478	17,227	20,223	20,972	74,900	83,888
3,675	3,675	3,710	3,815	35,000	8,239	8,614	10,112	10,486	37,450	41,944
40,528	0	0	40,528	162,113	41,538	41,538	41,538	41,538	166,150	186,451
3,430	3,430	3,430	3,430	41,164	11,018	11,018	11,018	11,018	44,072	49,361
25,000	25,000	25,000	25,000	300,000	75,000	75,000	75,000	75,000	300,000	300,000
136,308	101,630	113,600	160,789	1,163,277	282,920	289,982	318,230	325,292	1,216,422	1,326,756
58,353	118,701	138,818	123,715	584,394	340,048	172,083	260,807	364,894	1,137,830	1,247,134
203,160	321,861	460,679	584,394	584,394	924,442	1,096,524	1,357,331	1,722,224	1,722,224	2,969,358

business's liquidity. If not enough income is being generated from operating revenue to meet expenses, then the business's liquidity will be threatened. Additional revenue will have to be obtained either through financing or from the sale of investments. The cash flow statement provides a graphic look at how quickly cash is going out of the business compared with how promptly it is being collected. If cash is going out faster than it is being collected, you may want to review your credit collection policies.

Keep in mind that the cash-flow statement doesn't reveal a profit or a loss. Just because a company has positive cash flow doesn't mean that it generated more income from operating activities than it spent meeting its obligations. Additional revenue may have been obtained from investment and financing activities, both of which add to the business's cash position but not to its profitability.

On the other hand, a negative cash flow doesn't mean the company is unprofitable. The business can be producing a net profit for that accounting period, but may have additional obligations that do not effect the profitability of the company but does effect its cash position.

The cash-flow statement has three basic sections:

1. Income.
2. Expenses.
3. Cash flow.

The cash-flow statement begins with the income section. It shows all influx of revenue into the company:

- **Cash sales.** Income derived from sales paid for by cash.
- **Receivables.** Income derived from the collection of sales made by credit.
- **Investment income.** Income derived from investments, interest on loans that have been extended, and the liquidation of any assets.
- **Financing income.** Income derived from interest-bearing notes payable.

The second section includes all cash disbursements:

- **Material/Merchandise.** The raw material used in the manufacturing of a product (for manufacturing operations only). Or, the cash outlay for merchandise inventory during the accounting period (for merchandisers). In some cases, the material inventory used in a service will be included under this category.
- **Direct labor.** The labor required to manufacture a product (for manufacturing operations only), or the cost to service a client if this expense is not included under payroll.
- **Overhead.** All fixed and variable expenses required to operate a business. For manufacturing operations, the overhead costs related to the production of a product are included here as well.
- **Marketing and sales.** All salaries, commissions, and other direct costs associated with marketing and sales.

- **R&D.** All the labor expenses required to support the research and development operations of the business.
- **G&A.** All the labor expenses required to support the administrative functions of the business.
- **Taxes.** All taxes, except payroll, paid to the appropriate government institutions.
- **Capital.** The capital requirements to obtain any equipment elements needed for the generation of income.

The third section deals with the net and cumulative cash flow of the business. Net cash flow is the difference between income and expenses. This amount is carried over to the next reporting period through cumulative cash flow. To determine cumulative cash flow, the net cash flow of the current period is added to the cumulative cash flow from the previous period.

COMPARATIVE FINANCIAL RATIO ANALYSIS

Over the years, several analysis techniques have been developed that have proven to be valuable tools for financial management. They are used to illustrate the relationship between values drawn from the balance sheet and income statement as a ratio and are usually more accurate than using the dollar amounts. Financial ratio analysis enables owners of small businesses to gauge the financial weaknesses and strengths in the operation of their business, which enables them to take appropriate action. It also offers a view into the competitive performance of a company in relation to similar businesses in that industry.

Two areas within a company generally are measured through financial ratio analysis:

1. **Liquidity.** The amount of available liquid assets your business has at any given time to meet accounts or notes payable.
2. **Profitability.** The ability of the business to generate revenues, net income, and an acceptable return on investment.

Don't assume, however, that ratio analyses will tell you everything you need to know about the financial performance of your business. They won't. They provide a great deal of illumination, but they have their limitations. According to Jack Zwick in *A Handbook of Small Business Finance*,[1] those limitations are:

- **Not all businesses are the same.** When comparing ratios against industry averages, keep in mind that many businesspeople prepare their financial statements differently from others, resulting in financial ratios that may not present an accurate accounting of the average business in your industry.

---

[1] Jack Zwick, *A Handbook of Small Business Finance* (U.S. Small Business Administration, 1981).

- **Ratios are developed for specific periods.** If you operate a seasonal business, they may not provide an accurate measure of financial performance.
- **They are based on past performance of the company.** They don't offer any indications of present or future performance.

Despite these limitations, however, financial ratio analysis will be of great help to you in managing your financial situation.

Measures of Liquidity

The various measures of liquidity will tell you how much cash on hand you have, the amount of assets that can readily be turned into cash, and generally how quickly you can do so. In determining your financial health, a good rule of thumb is that the more liquid you are, the better.

Perhaps the most widely known ratio analysis is the *current ratio,* which is simply the ratio of your current assets to current liabilities, plus a safety margin for miscellaneous losses such as uncollectible accounts receivable. As discussed previously, you can find current assets and current liabilities on your balance sheet. For instance, suppose your current assets are $300,000 and your current liabilities are $100,000. The current ratio would be:

$$\$300,000 \div \$100,000 = 3$$

Generally, a current ratio of assets to liabilities that is at least 2 to 1 is good. You can compare your current ratio with that of similar companies within your industry by referring to surveys conducted by various trade associations and marketing companies.

After evaluating your current ratio and comparing it to the industry average, you may feel that it is too low. If so, you can use a number of strategies to increase it. For instance, you may be able to add to your current assets by raising capital through equity or debt financing. If you choose to borrow money through a debt financing route, make sure the loan has a maturity of at least one year in the future. You can increase your current ratio by paying off some of your debts that appear as current liabilities, or by turning some of your fixed or miscellaneous assets into current assets. As a last resort, you may have to funnel profits back into the business.

Another common ratio is the *acid test* or *quick ratio.* Like the current ratio, the acid test ratio measures the liquidity of your business. To find it, total all your liquid assets such as cash on hand plus any government securities and receivables, then divide these assets by your current liabilities. Suppose your current liquid assets are $30,000 cash, $50,000 in receivables, and another $20,000 in securities for a total of $100,000. You've determined your current liabilities are $50,000, so your quick ratio would be:

$$\$100,000 \div \$50,000 = 2.0$$

For most businesses, a quick ratio of 2.0 or better is more than sufficient. If, however, there are factors that will slow up payment of receivables or the due dates on your receivables exceeds the time stipulation of your payables, then you will need a higher ratio than 2.0.

An acid test ratio is a measure of exactly where you will be if there is a crisis and you don't have anything to correct your financial position. Try to keep your quick ratio at a level sufficient for your needs. Remember: Good financial management is the optimum use of your assets to increase the profitable operation of your business. If you have cash, receivables, and inventories that are not proportionate to your needs and lying idle, they are not working for you. You have to walk a tightrope between too much liquidity and not enough liquidity.

To help determine the right amount of liquidity for your business, conduct an evaluation of the *average collection period* of your receivables. You can do this by first taking your net sales found on your P&L or income statement and dividing this number by the days in your fiscal accounting period. This will provide you with your average sales per day. Now divide your average sales per day by your accounts receivables located on your balance sheet. This will result in your average collection period.

For example, say your annual net sales are $850,000, your fiscal accounting period is 365 days, and your accounts receivable are $50,000. This would result in the following:

$$\$850,000 \div 365 = \$2,328.77 \text{ (your average sales per day)}$$

$$\$50,000 \div \$2,328.77 = 21.5 \text{ (your average collection period)}$$

The average collection period in the preceding example shows 21.5 days or 22 days. If the credit terms are 30 days, then your accounts, or the people to whom you extend credit, are very dependable. However, if your average collection period is 60 days, then you may need to review your credit policies and institute a tighter credit collection strategy. Chapter 20 provides more information on collections of accounts receivable.

Inventory turnover is another measure to determine the amount of liquidity you should maintain. This measure will provide you with the amount of capital invested in inventory to meet your operation requirements. Turnover represents the number of times per year your inventory investment revolves.

Inventory turnover = Net sales (or cost of goods) ÷ the average value
of inventory on order and on hand

This ratio measures the efficiency of funds invested in materials and inventory and shows how often inventory is liquidated. To illustrate inventory turnover, let's say your cost of goods sold is $500,000 and the average value of inventory is $45,000. To arrive at inventory turnover, you would divide $500,000 by $45,000. This results in an inventory turnover of 11.1.

If inventory turnover is low in relation to the average for the industry (or in comparison with the average ratio for your business), it is likely that some obsolete or otherwise unsalable inventories continue to be carried. On the other hand, if the turnover is unusually high compared with the average figure, your business may be losing sales because of lack of adequate stock on hand.

It will be helpful to determine the turnover rate of each stock item so that you can evaluate how well each is moving. You may even want to base your inventory turnover on more frequent periods than a year. For perishable items, calculating turnover periods based on daily, weekly, or monthly periods may be necessary to ensure the freshness of the product. This is especially important for food-service operations.

Profitability Measures

Throughout your business lifetime, you'll rely on your business for several things. Making money, of course, is the topmost priority on that list. After all, it is the reason you went in to business in the first place. If your company isn't profitable, why put yourself through the headaches and long hours that usually accompany the business persuasion? You could be working for someone else secure in the knowledge of a weekly paycheck, benefits, and more free time.

Making money is what being in business is all about. In this section, we will discuss several methods that measure just how profitable your business is. These measures are asset earning power, return on owner's equity, net profit on sales, investment turnover, and return on investment (ROI). From these profitability measures, you'll learn:

- How much money you are making.
- Whether you are utilizing your present resources to maximize the profit potential of your business.
- Whether you are losing money or just breaking even.

Asset earning power measures how well your assets are preforming for you. In this measure, however, we are interested in the earning power of your total assets, not just your liquid assets. The *asset earning power* is a ratio that is calculated by taking your earnings before taxes and interest and dividing that number by your total assets. If you had total earnings before taxes and interest of $100,000 and total assets of $300,000, you would have an asset earning power of .33 or 33 percent. This shows you that your total assets are earning you 33 percent of their present marketable value.

The ratio known as *return on owner's equity* is used to determine what the return from the business is on the amount invested in your business. Equity in a company is usually based on capital investment and includes not only initial capitalization but ongoing as well. You can also include any intangible assets such as patents or trade secrets that have been contributed to the business in exchange for equity. If you are the only investor in your company, you control the total equity.

To compute the return on the owner's equity, you first have to calculate what your average equity investment in the business has been over a 12-month period. You can find this number on the balance sheet. Now divide your net profit by the equity and you will have computed your return on owner's equity. Therefore, if you have equity in the business of $75,000 and your net profit is $50,000, your return on the owner's equity would be .66 or 66 percent.

Net profit on sales is one of the most common ratios you can use to determine the profitability of your business. It measures the difference from what your net sales are against what you spend to operate your business. To determine the net profit on sales, you have to divide the net profit by the net sales. If we use the net profit of $50,000 from the preceding example and have net sales of $300,000, your net profit on sales would be .16 or 16 percent.

Most experts agree, and we concur, that if your percentage of net profit to net sales doesn't exceed the amount of money that can be earned from interest or dividends in securities, then you are not utilizing your assets to your best advantage. In this scenario you are earning .16 on every dollar the company spends. This is a very good return for most businesses. Check the average ratios of similar businesses within your industry and compare your net profit on sales against theirs. If your net profit on sales is substantially lower, you should reevaluate areas in your business that could be contributing to this reduced earning power. Those areas might be high operating costs, high shrinkage, or a price point that may not be producing sufficient profit or that might not be competitive enough.

Like inventory turnover, *investment turnover* can be used to determine the amount of times per year that your total investment or assets revolve. To calculate your investment turnover, divide your total annual net sales by your total assets. If your net sales are $500,000 and your total assets are $300,000, your investment turnover would be 1.6. Compare your investment turnover with similar businesses within the industry. In fairly investment-intensive businesses, your investment turnover may be lower than ones that don't require heavy capitalization.

Return on investment is the most common ratio used to determine a business's profitability. There are several ways to determine ROI, but the easiest and most popular method is to divide the net profit by total assets. If your net profit was $100,000 and your total assets are $300,000, your ROI would be .33 or 33 percent.

Return on investment is not necessarily the same as profit. ROI deals with the money you as the owner invest in the company and the return you are realizing on that money based on the net profit of the business. Profit, on the other hand, measures the performance of the business. Don't confuse ROI with the return on the owner's equity. This is an entirely different item as well. Only in very few enterprises (mostly sole proprietorships) does equity equal the total investment or assets of the business.

You can use ROI in several different ways to measure the profitability of your business. For instance, you can measure the performance of your pricing policies, inventory investment, capital equipment investment, and so forth. Some other ways to use ROI within your company are:

- Dividing net income, interest, and taxes by total liabilities to measure *rate of earnings of total capital employed.*
- Dividing net income and income taxes by proprietary equity and fixed liabilities to produce a *rate of earnings on invested capital.*
- Dividing net income by total capital plus reserves to calculate the *rate of earnings on proprietary equity and stock equity.*

Industry Averages

Not only can you use financial ratios to determine your company's strengths and weaknesses, you can also compare them against industry averages prepared by third-party companies. These studies provide industry averages for both financial and operating ratios.

We've already talked about financial ratios, but what about operating ratios? The operating ratio expresses the expenses of a firm as a percentage of net sales. It enables entrepreneurs to plan more efficiently by allowing them to designate their expenses as a percentage of projected net sales, and it points out any imbalances in the present performance of the business.

There are several sources of financial and operating ratios. Among the better known sources are:

- **Dun & Bradstreet, Inc.** Publishes its key business ratios in its monthly, *Dun's Review.* Operating ratios are published annually in the *Cost of Doing Business.* Contact Dun & Bradstreet's Public Relations Department, 99 Church Street, New York, NY 10007.
- **Robert Morris Associates.** A national association of bank loan and credit officers. Robert Morris Associates publishes an annual study on business ratios called the *Statement Study.* For more information contact the Executive Manager, Robert Morris Associates, Philadelphia National Bank Building, Philadelphia, PA 19107.
- **Accounting Corporation of America.** Publishes a semiannual study called *Barometer of Small Business,* which reports on operating ratios. Contact the Research Department, Accounting Corporation of America, 1929 First Avenue, San Diego, CA 92101.

Other sources of financial and operating ratios are those publications and organizations that report and support specific industries. These include accounting firms, trade magazines, universities, and trade associations.

The Resources section at the end of this chapter lists both trade magazines and associations. The government also publishes a number of studies with financial and operating ratios such as the *Statistics of Income Bulletin,* published by the Internal Revenue Service, and the *Census of Business,* published every five years by the Bureau of the Census.

RESOURCES

Associations

Financial Executives Institute, 10 Madison Avenue, P.O. Box 1938, Morristown, NJ 07962-1938, 201-898-4600; Fax, 201-898-4649

Financial Management Association, University of South Florida, School of Business, Tampa, FL 33620, 813-974-2084; Fax, 813-974-3318

Institute of Chartered Financial Analysts, P.O. Box 3668, Charlottesville, VA 22908, 804-977-6600; Fax, 804-977-1103

Magazines

Barron's National Business and Financial Weekly, 200 Liberty Street, 16th Floor, New York, NY 10281, 212-416-2700; Fax, 212-416-2829

Business Review, One Kwik Kopy Lane, P.O. Box 777, Cypress, TX 77429-2164, 713-373-3535

D&B Reports, 299 Park Avenue, New York, NY 10171-0102, 908-665-5000; Fax, 908-665-5430, David Monfried

Entrepreneurial Manager, 180 Varick Street, New York, NY 10014-4692, 212-633-0060

Entrepreneurial Manager's Newsletter, 180 Varick Street, Penthouse Suite, New York, NY 10014-4692, 212-633-0060; Fax, 212-633-0063

In Business, 419 State Avenue Emmaus, PA 18049-3717, 215-967-4135

Journal of Small Business Management, West Virginia University, College of Business Economics, Bureau of Business Research, P.O. Box 6025, Morgantown, WV 26506-6025, 304-293-5837

Nation's Business, 1615 H Street NW, Washington, DC 20062, 202-463-5650

Government Agency

U.S. Bureau of the Census, Public Information Office, U.S. Department of Commerce, Washington, DC 20233, 301-763-4040

Government Publication

Statistics of Income Bulletin, Superintendent of Documents, P.O. Box 371954, Pittsburgh, PA 15250-7954

17

Record Keeping

There are two reasons to keep records of a business operation: Records are required by law, and they are useful to you as a manager. Information about your business's financial condition will help you identify and correct any cash flow problems before they become major catastrophes.

You must also keep records to determine the tax liabilities of the business. Regardless of the type of bookkeeping system employed, the records must be permanent, accurate, and complete, and they must clearly establish income, deductions, credits, employee information, and anything else specified by federal, state, and local regulations. The law does not require you to keep any particular kind of records, but they must be complete and separate for each business.

When you start a business, establish the type and arrangement of books and records most suitable for your particular operation, keeping in mind taxes for which the business is liable and when they fall due. If you are not competent in this area, seek the aid of a professional accountant. Setting up a good system for record keeping need only be done once; doing it efficiently makes things much easier later.

ACCOUNTING METHODS

Two systems of accounting are used for record-keeping purposes—cash basis and accrual basis. Which one will be best for your business depends on your sales volume, the legal form under which you operate, and whether you extend credit.

Cash Basis

In cash basis accounting, you do business and pay taxes according to your real-time cash flow. Cash income begins as soon as you ring it up on the register or receive it by check. Expenses are paid as they occur. Both income and expenses are put on the books and charged to the period in which they are paid or received.

You can also defer income to the following year as long as it isn't actually or constructively received by you in the present year. A check received by you in the present year but not cashed until the following year is still income to you for the present year. Therefore, if you want to shift income to the following year, you will either have to delay billing until the following year or bill so late in the present year that a present-year payment is unlikely.

If you want to accelerate expenses to the present year, you should pay those bills received and log them as the present year's expenses. An expense charged to your credit card will count as an expense in the year it was charged and not when you pay the card company. Be careful about paying next year's expenses in advance. Generally, expenses prepaid in excess of one month have to be prorated over the specified payment period. However, dues and subscriptions can be currently deducted if prepaid for the forthcoming year.

Accrual Basis

With accrual basis accounting, income and expenses are charged to the period to which they should apply, regardless of whether money has been received. For instance, if you are a contractor using accrual basis accounting and have done work for which you haven't been paid, you recognize all expenses incurred in connection with that contract during the period in which it was supposed to have been completely paid and expensed, regardless of whether you have been paid for it yet. If an employee works for you this month but you haven't paid him or her, you still take the deduction for that expense because that person has earned the money.

You must use the accrual method to track purchases and sales if your business involves an inventory. Under the Tax Reform Act of 1986, if your gross sales exceed $5,000,000 per year and your business is a corporation, partnership, or trust, the IRS requires you to use the accrual accounting method. Several exceptions to this rule do permit some businesses to use the cash method of accounting no matter how large the gross receipts. These businesses are farming businesses, partnerships without corporate partners, sole proprietorships, and "qualified" personal service corporations. These include corporations performing services in the fields of health, law, accounting, actuarial science, performing, and consulting. A corporation must not only fall into these fields for the exception: 95 percent of its stock must be owned by shareholders who are performing services for the corporation.

In accrual basis accounting, it doesn't matter when you receive or make actual payment. Income is reported when you bill. Expenses are deductible when you are billed, not when you pay. This accounting method has more tax benefits for a company with few receivables and large amounts of current liabilities. Advance payments to an accrual basis taxpayer are considered taxable income in the year received.

Unlike payments for services rendered, advance payments for merchandise are reported by an accrual basis taxpayer when properly accruable under this method of accounting. But if you choose this accounting procedure, you must use it for all reports and credit purposes.

If you run two or more businesses at the same time, you may use different accounting methods for each business. Therefore, it is possible to run one business on the cash basis and the other on the accrual basis.

RECORD KEEPING

When developing a record-keeping system, your goal is to keep it as simple as possible. Your time is valuable, and if your records are too complex, you will spend too much time maintaining them. Also, you may need to hire an accountant or bookkeeper to maintain overly complicated records. You need to develop a record-keeping system that is both comprehensive and easily understandable.

The records you keep should have a direct bearing on the financial condition of your business. Don't maintain irrelevant and time-consuming records. Keep records you want to maintain up-to-date with current and pertinent information in a manner uniform throughout the entire system.

Bookkeeping Systems

Double-entry bookkeeping is the preferred method of keeping business records. You would first enter transactions in a journal, then post monthly totals of the transactions to the appropriate ledger accounts. There are five categories of ledger accounts:

1. Income.
2. Expenses.
3. Assets.
4. Liability.
5. Net worth.

The classification of ledger accounts sidebar provides a breakdown of the various ledger accounts found within the categories listed above.

Figures 17.1 and 17.2 show examples of two ledger accounts and how a transaction is posted and cross-referenced against each account. The transactions from these ledger accounts are then posted in the general journal,

Classification of Ledger Accounts Sidebar

Income
Retail Sales
Wholesale Sales
Sales—Services
Miscellaneous Income
Expenses
Salaries and Wages
Contract Labor
Payroll Taxes
Utilities
Telephone
Rent
Office Supplies
Postage
Maintenance Expense
Insurance
Interest
Depreciation
Travel Expense
Entertainment
Advertising
Dues and Contributions
Miscellaneous Expenses
Assets
Cash in Bank
Petty Cash
Accounts Receivable

Inventory
Materials and Supplies
Prepaid Expenses
Deposits
Land
Buildings
Accumulated Depreciation—Buildings
Tools and Equipment
Accumulated Depreciation—Tools and Equipment
Automotive Equipment
Accumulated Depreciation—Automotive
Equipment
Furniture and Fixtures
Accumulated Depreciation—Furniture and Fixtures
Organization Expenses
Liabilities
Accounts Payable
Notes Payable
Sales Taxes—Payable
FICA Taxes—Payable
Federal Withholding Taxes
State Withholding Taxes
Unemployment Taxes
Long-Term Debt—Mortgages Payable
Miscellaneous Accruals
Net Worth
Retained Earnings

Source: Small Business Administration—Office of Business Development. John Cotton, "Keeping Records in Small Business." Management Aids, Number 1.017 1986.

Figure 17.3. At the end of each fiscal year or accounting period, accounts are balanced and closed. The income and expense accounts are transferred to the income statement for use in the summary of revenue and expenses. The asset, liability, and net worth accounts are used to provide figures for the balance sheet (see Chapter 16 for more information about financial statements).

Although single-entry bookkeeping is not as complete as the double-entry method, you can still use it effectively for your small business, especially during its early years. The single-entry system can be relatively simple. The flow of income and expense is recorded through a daily summary of cash receipts, a monthly summary of receipts, and a monthly disbursements journal (such as a checkbook). This system is entirely adequate for the tax purposes of many small businesses.

Figure 17.1 General Ledger (Entry #1)

ACCOUNT Cash

ACCOUNT NUMBER 123

MONTH OF August

NUMBER Page 1

DATE	ITEM	TRANSACTION		BALANCE	
		DEBIT	CREDIT	DEBIT	CREDIT
August 3	Jones' Janitorial Payment	$500		$500	

Figure 17.2   General Ledger (Entry #2)

ACCOUNT Jones' Janitorial   **MONTH OF** August

ACCOUNT NUMBER 987   NUMBER Page 1

DATE	ITEM	TRANSACTION		BALANCE	
		DEBIT	CREDIT	DEBIT	CREDIT
August 3	Payment from Cash		$500		$500

Figure 17.3 General Journal

MONTH OF _____

NUMBER _____

DATE	ACCOUNT DEBITED	ACCOUNT NUMBER	AMOUNT	ACCOUNT CREDITED	ACCOUNT NUMBER	AMOUNT
August 3	Cash	123	$500	Jones' Janitorial	987	$500

Records to Keep

Your business will generate four basic types of records that you will need to track:

1. Sales records.
2. Cash receipts.
3. Cash disbursements.
4. Accounts receivable.

Sales records include all income derived from the sales of products or the performance of services. They can be grouped in one large category called gross sales or into several subcategories depicting different product lines so that you know what is doing well and what isn't. Figure 17.4 shows an example of a sales journal.

Cash receipts account for all monies generated through cash sales and the collection of accounts receivable. This is actual income collected and doesn't include earnings from your sales records unless you choose to operate a cash-and-carry business. In a cash-and-carry business, your cash receipts theoretically match your sales records. Figure 17.5 shows an example of a cash receipts journal.

Cash disbursements are sometimes referred to as operating expense records or accounts payable. All disbursements should be made by check so that business expenses can be well documented for tax purposes. If you need to make a cash payment, you should include a receipt for it, or at least an explanation of it, in the business records. All canceled checks, paid bills, and other documents that substantiate the entries in the business records should be filed in an orderly manner and stored in a safe place. Breaking the cash disbursement headings into different categories such as rent, maintenance, and advertising may be easier to deal with than one large category. Figure 17.6 shows an example of a cash disbursements journal.

You should establish a petty cash fund to disburse cash for expenses that are immediate and small enough to warrant payment by cash. The Small Business Administration suggests that you account for petty cash by cashing a check for the purpose of petty cash and placing the money in a safe or lockbox. Record items purchased from the petty cash fund on a form listing the date of purchase, the amount, and the purpose of the expenditure. When the petty cash fund is almost exhausted, total the cost of all the items and write a check to replenish the account. Figures 17.7 and 17.8 show examples of a petty cash voucher and a petty cash journal. Requests for petty cash are made using the voucher and are then recorded in the journal.

Accounts receivable are sales stemming from the extension of credit. Maintain these records on a monthly basis so you can age your receivables and determine just how long your credit customers are taking to pay their bills. If an account ages beyond a 60-day period, start investigating the reasons why the customer is taking so long to pay. We will cover the extension and collection of

Figure 17.4 Sales Journal

MONTH OF _____

NUMBER _____

DATE	INVOICE NO.	DESCRIPTION	ACCOUNT DEBITED	ACCT. NO.	AMOUNT RECEIVABLE	ACCOUNT DEBITED	ACCT. NO.	AMOUNT SALES TAX	OTHER

Figure 17.5   Cash Receipts Journal

MONTH OF _____

NUMBER _____

DATE	ACCOUNT CREDITED	ACCT. #	SALES	AMOUNT RECEIVABLE	OTHER	ACCOUNT DEBITED	ACCT. #	CASH	AMOUNT DISCOUNTS	OTHER

Figure 17.6 Cash Disbursements Journal

MONTH OF _____

NUMBER _____

DATE	CHECK NO.	PAYEE	ACCOUNT CREDITED	ACCT. NO.	CASH	AMOUNT DISCOUNTS	OTHER	ACCOUNT DEBITED	ACCT. NO.	AMOUNT PAYABLE	OTHER

Figure 17.7 Expense Report

DATE	BREAKFAST	LUNCH	DINNER	TIPS	LODGINGS	PHONE	TRAVEL	PARKING/TOLLS	GAS/OIL	ENTERTAINMENT	MISCELLANEOUS	DAILY TOTAL

NAME: _____   START DATE: _____

PURPOSE: _____   END DATE: _____

SUBTOTAL

LESS ADVANCE

TOTAL AMOUNT DUE

Figure 17.8   Petty Cash Voucher

DATE:_____

VOUCHER NUMBER: _____

FOR	ACCOUNT DEBITED	ACCOUNT NO.	AMOUNT
		TOTAL	

APPROVED BY:_____

RECEIVED BY: _____

credit in Chapter 20. Figures 17.9 and 17.10 are examples of journals where receivables and payables can be tracked.

Balancing and Bank Reconciliations

Every page of sales, cash receipts, and disbursements, the SBA notes, should be balanced to ensure the accuracy of your records, and every month you should reconcile your checkbook with your bank statement to make sure that your records match those of the bank. You should make any needed corrections or report any errors immediately. If there is a bank error, you usually need to notify the bank within 14 working days after receipt of the reconciliation statement.

OTHER RECORDS YOU SHOULD RETAIN

Records supporting entries on a federal tax return should be kept until the statute of limitations (ordinarily three years after the return is due) expires. You should keep copies of federal income tax returns forever.

Figure 17.9   Petty Cash Journal

REPORTING PERIOD

FROM: _____ **TO:** _____ **BALANCE ON HAND** [   ]

DATE	VOUCHER NUMBER	ACCOUNT	ACCOUNT NUMBER	PAYEE	APPROVED BY	TOTAL	BALANCE

TOTAL VOUCHER AMOUNT	$
TOTAL RECEIPTS	$
CASH ON HAND	$
OVERAGE/SHORTAGE	$
PETTY CASH REIMBURSEMENT	$
BALANCE FORWARD	$

AUDITED BY:

_____

APPROVED BY:

_____

Figure 17.10 Aging of Accounts Receivable

REPORTING PERIOD

FROM: _____ **TO:** _____

DATE	INVOICE NUMBER	ACCOUNT	ACCOUNT NUMBER	DESCRIPTION	AMOUNT			
					30 DAYS	60 DAYS	90+ DAYS	TOTAL

In addition to the four basic records and your tax documents, you should also maintain records for three other important items:

1. Capital equipment.
2. Insurance.
3. Payroll.

Capital Equipment

Keep equipment records for major purchases so you can determine what your depreciation expenses will be for tax purposes. Don't keep records on small items like staplers, tape recorders, and answering machines. Don't list leased equipment in this section. Keep records pertaining to leased equipment under the category of cash disbursements. Leased equipment is a liability that is payable each month.

Maintain records only on capital equipment you have purchased, whether outright, on a contract basis, or through a chattel mortgage. Major equipment you have purchased is considered an asset even though you may have financed it. As you pay off your loan obligation, you build equity in the equipment that you can enter on your balance sheet as an asset.

Your equipment records should include the following information: date purchased, the vendor's name, a brief description of the item, how it was paid for, the check number if appropriate, and the full amount of the purchase.

Insurance

Keep all records pertaining to your company's insurance policies. This includes auto, life, health, fire, and any special coverage you may obtain. List the policy carriers and the underwriting agents who issued the coverages. Also maintain records on any claims made against your policies to resolve any misunderstandings that may arise.

When updating your records, enter all information about the payment of premiums including the date the check was written, the amount, and which policy it was written for. This will help you in payment disputes and for tax purposes.

Payroll

Payroll records present another set of problems. An employer, regardless of the number of employees, must maintain all records pertaining to payroll taxes (income tax withholding, Social Security, and federal unemployment tax) for at least four years after the tax becomes due or is paid, whichever is later. Altogether, 20 different kinds of employment records must be maintained just to satisfy federal requirements:

Income Tax Withholding Records

1. Name, address, and Social Security number of each employee.
2. Amount and date of each payment of compensation.
3. Amount of wages subject to withholding in each payment.
4. Amount of withholding tax collected from each payment.
5. Reason that the taxable amount is less than the total payment.
6. Statements relating to employees' nonresident alien status.
7. Market value and date of noncash compensation.
8. Information about payments made under sick-pay plans.
9. Withholding exemption certificates.
10. Agreements regarding the voluntary withholding of extra cash.
11. Dates and payments to employees for nonbusiness services.
12. Statements of tips received by employees.
13. Requests for different computation of withholding taxes.

Social Security (FICA) Tax Records

1. Amount of each payment subject to FICA tax.
2. Amount and date of FICA tax collected from each payment.
3. Explanation for the difference, if any.

Federal Unemployment Tax (FUTA) Records

1. Total amount paid during calendar year.
2. Amount subject to unemployment tax.
3. Amount of contributions paid into the state unemployment fund.
4. Any other information requested on the unemployment tax return.

Payroll for a small firm is a simple task with a good pegboard or "write-it-once" system. Any office supply store can show you samples of different one-write systems. Most accountants recommend these systems because they reduce errors and save time in making payroll entries.

Business Papers

Carefully preserve all business papers. All purchase invoices, receiving reports, copies of sales slips, invoices sent to business firm customers, canceled checks, receipts for cash paid out, and cash register tapes must be meticulously retained. They not only are essential to maintaining good records but also may be important if legal or tax questions are ever raised.

How Long Should I Keep These Records?

The accounting firm Price Waterhouse offers the following guidelines:

1. Income tax, revenue agents' reports, protests, court briefs, and appeals: Retain indefinitely.

2. Annual financial statements: Retain indefinitely. Monthly statements used for internal purposes: Retain for three years.
3. Books of account, such as the general ledger and general journal: Retain indefinitely. Cash books: Retain indefinitely, unless posted regularly to the general ledger. Subsidiary ledgers: Retain for three years. ("Ledgers" refer to the actual books or the magnetic tapes, disks, or other media on which the ledgers and journals are stored.)
4. Canceled, payroll, and dividend checks: Retain for six years.
5. Income tax payment checks: Retain indefinitely.
6. Bank reconciliations, voided checks, check stubs, and check register tapes: Retain for six years.
7. Sales records such as invoices, monthly statements, remittance advisories, shipping papers, bills of lading, and customers' purchase orders: Retain for six years.
8. Purchase records, including purchase orders, payment vouchers authorizing payment to vendors and vendor invoices: Retain for six years.
9. Travel and entertainment records, including account books, diaries, and expense statements: Retain for six years.
10. Documents substantiating fixed asset additions, such as the amounts and dates of additions or improvements, details related to retirements, depreciation policies, and salvage values assigned to assets: Retain indefinitely.
11. Personnel and payroll records, such as payments and reports to taxing authorities, including federal income tax withholding, FICA contributions, unemployment taxes and workers' compensation insurance: Retain for four years.
12. Corporate documents, including certificate of incorporation, corporate charter, constitution and bylaws, deeds and easements, stock, stock transfer and stockholder records, minutes of board of directors' meetings, retirement and pension records, labor contracts, and licenses, patents, trademarks and registration applications: Retain indefinitely.

Recording Transactions

In a manual or one-write system of recording financial transactions, each check you enter is recorded automatically in the cash disbursements journal. This is popular with many small businesses because it saves time. If you only write a few checks each month, it makes sense to use a manual or one-write system. Maintaining your general ledger on a regular basis should give you all the financial information you need to make good business decisions.

If you write a large number of checks each month, consider changing to batch processing of your general ledger postings. Data processing services will handle this for you. You would need to develop expense codes for the types of checks you write. Then make an adding machine tape of the totals and send that to the data processing center. You will then get a computer printout of your general ledger, with all your checks listed according to expense code.

If you are spending a lot of money in cash, you should list these expenditures on an expense report form. Such forms are readily available at stationery stores and are designated by category, such as travel, entertainment, office supplies, and so on. Attach the receipts to the entry on the form corresponding to the expenditure. Now the bookkeeper adds the expense codes and writes you a check for reimbursement of expenses. Ultimately, therefore, all cash disbursements are handled by check—even out-of-pocket expenses. For example, you spend $200 out of pocket, fill out an expense report, and pay yourself for what you spent. This way you know those expenses were entered into your bookkeeping system. Figure 17.11 shows an example of an expense report.

We cannot stress enough that you should try to pay as much as you can by check. This gives you a record of all debits to your company. Additionally, most bookkeeping veterans agree that it is best to work out of one checkbook for the business, if at all possible. Nothing is more annoying to an accountant than tracking interaccount transfers. This is where the financial problems of many businesses begin. You run the risk of recording an investment in the business as income, or of making a similar error.

In some lines of business, legal restrictions prevent you from using just one checkbook for your business. Lawyers and collection agents are usually required by law to maintain trust accounts on behalf of their clients. These accounts represent money held in trust on the client's behalf until it is disbursed in the form of client receipts (for example, court-awarded damages or collection monies) or, ultimately, service fees.

PROFESSIONAL FINANCIAL ADVISORS

If you choose your banker wisely, you will have at your service a skilled professional consultant who will not, under normal circumstances, charge for his or her services. You will also require the help of other specialists, including an accountant, an attorney, and one or more consultants who are experts in your field. You will rely on some of these experts only sporadically, such as during the start-up phase or when problems arise. Your accountant, however, will serve you on a regular basis.

Discuss bookkeeping and accounting fees early in your relationship with all professional financial experts and consultants, making certain you understand what services you will receive for the agreed-on fee. Fees charged by professionals vary enormously, depending in large part on their experience and their expertise in the field. Geographic area is also a major determinant for the cost of professional advice.

Accountants

A good accountant is the most important outside advisor the small-business owner has. The services of a lawyer and consultant are vital during specific

Figure 17.11 Aging of Accounts Payable

REPORTING PERIOD

FROM: _____ **TO:** _____

DATE	INVOICE NUMBER	ACCOUNT	ACCOUNT NUMBER	DESCRIPTION	AMOUNT			TOTAL
					30 DAYS	60 DAYS	90+ DAYS	

periods in the development of a small business or in times of trouble, but it is the accountant who, on a continuing basis, has the greatest impact on the ultimate success or failure of a small business.

Once you are in operation, you will have to decide whether your volume warrants a full-time bookkeeper, an outside accounting service, or merely a year-end accounting and tax-preparation service. Even the smallest unincorporated businesses employ an outside public accountant to prepare their financial statements. When you borrow money, your bank manager will want to see your balance sheet and your operating statement. If these statements are prepared by a reputable public accountant, they will be more credible than if you prepare them yourself. (If you are borrowing less than $500,000, many banks will accept unaudited financial statements prepared by a public accountant.) Accountants can be useful in several ways:

- If you are organizing a corporation, your accountant should counsel you in the start-up phase to determine how you can save the most money in and from taxes.
- If you are starting a sole proprietorship or a partnership, you won't need an auditor at this point. Instead, you'll want the accountant to set up a bookkeeping system you can operate internally.
- An accountant should help you organize the statistical data concerning your business, assist in charting future actions based on past performance, and advise you on your overall financial strategy for purchasing, capital investment, and other matters related to your business goals.

In addition to these tasks, accountants help business owners comply with a number of laws and regulations affecting their record-keeping practices. If you spend your time trying to find answers to the many questions that accountants can answer more efficiently, you will not have the time to manage your business properly. Spend your time doing what you do best, and let accountants do what they do best.

Of course, you need to use the services of your accountant, as well as of other outside professionals, as efficiently as possible. If you consult the accountant sparingly but wisely, it doesn't have to cost you much money.

Choosing and Using Financial Advisors

Where do you find a good accountant? Ask other small-business owners, your banker, or your lawyer for recommendations.

Use your financial advisors wisely. Decide that you are going to spend at least one hour of every quarter with a CPA to have your financial statements either prepared or reviewed. Take the time away from your business to do this if necessary.

How much does a good accountant charge? Their fees, like those of lawyers, doctors, and other professionals, vary widely. Small-town accountants in business for themselves may charge $10 or $15 per hour, while some of the large, nationally known firms might charge $50 to $100 per hour for their service. An independent bookkeeper's fee can range from $7.50 per hour to $25, depending on the region where the bookkeeper operates.

If you see your accountant four times a year and pay $50 each time, then you will spend $200. Assuming you have a CPA prepare your taxes, you will spend another $100 to $200 to file your tax return. If the CPA can save you $400 in tax liability, then the money is well spent.

How to Pick a Professional Accountant

Because it is so important for you to work with a good accountant, we offer a few suggestions on how to find one. First, look at the personality of a CPA before you decide to hire him or her. You must feel comfortable with the person who will help direct your business and personal finances. To find out if you would be comfortable working with a particular CPA, arrange for an initial interview, which most firms provide without charge.

Get a list of services available. You should find a firm that can offer the types of services you will need. Equally important is the CPA's experience, particularly in your type of business.

Another factor to consider is the CPA's standing in the business community. An accountant's connections and professional relationships can be of benefit to you. If you need a business loan, the whole process will be easier if the CPA is respected by members of the local banking and financial community. To assess a CPA's professional standing, inquire into his or her certification, license status, educational background, and involvement in professional organizations. A CPA's reputation can be a good measure of performance. Take the time to question peers, clients, associates, and others.

Once you have found a CPA who can meet your needs, ask for an accurate assessment of the cost of services. George Johnson, head of a Detroit-based accounting firm, advises inviting the CPA to conduct an initial diagnostic review of your business's finances. Then ask for a proposal letter to find out what kind of work needs to be done and what it will cost to do it. Finally, you should look for a firm that offers sufficient personnel to meet your needs if the principal CPA is not available.

Having said all that, let us caution you not to expect too much from a CPA. The CPA is not a miracle worker and cannot turn a troubled business around overnight.

When to Use National Accounting Firms

Whether you use a local CPA or a national firm depends on how large you expect your business to grow, and on what type of business you will operate. If you have a small shoe shop and don't plan to build a chain of stores, then stay with a local CPA. If you have an investment business and expect your customers to look closely at your financial stability, it may be worthwhile to have an audited statement prepared by a well-known national firm; the added prestige could enhance your sales efforts. If you think the business will require large-scale financing, or if you plan to go public with a stock offering, using a big CPA firm is definitely a plus. You also need to consider the price difference between an audited statement and an unaudited one. Whether you use a small local firm or a national one, auditing can be costly but necessary if you fit in one of these categories.

Large accounting firms used to be reluctant to work with small companies. But as the number of corporate giants has decreased due to mergers and acquisitions, some of the Big Eight (the nation's largest accounting firms) have gone after the small-firm market with a vengeance. That's good news for entrepreneurs who can now get those firms' resources at competitive prices.

Calling in the accountant before it's time to do the books could make the bottom line of those books look a lot better. An audit is essentially after the fact, and some things can't be changed no matter how skillful or experienced the accountant may be. For example, how a firm obtains something—whether it's rented, leased, or bought—can determine how it is taxed. Acquiring an asset one way can cause you to lose tax benefits you would enjoy if you acquired it another way.

Streamline Your Accounting System

You can make the most efficient use of your accountant, and reduce your accountant's fees, if you handle a number of routine bookkeeping tasks yourself. Do you produce neat, efficient records for monthly accounting work and taxes? If not, you are probably paying for more accounting hours than you should.

Ask your accountant for a list of the specific records required for routine accounting work. Make sure you provide these records on time and in good form each month. If your accountant spends many hours each month deciphering unreadable records or adding up columns of daily figures, you will pay for it. If your accountant has to call you two or three times each month to get all the information needed, you will probably pay a quarter-hour fee for each call. Don't take a paper bag full of canceled checks, invoices, bank deposit slips, and bank statements to your tax preparer each year, or you will pay up to $60 per hour to have those documents compiled into income-and-expense figures.

If you have organized your accounting system correctly and have an orderly filing system for important documents, your records should be ready at tax time. For taxes, you need careful records of assets and depreciation, income and expense, capital gains and losses, inventory, and costs of goods sold.

If your accounting system does not provide the information you and your accountant need—when it is needed and in an understandable form—you are increasing your accounting costs needlessly.

RESOURCES

Associations

American Accounting Association, 5717 Bessie Drive, Sarasota, FL 34233, 813-921-7747

Independent Accountants International, 9200 S. Dateland Blvd., Suite 510, Miami, FL 33156, 305-670-0580

Magazines

Accounting Office Management & Administration, 29 W. 35th Street, 5th Floor, New York, NY 10001, 212-244-0360

Barron's National Business & Financial Weekly, 200 Liberty Street, New York, NY 10281, 212-416-2700

The Business Owner, Thomas Publishing, Inc., 383 S. Broadway, Hicksville, NY 11801, 516-681-2111

Business Week, 1221 Avenue of the Americas, 39th Floor, New York, NY 10020, 212-512-3896

In Business, 419 State Ave., Emmaus, PA 18049-3717, 215-967-4135

Institute of Management Accountants, 10 Paragon Drive, Montvale, NJ 07645, 201-573-9000

18

Pricing

Entrepreneurs often neglect the area of pricing because they simply do not understand the concepts associated with this business function. Many small business owners tend to take the cost of the product or of providing the service and multiply that number by an arbitrary figure, reasoning that the end price will produce a sufficient profit.

Well, that may or may not be true. Under this type of system, the costs of operating the business may not have been covered and an appropriate profit produced. Since the pricing was arbitrarily figured, the results will be just as arbitrary.

Costs and desired profit are just a few things entrepreneurs fail to calculate in their pricing scheme. They also pay little attention to the competition and to the image the end price will produce for your company—all of which are elements that you should consider in conjunction with your overall business or marketing plan.

This chapter is designed to familiarize you with the various fundamentals involved in pricing as well as the methods employed. As you read through this chapter, however, keep in mind that pricing is subjective. What works for one company may not be entirely correct for another. The important thing to remember is that pricing almost always follows the same basic rules and guidelines from one situation to the next.

PRICING GUIDELINES

Whether your company sells a product or provides a service, the price you charge your customers or clients will have a direct effect on the success of your business. Though pricing strategy and computations can be complex, the basic rules of pricing are straightforward:

1. All prices must cover costs.
2. The best and most effective way of lowering your sales prices is to lower costs.
3. Prices must be changed frequently to assure that they reflect the dynamics of cost, demand, changes in the market, and response to your competition.
4. Prices must be established to assure sales. Do not price against a competitive operation alone; price to sell.
5. Product utility, longevity, maintenance, and end use must be judged continually, and target prices adjusted accordingly.
6. Prices must be set to preserve order in the marketplace. In other words, if you increase your marketing budget and raise your prices to offset that increase but the competition doesn't follow suit, your price will not be consistent with the market.

Although there are many different methods to establish prices, the rules are universal and should be adhered to when forming and maintaining pricing strategies. To understand these rules better, you should first become familiar with the basic structure of pricing.

The Relationship between Prices and Costs

Before you can set a price for your product or service, you have to recognize the cost of running your business. You derive all of your revenue from one source—the sale of your product or service—yet that must cover all of your expenses, no matter how or why you incur them. If the price you set for your product or service doesn't cover your costs, you will have to infuse more cash into the business until your resources are depleted and your business fails.

So just how much does it cost to run your business? You must add fixed costs, such as property/equipment leases, loan repayments, management costs (i.e., salaried employees), and depreciation to the variable costs of raw materials, inventory, utilities, and hourly wages/commissions. You must also calculate the cost generated by markdowns, shortages, damaged merchandise, employee discounts, cost of goods sold and desired profits, and add them to the previously listed operating expenses to arrive at an initial price for your product.

But the most important aspect of cost versus price—a factor that you must grasp if you are to learn how to price correctly—is that, ultimately, the market dictates the price you may charge for your product or service. Your cost of providing customers and/or clients with that product or service simply establishes a minimum or break-even point. You must work within the range between that break-even figure and the maximum price you could demand (and get) for your product or service.

Pricing and Repricing Considerations

Don't make the mistake of thinking that your prices are set in concrete. They aren't. Just because you've established a price doesn't mean you can simply forget about it. Many first-time small-business owners commit that error. Because pricing is so important—and can be so confusing—many entrepreneurs set prices once and "hope for the best." In reality, they are merely consigning themselves to lost profits. Or, in effect, they are putting profits directly into the pockets of their competitors. As such, the smart entrepreneur must check pricing continuously, to make certain that his or her company always makes the best price available.

According to William Cohen, in *The Entrepreneur and Small-Business Problem Solver*,[1] certain circumstances warrant pricing or repricing consideration such as when:

- You introduce a new product or product line.
- You're testing for the best price.
- You decide to pursue a new market.
- Your competitors change their prices.
- There is high inflation/recession.
- You plan to change your overall sales strategy.

As a rule of thumb, if there are changes in the economic situation, competition, the product mix, the market, or any other factor affecting your business, you should reconsider your previous pricing decisions in light of these new factors.

Price should also reflect a good-better-best relationship among similar or competing products for the market to retain some resemblance of order. Your creativity in merchandising, flair for the inventive, product selection, and motivating management style are all significant factors in this market balance. You must monitor those activities you perform to create customers and evaluate them against your actual costs and how they relate to price. It's vital to the success of your business for you to recognize that too high a price cannot compensate for overly high promotional costs. Simply raising your prices does not solve a cost problem—it only compounds it.

Covering your costs is important, but it is only one aspect of pricing. Overcompensating (by raising your prices) is quite another matter and will ultimately upset the market balance. This is particularly dangerous for businesses that seem to be in noncompetitive markets. All too often, the company without competition will price its products or services so high that it creates the perfect environment for a competitor to undercut it.

---

[1] William A. Cohen, *The Entrepreneur and Small-Business Problem Solver,* 2nd ed. (New York: John Wiley & Sons, 1990).

Figure 18.1   Demand and Price Game—Lower Price Means Higher Demand

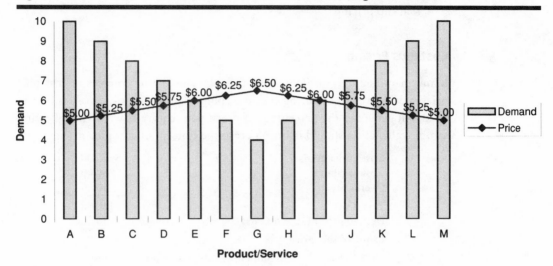

PRICE, QUANTITY, AND THE THEORY OF DEMAND

What is the relationship between the price you set for your product or service and the quantity of goods you can sell at that price? According to general economic theory, the higher the price you establish, the lower the customer demand for that product at that price. You can visually depict this ratio as a graph, table, or even an algebraic equation (see Figure 18.1). Among businesspeople, it is usually referred to as the *demand curve,* and it graphically depicts how revenues (i.e., price × units sold) change as price changes.

Quite often, new entrepreneurs learn of the demand curve and automatically infer that the *only* way to stimulate higher sales volume is by lowering prices. This is not always the case, either. Changes in the market can also affect the demand curve. Occasionally, these changes may enable a particular company to both charge more and sell more—which seems to violate the theory. Actually, it does not. If the public perceives that a particular product has a significant value, consumers are generally willing to pay more for that product. That's why people are willing to pay more for a name brand than good old Brand X, even though there may be absolutely no difference in the quality of the two products.

PRICING METHODS

Several methods of establishing prices are available to you:

- Cost-plus pricing.
- Demand pricing.

- Competitive pricing.
- Markup pricing.

Cost-Plus Pricing

Many manufacturers use cost-plus pricing. The key to employing cost-plus pricing effectively is ensuring that the "plus" figure not only covers all overhead, but generates the percentage of profit you require as well. The following sample calculation should help you grasp the concept of cost plus pricing:

Cost of materials	$ 50.00
Cost of labor	30.00
Overhead	40.00
Total Cost	$120.00
Desired profit (20% on sales)*	30.00
Required sale price	$150.00

*To calculate 20 percent profit on *sale*, simply multiply total cost [$120] $\times$ 1.25, which equals the required sale price of $150.

Should you decide to employ cost-plus pricing, you must ensure that *all* costs are accounted for in overhead. Should you fail to include a cost in the overhead category when calculating price, that cost will reduce profit.

Demand Pricing

Demand pricing is determined by the optimum combination of volume and profit. Products usually sold through a variety of sources at differing prices—such as those sold at retailers, discount retailers/chains, wholesalers, or direct mail marketers—are good examples of goods whose price is set based on demand. A wholesaler might buy significantly greater quantities than a retailer, and as such, purchase at a markedly lower unit price. The wholesaler then seeks to generate profit from a greater volume of sales on a product priced lower than the retailer's price to his or her customers. The retailer must pay more per unit as a result of stocking (and selling) significantly fewer units than the wholesaler. Obviously, the retailer cannot sell at the wholesaler's price, but must charge a higher price to customers. The direct mail company can charge yet more for its product, but this higher price is offset by the firm's higher promotion cost.

This is a difficult method of pricing to master because you must correctly calculate *beforehand* what price will generate the optimum ratio of profit to volume.

Competitive Pricing

Competitive pricing is generally used when there is an established market price for a particular product or service. If all your competitors are charging $100 for a replacement windshield, for example, that's what you should charge. Competitive price is used most often within markets where it is difficult to differentiate one product from another. If there is a major player in the market that acts as the market leader, that company will often set the price that other, smaller companies within that same market will be compelled to follow.

To employ competitive pricing properly and effectively, it is imperative that you know exactly what prices each competitor has established. Determine the price you would like to set in an optimum situation. You must then gauge your prices against the market as a whole and decide, based on direct comparison, whether you can defend the prices you have set. Should you wish to charge more than your competitors, you should be able to make a case for a higher price, such as providing a superior product. Before making a final commitment of your prices, it is also advisable to determine the level of price awareness within the market.

If you wish to use competitive pricing to set the fees for a service business, be aware that unlike a situation in which several companies are selling essentially the same products, services vary widely from one firm to another. As such, you could conceivably charge a higher price for a better quality of service and still be considered competitive within your market.

Markup Pricing

Used by manufacturers, wholesalers, and retailers, markup is calculated by adding a set amount to the cost of a product, which results in its price to the customer. For example, if the cost of the product is $100 and your selling price is $140, the markup would be $40. To find the percentage of markup on *cost*, divide the dollar amount of markup by the dollar amount of product cost, or:

$$\$40 \div \$100 = 40\%$$

This pricing method often generates confusion—not to mention lost profits—particularly among first-time small-business owners because markup (expressed as a percentage of cost) is often confused with gross margin (expressed as a percentage of selling price). The next section discusses the difference in markup and margin in greater depth.

PRICING A PRODUCT

To price products, you need to be completely familiar with pricing structures, especially the difference between margin and markup. As mentioned already, every product should be priced to cover its production or wholesale cost, freight charges, a proportionate share of overhead (fixed and variable operating expenses), and a reasonable profit. Such factors as high overheads (particularly when renting in prime mall or shopping center locations), unpredictable insurance rates, shrinkage (shoplifting, employee or other theft, shippers' mistakes), seasonality, shifts in wholesale or raw material product costs and freight expenses, and sales or discounts will all affect the final pricing.

Overhead Expenses

We use "overhead" to refer to all nonlabor expenses required to operate your business. Expenses can be divided into two types:

1. **Fixed expenses.** No matter what the volume of sales is, these costs must be met every month. A good example is the flat rent paid for the business premises. If the rent is $1,000 per month, irrespective of profits, it is a true fixed expense. Other fixed expenses are depreciation on fixed assets (such as cars and office equipment); skeleton-staff salaries and associated payroll costs; liability and other insurance; utilities; membership dues and subscriptions (which can sometimes be affected by sales volume); and accounting and legal costs. All of these continue at the same rate with little or no relation to the firm's revenues.
2. **Variable expenses.** Most so-called variable expenses are really semivariable. They will fluctuate from month to month in relation to sales and other factors, such as promotional efforts, seasons, and variations in the prices of suppliers' products and services. Fitting into this category are phone calls, office supplies and business forms (the more business, the greater the use of these items), printing, packaging, mailing, advertising, and promotion. In estimating variable expenses, it is common to ignore month-to-month variations (unless they are large and can be accurately predicted in advance) and use an average figure based on an estimate of the yearly total.

Cost of Goods Sold

Cost of goods sold, also known as *cost of sales,* refers to your cost of purchasing products for resale, or to your cost of manufacturing the products. Freight and delivery charges are customarily included in this figure. Accountants segregate cost of goods on an operating statement because it provides a measure of gross profit margin when compared with sales, an important yardstick for measuring the business's profitability. Expressed as a percentage of total sales, cost of goods sold will vary greatly from one kind of business to another. But within a given line of business, it should fall within a relatively narrow range.

Normally, the cost of goods sold bears a close relationship to sales. It will vary, however, if increases in the prices paid for merchandise cannot be offset by increases in sales prices, or if special bargain purchases increase profit margins. These situations seldom make a large percentage change in the relationship between cost of goods sold and sales. Therefore, the cost of goods sold is a semivariable expense.

Pricing Your Product

How do you price a new product or service? As you are starting your business, this is one of the most important questions to answer.

You know your costs. One easy way is to decide "Because this widget cost me two dollars to make, I will retail it for five times its cost, or ten dollars." Although this is easy to calculate, when you determine your prices according to how much the parts cost you, you forget about your consumer. In determining prices, user benefits are a better criterion.

To illustrate this point, many products consist of inexpensive parts, but they have an important use. For example, a heart valve may contain less than $20 worth of parts. However, because of its use, the valve is priceless to the patient and the surgeon. If you own a computer and you need a piece of software to solve a problem, that software becomes very precious.

To know how much to price an item, you should do a lot of consumer testing. Try different prices in isolated geographic areas. Because you'll incur a lot of extra start-up costs, we recommend starting high as you enter the market. It's easier to lower your prices later. However, because every product competes for your customers' hard-earned dollars, it is necessary to accurately measure the value of your product.

As a budding entrepreneur, ask these questions:

- *Is my product faster, cleaner, smaller?*
- *What will the customer pay for the benefits my product offers?*

  If you have a reseller, you need to ask:

- *What margins do the resellers need?*

  Finally, if you are the manufacturer, you need to know:

- *What about warehousing, transportation, and packaging?*
- *What kind of warranties and return policies should I have?*
- *How much will liability insurance, credit, labor, advertising, and sales cost me?*

As you can see, there are a lot of questions to answer when you are preparing to price your product. If you answer these questions through research, marketing, and testing, you can anticipate how much people will pay to become your customers.

Computing Margin

Margin, or gross margin, is the difference between total sales and the cost of those sales. For example, if:

$$\text{Total Sales} = \$1{,}000$$
$$\text{and Cost of Sales} = \$\ \ 300$$
$$\text{then Margin} = \$\ \ 700$$

Gross profit margin can be expressed in dollars or as a percentage. As a percentage, the GP margin is always stated as a percentage of net sales. The equation is:

$$(\text{Total Sales} - \text{Cost of Sales}) \div \text{Net Sales} = \text{GP margin}$$

In the preceding example, the margin would be 70 percent.

$$(\$1{,}000 - \$300) \div \$1{,}000 = 70\%$$

When all operating expenses (rent, salaries, utilities, insurance, advertising, and so on) and other expenses are deducted from the GP margin, the remainder is your net profit before taxes. If the GP margin is not sufficiently large, there will be little or no net profit left.

Some businesses require a higher GP margin than others to be profitable because the costs of operating different kinds of businesses vary tremendously. If the operating expenses in one line of business are comparatively low, then a lower GP margin will still yield the owners an acceptable profit.

The following comparison illustrates this point. Keep in mind that operating expenses and net profit are shown as the two components of GP margin; that is, their combined percentages (of net sales) equal the GP margin:

	Business A	**Business B**
Net Sales	100%	100%
Cost of Sales	40	65
Gross Profit Margin	60	35
Operating Expenses	43	19
Net Profit	17%	16%

Computing Markup

Markup and (gross profit) margin on a single product, or group of products, are often confused. The reason for this is that when expressed as a percentage, margin is always figured as a percentage of the selling *price*, while markup is traditionally figured as a percentage of the seller's *cost*. The equation is:

$$(\text{Total Sales} - \text{Cost of Sales}) \div \text{Cost of Sales}$$

Using the numbers from the preceding example, if you purchase goods for $300 and price them for sale at $1,000, your markup *in dollars* will be $700. As a percentage, this markup comes to 233 percent:

$$(\$1{,}000 - \$300) \div \$300 = 233\%$$

In other words, if your business requires a 70 percent margin to show a profit, your average markup will have to be 233 percent.

You can now see from the example that although markup and margin may be the same in dollars ($700) as percentages (233% vs. 70%), they represent two different concepts. More than a few new businesses have failed to make their expected profits because the owner assumed that if his markup is X percent, his or her margin will also be X percent. This is not the case.

Table 18.1 shows what the markup on cost must be to give the desired margin in a number of more common cases. To use this table, find your margin or gross profit percentage in the left-hand column. Multiply the cost of the article by the corresponding percentage in the markup column. Add this result to the cost to give you the correct selling price.

PRICING A SERVICE

How should you set the price(s) for your service business? Procedures vary with the business, but the same three elements must be considered in every situation:

1. Labor and materials costs.
2. Overhead.
3. Profit.

Table 18.1   Markup Table—Pricing a Product

MARGIN % OF SELLING PRICE	MARKUP % OF COST	MARGIN % OF SELLING PRICE	MARKUP % OF COST	MARGIN % OF SELLING PRICE	MARKUP % OF COST	MARGIN % OF SELLING PRICE	MARKUP % OF COST
4.8	5.01	18.0	22.0	32.0	47.1	50.0	100
5.0	5.3	18.5	22.7	33.3	50.0	52.4	110
6.0	6.4	19.0	23.5	34.0	51.5	54.5	120
7.0	7.5	20.0	25.0	35.0	53.9	56.5	130
8.0	8.7	21.0	26.6	35.5	55.0	58.3	140
9.0	10.0	22.0	28.2	36.0	56.3	60.0	150
10.0	11.1	22.5	29.0	37.0	58.8	61.5	160
10.7	12.0	23.0	29.9	37.5	60.0	63.0	170
11.0	12.4	23.1	30.0	38.0	61.3	64.2	180
11.1	12.5	24.0	31.6	39.0	64.0	65.5	190
12.0	13.6	25.0	33.3	39.5	65.5	66.7	200
12.5	14.3	26.0	35.0	40.0	66.7	69.2	225
13.0	15.0	27.0	37.0	41.0	70.0	71.4	250
14.0	16.3	27.3	37.5	42.0	72.4	73.3	275
15.0	17.7	28.0	39.0	42.8	75.0	75.0	300
16.0	19.1	28.5	40.0	44.4	80.0	76.4	325
16.7	20.0	29.0	40.9	46.1	85.0	77.8	350
17.0	20.5	30.0	42.9	47.5	90.0	78.9	375
17.5	21.2	31.0	45.0	48.7	95.0	80.0	400

Table 18.2   Markup Table—Pricing a Service

NET PROFIT PERCENT OF SELLING PRICE	MARKUP PERCENT OF OPERATING COST	NET PROFIT PERCENT OF SELLING PRICE	MARKUP PERCENT OF OPERATING COST	NET PROFIT PERCENT OF SELLING PRICE	MARKUP PERCENT OF OPERATING COST	NET PROFIT PERCENT OF SELLING PRICE	MARKUP PERCENT OF OPERATING COST
4.8	5.01	18.0	22.0	32.0	47.1	50.0	100
5.0	5.3	18.5	22.7	33.3	50.0	52.4	110
6.0	6.4	19.0	23.5	34.0	51.5	54.5	120
7.0	7.5	20.0	25.0	35.0	53.9	56.5	130
8.0	8.7	21.0	26.6	35.5	55.0	58.3	140
9.0	10.0	22.0	28.2	36.0	56.3	60.0	150
10.0	11.1	22.5	29.0	37.0	58.8	61.5	160
10.7	12.0	23.0	29.9	37.5	60.0	63.0	170
11.0	12.4	23.1	30.0	38.0	61.3	64.2	180
11.1	12.5	24.0	31.6	39.0	64.0	65.5	190
12.0	13.6	25.0	33.3	39.5	65.5	66.7	200
12.5	14.3	26.0	35.0	40.0	66.7	69.2	225
13.0	15.0	27.0	37.0	41.0	70.0	71.4	250
14.0	16.3	27.3	37.5	42.0	72.4	73.3	275
15.0	17.7	28.0	39.0	42.8	75.0	75.0	300
16.0	19.1	28.5	40.0	44.4	80.0	76.4	325
16.7	20.0	29.0	40.9	46.1	85.0	77.8	350
17.0	20.5	30.0	42.9	47.5	90.0	78.9	375

These factors must be considered not only during your start-up phase, but also when you decide to increase the level of service-fee income in your business. Table 18.2 shows the markup cost to give the desired margin for service businesses.

Labor and Materials

Labor costs are wages and benefits you pay your employees and/or subcontractors who perform, supervise, or manage your service business. If you as the owner are even partly involved in executing a job, then the cost of your labor, proportionate to your input, must be included in the total labor charge. This will be quite significant during the first year or so (at least).

Labor cost is usually expressed as an hourly rate. Check in your library's reference room for government publications giving national and state salary ranges for different occupations. The editors of trade publications might have such information. Also check for current rates in classified newspaper ads and with your local chamber of commerce.

Labor can also be subcontracted. Under this system, you do not put a worker on the payroll as an employee. The owner thus eliminates the time and expense associated with timekeeping, payroll preparation, payroll taxes, and benefits. Also, when labor is purchased for each job on a contract basis, the full cost is agreed on in advance; therefore, you as the owner know exactly what your cost for that particular project will be.

Carefully estimate the labor time it will take to accomplish each job on which you bid. For example, if you estimate that your service contract will take two hours of labor each 24-hour period, five days a week, with two hours of supervision each month, you would compute your labor and materials cost for a month as follows:

Hours/Month	Rate	Cost
Labor (2 workers × 21 days)	at $4.50/hr.	$189
Supervision (2 hrs)	at $6.00/hr.	12
Total Labor Cost*		$201
Supplies (@6% of labor costs)		12
Total Labor & Materials		$213

*If you put people on payroll instead of subcontracting labor, add 10 percent to this total to cover payroll taxes, worker's compensation, and any other related costs.

Overhead

Overhead refers to all the indirect expenses required to operate your business. These expenses include insurance premiums, legal and accounting fees, telephone, advertising, vehicle maintenance, equipment depreciation, management salary, business forms, office supplies, dues, and memberships.

Overhead expenses can vary substantially from one business to another depending on the way you operate. If you have past operating expenses to guide you, overhead is not difficult to calculate. Simply total all your expenses for one year, excluding labor and materials. Divide this number by your total cost of labor and materials to determine your overhead rate. For example, suppose your costs and expenses for a one-year period were as follows:

$$\text{Overhead Expenses} = \$31,200$$
$$\text{Labor-and-Materials Cost} = \$52,000$$
$$\text{Overhead Rate } (\$31,200 \div \$52,000) = 60\,\%$$

Overhead may cost anywhere from 30 to 60 percent of your labor-and-materials cost. You can raise or lower that figure to suit your own kind of operation. This will vary greatly from one industry to another. Using an arbitrary overhead rate of 60 percent as just computed, and continuing with the same example, you now have:

Labor and Materials Cost	$213
Ovehead (60% of 213)	111
Subtotal of Operating Costs	$324

Profit

Profit is the amount of income earned after all costs for providing the service have been met. When calculating the price of a service, profit is applied in the same manner as markup on the cost of a product. For instance, if you plan to net 20 percent before taxes on your gross sales, you will need to apply a profit factor of about 25 percent to your labor and overhead to achieve that target. Doing this in our example, you have:

Subtotal of Operating Costs	$324
Profit (25% of $324)	81
Price you quote your customer	$405

If you compare the price of $405 with the cost of labor ($201) already estimated, you will notice that one figure is more than double the other. Some contractors use this ratio as a basis for determining price: They estimate their labor costs and then double that figure to arrive at their bid price. Pricing can be tedious and time-consuming, especially if you don't have a knack for it. Some contractors seem to have a "sixth sense" when it comes to pricing and estimating; they know what they need to ask to make a job profitable to them.

If you're just starting out, you obviously won't have the skill of a seasoned pro. If your quote is too low, you will either rob yourself of some profit or be forced to lower the quality of your work to meet the price. If you estimate too high, you may lose the contract altogether, especially if you are in a competitive bidding situation. Make it your business to learn how to estimate labor time accurately and how to calculate your overhead properly so that when you quote a price, you can be competitive and still make the profit you require.

RESOURCES

Associations

American Management Association, 135 West 50th Street, New York, NY 10020, 212-586-8100

American Production and Inventory Control Society, 500 West Annandale Road, Falls Church, VA 22046-4274, 703-237-8344

Center for Entrepreneurial Management, Inc., 180 Varick Street, New York, NY 10014, 212-633-0060

National Management Association, 2210 Arbor Boulevard, Dayton, OH 45439, 513-294-0421

Small Business Service Bureau, 554 Main Street, Worcester, MA 01601, 508-756-3513

Magazines

Business Review, One Kwik Kopy Lane, P.O. Box 777, Cypress, TX 77429-2164, 713-373-3535

The Pricing Advisor, 3277 Roswell Road, Suite 620, Atlanta, GA 30305, 404-252-5708

19

Taxes

The purpose of this chapter is to make you aware of the current tax environment and raise some basic tax issues important for every small-business owner. Even if you have a bookkeeper or CPA to advise you in tax matters, this person will not be at your business every day. All owners of a small business should have some understanding of the tax system so that they may take advantage of the opportunities available for deductions, credits, and tax savings.

Periodically, the federal government revises the Internal Revenue Code; the laws in your state may also change over time. Consequently, if you find that you need answers to specific or complex tax questions, contact your accountant or the Internal Revenue Service (IRS) office in your region. The IRS will be only too happy to tell you whether you should pay additional tax.

TAXATION BASICS

At the turn of the century, 1 out of 100 people worked for the government. Today, 1 out of 5 persons works at some level of government—federal, state, or local. That's approximately 17 million people out of a 90-million-odd workforce. The payroll and administrative expense for this bureaucracy that provides government authority or service is funded by the payment of taxes in one form or another. For a variety of reasons, the amount of ready cash available to the government has dwindled. The effect has been the creation of a high deficit, which must be financed to meet payroll and overhead expenses.

The deficit the U.S. government incurred during the 1980s and early 1990s has been greater than the total amount of debt in the prior two centuries of the

---

This chapter was written by Dave Juedes, CPA.

country's history. The trend toward higher deficits has, in the opinion of many observers, reached a dangerous level.

The government has two ways to pay for its deficit:

1. It can create money or increase the money supply by printing new bills and putting them into circulation.
2. It can borrow money from the existing money supply.

If the government increases the money supply, there is a danger that there will be too much currency in the economy relative to the amount of goods and services; this is a generally accepted definition of *inflation*. If the government borrows, it will obtain its loan from banks, other lending institutions, or the public. When it borrows, money tightens up and the public is unable to borrow. Interest rates rise. The economy tends to slow down because there is not enough money to buy whatever goods and services may be available; this is a definition of a *depression* (also called *panic* and *recession*).

The economy seems caught in a vicious cycle in which government is taxing at what appears to be an oppressive level. The government collects revenue in the form of taxes it levies on the same people it squeezes out of the lending markets. And alas, the taxes are not enough for the government to cover its bills.

Who pays for all this? Typically the businesses and its employees are destined to pay a large share of the government's bill.

Because one of the primary motives for going into small business is to take advantage of some of the deductions available to the self-employed, and perhaps pay less tax, we want to create an awareness of tax-related issues that can be used to your advantage. If you learn one thing that will result in an allowable deduction you otherwise would have missed, the time you spend with this material will have been worthwhile.

Taxes You Collect

As a business owner and employer, you will be responsible for collecting various state and federal taxes and remitting these to the proper agencies. In addition, you will be required to pay certain taxes yourself. When reading the following sections, remember that at the time this went to press, all tax information reflected current law. But Congress has been passing tax legislation at the rate of one major act every six years. Therefore, it is important that you check for any major tax changes before making a decision that will affect the tax structure of your business.

Employer Tax Identification Number

If you employ one or more persons, you are required to withhold income tax and Social Security tax from each employee's paycheck and remit these amounts to the proper tax-collecting agency. You will need to obtain an employer tax number from the federal government using IRS form SS-4 and—if your state has an income tax—from the state as well. Call the local numbers of the federal and state agencies listed in the white pages under "United States" and the name of your state. The federal agency will send you your number as well as charts to determine payroll tax deductions, quarterly and annual forms, W-4 forms, tax-deposit forms, and an instruction manual (you guessed it) on filling out forms. No advance fees or deposits are required.

Income Tax Withholding

The amount of "pay-as-you-go" tax you must withhold from each employee's wages depends on the employee's wage level, the number of exemptions he or she claims on the withholding exemption certificate (Form W-4), marital status, and length of the payroll period. The percentage withheld is figured on a sliding basis, and IRS percentage tables are available for weekly, biweekly, monthly, semimonthly, and other payroll periods.

Social Security (FICA) Tax

The Federal Insurance Contributions Act, or FICA, requires employers to match and pay the same amount of Social Security tax as the employee does. Currently, the FICA tax for both employers and employees is 6.2 percent for Old-Age, Survivors, Disability, Insurance (OASDHI), commonly known as Social Security, for wages through $60,600, and 1.45 percent for Medicare on earnings without limit. For self-employed individuals, the OASDHI tax rate for 1994 is 12.4 percent on self-employment income through $60,600 and 1.45 percent for Medicare on all self employment income.

Charts and instructions for Social Security deductions come with the IRS payroll forms. Congress has accelerated the requirements for depositing FICA and withholding taxes. Failure to comply subjects a business to substantial penalties. Four different reports must be filed with the IRS district director in connection with the payroll taxes (both FICA and income taxes) that you withhold from your employees' wages:

1. Quarterly return of taxes withheld on wages (Form 941).
2. Annual statement of taxes withheld on wages (Form W-2).
3. Reconciliation of quarterly returns of taxes withheld with annual statement of taxes withheld (Form W-3).
4. Annual Federal Unemployment Tax return (Form 940).

State Payroll Taxes

Almost all states have payroll taxes of some kind that you must collect and remit to the appropriate agency. Most states have an unemployment tax that is paid entirely by the employer. The tax is figured as a percentage of your total payroll (up to a specified limit of annual wages per employee), and remitted at the end of each quarter. The actual percentage varies with the state and the employer.

Some states impose an income tax that must be deducted from each employee's paycheck. As an employer, you have the responsibility of collecting this tax and remitting it to the state. A few states have a disability insurance tax that must be deducted from employees' pay; in some states, this tax may be split between employee and employer.

Most states have patterned their tax-collecting systems after the federal government's. They issue employer numbers and similar forms and instruction booklets. As discussed, you may apply for the employer number and various forms and booklets by calling the local office of the appropriate state agency.

Independent Contractors

Hiring individuals as independent contractors requires filing an annual information return (Form 1099) to report payments totaling $600 or more made to any individual for rents or services performed in the course of trade or business during the calendar year. If this form is not filed, you may be subject to penalties. Be sure your records list the name, address, and Social Security or Federal Identification number of every independent contractor you hired, along with pertinent dates and the amounts paid each independent contractor.

Other than licensed real estate agents and insurance agents, very few people who perform services on your business premises qualify as independent contractors. If the IRS feels an individual should have been treated as an employee, you will be liable for payroll taxes that should have been withheld and paid, plus penalties and interest.

Some factors that are reviewed by the IRS to determine if an individual is really an "independent contractor" include:

1. Does the person have his or her own business license?
2. Does the person have cards, stationery, and a real business address?
3. Does the person have a business bank account?
4. Does the person sell services regularly to various customers?

Personal Income Tax

Operating as a sole proprietor or partner, you will not be paid a salary like an employee; therefore, no income tax is withheld from money you take out of your business for personal use. Instead, you must estimate your tax liability each year and pay it in quarterly installments on Form 1040 ES. You may request from your local IRS office the forms and instructions for filing estimated tax returns. When applying for the forms, also request the *Tax Guide for Small Business* (Publication 17).

At the end of the year, you must file an income tax return as an individual and compute your tax liability on the profits earned in your business for that year. Partnerships are required to file a partnership return (Form 1065). Each partner's share of the net income or expense of the partnership is reported to the partner on a Schedule K1.

Corporate Income Tax

If your business is organized as a "C" corporation, you will be paid a salary like other employees. Any profit the business makes will accrue to the corporation, not to you personally. At the end of the year, you must file a corporate income tax return. Corporate tax returns may be prepared on a calendar- or fiscal-year basis. If the tax liability of the business is calculated on a calendar year, the tax return must be filed with the IRS no later than March 15 each year; however, the corporation may file a request for extension of due date.

Reporting income on a fiscal-year cycle is more convenient for most businesses because they can end their tax year in any month they choose. A corporation whose income is primarily derived from the personal services of its shareholders must use a calendar-year end for tax purposes. In addition, most Subchapter S corporations are required to use calendar-year ends.

Sales Taxes

Sales taxes are levied by many cities and states at varying rates. Most provide specific exemptions, as for certain classes of merchandise or particular groups of customers. Service businesses are often exempt altogether. Contact your state and/or local revenue offices for information on the law for your area so that you can adapt your bookkeeping to the requirements.

Levying taxes on all sales would present no major difficulties, but since this is not the case, your business will have to identify tax-exempt sales from taxable sales. Then you can deduct tax-exempt sales from total sales when filing your sales tax returns each quarter. Remember, if you fail to collect taxes that should have been collected, you can be held liable for the full amount of uncollected tax.

Advance Deposits

Some states may require an advance deposit against future taxes to be collected. In lieu of a deposit, some states will accept a surety bond for that amount from your insurance company. If you have a fair credit record, the bond is usually simple to obtain through your insurance agent. The cost varies according to the amount and the risk; 5 percent is a rule of thumb, but 10 percent is not unusual for small dollar amounts.

If your state requires a deposit or bond, you can keep the amount down by estimating sales on the low side. This is a wise tactic, because most new business owners tend to overestimate early sales.

Tax-Reporting Summary

Every government entity, bureau, or agency that has any legal jurisdiction whatsoever over your business requires that you submit something in writing—usually accompanied by a payment—on a monthly, quarterly, or annual basis. These taxes don't apply in every state, county, or city. We have covered the important ones in the previous pages. Any other taxes you must pay in your area will come automatically to you. In other words: The agencies doing the collecting will find you.

TAXES AND YOUR BUSINESS FORM

The first tax issue you are confronted with when you go into business for yourself is the legal form of operation you choose. You can be a sole proprietor, a general partner, or the head of your corporation. The choice of business organization you make can strongly affect your tax liability.

Sole Proprietor

A sole proprietorship is a one-owner business. You may have many or few employees, but if you are its one owner, you are its sole proprietor. This form of organization is simple. It requires no fancy legal work. You name your business in accordance with licensing laws. You apply for a federal ID number, and you're all set. The income from a sole proprietorship flows through the owner into an individual tax return.

Suppose a husband and wife are filing a joint return. The husband has his own business; the wife works for the government and makes $15,000 a year. The husband's gross from this business was $100,000, and his business made him $15,000 after business expenses were deducted. His $15,000 is integrated into the individual return just as the wife's $15,000 is. The business income flows through the personal income. There are no special business-income taxes other than self-employment taxes.

Partnerships

A partnership is a business with two or more owners. Like a sole proprietorship, it is not a taxable entity. The income or loss from a partnership flows through the personal income of the individual general partners. If Owner A and Owner B are in a partnership that makes $20,000 and they divide everything evenly, the $10,000 Owner A gets and the $10,000 Owner B gets will go on their individual returns with whatever other income they have. Itemized deductions and credits are taken from that figure. A partnership agreement must be well defined as to capital investment, return, salaries, duties, responsibilities, losses, and so on. What if you are in a partnership with someone who isn't as reliable and hard-working as you are? Whatever mistakes your partner makes, you will also pay for because of the rule known as "mutual agency." Mutual agency means that you are responsible for the actions of your partner because he or she is an agent for the partnership. If your partner does something stupid that costs you all your money or causes you to suffer great losses in the business, you will bear the responsibility equally. The same is true if your partner does something that results in tax liability for your company. You may very well sue your incompetent or unscrupulous partner, but that is a separate matter.

A corporation is different. It is a separate, taxable entity and requires detailed attention.

Taxes on Corporations

For fiscal years beginning after January 1, 1993, corporate tax rates are as follows:

- 15 percent on the first $50,000 of net income.
- 25 percent on the next $25,000.
- 34 percent on the next $25,000.
- 39 percent on the next $235,000.
- 34 percent on the next $9,665,000.
- 35 percent on the next $5,000,000.
- 38 percent on the next $3,333,333.
- 35 percent on income over $18,333,333.

Your corporation may be subject to several other taxes, such as the personal-holding-company tax or the accumulated-earnings tax. A special tax is imposed on any personal holding company. The additional tax is 39.6 percent of undistributed personal holding company income. You should ask your tax consultant if any of these special taxes apply to your corporation.

A corporation's income is taxable, and any distribution of income to individual stockholders, known as dividends, would be taxable again as ordinary dividend income. If General Motors earns $1, it will in theory pay 34 cents in federal tax, and the remaining 66 cents will be distributed as dividends. If you are the stockholder, you pick it up as dividends-and-interest income on Schedule B of your 1040. That's income for you, and you will pay the tax on that 66 cents. If your tax rate is 28 percent, you'll pay another 19 cents tax. That means $1 of corporate income could be reduced to less than 47 cents for the individual. Of course, with that 47 cents you'll also pay your property tax, sales tax, and whatever other taxes that may be credited to you or deducted by you from your taxable income.

Subchapter S Corporations

The disadvantage of double taxation is effectively eliminated if you file a Subchapter S Election with the IRS. The qualifications for electing Subchapter S were changed in 1982. The Subchapter S Revisions Act of 1982 liberalized many of the old rules and the new flexibility of these corporations makes them popular with small and medium-size businesses. Subchapter S allows profits or losses to travel directly through the corporation to you and your other shareholders. If you earn other income during the first year and the corporation has a loss, you can deduct the loss against the other income, thereby reducing or possibly wiping out your tax liability completely.

Subchapter S corporations are corporations that elect not to be taxed as corporations; instead, the shareholders of a Subchapter S corporation include in their individual gross incomes their proportionate shares of the corporate profits and losses. This type of business organization combines some of the advantages of proprietorships, partnerships, and regular corporations.

To qualify under Subchapter S, the corporation must be a domestic corporation, must not be a member of an affiliated group, must not have more than 35 shareholders, must have only individuals or estates as shareholders, and must not have a nonresident alien as a shareholder. Under current law, an unlimited amount of passive income from rents, royalties, and interest is now allowed. When profits exceed 25 percent of the gross receipts, Subchapter S corporations may be taxed on passive income, according to Section 1375(a) of the Internal Revenue Code (IRC). Pension restrictions have been eased. Call your local IRS office for the appropriate election forms.

The Fiscal Year

The corporation's fiscal year may be different from the calendar year. You can elect any day of the year as the year end for your corporation. Why would that be important for tax-saving purposes? Many people begin their small business operating as a sole proprietorship or partnership and later choose to incorporate. They gain some flexibility in reporting the income of the business by having a corporate year different from the calendar year, which ends on December 31.

There are some limits on the ability of many corporations to use fiscal years different than calendar years. The general rules are as follows:

1. If a corporation derives most of its income from the personal services of its shareholder/employees, it must use a calendar-year end. This would apply to the businesses of accountants, lawyers, insurance agents, and so on.
2. A Subchapter S corporation must generally use the same year end as its shareholders, which, if they are individuals, will usually be the calendar-year end. As an alternative, the Subchapter S corporation can show a business purpose for a different year end if the IRS approves it. If you choose to have your fiscal year begin on July 1 and end on June 30, you could cut off income from your original sole proprietorship at six months. If you don't want your income to go up much for the second half of the year, give yourself a low salary. For the remainder of the year, June 30 to December 31, your total income will be the income from the sole proprietorship, plus whatever salary the corporation paid you, which may not be its entire profits.

The corporation has only until the next June 30 to file its tax return, which means you have to empty it out before June 30 of the following year. You can do that by paying out its profits to you as owner and into a qualified pension/profit-sharing plan. This is a one-time bonus of incorporating. You are cutting off income in mid-year and deferring a portion of it, which allows you to make some allocations that you and your accountant determine may be useful to your tax position.

Tax Planning for Corporations

The importance of tax planning in this regard cannot be overstressed. Consider the case of Mr. X, who was working for $20,000 a year and never had a tax problem. He had a house and lots of itemized deductions for his six children. He quit his job and went into business for himself. To finance the business, he sold his home and collected his vested pension and profit-sharing interests in a lump sum. He sold the stock he had in his own company for a profit. He also collected accumulated vacation and sick pay.

With the profits from the sale of his home (over $50,000), the income from his new company that first year, and the sale of his other property, he had about $100,000 in income that year. He set up his company as a corporation, of course, because he'd heard of the tremendous tax advantages to the corporate structure. He didn't do much business in those first few months of start-up and had a lot of expenses. His company showed a $15,000 loss that first year. Initially, his reaction was, "At least I have this $15,000 deduction to offset the $100,000." *Wrong.*

Mr. X had formed a conventional corporation or "C" Corporation, a separate taxable entity, and the business loss didn't do him a bit of good as far as his personal income tax was concerned. He had to pay a huge tax bill. But had he elected to form a Subchapter S corporation, the loss from the corporation would have passed through the corporation—as it would have in a partnership—and would have been deductible at the personal level.

It is not unusual for a new company to lose money in the first year or two. This is why it might make sense to make the Subchapter S election when the corporation is first formed. You can take the corporation's losses on your tax return to the extent of your investment in the corporation and any loans you made to it. If the business becomes profitable and you and your accountant feel you should switch to the conventional form, then it is a simple matter to convert. The only catch is that once you switch from Subchapter S to conventional status, it's difficult to switch back again and usually disallowed.

There are other techniques for reducing your tax liability if your small business is incorporated. You may set up a staggered fiscal year that may be different from the calendar year by which individuals are typically taxed. You may accrue or defer income between the corporation and yourself so that you can stay in the lower tax bracket consistently. You can zero out the income of the company by making sure the corporation doesn't have any income outstanding at the end of the year.

How can you achieve this? Pay salaries that will absorb whatever profits there are in the company. There is a limit to how much of this you can do, and in most states you have to document this process with appropriate resolutions and director meetings. But for most small companies not making a tremendous amount of money, it makes sense to pay income out of the corporation in the form of salary. There may come a time when you want to keep some of the income of the corporation and get a lower tax break by splitting income between corporation and individual, especially if you are reinvesting the money for expansion purposes. But this, in any event, will be something complex enough to structure with the advice of your tax accountant and/or attorney.

Other items that may be deducted from a corporation's tax bill include group life insurance that is purchased on the lives of major employees or medical plan for all personnel and their families. Perhaps the most significant benefit in this area is the deduction for contributions to pension or profit-sharing plans. Of course, planning and paperwork are essential in implementing plans of this type. The point for present purposes is that the cost of such programs can be set against corporate tax liability.

Business veterans know that there are many reasons to form a corporation aside from tax savings. One is that a corporation limits the legal, personal liability of its principal shareholders. Suppose you've invested $20,000 to begin a business that you incorporate. Should your company get sued or suffer irreversible losses, the liability extends only to the assets of the company. Your home and other personal assets and investments would be protected from any litigation against the corporation. That's not true of a sole proprietorship or a partnership, in which you are liable for the full extent of everything you own—your entire net worth.

In some instances, even though you form a corporation, you cannot assume that your personal assets will always be protected. Often, a lawsuit or losses come up in connection with fraud or product liability. If this occurs, lawyers will sometimes sue you as an individual and claim that there was some irregularity in the way you maintained the company. Thus they "pierce the corporate veil" and go after you personally. To avoid this problem, you must keep good corporate minutes and records. Also you should not commingle personal assets with corporate assets. You must, in addition, be certain your corporation is sufficiently capitalized.

STANDARD BUSINESS DEDUCTIONS

General and Administrative Expenses

There are deductible general and administrative (G&A) expenses in your business. These include all office expenses such as telephone, utilities, office rent, salaries, legal and accounting expenses, professional services, dues, and subscriptions to business publications.

Many people working out of their home want to claim a home office expense. There are severe limitations to the home office deduction. One can only claim a home office if it was the sole and primary place of doing business. If you have another office somewhere, you will not be able to deduct the cost of a home office as well. You might still deduct some business-related telephone charges made from your home, as well as business equipment and supplies, but you will not be able to deduct any part of your rent or depreciate any part of the property as a business expense.

A deduction is allowable to the extent that a portion of your home is used "exclusively" and "regularly" as your principal place of business for any business that you operate. Normally that portion of your residence must be used to meet clients, store inventory and perform your work. If you perform the majority of your work somewhere else, the home office may not be deductible.

Home office expenses that are eligible for deduction would include all normal office expenses plus interest, taxes, insurance, and depreciation on the portion of your home used exclusively as your office. The total amount of deduction is limited by the gross income derived from that business activity reduced by all of your other business expenses other than those connected with the home office. Therefore, a home office cannot be used to produce tax losses for an otherwise profitable business. Any disallowed loses can be carried over and used in a year when the limitation is not exceeded. Allocation of home-office expenses is generally made on the basis of the ratio of square footage used exclusively for business to total square footage of the residence.

Although computers are becoming part and parcel of virtually all business, the Deficit Reduction Act of 1984 severely limited the conditions under which home computers can be used to limit tax liability. Actually, the test is simple; a home computer used for business over 50 percent of the time can qualify for appropriate business deductions or credits. In this connection, business owners using home computers will have to document business and personal use of the machine in writing.

Automobile Expenses

Almost everybody doing business in the United States has to drive an automobile to conduct that business. At this writing, business-related automobile mileage is deductible at 28 cents a mile. Keep abreast of any changes the IRS may make in this regard in any given year.

To calculate the deductions you could take based on straight mileage is very simple. Suppose you drive a car 20,000 miles a year. Of those, 12,000 were for business purposes. Your deduction would be 28 cents × 12,000 miles, or $3,360. Under the straight-mileage approach, you would get a deduction of this amount.

What constitutes a business mile? The distance you drive from your home to your place of business is not deductible, but mileage you drive from your place of business to any other location for business purposes is. Not only is a business mile driven for the purpose of doing business, but also for the purpose of seeking business. Going to talk to a client prospect or doing something related to the promotional aspects of your business would be considered business mileage. Keep in mind that you are required to maintain a log of your business miles for tax purposes; on your appointment calendar enter your miles at the end of each day.

There is another method of deducting the cost of driving using actual operating expenses. The normal deductions in this area would be gasoline, maintenance, insurance, and deprecation. For example, assume that you are going to take a depreciation deduction of $2,800. Add to this the following expenses for operating your car: insurance, $400; maintenance, $500; gasoline, $1,600. You have $5,300 in deductions. Take this number and multiply it by the fraction of business miles over total miles driven: 12,000 business miles divided by 20,000 total miles, or 60 percent business mileage. Sixty percent of $5,300 is $3,180. If you elect the second method, then, you get a deduction of $3,180 for the same mileage versus the $3,360 for straight-mileage calculation.

If you use this second method, you must stick with it for the life of the car you use for your business. If you sell the car for a profit, you have to take the depreciation off its cost to determine its tax basis. If you sell it for more than its base, you'll have a gain that will result in a tax at your regular income tax rate.

Generally, straight mileage is best if you are driving an older car many miles. If you are driving a fairly new car with a fairly high cost (over $14,000), the operating expenses/depreciation method might give you more deductions.

Entertainment and Travel

If in your business you entertain clients for promotion, you have to maintain a log to deduct for entertainment, travel, and related expenses. Use a standard appointment calendar to write in whom you were entertaining, the nature of the business, where you were, and how much you spent. Contrary to popular belief, you do not need receipts for expenditures on entertainment under $25—but you must maintain your log. In certain instances, you can even claim business-related home entertainment; have clients or prospects sign a guest log. If you prepare a meal or serve drinks, your expenses are deductible as part of the expense of doing business.

After December 31, 1993, only 50 percent of entertainment expenses are deductible. The remaining 50 percent are not deductible, even if your business is incorporated. For entertainment expenses, all these elements must be proved:

1. The amount of expenditure.
2. The date of expenditure.
3. The name, address, and type of entertainment.
4. Reason for entertainment and the nature of the business discussion that took place.
5. The occupation of the person being entertained.

A deduction is not permitted for travel, food, and lodging expenses incurred in connection with attending a conference, convention, or seminar related to investment activities such as real estate investment or stock investments. However, the cost of the actual seminar is still deductible.

Travel deductions would include the cost of air, bus, and auto transportation; hotels; meals; and incidentals including dry cleaning, tips, and taxis. However, the rule is that you must stay overnight to claim travel-incidentals deductions.

The things you do to expand your awareness of and expertise in your field of business are tax deductible. Accordingly, deductions are allowed for convention expenses. However, rules limit the amount that can be deducted for attending conventions in foreign countries. Also, there are limits to the deductibility of conventions held on cruise ships. The cost of getting to and from the convention and the cost of your stay are deductible, but if you stay three days after the convention ends, those expenses would not be deductible. Deductions for your spouse are not allowed unless he or she is active in the business.

RECORD KEEPING FOR TAX PURPOSES

An especially important area of tax planning is the need for adequate records. Most people who run small businesses, especially for the first time, have no understanding of accounting, don't appreciate what it can do for them, and lose many of their deductions and credits simply because their records don't support their transactions during the year. When people start a business, they are concerned with decorating the store, getting new clients, or advertising. The last thing they think about is the kind of accounting system they want. Yet, without a proper accounting system, you could lose the very tax benefits that you may have started your business to obtain.

To take advantage of business deductions, you need to be transformed into a bookkeeper expert. It is the frustration of even the most highly paid executives that they have to maintain these records for themselves, but failure to do so means they will not receive the benefit. In the event of an audit, you will be unable to support the expenses you claimed unless you have a journal.

It doesn't mean you're going to go to jail for not recording the $12.50 you spent at the diner on entertainment; it can mean, however, that the IRS may disallow a portion of the entertainment deduction, take it out of your deduction total, and raise your taxable income. It also means you would have to pay taxes and any accrued interest from the year in which the assessment was made. The IRS may also impose negligence penalties.

One accountant's rule is that the money you invest in sound bookkeeping and accounting procedures is going to be worth 10 times that investment in tax savings. From a management point of view, it's just plain good sense to have a good set of records you can rely on.

Bookkeeping Methods

Good bookkeeping does not have to cost a lot of money, but it cannot, must not, be the very last thing you take care of in your business if you expect to obtain tax benefits from it. Remember this: If you have spent money in the business and cannot adequately support your expenditures, you will lose tax credits and deductions. In the event of an audit, accurate and timely records will lend support to your deductions. Disorganized records will result in audit adjustments, more taxes, and possibly more penalties.

Your bookkeeping system should include a cash receipts journal, a cash disbursements journal, a general journal, and a general ledger for assets, liabilities, capital, revenue and expense accounts. You may need a purchases-and-sales journal. You will also need a payroll record. Your accountant knows what these things are and should set them up for you and your bookkeeper. One-write or "pegboard" accounting systems are excellent for new and small businesses. Many accounting programs are also available for use on a personal computer.

Remember to maintain your logbook. If you spend money in the field, prepare a summary of the expenses listed in the log for the period covered and write yourself a check from the business bank account. Have the bookkeeper record expenses so you can deduct all cash disbursements made during the period. Suppose your log shows you spent $5 for a stapler, $6 for other supplies, and $40 on entertainment. You could write a check for $51, indicate what items the check was for, and then have the bookkeeper post them in the individual expense columns in the record.

One of your goals should be to compile financial statements for your business at least once a quarter, and ideally once a month. A financial statement shows your assets and liabilities as of a certain date. This document provides useful information that allows you to evaluate your financial condition and the health of your business for both tax and management purposes. For more information on records and bookkeeping methods, see Chapter 17.

Payroll Records

It is essential that you keep accurate employee compensation records. Be particularly vigilant about your payroll tax returns. Information you need in this area is contained in the *Employer's Tax Guide* available from the IRS. The guide also has a tax calendar showing you exactly when you must file various forms. The paperwork in this area is annoying and can take a large part of a day, but do not ignore it. Even if you are working with an accountant who knows all the ins and outs of these filings and can take care of them for you, it wouldn't hurt you to know about them.

With respect to Social Security (FICA), federal unemployment insurance, state unemployment insurance, federal withholding, state withholding, and state disability taxes, you are responsible for collecting and withholding from employee paychecks all relevant amounts, contributing whatever the employer's portion may be, and depositing those amounts monthly with the appropriate agency. In particular, you must file quarterly state and federal tax returns. In all cases, with all employee-compensation-related taxes of this type, penalties and interest may be assessed if you file late.

Whatever your financial squeeze may be in your business, don't get behind on payroll taxes. A story is told of an employer who got behind on his payroll taxes, went out of business, yet owed that tax money for the rest of his life. The money that he had failed to remit to the appropriate government agencies had never belonged to him, and he was assessed interest and penalties on the amount that he had kept back.

DEPRECIATION

Section 179 Expense Election

Under the current federal tax law, you can generally write off the first $17,500 of equipment purchased for use in your business. If a piece of equipment costs more than $17,500, the balance of the amount over that point can be depreciated over a five- to seven-year life as provided by the IRS.

An enterprise zone business is entitled to an increase in the annual limitation of the lesser of $20,000 or the cost of the Section 179 property that is qualified zone property.

Depreciation

There are two kinds of depreciation: financial statement and tax-related. Tax-related depreciation is purely an accounting device to take advantage of the maximum allowable deduction permitted by law when figuring your annual net taxable income. Tax-related depreciation is determined by a formula laid down in the Internal Revenue Code. It has nothing to do with the actual condition of your equipment or its loss in value at the end of each year's use.

If you buy a piece of equipment, depreciation of its original cost should be included as an expense on your monthly operating statement. If you lease a piece of equipment, the monthly lease payment will be a part of your monthly operating expenses (cash-value depreciation is frequently figured into the cost of an equipment lease and need not necessarily be figured separately by you).

Many equipment-leasing agreements have a clause providing for what is known as a depreciation reserve. This consists of money set aside to correspond with the declining value of the vehicle. When the lease is up, the equipment is going to be sold either to the lessee or to a third party. If it goes for a price over and above its depreciated value, the difference can be refunded to the lessee. If, however, the equipment is sold for a price under its depreciated value, the lessee must pay the difference to the lessor. This is where the depreciation reserve comes in. It is usually a part of the lease and should be considered a monthly expense of running the business.

Straight-line or uniform depreciation is the most frequently used method of depreciating new equipment for financial statements. In straight-line depreciation, the equipment loses an equal part of total value in every year of its life. The depreciation method used on financial statements often is different from that used on your tax return. For your tax return, your accountant will most often use a tax-approved depreciation that will give you the largest deduction on your tax return (and, therefore, reduce your taxes).

Suppose you buy a $15,000 printing press with a 10-year useful life according to your accountant's schedule. The straight-line depreciation rate would be calculated by dividing its 10 years of useful life into the $15,000, or $1,500 a year. If you are in the 28 percent tax bracket, $1,500 in depreciation will save you $420. Suppose you only need 20 percent down to buy a $15,000 machine. Suppose, too, that you financed your machine on the installment plan. The interest you pay on any amount owed is going to be another deduction for you. So if you have a $12,000 loan that costs you $1,200 in interest, you will wind up with another $336 (in the 28 percent bracket) in savings.

The current methods of depreciation are often referred to as "MACRS" (modified accelerated cost recovery system) whereas the method used for assets acquired before December 31, 1986 is often called "ACRS" (accelerated cost recovery system). Assets used in your trade or business that were purchased before that time are depreciated using different methods than those discussed here. Those earlier methods generally give you a larger depreciation deduction than the current rates. You should also keep in mind that in many states, a set of rules entirely different from those used on your federal income tax return are in effect for allowable depreciation methods on state tax returns.

You can learn the rules for depreciation of assets used in your trade and business by ordering Publication 17 from the Internal Revenue Service and ordering Form 4562 with the accompanying instructions.

Real Estate

If you are depreciating real estate used in your business or held for investment, the time period over which it is depreciated depends on whether it is residential property (e.g., apartments) or commercial property (e.g., stores, offices). Residential real property is depreciated over 27.5 years using the straight-line method. Commercial real property placed in service after May 12, 1993, is depreciated over 39 years using the straight-line method (31.5 years if it was placed in service prior to May 12, 1993).

Personal Property Used in Trade or Business

Several different depreciable lives are possible for depreciable personal property used in your trade or business. Those lives include 3, 5, 7, 10, 15, and 20 years. Almost all equipment such as automobiles, trucks, typewriters, desks, and machines, will be depreciated using either a 5-year or 7-year life. You should consult IRS publications to determine what types of assets use other lives.

Equipment that fits into the 5- or 7-year lives class can be depreciated using the 200-percent declining balance rate. This means that the equipment is depreciated using twice the straight-line rate. However, in years of acquisition and disposition of the property, you can only take one-half of a full year's depreciation, no matter in what month of the year the property was purchased.

Some of the items included in the 5-year depreciation class under MACRS include:

1. Automobiles and light trucks.
2. Computer-based telephone central office switching equipment.
3. Research of experimentation property.

The 7-year MACRS depreciable life property includes most forms of equipment used in business such as typewriters, computers, desks, chairs, and fixtures.

For example, if you purchase a $1,400 computer that has a 7-year MACRS depreciable life, the depreciation in the first year would be $1,400 divided by 7 = $200. You can take twice the straight-line rate depreciation of $400, but it is limited to one-half year's worth of depreciation, which would mean $200 depreciation in the first year.

After the initial year's depreciation, you would calculate your depreciation for each subsequent year using the following formula:

$$\text{Initial cost} - \text{Prior year's depreciation} \times [1 \div 7] \times 2$$

Generally light trucks, automobiles, research equipment, and computerized central telephone switching equipment are depreciated using a 5-year life. Most other machinery, office equipment, fixtures, and so on are depreciated using a 7-year life. Since only one-half a year's depreciation is allowed in the year of acquisition, in reality it usually takes one year more than the depreciable life to fully depreciate any personal-property asset.

Certain properties such as luxury automobiles used less than 50 percent for business use are limited to straight-line depreciation. Automobiles used for business that cost more than $14,300 are limited to $2,860 depreciation in the first year, $4,600 in the second year, $2,750 in the third year, and $1,675 for all subsequent years.

Under Section 179, you can immediately deduct up to the first $17,500 of equipment purchased for your business each year and avoid depreciating it over a period of time. However, if you place in service personal property in excess of $200,000 in any one year, the $17,500 is reduced dollar for dollar for all property purchased in excess of the $200,000. In addition, this $17,500 deduction is limited to the taxable income of your trade or business before taking this deduction. If the equipment is sold, this deduction must be recaptured.

We emphasize that these points are current at the time of publication but may change from year to year. So make sure your financial advisor(s), particularly your tax advisor(s), will keep abreast of any changes in tax-related depreciation guidelines and pass relevant information on to you without prodding.

PENSION AND RETIREMENT PLANS

Often, a small business is a family operation with part-time help or just one or two employees. Retirement plans exist that provide deductions not available to you as an employee of a company but that are available to you as a self-employed person. The area of pension and profit-sharing plans is highly complex. Many small-business owners do not have such a plan in place, and others are not even aware of them.

CPAs and pension-administration companies can give you details of various programs if you tell them you have a business and are interested in setting up a plan. Typically, they will counsel you for free because they want to sell you a plan. Be prepared to be confused in this area if you have no information before contacting them. We cannot make you a pension expert, but can create an awareness of options available to you. And under the right circumstances, a pension plan can be a valuable source of tax deductions for you.

New Keogh Plan Rules

Owners of unincorporated businesses now have important new options available to them to reduce current taxes while planning for their long-term retirement security. The familiar Keogh plan used by unincorporated individuals and partnerships is a valuable tax-saving and retirement-planning device.

The maximum contribution to a Keogh plan is $30,000, or 25 percent of annual compensation, whatever is less. If you adopt a defined-benefit Keogh plan, the maximum contribution limit was raised to $115,641 as of 1993, or 100 percent of the average of your three highest years of compensation, whichever is less. Your earned income from which you may make and deduct a Keogh plan contribution does not include investment income or salary received as an employee. Directors' fees are considered self-employment income from which you can make Keogh plan contributions.

The most common type of Keogh plan is a profit-sharing plan. This type of plan permits you to determine the amount of contribution you make each year based on the profits of your business as shown on your tax return prior to deducting the Keogh plan contribution. You are limited, however, to 15 percent of your profits (which is actually 13 percent of your profits before making the deduction for the maximum contribution). You can also make a smaller contribution if you choose not to make the maximum one.

In addition to a profit-sharing Keogh plan, a "defined contribution" plan is available that allows a flat percentage contribution each year of up to 10 percent of your net profit. Another type of Keogh plan is a "defined benefit" plan where an actuary determines the contribution to be made each year. The actuary calculates the amount of contribution needed to yield a desired amount of savings at the time of retirement. The actuary bases this amount on the participant's remaining years until retirement and the expected earnings of the contributions. This type of plan is usually the most expensive to administer due to the additional cost of the actuary.

You must sign all the papers to open your Keogh plan on or before December 31 of the year you open it. However, you need not make the actual cash contribution until the due date plus extensions of your tax return. Many stockbrokers, insurance companies, and some banks offer Keogh plans for nominal installation charges (of less than $200) and with modest yearly administration fees (from $0 to $100 per covered individual). These institutions administer the plan while you direct them—as trustee of the plan—concerning its investments. The earnings of the Keogh plan are tax-free until withdrawn by the participants.

Generally the plan must cover all employees who are at least 21 years of age and who have one year of service with the employer. You can usually exclude part-time employees from your plan. Benefits of the plan must be nondiscriminatory.

Plans that benefit owners to a much greater extent than they do employees are deemed to be "top-heavy" and may be disqualified. The rules governing when a plan is top-heavy and how to avoid this problem are too complex to discuss here. You must review your plan with a Keogh plan expert to make certain it is not top-heavy and to take the steps necessary to remedy the situation if it exists. Most plans also permit voluntary employee contributions to the plan—which are not deductible to the employee—of up to $2,500 per year.

Individual Retirement Accounts

You've probably seen at least one or two of the hundreds of advertisements for Individual Retirement Accounts (IRAs). Banks, stockbrokers, insurance companies, and mutual funds have stepped up their ad campaigns since January 1, 1982, when the law changed to allow anyone who earns money from a job to open an IRA.

There's no question that the financial-services industry has benefited from the new business brought on by this legislation. But what about the members of that expanded market?

How an IRA Benefits You

An IRA is an investment for your retirement with two tax benefits: one immediate and one long-term. First, your contribution to an IRA is tax deductible subject to limitations. It is deducted from your gross income, thereby lowering your net taxable income. Second, the interest or dividends earned on your IRA investment are tax deferred. You pay federal taxes on your IRA investment earnings only when you take the money out of your IRA. IRA earnings are tax deferred in many states, too.

When you consider that most people's tax brackets drop appreciably when they retire, you understand the benefits of an investment that accumulates compounded interest over the years, unfettered by taxes, and then is taxed at the rate for the lower retirement tax bracket. All in all, an IRA is a very good way to build a retirement nest egg.

If you are not covered by any other type of pension plan offered by your employer (or by a Keogh plan if you are self-employed), you can deduct the lesser of 100 percent of your earned income or $2,000 contributed to an IRA each year. However, if you are covered by another type of qualified plan, there are limits on the amount of contribution you can make to an IRA and still take a deduction on your tax return.

A taxpayer with earned income can now make a fully deductible contribution to an IRA if his or her adjusted gross income (AGI) is less than $25,000 per year for a single person or is less than $40,000 on a joint return (AGI on a joint return includes income earned by the spouse).

The deductibility of the IRA contribution is phased out until it reaches zero, as the adjusted gross income increases up to $10,000 over the applicable $25,000 or $40,000 AGI figures. Therefore, if you are single and your AGI is $30,000 and you make a $2,000 contribution to an IRA, $5,000/$10,000 or 50 percent of your contribution ($1,000) is deductible.

You can open an IRA at any point before age 70 and you may begin to withdraw your savings at age 59. But you *must* begin to withdraw by age 70 or face stiff penalties. You can contribute (invest) up to $2,000 or 100 percent of your earned income (whatever is less) every year. If you are married, filing jointly, and only one of you earns an income from a job, you can open a second IRA (called a "spousal IRA") to cover the non-wage-earning partner. The maximum contribution for the two IRAs is $2,250—that's $2,000 allowed the wage-earning spouse plus an additional $250. If both of you are employed, you may contribute up to $2,000 to an IRA every year and deduct $4,000 from your combined gross income at tax time.

Your contributions to an IRA don't have to be regular. If money is tight, you can skip a year, or contribute less than $2,000. With many investments, you have the option of monthly contributions if the $2,000 in a lump sum is a daunting figure. If you happen to contribute more than the maximum allowed, the IRA will fine you a percentage of the amount you overcontribute, and you will be liable for the taxes on that, too.

But can you get to your money in case of a financial emergency? Although it's not encouraged by the IRS or institutions offering IRA investments, you can get your money—if you're willing to pay for it. The IRS will levy a 10-percent penalty on the amount you withdraw prematurely from your IRA, and you're also liable for the taxes on that money. If you are over age 59, the IRS does not charge the 10-percent penalty. Some investments, however, charge fees for early withdrawal of IRA funds. Be sure to read the fine print on your depositor or shareholder agreement.

In an emergency, you could exercise the IRA's "rollover" option and use that money without penalty for 60 days. With a rollover, you receive a check made out to you for the amount of your investment to date. You have 60 days to reinvest that money somewhere else before the IRS penalizes you 10 percent in addition to making you pay the taxes due on the money. A rollover may be exercised only once a year but could be useful in the event of a crisis.

Let's return for a moment to those endless IRA ads. Just who is competing for your IRA dollars? You can open an IRA at a bank, savings and loan institution, federal credit union, mutual fund company, brokerage firm, or insurance company. You can choose among bank certificates or accounts, mutual funds, stocks, bonds, annuities, a particular security, or any combination of a number of different investments. There is no limit on the number of IRAs you can open or the combination of investments, as long as you do not exceed the maximum annual allowable contribution.

What You Can Do

Most financial-services experts caution against attempting to play the market with your IRA, which you could do if you opened a "self-directed" IRA at a brokerage firm. You are making the right investment decision if you choose an IRA investment to buy and hold for the long term, an investment with a reasonable amount of stability, and most important, one you are comfortable with. Consider a mutual fund that invests in a mix of stocks and bonds, a diverse, so-called "growth-income fund" that provides a buffer against the swings of inflation and the market. The pros and the lucky amateurs are in the minority in the stock market. If you want to time the markets and play the odds, don't use money that's earmarked for your retirement.

You can switch your IRA investment to another type of investment if you are not happy with its performance. Simply request a transfer form from the sponsoring institution of the new investment you have chosen, and notify the custodian (usually a bank or trust company) of your present IRA investment. You may transfer your IRA between investments as often as you wish. The difference between this type of transfer and the rollover is that with a transfer you never actually receive a check for the amount of your IRA investments. The IRA simply changes custodians.

If you are invested in a mutual fund that is part of a mutual fund family, you can switch your investment from one fund to another with a different investment objective by notifying your mutual fund customer service representative. In this case, the transfer may be simpler to complete because there is usually no change in custodian. Because you never actually take possession of your IRA money, a transfer is tax- and penalty-free and not subject to a time deadline.

The best investment choice for your IRA is the investment that you are most comfortable with. Consider the old "sleep factor" when making your choice.

Can you sleep at night, free from worry about the safety of your retirement funds? If so, you've chosen the right investment for your IRA. The competition in the IRA investment market may be confusing at first, but in many cases that increased competition benefits you.

Do some rate shopping and determine how often interest is compounded: daily, monthly, annually. Your interest will pile up more quickly if it is compounded daily. Also shop for services. What kind of statement is provided, and how often? Is it clear and easy to understand? A statement that acknowledges your investments as they are made may help you avoid overcontributing to your IRA. Fees for maintaining your IRA can range up to $35 annually; be sure to check that fine print. Brokerage firms often charge an additional fee (up to $30) to open an IRA. Some mutual funds charge an up-front fee (or "load") to invest in their fund. And if a bank CD or other investment charges an early-withdrawal penalty—think twice. In an emergency, that additional penalty could take quite a chunk of your earnings.

Minimum initial investments also vary from plan to plan. Some require the entire $2,000 at once, while others allow weekly or monthly investment minimums to fit your budget.

Corporate Pension Plans

If your business is incorporated and you wish to install a corporate pension plan, the plan must be adopted before the end of your fiscal year. Like the Keogh plan, the contribution need not be made until the due date of your corporate tax return. Also, as with the Keogh plans, you can adopt a defined contribution plan, a profit-sharing plan, or a defined benefit plan. Since the rules are quite complex, you should consult experts before adopting the plan.

Plans can be designed so that they are integrated with benefits employees will receive from Social Security so that higher-paid executives may receive more benefit than other employees. However, you must comply with all the rules governing top-heavy plans.

The same maximum contribution rules that govern Keogh plans also govern corporate plans. The maximum contribution for an employee cannot exceed 25 percent of his or her earnings. In the case of participants in both a defined contribution and defined benefit plan, special limitations must be calculated. An alternative is a defined contribution plan in which an actuary determines the maximum allowable contribution per employee.

There are also other types of plans available to corporations, including Employee Stock Ownership Plans in which the contributions are the employer corporation's stock, and Section 401(k) plans in which an employee may elect to defer up to $8,994 of his or her earnings (after 1993) per year tax-free. With a 401(k) plan, the employee generally has the option to direct the type of investments and benefits in which the deferred amount is placed.

Objectivity is a key consideration in choosing a pension-services organization or administrator. If an institution does not have extensive design capability and flexible prototype plans, it may not be able to meet the financial needs of both the business and its owners. Similarly, if the institution's investment choices are limited, it may structure a plan to accommodate only those investment vehicles it has to offer. "Look for a company with the resources and expertise to keep it completely objective," one expert advises. "Make sure the plan accommodates your needs, rather than accommodating your needs to the plan."

Two of the biggest obstacles to getting the right pension plan are inertia and the demands of running a business. Studies have shown the average business owner devotes less than 5 percent of his or her time to the company pension plan. Many will not even think about amending their pension plan until the last minute, and then they must accept whatever comes off the shelf from the nearest supplier.

If your design, administration, and investment services are all managed in a single place, you have complete control without administrative burdens. So instead of spending your time managing your pension plan, you are free to manage your business. Then all you have to do is reap the benefits.

Real Estate Tax Shelters and TEFRA

Supreme Court Justice Oliver Wendell Holmes once said, "It is the right of every citizen to pay the least amount of taxes." Under existing law, a properly structured real estate tax-sheltered investment can yield an investor very reasonable returns and extensive tax benefits. The Tax Equity and Fiscal Responsibility Act (TEFRA) has given prospective investors interested in tax shelter types of transactions the benefit of providing stiff penalties against developers, promoters, lawyers, and investors who attempt to take unfair advantage of the tax code using fraudulent or unlawful tax shelters.

A tax shelter is an investment that is designed primarily to take legitimate advantage of existing tax law. The benefits of the investment come mainly from tax deductions generated by the transaction that are used to reduce an individual's reportable net taxable income, thereby reducing taxes. In fact, these laws were intentionally written to encourage investment in socially beneficial areas determined by Congress, such as real estate, oil and gas development, and capital equipment. The 1986 Tax Reform Act has substantially curbed many tax shelters that were popular before 1987.

These investments can be an appropriate part of a well-rounded investment portfolio. However, is a tax shelter for everyone? The answer is "no." The first criterion is the potential investor's federal income-tax bracket. The investor's tax bracket must be high enough to properly utilize the tax benefits generated by the investment. In addition, the investor must be comfortable with the risks inherent in all tax shelters.

It is important to understand that tax shelters provide tax *deferral—not avoidance.* Investors in a 33-percent tax bracket enjoy a tax reduction at that rate during the greater part of the life of the project. After a period of some years, when these tax benefits have been exhausted, it can be anticipated that the property will be sold. The bulk of the gain realized on sale is then taxed at the maximum 28 percent rate on capital gains. The investment, therefore, defers taxes due now and repays the tax at a later date. Providing the property has intrinsic economic value, the tax due can be paid out of the buildup in residual value of the asset. The rules that became effective in 1987 have diminished the appeal of tax shelters. In addition, since the maximum tax rate for individuals is 33 percent, tax shelters now have less value. More and more investors will be investing based on the prospect of pure economic return, rather than the tax savings that might be secured.

How can sponsors help inexperienced investors? Investors should realize that it's actually against the law for a sponsor to sell a tax shelter transaction to an unqualified investor. Reputable sponsors will insist the investor demonstrate the sophistication necessary to understand the deal or be represented by someone who can. Your broker, lawyer, or accountant is a good place to start. Take time to find someone in whom you have faith and confidence.

The law protects the investor. Legislation is punitive not only to the sponsors of a bogus tax shelter deal, but also to any advisors involved in preparing the deal (lawyers and accountants), and ultimately to participating investors themselves. The investors may be liable not only for back taxes that were originally due, but for a 20 percent penalty as well. Needless to say, it pays to be well informed on all aspects of a particular deal.

What, then, are the basic components of a good tax-shelter investment? The investor must remember that he or she is assuming some risk. So, as in any investment, the economics of the project must be substantive.

Always attempt to learn something definitive about the quality of the real estate. A residential property, for instance, must have some intrinsic value that will ensure the generation of rental income to pay its ongoing expenses and service debt. Also, there should be a reasonable likelihood of residual value sufficient to fund the capital gains tax due at sale and provide the investor with some additional cash. Obtaining an independent appraisal, as well as inspecting the property yourself, is a good protective measure.

It is important to investigate the track record, experience, and success of the sponsor and the developer involved. You should be specifically concerned with actual performance of particular projects compared with initial projections. Try to find out any bad news, such as lawsuits brought against the promoter by disappointed limited partners. Financial delinquencies on any past properties indicate weakness on the part of particular properties and on the developers themselves. Such revelations should be carefully investigated and all questions completely answered before proceeding to invest.

You should obtain guarantees from the developer. In the case of construction, the developer should pick up cost overruns and have the proven net worth to do so. The developer should also be obligated to buy back your investment if specified events occur, such as losing the project financing. Guarantees against operating deficits for a period of years are another protective measure.

What prevents a developer from bailing out of a project early? The best protection here is to ensure that he or she has a large financial interest on the back end in addition to the front-end position. This will give the developer the motivation to stay on to manage the project well and be entitled to residual benefits at resale along with the limited partners.

Fees vary from one deal to another; however, certain benchmarks can serve as a guide. Fees paid to the promoter and selling broker shouldn't exceed 25 to 30 percent of cash raised (depending on timing of payments). Management fees shouldn't surpass 6 percent of annual gross rents. Finally, on the sale of the real estate, a portion of any profits ranging from 25 to 50 percent above the investor's return on capital is considered typical.

Investors are liable only for their investment. This is legally true. However, limited partners occasionally find themselves in situations where additional cash is needed to prevent a property failure. To avoid recapture of their previous deductions and loss of property, the partners end up loaning additional cash to save the project. Although such contributions are optional, the tax consequences of not contributing make additional expenditure virtually mandatory.

How can an investor keep on top of what's happening during the life of the project? Any good sponsor provides regular reporting services to keep the investor informed. It is important to find one whose services are meaningful, comprehensive, and timely. The investor and his or her broker should receive a report on the physical and financial condition of the property approximately every 90 days. Services should also include a yearly review of anticipated deductions that are crucial to the investor's financial planning. In addition, the sponsor can orchestrate any offers to purchase the real estate. Also, if the deal gets in trouble, the sponsor should act as a mediator or facilitator, with the ultimate purpose of turning the project around.

One good investment with tax-shelter advantages (for all but wealthy taxpayers) remains. If you own rental real estate and have an adjusted gross income on your tax return of $100,000 or less, you can still deduct up to $25,000 of the tax losses generated by that real estate (usually from depreciation) against all of your other income of any type. That deduction is phased out 50 cents on a dollar as your adjusted gross income increases to $150,000, after which you can only deduct your real estate losses against your "passive" income. All real estate rental losses in excess of $25,000 are subject to the same rules and phased-in disallowance as previously mentioned for limited partnership tax shelters.

If you qualify under the rules mentioned, you still must actively participate in the operation of your rental properties. If you make significant and bona fide management decisions concerning the property, you are deemed to be actively participating. You can use a rental agent to manage the property and still qualify. Your deductions are also limited to the amount you have "at risk" in the rental property, which usually includes the amount you paid down on the property and certain loans taken out to acquire the property that are secured by the property.

Prior to 1987, real estate investments could be depreciated at an accelerated rate over either 18 or 19 years. However, now residential rental property must be depreciated using a straight-line rate over 27.5 years, and commercial property must be depreciated in a straight line over 39 years (31.5 years if it was placed in service prior to May 12, 1993). These increased depreciation periods substantially lessen the tax losses that can be taken from rental properties.

TAX PLANNING

Good tax planning not only minimizes your taxes, but also provides more money for your business or investments. As an entrepreneur, you should view tax savings as a potential source of working capital.

From a working capital perspective, there are two important rules to follow in your tax planning. First, don't incur an additional expense solely for the sake of getting an extra deduction. For instance, suppose your accountant tells you that you are in the 36-percent tax bracket and need more deductions. To get an extra $1,000 interest-expense deduction, you incur $1,000 in finance charges for credit-card purchases for business purposes. These finance charges are incurred not because of a cash-flow problem or for business reasons, but solely for the benefit of writing off $1,000. If you think you are ahead because you saved $310 in taxes, think again. You actually lost money. In effect, you avoided paying one party $310 by giving another party $1,000. You just spent $690 out-of-pocket.

The second rule to remember is that immediately deferring taxes allows you to use your money interest-free before paying it to the government. Interest rates may justify deferring taxes for even a year, though this may cost you more taxes in a later year.

Estimated Tax Underpayments

If you have not paid sufficient amounts of estimated income tax, you may be able to avoid or reduce penalties for underpayment by arranging to increase the amounts withheld from the paychecks remaining in the present year. All withheld income tax is treated as if spread equally over the calendar year, even when a disproportionately large amount is withheld in December. Individuals required to make estimated tax payments should pay special attention to other techniques that may be beneficial, especially if their income is irregular or seasonal.

Careful planning and analysis of required tax payments is warranted in all categories of small business because of the high nondeductible penalty rates in effect.

Accounting Methods

Without incurring any additional expense, you can save taxes by your choice of accounting method. In cash-basis accounting, you report the income in the year you receive payment or have an unrestricted right to it. Generally, you can deduct an expense in the year you pay it. If you send payment on December 31, 1994, the expense is deductible in 1994 even though your payment won't be received until 1995.

If your gross sales receipts exceed $5,000,000 per year, and your business is a corporation, partnership or trust, the IRS will not permit you to use the cash method of accounting. You must use the accrual accounting method. There are several exceptions that permit some businesses to use the cash method of accounting no matter how large the gross receipts. Those are the farming business, partnerships without corporate partners, sole proprietorships, and "qualified" personal-service corporations performing services in the fields of health, law, accounting, actuarial science, performing, or consulting. In addition, 95 percent of the stock of the corporation must be owned by shareholders who are performing services for the corporation.

In accrual basis accounting, it doesn't matter when you receive or make actual payment. Income is reported when you bill. Expenses are deductible when you are billed, not when you pay. This accounting method has more tax benefits for a company with few receivables and large amounts of current liabilities. Advance payments to an accrual-basis taxpayer are generally held to be taxable income in the year received.

Unlike payments for services rendered, advance payments for merchandise are reported by an accrual-basis taxpayer when properly accruable under their method of accounting. If you choose this accounting procedure, you must use it for all reports and credit purposes. If you run two or more businesses at the same time, you may use different accounting methods for each business. Therefore, you can run one business on the cash basis and the other on the accrual basis.

Equipment Purchases

Due primarily to tax incentives, the year end is the time to consider buying business equipment. The tax incentive is the $17,500 expense deduction. Under Section 179 of the Internal Revenue Code, this deduction is not prorated for the period of the year that you hold and use the equipment. Consequently, you will get the same deduction whether you buy and put into service the equipment at the beginning or the end of the year.

You can only take this deduction for tangible personal property used in your business. It is not available for real estate or automobiles. You can expense up to $17,500 in equipment costs that were purchased for a trade or business. The expending deduction may be deducted in full even though the property is acquired and used in the last days of the year. If you purchase the equipment in the present year, but don't use it until the following year, the expending deduction won't be allowed for the present year. To the extent you take the deduction, you must reduce the cost basis for the equipment in computing its depreciation with the methods previously discussed.

Inventory Valuation

You don't automatically get a deduction for purchasing inventory items for your business. You must reduce the amount paid for inventory purchases by the value of the inventory at the end of the year. For example: If you paid $10,000 for merchandise in one year, and your inventory at the end of the year is $7,000, you can only deduct $3,000 for purchases in the year, even though you paid $10,000.

A change in how your inventory is valued can save a substantial amount of taxes. Under FIFO (first in, first out), inventory is valued at the latest current cost. Under LIFO (last in, first out), inventory is valued at the beginning of the year in which LIFO is adopted. In periods of rising costs, LIFO applies the most recent, higher cost of goods to current income, thus reducing the stated profit and resulting tax. Given the trend toward rising costs, a switch to LIFO in a typical year will give your company a one-shot loss deduction for the increase in prices of the items in your inventory. The switch to LIFO is made by filing Form 970 with your tax return. Once you adopt the LIFO method, it is irrevocable, and IRS approval is required to return to FIFO.

Electing LIFO will not be beneficial in long periods of deflation. The lower costs will be applied to revenues, thus increasing your stated profit.

Research and Development Expenses

Your research and development (R&D) expenses may both be deducted and also used to qualify for a 20 percent incremental research tax credit. In effect, you are allowed to take special benefits. The research expenses must be incurred from June 30, 1992, to June 30, 1995.

The R&D expenses must be incurred in a trade or business. The 20 percent tax credit is applied to the excess of your present year's R&D expenses over your average R&D expenses in accordance with a specified formula. Even if you were not in business before, your R&D expenses could still qualify based on a formula established in the tax code.

"Qualified research expenses" consist of certain wages and supplies for in-house research and 65 percent of amounts paid to certain nonemployees for contract research expenses. Generally, "qualified" expenses must be paid in cash during the year they are claimed. Qualified research could include development of an experimental or prototypical model, a product, formula, invention, or plant process. Research conducted outside the United States or in the social sciences or humanities fields is not eligible for the credit.

Employing Family Members

Employing your spouse or children in your business has several tax advantages, especially if your business is not a corporation. In fact, you can reduce three different taxes at the same time.

If you are self-employed and pay wages to your spouse or your son or daughter under 21 years of age, these wages are not subject to Social Security taxes and federal unemployment taxes. Wages paid your children will be taxable to them at their tax bracket, which is normally lower than yours. As long as their wages are reasonable and for actual services rendered, you can deduct their wages as a business expense.

You should note that if your children are under 14 and have unearned income (income not derived through the child's employment), that unearned income will be taxed at the same rate as the child's parent. Unearned income includes interest, dividends, capital gains, and any other sort of income that is derived from any source other than the child's personal labors.

Normally, you won't achieve this type of income splitting by paying wages to your spouse. Your taxable income, hence your income tax, will be the same whether you pay your spouse a wage or not. However, you have a potential reduction in your self-employment tax.

As a self-employed individual, you are subject to two taxes—the income tax and the self-employment tax. The maximum amount subject to the OASD portion of the self-employment tax is $60,600 (there is no maximum for the Medicare portion). Therefore, any wage you pay to your spouse that reduces your net business income below $60,600 will reduce the OASD portion of your self-employment tax even though it won't reduce your income tax because you are filing a joint return.

Income Rollover: Postponing Taxes on Compensation

If you are employed by someone else and expect to receive a year-end bonus or other additional compensation, you may want to defer receipt until the succeeding year, especially if you will be in a lower tax bracket in the following year. This is often the case with first-time entrepreneurs who quit their job and do not have a steady income during the time needed for their new business to break even. If your employer uses the accrual method of accounting, the bonus should still be deductible in the current year, provided it is fixed by year end and paid shortly thereafter, and the employer is legally obligated to pay it.

As to compensation expected to be received for future services, you may want to negotiate an agreement with your employer whereby part of your earnings will be deferred and paid either in one or several future years. Since the employer will have the use of the funds during the deferral period, an interest factor may be added. If certain requirements are met, deferred compensation will generally not be taxed to you, and similarly it will not be deductible by your employer until actually paid.

Computations of projected tax liability are needed to evaluate the desirability of postponing compensation. Any potential tax advantage of deferring compensation will be offset, at least in part, by the loss of interest or other income that can be earned if the compensation is received currently, unless the deferred compensation is increased. Credit risk is another important factor to consider. You should seek consultation prior to entering into deferred-compensation agreements. Deferring compensation may reduce your retirement or other benefits since it may reduce the base period figure used in calculating the benefits. Also, special rules apply for employees of state or local governments or tax-exempt organizations.

Tax-Postponed Investment Income

Postponing the reporting of taxable income, if possible, is almost always advantageous since it enables you to defer taxes and use funds for an additional period of time. However, tax-rate prospects for future years must be evaluated.

The following are widely used methods for postponing investment income:

- **Treasury bills and bank certificates.** Investors in short-term securities can shift interest income forward into a succeeding year by buying Treasury bills or certain bank certificates with a term of one year or less that mature in the next year. This applies not only to businesses but also to individuals.
- **Savings bonds.** U.S. savings bonds have become a more viable investment for some investors. Bond holders may elect to postpone the tax on the interest until the bonds are cashed in, which may be 30 years or more if the Treasury continues to extend maturities as it has in the past. Alternatively, the income tax may be reduced or avoided by giving the bonds at the time of purchase to minor children in low tax brackets and having them elect to report the interest currently. This election, once made, applies to all savings bonds owned now or in the future, and the election cannot be reversed. The election by the children will not be considered an election by the donor. If you have accumulated untaxed savings-bond interest for many years and now require current funds, you can extend the tax postponement if you exchange the bonds for Series HH bonds, which pay interest semiannually.
- **Deferred annuities.** Taxes can be postponed on earnings from capital put aside for long-range goals by purchasing a deferred annuity. Annuities are arranged by contract with an insurance company. While there is not tax deduction for the amount contributed, all interest earned and compounded will be tax-free until it is withdrawn, which may be as late as age 70 for some plans. Deferred annuity purchases may be made in installments or with a single payment. Early withdrawals will be deemed taxable to the extent the cash value of the contract exceeds the investment in the contract. Only after any excess has been withdrawn as taxable income will it be possible to receive nontaxable early withdrawals of principal.

Distributing Expenses and Profits

If you start a business this year, incur expenses, but your business does not become active, can you write off your expenses? The answer: Yes and no. If the expenses are related to the organization of the business, you must capitalize and amortize those expenses. This means listing organization expenses as an asset, like a piece of equipment. Then amortize the expense of the organization over a five-year period. If, for example, you spend $1,000 to incorporate your business, that expense is not deductible as a single legal fee in the first year of business. It is considered a start-up cost and is amortized over a five-year period. You would thus take a $200-a-year deduction over the period.

Even if you do not actively engage in business in your first year, many items will be write-offs, provided you are in business in the subsequent fiscal year. You would have some expenses with no income and some deductions against your salary or other income. However, you must not only be reasonable in your approach to write-offs, but also use thorough documentation. If you were planning a business, you would get the fictitious-name statement, open a business bank account, and start spending well-documented money out of that account.

Showing your new business with no income, but with deductions, in the first year may substantially increase the possibility the IRS may audit your tax return. In addition, the IRS may, on audit, attempt to disallow your loss deduction using the "Hobby Loss" rules that limit deductions on your activity to the amount of income derived from it. The presumption is that your business is a "hobby" if it does not make a profit in three out of every five years of business. To avoid the IRS determining your business as a "hobby," you must show that you have entered it with the intent to make a profit and not just to reduce your taxes. You can overcome the "hobby loss" presumption with factual evidence of being seriously engaged in business such as having a business license, stationery, a bank account, an office, sales literature, a business phone, and advertising.

Partnerships present special problems in the area of expenses and profits. If two persons form a partnership, losses may be allocated in any manner agreed on between the partners subject to some complex restrictions and rules in the tax code. If Partner A does not have a tax problem and Partner B does, and if the partnership is going to lose money that year, Partner B can take the entire loss for tax purposes. That doesn't mean Partner B has to pay all the money—just that he or she could take the entire loss. One way to raise money for a business is to approach someone who anticipates a large tax bill with the proposal to invest in your business. Tell the person that you are going to form a business and expect to lose X amount because you are just starting up. This person's investment of X amount would provide him or her with that much write-off. A person in the 33 percent tax bracket, could save $\frac{1}{3}$ of the investment in taxes, which means that the investor has a 33 percent return on investment. When the business becomes profitable, you two can work out a new profit-and-loss arrangement.

Whether or not such an arrangement is successful for tax purposes depends on whether the allocation of the partnership's profits and losses has a "substantial economic effect." Due to the complexity of the tax law in this area, you will need the services of an expert tax attorney or CPA to structure your partnership agreement in a manner that would successfully allocate all the partnership losses to one partner.

With respect to profits in a partnership, you have to define just how income is going to be distributed. It is not always straightforward and simple. Suppose Partner A puts up $100,000 but is not going to be active in managing the business. Partner B is going to do all the work. Do they split profits evenly? Perhaps Partner B could be guaranteed a salary of $10,000 a year. Then Partner A who put up the $100,000 would receive a 10 percent return on investment, which comes to $10,000. They could agree to split additional profits in any manner they choose.

What if the business only earned $15,000 before salaries and interest paid to the investor (Partner A)? Would $10,000 still go to Partner B and only $5,000 as a return to the investor? Is there going to be an even distribution of revenue until each partner receives their limit? This, too, must be decided.

Suppose the business loses money. Is Partner A, who put up the $100,000, entirely responsible? Or is Partner B, who is doing all the work and has very little cash investment in the business, partly responsible for the losses? They have to define the consequences of profits and losses in the partnership agreement.

Suppose the spouse of Partner A claims that if it weren't for Partner A the business wouldn't be going at all and that Partner A should get a bigger share than Partner B. Or suppose the partnership is doing very well, with Partner B spending a lot of money on travel and entertainment, charging it all to the partnership; Partner A isn't going to like that. Such matters must be dealt with in advance of business operation to receive the proper tax benefit from them. Experts recommend having them built into the partnership agreement.

Tax Adjustments

If the IRS wants to look at one of your tax returns, it must do so within three years of your filing that return. Allegations of fraud are an exception to this rule. In such cases (e.g., deductions claimed with the intent to defraud the government out of tax revenues, or unreported income), the IRS may look at tax returns that have been filed at any time. Assuming, however, that you are doing a proper job of tracking your tax credits and liability, the IRS has three years to look at your records.

The statute of limitations for assessment of taxes starts from the date you file your tax return. If you fail to file your tax return, the statute does not start to run. If you omit from gross income an amount in excess of 25 percent of the gross income reported on your return, the statute of limitations for an audit and assessment is six years.

Conversely, this means you have three years to straighten out tax matters as they arise. If you discover something that results in a change in your taxable income in any of three previous years, you may file a one-page amended return form, known as a 1040X, and indicate whatever changes there are on the amended return. It may mean you'll be paying more taxes. On the other hand, if you've had business deductions you didn't take, you can file an amended return and claim a refund—plus interest.

Tax Advisors

A commonly asked question is where a CPA fits into all of this. If you know enough about fundamental tax requirements for your small business, you can use a bookkeeper to maintain day-to-day, month-to-month books. Or, if you are familiar with standard bookkeeping procedures, you can do this yourself.

Nevertheless, in most small businesses, it's good business to see a CPA twice a year—once when you prepare your taxes, and once in midyear when you do your tax planning for the rest of the year. Additionally, many business veterans believe that a CPA should summarize the transactions of your business every three months, preparing quarterly financial statements. These financial statements can also be used for the preparation of your business tax return and are often useful when dealing with bankers for loans.

Use financial advisors prudently, working with them to determine realistically where your business is going and how you can adjust your tax-related decisions to help it get there. Based on the financial information they organize for you, you should be able to plan the purchase of equipment that will benefit you in the area of deductions or in the estimation of your taxable income for the year.

State Income Taxes

Though many states base their income taxes on the federal tax law, some states (California is one) partially base their tax system on federal law and also have many unique variations of their own. Only federal tax rules have been reviewed. You should secure information from your state concerning the rules and regulations taxing individuals, partnerships, and corporations. Though state taxes are substantially lower than federal taxes, you will still be able to save state taxes by planning ahead based on state tax rules.

Omnibus Budget Reconciliation Act of 1993 (OBRA '93)

On August 10, 1993, the Omnibus Budget Reconciliation Act of 1993 (OBRA '93) was signed into law by President William Clinton. The provisions of the law were projected to increase tax revenues by more than $250 billion over the following five-year period. Many provisions of OBRA '93 are effective for tax years beginning on or after January 1, 1994; however, increases in the top individual and corporate marginal tax rates, AMT rates, and estate and gift tax rates were retroactive to January 1, 1993.

Due to the provisions of OBRA '93, the top individual rates (39.65%) are higher than the top corporate rates (35%) for the first time since 1987. In addition, there is now a 10% surtax on individuals with taxable income in excess of $250,000 and on estates and trusts with taxable income in excess of $7,500. These thresholds will be indexed for inflation beginning in 1995.

OBRA '93 established nine empowerment zones and 95 enterprise communities to be designated in 1994 and 1995. Tax incentives are available to businesses located in the empowerment zones. The Section 179 expense election is increased to $37,500 of qualified zone property. An employment credit equal to 20 percent of the first $15,000 of "qualified wages" paid each year to each employee who both lives and works in the zone is available to employers. You should check with your CPA to determine if you can qualify for empowerment zone tax incentives.

Other OBRA '93 revisions to the tax laws have been reflected throughout this chapter.

RESOURCES

Government Agencies

U.S. Department of the Treasury, Internal Revenue Service, 800-829-1040. Call this number for answers to any tax-related questions.

Associations

American Institute of Certified Public Accountants, 1211 Avenue of the Americas, New York, NY 10036, 212-596-6200

Association of Tax Consultants, 1313 12th Avenue SE, Suite 100, Portland, OR 97214, 503-238-0834

CPA Associates, 230 Park Avenue, Suite 1545, New York, NY 10169, 212-818-9700

Independent Accountants International, 9200 South Dateland Boulevard, Suite 510, Miami, FL 33156, 305-670-0580

Institute of Tax Consultants, 7500 212th Street SW, Suite 205, Edmonds, WA 98026, 206-774-3521

National Association of Tax Consultants, 454 North 13th Street, San Jose, CA 95112, 408-298-1458

National Office Systems Association, P.O. Box 8187, Silver Spring, MD 20907, 301-589-8125

Magazines

The Tax Adviser, Harborside Financial Center, 201 Plaza 3, Jersey City, NJ 07311-3881, 201-938-3447

Tax Law Review, Warren, Gorham, and Lamont, Inc., 31 St. James Avenue, Boston, MA 02116, 617-423-2020

Taxes: The Tax Magazine, 4025 West Peterson Avenue, Chicago, IL 60646-6001, 312-583-8500

20

Credit Management

" "In God we trust. All others pay cash." "Yes, we accept checks and all major credit cards." ·

You have seen these signs in professional offices and retail outlets all over the country. They spell out the very real confusion that you as an entrepreneur face when you consider granting credit to your customers.

Virtually any business beyond the level of street vending relies heavily on credit for its success. Whatever business you are in—manufacturing, wholesaling, retailing, or services—you have an automatic sideline: loaning money. Any time you extend credit to a customer or any time goods or services are not paid for in cash, your customer is using your money interest-free.

Maintaining tight control is the only way to profitably run this sideline business of loaning money. However, since you're trying to control the human factor (risky at best), you face certain hazards. How will you know if the customer is as good a credit risk as you are? How can you tell if credit will actually increase your sales? Will it cost a lot to sell on credit?

THE ADVANTAGES OF EXTENDING CREDIT

Cash and carry is definitely the cleanest, most efficient way to do business. It eliminates the need for credit checks and costly accounts managing, and it minimizes the chances of operating loss.

Certain types of business by their very nature—custom manufacturing, one-time professional services, low-ticket items—demand a straight cash transaction. The decision to offer credit will depend totally on the business you are in. There is no magic formula to determine which businesses should offer credit, so you have to make the decision on your own.

A good argument for installing credit is found in past success stories of businesses that have offered credit. Almost every business that has extended credit

417

finds that sales volume increases simply because it becomes easier for the customer to buy.

The spending ceiling for a cash-only customer is limited to cash in hand. Your ad might have gotten that person into the store, but once there, his or her spending power is limited by the amount of cash the individual is carrying. And since we live in a credit economy, that's usually not too much—twenty dollars on the average. However, if that customer is allowed credit, the ceiling is raised to the available credit allowed.

Case histories from leading merchants prove that offering credit can:

1. Encourage your customers to spend more and increase total sales.
2. Express friendliness and trust making your operation a pleasant place to visit; customers may respond with goodwill toward you.
3. Make your customers less concerned about price.
4. Help you attract a more financially stable group of customers.

A case history of a small retail operation will illustrate this. In 1972, a small bookstore opened in Minnesota selling books to college students on a cash-only basis. After one year of operation, the store had fallen 60 percent below its projected first-year volume and was facing a loss of several thousand dollars.

Then the owner did a simple study of the store's customers, and discovered that most operated on a monthly budget (either from scholarship funds or money from home). In this particular rural area, people traditionally sent money to their children on the first of the month.

For three or four days around the first, sales volume and foot traffic were good. But for the remaining days, sales bottomed out. The owner tried everything—more advertising, sales promotions, discount offers—but nothing worked.

In the bookstore's second year of operation, the owner began accepting checks and credit. Business zoomed. His first-quarter sales were up over 200 percent, and he finished the year with $180,000 gross sales.

THE DISADVANTAGES OF EXTENDING CREDIT

There are certain costs involved in granting credit. The major gamble is that the customer might not pay you. Statistics indicate that 97 to 98 percent of all credit bills in America are paid on time. However, that remaining 2 to 3 percent can sink you if you are not careful.

Make no mistake about it: It can and will happen. It happens to everyone from Avco Finance to Bank of America, even to Sears and Macy's. All customers are mortal, and as the saying in the credit field goes, the road to bankruptcy is paved with good intentions. Things don't always go as planned. That is why pencils have erasers, and why some creditors lose money.

Credit costs you money. When you offer credit, you are selling an item you've already paid for on the premise that you will be paid by the buyer tomorrow.

The dollars to pay for the product come from operating capital that you don't then have on hand to reinvest in the business.

Your customer is using your product on loan, yet you still have your operating expenses and cash needs. Offering credit will force you to invest more money in your operation. If you decide you can safely carry receivables of $20,000, then one way or another you are going to have to replace that $20,000 in your cash flow.

Credit costs you time. This is a strong disadvantage. As you know, time is your most valuable commodity. As an entrepreneur, you have doubtlessly discovered that running your own business takes time and energy in dealing with customers and paperwork, balancing bank statements, and so on. When you add credit decisions to this workload, you use more time. You spend time making some credit decisions that could be spent running other aspects of your business.

Other major disadvantages of offering credit are the potential losses when a customer fails to pay, and the additional expense of credit checking, credit-bureau memberships and fees, discounts on sales, and costs of collection agencies and lawyers.

When all is said and done, however, your competitors may simply force you to offer credit. You may have to provide credit options not just to increase sales but to maintain them. You will be in a situation of running just to stand still.

EXTENDING CREDIT

When you offer credit, you are making four basic assumptions:

1. You assume that your customer has every intention of paying.
2. You assume that your customer is able to pay.
3. You assume that nothing will happen to prevent payment.
4. You assume that your judgment about the character and integrity of your customer is accurate.

As a business owner, you are used to dealing in facts and figures. Notice that in the four assumptions noted here, nothing is particularly scientific to help you in making your judgments.

Credit data and a past history will give you a good initial indication of your customer's intention and ability to pay for the purchase (see Figure 20.1). Past payment history nationwide will help you with the third assumption. The fourth assumption can only be dealt with by calling on your own years in business, what you know about your customers, and your gut feelings.

Verifying credit is fairly easy. On your credit application form, request three trade references and the name and branch of the applicant's bank. Call the bank, give your name and company name, and ask for a credit rating on your customer. Ask how long the account has been open, the average balance, and whether the bank has credit experience with this account.

Figure 20.1   Consumer Credit Application

NAME/ADDRESS

Last:	First:	Middle Initial:	Social Security Number
Address:			
City:	State: Zip:		Telephone:

EMPLOYMENT HISTORY

Employer	Job Title:
Address:	Supervisor:
City: State: Zip:	Salary:
Phone: Date From:	Date To:
Employer	Job Title:
Address:	Supervisor:
City State Zip	Salary
Phone: Date From:	Date To:

SOURCE OF INCOME	TOTALS	EXPENSES	TOTALS
Salary		Loans	
Bonuses & Commissions		Charge account bills	
Income From Rental Property		Monthly bills	
Investment Income		Real estate mortgages	
Other Income *		Other debts—Itemize	
TOTAL INCOME		TOTAL EXPENSES	

BANK REFERENCES

Institution Name:	Institution Name:	Institution Name:	
Checking Account No.	Savings Account No.	Home Equity Loan No.	Loan Balance:
Address:	Address:	Address:	
Phone:	Phone:	Phone:	

STATEMENT OF ACCURACY AND PERMISSION TO VERIFY

I hereby certify that the information contained herein in this credit application is complete and accurate. This information has been furnished with the understanding that it is to be used to determine the amount and conditions of the credit to be extended. Furthermore, I hereby authorize the financial institutions listed in this credit application to release necessary information to the company for which credit is being applied for in order to verify the information contained herein.

_____   _____
                  Signature   *Date*

Contact each of the trade references and tell whoever answers that you would like a credit rating on one of their customers. Ask how long the account has been open, what the highest credit granted is, and how the customer pays. Once you have reached the bookkeeper, you usually don't even have to ask these questions; the needed information will be volunteered. You might also obtain membership in your local credit bureau and draw reports on each account or utilize one of the financial rating services for businesses such as Dun & Bradstreet (D&B). This way, if the customer has any judgments against him or her or a record of slow payments with anyone, you will know.

RETAIL CREDIT

You may need to extend three kinds of credit:

- Check cashing.
- Credit cards.
- Installment loans.

Each of these three areas have certain risks inherent in them, but there are also proven techniques to cut your risks without losing customers.

Check Cashing: First Step to Credit

According to the American Collectors Association (ACA), in 1992 alone, there were approximately 533 million checks, totaling $16 billion, returned to U.S. banks for nonsufficient funds, closed accounts, and stop payment requests.

How can you minimize your risks in accepting checks? The answer is careful screening and use of modern technology. It is possible to get insurance against bad checks from check-verification and guarantee services such as Telecheck Services, Inc., Equifax Check Services (formerly Telecredit Inc.), and NPC Check Services. A number of smaller services also offer just verification-only services or verification and guarantee.

These companies will verify checks by phone, simply with one identification: the customer's driver's license or state ID (from United States or Canada) or a military ID. Telecheck also offers a new device called a check reader, with which a merchant may not even need to ask for an ID. The merchant runs the check through a terminal, which will pick up the check's microline and determine (1) if it's printed in magnetic ink (all bank-authorized checks are); and (2) if the account is valid and the check good. A verification code or a decline on the check is provided within seven seconds. Once Telecheck authorizes a check, they will guarantee it; that is, if it is bad, they will buy the check from you at face value. Typically, the fee for check-verification and guarantee services varies according to the kind of service you choose, your total check dollar volume, and the kind of business you are in. Expect fees to range anywhere from .7% to 4% of the check's face value. Some high-risk businesses whose fees generally fall toward the higher end of the range include electronics stores, mail and telephone order (which have a high propensity for fraud), and operations that sell fenceable goods such as computers and shoes. Their fee can be offset though, by the volume of checks you take in. For example, a small electronics store would pay a higher per-check fee for Telecredit's service than say, a large Circuit City store. Still, most merchants use some kind of check verification service. It's too risky not to. The amount spent, say $24 for a $600 check, is often worth the risk of losing the whole $600. Also, the fee will often be lower than the merchant's discount rate (fee) for accepting credit cards.

Whether using a service or not, any time a check is presented to you or your clerks, look for several key items:

- Make sure the check is drawn on a local bank.
- Check the date for accuracy: the month, day, and year.
- Do not accept a check that is undated, postdated, or more than 30 days old.
- Be sure the written amount and the numerical amount agree.

We also suggest that you post your check-cashing procedures in a highly visible place. Most customers are aware of the problem of bad checks and are willing to follow your rules, but if your rules are not known until the customer reaches the checkstand (e.g., that you require certain forms of ID), it can cause ill feelings.

Your main reason to ask for identification is so you can locate the customer if something is wrong with the check. The most valid and valuable piece of identification is a driver's license, which in some states, includes a picture, signature, and address. If the signature, address, and name agree with the check, then the check is probably safe.

The driver's license is a valid ID, thanks to computer technology. In each state, the license is recorded and registered on a computer system. Each driver's license is also registered in a series of computers that can tell instantly whether it is valid, stolen, or has been connected with some fraudulent credit or check procedures.

If you are not connected with one of these check-verification systems, you may want to ask for a second piece of ID, such as a check guarantee card, major credit card, or department store credit card. Keep in mind, though, that in many states now it is illegal to copy down any numbers off credit cards. You can only ask to see them. Retail merchants' associations often provide lists of stolen drivers' licenses and credit cards so if the customer is unknown to you, it makes sense for you to check the list.

The following pieces of ID are not acceptable:

- Social Security cards (anyone can apply for one by mail).
- Business cards (anyone can have them printed).
- Club cards (membership does not imply honesty).
- Bank books (easily forged or stolen).

- Birth certificates (they prove someone was born but not that this is the person in front of you).
- Voter registration cards (they simply prove that the customer lives or lived at a certain location).

Without a check-verification service, if you have any question about the validity of the ID, don't accept the check! Remember, you are loaning that person your money when you take a check, and if the loan doesn't look good, forget it.

Credit Cards: Plastic Money in Your Till

The number of credit cards in use is staggering. In 1991 there were 111.3 million credit card holders in the United States, says *The Nilson Report*.[1] Also, most people carry more than one card; in fact, the average executive has 5.3 cards. In addition to various department store, phone company, and miscellaneous credit cards in their wallets, these 100 million-plus consumers carry either one or both of the two main credit cards in the United States—MasterCard and Visa (formerly BankAmericard).

Visa and MasterCard are not actually credit card companies. Instead, they are interchange and clearing house systems for the credit-card activities of their bank members. All major cities and most smaller ones have one or more banks participating in both these programs.

When you accept credit cards, you increase sales because you are offering convenience and the chance for the customer to buy on "float." Yet the money isn't coming out of your pocket—quite.

A hardware store in Atlanta might take a Visa card purchase from a customer who lives in Milwaukee. The sales slip is deposited along with the other receipts in the hardware store's bank account.

The Atlanta bank credits the amount of the sales less a handling fee, generally 4 to 7 percent. Assuming the sale was for $20 and the handling fee is 5 percent, the Atlanta hardware-store owner actually receives only $19. The loss of the $1 is built into the store's pricing and profit structure and passed along to the customer.

Then the Atlanta bank transfers the debt to the customer's Milwaukee bank, which stands behind the debt and transfers the necessary funds to the Atlanta bank. The Milwaukee bank then bills the customer for the $20 plus interest. The bottom line is that the store owner in Atlanta offered credit without much risk, the Milwaukee customer received the merchandise, and the banks in both cities made a profit.

Since the card companies are taking the risks in granting credit, they expect the merchants to help them cut their losses. Both major cards publish regular lists of card numbers that are unacceptable for some reason, and they expect you to look at this list before granting credit.

[1] H. Spencer Nilson (HSN) Consultants, *The Nilson Report*, Oxnard, CA, 1991.

You are also required to check the signature on the sales slip with the signature on the card. If they don't look the same, ask the customer to sign again. Both companies will establish a house limit (say $50 to $100), requiring you to check by telephone before writing a ticket in excess of that amount. Failure to do any of these three steps can result in a dispute between you and the major credit card companies if the account is fraudulent.

American Express, Carte Blanche, Diner's Club, and the Discover Card are four credit cards you may decide to accept. They differ considerably from bankcards because their credit requirements are generally higher. Most bank cards grant credit if a person has a job, a permanent residence, and no derogatory information in a computer credit file. Entertainment cards, as American Express and the others are called, require a more complete credit history: bank references, type and size of account, minimum income (usually $15,000 or more), and they charge an annual membership fee in excess of the typical membership fee for a bank card.

Another main difference is that the entertainment cards generally have a higher credit ceiling. Bankcards will put a credit line to a customer's account and hold the person to that limit. Entertainment cards are geared to the more affluent consumer with discretionary dollars to spend.

The final difference is that entertainment card companies expect to be paid in full each month (with the exception of certain purchases such as plane tickets), while the bankcards give the customer two options: Pay the balance in full or pay 3 percent of the total balance plus interest monthly.

Banks tend to discourage people from paying off their entire bankcard bill at once. The thinking is that since they've gone to all the trouble to establish this credit for a customer, the least that customer can do is stretch payments out and let the bank rake in the interest.

If you have not already been approached by one of the major credit-card representatives, you may approach them. They have a sales force that works on commission and is geared to pitch the advantages of the various programs. One advantage they state is that sales will increase because of the sheer volume of credit-card users. With over $480 billion spent using credit cards in 1991 (according to HSN Consultants),[2] this argument seems to have plenty of strength behind it.

Offering a credit card program will eliminate the time you waste handling credit sales. When you consider that certain costs of credit are fixed (posting accounts, billing, etc.) and will cost you the same for a $10 sale as for a $500 sale, this argument also makes sense.

A marketing benefit that helps your advertising plans is the automatic mailing list the credit-card sales slip provides you with. You can (if you ask customers to fill in name and address) have a day-by-day record of that customer's purchases and use this list to promote future sales by mail.

[2] H. Spencer Nilson (HSN) Consultants, *The Nilson Report,* Oxnard, CA, 1991.

Another benefit you will hear about is the security of the sale. You will (if you follow other guidelines mentioned herein) be able to collect even if the bill payer skips town. The credit card operation assumes the risk and pursues collection. Since your time can be more profitably used making sales than tracking down nonpayments, this aspect is valuable.

A little-publicized but well-known part of the sales pitch is the psychological one of security. Burglars tend to stay away from stores that offer credit cards since they know there is generally less cash on hand.

Installment Credit

Certain kinds of businesses demand installment credit. Companies selling cars and RVs, major appliances, televisions, high-ticket cameras, sound equipment, and carpeting are good examples.

Basically, installment credit means that your customer is willing to sign a contract agreeing to pay, over a set period of time, the purchase price plus accrued interest and carrying charges. The key concept is the phrase "sign a contract." This makes your customer liable for full payment of the debt and gives you the power to exert legal steps to extract overdue payments. If you do not want to spend the time and money to manage an installment credit program, you may want to sell your credit contracts to a factor.

Factoring Receivables

You're in the business of selling, not bookkeeping. Finance companies, however, are in the business of bookkeeping—for business. Commercial and consumer finance companies and certain banks are willing to buy the signed customer "contract" from you at a discount. You sell your product to a customer, they sign the sales contract, then you sell a contract to a company geared to handling billings and collections.

This system costs you money in terms of the discount, but can save you money in bookkeeping. Finance companies generally work this way: If a total sales figure is $650 (including your profit, the interest, and carrying charges), the finance company will discount that figure (ranging from about 3 to 6 percent) and pay you that discounted figure. But you still come out ahead.

In that $650 figure, you add your interest charge, insurance, and carrying charge of $125 (18 percent interest or more). Those figures equal the financed price of an item you retailed for $525. Assuming a keystone markup (twice wholesale) on that $525 item, its raw cost was $262.50.

By selling the contract on that $262.50 raw cost item that had escalated to $650, you would lose 10 percent of the finance company discount. That would leave you with a $595 sale, or a $330 gross profit, and no bookkeeping headaches.

Before you embark on installment selling, get in touch with a finance company in your area. You can work a deal with them whereby you send them the business and they do the work. When discussing future terms with the finance company, make sure you find out their policy on recourse paper.

Installment credit has a higher risk factor than checks or credit cards. At the same time, it allows you tremendous volume growth with high-ticket items. The secret to profitable installment credit is careful step-by-step management.

Because you are in business, you have undoubtedly filled out dozens of credit applications in the past. But unless you are heavily involved in professional credit management, you probably never realized the wealth of information a credit application obtains. No matter what kind of data you have before you, you will still be making a subjective decision. That's why most credit experts also call on the "Three Cs" of good credit:

- Capacity (to repay).
- Character.
- Collateral.

Armed with the credit application your customer filled out, you can learn a lot about your customer's creditworthiness. First, confirm employment. A phone call to the employer will give you beginning information. Don't ask for the exact salary. Phrase the question in terms of range. "Does he earn in the low to mid-teens?"

If the switchboard operator has trouble recognizing the name, then check the length-of-time blank on the application for credit. If the customer has been employed for two years and someone has trouble recognizing the name, a siren should go off.

Next, call the bank(s) the customer listed. A bank's first priority is to its customers, but it will provide certain information. You might hear that a customer's average checking balance is an "L-3" or an "H-4." This translates to "low three figures" or "high four figures." A low three figure would be in the $100 to $300 range, while a high four figure would be in the $7,000 to $9,900 range.

Several experts suggest that you involve your own bank in this process. Tell your banker you need a credit "suggestion" on a certain customer. Banks tend to speak more freely with one another, and you can get a fairly realistic appraisal, not only of general balances, but of any trends such as slow payments or insufficient funds.

After you've made your preliminary investigations, then enlist the aid of one of the major credit reporting houses. TRW is a good example. With this operation, giant computers store millions of records on millions of customers. For a fee, you can receive an in-depth credit history (if available) that will greatly help in your decision (see Figure 20.2). Armed with this information, you will be ready to grant your customer's credit and watch your sales expand.

Your analysis of an individual's creditworthiness should help you decide the kind and amount of credit to offer. Experts generally agree that you should be cautious about going into the installment credit business yourself, unless you have done your homework. Here's why:

- **Protect increased capital.** You will need to increase your capitalization. The merchandise you are selling on credit has already been paid for by

Figure 20.2 Sample Credit Report

The Updated Credit Profile Report

TRW's Credit Profile report is designed to display information in a standard, objective, easy-to-read manner. An illustration and description of a sample Profile report for a fictitious person follows.

(1) Name and address as recorded on automated subscriber tapes, including date of most recent update.

(2) Employment name and address as reported by a subscriber through an inquiry on the date shown.

(3) A code designating the TRW or Credit Bureau office nearest the consumer's current address, for your use in consumer referrals.

(4) Consumer's social security number.

(5) Three columns indicating positive, nonevaluated, and negative status comments.

(6) A (Automated) and M (Instant Update or Manual Form) indicate the method by which the credit grantor reports information to TRW.

(7) Name and number of reporting subscriber.

(8) Association code describing the legal relationship to the account.

(9) Account or docket number.

(10) Status comment reflecting the payment condition of the account as of the status date.

(11) Date the account was opened.

(12) Scheduled monthly payment amount.

(13) Estimated monthly payment amount.

(14) Date last payment was made.

(15) Type and terms of the account.

(16) The original loan amount (ORIGL), credit limit (LIMIT), historical high balance (HIBAL), or original amount charged to loss (C/OAM), represented in dollar amounts.

(17) Balance owing, balance date, and amount past due, if applicable.

(18) The applicant's payment history during the past 24 months. The code reflects the status of the account for each month, displayed for balance reporting subscribers only.

C	—	Current
N	—	Zero balance reported/current account
1	—	30 days past due
2	—	60 days past due
3	—	90 days past due
4	—	120 days past due
5	—	150 days past due
6	—	180 days past due
— (Dash)	—	No history reported for that month.
Blank	—	No history maintained; see status comment.

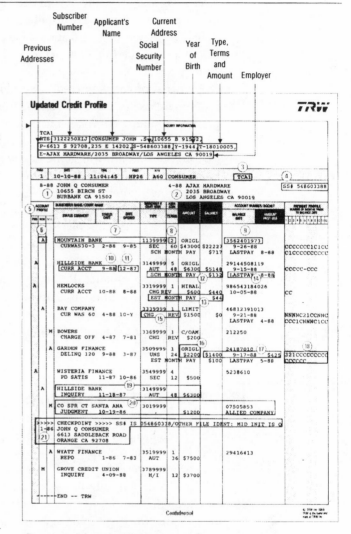

(19) Inquiries indicate a request for the applicant's credit information — inquiring subscriber; date of inquiry; and type, terms and amount, if available.

(20) Public Record: Court name, court code, docket number, type of public record, filing date, amount, and judgment creditor. This information may include bankruptcies, liens and/or judgments against the applicant.

(21) Profile report messages alert the subscriber about a credit applicant's social security number, name, address, generation, or year of birth. See back of page for further explanation.

you. Installment credit will involve an initial cash drain. For instance, assume you buy a refrigerator for $200. Depending on your credit arrangements with the manufacturer, you will have to put $50 to $100 up front for that refrigerator. If you mark that refrigerator up to $450 and sell it for that in cash, you will have a guaranteed cash flow. You pay the manufacturer $200, and you reinvest your $250 gross. But if you sell that refrigerator on time, in 12 monthly installments, you will have one-twelfth of the $450 plus interest in the till at the time of the sale. You will have to pay the manufacturer the full $200 before you collect all the money from your customer.

- **Project cost of carrying credit.** By adding interest and carrying charges to the purchase of the $450 refrigerator, you would arrive at a financed price of around $550 (figuring 18 percent interest, insurance, and overhead charges). That will increase your profit from the original price projection. But that profit is going to cost you. You will need to hire one or more persons to handle paperwork—the bookkeeping, mailing statements, aging accounts receivable, and collecting.

- **Recourse paper: Big decision.** Recourse paper means that the customer's credit appears good, but there is not enough credit data to take the entire risk; therefore, it is processed through a commercial finance company or bank. If the customer defaults, however, you will have to buy back the contract or the product. Recourse paper generally gets a lower interest charge since the lending institution has cut its risks. The decision for recourse and no recourse paper is based on the credit application, the credit investigation, the amount of credit asked for, and the expected volume of business.

TRADE CREDIT: TIPS AND TRAPS

How would you like an interest-free business loan without the hassle of credit checks and filling out papers? Sound too good to be true? Well, businesses do it every day by using payables financing. In a nutshell, this means that businesses big and small can skillfully use trade credit (sometimes called commercial credit) to keep their businesses going. Just as consumer credit is the fine art of keeping someone from using your money carelessly, trade credit is the fine art of using other people's money.

Almost 90 percent of American businesses operate on trade credit, generally in the form of *invoices* or *promises to pay.* Yet most of the information on trade credit available to small-business owners is written in a style that would require an MBA from Harvard to decipher. Also, most of the information is based on the ideal situation, imagining a company big enough to have credit managers, collection departments, payables divisions, and so on.

This is probably not your case. You are generally involved in opening and closing your doors, handling employee problems, making inventory decisions, answering advertising questions, and filling out government forms. Credit is just one of the many hats you wear daily, so this field of trade credit needs to be quickly and easily understood.

Your Credit Policy

The biggest problem most small businesses face with their credit policies is that they have none. Credit decisions—whether asking for credit or granting credit—are generally made on the spur of the moment, relying on a gut feeling. But sharp businesspeople realize that credit is one of the most important aspects of business financing. It must be managed with a successful game plan. That game plan must have two definite aspects—what you will do as a borrower, and what you will do as a lender.

The first step in determining your long-range credit policy is to get a fix on the exact status of your credit rating. Just as you turn to consumer credit bureaus to get a picture of the customer, so can other businesses turn to financial rating services to get a picture of you. Dun & Bradstreet is just one major company, among others, that produce various reports on businesses.

These reports give a detailed picture of your operation, including types of credit, payment history, size of operation, capitalization, net worth, and so on. Your listing with credit-reporting companies is of utmost importance in determining your policies. Ask these agencies for copies of their reports on you. If you are not listed, take steps to become so. Their books are the bible of the trade-credit business, so you have to be listed here to successfully use trade credit to make your business grow.

Once you have a record of the exact public appraisal of your credit rating, then you will be able to plan your long-range strategy with accurate data. If there is inaccurate information in these reports, you must have it investigated, and make sure that your side of the story is included in future credit reports.

Types of Trade Credit

Basically, there are two types of trade credit:

1. **Promises.** Also known as promises to pay, they are of two kinds: invoices and promissory notes. Any time you order goods and don't want to lay out the cash at that time, you get them on an invoice. If the amount of goods involves a high price, you may, on occasion, be asked to sign a promissory note guaranteeing payment.
2. **Orders.** Also known as orders to pay, they differ from promises in that you sign a document specifying the rate of payment, the dates of payment, and the method of transaction. Once an order to pay is accepted, it then becomes known as a trade acceptance. This term allows the company that is granting you credit to use your trade acceptance as a guaranteed source of

receivables income. This practice generally occurs when the amount of cash is considerable, usually over $10,000.

When you order goods, you will probably receive them on an invoice. This simply means that the supplier has checked your credit, believes you to be a good risk, and lets you have the goods. Many small businesses slip up at this point by not specifying their terms when ordering. One major term to always ask for is "ROG as of the 25th." This means you want the billing date to start upon receipt of goods (ROG). The reason you ask for the 25th is that most American businesses consider the 24th to be the end of the billing and shipping month, a custom that has solidified over the years.

Say you order a line of t-shirts on June 8 and you receive them on the 15th. If you had not specified ROG, your billing obligation would be the 8th instead of the 15th. If you specified "as of the 25th," and this was accepted, then you would not be billed until the 25th or later. When you are billed, your net payment would not be due for 30 days, or July 25. So the effect of this technique is that you get the t-shirts to sell for 45 days, interest-free.

It makes sense to request shipping terms. Many business owners ignore the money-saving aspect of "FOB" terms. This abbreviation stands for "Free on Board" and simply designates who pays the freight. If you request in your order "FOB destination," the supplier pays the freight. If you don't specify this, chances are you'll be paying it.

FOB terms are always negotiable. Remember, most suppliers want your business and will make exceptions. This is a point worth haggling over. So, the money-saving initials to include in your order are "ROG as of the 25th," and "FOB destination."

Spell Out Credit Terms

Spell out credit terms exactly so there's no chance for confusion. Most businesses, on one hand, will ask for "ROG as of the 25th, FOB destination," and on the other hand will reject or renegotiate any orders coming in like that. Their view is that they should not let anyone else use their money even though they want to use that of others!

Make sure that all the credit you grant is "EOM," otherwise known as "end of the month." This is generally written up as "net 15 EOM"—you expect the customer receiving your goods to pay you by the 15th of the following month. If you ship radios out on June 20, using this phrase will guarantee payment by July 15. In other words, you've cut the maximum time someone else can use your money down to 25 days.

To see just how important this aspect is, consider this: If you carry someone for three months, you have lost 10 percent of your net profit. Carrying them for four months results in a 14-percent loss; five months brings the loss to 19 percent. Generally if a bill is not paid in 5 years, you can write it off as a 100 percent loss.

To eliminate this potential loss of business revenue, you must spell out your credit terms exactly and stick to your guns. If someone else is using your money, you want to cut your risks to a minimum.

Expensive Discounts

Often a customer will ask if there is a cash discount for fast payment. Although this is a standard practice, you should decide for yourself whether to allow this. It is an expensive proposition. If you give a customer terms of "2 percent 10, net 30," then that customer can deduct 2 percent from the cost of goods if they pay you within 10 days. If you go along with this, then you are letting the customer use your money for a very low interest rate.

In effect, the customer is paying you only $2 interest for the use of $98, based on a $100 order. On the other hand, quick-paying customers will boost your cash flow and cut down on your bookkeeping chores, so weigh both sides of the coin.

If a customer applies for credit and your research tells you that their credit history is bad but the business picture looks bright, then you will move from "promises to pay" into the realm of "orders to pay."

You get the customer to sign a promissory note that on a certain date, a specified amount of cash is due. Businesses signing these documents know you have recourse with this kind of document. If all else fails, you can have your bank draft an order to pay which is then transferred to the other business's bank. Businesses don't like this to happen because it tips off the bank that the customer isn't paying bills when they are due.

Establishing Credit

The best credit managers have predetermined lines of credit available to their customers. This simplifies bookkeeping and makes it easier for credit arrangements. If a certain store has a $1,000 line of credit with a manufacturer, then goods up to that $1,000 can be ordered and shipped out quickly. Figure 20.3 shows a sample credit application for a business.

When you start your credit policy, you want to establish a good line of credit with your suppliers. Make sure that in your first six months of operation you pay according to the terms of the agreement. Because of the unpredictability of the mail, you always have room to maneuver. The check has to be dated the date the payment is due. If it is dated after that, your creditor will correctly assume that you have not met your obligation.

Once your credit line is established, you can begin using other businesses' money. The key to doing this is to make sure that you keep in touch with your creditors. If you are going to be late in paying, let them know ahead of time. If you can't make full payment on the first month, make a partial payment. If you are going to have to be carried for a longer period of time, make sure that the creditors always know.

Figure 20.3 Business Credit Application

NAME/ADDRESS

Last:	First:	Middle Initial:	Title:
Name of Business:			Tax I.D. Number
Address:			
City:	State:	Zip:	Telephone:

COMPANY INFORMATION

Type of Business:		In Business Since:	
Legal Form Under Which Business Operates: Corporation ☐ Partnership ☐ Proprietorship ☐			
If Division/Subsidiary, Name of Parent Company:		In Business Since:	
Name of Company Principal Responsible for Business Transactions:		Title:	
Address:	City:	State:	Zip: Phone:
Name of Company Principal Responsible for Business Transactions:		Title:	
Address:	City:	State:	Zip: Phone:

BANK REFERENCES

Institution Name:	Institution Name:	Institution Name:	
Checking Account No.	Savings Account No.	Loan No.:	Loan Balance:
Address:	Address:	Address:	
Phone:	Phone:	Phone:	

TRADE REFERENCES

Company Name:	Company Name:	Company Name:
Contact Name:	Contact Name:	Contact Name:
Address:	Address:	Address:
Phone:	Phone:	Phone:
Account Opened Since:	Account Opened Since:	Account Opened Since:
High Credit:	High Credit:	High Credit:
Current Balance:	Current Balance:	Current Balance:

STATEMENT OF ACCURACY AND PERMISSION TO VERIFY

I hereby certify that the information contained in this credit application is complete and accurate. This information has been furnished with the understanding that it is to be used to determine the amount and conditions of the credit to be extended. Furthermore, I hereby authorize the financial institutions listed in this credit application to release necessary information to the company for which credit is being applied for in order to verify the information contained herein.

_____ _____
Signature   *Date*

The availability of trade credit helps you reduce the amount of cash you have to borrow from other institutions. Since no interest is charged for such credit, this amounts to free money. To be a successful entrepreneur, you must make yourself aware of the intricacies of trade credit. A visit to your local banker can be a big help here. Make sure you establish a definite policy for your trade credit operations. The most sound business practice is to pay all your bills in a timely manner. But should conditions prohibit this, you can safely use the secrets of trade credit to tide you over the rough times.

COLLECTIONS: THE OTHER SIDE OF THE CREDIT COIN

The moment you decide to extend credit to your customers—whether to consumers or to another business—you automatically inherit another hat to wear in your entrepreneurial venture, that of bill collector. Most entrepreneurs realize that bad debts cost money, but few realize exactly how much. If your business averages 7 percent net profit after taxes, and you have $100 in bad receivables, you have to gross $1,429 more to make up for it.

Bill collecting is a combination of scientific procedure, good management, and regular control. There are dozens of laws spelling out what you can and cannot do when going after money that's owed you. The first step is to set up a clear, well-ordered collection policy. There are basically two possible policies: the "100 percenters" and the "pay when you can." The "100 percenters" have a firm, rigid collection policy that shoots for everything owed on the exact date due. The "pay when you can" school uses a more flexible approach, taking into consideration the many possible reasons for slow paying.

Your policy should fall somewhere between these two extremes. If you are dealing with perishable products like food, you need a strict policy. If you are dealing with products that have a long life, then you can have a more relaxed policy. You should decide up front what kinds of collection procedures to use, the time period of a collection, and the various approaches you will use. The most important thing is to think your policy through, then make sure all your employees know exactly what it is. This will save you time in the long run since you won't have to be called to solve every collection problem.

A full 80 percent of collection and payment problems revolve around invoicing difficulties. A recent study showed that costly mistakes on invoices occur in several areas. The major errors are wrong addresses, wrong person billed, payment terms not spelled out, and due dates not clearly specified.

The invoice you send out should always be typed or computer-printed. Illegible handwriting accounts for many of the errors. It should be written in terms understandable by everyone, especially your customers (see Figure 20.4).

If you invoice a customer on an irregular basis, always have the payment terms spelled out. If you do regular business with a customer, keep a "statement of account" that you send out monthly. A statement of account is

Figure 20.4 Invoice

BILL TO: _____

_____

_____

_____

Date: _____

Invoice No.: _____

Salesperson: _____

P.O. NO.	QUANTITY	DESCRIPTION	PRICE	DISCOUNT	TOTAL

Sub Total	
Sales Tax	
Total	

STATEMENT OF ACCOUNT

Payments	
Balance	
Current Charges	
New Balance	

Current	30 Days	60 Days	90+ Days

simply a recap of all the invoices sent to a customer during a given month. This statement should list each invoice by number, date shipped, and amount due.

Whether using a computerized or a manual system, be sure to stay organized and know how your system works. In a manual system, many businesspeople lump all the invoices together, then spend time at the end of the month sorting them out. This system presents several problems. If you are a one- or two-person operation, there's a chance of losing an invoice. If you wait until the end of the month, you may also face other end-of-the-month bookkeeping problems and want to put off the invoicing. Remember that if you don't promptly bill your customers, they will be using your money interest-free, so you should keep up to date with them.

When you prepare an invoice (and are not using computerized filing), immediately file it in a special folder clearly marked with the customer's name. This folder should have a ledger sheet so that when you file the original invoice, it can easily be checked.

Aging Receivables

There are many different techniques for setting up an aging system. You can either automate and purchase appropriate accounting software with this function or set up your own manual system—with code letters, different colored folders, and so on. The key is to make sure that anyone in your business can tell at a glance the status of any account at any given time.

The best operators have their accountants provide them with recaps of receivables on a monthly basis, so that they can structure their collection efforts in a logical, orderly way. We can't recommend strongly enough that you regularly review your receivables. Good receivables can quickly turn into overdue ones, and from there into collection problems and then into losses, while you're preoccupied with other aspects of running your business.

If you have a customer's history in front of you, you will be able to immediately spot any problems you're likely to have. If a customer traditionally pays 10 days after a due date, that person is probably taking advantage of an implied grace period. You would see this reflected on their payment ledger and know that it isn't cause for worry.

On the other hand, if a customer has traditionally been prompt with payments and is suddenly overdue, you have a problem. Problems with overdue accounts seldom go away by themselves. The further behind you let a customer get, the greater the risk that you will never collect.

If a bill isn't paid when it's due, it's costing you money. Even levying a 1 percent surcharge doesn't begin to compensate for the worker hours and cost you face when trying to collect. Adding a service charge can serve as a warning to the slow payer. It lets the customer know you aren't going to allow your business to be treated in this manner. If the customer continues to do so, they're going to have to pay more. So the service charge may not improve your profit situation but it will help prod the slow-paying customer.

Before proceeding with firm collection procedures, you owe it to your customer to determine why he or she is slow to pay. The customer could be confused, negligent, delinquent for reasons beyond the person's control, seasonally delinquent, chronically slow, or simply unable to pay. Each situation must be dealt with differently.

Confused customers have lost the invoices, are unclear about the terms, or do not want to pay because the balance is too small. This type of delinquent account will pay once these confusions are cleared up. These accounts should be sent a form note that is pleasant and to the point.

A negligent customer has the money and the intention to pay, but needs reminding that the bill is past due. Companies often instruct their employees not to process bills until "past due" notices are sent. To speed up payment of these accounts, mail the past due notices early. You must keep on top of negligent accounts because they can quickly become delinquent and cost you money.

Not-at-fault delinquent customers have faced some sort of disaster—fire, flood, earthquake, loss of key employee(s), and so on. If this is the situation, we recommend that you don't press for payment; let such customers know that you will carry the account for a reasonable time until they are back on their feet.

Seasonally delinquent accounts will fall behind during the slow seasons. When the income of these customers is reduced, they still have fixed expenses to meet, and you must make allowances for this. Check to see if other suppliers are getting paid. If they are, proceed with your collections.

THE COLLECTION PROCESS

The collection process is a step-by-step procedure that starts with friendly reminders, then firm requests, then demands for payment, and finally threats of legal action. Each step has proven techniques that will pay off. The important thing to remember is to organize your approach, then follow through.

The most effective pattern is to begin with written reminders, followed by collection letters, followed by phone calls. Most operators prepare and print a series of collection form letters that are mailed regularly, generally 10 days apart. As an entrepreneur, you have many jobs to do each day. If you run your business by yourself, your first reaction probably is, "I can't take time out to write collection letters. I don't even have a secretary." That's a valid problem, but collection letters can be effective in a planned form.

The first step in your letter campaign is to send another copy of the bill along with a handwritten note on the bill saying, "In case you forgot," or "past due." This reminds the customer without questioning the person's creditworthiness. It gives the customer the benefit of the doubt. The tone of the letters gradually moves from friendly persuasion to firm demands.

Personalized Letters

With accounts that are three months old, you will have to adopt a slightly tougher policy. This is an area where form letters aren't as effective as personalized letters. Seasoned veterans use a number of standard techniques to elicit responses:

- First and most important, be brief. Letters that appear long and complicated go to the bottom of the stack, especially if the recipient is loaded with work. Think how you act when you get your morning mail. If a letter looks as if it's going to take a while to study, it will be set aside.
- Make sure the letter is clear. When your reader can't grasp right away what your letter is about, he or she will ignore it. We're not suggesting that you start off with, "Pay up or we'll break your knees," but you should get to the topic at hand quickly.
- Keep it brief, keep it clear, and finally, keep it accurate. Nothing destroys the effectiveness of a collection appeal faster than being wrong. The letter must have the correct invoice (or statement) number, date, and amount. It should also accurately reflect the status of the account on the date it was written.

Using the Phone

With the cost of business letters spiraling, many collection pros are turning to the telephone. If you decide to do this, first make sure you review the situation thoroughly before calling. You want to have all the facts and figures at hand. When you call speak in a warm, cordial, yet firm voice. Finally, make sure that you listen. Nothing makes phone techniques fail more quickly than a caller who is not listening.

Following is a list of excuses commonly used by debtors along with suggestions on how to react to each excuse, which may or may not be applicable to a particular account.

1. **"I paid the bill."** Ask the debtor to send you a copy of the canceled check, money order receipt, or any other receipt that can prove payment.
2. **"I never got a bill."** Ask the debtor to tell you their residence address to verify the one on your records.
3. **"Business is slow right now."** Ask the debtor the place of employment and type of business. If self-employed, ask the name of the person's company. Also find out when business is expected to pick up.
4. **"I sent it yesterday."** Find out who mailed the payment, the time of day it was mailed, and where it was mailed. Find out if it was a personal check or money order. If it was a money order, ask where it was purchased and the receipt number.
5. **"The insurance company was supposed to pay for this."** Ask the debtor the name of the insurance company. Also find out if the debtor had a group

or individual policy. If it was a group policy, get the name of the employer and the name of the insured employee, which may be different from that of the patient. In addition, you may need to know the name of the insurance agency where the insurance was purchased. Further, ask the debtor for the policy number and any other identifying or claim number. Investigate why the insurance company did not pay.

6. **"I am out of work."** Ask for the last place of employment and how long the debtor has been unemployed. Find out the type of employment and if the debtor expects to be working soon. Have the debtor call you at least once every two weeks to advise you of any change in his or her financial situation.

7. **"I did not get what I ordered."** Ask the debtor what was wrong with the merchandise. If the debtor claims that the right number of items was not received, that it was a different product, or that part of the merchandise was damaged, ask for payment for the part of the order that was correct and then try to reach an agreement on the disputed portion.

8. **"My signature was forged."** Ask the debtor to come to your office and write a statement proclaiming that the signature was forged and have the person sign it. Be sure the debtor brings identification with a signature on it. If he/she lives too far to travel to your office, ask for a letter stating that the signature was forged and be sure it is signed. If the debtor has a driver's license, ask for a photostat copy showing the signature.

9. **"The balance is wrong."** If you cannot resolve the dispute at the time, advise the debtor that you will send an itemized statement and a copy of the payment record. Check the debtor's mailing address to be sure it is correct. Send the statement by registered mail, return receipt requested.

If a customer still hasn't paid after collection letters and phone calls, then you should turn the account over to a collection agency. Most agencies won't accept bills for amounts less than $50, so some operators wait until they have several overdue accounts before turning them over to a collection agency.

As soon as you start offering credit, familiarize yourself with the reputable collection agencies in your community. In 1991, according to the U.S. Census Bureau, there were 6,580 "credit reporting and collection establishments" in the country.[3] Credit agencies differ in operations and levels of success, so test several of them before you commit yourself. You may want to find out if they are affiliated with a reputable national organization, such as the American Collectors' Association (ACA), or the American Commercial Collectors Association (ACCA).

Small Claims Court

An alternative to the collection agencies is to file a complaint with a small claims court. This is a simple procedure that forces a hearing between you and

[3] U.S. Census Bureau, *County Business Patterns, Cendata* (Online Service) (June, 1991).

Effective Phone Collection Technique

The following sample phone call illustrates the elements of good collection techniques:

You: *Hello, may I speak to Mr. Joe Jones, please?*
Debtor: *This is Joe Jones.*
You: *Mr. Jones, this is Mr. Smith of the XYZ Company. I am calling about your bill. (Pause up to 8 seconds to allow the debtor to respond.)*
Debtor: *I won't be able to pay anything until the 20th.*
You: *Do you still work at Acme?*
Debtor: *Yes. (If the answer is yes, confirm the street location and phone number. If the answer is no, find out the new place of employment.)*
You: *So you will pay on the 20th?*
Debtor: *That's right.*
You: *How much will you be paying?*
Debtor: *(The customer will give an amount.)*
You: *Then will you bring in a check on the 20th in the amount of $_____?*
Debtor: *I can't do that. I have to work.*
You: *Then will you mail it today?*
Debtor: *Yes.*
You: *Do you have our address?*
Debtor: *Somewhere.*
You: *Let me give it to you again. (Repeat address and have him repeat it back to you.) I will expect a check from you on the 20th in the amount of $_____. If you mail that today, I should receive it by the day after tomorrow. If I don't receive your check, I will call you back.*
Debtor: *You'll get the check.*
You: *Thank you very much.*

---

your debtor and generally results in a judgment in the creditor's favor. In many states, debts up to $1,000 can be handled in this manner, but policies differ from state to state. Check with appropriate local government agencies to determine the best way to handle any small claims accounts.

Laws on Collection

Like most consumer-oriented legislation, laws on credit and collection tend to be complex in their wording. The following is a brief summary of the main points of some of the most important laws:

- **The Robinson-Patman Act (1936).** This act makes it illegal to discriminate among customers on the basis of price if it would injure competition among sellers. This means that cash discounts for customers who pay promptly are legal. Discounts for customers who buy from another company are illegal.

- **The Assignment of Claims Act (1940).** This act permits the assignment of proceeds from contracts to institutions solely involved in banking or financial activity. In effect, this allows businesses to replenish their supply of operating capital immediately on shipment of a product and opens the door to receivables financing.
- **Uniform Commercial Code (1972; frequent revisions).** This provides the basis for all commercial transactions. Of particular interest to you as an entrepreneur are Articles 4 (bank deposits and collections) and 9 (secured transactions, sales of accounts, and chattel paper).
- **The Consumer Credit Protection Act (1968).** This is popularly known as the Truth in Lending Act and protects consumers from unfair credit practices. Although it currently applies only to consumers, it is predicted that it will carry over to commercial dealings as well.
- **The Fair Credit Billing Act (1975).** This act regulates the methods and procedures firms may use in billing credit card accounts and other revolving accounts with a finance charge.
- **The Fair Credit Reporting Act (1970; added to the Truth in Lending Act).** This regulates consumer credit information in regard to the confidentiality, accuracy, relevancy, and proper utilization of customers' credit histories.
- **The Equal Credit Opportunity Act (1977).** This act prohibits discrimination on the basis of sex or marital status in granting credit.
- **The Fair Debt Collection Act (1978).** This eliminates abusive collection practices by debt collectors.
- **Postal regulations.** This legislation requires that no words, illustrations, or codes identifying an addressee as delinquent in payment of a debt may appear on the outside of an envelope or postcard where they might be seen by a third party.
- **Internal Revenue Service.** The IRS governs writing off bad debts.
- **State regulations.** Each state has its own laws regarding collection processes. Discuss these with legal counsel before setting up your long-range collection program.

Organization

All collection procedures are, by nature, after the fact. If you have been thorough in your credit checking and have kept on top of each account, then your collection problems should be minimal.

Millions of dollars are lost each year by creditors. A portion of this money could have been recovered with the use of thorough, well-managed collection systems. Granting credit to your customers is a proven way of building sales volume. Following collection procedures like those included in this book are proven ways of making sure that sales volume is profitable. A good credit and collections policy will remove many of your headaches.

RESOURCES

Associations

CWI: Credit Professionals, 50 Crestwood Executive Center, Suite 204, St. Louis, MO 63126, 314-842-6280

International Credit Association, 243 North Lindbergh Boulevard, St. Louis, MO 63141, 314-991-3030

Magazines

Barron's National Business & Financial Weekly, 200 Liberty Street, New York, NY 10281, 212-416-2700

The Business Owner, Thomas Publishing, Inc., 383 South Broadway, Hicksville, NY 11801, 516-681-2111

Business Review, One Kwik Kopy Lane, P.O. Box 777, Cypress, TX 77429-0777, 713-373-3535

D&B Reports, 299 Park Avenue, New York, NY 10171, 212-593-6723

Entrepreneurial Manager, 180 Varick Street, New York, NY 10014-4692, 212-633-0060

Entrepreneurial Manager's Newsletter, 180 Varick Street, Penthouse Suite, New York, NY 10014-4692, 212-633-0060

In Business, 419 State Avenue, Emmaus, PA 18049-3717, 215-967-4135

Journal of Small Business Management, West Virginia University, College of Business Economics, Bureau of Business Research, P.O. Box 6025, Morgantown, WV 26506-6025, 304-293-5837

Nation's Business, 1615 H Street NW, Washington, DC 20062, 202-463-5650

Credit Organizations

Dun & Bradstreet Inc. Credit Services, 1 Diamond Hill Road, Murray Hill, NJ 07974-0000, 908-665-5000

TRW Business Credit Services, 505 City Parkway West, Suite 150, Orange, CA 92668, 714-385-2102

21

Bootstrap Financing

W hen you're thinking about how to raise money, one of the first things you should consider is bootstrap financing—using your own money to get your business off the ground. This is one of the most popular forms of internal funding because it relies on your ability to utilize all your company resources to free additional capital to launch a venture, meet operational needs or expand your business.

A long time ago, bootstrap financing was the major way new businesses got started. This was before the government was guaranteeing loans. But the SBA is now perceived by some as "the lender of last resort," and Small Business Investment Companies (SBICs), which are partially funded by the SBA, have become more conservative in their lending policies. As a result, many entrepreneurs have had to become acquainted once again with the concept of bootstrap financing.

Bootstrap financing is probably one of the best and most inexpensive routes an entrepreneur can explore when raising capital. It enables you to utilize unused opportunities within your own company by simply managing your finances wisely. Bootstrap financing is a way to pull yourself up without the help of others. You are the one financing your growth by your current earnings and assets.

There are a number of advantages to using the various methods of bootstrap financing outlined in this chapter:

- Your business will be worth more because less money has been borrowed, and therefore, no equity positions had to be relinquished.
- You won't have to pay the high interest on borrowed money.
- Coming from a stronger position (with less debt on hand), you look more desirable to external lenders and investors when the time does come to raise money through these routes.
- You can be creative in finding ways to raise profits, without having to look to external sources.

TRADE CREDIT—USES AND COSTS

The first source of business money we'll discuss is *trade credit.* Normally, suppliers will extend regular customers credit for 30, 60 or 90 days, without charging interest. For example, suppose that a supplier ships something to you, and that bill is due in 30 days but you have trade credit or terms. Your terms might be net 60 days from the receipt of goods, in which case you would have 30 extra days to pay for the items.

However, when you're first starting your business, suppliers are not going to give you trade credit. They're going to want to make every order COD (cash/check on delivery) until you've established that you can pay your bills on time. While this is a fairly normal practice, to raise money during the start-up period you're going to have to try and negotiate a trade credit basis with suppliers. One of the things that will help you in these negotiations is a properly prepared financial plan.

When you visit your supplier to set up your order during your start-up period, ask to speak directly to the owner of the business if it's a small company. If it's a larger business, ask to speak to the chief financial officer or any other person who approves credit. Introduce yourself. Show the officer the financial plan that you have prepared. Tell the owner or financial officer about your business, and explain that you need to get your first orders on credit to launch your venture.

The owner or financial officer may give you half the order on credit, with balance due on delivery. Of course, the trick here is to get your goods shipped to you and sell them before you have to pay for them yourself. You could borrow the money to pay for your inventory, but you would have to pay interest on that money. So trade credit is one of the most important ways to reduce the amount of working capital you need. This is especially true in retail operations.

Despite the urge to use trade credit on a continual and consistent basis, you should consider it as a source of capital to meet relatively small, short-term needs. Do not look at it as a long-term solution. By doing so, you may find your business heavily committed to those suppliers who accept extended credit terms. As a result, the business may no longer have ready access to other, more competitive suppliers who might offer lower prices, a superior product, or more reliable deliveries.

Depending on the terms available from your suppliers, the cost of trade credit can be quite high. For example, assume you make a purchase from a supplier who decides to extend credit to you. The terms the supplier offers you are 2 percent cash discount within 10 days and a net date of 30 days. Essentially, the supplier is saying that if you pay within 10 days, the purchase price will be discounted by 2 percent. On the other hand, by forfeiting the 2 percent discount, you are able to use your money for 20 more days and it will only cost you that 2 percent discount. On an annualized basis, this is actually costing you 36 percent of the total cost of the items you are purchasing from this supplier (360 days/20 days = 18 times per year without discount; 18 times × 2% discount = 36% discount missed).[1]

Cash discounts aren't the only factor you have to consider in the equation. There are also late payment or delinquency penalties should you extend payment beyond the agreed-on terms. These can usually run between 1 and 2 percent on a monthly basis. If you miss your net payment date for an entire year, that can cost you as much as 12 to 24 percent in penalty interest.

Effective use of trade credit requires intelligent planning to avoid unnecessary costs through forfeiture of cash discounts or the incidence of delinquency penalties. But every business should take full advantage of trade credit that is available without additional cost to reduce its need for capital from other sources.

FACTORING

In this financing method, you actually sell your accounts receivable to a buyer such as a commercial finance company to raise capital. A "factor" buys accounts receivable, usually at a discount rate that ranges between 1 and 15 percent. The factor then becomes the creditor and assumes the task of collecting the receivables as well as doing what would have been your paperwork chores. Factoring can be performed on a non-notification basis. That means your customers are not aware that their accounts have been sold.

There are pros and cons to factoring. Many financial experts believe that you should not attempt factoring unless you cannot acquire the necessary capital from other sources. Our opinion is that factoring can be a useful financial tool. If you take into account the costs associated with maintaining accounts receivable such as bookkeeping, collections, and credit verifications, and compare those expenses against the discount rate you'll be selling them for, sometimes this financing method can even be profitable. After all, if the factor takes on only part of the paperwork chores involved in maintaining accounts receivable, your internal costs still will shrink significantly. Most of the time, the factor will assume full responsibility for the paperwork.

In addition to reduced internal costs, factoring also frees up money tied to receivables, especially for businesses that sell to other businesses or to government, where there are often long delays in payment. This money can then be used to generate profit through other avenues of the company. Factoring can be a helpful tool for raising money and maintaining cash flow.

According to Mace Edwards, publisher of the *Edwards Directory of American Factors* in Newton, Massachusetts, (as quoted in a recent *Wall Street Journal* article), factoring firms financed at least $62 billion in receivables in

---

[1] U.S. Small Business Administration Office of Management Assistance, "Understanding Money Sources," Self-Instructional Booklet (Washington, DC: U.S. Government Printing Office).

1993, up from $46 billion in 1987. He adds that much of that capital went to small business.[2]

CUSTOMERS

Customers are another source of bootstrap financing, and there are several ways to take advantage of these valuable assets. One way to use your customers to obtain financing is by having them write you a letter of credit. For example, suppose you're starting a business manufacturing industrial bags. A large corporation has placed an order with your firm to supply them with a steady flow of cloth bags. The major supplier that you will source the material through to make the bags is located in India. In this scenario, you obtain a letter of credit from your customer when the order is placed, and the material for the bags is purchased using the letter of credit as security. You don't have to put up a penny to buy the material.

In your personal financial dealings, you may have had a builder, or someone else working for you, ask for money up front in order to buy the materials for your job. That contractor used your money to get started on the job. You were actually helping to finance that business. This is how customers can act as a form of financing.

REAL ESTATE

Real estate is another bootstrap financing source that can be accessed in several ways. The first is to simply lease your facility. This reduces start-up costs because the expense to get into a lease is not usually as much as the outright purchase of the property. Also, when negotiating a lease, you may be able to arrange payments that correspond to seasonal peaks or growth patterns.

If you enter into a business where you will need to buy the facility, your initial cost will increase but the building's cost can be financed over a long-term period of 15 to 30 years. Again, the loan on the facility can be structured to make optimum use of your planned growth or seasonal peaks. For instance, you can arrange a graduated payment mortgage that initially has very small monthly payments with the cost increasing over the lifetime of the loan. The logic here is that the low monthly payments will give your business time to grow. Eventually, you can refinance the loan when time and interest rates permit.

Another advantage that the outright purchase of the facility will provide you is continuing appreciation of the property (hopefully) and the decrease of your

[2] Udayan Gupta, "Factoring and Venture Firms' Roles in Financing Growth," *The Wall Street Journal* (June 1994).

principal amount to create a valuable asset called *equity*. You can borrow against this equity. Lenders will often loan up to 75 or 80 percent of the property's value once it has been appraised.

This applies to any private real estate you might own. If you have a desire to go into business and you need a certain amount of money that you can't get any other way, you may have to borrow against the equity in your home or sell it altogether. If your home is appreciating in value, real estate is a good venue to choose. If it is depreciating, it won't be quite as attractive.

EQUIPMENT SUPPLIERS

If you spend a lot of money on equipment, you may find yourself without enough working capital to keep your business going in its first months. Instead of paying out cash for your equipment, the manufacturers of the equipment can loan you the money; that is, they sell the equipment over a period of time. In this way, equipment suppliers are a source of bootstrap financing.

Two types of credit contracts are commonly used to finance equipment purchases:

1. **The conditional sales contract.** With this contract, the purchaser does not receive title to the equipment until it is fully paid for.
2. **The chattel-mortgage contract.** In this contract, the equipment becomes the property of the purchaser on delivery, but the seller holds a mortgage claim against it until the amount specified in the contract is paid.

By using the equipment suppliers to finance the purchase of your equipment, you reduce the amount of money that you need up front. There are also lenders who finance 60 to 80 percent of the equipment value. And then, of course, the balance represents the borrower's down payment on a new purchase. The loan is repaid in monthly installments, usually over one to five years, or the usable life of that piece of equipment.

LEASING

Another thing for you to consider is leasing instead of purchasing. Generally, if you are able to shop around and get the best kind of leasing arrangement when you're starting up a new business, it's much better to lease. It's better, for example, to lease a photocopier, rather than pay $3,000 for it; or to lease your automobile or van instead of paying out $8,000 or more.

Leasing has been around for a long time. It is common for businesses to lease real property for a retail facility, office space, production plant, farmlands, and so on. Although many people do not consider leasing a true form of financing, it has the following characteristics:

- The lessor owns the property for a specific term at a predetermined cost paid in installments.
- The lessor is responsible for all costs associated with the ownership of the leased property such as property taxes, insurance, and so on.
- As the owner, the lessor either benefits from the capital appreciation of the property or loses from any depreciation in value.
- Finally, the lessor enjoys all the tax benefits of owning the property such as depreciation, interest, and property taxes.

Because of the question of cash flow, it is usually better from a dollars-and-cents standpoint to lease rather than buy. There are many ways that a lease can be modified to increase your cash position. These modifications include:

- A down payment lower than 10 percent or no down payment at all.
- Maintenance costs that are built into the lease package, thereby reducing your working capital expenses. If you needed employees or a repair person to do maintenance on purchased equipment, it would cost you more than if you had leased.
- Assignment of all executory costs such as insurance and property taxes. While this will initially increase your cash flow, from a tax standpoint it will reduce the amount of taxable income the business generates.
- Extension of the lease term to cover the entire economic life of the property (or use of the property can be guaranteed for as long as you wish to use it).
- A purchase option that can be added to the lease allowing you to buy the property after the lease period has ended. A fixed purchase price can also be added to the option provision.
- Lease payments that can be structured to accommodate seasonal variations in the business or tied to indexes that track interest to create an adjustable lease.

MANAGING CASH FLOW

Bootstrap financing really begins and ends with your attention to good financial management so that the company can generate the funds it needs. Be careful and aware when you buy. Make sure that when you go top dollar you can justify the expense, and that you aren't in an overly expensive office or location, unless it's really going to pay off in dollars and cents. If a new desk is not necessary for your business front, and you have an opportunity to buy a used desk, then by all means do so. Such actions reflect the meaning of the statement that bootstrap financing requires you to buy carefully at the beginning to reduce the amount of money that you need.

Also, keep a close watch on operating expenses. If interest rates are high, it won't take too many unpaid bills to wipe out your profits. At an 11 to 12 percent interest rate, carrying an unpaid $10,000 is costing you as much as $120 per month. Tight, competitive profit margins mean more money can be lost trying to collect bills than was originally made on the production line.

You can get profitable cash flow for your firm by starting each production order off on the right track. Implement a four-step payment plan. Negotiate terms and conditions that require payments when *you* want them. Profitable cash flow will happen when you establish and execute timely cash flow concepts into every order.

Many firms totally overlook the following critical factors:

1. Identifying a billable event—other than delivery.
2. Setting payment due dates.
3. Establishing penalties for late payment.
4. Determining place of payment.

The result: great sales but no cash.

Be prepared to consider these steps before accepting an order. You need a negotiation plan. It should be prepared and followed with the same care you use to document your production process. Time invested in obtaining favorable cash flow terms and conditions can mean added profit and higher returns on your investment. Never forget the fact that your cash flow will never get any better than the terms defined in the negotiation process. Take steps to get the best available payment terms.

Identifying a Billable Event

Try to bill before delivery. There are three ways you can issue an invoice before you ship the final product:

1. **Milestone billing.** This is fairly common where heavy up-front investment is required for a new product or job. In this case, the completion of a certain event or milestone (placing a subcontract, passing a critical design review, completing a set of test/equipment/tools, or receiving a large amount of material), is given a billing value. This authorizes you to issue an invoice when the event occurs—often long before completion of a deliverable item.
2. **Progress billings.** This is fairly common in the defense and aerospace industries. Progress billings allow you to invoice costs, as incurred, on a routine bimonthly or monthly basis. This way your customer finances your inventory. The advantage is that while a job is in process your investment is reduced. In effect, you recover your costs before you deliver anything. (In this case, your customer has a lien against the inventory.)
3. **Subline item billings.** This is fairly common in the construction industry. This billing term recognizes the times when an entire item cannot be completed, but main elements of it are. Examples of subitems are foundation, plumbing, frame, and roof. Each could be subitems of an apartment

complex. The advantage here is that as each major subelement is completed, an invoice can be issued, thus speeding cash flow.

Setting Payment Dates

Define *when* you will be paid by setting payment dates. Why take an order if you don't make an effort to assure payment? Bear in mind that extending credit to customers has a real cost to you, and be sure your contract (and price) provides for that cost. Sales to poor credit risks should be COD. Discounts can be offered but tied to the shipment date, customer acceptance date, your invoice date, or a calendar date. The point is, once the payment date is established in your contract (purchase order, etc.) you have a legally enforceable document.

Establishing Late-Payment Penalties

Enforcing penalties for late payment will help get timely payment. What happens today if a customer pays you 30 days late? Do you collect interest, or are you just happy to get paid? If your terms and conditions require a penalty for late payment, you improve your chances for timely payment—and based on contract terms, you have legal remedies available to use to collect interest from delinquent accounts.

Determining Place of Payment

The place of payment can make a two- to five-day difference in cash receipts. Firms that sell throughout the United States use geographically dispersed deposit lockboxes. Each order requires payment to the lockbox closest to the customer. Other firms require payment directly to their bank. This makes the money available for use faster. These firms let their accounting department figure out who paid what after the deposit—rather than delaying it while they do their thing.

You can negotiate profitable cash flow to save collection time and effort. You must place extra emphasis on payment provisions if you want to keep the profit you earned on the production line *as your own.*

RESOURCES

Associations

National Commercial Finance Association, 225 West 34th Street, Suite 1815, New York, NY 10122, 212-594-3490

National Corporate Cash Management Association, 7315 Wisconsin Avenue, Suite 1250 West, Bethesda, MD 20814, 301-907-2862

Magazines

Business Credit, 8815 Centre Park Drive, Suite 200, Columbia, MD 21045, 301-740-5560

Corporate Cashflow, 6151 Powers Ferry Road NW, Atlanta, GA 30339-2941, 404-955-2500

Corporate Finance, 1328 Broadway, New York, NY 10001, 212-594-5030

Credit, 919 18th Street NW, Suite 300, Washington, DC 20006, 202-296-5544

Journal of Cash Management, 7315 Wisconsin Avenue, Suite 1250 West, Bethesda, MD 20814, 301-907-2862

22

Legal Matters

Although the law of the United States is based on precedent (*stare decisis*), different locales and cultures demand modification. The information provided in this chapter is the law generally across the United States. Even with the advent of CD-ROM, the amount of volumes required to cover each state's idiosyncrasies is beyond the scope of this chapter. So, please consult with your local lawyer or government agency to determine if you happen to be in one of those jurisdictions with an odd twist to the law.

Use the material provided here to help you identify what you need to be concerned about, and to help you know what's important enough to cost you large sums of money if you don't pay attention to it. The first six sections of the chapter discuss laws that assist you in bringing money into your company (*money coming in*); the remaining sections consider laws that you must heed to avoid paying out inordinate amounts of money with no hope of a return (*money going out*).

The following sections do not cover information that you could pick up from any book on common legal subjects at your local library. They instead cover specific issues that seem to affect many business owners.

RAISING MONEY

Money . . . Money . . . Money . . . who's got the money, and how do you get some to run your business? There are two ways to raise money for your business: (1) debt capital and (2) equity capital. Debt capital is money that you must pay back no matter how well or how badly your company is doing (e.g., loans). Equity capital is money that is returned based on the success of your company (e.g., stock or partnership interests). An investor receives a portion of your

This chapter was written by Barbara Frantz.

company ownership for the money he or she puts in, and then takes the risk that there will be a high rate of return on the investment.

Debt Capital

Although banks traditionally provide loans to businesses, other groups have jumped on the bandwagon. Credit card companies offer lines of credit. The Small Business Administration (SBA) state commerce and trade agencies have joined forces to provide miniloans of about $25,000 for working capital, and local areas in which there may have been a disaster or where there is a commitment to economic recovery will provide loans to certain classes of business owners. A loan is either secured or unsecured. If it is secured, you will be required to sign a security agreement in addition to your promissory note. The security agreement typically requires you to put up some form of collateral (tangible things you own that the lender could sell to get some of the money back if you don't pay). If you sell the specified collateral, the agreement usually allows the Lender to take whatever new collateral you may have received for the old. In other words, if you put up a car as collateral, then sell the car for another car of more value, the new car becomes the collateral even if it is worth more. However, you must receive credit for the difference if the lender seizes your new car and sells it in order to be paid.

Equity Capital

Since banks don't take kindly to other loans when you ask for money from them, many start-up companies raise their first round of capital from investors. Typically, this is accomplished through selling shares in a corporation or units in either a general or limited partnership. Because of misuse of these vehicles for raising capital, the government stepped in with some regulations. On a federal level, the agency is the Securities and Exchange Commission (SEC). Broadly speaking, securities includes both shares of stock and partnership interests. On a state level, the rules are called "Blue Sky" laws and are enforced by the Attorney General's office.

The highest form of regulation—registering your securities—involves attorneys, accountants, underwriters, and hundreds of thousands of dollars. In this situation, you're most likely going public. The only motive to justify the cost is the need to raise millions of dollars. You are preparing a "prospectus" that in essence is a business plan that meets the SEC requirements and a "subscription" that tells the investor the details of the investment.

Very few businesses go public in their first five years of operation. The government recognized how onerous these rules and regulations would be, so it carved out a series of exemptions depending on how much money is to be raised in a certain time frame, how many investors are involved, how sophisticated the investors are, and how closely related to the business owner the investors are. The process becomes very simple if investors all reside in one state.

The most common exemption is the Rule 504 exemption through the federal government. Most state laws are compatible with the requirements of this rule so it saves time and money. It permits you to raise $1 million in a 12-month period by filing a few simple forms. Your local SBA can help you through the process.

If you are offering equity to partners who will share in the management of your company, and you are all putting in your money at the same time, the federal government won't bother with you, but you will still have to file for an exemption at the state level. Most incorporation kits include a one-page form that is most concerned about how much money is coming in cash, how much in services, and how much from outside the state. The fee you pay is typically based on how much money is being put in.

Some states have adopted "ULOE," the Uniform Limited Offering Exemption. This law permits a form of mini-registration for raising up unlimited amounts of money to a limited number of investors on forms created by the state government. The forms are designed to simplify the process so that you do not require as many attorneys or as much money. The success of this program has still not been proven. The number of successful candidates is small. Most companies' offerings do not meet the criteria to fit into this program. An excellent book dealing with this program is James Daley's *Scoring Millions* (see Resources).

MARKETING LAWS

Having a great product or service is not enough to assure success in a competitive economy. People must know how to get your product or service, which is the business of marketing. The laws related to marketing your product cover many areas such as contracts, patents, trademarks, copyrights, packaging and labeling laws, product liability, and various consumer laws designed to protect customers who order by mail. This chapter covers some of these areas separately. Successful business owners are at least aware of the issues, so that if a dilemma arises, they know how serious the problem is and whether they need to get help. The following sections describe the tip of the iceberg on the laws relating to marketing your products or service. A comprehensive treatment is covered in Robert Posch's book *The Complete Guide to Marketing and the Law* (see Resources).

Patents, Trademarks, and Copyrights

Patents
A patent is a government grant of the exclusive right to make, use, or sell an invention. Its value is proportional to its commercial importance. A U.S. patent is good for 17 years. A U.S. design patent is good for up to 14 years on new, original, ornamental shapes, or configurations.

Generally speaking, the following are excluded from patenting: printed matter; naturally occurring substances; methods of doing business; ideas; scientific principles; and mental processes. You must file for patent protection before exposing your product to the marketplace or you run the risk of someone taking it apart and copying it.

Some examples of what's patentable: certain types of computer software; fabric designs; furniture designs; a drink holder with a unique configuration to prevent spillage, or an automated machine that analyzes blood components.

Patents are the best form of protection for your product because even if someone can prove that he or she invented it first, your application will take precedent. The Patent and Trademark Office (PTO) is located in Washington, DC. You can obtain a basic search for prior patents for a similar invention through computer or through major cities. However, if not extensive, these searches can lead to false results. If a large sum of money is at stake, it is best to request a patent attorney who is trained in your area of invention to conduct a search through the patent office.

Trademarks

Trademarks and service marks are a shorthand designation of the origin or source of a product or service. Trademarks are used for products; service marks are used for services. Trademarks and service marks are applied to a manufacturer's or a seller's products and services to distinguish these goods and services in the marketplace. A trademark or service mark prevents another person from offering a similar generic product or service confusingly similar to yours. For example, a "Sany" TV would be prohibited because it sounds and looks too much like a "Sony ™" TV. If you do not register your trademark, you may be prohibited from using it by someone who has.

While only federal government statutes can provide patent and copyright protection, trademarks can either be federal or state by state; federal statutes supersede those of states. Tradenames are a company's name and are not registered unless they are part of a mark but may nonetheless be protected.

Trademarks when representative of quality or some feature of the products sold are an invaluable tool to market your product.

Copyrights

A copyright does nothing more than protect against unauthorized duplication of certain classes of original works of art including writings, toys, art, films, photography, music, and computer software. The federal copyright law does not protect individual words and may or may not protect character configurations, depending on the focus. For example, the courts held that the Disney character, Mickey Mouse, being the focus of many pieces, was protected. Also the courts looked at Mickey Mouse as a work of art rather than a functional item that is not protected. In contrast, exotically designed light fixtures have not obtained copyright protection, because it is too difficult to separate the aesthetic element from the functional element.

You should place the © with the year and "All rights reserved" on your materials to provide your company with minimal protection. Registering your copyright will be necessary if you want to file suit for infringement.

Consumer Laws

Various states adopt laws in response to customers who have been taken advantage of by misleading advertising, bogus products or services, and other rip-offs. Unfortunately, these laws then add to the cost of sales for honest and ethical business owners. The following sections describe the most common areas in which business owners are caught off guard when they assume that the logical way to do business is the legal way of doing business.

Truth in Advertising

Especially in retail businesses, competitive advertising can be cutthroat. Often you will see companies refer specifically to their competitor's product in pointing out deficiencies, do a price comparison, or make their own grandiose claims about the superiority of their products.

Advertising is regulated primarily by the Federal Trade Commission (FTC), and by various state laws too numerous to mention. Commonly, complaints against your company for false or misleading advertising will originate from a disgruntled customer or from your competitor. The agencies that regulate this area most often are responding to complaints in determining what company they go after. They look to see if you can substantiate your claims in an objective way (lab tests, etc.). They will actually review your lab results for adequacy in both scientific principles and consistency of implementation of test studies. If you make a true statement that is misleading within the context of the entire ad, you have violated the law. If you claim that your price for an item is less than that of your competitor, but your competitor has one store in a remote location with a lower price, you have violated the law. If "sales puffery" is presented as factual information, you have violated the law.

Direct Mail

In addition to general advertising rules, business owners who send products through the mail must also comply with the direct marketing laws. The U.S. Postal Service controls this area with the use of a criminal mail fraud statute. Anything that travels through the mail is subject to this review. The Postal Service can issue a stop order to terminate the distribution of your product through the mail.

The Mail Order Rule states that it is a deceptive act (violation of FTC rules) to solicit an order for merchandise unless you believe that you can ship the merchandise after receipt of a properly completed order within the time period that you advertise or, if none is stated, then 30 days. Some states are more stringent and require that you be able to deliver within the time periods specified.

You must notify the buyer within 15 days that their order has not been properly completed. Keep records of your correspondence with your customers.

If you unavoidably have to delay a shipment, you must send a postage-paid return notice offering the buyer the option of either terminating the order or extending the time for shipment to a revised shipping date. If they cancel, you must send them a prompt refund (within seven business days).

Product Liability

Product liability is a special area of the law that implies that just the mere manufacturing and distribution of your product gives you certain responsibilities to the consumer who buys the product. Marketing is crucial in minimizing the risk that you could experience. For example, an elaborate customer-oriented recall program on parts that you manufacture may save you thousands in government intervention and consumer lawsuits. The education of your distributors, and the instruction manuals that you generate, can eliminate risk. Your warranties can cause you to be liable for a method of using your product that you never anticipated. You may be required to prepare hazard warnings. You will be held responsible if you had a duty to warn, did not do so, and as a result your customer became injured. You may be responsible based on the market share of your product in the case of mass distribution such as in pharmaceuticals. The key is to have product teams work together at the very start of a concept to develop proper documentation that is easily readable by your target market and that is updated regularly.

CONTRACTS

Relationships between businesses and consumers are controlled by contracts, whether oral or written. Although no contract can be enforceable against a truly dishonest person, contracts serve to clarify what each party expects, and what each party is willing to give in exchange for the expected results. I often tell clients that a hotly negotiated contract in which the other side feels taken advantage of will result in fewer lawsuits than a haphazard agreement in which the other side has a sense of being conned. Many books and articles exist on standard contract law, so it will not be dealt with here. A few topics that often lead to lawsuits or at the very minimum to a lot of confusion will be discussed.

Agency

"Agency" is the theory that people who work for you or represent you are you for purposes of the law. Another way this is expressed is *Respondeat Superior,* or the acts of the agent are the acts of the owner. For example, assume your secretary signs a one-year contract for a postal machine. It seems innocuous enough, less than $100 per month, and it saves the secretary from having to go to the post office all the time. Unfortunately, she did not check with your budget, and now you find you can't afford this luxury (in your eyes, not hers). You try to cancel the agreement, and you are informed that it is a one-year commitment. Do you have an out?

Agency theory says that if the secretary was in a position of apparent authority and had a history of signing other documents on your behalf, then you are responsible for her actions. However, if you are a corporation, and you have very clear written policies that only corporate officers can bind the company, then you have a case that the secretary was acting outside the scope of her authority, and you may get out of the contract. Another area in which agency comes into play is when one of your staff leaves work in the morning to pick up donuts for the employees and has an accident on the way back. The car she hit can sue your company in that she was acting in the scope of her employment so that her negligence is your negligence. At the same time, your company liability insurance, unless it has a specific exclusion, will cover the damage related to the lawsuit.

Warranties

Warranties are typically part of contracts because otherwise you can be held to another standard based on your industry. Warranties are express or implied. Express warranties are those in writing or directly given by you to your customer or client. Examples of express warranties are "Parts and labor warranted for 90 days on moving parts," or "This product is guaranteed free from defects in workmanship for 90 days." Implied warranties are not expressly stated but can be derived from advertisements and literature. Examples are "You'll never have to paint again if you use this product," or "Use this rust-free compound to save you time and money." The implication is that no rust will form on the item, and that you will never have to redo your project. From a business owner's point of view, it is important to make sure that the person writing your advertising or brochures doesn't inadvertently give a warranty that you can't pay for. Breaches of warranties usually mean that you have to give the cost of the product back or at least replace or repair it. This can be very costly.

You might also see in large print "NO OTHER WARRANTIES INCLUDING BUT NOT LIMITED TO WARRANTIES FOR MERCHANTABILITY OR FITNESS FOR AN INTENDED PURPOSE ARE MADE." This language is crucial when your product is being used with someone else's to solve a customer's need. For example, a printing company requires two major types of computer equipment to automate its printing of large jobs. Your sales representative says that your equipment is compatible with the other company's. But you don't really know if this is true. It turns out that it's not. The printing company lost several large jobs because your equipment was not compatible. You can be held liable for their losses because you didn't have the limiting language in your purchase contract, and your salesperson "gave a warranty of fitness for an intended purposes or particular use." The law also requires that these exclusions are of a certain size print. If you do not comply you can be held liable even though you had the language in your contract.

Purchase Orders

A great deal of confusion surrounds the exchange of company's purchase orders back and forth. This happens when a sales rep contacts a customer and strikes a deal. The sales rep typically hands the standard terms and conditions from the company to the customer. The customer then issues a purchase order that has its own standard terms and conditions on the back. The company then issues an invoice with the company's terms and conditions on the back. Many times, one or two clauses between the parties are at odds with each other. Whose terms rule? The theory of law affecting purchase orders is standard contract law. An offer that is accepted with "consideration" (money, usually) transferred is a contract. An offer can be met with a counteroffer. A counteroffer is not a contract until the counteroffer is accepted. The sales rep's standard terms and conditions are the offer. The purchase order with conflicting terms and conditions is the counteroffer. The invoice is the counter-counteroffer. So if the item is delivered, the customer can reject the delivery because no contract exists yet. A business owner resolves this problem in the initial terms and conditions stating that a contract does not exist until the owner's company has signified its acceptance of the contract by a signature on the initial billing. Additional language can state that terms and conditions of a customer's purchase order are superseded by the owner's terms and conditions if in conflict. Then customers who have paid can't come back later and say that their terms and conditions were to apply. Their payment is conduct signifying that they agreed to the owner's terms and conditions.

Uniform Commercial Code

You can imagine the amount of delay that would occur if businesspeople exchanging goods and services had to wait for fully executed contracts with all details specified. Commerce would slow to a stop. The legislature recognized this, as well as the difficulty in dealing with companies in another state with different state laws. They adopted a set of standardized laws among business owners who exchange goods to short-cut the need for detailed writing. It's called the "UCC" or "Uniform Commercial Code." It's divided into sections on sales, secured transactions, letters of credit, bulk transfers, warehouse receipts, bills of lading, investment securities, bank deposits, and collections. It is designed to fill in the gaps if two owners have not committed to something in writing. Article 2 on sales is most relevant to contracts. The following important issues are dealt with in detail in the code:

- What constitutes an offer?
- What constitutes acceptance?

- What happens when you allow the other side to modify its performance?
- How is risk allocated during shipment?
- What is "open price" term?
- What happens when partial shipments are defective?
- What is the warranty of good title?
- What is CIF, C&F, FOB, and FAS?
- What is the importance of a letter of credit?
- What is sale on approval; sale or return?
- When does title pass?
- What are different legal methods of payment; when can you withhold payment?
- When can the buyer reject goods?
- What are the sellers' and the buyers' remedies for breach?

Certain states have not adopted all these provisions, but most have adopted a number of them. If you take the time to read the code in your state, you will find that many of the items that you presently commit to writing while dealing with your suppliers may be unnecessary.

PURCHASING A BUSINESS OR FRANCHISE

Nothing is more exciting than purchasing a business. This is your dream come true, your chance to live the lifestyle you always dreamed about. Nothing can be more devastating than to have that purchase be so complicated, you're lost in a morass of laws, liability and insecurity.

If you purchase a sole proprietorship, you are purchasing assets. If you are purchasing a corporation, you could be purchasing either the assets or the stock. If you are purchasing a partnership interest, it is similar to purchasing stock (also known as shares or securities) in a company. You could also purchase the partnership's business, which is like purchasing assets. Along with the assets (the plus side of the business), you have the option of purchasing all, some, or none of the liabilities (the negative side of that business). When you purchase stock, you automatically receive a portion of the assets and liabilities.

The tax ramifications to purchasing stock in a business can be very complicated, so it is wise to seek an accountant who is familiar with your personal tax profile to help you decide whether to purchase assets and liabilities or stock.

The four primary objectives to keep in mind in purchasing any business are:

1. What are the true account receivables? That is, how many of them listed are really bad debts at this point?
2. For guaranteed business that supposedly represents ongoing relationships, how many are committed to writing? Ask the seller to send a letter to the customers verifying that the terms the seller has represented to you about the customers are what the customer understands to be true.

3. Leave about 15 to 25 percent of the purchase price to be paid six months to one year from the close of sale. The money should be deposited into an escrow account. The money should be used to pay unexpected liabilities that the seller may have forgotten about such as unpaid sales tax, payroll taxes, and amounts due on open-ended leases of equipment.
4. Pay for an asset tracker to do a basic search that includes a Dun & Bradstreet search, a TRW search, local courthouse information, the secretary of state, the Department of Motor Vehicles, and the county recorder. These can be very enlightening.

Some parties prepare a "letter of intent" that outlines the business parts of the transaction. In most states, letters of intent are not contracts and therefore are not worth much to the party who wants to enforce its terms. However, letters of intent make it easier for an attorney to draft a purchase and sale agreement.

The purchase and sale agreement, besides detailing legal release requirements with taxing authorities, and formulas for transitioning accounts receivables and payables, is usually accompanied by a series of exhibits that form the "due diligence" of the purchase. In other words, while the concepts have been expressed in the body of the agreement, the exhibits include actual sales contracts, employment contracts, inventory lists, customer lists, equipment lists, tax clearance certificates, and rental contracts. Typically the sales agreement is signed with a 30- to 60-day escrow. During the escrow, the documents to complete the exhibits are collected.

Purchasing a franchise is somewhat more structured. Franchises are regulated by the Federal Trade Commission. The Franchise Agreement must be in a particular format to meet legal requirements. The format is divided into the offering circular and the contract. Franchises must be registered in most states with the government. Franchisors must give the offering circular to the franchise before a sale occurs. These documents are usually 30 to 40 pages long and should be reviewed by an attorney.

NEW WAYS OF DOING BUSINESS

Information Superhighway

The development of the information superhighway in communications is similar in impact to humans learning to make fire. The explosion of information availability will create new industries, new job descriptions, and new opportunities for entrepreneurs. What is the information superhighway and how does it differ from multimedia?

The information superhighway is presently composed of several commercial on-line services and local bulletin board services (BBS) in which the master network is accessible without restriction as long as you're willing to pay the price. Presently, Internet is the major such master network. It is available on a narrowband wave. It is anticipated that technology will advance to a broadband width to eliminate the distribution bottleneck that will occur as more and more people enter the system. Advancing to a broadband will permit video, text, and digitized sound to be transmitted concurrently. This is multimedia.

Vice President Gore in a speech at the National Press Club on December 21, 1993 described four components of this industry:

1. Owners of the highways because unlike the interstates, the information highways will be built, paid for, and funded by the private sector.
2. Makers of information appliances, such as televisions, telephones, and computers, and new products of the future that will combine the features of all these appliances.
3. Information providers such as local broadcasters, digital libraries, information service providers, and millions of individuals who will have information they want to share or sell.
4. Information customers, justly demanding privacy, affordability, and choice.

The key is that the same number of consumers will be available to purchase your products, but now your competition may be living in France. Since there is still much to be decided on how these forms of communication will be put together, the related laws are also up in the air. For example, since the communications may be coming via satellite dishes, the postal service can only become involved when a product is shipped. The Federal Communications Commission (FCC) would regulate the transmission, but it is not set up for individual customer complaints requiring immediate response. Because products may be shipped from a foreign country, treaties regarding prosecution of foreign fraud will become crucial. Very few are presently in place. Also, the same treaties must assure that if a product shipped to a foreign country gets waylaid when it lands in port, there will be some recourse for the business owner. Business owners will be required to be far more careful regarding how products are delivered and paid for when using the information superhighway.

Another ramification is that consumers will be in control on when and how they receive the information they require to make purchasing decisions. The entertainment value of a marketing message will become a necessary component of the message. This means that the laws related to entertainment will take an active role in the industry. For example, imagine selling widgets using a famous movie star who has died. A computer whiz could completely and easily reproduce that star's likeness to sell your widget. *But* you will be required to negotiate with the star's estate for the rights to do so. Another example is someone who wants to read the *Far Side* cartoon series but does not want to purchase the newspaper it appears in. Companies will arise that do nothing more than negotiate value and rights for the components of what are now bundled together. This will probably generate the need for enhancement of consumer laws.

There will be a higher incidence of plagiarism, whether intentional or due to the mere facile use of the electronic scissors. Consequently, rather than users needing more protection, copyright holders will have to be more vigilant.

Timothy King, Vice President of John Wiley & Sons, testifying in public hearings on the subject said, "While at present, a software company can police an electronic bulletin board system because it takes time to download a pirated piece of software, when broadband becomes widely available, thousands of non-paying users can download in a few minutes."

The good news is that the present intellectual property laws protecting materials through patents, trademarks, and copyrights are flexible enough to give the kind of protection business owners will need for the information superhighway materials. In the licensing arena, an excellent case to show the issues that arise with multimedia is *Rey v. Lafferty,* 990 F.2d 1379 (1st Cir. 1993). It is important to draft an agreement that at least limits the media for which rights are granted so that if future forms of media are invented, they don't automatically become vested in the licensee.

In terms of future trends, the industry could develop a form of electronic contracting that would involve digital signatures, headers to limit the uses to which the information can be put, and companies whose purpose is to track who is using what information and whether its access is being paid for.

THE NORTH AMERICAN FREE TRADE AGREEMENT AND EXPORTING

The North American Free Trade Agreement (NAFTA) is designed to create a single trade entity among the North American countries: the United States, Mexico, and Canada. It is anticipated to take 15 years to implement all the portions of the plan. The United States has been reluctant for many years to sign such a plan for fear of losses to American business. However, through extensive lobbying and threats of Japan moving in on Mexican commerce, the United States has chosen to lead the way for this agreement.

Once in place, import duties that affect the flow of goods from the United States to both Canada and Mexico will be eliminated. Many companies have already negotiated agreements in anticipation of the adoption of this agreement.

However, there remains a significant opportunity for the business owner who will take some time to learn the ins and outs of NAFTA and commence business with Mexico, especially. One key element of Mexican commerce will remain the same: relationships. With a very small elite upper class, a very large lower class, and few people in the middle class, connections remain important.

There are groups that assist in creating the proper relationships. One such group is the Americas Law Group in San Francisco, California, headed by one of the lobbyists for NAFTA, Alina Aldape. You should not do business with anyone whose facility you have not seen and confirmed ownership.

Although proprietary protection laws are now in place in Mexico, their enforceability is still questionable. Companies have received inconsistent results from the Mexican courts. Remember that even though trade barriers are coming down with NAFTA, basic exporting principles remain the same. You must verify that a difference in culture will not require changes in your product formula, packaging, or marketing.

Books and seminars are coming out in droves on NAFTA. A bibliography of the information is in the works. Meanwhile, the U.S. Department of Commerce and the SBA have relevant sources of information. The Export Small Business Development Center specializes in assisting companies to do business in a foreign country and professes many success stories from their assistance.

The U.S., Canadian, and Mexican embassies and consulates are another good source of information. Some differences, however, are hard pressed to change. While incorporating in California can be done in 24 hours, in Mexico the process can take months unless you can get assistance from an organization with connections in Mexico.

Another issue is banking and capital. I have had discussions with clients who state that they still demand money up front even after years of receiving Mexican customers' prompt payments. The Export SBDC recommends letters of credit with one of the better known Mexican banks. In a letter-of-credit situation, a bank acts as an escrow agent holding money pending delivery and acceptance of merchandise. The customer's bank verifies with the seller's bank that the funds are available. It is important to ask for an "irrevocable letter of credit."

The key to getting started in Mexico is just to start small and work your way up. Vendors are selling everything from twist-tie machines to paper covers for dry cleaners' clothes hangers.

COLLECTIONS

The pain of doing a really good job for a client, only to have the person not pay me is one of the worst feelings in business. The reasons always seem good enough: "Business is bad"; "my client didn't pay me"; "I just don't have the money." Fortunately, most people believe in paying their attorney first, because they know they will need an attorney for their other problems. But it happens to the best of us. Collections is another element of conducting business.

Checks Written on Nonsufficient Funds

A customer writes a check that does not clear the bank. Most banks will put the check through a second time approximately 48 hours after the first submission before bouncing the check. There are two reasons that the check bounced. Either "nonsufficient funds" (nsf) were available to cover the check, or the customer stopped payment on the check. If nsf is the reason, most jurisdictions permit the recipient to obtain three times the face value of the check up to $500 in addition to the value of the check as damages. If a person does not have the money in the first place, what good is awarding triple the amount that cannot be paid? Sometimes for large checks, you can show that criminal fraud is present and the vice section of the police department will follow up for you. In that case, when the customer is being charged, the judge will give the person the opportunity to pay back the money (restitution).

If a stop payment is placed on a check, or even on a credit card, it is much more difficult to recover. Typically, you would go to small claims court, show that the merchandise was delivered and that there was no reason to stop payment.

A stop payment is good only for six months. I actually had a client who stopped payment on a check. The vendor after six months redeposited the check. Because it did not show up on the bank computers as a stop payment (even though it was marked on the check itself), the bank put it through. The bank debited my client's account. This was in error. Checks are no longer redeemable after six months. If a bank does so, it does so at its own peril.

Enforcement of Judgments

You've gone to court, obtained a judgment, and now it's time to collect. Thought you were through after court did you? Think again! Enforcement of judgments is like an entirely new lawsuit. There are legal procedures that you must use to obtain the money that the court said you were entitled to. They include writs of execution, levy, garnishment, judgment debtor exam, and abstract of judgment. You must identify a debtor's bank account numbers, the person's place of employment, and the exact description of the real property he or she owns. A judgment debtor's exam is a place where all of this can happen. Debtors are given one opportunity to provide this information voluntarily, and then they must appear in court. You can drag the debtor into court every six months. If the person walks in with money in his or her pocket, you can demand it. At each exam, you have the right to ask as many questions as you wish regarding the debtor's assets. The local library typically has a form book with the questions available to ask. Table 22.1 lists sample questions for a business.

Table 22.1   Postjudgment Interrogatories

1. Please state your full name and address.
2. Please state the name and address of your employer, your job title, and responsibilities.
3. Please state the amount of your wages and full description of how all other compensation is computed and paid to you (whether commission, bonus, etc.).
4. Please state the full name and address of all businesses in which you have had an interest in the preceding five (5) years, together with a description of the business and your interest therein.
5. Describe all income by amount, source, and name of payor of all income received by you or your spouse from every source other than wages, in the past five (5) years.
6. Please identify all bank accounts in which you have an interest indicating name and address of bank, account number, name of account owner, and current balance.
7. If you and your spouse have authority to sign checks or other instruments on any bank account not identified in response to Interrogatory 6, please state the bank, account numbers, and owner of the account.

Table 22.1 (continued)

8. Please state the institution name and identifying number of all institutions in which you have a safety deposit box or other depository for valuable goods.

9. Please state the legal description, name of record owner, and common address of all real property or oil and gas leases that you or your spouse own, or have any interest in.

10. Itemize in detail all assets, whether tangible or intangible, owned by you or your spouse stating the owner, a description of the assets, its fair market value, and location.

11. Fully describe all commodities, stock, and other securities owned by you or your spouse. Please state the number of shares, corporation, present location, description of certificates or other evidence of ownership, serial or identifying number of each, and current market value.

12. Please identify all jewelry and antiques owned by you or your spouse, including the fair market value and location of each.

13. If you or your spouse own any interest in a boat, motor vehicle, trailer, airplane, gun, or animal, please state the purchase price, current indebtedness, location, serial or model number of each, and a complete description of each item.

14. Please list all persons who owe you money, including name and address of debtor and amount owed.

15. Describe in full all mortgages, liens, promissory notes or other encumbrances held by you or your spouse, or attach a copy of each to your answers. Include in your answer all amounts still owing to you and when the obligation is anticipated to be retired.

16. As to each policy of insurance you have had in the past five (5) years, please state the name of each carrier, policy number, term, and current cash value.

17. If you or your spouse is entitled to any money from any governmental agency, please state the name of the entity from which you are entitled to this money, the amount, and the circumstances surrounding such entitlement.

18. If you have prepared or issued any financial statement within the past ten (10) years, attach a copy of each such financial statement to your answers of these Interrogatories, or set forth the contents of such verbatim.

19. Set forth verbatim the contents of your income tax returns for each of the past three (3) years, or attach a photocopy of each such return.

20. If within the past thirty-six (36) months any of your accounts receivable or other assets have been assigned, please describe account or item assigned, date of assignment, the name and address of each assignee and the consideration received.

21. If during the past ten (10) years, you or your spouse have been a beneficiary of, or contributed to any trust, please state when the trust was created, the name and address of each trustee and beneficiary, and the property contributed to the trust.

22. If you or your spouse are a beneficiary under the terms of the will of any person now deceased, please state the name of the decedent as well as the court in which such estate is pending.

23. If you or your spouse have received any property or money by way of inheritance, please state the name of the decedent and the court having jurisdiction of said estate. Also, fully describe any distribution made to you.

24. If at any time in the past five (5) years, you have entered into any transaction with your spouse or any other relative involving the transfer of any of your real or personal property, fully describe the transaction and the property transferred.

25. If you or your spouse have ever received a court settlement or judgment in your behalf or have lawsuits pending, please identify each by court and case number.

Once you have the bank account information from the debtor, writs of execution and levy are what you use to force the bank to give you, the creditor, some of the debtor's money. Remember, a judgment is good for 10 years. So if you wait long enough, the debtor will forget about you, and you can probably get some money at that point. If the debtor is an employee somewhere, you can also garnish up to 25% of the debtor's paycheck to pay you back. Finally, abstracts of judgment are placed on real property. If the debtor ever tries to sell property, the money will stay in escrow until you are paid.

Collection Letters

The Complete Book of Contemporary Business Letters contains excellent examples of three levels of collection letters (see Resources). You must make a demand before you can take any further action on collecting money. Some people find this amazing. Isn't the invoice a demand note? Most of the time, yes, depending on how specific it is. But I advise clients to play it safe. Within a very short time after money is due, you should send a separate letter stating how much is owed, for what, the due date, the interest rate, and when you expect it to be repaid.

Credit collection agencies are not permitted to call a debtor at work to discuss collections. They are also not permitted to tell the person's employer. If he or she hires an attorney and notifies the collection agencies, they must speak to the attorney, not to the debtor.

If you are demanding payment, only give the customer a few days to respond to you in writing before taking further action and always follow up with a phone call. Although my clients can achieve about 80% success rate in collections obtaining judgments, they have about a 25% success rate in actually getting paid. Usually, in one phone call it is clear whether a letter will be effective or if the business owner must go directly to court. When a debtor does not respond to the letter, or starts arguing about what services were provided in the same breath as not having any money, don't waste time negotiating: Go to court.

Bankruptcy

Many business owners are in total shock that a debtor can owe them money and that they can pay thousands of dollars in attorney's fees to pursue payment only to find out that they will not get a penny because the debtor has filed bankruptcy. Unless you can show that the debtor intended to defraud you, the debt to you will be satisfied by the debtor being adjudicated a bankrupt. An even worse scenario occurs when you deliver merchandise, the recipient doesn't pay, is adjudicated bankrupt, and gets to keep your merchandise.

Individuals file Chapter 7 or Chapter 13 bankruptcy. Chapter 7 is total liquidation. The court receives a complete listing of all the debtor's assets and liabilities and divvies up the assets. Priority is given to taxing authorities first, secured creditors second, and unsecured creditors last. Usually by the time the unsecured creditors are considered, there are no assets left. Chapter 13 bankruptcy is a consolidation plan offered to individuals who have some means of paying the debt off, but perhaps cannot handle the high interest rates on the principal debt or find the payment amounts are too steep. The court forces creditors to take the amount and payment plan directed by the court.

Businesses have the option of filing Chapter 11, reorganization. Technically, Chapter 11 is not formal bankruptcy. A plan is submitted to the court, creditors are notified and given the opportunity to appear to state relevant facts about the debtor's ability to reorganize, and then the debtor is given the opportunity to pay back the creditors. A creditor may get 50 cents on the dollar or may be told that interest cannot be charged on the remaining debt.

As a creditor, your first notice that your customer filed bankruptcy will be a notice to creditors that comes from the bankruptcy court. A court-appointed trustee in bankruptcy will be listed. The trustee, who is a lawyer, represents the court and oversees the procedure to make sure that all the details are flushed out. They are very helpful in explaining where the debtor is in the process, if other creditors have filed fraud claims, and how many assets are available. They are also for the most part very patient and will explain the process to you in detail. Then there is the attorney for the debtor. The attorney is being paid out of the remaining assets of the debtor. Fees are regulated by the court. You will receive reams of paper regarding the bankruptcy. The one crucial paper to complete is the document confirming that you are owed money. It is self-explanatory, and the trustee can assist you in completing it.

Go to a creditor's meeting if convenient and if it won't cost any money. It's interesting, but you are not obligated to be there to receive protection. Once the debtor is "discharged in bankruptcy" all debts are considered resolved in accordance with the court order.

Sometimes clients have successfully proven fraud by the debtor. This is especially true when the debt is incurred right before the filing, such as a couple of days. In this case, the judgment you get stands and is enforceable for 10 years, with the option to renew it if the debt has not been paid in full. The real problem is that the debtor who is otherwise successful in bankruptcy probably doesn't have the money to pay.

If a debtor owes you more than $25,000, it's worthwhile to see a bankruptcy attorney who represents creditors. The attorney should tell you up front what side he or she represents.

Even if you believe that you will never be paid, you should file the court document regarding confirmation of your debt. With the discharge in bankruptcy, it is evidence of bad debt that you can write off on your taxes.

One final note: The law provides for a "60-day preference" rule. This rule is designed to prevent debtors from paying off their friends right before they file bankruptcy while leaving others stiffed. The 60-day rule allows the court to set aside any payments made up to 60 days before the actual filing of bankruptcy. Creditors who have been paid must return the money to the bankruptcy court for it to be placed in the pot. Business owners should keep in close contact with their ongoing customers so that they will have a good enough relationship to know far in advance to avoid being caught up in this rule.

KEY EMPLOYEE PROMISES

When you are starting your own business, you are full of dreams, aspirations, goals, and enthusiasms, but usually not very much money. However, you realize that if you just had that special person who could assist you in sales or finance or marketing, you'd be on easy street. Maybe it's even a couple of people. Those people through sheer luck arrive at your doorstep while you're working really hard, only you're not prepared for them . . . you still don't have much money. *So,* you offer them the sun and the moon if they will just sign on with you. Your business grows rapidly, and you now have outgrown those key employees, yet they own a fairly significant portion of your business. Does this scene sound familiar? It happens too many times . . . and it all could have been avoided with legal documents up front:

Rule 1.   Never underestimate how large your business will grow and in how short a time frame. Once a business gets to a critical mass, it takes on its own personality, its own growth patterns, and you're pretty much along for the ride. Daily, the business teaches you as much or more as you put into it in terms of direction.

Rule 2.   Never give away more than 10% of your company collectively unless you have a strategic plan and a business plan that in detail shows otherwise with the ramifications. The more successful you are, the more working capital you will need for your growth. That's typically how you end up with investors who are usually your key employees. They see your vision, they see the company growing, and they want to be part of it. A cavalier promise made during a time when everyone is working hard can end up in a lawsuit. Even though it is unlikely that your key employee will prevail based on an oral promise, you must still go through the cost and emotional drain of defending a lawsuit.

Rule 3.   Don't give away any of your company ownership even in jest without a written document. Most business owners do not understand the difference between profit sharing, giving up equity interest in a company, and giving stock either as a bonus or through a stock option plan. Profit sharing allows employees to receive a portion of the profits of a company. They do not necessarily receive company ownership in a profit-sharing plan. However, many business owners will give stock as an easy way to monitor profit. This is not a wise idea. If you want to have your key employees receive a portion of the profits of your company, see an accountant first and then a lawyer to draft a formal plan that you feel comfortable showing your employees. You and your employees can end up paying unnecessary taxes if the plan is not structured properly. If your company is a corporation, giving an equity interest and giving stock are one and the same. The stock is evidence of how much equity you are giving. Stock is either "authorized" or "issued." Authorized stock is how many shares you can give out totally. The only way to increase the number of authorized shares is by amending your articles of incorporation, which takes usually a two-thirds vote of all your stockholders. A stock certificate can reflect one share or hundreds or thousands of shares. You do not receive a single stock certificate for each share that you own. Issued shares collectively represent 100% ownership of the company. Often, issued shares are some portion of authorized shares. If you remember that shares are a financing vehicle for your company, this will make sense. You always want to have authorized but unissued shares available to sell in case you need more money. The key is to sell those shares for a higher price than the initial shares so that everybody who bought initial shares now has a higher value to their shares. Also, when you sell shares for money, the money should in some way increase the net worth or potential net worth of your company so that shareholders, if bought out, receive a profit from their sale. The problem with comments to key employees in the heat of hard work about company ownership is that years after the promise was made, no one quite remembers what was said. Maybe you didn't intend your comment to be a promise, or maybe you didn't understand the significance of that promise while your company was so small. If you outgrow your key employee, you usually now have to contend with a lawsuit over what was said, whether it was indeed a promise, and what was it a promise for (e.g., company ownership, profit sharing).

Rule 4. Make your promises conditional on continued performance. Your job as company president is unenviable. Your company has outgrown employees, of if they refuse to take a lesser position, you must terminate people that you have relied on, built your business with, become close to. When you are just starting out, you are probably unclear on what you expect, but you do believe that there is an implied good faith, loyal and conscientious effort on the part of your key employees. If a key employee has stopped performing in this manner, you must document it immediately. Don't believe that you are doing anyone a favor by trying to handle it informally. The truth is that if you are a true entrepreneur, you will come to a point where you must replace yourself as president. This honesty up front will foster the continued success of your company.

Rule 5. Invest in an employment agreement. Employment agreements for key employees and executives are important in clarifying what their positions require. Seek a labor or business attorney to assure that for your particular circumstances you have all your bases covered.

Rule 6. If you do wish to give your employees part ownership of the company, plan on ultimately having a qualified plan with all your employees participating. Don't give away the store. If you compare Bill Gates who started Microsoft with Steve Jobs who started Apple, why is one a billionaire and the other one trying to recover from a corporate blood bath? I believe that Bill Gates was prepared for the size his company ultimately achieved and Steve Jobs was not. It was the structure set in place up front that made the difference. The bare minimum to start with is a shareholder agreement that allows you to buy back stock personally first, then through the company for employees who terminate for any reason. With that document in place, you can pay to have a qualified plan put in place when your company grows large enough. However, when you create your shareholder agreement, have an accountant who understands your long-range goals look at what you have set up to assure a smooth transition.

THEFT OF INFORMATION

Example 1.   You have just spent $10,000 for a special mailing list. Your business is in a highly competitive industry. You are hiring salespeople because you believe that saturating the market with your product information will allow you to dominate the market share. Your existing subcontractor and supplier list took you five years of cold-calling and testing to develop. You spent thousands on new graphics because you were told this would do the trick. You are poised for success—and a highly aggressive sales rep starts a competing business out of their house with your information.

Example 2.   You learn a method of doing business that no one else knows; your partner of five years becomes disillusioned with your business philosophy now that you are beginning to achieve major success; and she starts her own business in competition with you, using that same method.

Example 3.   Your archrival hires away one of your popular computer software programmers who happens to be familiar with the design and code of an existing product that has paid your overhead for many years. They call up three of your programmers who all go work for the archrival. Your programming staff has just been halved.

All these situations are depressing for a business owner, but which actions are illegal, if any? Almost all states distinguish between the duties of an employee, a partner, and independent contractor toward an owner. The issues involve noncompetition, nonsolicitation, nondisclosure, unfair business competition, and a duty of loyalty.

Business partners who split up are entitled to prohibit each other from competing if they pay for it. This is usually done with a noncompetition clause that exists in the buyout contract. A portion of the purchase price is allocated to goodwill that can be paid out over the time period of the noncompete. If the partner sets up a competing business, you can—presuming the contract is drafted correctly—stop the payments and obtain an injunction against your previous partner to prevent the person from competing for the time specified.

The geographic area of noncompetition and the time period must be reasonable for your particular business and the industry. In other words: You cannot prohibit worldwide competition for a local deli.

Employees are a different matter. There is a presumption in the law that all people are entitled to gainful employment. Companies that have tried to pay their exemployees not to complete have been unsuccessful unless they were paid the equivalent of their salary not to work. Even then, an employee can choose to not receive the payment and find a job elsewhere. The employee does owe the owner a duty of loyalty while employed. This means that if the employer finds the employee calling about another job while still employed, or trying to solicit coworkers to work somewhere else, the employer has a right to damages if it can prove its case. However, the day after the employee leaves, he or she can call coworkers on the phone and solicit them.

But how about those customer lists? Do exemployees have the right to take those with them? This leads to the issue of confidential information. The basic law is that exemployees are entitled to use those skills and resources that formed the basis of their experience in the profession at a new job. However, employees are not entitled to steal confidential trade secret information from a previous employer. The most common reason that business owners lose these cases against their exemployees is that the owner has never identified the company's confidential or trade secret information. The receptionist on the computer network has access to the customer lists. None of the computers have passwords. Anyone walking by can sit down to a computer and retrieve the information. An exemployee does not have the right to steal company confidential information or trade secrets that are identified as such; however, the ownership of information developed through company procedures must clearly differentiate what belongs to the employee and what to the company. The easiest way to accomplish this is through nondisclosure agreements.

Nondisclosure Agreements

Nondisclosure agreements should be signed by anyone who has access to sensitive company information. I recommend that outside consultants receive them if you are considering a business relationship, that employees get them prior to starting (their signing is a condition of employment), and that clients sign them before receiving unpublished information about the future direction of your company.

A nondisclosure agreement identifies confidential information by category, states what actions will be required to maintain confidentiality, and identifies ownership rights in the material disclosed. It is not a substitute for establishing a hierarchy of access among your employees to sensitive information. Prudent measures include allowing sales reps to have access only to the territory that they are responsible for, instituting passwords for computer access, hiring outside consultants to assemble certain portions of information so that no one person has the entire picture except you, intentionally putting misspellings in some parts of your documentation so it is easy to prove an unauthorized copying, and always using copyright and trademark symbols as appropriate to establish ownership.

LAWSUITS

It is often said that you haven't really made it until you've been sued. It means that you are taking the risk necessary for great strides in business success. The key is to not let a lawsuit (litigation) affect the forward motion of your business. Lawsuits are costly. Even the prevailing party, if attorney's fees are paid and judgment received, loses much in emotional energy and in actual time spent for various aspects of litigation. As a result, alternatives have arisen in the form of arbitration, mediation, and small claims court to solve nonnegotiable situations.

Litigation and an Overview of the Court System

The system of justice in the United States is somewhat complicated because there are two systems that at times duplicate each other and at times do not.

Basically, if a federal question exists such as gun control or violations of federal statutes, the case may be heard in a federal court. In addition, a case will be heard in federal court if the damages exceed $50,000 and the parties come from separate states. You always have the option of hearing the case in the state courts, but they will apply federal law if appropriate.

Typically, it costs more to bring a lawsuit in federal court than in state court because the procedural part of the court is done in a very fast pace (i.e., no continuances are permitted for just about any reason). Therefore, the time that your case is heard is compressed into a shorter time span. So the attorney is spending 100 hours in a one-week period instead of a six-month period. That means that you pay the same fees in one week that you would have paid in six months had you been in state court.

Attorneys rely on published cases to prove that your facts match the facts of case in which your equivalent party prevailed. Only cases that have been appealed from the trial court to the appellate or supreme court are published. This means that many of the most common cases decided in the lower courts are never recorded, which in turn means that it is very important to have a trial attorney who has experience in your local court system.

Arbitration

A clause invoking arbitration must be included in a writing for the parties to have arbitration available. If a dispute arises, and no arbitration clause exists, either party may opt for litigation and the other party is stuck. Why would someone want a lawsuit in court instead of the more informal proceeding of arbitration? Most likely to draw out the time in which money would be paid, or to wear down a smaller company that may have a right but does not have the money to enforce that right.

The difference between arbitration and a lawsuit is primarily in formality. For example, in arbitration the formal rules of evidence do not apply. Each side can go on and on with narrative discussions, drawings, and charts, and the arbitrator will take in all of it and make a decision. There are no juries in arbitration. Instead, usually one to three people specially trained in the subject matter of the arbitration will hear the case. Arbitrations are heard much sooner than lawsuits can be scheduled. This can be either good or bad, depending on what side you're on. Prior to the trial, there is no "discovery" in arbitration. You present your case from the information you have available. This means that the person with the better paper trail has an advantage.

Unless so specified in the arbitration clause, arbitrations *are not* final and binding. Either party can decide that they do not like the outcome. Once an arbitration award is made, and a binding clause is in the contract, you must take the arbitration award to court to have it made into an enforceable judgment.

Mediation

Sometimes you just want to know you're right. But your relationship with the person that you are suing is one that you depend on for the long run. In these cases, it pays to mediate if you have a dispute.

Unlike arbitration, mediation is never final or binding. It is heard in front of a person who has expert advice on the subject matter in question. The arbitrator can share the law in a way that allows both parties to have their day in court, vent their position, and work toward a resolution, so that the relationship is not lost over the threat of a lawsuit. Mediation is very effective in this situation.

Small Claims Court

Small claims court is fast becoming a method to resolve differences quickly and efficiently. Attorneys are not permitted to be present until the appeal stage. Cases are usually heard within 30 days; you need to complete only a one-page form, and the fee for filing is minimal. In some states, the amount you can sue for has been raised to $5,000 under certain conditions. Each state—and many times each county—has different rules about the allowable sum. The key commonality is the simplicity and speed in which minor matters can be handled.

STEPS IN FILING A SMALL CLAIMS ACTION

The following list outlines the steps in filing a small claims action.

1. Determine the jurisdictional dollar-limit on small claims actions for the jurisdiction in which you will bring the action.

2. Determine in which jurisdiction the defendant resides or does business. This is the jurisdiction in which you will generally bring the action.

3. Visit the court clerk for the above jurisdiction. The clerk will give you the appropriate forms for filing the claim. Follow the instructions on these forms.

THE CORPORATE VEIL

Business owners are often fooled by the statement, "If you are a corporation, your assets are untouchable." This statement has many disclaimers and conditions that you must be aware of before you take those business risks.

A corporation is its own entity that can sue and be sued presuming that it is in good standing. If you have a validly established corporation, your personal assets usually cannot be touched if a judgment is awarded against the corporation.

The first exception to the rule relates to personal guarantees. Sometimes when you apply for a line of credit with a bank, especially if your corporation is newly formed, the bank will require you to sign a personal guarantee. If you don't pay on your loan, although the bank will look first to the corporation to pay, you will be on the hook individually as well. This also occurs in equipment leasing and on the lease of your premises. I tell my clients to always negotiate up front or at least sometime in the first year after paying promptly on a regular basis, that some time in the first three years the personal guarantee comes off. After all, IBM doesn't give personal guarantees. Another personal guarantee that is implied when you set up your corporation is the payment of taxes. The Franchise Tax Board will always hold you personally responsible for the payment of corporate taxes as an officer and director of the corporation. It is important to explain this potential liability to your best friends, who may be your new directors.

The next exception is for specific statutes that hold directors and officers personally liable for the criminal acts of the corporation. The CEO of a large aerospace corporation is in the federal penitentiary for selling $21,000 toilet paper rolls to the government. Other directors have been incarcerated for failing to correct workplace hazards for their employees, or for gross negligence in toxic spills. Trade association newsletters will inform you of the pitfalls for your particular industry. If your corporation has committed a fraud, even if you are not directly aware, you may individually be held responsible. In addition, professionals such as lawyers or doctors are not protected from malpractice by the "corporate veil."

The next exception is when a director or officer acts outside the scope of their duties. For example, a general contractor is angered by a homeowner and gets into a fist fight. The corporation cannot in most cases protect against an action of this sort.

Protection can be lost in divorce situations or through inadvertence. In community property states, unless your share certificate specifically states that the shares are held as separate property, if joint funds started the company, it is presumed that the shares are held as community property. Or in a fit of tax-avoidance zeal, a piece of property could be titled in the corporate name. In both of these situations, your personal assets have been diminished.

Finally, if the corporation is not established and maintained properly, a plaintiff may claim that the corporation and you are one and the same, and therefore your personal assets can be used to satisfy the judgment. This is called "piercing the corporate veil." What constitutes establishing and maintaining? First, you must have good standing with the secretary of state. That means that you have paid your taxes to date and that you have completed the yearly forms that they require. Second, you must have your corporate minutes up to date, and you must have complied with your bylaws regarding holding of annual meetings, and so on. Third, you must properly capitalize your corporation. That is, you must have sufficient capital in the corporation to pay its bills. The states usually use a debt-to-equity ratio of 2:1 as a guideline. That means that your debts can be no greater than twice your equity. In a service corporation, this is no easy task unless you have cash in the bank. In most states, another element that the plaintiff must show to pierce the corporate veil is that you have set up the corporate shell with the intent to defraud creditors. This is usually proved by showing the commingling of assets and liabilities. Thus, you must keep your personal and corporate business separate. If you loan money to the corporation or borrow money from the corporation, you must complete written promissory notes with the going rate of interest and a reasonable payback schedule. Never write checks for personal debts such as your house payment, out of your corporate account. Finally, when you sign documents, you must use the proper format as follows:

CORPORATE NAME

BY: _____
    Your Name, President

The word "BY" is important, as is your title.

Most plaintiff's attorneys will try to always sue you personally when suing the corporation, just as a scare tactic. Most states now require some prior basis for claiming the right to pierce the corporate veil. The plaintiff cannot just make the claims and hope that something to hook you in will show up during discovery. I recommend to my clients to have personal suits removed right at the beginning of the lawsuit through a summary judgment action. It costs a little more money up front, but it keeps your personal credit profile clean and allows your spouse to sleep at night.

RESOURCES

Associations

American Management Association, 135 West 50th Street, New York, NY 10020, 212-586-8100

Center for Entrepreneurial Management, Inc., 180 Varick Street, New York, NY 10014, 212-633-0060

Small Business Network, P.O. Box 30149, Baltimore, MD 21270, 301-581-1373

Small Business Service Bureau, 554 Main Street, Worcester, MA 01601, 508-756-3513

Books

Daley, James H., *Scoring Millions,* Aim Press (1993)

Elliot, Stephen P. (Ed.), *The Complete Book of Contemporary Business Letters* (Round Lake Publishing, 1988)

Enkelis, Richard L., *Enforcing Civil Money Judgements/Here's How and When to Do It* (Continuing Education of the Bar, 1993)

Frantz, Barbara A., *What You Need to Know about Business Law* (Business Advisement Center™, 1992)

Mancusco, Anthony, *Doing Your Own Corporation,* 8th ed. (Nolo Press, 1994)

Posch, Robert J., Jr., *The Complete Guide to Marketing and the Law* (Prentice Hall, Inc. 1988)

Pressman, David, *Patent It Yourself* (Nolo Press, 1994)

Scott, Michael, and Talbott, James, *Multimedia Law and Practice* (Prentice Law and Business, 1993)

Magazines

Barron's National Business and Financial Weekly, 200 Liberty Street, New York, NY 10281, 212-416-2700

The Business Journal, 101 2nd Place SE, Suite 202, P.O. Box 2879, Gainesville, FL 32601-6592, 904-371-9228

The Business Owner, Thomas Publishing, Inc., 383 South Broadway, Hicksville, NY 11801, 516-681-2111

Business Review, One Kwik Kopy Laine, P.O. Box 777, Cypress, TX 77429-2164, 713-373-3535

D&B Reports, 299 Park Avenue, New York, NY 10171-0102, 212-593-6723

Entrepreneurial Manager, Center for Entrepreneurial Management, 180 Varick Street, New York, NY 10014, 212-633-0060

Entrepreneurial Manager's Newsletter, 180 Varick Street, Penthouse Suite, New York, NY 10014-4692, 212-633-0060

In Business, 18 South Seventh Street, P.O. Box 323, Emmaus, PA 18049-3717, 215-967-4135

Journal of Small Business Management, West Virginia University, College of Business Economics, Bureau of Business Research, P.O. Box 6025, Morgantown, WV 26506-6025, 304-293-5837

Nation's Business, 1615 H Street NW, Washington, DC 20062, 202-463-5650

Small Business Report, 203 Calle Del Oaks, Monterey, CA 93940, 408-899-7221

Growing Your Business

Growth! Some small businesses never experience it. Their owners are either content with the status of their business or they don't know what it takes to grow a company. Either way, their businesses inevitably suffer by failing to reach their full potential.

The flip side to this scenario is that some businesses grow too rapidly. This uncontrolled growth creates internal problems that eventually filter outward to customers. Other businesses pursue growth strategies that are either faulty, misguided, or too ambitious, thereby overextending their resources and placing a great deal of pressure on the business just to survive.

Growing your business can be like walking through a minefield if you haven't properly planned for expansion. For instance, more staff may need to be added, additional equipment may need to be purchased, proper marketing support has to be in place, and the appropriate amount of financing needs to be present. When you are growing your business, you need to address and plan out each of these factors so you know what resources you will have to devote to these areas.

Although growing your business can certainly be risky, the rewards of a successful enterprise, can be enormous. To measure the potential return for your effort, all you have to do is look at entrepreneurs who have achieved their goals. Some of the more recognizable names are Bill Gates (Microsoft), Lillian Vernon (catalog sales), Dave Thomas (Wendy's), and Calvin Klein (ready-to-wear), to name just a few. All these entrepreneurs started small with a dream that they have grown into a large, thriving business. Some of these companies dominate the industries they operate within.

This kind of entrepreneurial success comes not only from hard work and good ideas, but from careful planning and skill in recognizing growth opportunities. The goal of Part III of the *Entrepreneur Small Business Advisor and Desk Reference* is to provide you with the information you need to take advantage of strategic opportunities and execute those plans. The chapters in Part III cover the following subjects:

- **Marketing plan.** The differences between a business plan and a marketing plan; structuring a marketing plan; incorporating long-term objectives and short-term goals in the marketing plan; sample marketing plan.
- **Sales.** Developing and structuring a sales force; how to prospect potential customers; closing strategies.
- **Advertising.** Structuring an effective advertising campaign; elements involved in developing a media plan; the characteristics of successful creativity in advertising; elements of designing a strong ad.
- **Telemarketing.** Using telemarketing in your sales strategies; types of phone systems; prospecting over the phone; how to close over the phone; the impact of new technology.
- **Expansion capital.** When you will need expansion capital; determining your financial requirements; the different types of loans available through debt financing and the various lenders you can approach; what banks and other debt financing sources will require; how equity financing works and the sources available for this type of capital; seven common sources of venture capital; how to put together a venture capital proposal.
- **Public offerings.** The advantages and disadvantages of going public; the major steps associated with the process of going public; reporting requirements; what is involved in closing the initial public offering.
- **Selling a business.** Things to consider before selling a business; common methods used to price a business; what's involved in making the sale; checking the buyer's track record.

23

Marketing Plan

The business plan is the only strategic planning tool many entrepreneurs use to document their company's strategies. They'll create it once and most likely update it on an annual basis; as the company grows, so will the thickness of the business plan. But there is another strategic planning tool to document a company's strategy that entrepreneurs either don't know about, or fail to utilize. It's called the marketing plan.

During the formative stages of a small business, the marketing plan isn't that critical to the success of the venture and it can easily be incorporated into the business plan; however, as the company grows and adds new concepts to its business, the marketing plan then becomes a very important tool because it charts the strategies and goals of those new concepts. The primary difference between a business plan and a marketing plan is that the business plan deals with the entire business, whereas the marketing plan focuses on expanding a specific product or service of the company. Ideally, the business and marketing plans will work hand in hand. The goals and strategies that the marketing plan documents for a new product or service can readily be transferred to the business plan during its revision. Since the two plans have a similar structure, they are compatible tools for the strategic planning process.

The marketing plan formalizes the strategic planning process by providing a written format for the business's plan to diversify into other product areas. More than this, however, it forces the entrepreneur to do the following:

- Chart industry growth.
- Define the market(s).
- Determine the strengths and weaknesses of the competition.
- Project sales.
- Chart the marketing strategies to achieve its sales goals.
- Identify capital equipment requirements.
- Determine investment requirements.

- Provide direction for the assignment of responsibilities.
- Produce financial projections.

As mentioned, many entrepreneurs fail to use a marketing plan. They either don't understand the marketing plan concept, feel their business plan is more than adequate to deal with new production development, or think that they can undertake an ambitious project simply with a plan in their head. But, just as you wouldn't start a business without first planning it out and writing down your agenda, you shouldn't start expanding your product line or arena of services without mapping out your goals and strategies.

THE CONCEPT

The first thing you should do when forming a marketing plan is define its structure. It should allow the presentation of strategic information in a logical and progressive manner. The best approach is to prepare a written outline detailing the progression of topics and how they will appear. The structure of a marketing plan will usually vary according to the business, its objectives, and its product or service. Generally, however, the plan will include the following topics:

- Executive summary.
- Product description.
- Market analysis.
- Competitive analysis.
- Product development.
- Operations.
- Goals and objectives.
- Marketing tactics.
- Financial projections.
- Summary.

Keep in mind that the preceding list is just an example. Go through and determine just what topics will be appropriate for your own marketing plan. You'll find that some of the items listed here will not be relevant to what you are proposing or will require a different approach.

The following sections explain each topic's significance to the overall marketing plan and will help you determine just what you need to include in your own plan.

EXECUTIVE SUMMARY

The executive summary is a brief synopsis of the entire marketing plan. It provides the following information:

- A short description of your product or service.
- Why it is different from your competitors' products.
- Your objectives and goals.
- The competitive advantage your product or service has over your competitors.
- The amount of expansion capital needed to meet your objectives.
- Financial results (e.g., return on investment, sales, profits, market share) and strategies that will be utilized to reach your objectives.

A solid, hard-hitting executive summary is an important element of a marketing plan, especially if you are trying to raise capital. It provides busy investors and lenders with a quick view of your proposed idea. It can be a few paragraphs, but should be no more than a page and a half. The idea is to present a well-thought-out and succinct executive summary that will grab the reader's attention within the few minutes allotted to review the plan. It must convey the feeling that you are a responsible individual who can get things done and that your plan has good potential for success.

Although the executive summary is usually prepared after the plan has been drafted, we are starting with it because it will appear at the beginning of the completed marketing plan. You will want to write your executive summary after you have finished the rest of your plan—it is impossible to summarize a plan you haven't yet formed.

An executive summary is developed by reading through your presentation and extracting the key factors in the success of your proposal such as size of the market, growth forecasts, relative competition, and your objectives. Start your summary with an attention-grabbing statement that describes your market, product, and any unmet customer needs. Follow this up with the specific thrust of your marketing strategy. What are you trying to accomplish?

For instance, suppose you're in the business of manufacturing disposable diapers. It's a huge market with several major players and many minor ones including private label manufacturers and direct marketing companies. This doesn't even take into account periphery competitors like diaper services and cloth diaper manufacturers. Through your research, you've come across a little-exploited gap in the market, and based on that information have developed a biodegradable disposable diaper. You want to act fast and place this product on the market to develop product brand association with your company before your competitors launch themselves into this market segment.

Given this situation, your executive summary might look like the following:

EXECUTIVE SUMMARY (Sample)

With over 1.6 million pounds of nondegradable disposable diapers finding their way to dumps across the United States each year, many Americans are seeking a more environmentally safe baby diaper that will reduce this continued buildup. Americans spend approximately $2.7 billion dollars per year for disposable diapers, but that number has been shrinking due to the encroachment of cloth diapers and delivery services with an estimated $400 million in sales each year.

The huge disposable diaper market is especially attractive to dual-income earners and single parents who don't have the time to wash cloth diapers and don't want to spend the extra money for a diaper delivery service. Competitors in the market all offer the same kind of product consisting of an absorbent pad, surrounded by a snug-fitting plastic diaper that is secured with tapes. Except for some product differentiation in packaging, nonallergenic claims, and pad size ranging from ultrathin to thick, there is very little difference among products. Despite the popularity of disposable diapers, however, many consumers are turning away from them because they are not biodegradable.

Given this gap in the market, Bio-Diapers have been developed to provide ecology-minded consumers with an environmentally safe disposable diaper. This new line of biodegradable disposable diapers will feature all the elements that are popular among users of disposable diapers, but will add the benefit of biodegradability. This revolutionary new advancement in the disposable diaper market will attract consumers who are concerned about the environment as well as those consumers using cloth diapers and diaper services due to the non-degradability of current disposable diapers.

Bio-Diapers will be available for babies ranging from newborns all the way up to 30 pounds and over. We will offer them in a variety of colorful designs and pad sizes. Our marketing objectives and strategies are highlighted in the following pages. We anticipate placing Bio-Diapers on the market by the summer of 1995.

As you can see, the executive summary for Bio-Diapers is not a drawn-out account listing all the profit projections, strategies, and tactics. The plan itself will deal with those factors. It does provide a descriptive summary that grabs the reviewer's attention and creates the necessary curiosity to move to the next section of the marketing plan.

PRODUCT DESCRIPTION

Unlike the executive summary, the product description is not a synopsis of the overall plan, but a detailed preface of your proposed project. In the product description, you need to explain what your product or service is, the specific thrust of your plan, and the main strategies that you will use to accomplish your objectives. The product description should communicate to readers the purpose of your plan—what your product or service is and what you intend to do with it.

Like the executive summary, the product description can be a few paragraphs in length to a few pages depending on the complexity of your plan. If your plan is not too complicated, keep your product description short, describing your product or service in one paragraph and your objectives and strategies in another. While a lengthy product description may be necessary in some cases, a short product description that conveys the required information in a succinct manner is the most effective. It doesn't attempt to hold the reader's attention for a extended period. If your product description is long and overly detailed, you will lose the reader's attention, and possibly any chance of receiving the necessary funding for the project.

When writing your product description, you should use any support statistics from the body of your plan. Make sure that you credit any secondary or primary sources so the reader knows they weren't formed arbitrarily.

In our example of the biodegradable diapers, the product description would look like this:

PRODUCT DESCRIPTION (Sample)

The purpose of this plan is to demonstrate the need for a high-quality, biodegradable disposable diaper that will fill a gap left in the marketplace by large disposable diaper manufacturers. From a survey of 1,000 parents commissioned by Softie Baby Care, Inc. and conducted by Timmons Research, over 60 percent of the respondents were extremely concerned about the environment and the effects of nondegradable diapers; 20 percent were mildly concerned; 15 percent were concerned, and 5 percent used cloth diapers or a service. These figures indicate the importance parents are placing on the ecology.

The solution we are providing to these consumers is a biodegradable disposable diaper at a price point that is just 20% above regular disposable diapers. The "Bio-Diaper" will be produced in all normal diaper sizes and will feature various nursery designs to appeal to a more affluent, brand-name-oriented consumer. To reach these consumers, we will introduce the Bio-Diaper through specialty stores and mail order to begin with, slowly moving to large retail chains and supermarkets. It is our goal to eventually supplant the need for regular disposable diapers.

As you can see, this example starts by explaining the purpose of the plan and quickly moves into supporting evidence that plainly illustrates the need described in the preceding sentence. The second paragraph details the whole thrust of the plan. The readers learn that the proposed product is a biodegradable diaper that is very price competitive with regular disposable diapers on the market. It goes on to specify an entry point into the market that introduces the probable marketing strategy to reach the goal described at the end of the paragraph.

MARKET ANALYSIS

Within the market analysis section, you need to define the market that the product targets. The market definition will start from a broad study of the industry and eventually conclude with a narrow definition of the market share that the product can reasonably sustain. The basis for this information will be drawn from your market research (see Chapter 3). Through the market analysis, you want to chart items such as sales history, current demand, and future trends for your product or service based on the customer base you have targeted. From this information, you need to draw conclusions regarding the demand of the product or service: Is the demand for your product or service increasing, leveling off, or declining?

In addition to defining demand, you will have to identify the decision makers who will buy your product or service. For instance, with disposable diapers, the mother is often the decision maker as well as the buyer. You also need to address motivating factors behind a purchase. Why do these potential customers buy this particular product or service? How do they buy it? When do they buy it? Where do they buy it? And what brands do they buy?

With these questions answered, you need to include information about the social and cultural aspects of the industry including the demographics of age, sex, income, educational background, housing (owner or renter), and the economic conditions of the period covered by the plan. The industry discussion should cover the technological condition of your product class within the industry. Is your product high-tech, low-tech, or no-tech? If high-tech, how often are new products introduced? This will have a direct bearing on the product life cycle, which you need to cover in this section of the marketing plan. In general, you want to provide a clear idea of just how technology affects the product or service and its marketability. The distribution channels used in the industry should be described in detail, along with any applicable laws and regulations.

The market analysis section should also define the target market. This can be done in the same fashion as described for the business plan in Chapter 8, where we used a market equation to define market share. This equation can also be used for the marketing plan. Much of the market equation is based on defining specific market segments that fit the demographic profile of your prospective customers. Within the scope of the marketing plan, concentrate on describing these segments, providing a complete description of just exactly who these people are. It may help to answer the following questions before proceeding with a segmentation of the industry:

1. What is the geographic location of the target market?
2. Is the geographic location subject to any special climatic changes or topography?
3. What are the prominent cultural, ethnic, religious, and racial characteristics of your target customers?
4. What is the social class of your target customers?
5. What is the sex of your target customer base?
6. What is the age range of your target customer base?

7. What is the education of your target customer base?
8. What is the income range of your target customer base?
9. What is the average household size of your target customer base?
10. What is the marital status of your target customer base?
11. What is the work status of individuals within the household?
12. What is/are their occupation?
13. What member of the household is the decision maker for your particular product or service?
14. What member of the household does the actual buying for your particular product or service?
15. How much disposable income is available to the average household?
16. What are the wants and needs of the target market?
17. What are the key traits of your product or service?
18. How frequently do customers use your product or service?
19. What is the size of the market?
20. What are the growth trends of the market?
21. What is the technological environment of your product or service?
22. Are new products introduced frequently in this industry?
23. Are there any laws or regulations that will affect the marketing of the product or service?

Confining the description of your target market to a segment of the industry that is most desirable for your proposed product or service will also allow you to maximize your resources more effectively. If you try to market your product or service toward too many market segments, you will squander your resources without effectively reaching any of them.

Your target market analysis should include arguments indicating the advantages of this market over other segments. You should also include the overall size of the target market in relation to the industry, as well as demographic characteristics, geographics, psychographics, and lifestyle. Developing a thorough understanding of your customers is as important as knowing your own capabilities and those of your firm or department.

The following market analysis section was developed for the biodegradable diaper example:

MARKET ANALYSIS (Sample)

Today, babies mean big business. Over the past few years, retailers of baby products have witnessed sharp increases in their profits. According to the latest figures at Juvenile Products Manufacturer's Association (JPMA), sales of infant products have topped $1.6 billion. And that excludes clothing and some $12 billion worth of toys. It also doesn't account for the baby-food market ($750 million) and the

Figure 23.1 Sales of Children's Products

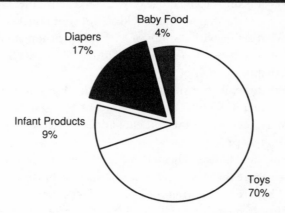

diaper industry ($3 billion). Altogether, sales have approached $17 billion a year. Industry sales breakdowns are shown in Figure 23.1.[1]

Sales seem to be linked more to changing needs than to a true boom in population, although baby boomers have reached their peak childbearing years. But beyond these demographic factors, changing attitudes and spending patterns of millions of baby-boomer parents are fueling the surge in the infant retail industry. Closely linked to this surge is an increase in disposable diaper sales. In 1994, the disposable diaper market accounted for $2.7 billion according to the JPMA, up from 1979 when disposable diaper sales were only $700 million. That means that the disposable diaper market has grown close to 400 percent since 1979. With projected growth for 1995 pegged at 15 percent, sales will reach an estimated $3.1 billion. Market growth in revenue is shown in Figure 23.2.

While the overall disposable diaper market is projected to continue its growth in the foreseeable future, the market is beginning to level off and enter a mature stage. The primary concern of producers in the industry is to find gaps in the market that will create future trends. Studies commissioned by Softie Baby Care, Inc., and conducted by Timmons Research have revealed that both existing parents and prospective parents have a deep concern over the impact of regular disposable diapers on the environment. Over 60 percent of the respondents were extremely concerned about the environment and the effects of nondegradable diapers, 20 percent were mildly concerned, 15 percent were concerned, and 5 percent used cloth diapers or a service. This survey underscores the importance parents are placing on the ecology. The results of the Timmons Research Survey are shown in Table 23.1.

---

[1] For convenience of presentation, tables and figures in this example have been assigned numbers following the style used throughout this book. In creating your own marketing plan, you should choose an identification system appropriate for your illustrative material.

Figure 23.2 Disposable Diaper Market Growth

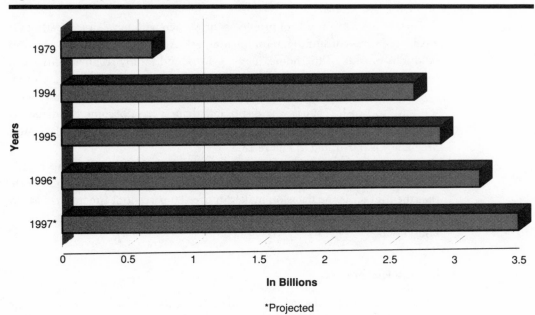

In Billions

*Projected

Using 1,000 parents as total population: 60 percent = 600 parents who are extremely concerned about the effects of nondegradable diapers on the environment.

Based on statistics from the Census Bureau, over 1.6 million pounds of nondegradable disposable diapers are ending up in the waste disposable dumps across the United States each year. This alarming fact is a real concern for many parents, so much so that some are turning to cloth diapers and diaper delivery services.

Working Mothers

One of the reasons disposable diapers are enjoying an overwhelming popularity compared with the $300 million diaper delivery and cloth diaper market is the increase in the number of working mothers. According to the Bureau of Labor Statistics, 50.4 percent of all married mothers return to work before their children's second birthdays. The percentage of working women continues

Table 23.1   Timmons Survey

EFFECTS OF NON-DEGRADABLE DISPOSABLE DIAPERS—PERCENTAGE			
EXTREMELY CONCERNED	MILDLY CONCERNED	CONCERNED	CLOTH DIAPERS
60%	20%	15%	5%

to rise, and by the end of the 20th century, women should make up 47 percent of the U.S. workforce.

This creates a multitude of problems for women with new babies. Caring for a baby is a time-consuming, monumental task. And for new mothers who also hold jobs outside of the home, juggling work and family responsibilities can often prove overwhelming. When both the mother and father are employed, time is at a premium and parents can no longer afford to sit around waiting for the wash to finish. That is why disposable diapers have become the diaper of choice for parents. The increase in numbers of women in the workplace after pregnancy is illustrated in Figure 23.3.

Industry studies indicate that over 70 percent of disposable diaper purchases are made by households in which the mother works. They also indicate that the mother is the decision maker in over 80 percent of the households in terms of the choice of diaper used, and are also the buyers in 95 percent of the households.

Income Factors

Diapers are considered a necessity and not a luxury item to parents. Income is not a consideration in terms of buying diapers, but it is a determinant of the kind of diapers that are purchased. In the Timmons Survey, a definite income-to-price variable influenced the purchase decision of the household. In more affluent homes with income above $30,000 annually, over 90 percent purchased name-brand disposable diapers, 9 percent purchased cloth diapers, and

Figure 23.3   Women in the Workplace

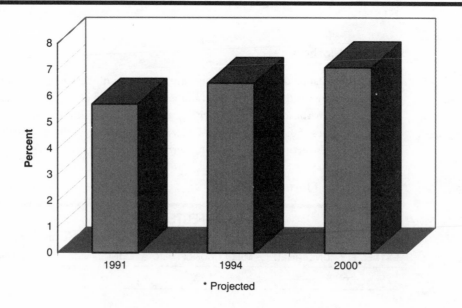

* Projected

approximately 1 percent utilized a diaper service. On the other hand, in households with incomes below $20,000 annually, the choice of 40 percent of the respondents was generic or store-brand disposable diapers, while the remaining 60 percent used cloth diapers.

Purchasing Factors

Equally important to the purchase decision, according to the Timmons Survey, is the place where disposable diapers are purchased, as well as the frequency, average number, and how they are purchased. As shown in Figure 23.4, 41 percent of respondents made the majority of purchases for disposable diapers in supermarkets, 19 percent made their purchases in specialty stores, 18 percent bought diapers in discount stores, 13 percent went to chain stores, and 9 percent used miscellaneous avenues such as membership warehouses.

Disposable diapers are purchased on an average of once a week by 92 percent of the buying market. The other 8 percent purchase disposable diapers on an average of two times per week. In addition, the Timmons Survey also indicates that coupons are used heavily in supermarket purchases of disposable diapers with over 70 percent of those households purchasing through this distribution channel using coupons.

The Product

Introduced in the 1960s, disposable diapers have gone through a number of changes including changes in fasteners, liner material, sizes of the pad, and even colored patterns, but the main appeal of disposable diapers is still the convenience, and this is very important to working mothers. Made of non-degradable plastic, disposable diapers are used once then thrown away. This eliminates the chore of washing cloth diapers.

Plastic is by far the most expensive ingredient in the production of disposable diapers. The plastic is a durable material that is highly resistant to weather and chemicals. Because of the structure of disposable diapers, they cannot be

Figure 23.4 Distribution Channels

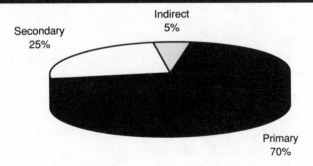

broken down by sunlight or through natural deterioration, creating a huge amount of nondegradable waste.

Biodegradability, therefore, becomes a highly desirable added benefit to consumers. In fact, the major trend among manufacturers is the development of a cost-effective agent that can affect the molecular structure of the plastic diaper upon extended exposure to environmental elements. This development would promote a significant change in the disposable diaper industry and how it is viewed by consumers.

THE COMPETITIVE ANALYSIS

The competitive analysis section identifies your competitors and evaluates their strategies to determine their strengths and weaknesses in comparison with your product. With this evaluation, you will be able to focus on what makes your product unique. This is important because in this section of the marketing plan you want to illustrate the distinct advantage your product will have over the competitors you have identified. As detailed in Chapter 3, you can evaluate your competitors by placing them in strategic groups according to how directly they compete against you for a share of the customer's dollar. Under each competitor or strategic group list the product or service, size, profitability, growth pattern, objectives, assumptions of the market, current and past strategies, organizational and cost structure, and strengths and weaknesses.

Once again, it may be helpful to ask questions that will further define your competitors:

1. What type of media is used to market the product or service?
2. How many hours per week are purchased to advertise through the media used in this market?
3. Who are your competitors?
4. What products do they sell?
5. What is the market share of your competitors?
6. What are their past strategies?
7. What are their current strategies?
8. What are your competitors' strengths and weaknesses?
9. What potential problems face the marketing of the product or service?
10. What potential threats from your competitors face the marketing of the product or service?
11. What potential opportunities are available for the marketing of the product or service?

You may even want to chart the strengths and weaknesses of your competitors against your product by weighing specific product and organizational factors within the context of a competitor strength grid as detailed in Chapter 8.

Using the biodegradable diaper example, the competitive analysis section would look like the following:

COMPETITIVE ANALYSIS (Sample)

The disposable diaper market can be divided into several strategic groups starting with the primary competitors that make up the bulk of the market: Pampers, Huggies, and Luvs. These three companies control 70 percent of the entire disposable diaper industry and target the middle- to upper-income markets. The second strategic group is made up of secondary competitors such as private-label marketers and smaller brand-name manufacturers who control 25 percent of the market and target the discount shopper. The generic-brand marketers form the last group of competitors in the disposable diaper industry; they represent 5 percent of the market and target primarily the low-income consumers. Refer to Figure 23.5 for a complete breakdown of the disposable diaper market by market share.

Peripheral strategic groups consist of cloth diaper marketers and diaper services. The cloth diaper marketers are important because, as sales increase in this sector of the industry, volume in the disposable diaper sector may be affected. Cloth diaper marketers are geared mainly toward budget-conscious shoppers where the head of the household and the only wage earner in the family is a man. Diaper services, on the other hand, directly encroach on the disposable diaper market because they offer convenience as well as the benefit of the safer, nonpolluting cloth diapers. Due to this, they target middle- to upper-income families with working mothers and a preference for an environmentally safe diaper.

Primary Competitors

By far, the companies with the greatest market share in the industry are Pampers, Huggies, and Luvs. All three target a more affluent customer and their price structure reflects this strategy. In a survey of five major supermarket chains in the southern California area, the price differentiation between the three is minimal with Pampers leading the pack most of the time.

Figure 23.5 Disposable Diaper Market by Share

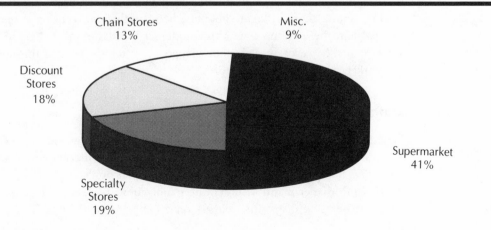

These companies also distribute their products through the same channels, with supermarkets and specialty stores being the most prominent. All three attack the market aggressively through promotional campaigns that place a large portion of their advertising dollars in television and magazines. Direct-mail campaigns featuring coupons and giveaways as well as cooperative advertising programs with hospitals that sponsor Lamaze programs offer additional marketing support.

Secondary Competitors

This strategic group consists of smaller disposable diaper marketers as well as store-brand product lines. This group appeals to discount shoppers, who don't care about decorative designs on the diapers or the packaging. Instead, they look for quality and price relationships. Competitors in this strategic group offer consumers a good-quality diaper at a price significantly below the major competitors.

Store-brand diapers are distributed through the chain of stores producing them. For instance, Toys 'R Us produces private-label disposable diapers that are sold exclusively through its own stores. The major advertising for store-brand diapers is through the chain's weekly flyers in local newspapers featuring items that are currently on sale.

Smaller manufacturers differ in their distribution strategy and promotional campaigns. These brands are sold mainly through specialty stores and selected supermarkets. They generally rely on point-of-purchase displays and coupon offerings in the local newspapers. Rarely will you see them advertise on television or in magazines.

Generic Brand Marketers

Geared toward the low-income, budget-conscious shopper, generic-brand disposable diapers are the ultimate no-frills diaper. Their price points are very attractive to budget-conscious shoppers because they are often priced 45 percent below name brands and 25 percent below store brands.

The problem with these disposable diapers is their association with poor quality among more affluent shoppers; because their advertising support is nonexistent, there are no claims to counteract this assumption. Due to their price points, however, these brands diapers are often distributed through supermarkets and large discount stores.

Cloth Diapers and Delivery Services

Together, these two strategic groups equal a $300 million segment of the diaper industry. They are significant because both groups offer alternatives to parents and fulfill many of the needs that disposable diapers don't.

For cloth diaper manufacturers, the major competitive advantage is price. The cost of using disposable diapers on a baby for 30 months is $2,000 to

$2,600 more than using cloth diapers. In addition, some babies are allergic to components in disposable diapers and some people object to the waste generated by disposable diapers; thus, cloth diapers become a considerable competitive force. Cloth diapers are distributed through specialty stores, chain stores, membership warehouses, and mail order. Because of their cost advantage, cloth diapers are marketed mainly to low-income consumers and households where only one parent works. They are also finding ready acceptance among the affluent households that have a deep concern over the environmental problem created by disposable diapers.

Diaper services are in direct competition with disposable diapers and are very price competitive with the primary competitor group of disposable diaper marketers. They deliver freshly laundered cloth diapers on a weekly or biweekly basis and collect used diapers. Customers can request more diapers if they choose. Diaper services usually target affluent households in which both parents work and are very selective about what diaper they use, and are very concerned about the environment.

PRODUCT DEVELOPMENT

As with the business plan, the purpose of the product development section is just what the name implies: It details the development of the product or service. This requires placing that development in the context of charting development goals, placing time lines on those goals, and associating costs with the development of the product or service. The product development section also needs to define the expertise required to develop the product or service and state whether it is currently available on staff or the necessary human resources must be recruited to produce the proposed product or service.

The first thing you have to detail is the current status of the product or service. Explain exactly what stage of development your product or service is in. You may have a laboratory prototype of the product or a rough idea of what type of equipment and materials will be required for a service concept, but have saved ironing out all the "wrinkles" until you acquire adequate financing. In this event, the potential investor or lender will want to know just how far along you are in the development of the product or service concept.

After you have provided information about current status, you then need to detail the goals associated with its development. When forming your goals, do not underestimate time lines, costs, and personnel requirements, or you may not cover the expense of production adequately. If you say you can develop a product in three months and it will actually take closer to four months, that raises the costs beyond your specified requirements, thus jeopardizing the completion of your product.

The goals you set for product development must meet the *technical* as well as the *marketing* aspects of the product; so the development team can work with a focused outline. We stress technical as well as marketing aspects because the product must be developed with an eye toward marketability. If the product doesn't meet the needs of the target group of customers and doesn't offer the key strengths defined in your competitive analysis, then there is no sense in developing it. It is nice to set goals, but for them to work, a certain level of expertise has to exist within the company. For instance, to create a biodegradable disposable diaper, you have to have expertise in the realm of plastics that deteriorate with prolonged exposure to the sun. If the development team does not include someone with that expertise, the product may never make it to market. Your goals must also provide a set of general procedures with schedules and delegated personnel for each task to ensure completion of the goals by the specified deadlines.

The work assignments created from the broad procedures will break down the various tasks into stages that will achieve the goals outlined in this section. These stages usually include a completion date for delivery of the preliminary product, a time line for preliminary product review and revision, and final delivery of the product.

Within the product development section, you should also produce a development budget. When forming your development budget, you need to take into account all the expenses required to develop the product, from prototype to production. As detailed in Chapter 8, these costs usually include:

- **Material.** All raw materials used in the development of the product.
- **Direct labor.** All labor costs associated with the development of the product.
- **Overhead.** All overhead expenses required to operate the business during the development phase such as taxes, rent, phone, utilities, and office supplies.
- **General and administrative costs.** The salaries of executive and administrative personnel along with any other office support functions.
- **Marketing and sales.** The salaries of marketing personnel required to develop prepromotional materials and plan the marketing campaign that should begin prior to delivery of the product.
- **Professional services.** Those costs associated with consultation of outside experts such as accountants, lawyers, and business consultants.
- **Miscellaneous costs.** Costs that are related to product development.
- **Capital equipment.** Equipment requirements related to product development. To determine capital requirements, first establish the type of equipment you will need; decide whether to acquire the equipment or use outside contractors; and finally, if you decide to acquire the equipment, whether to lease or purchase it.

The last element you need to discuss in the product development are risks involved in the development of the product or service. Identifying these risks is important because it will help you address these concerns. It will also show any potential investors or lenders that you have completely thought out the development process and have already come up with a plan to solve any problems that may occur.

PRODUCT DEVELOPMENT (Sample)

The design and development effort of Softie Baby Care's biodegradable diaper, Bio-Diaper, will include the development of the product to the final version for marketing, a distribution system and sales promotion program to establish a solid customer base, and recruitment of key organizational team members.

Product/Market Development

1.0 Development of biodegradable plastic
- **1.1** Research
- **1.2** Development of plastic biodegradable shell in three sizes: small (up to 12 lbs.), medium (up to 24 lbs.), large (up to 36 lbs.)
- **1.3** Testing
- **1.4** Delivery

2.0 Pad development
- **2.1** Delineation of pad thickness and sizes for production of a thin and thick pad in three sizes: small (up to 12 lbs.), medium (up to 24 lbs.), large (up to 36 lbs.)
- **2.2** Delivery of raw material
- **2.3** Development of odor reduction agent
- **2.4** Testing of pads for absorbency and odor reduction
- **2.5** Delivery of the three specified pad sizes
- **2.6** Integration of pads into plastic shell for working prototype

3.0 Package creation
- **3.1** Creation of imprint designs (will require the recruitment of a marketing director to oversee the operation)
- **3.2** Integration of imprint designs onto working prototype
- **3.3** Creation of shelf packaging that will include the design, color scheme, and manufacture

4.0 Integration/Delivery
- **4.1** Component tests of shell, pad, and packaging
- **4.2** Product test of working prototype
- **4.3** Alpha test
- **4.4** Beta test

5.0 Manufacturing
- **5.1** Design modification as a result of alpha and beta tests
- **5.2** Preproduction run
- **5.3** Cost reduction check to achieve pricing goal of $8.40 per package for sale to wholesale distributors.
- **5.4** Manufacturing run

6.0 Final delivery
- **6.1** Distribution development that will include the recruitment of a sales manager and sales force to obtain purchase orders from five national distributors that service major supermarket and drugstore chains, and

enlist the aid of manufacturer representatives in the 10 major regional territories of the United States.

6.2 Delivery of initial orders for distributors and retailers

6.3 Implementation of sales promotion campaign that is budgeted at $15.3 million during the first year of operation and is geared toward raising consumer awareness at the supermarket and specialty store level.

The major benchmarks include:

- A disposable plastic diaper shell that is biodegradable and available in three sizes: small (up to 12 lbs.), medium (up to 24 lbs.), large (up to 36 lbs.).
- A thin and thick pad in three sizes (to fit the plastic shells) with effective odor control and high absorbency.
- Imprinted designs of favorite nursery characters in pastel colors.
- Attractive pastel package designs.
- A suggested distribution price point of $12 per package.
- A manufacturer's price of $8.42 per package.

The development effort for Bio-Diapers will be spearheaded by the following executives of Softie Baby Care:

- **Vice President of Production—Roger Smith.** Reporting directly to the CEO, responsibilities include the management of the research and development arm of the company. Mr. Smith has a strong background as a research and development director in the realm of industrial plastics.
- **Vice President of Operations—Steve Smith.** Reporting directly to the CEO, responsibilities include the management of all purchasing and inventory control operations. Mr. Smith has considerable experience in purchasing and inventory control operations for large manufacturers.

Risks

Since the development effort of Softie Baby Care is phased over a period of time, the risks are very few and controllable; they include:

- **Product acceptance by consumers.** Based on surveys commissioned by Softie Baby Care, Inc., we feel consumer acceptance will be high and present minimal risk.
- **Technical delays.** The expertise already present within the principal owners of the company, will greatly reduce this risk.
- **Increased competition from major competitors.** Most of the major players are in the process of developing their own biodegradable diaper. The risk of increased competition will be reduced through superior product quality and consumers' association of Bio-Diapers as the first biodegradable diaper.

Table 23.2   Development Expenses

ITEM	BUDGETED AMOUNT (000)
Materials	$ 7,133
Direct labor	7,254
Overhead	9,992
G&A	1,088
Equipment	806
Marketing and sales	1,500
Professional services	400
Miscellaneous	300
Total	$28,473

Financials

The major development expenses are shown in Table 23.2.

OPERATIONS

In the operations section of the marketing plan, you need to describe how the product will be integrated into the company's continuing operations. Start by listing all the various products or services your company offers and the motivating factors behind your current proposal. After you've done this, provide some background information on yourself and your management team. Include your experience, projects you've supervised, education, and so on. Give the reader a good idea of whom he or she will be dealing with and what type of expertise this proposal is based on. You want to make your investors comfortable with you and your track record so they will feel confident about funding your project.

You should also discuss your business's financial resources, human resources, and strengths and weaknesses. It is essential to let the reader know how solvent your company is, what type of expertise you have available to implement your marketing plan, and how you perceive your company's strengths and weaknesses.

As with the business plan, you should include tables showing operating expenses, capital requirements, and the cost of goods. Operating expenses should include all fixed and variable expenses associated with the operations of business. This is important because it will illustrate how the introduction of the new product will impact the company from an operating expense viewpoint. The same is true of the capital requirements table. It will show the required investment for new equipment to produce the product. If this equipment is already in place, the investment shown in this table might be nominal or even nonexistent. Most companies, however, will need to purchase new equipment to produce the new product.

The cost of goods table is mainly for manufacturers, merchandisers, and service companies that utilize a great deal of material to service their clients. This table will show the material, labor, and overhead expenses associated with the production of the product on a continuing basis.

For a more thorough explanation regarding these three financial tables, see Chapter 8.

Before you begin writing this section, you may want to answer the following questions:

1. What are your strengths and weaknesses?
2. Are you asset rich?
3. What type of expertise do you have in this industry?
4. What is your past track record like?

OPERATIONS (Sample)

Softie Baby Care, Inc., is a disposable diaper manufacturer that has been in existence for 10 years. We currently produce a product line of disposable diapers featuring three sizes and two pad thicknesses—thin and thick. Our line of disposable diapers is very price competitive with current store-brand prices while offering the same packaging amenities associated with the industry's primary competitors.

Through aggressive marketing campaigns that include direct mail giveaways, coupon offers, price discounts to retailers, and distribution through large and small specialty stores, chain stores, membership warehouses, and selected supermarkets, we have been able to build sales of $200 million. Currently we control 7.4 percent of the disposable diaper market.

Softie Baby Care, Inc., is a privately held company that has grown very conservatively over its ten-year history. The principal officers of the firm include its three founders: John Smith, CEO, Roger Smith, president, and Steve Smith, vice president of marketing. Before starting Softie Baby Care, Inc., all three principals had been involved in the diaper industry for 10 years. Combined, they have 30 years of experience in the industry.

With this expertise, we have been able to build a company with over $300 million in total assets. Our company's strengths include strong quality-brand association with consumers, a firmly entrenched national distribution system, and the experience of upper management. Our weaknesses include limited capital resources as well as a limited product line.

The following sections describe the structure for the operations of the business.

Marketing

Managed by the president and marketing art director, the scope of responsibilities that this department will cover revolve around sales promotional support at the wholesale and retail level. The marketing department will define the markets, outline the prospective customers within those markets, plan the various sales and promotional campaigns, measure response and analyze the market to produce competitive strategies that will generate sales leads, and supervise the development of the product to meet the needs of the customer base.

Sales

As a manufacturer, sales for Bio-Diapers will take place on three levels: manufacturer to distributor, distributor to retailer, and retailer to consumer. At the manufacturer-to-distributor level, an inside sales force of 13 will be responsible for sales to distributors on a national level from the company's headquarters in Sherman Oaks. Territories will be divided into the 10 major regions of the United States, and their responsibilities will include initiating sales contact, closing the sale, and servicing existing accounts.

At the distributor-to-retailer level, manufacturer's representatives will be recruited and serviced by the sales manager to cover the 10 major regions of the United States. The manufacturer's representatives will concentrate mainly on specialty stores and small grocers, while the distributors will handle chain supermarket accounts.

Customer Relations/Service

Customer service will involve two layers of personnel: one layer to deal with problems originating at the manufacturer-to-distributor level, and another layer to handle problems originating at the retail level. The sales manager and account executives will service their accounts to assure that the distributors and reps receive their shipments and that the billing and payment schedules are consistent with the agreements signed between both parties.

The second layer of personnel will handle problems originating at the retail level. Most complaints from consumers will be handled at the retail level and passed along through the distribution channel. That means the distributors and reps will interface with the manufacturer, Softie Baby Care, Inc. The customer service staff will handle all these problems.

Production

The function of production is to coordinate the actual manufacturing of the product. The production requirements for Bio-Diapers can be broken down into several operational procedures:

1. Purchasing of raw material and inventory control.
2. Pad and shell production—cutting, integration of components, attachment of tape fasteners, and imprinting of the shell.
3. Packaging—counting, stuffing, and sealing.
4. Shipping to the designated distributors and retailers.

Table 23.3   Cost of Goods

	YEAR		
	1995	1996	1997
Units sold (000)	18,400	53,875	108,875
Begin FA (000)	0	11,040	32,325
FA% sales (units)	60	60	60
End FA (000)	11,040	32,325	65,325
Change/FA (000)	11,040	21,285	33,000
Begin PA (000)	0	4,600	13,469
PA% sales (units)	25	25	25
End PA (000)	4,600	13,469	27,218
Change/PA (000)	4,600	8,869	13,749
Begin U (000)	0	2,760	8,081
U% sales (units)	15	15	15
End U (000)	2,760	8,081	16,331
Change/U (000)	2,760	5,321	8,250
Units sold (000)	18,400	53,875	108,875
Units FAI (000)	11,040	21,285	33,000
Units PAI (000)	4,600	8,869	13,749
Units UI (000)	2,760	5,321	8,250
Total units mat (000)	36,800	89,350	163,874
Mat/unit ($)	1.19	.97	.97
Mat costs ($000)	43,792	86,670	158,958
Units sold (000)	18,400	53,875	108,875
Units FAI (000)	11,040	21,285	33,000
Units PAI (000)	4,600	8,869	13,749
Total L&OH units (000)	34,040	84,029	155,624
Labor/PA% (units)	50	50	50
Labor/unit ($)	.52	.52	.52
OH/unit ($)	2.49	2.49	2.49
Labor costs ($000)	16,505	41,389	77,350
OH costs ($000)	79,033	198,190	370,386
Total L&OH ($000)	95,538	239,579	447,736
Change/U ($000)	3,284	5,161	8,003
Man costs ($000)	136,046	321,088	598,691
Change/PAI ($000)	12,397	21,951	34,029
COG man ($000)	123,649	299,137	564,662
Change/FAI ($000)	46,368	84,714	131,340
COG sold ($000)	77,281	214,423	433,322
COGS/unit ($)	4.20	3.98	3.98
Begin UI ($000)	0	3,284	8,445
Change UI ($000)	3,284	5,161	8,003
End UI ($000)	3,284	8,445	16,448
Begin PAI ($000)	0	12,397	34,348
Change PAI ($000)	12,397	21,951	34,029
End PAI ($000)	12,397	34,348	68,377
Begin FAI ($000)	0	46,368	131,082
Change FAI ($000)	46,368	84,714	131,340
End FAI ($000)	46,368	131,082	262,422
Begin inventory ($000)	0	62,049	173,875
Change inventory ($000)	62,049	111,826	173,372
End inventory ($000)	62,049	173,875	347,247
Revenue/unit ($)	8.42	8	8
Revenue ($000)	155,000	431,000	871,000
Inventory turn	2.49	2.47	2.50

Embedded within the production process is a commitment to quality control that is measured by designated quality assurance agents who are employees of the company.

The costs associated with the production of the product are detailed in Table 23.3. The cost of goods breakout is based on two elements: materials and labor. During the manufacturing process, the product may be in any one of four stage:

1. Unassembled or just raw material (U).
2. Partially assembled (PA).
3. Fully assembled (FA).
4. Sold (S).

Merchandise that is sold is expensed as a cost of good, while merchandise that isn't sold is placed in inventory.

Much of the production process for Softie Baby Care will be automated through the use of cutting, pressing, assembly, and packaging machines. A staff of 27 will control the entire production process during the first year of operation. The investment costs for the manufacturing equipment are shown in Table 23.4.

Table 23.4   Capital Requirements

	YEAR		
	1995	1996	1997
Initial capital	$0	$0	$0
Net capital	$0	$1,111	$3,989
Testing equipment			
No. units	18,400	53,875	108,875
TE/unit	12,000	12,000	12,000
TE cap	$161	$161	$161
TE cap req	$247	$721	$1,460
New TE cap	$247	$474	$739
Assembly equipment			
No. units	18,400	53,875	108,875
AE/unit	12,000	12,000	12,000
AE cap	$403	$403	$403
AE cap req	$617	$2,764	$3,655
New AE cap	$617	$2,147	$891
Packaging equipment			
No. units	18,400	53,875	108,875
PE/unit	12,000	12,000	12,000
PE cap	$242	$242	$242
PE cap req	$370	$1,084	$2,195
New PE cap	$370	$714	$1,111
Total new cap	$1,234	$3,335	$2,741
Total capital	$1,234	$4,446	$6,730
Depreciation	$123	$457	$731

Table 23.5   Operating Expenses

| | YEAR | | |
	1995	1996	1997
M&S Expense	$16,690	$ 47,405	$ 94,375
Prod Expense	9,615	28,115	56,815
R&D Expense	3,216	6,240	9,648
Admin Expenses	3,828	8,164	16,848
Overhead	45,859	121,741	249,876
Total Expenses	$79,331	$212,655	$428,282

Research and Development

Research and development will be in charge of improving the existing product and developing new ones to expand the product line of the company. This division of operations will continually test new technology for applicability and then define the new prototype.

Administration

Administration is in charge of those overhead functions that support operations such as accounting, legal, human resources, and other functions related directly to internal operations.

The expenses for Softie Baby Care are illustrated in Table 23.5. They are divided according to the functional lines detailed earlier.

OBJECTIVES AND GOALS

Objectives and goals are important to a marketing plan because they provide a direction in terms of your strategy for growth. You will gear your company and its resources toward these precise targets. They are specific in nature, measurable over time, and within the realm of feasibility. And, they are linked to the company's basic mission and purpose.

Your objectives and goals should spell out exactly what you intend to accomplish. Long-range objectives are usually linked to the performance and prosperity of a company and involve financial targets such as overall sales, return on investment, and increased profit margins. Your long-range objectives don't have to be confined to financial goals, but can include other areas of growth such as market share, personnel, productivity, research and development, and/or any other objective you deem suitable for your company or the division you manage. You can have a single objective, or two, three, or more. As long as these objectives do not conflict, there should be no problem listing more than one task in the objectives and goals section of your marketing plan.

Short-term goals should interact with your long-range objectives. They should be viewed as a series of building blocks that eventually will lead to the achievement of your long-range objective(s). Short-term goals let you know whether you are on the right course or not. These goals are often developed around financial targets but, like long-range objectives, should not be confined solely to these items. In fact, a well-developed short-term goals section takes into account the various elements within your organization that need to be accomplished to achieve your long-range objectives such as an increase in production staffing, introduction of modernized equipment, and increased productivity. The whole idea is to further define just how you will reach your long-range objective.

Before you begin writing your marketing plan, you should prepare your long-range objectives and short-term goals. The previous sections of your marketing plan should have presented the facts and ideas that support the logic behind your objectives and goals. The objectives and goals section should tie all this information together in a plan of action with a specified time frame.

Start your objectives and goals section by stating your long-range objective(s). Then describe the various short-term goals that must be accomplished by a certain time period to reach your objectives. Some consultants believe it is necessary to include the actual supportive evidence used to formulate your stated objectives. This may simply be a table showing the growth of the company to meet your long-range objective or it may be an equation showing exactly how you determined your stated targets. However, supportive evidence is not essential as long as you clearly state your objective(s) and goals and explain why you think they are feasible. Our view is to use intriguing supportive material whenever it is possible to do so while maintaining brevity. Remember, you're dealing with busy people who are usually considering more than one marketing plan for funding. You must relay your facts and ideas in an economic format: Your presentation needs to be concise and it needs to stand out.

Following is a sample objectives and goals section for the biodegradable diaper example.

OBJECTIVES AND GOALS (Sample)

The objective of Softie Baby Care, Inc., is to obtain 25 percent of the disposable diaper market within a three-year period with the introduction of its new biodegradable disposable diaper line, Bio-Diapers. During the first year of business, our goal will be to concentrate on marketing and distribution to raise awareness among consumers and retailers. Projected sales goals for the first year at an average retail cost of $12 for a large bag of Bio-Diapers is $155 million, which is a 5 percent market share. To reach this goal, it will be necessary to increase our marketing staff by 10 percent and our production staff by 3 percent.

Our second-year goals are to reinvest profits to increase our marketing staff by close to 200 percent and our production staff by close to 300 percent while continuing with a strong research and development program aimed at reducing the component costs of the Bio-Diaper product by 5 percent, leading to a 5 percent reduction in the suggested retail price. With these elements in place, our goal is to increase sales from the first year by 7 percent, resulting in $431 million of sales and a 13 percent market share.

With volume expected to double in the third year, our goals are to increase our production staff by 100 percent and marketing by another 100 percent. Our goal in the third year is to increase sales by 12 percent to $871 million with the objective of a 25 percent market share.

First-Year Sales Goals

*Industry sales	$3,100,000,000
Bio-Diapers sales	$ 155,000,000
Market share	5%
Marketing costs	$ 15,500,000
Unit sales	18.4 million

Second-Year Sales Goals

*Industry sales	$3,317,000,000
Bio-Diapers sales	$ 431,210,000
Market share	13%
Market growth	7%
Marketing costs	$ 41,300,000
Unit sales	53.9 million

Third-Year Sales Goals

*Industry sales	$3,482,850,000
Bio-Diapers sales	$ 870,712,500
Market share	25%
Sales growth	12%
Marketing costs	$ 85,000,000
Unit sales	108.9 million

*Projected industry sales. See Figure 23.2.

MARKETING TACTICS

Through the analysis of your customers, competitors, industry, and company, you should have a good idea of your marketing strategies. Your strategies should primarily revolve around establishing the point of entry in the product life cycle and a distinct competitive advantage. This involves defining the elements that will set your product or service apart from your competitors or strategic groups. You need to detail this competitive advantage so the reader understands not only how you will accomplish your goals, but why your strategy will work. For example, marketers can enter first, early, or late when attacking a new market. They can also penetrate vertically or horizontally, or through a market niche.

In the strategies section you should not only detail your market strategy, but how your competition will react. Many marketing plans overlook this area. Don't make the same mistake. For every action you take, your competitors will respond with a countermove to maintain their present position in the market or expand it. Provide the reader with an outline of your competitors' probable reactions to your plans, and how you propose to counteract them.

To develop the information you will need for the marketing tactics section, you should ask yourself a series of tactical questions and write your answers down in a notebook under the correct subject headings.

Product

1. How does your product or service differ from the competition?
2. What are the main features of your product or service?
3. At what point is your product entering the life cycle?
4. What message will you include on your package?
5. What will be the size, shape, color, and material of the package?
6. What is your sales and production forecast?

Distribution

1. What channels will you use to distribute your product or service?
2. How will you time your distribution?
3. Will your distribution be intensive, selective, or exclusive?

Price

1. What are your pricing objectives?
2. What will be your basic per unit cost of acquisition?
3. Will you offer a discount policy?
4. What will be your per unit price?
5. What do you project your revenue and profit to be?

Sales Promotion

1. What are your constraints?
2. How will you position your product or service?
3. Will your promotions be coordinated with distribution schedules?
4. What are your sales promotion objectives?
5. Will you employ extensive personal selling?
6. How large will your sales staff be?
7. Will you define sales territories?
8. How will you compensate your sales force?
9. What type of publicity will you seek?
10. What are your publicity objectives?

Advertising

1. What will your campaign theme be?
2. What will your copy theme be?

3. What media do you plan to use?
4. How frequently will you use these avenues?
5. What will be the size of your commercials or ads?
6. What will their cost be?
7. What is your advertising budget?

After you've answered all these questions, review your answers and start forming your thoughts for the marketing tactics section. Start each segment of this section with your marketing strategy and its objectives and explain the actions you will use to reach these objectives. Include supporting information whenever possible. This may be in written form; in a graph, table, or illustration; or it may include all these techniques. Be as clear and concise as possible so that the reader can grasp the tactics behind your objectives quickly and identify what you believe it will take in terms of costs and timing to accomplish them.

MARKETING TACTICS (Sample)

To reach our projected objectives and goals Softie Baby Care, Inc., must be guided by the following key items of our marketing strategy.

Product

The main emphasis of our product strategy will be the added value of a biodegradable diaper. This fulfills an unmet need of consumers of disposable diapers: to be environmentally safe. Bio-Diapers will eliminate the continued buildup of nondegradable waste as a result of disposable diapers. At the same time, all the key elements that have made disposable diapers so attractive to the modern generation of parents will still be firmly in place. Therefore, our product strategy is to strongly enter the market with an emphasis on creating brand loyalty through the benefit of our environmentally safe diaper.

To build the brand loyalty of Bio-Diapers, we will take advantage of this distinct feature by implementing the following:

- Obtain support from environmental protection groups (Sierra Club, EPA, Green Peace).
- Invite product testing from consumer groups to substantiate our claim.
- Place one of our campaign slogans on the package: "The First Biodegradable Diaper."

A secondary emphasis will be placed on the colored designs printed on the actual diapers. Many parents like to maintain a color scheme and motif throughout their nursery such as ducks, bears, or kangaroos. Bio-Diapers will be available in a number of colored prints that correspond to the popular colors and themes used in children's nurseries. This added feature to the actual product design has a crucial appeal for our primary consumers, who are mothers of upper-income households.

Packaging will also appeal to upper-income groups. Bio-Diapers will come in a cardboard box with a convenient plastic handle. The boxes will come in three colors to denote the size and quantity of the package:

- A pastel yellow will signify sizes of newborn to 14 pounds.
- A pastel green will signify 14 pounds to 25 pounds.
- A pastel purple will signify 25 pounds and up.

While Bio-Diapers will be vastly different from the diapers produced by our competitors, we will be entering into competition with the major brand-name producers such as Pampers, Huggies, and Luvs. Although many of these manufacturers have plans in the works for their own biodegradable diapers, they will try to counteract Bio-Diapers through claims of poor quality. This will appear mainly in print ads attacking the pad absorbency of Bio-Diapers. We will counteract this strategy by commissioning pad absorbency tests of Bio-Diapers and our major competitors. We will then publish the results using a direct-mail campaign.

Distribution

Bio-Diapers will be marketed primarily as a convenience item in the same way as regular disposable diapers. Distribution, therefore, is critical in obtaining the coverage we will need to effectively reach our primary customers. Our research has indicated that the most effective distribution strategy to reach the primary customers of Bio-Diapers is through large grocery and drugstore chains, independent baby goods stores, department stores with baby departments, major toy store chains, and membership warehouses. Since Softie Baby Care, Inc. is a small manufacturer compared with giants like Kleenex (the manufacturer of Huggies), we will employ a four-tiered channel of distribution to assure the presence of Bio-Diapers in the right place at the right time and in the right quantities. Our four-tiered approach will flow from manufacturer to wholesaler, from wholesaler to retailer, and from retailer to consumer.

To achieve our stated first-year sales goals, we will need to build national distribution in quarterly stages that will span the entire year. During the first quarter, we will concentrate on distribution through all major grocery and drugstore chains, as well as the larger independent baby goods stores. This will produce the national range of coverage needed to properly capitalize on the aggressive advertising campaign we will undertake to create shelf awareness. To meet initial production quotas, the production staff will have to be increased at this point. To assure sufficient stock is on hand to meet expected consumer demand, retailers will be offered stock allowances.

During the second quarter, we will expand our distribution from major grocery and drugstore chains to smaller independent baby goods retail outlets.

Due to increased market coverage, we will need to increase our marketing staff at this time and add more wholesalers.

During the third and fourth quarters, we will continue to expand our distribution to the remaining outlets such as department stores, membership warehouses, and major toy store chains. We will need to add more wholesalers to handle the increased distribution.

Pricing

Our pricing strategy will correspond with our product strategy. Since Bio-Diapers will enter the market as a premium-brand product targeted toward upper-income groups, we will employ a premium price for Bio-Diapers based on the added value of a biodegradable agent that will make the diapers environmentally safe. The suggested retail price for the product will be about 20 percent higher than the price of regular disposable diapers. A premium price for the product will be applied for these reasons:

1. The distinct product differentiation between Bio-Diapers and other brands will warrant a higher price based on its premium value.
2. Due to high research and development costs to produce the patented agent responsible for the molecular breakdown of diapers on prolonged exposure to the sun, initial prices will be higher.
3. Since Bio-Diapers will be a new concept, there will be a need for considerable advertising support to introduce the product; the price will reflect that cost.
4. Higher initial component costs will also demand a higher price.

Through the first sales year, the prices for Bio-Diapers will remain stable due to lack of competition from the major disposable diaper producers. Starting in the second year of sales, the price for Bio-Diapers will drop roughly 5 percent. We will incorporate this pricing strategy for several reasons:

1. Lower material costs in the production stage due to higher volume.
2. Reduced costs in key components from continued research and development.
3. Introduction of biodegradable diapers from major competitors at a higher price. Undercutting them will help increase sales and market share.

The Bio-Diaper price will remain steady at this point for the second and third sales years.

Sales Promotion

The promotional strategy Softie Baby Care, Inc., will use is to obtain maximum reach within our target market group to promote initial purchases and sustain repurchases. Our strategy to stimulate initial purchases will revolve around in-store displays in major grocery and drugstore chains, coupon programs initiated through print advertising and direct mail, and a giveaway program targeted toward existing and prospective parents, hospitals, and baby-care education classes.

During the first year of sales, 10 percent of projected sales will be set aside for promotional purposes. This will total $15.5 million. Of this, 65 percent will be budgeted for advertising, 30 percent for sales promotion, and the remaining 5 percent will be held in a contingency fund.

Through our sales promotions, the objectives of Softie Baby Care, Inc., is to stimulate initial purchases of the product and maintain those customers through repurchases. Our sales promotion strategies to achieve these objectives are:

1. Obtain in-store display and price feature support from retailers by implementing a merchandising allowance program where we will make contractual payments of $15 for a 10-package, in-store display. This merchandising allowance program will only be established at major grocery and drugstore chains, and at larger independent specialty baby goods stores.
2. A coupon program will be instituted through advertisements in local newspapers and baby magazines, a direct mail campaign, and through Lamaze classes. The coupons will offer a discount of 75 percent off the regular price. Twenty million coupons will be distributed through newspapers, magazines, and the mail.
3. Along with the coupon program, we will initiate a giveaway program to existing and prospective parents of babies. They will be mailed a free sample of the diaper along with their coupons. In addition, we will supply hospitals and baby care education classes with free samples. This giveaway program will create greater product awareness and stimulate product use.

Competitor reaction to our aggressive sales promotion campaign will be to increase their own efforts, mainly through point-of-purchase displays. This will be done through merchandising allowance programs designed to provide incentive for retailers to provide more in-store display space. We feel this can be easily counteracted by our own merchandising allowance programs in major grocery and drugstore chains.

Advertising

Our advertising strategy will be an aggressive campaign geared toward accomplishing the following objectives:

1. To effectively reach our primary purchase group of married women between the ages of 26 and 34 with one or more children still in the diapering stages and household incomes above $30,000. These customers are not only the decision makers when it comes to diapers but also the purchasers.
2. To increase awareness by attaining a 60 percent penetration level among our target market. We will commission a penetration study one year after the introduction of Bio-Diapers.
3. To generate product awareness and support among wholesalers and buyers, merchandisers, and store managers of retail outlets.

The total advertising budget for the first year will be $10 million. The goal in our advertising strategy is threefold:

1. Advertising support will be used aggressively throughout the first and second years with major pushes during the introductory period and major sales promotion activity—January through July 1995. From August to the end of the year, advertising will be reduced to evaluate results from earlier efforts.

2. We will concentrate our efforts on a print-only media format. Ads for our print copy will consist of a full-page, four-color format that will emphasize the comfort, absorbency, and snugness of the diaper and its primary advantage of environmentally safe waste. The head will read: "Finally, a diaper that is truly disposable." In the bottom right-hand corner of the ad, we will include a coupon. Production expenses will be limited to 1 percent of the total advertising budget.

3. Our media strategy will be to purchase space in national and regional baby care magazines, which total 18 publications. We will purchase a minimum of nine insertions in monthlies, six insertions in bimonthlies, and four insertions in quarterly magazines to generate frequency and provide support throughout the year (see Table 23.6). Whenever possible, we will try to secure preferred positions in the magazines to increase our total reach. Total exposure is estimated at 92.6 million with a net unduplicated coverage of 45 percent of the primary target group.

Table 23.6 Advertising in Baby Magazines

MAGAZINE	NO. INSERTS
American Baby	9
Baby Talk	9
Baby Times	6
Baby!	3
Chatelaine's New Mother	4
Chicago Parent News	6
Child	6
Dallas Child	9
Expecting	4
Lamaze Parents' Magazine	3
Metro Parent	2
Mothers Today	6
Parenting	9
Parents' Magazine	9
Rodale's Children	6
Today's Parent	6
Twins	6
Working Mother	9
Working Parents	6

FINANCIAL PROJECTIONS

This section is perhaps the most critical in the whole marketing plan because it will be the one most closely scrutinized by the reader. The financial projections section will include all the financial information relevant to the project. Although each plan differs, most will require you to include a three-year income statement, a three-year cash flow projection, and a three-year summary of the balance sheet. You may also want to include an implementation schedule and balance sheet.

Through your research and from the body of the marketing plan, you should already have solid numbers on which to base your projections. Your financial information is not only important to investors to determine whether or not they want to fund the proposal, but it is also important to you because it provides you with yet another crucial tool that will aid you in controlling the course of the project.

Chapter 16 of this book discusses in detail what's involved in generating the financial control tools and statements required for this section of the marketing plan. A three-year income statement is a month-by-month look at projected sales, fixed and variable expenses, and profits. It provides a quick look at how you believe your project will perform over a three-year period. See Table 23.7. Whereas the income statement takes a close look at sales and expenses, the cash flow projection summarizes this information and displays the availability of cash on a month-to-month basis. A cash flow projection is usually divided into two sections: income and total expenses. When expenses are subtracted from income, you wind up with your cash flow excess or deficit.

The cash flow projection is an important barometer because it shows when you will need additional money to keep the project going. Although we recommend you perform a three-year profit/loss and cash flow projection, you can generate them for a one- or two-year period or even up to five years. The choice is yours. A three-year period, however, is generally the norm for marketing plans. See the sample cash flow projection in Table 23.8.

A balance sheet is a table of assets and liabilities (i.e., summary of credits and debits) as well as capital, or owner's equity, of a business at one point in time. A balance sheet is typically generated when books are closed after a specific period of time, either monthly, quarterly, or annually. For the marketing plan, we suggest you provide balance sheets on a yearly basis. You will be able to generate a balance sheet for year one, year two, and year three. Information for the balance sheet will be available from your profit and loss statement and cash flow projection. See the sample balance sheet in Table 23.9.

You may also want to include an implementation schedule in your marketing plan. The implementation schedule lists the major goals and tasks necessary to complete the project and the capital outlay for each period. You can base your schedule on weekly, monthly, or quarterly periods. If your project is a lengthy one with projections up to five years, we recommend basing your

Table 23.7   Sample Income Statement

INCOME STATEMENT (000)	JANUARY	FEBRUARY	MARCH	APRIL	MAY	JUNE	JULY	AUGUST
INCOME	4,650	6,200	6,200	9,300	10,850	10,850	13,950	15,500
COST OF GOODS	2,318	3,091	3,091	4,637	5,410	5,410	6,955	7,728
GROSS PROFIT	2,332	3,109	3,109	4,663	5,440	5,440	6,995	7,772
MARGIN %	50%	50%	50%	50%	50%	50%	50%	50%
EXPENSES	2,080	2,784	2,784	4,176	4,872	4,872	6,263	6,959
NET PROFIT	252	325	325	487	568	568	732	813
MARGIN %	5%	5%	5%	5%	5%	5%	5%	5%
DEPRECIATION	17	17	15	12	12	11	9	9
NET PROFIT BEFORE INTEREST	235	308	310	475	556	557	723	804
MARGIN %	5%	5%	5%	5%	5%	5%	5%	5%
INTEREST	17	17	14	12	12	11	8	8
NET PROFIT BEFORE TAXES	218	291	296	463	544	546	715	796

Table 23.8   Sample Cash-Flow Projection

CASH FLOW STATEMENT (000)	JANUARY	FEBRUARY	MARCH	APRIL	MAY	JUNE	JULY	AUGUST
CASH SALES	3,488	4,650	4,650	6,975	8,138	8,138	10,463	11,625
RECEIVABLES	0	0	1,550	2,325	2,713	2,713	3,488	3,875
OTHER INCOME	0	0	0	0	0	0	0	0
TOTAL INCOME	3,488	4,650	6,200	9,300	10,851	10,851	13,951	15,500
MATERIAL	0	1,752	1,752	2,628	3,065	3,065	3,941	4,379
DIRECT LABOR	495	660	660	990	1,155	1,155	1,485	1,651
OVERHEAD	2,371	3,161	3,161	4,742	5,532	5,532	7,113	7,903
MARKETING & SALES	501	668	668	1,001	1,168	1,168	1,502	1,669
R&D	96	129	129	193	225	225	289	322
G&A	115	153	153	230	268	268	345	383
TAXES	0	0	670	0	0	670	0	0
CAPITAL	173	173	148	123	123	111	86	86
LOANS	35	47	47	71	83	83	106	118
TOTAL EXPENSES	3,786	6,743	7,388	9,978	11,619	12,277	14,867	16,511
CASH FLOW	-298	-2,093	-1,188	-678	-768	-1,426	-916	-1,011
CUMULATIVE CASH FLOW	-298	-2,391	-3,579	-4,257	-5,025	-6,451	-7,367	-8,378

SEPTEMBER	OCTOBER	NOVEMBER	DECEMBER	1995	1ST QTR	2ND QTR	3RD QTR	4TH QTR	1996	1997
15,500	18,600	21,700	21,700	155,000	47,410	86,200	124,990	172,400	431,000	871,000
7,728	9,274	10,819	10,819	77,280	23,587	42,885	62,183	85,769	214,424	433,322
7,772	9,326	10,881	10,881	77,720	23,823	43,315	62,807	86,631	216,576	437,678
50%	50%	50%	50%	50%	50%	50%	50%	50%	50%	50%
6,959	8,351	9,743	9,743	69,586	20,191	36,710	53,230	73,420	183,551	370,747
813	975	1,138	1,138	8,134	3,632	6,605	9,577	13,211	33,025	66,931
5%	5%	5%	5%	5%	8%	8%	8%	8%	8%	8%
7	5	5	4	123	183	133	91	50	457	731
806	970	1,133	1,134	8,011	3,449	6,472	9,486	13,161	32,568	66,200
5%	5%	5%	5%	5%	7%	8%	8%	8%	8%	8%
7	5	5	4	120	47	34	24	13	118	118
799	965	1,128	1,130	7,891	3,402	6,438	9,462	13,148	32,450	66,082

SEPTEMBER	OCTOBER	NOVEMBER	DECEMBER	1995	1ST QTR	2ND QTR	3RD QTR	4TH QTR	1996	1997
11,625	13,950	16,275	16,275	116,252	35,558	64,650	93,743	129,300	323,251	653,250
3,875	4,650	5,425	5,425	36,039	11,321	20,584	29,847	41,168	102,920	207,338
0	0	0	0		0	0	0	0	0	0
15,500	18,600	21,700	21,700	152,291	46,879	85,234	123,590	170,468	426,171	860,588
4,379	5,255	6,131	6,131	40,726	9,392	17,077	24,761	34,154	85,384	156,789
1,651	1,981	2,311	2,311	15,350	4,553	8,278	12,003	16,556	41,390	77,350
7,903	9,484	11,065	11,065	79,032	21,801	39,638	57,475	79,276	198,190	370,386
1,669	2,003	2,337	2,337	16,691	5,215	9,481	13,747	18,962	47,405	94,375
322	386	450	450	3,216	686	1,248	1,810	2,496	6,240	9,648
383	459	536	536	3,829	898	1,633	2,368	3,266	8,165	16,848
670	0	0	670	2,680	2,759	2,759	2,759	2,759	11,036	22,468
74	49	49	37	1,232	1,334	967	667	367	3,335	2,741
118	142	165	165	1,180	130	236	342	472	1,180	1,180
17,169	19,759	23,044	23,702	163,936	46,768	81,317	115,932	158,308	402,325	751,785
-1,669	-1,159	-1,344	-2,002	-11,645	111	3,917	7,658	12,160	23,846	108,803
-10,047	-11,206	-12,550	-14,552	-11,645	-11,534	-7,617	41	12,201	12,201	121,004

Figure 23.6   Sample Balance Sheet

BALANCE SHEET (000)

ASSETS	1995	1996	1997
Current Assets			
Cash	$166,250	$323,250	$653,250
Account Receivables	36,038	102,920	207,338
Inventory	62,049	173,875	247,247
Total Current Assets	$264,337	$600,045	$1,107,835

	1995	1996	1997
Fixed Assets			
Capital/Plant	$1,111	$3,989	$5,999
Investment	0	0	0
Miscellaneous Assets	0	0	0
Total Fixed Assets	$1,111	$3,989	$5,999

	1995	1996	1997
Total Assets	$265,448	$604,034	$1,113,834

LIABILITIES

Current Liabilities	1995	1996	1997
Account Payables	$43,792	$86,670	$158,958
Accrued Liabilities	119,272	301,388	568,607
Taxes	2,681	11,034	22,468
Total Current Liabilities	$165,745	$399,092	$750,033

Long-Term Liabilities	1995	1996	1997
Bonds Payable	$0	$0	$0
Notes Payable	1,298	1,298	1,298
Total Long-Term Liabilities	$1,298	$1,298	$1,298

	1995	1996	1997
Total Liabilities	$167,043	$400,390	$751,331

OWNER'S EQUITY	1995	1996	1997
Owner's Equity	$98,405	$203,644	$362,503

	1995	1996	1997
Total Liability/Equity	$265,448	$604,034	$1,113,834

schedule on quarterly periods. If it ranges between one year and three years, implement a monthly schedule. If it is a year or less, you may want to consider a weekly schedule.

Keep in mind while you are forming your projections that market potential, sales potential, and sales forecast all mean different things when it comes to forecasting. Market potential pertains to the total potential sales for a product or service within a specific geographic area over a fixed period. Sales potential refers to the capability of the market to absorb the volume produced by a specific company within the industry, supposedly yours. For instance, market potential for the first year for the entire disposable diaper industry is $3.1 billion, but the ability of the market to purchase Bio-Diapers during that period is only $248 million.

Your sales potential, however, is not the same as your sales forecast. Sales forecast is the actual sales you believe your company will generate during the year based on your market research. In the Bio-Diapers example, the sales forecast for the first year is $155 million, far short of the $248 million potential. There are reasons companies don't achieve the total sales potential within a market:

- Limited resources.
- Margin of return on the investment.
- Unforeseeable market factors.

Perhaps the greatest reason, however, that companies don't achieve total sales potential is the law of diminishing returns. This means the more aggressive you are in achieving total sales potential, the greater your marginal cost will be for each additional percentage point above your sales forecast. In the Bio-Diapers example, we've forecasted sales of 62 percent of the total sales potential. To achieve the goal, $15.5 million has been budgeted for marketing. That's $250,000 for each percentage point of sales in the forecast. To increase our sales forecast beyond this point and achieve our total sales potential, we would have to raise the cost per point aggregately. This may be $300,000 per point, $350,000, or as much as $500,000. If the cost per point goes up to $300,000 for instance, you would need a total marketing budget of $30 million. That's almost double the original budget to achieve the additional 38 percent. Most companies won't be able to sustain this expenditure, and it is not very good planning to try to do so. The return on investment will decrease while your overhead increases. Your break-even point will be extended dramatically and you won't reach your profit goals. All this has to be considered when forecasting sales.

SUMMARY

The summary concludes your marketing plan; therefore, it should highlight the significant points in your plan such as the advantages your product has over your competitors, cost structure, and profits. Strongly emphasize the differential advantage of your product. This is something your product or service has that your competitors don't. It is the key to your marketing plan's success.

The summary doesn't have to be long. A few paragraphs should allow you to encapsulate all the major points within your marketing plan so it is readily available for readers who bypass the body of the plan and go straight to the summary. Don't skimp on this section of the marketing plan. Just because you're at the end doesn't mean you should be lazy.

Your summary statement should start off by explaining the purpose behind the marketing plan. Since most are formed for the purpose of raising capital, you should include the amount of the investment you will need to accomplish your goals. Next, provide the reasons this investment is justified such as your differential advantage and any other main elements that will contribute to its success. To make sure you include all the necessary information, you may want to write down all the major points you've discussed.

You should include an implementation schedule in the summary outlining all the major tasks and when they will be executed. You can base your schedule on weekly, monthly, or quarterly periods. If your project is a lengthy one with projections up to five years, we recommend basing your schedule on quarterly periods. If it ranges between one year and three years, implement a monthly schedule. If it is a year or less, you may want to consider a weekly schedule.

SUMMARY (Sample)

This marketing plan has presented the logistics behind the introduction of Bio-Diapers—the first disposable diaper that is completely biodegradable. Because it is a unique concept within the disposable diaper industry, we strongly believe that an initial investment of $80.6 million dollars to cover start-up inventory costs would provide Softie Baby Care, Inc., with the additional strength needed to strongly enter the market.

Given this capital and the successful execution of this marketing plan, a market share of 25 percent over a three-year period is more than possible.

RESOURCES

Associations

Association of Small Business Development Centers, 1313 Farnam, Suite 132, Omaha, NE 68182, 402-595-2387

Center for Entrepreneurial Management, Inc., 180 Varick Street, New York, NY 10014, 212-633-0060

National Small Business United, 1155 15th Street NW, Suite 710, Washington, DC 20005, 202-293-8830

Small Business Network, P.O. Box 30149, Baltimore, MD 21270, 301-466-8070

Small Business Service Bureau, 554 Main Street, Worcester, MA 01601, 508-756-3513

Magazines

Barron's National Business and Financial Weekly, 200 Liberty Street, New York, NY 10281, 212-416-2700

The Business Journal, 101 Second Place SE, Suite 202, P.O. Box 2879, Gainesville, FL 32601-6592, 904-371-9228

Business Marketing, 740 North Rush Street, Chicago, IL 60611, 312-649-5260

The Business Owner, Thomas Publishing, Inc., 383 South Broadway, Hicksville, NY 11801, 516-681-2111

In Business, 419 State Avenue, Emmaus, PA 18049-3717, 215-967-4135

Journal of Small Business Management, West Virginia University, College of Business Economics, Bureau of Business Research, P.O. Box 6025, Morgantown, WV 26506-6025, 304-293-5837

Marketing News, 250 South Wacker Drive, Suite 200, Chicago, IL 60606-5819, 312-648-0536

Nation's Business, 1615 H Street NW, Washington, DC 20062, 202-463-5650

Small Business Report, 203 Calle Del Oaks, Monterey, CA 93940, 408-899-7221

24

Sales

Business strategy is usually a four-letter word—we're in it for *cash*. And other than liquidating the business, the sole source of cash for a business is sales. In fact, it is often referred to as the lifeblood of any business. Is it little wonder then, that the common goal for each and every business owner is the pursuit of *sales*. Keep in mind, though, that making the sale is only half the picture. Your goal should not only be *the sale*, but the experience of the customer before, during, and after the sale. A satisfied customer who has had a positive experience with your company will recommend you to other potential customers and, more important, will continue to buy from you. That is when you *really* begin to profit from a sale.

It is extremely important to realize that the apparently subtle difference between selling something and getting someone to buy something is a significant business philosophy. Salespersons sell, and you hire a sales force to sell. But your ultimate task is rather different: to get people—customers—to buy. You must build a responsive program that will attract customers who are solvent and who will respond to your offer by laying down hard cash—more than once, if possible.

Building a selling attitude in your business is difficult to accomplish. It is usually the culmination of concepts, plans, programs, and actions all designed not only to make the sale, but to keep the customer. The issues you face and the decisions you make before attempting to sell are far more important to your success and survival than the actual execution of a sale.

PLANNING FOR SALES

Successful sales don't happen by chance. They are a product of hard work, not only by the salespeople but by you, the entrepreneur, as well. To achieve a high level of sales, the entrepreneur and his or her company's sales staff has to work that much harder to compete with companies that are often larger and have greater resources.

To attain effective sales, the owner of a small business must be familiar with the entire selling process. That is actually the first step when organizing for sales: recognizing that sales, like any strategic marketing tool, is the product of careful planning and organization. Once the entrepreneur has crossed that hurdle, the actual *sales management process* begins.

Sales Forecasts

One of the first elements that you need to handle when organizing for sales is to determine an accurate sales forecast from which you can form a budget and plan. There are many ways to produce a sales projection for your business. Two of the most common are:

1. **The sales force survey.** Each salesperson is asked to develop individual sales projections for the upcoming year that take into account past performance, including number of customers sold, revenue per customer, and total sales generated. Using past performance as a basis, the salesperson would then project increases, if any, in the number of customers and the average revenue generated by the total number of clients. For instance, if a salesperson had been servicing 750 customers the previous year at an average of $500 per customer for a total of $375,000 and projects that his customer base will increase by 100 new customers in the upcoming year to 850 with average revenue pegged at $520, then the sales projection would be 850 × $520 = $442,000. That would be an increase of 18 percent in sales from the previous year. If your business sells more than one product, the sales projection should take into account all revenue streams generated through sales efforts.

2. **The executive committee survey.** The entrepreneur forms a committee, usually consisting of him- or herself and those managers involved in the sales process, who are responsible for compiling the market analysis and developing a quantitative outlook concerning the sales potential of the business. Like the *sales force survey* method, the *executive committee* method should base the sales projection not only on industry, competitor, customer, and overall market conditions, but on past sales performance and the internal climate of the business. For instance, if you have sold 10,000 units of product A at an average price of $8 per unit, the total sales for that product would be $80,000. Based on market conditions and the internal support from the business, the executive committee projects unit sales to increase by 10 percent to 11,000 at an average price per unit of $8.20 for total projected sales of $90,200 for product A. If your company sells more than one product, you would have to conduct this type of sales projection for each to arrive at a total projected sales figure.

While the *executive committee* method of projecting sales is a nice way to centralize the planning process, it doesn't take full advantage of the practical experience and understanding of the market that salespeople bring to the forecasting process. Since salespeople constantly deal with customers and obtain feedback from them, their input is of great importance to the planning process.

Including the salespeople in the planning process also is valuable from a motivational standpoint. It lets them know that you appreciate their opinions and talents, and that awareness is critical because they are the ones who have to go out and sell the product. They have to feel good, not only about the product, but about the company as well.

By combining the *survey* and *executive committee* methods, you can build a better consensus among your executive managers and salespeople as to what constitutes an accurate sales projection for the company. Have each salesperson submit an individual sales projection to you or the sales manager, and then have the executive committee form its own forecast. Compare the two to develop a final projection (see Figures 24.1 and 24.2).

The Sales Plan and Budget

Once the sales projection has been finalized, you need to develop a strategy or plan that will enable the company to reach that goal. The main focus of the sales plan is to determine *how sales will occur* and the *cost*. The question of "how" encompasses many different elements such as the flexibility a salesperson will have in pricing, how to handle returns, policies for the servicing of products, salesperson compensation, and salesperson market responsibilities. But perhaps the foremost consideration here is whether to employ a sales force or conduct sales efforts through independent representatives.

Closely related to this aspect of the sales plan is *cost*. How much can you afford to spend to make the sale? Some entrepreneurs feel that they can spend whatever it takes. If the market is willing to bear an inflated price for the product, that strategy might be applicable. Most businesses, however, especially small businesses, operate within a very competitive environment where pricing is integral to sales, along with service, support, and other marketing elements. So most companies can't spend whatever it takes to make a sale. They have to work within a budget (see Figure 24.3 for a sample budget).

The costs incurred to make the sale are a large part of the sales budget. For instance, it will cost you more to employ a sale force than it would to contract with independent reps or to sell through direct marketing; however, while employing a sales force is costly, it allows you to control the sale more effectively and provide better service to your customers.

To determine if, and how many, salespeople you can afford, you can utilize a fairly standard measurement tool called the "cost method," in which the average amount to employ a salesperson is divided into a specific amount budgeted for sales. For instance, if projected sales for the upcoming year are calculated at $3 million and 8 percent is budgeted for sales, that would be a total of $240,000. If sales supervision is 30 percent of the sales budget, $72,000 would be allocated for this purpose. That would leave $168,000 for the sales staff. If

Figure 24.1 Sales Projection by Customer

DATE: _____

SALESPERSON: _____

APPROVED BY: _____

TITLE: _____

CUSTOMER	TYPE OF INDUSTRY	SALES CALLS PER YEAR	TOTAL CURRENT SALES	PROJECTED SALES INCREASE	TOTAL PROJECTED SALES	PRODUCT A	PRODUCT B	PRODUCT C	PRODUCT D
TOTAL									

Figure 24.1 Sales Projection by Customer

DATE: _____

MANAGER: _____

FOR PERIOD ENDING: _____

CUSTOMER	TOTAL NO. OF CUSTOMERS	REVENUE PER CUSTOMER	TOTAL CURRENT SALES	PROJECTED CUSTOMERS SOLD	PROJECTED NO. OF CUSTOMERS	TOTAL PROJECTED SALES
TOTAL						

Figure 24.3 Sample Budget

DATE: _____

MANAGER: _____

FOR PERIOD ENDING: _____

ITEM	JAN	FEB	MARCH	APRIL	MAY	JUNE	JULY	AUG	SEP	OCT	NOV	DEC	TOTAL
TOTAL													
PROJECTED SALES													

the average cost to employ a salesperson is $42,000 per person, the total number of salespeople the company can afford would be:

$$\$168,000 \div \$42,000 = 4 \text{ salespeople}$$

When doing a cost analysis for sales, you must include base salaries and commissions in the average cost to employ a salesperson. After you have completed the cost analysis, you will have a concrete idea of whether hiring a sales force is compatible with your marketing strategy. This is extremely important, because if your marketing strategy is to have nationwide distribution, you would be hard pressed to do that with only four salespeople as illustrated in the preceding example. If all you had was $240,000 to spend on sales, that money might be better spent contracting with independent reps or by mounting a direct mail campaign (if your products are compatible with this type of strategy).

Whatever the decision, the cost must be included in the *sales budget.* Four major sections need to be accounted for within the sales budget:

1. Projected sales.
2. Salaries and commissions.
3. Advertising and special promotions.
4. Sales administration.

We have already described the process involved in developing a sales projection. After finalizing the sales projection, you should include all the details regarding company sales in the sales budget and allocate these figures in months, with estimates of seasonal variations. The same is true of the remaining components of the sales budget. These costs should be estimated based on the sales projections and divided into monthly segments as well.

Defining the Sales Organization

Most firms spend, as a general rule, between 5 and 10 percent of sales on sales force costs. Large firms often spend more. Basically, sales force costs are broken down into two categories: compensation and expenses.

When the funds are available, most entrepreneurs prefer to build an in-house sales force for their company. The main advantage to this is the control you have over your sales force, which allows you to train them your own way and ensures that all the salespeople's efforts will be concentrated solely on your product.

When building a sales force, however, you must define an appropriate sales organization that will allow the company to meet its marketing objectives. This means defining the positions which will be required when developing the sales organization, the objectives and responsibilities of each position, the hierarchy that will be needed to develop effective communication channels, and the organizational format.

Defining the Sales Positions

In most cases, the sales force consists of a number of different positions. Which ones you institute will depend on the sales-delegated funds you have available, your sales goals, and the mode by which you distribute your product. Some positions consist only of taking orders from customers who have already decided to buy, while others involve persuading an individual to buy in a cold-call sales situation. William Cohen in his book *The Entrepreneur and Small Business Problem Solver,*[1] divides sales positions into seven groups:

1. **Delivery persons.** Don't generate sales but are responsible for the prompt and safe delivery of the product and are, therefore, important to the sales force from a service point of view.
2. **Inside order takers.** Passive salespeople who are present to assist the customer and make the buying experience a pleasant one.
3. **Outside order takers.** Passive sales position where the emphasis is placed on servicing customers throughout a specific geographic territory.
4. **Missionary or public relations salespeople.** Responsible for performing promotional activities and providing other services for the customer.
5. **Technical salespeople.** Often referred to as sales engineers. These people have a great deal of technical knowledge along with superior selling skills and can discuss the product or service in depth with the customer demonstrating it if necessary.
6. **Creative sellers of tangibles.** Responsible for outside sales of a physical product line using creative selling techniques to educate customers and persuade them to buy. Persuasiveness, product knowledge, honesty, and the ability to pinpoint and fill a customer's needs are crucial for this position. Depending on the technical complexity of the product, this position can overlap that of the sales engineer.
7. **Creative sellers of intangibles.** Similar to creative sellers of tangibles except these salespeople deal in products that cannot be easily demonstrated such as insurance, advertising, and consulting services.

Organizing the Sales Force

Once you have decided which positions you will include on your sales force, you must develop an organizational plan. It should address several basic issues that will define communication channels, the flow of authority, and the criteria for organizing the sales force.

When developing a plan, you must first determine your sales organization criteria. Possible criteria are:

- **Territories.** The most common way of organizing a sales force is by physical territories. In this type of structure, a territorial manager supervises a number of reps, each of whom has a specific geographic territory in which

[1] William A. Cohen, *The Entrepreneur and Small Business Problem Solver,* 2nd ed. (New York: John Wiley & Sons, 1990).

to operate. The first step in instituting a territorial format is to divide your market into territories making sure that all districts provide the sales representatives with equal sales potential and workloads. This will eliminate jealousy on the part of reps who might otherwise feel they have not gotten a fair chance to make money. Equal sales territories will also make it much easier for you to evaluate sales performance. In establishing your territories, take into account indexes such as buying power of the population, number of businesses in an area, and trading areas within the territory.

- **Product line.** Organizing by product line is especially attractive to companies that offer a good mixture of diverse products or services, or products or services that are sold to a variety of different markets. Organizing your sales force by product line allows each of the various products or markets to receive the type of attention needed for successful sales. For instance, if your company sells computer hard drives and stereo CD players, it would be very difficult for one salesperson to sell both products within a territory. A more effective strategy would be to have a different salesperson in charge of selling each product, who could bring a higher level of expertise to the sales of that product line.

- **Types of customer or size of the account.** Organizing your sales force by customer or size of account would be beneficial when your company deals with only a few major accounts that represent a large portion of your business. Assigning salespeople by account or customer provides the type of attention required for major customers. For instance, advertising agencies often assign each major account to an account executive, who does nothing but satisfy the concerns and needs of that one particular client.

- **Functional organization.** Organizing sales by function is desirable when a product or service requires a great deal of after-market maintenance. If you sell a product or service that requires a great deal of hands-on care by salespeople after the sale, such as counting stock or constantly setting up and refilling point-of-purchase displays, these chores will take away from the time spent developing new accounts. Therefore, it may make sense to organize sales so that one salesperson is developing new accounts and another is servicing existing accounts.

When organizing for sales, keep in mind that most businesses selling consumer services don't apply restrictions to their salespeople. They are free to sell the company's services to any account in any geographic region since the main goal is to build volume within the available trading area.

As a small business, you may want to organize your sales staff by combining some of the structures mentioned earlier. Most small businesses are limited in their resources and rely on the existing expertise of their salespeople. For instance, suppose one of your salespeople has extensive knowledge of a specialized and important product you sell to a few major accounts, but the rest of your products are more consumer oriented. A good way to organize your sales force would be to assign the salesperson with the specialized expertise to the major accounts purchasing that product, while dividing the rest of the sales-people by territories to handle the remaining products. Or if one of your sales-people is more comfortable handling large accounts while another is more effective with smaller accounts, organize your sales force to take advantage of these strengths; you'll experience greater sales.

When picking an organizational format, you need first to achieve economy in the cost of marketing your product, and second, to ensure that each sales-person has the chance to make a decent living. You must evaluate both your sales objectives and the costs of implementing them. Then choose the organizational formula that is simplest and most efficient for your product, your industry, and your customer base.

Structuring Territories

After you have decided on an organizational method, the next step is to define boundaries for each territory. This can take a great deal of time and research, but the result should be the assignment of territories that will allow your sales-people the potential to produce a satisfactory income.

When structuring territories, you need to consider several factors:

- **Current sales and customers.** By reviewing your current sales and customers, you can determine several factors that will influence how you structure a territory: size of accounts, location, demographics, any shifts or trends in sales and customer characteristics, number of calls needed to service an account, and number of accounts per territory. To analyze your current sales and customers, refer to internal records such as customer files, sales reports, and financial statements. This should provide you with a detailed picture of how sales are currently distributed, which customers account for those sales, and the amount of effort it takes to service those accounts.
- **Potential sales and customers.** To gauge potential sales and customers, you need to compile research that can best illustrate the market opportunities for your product or service. Sales potential within a specific market can usually be determined by analyzing the area's potential spending characteristics, purchasing power, present sales volume of the type of product or services you will be offering, and the proportion of the total sales volume you can reasonably obtain. There are many helpful sources of previously compiled information including the Census Bureau, which publishes statistical information in a series of reports titled *Economic Censuses*. The Economic Censuses cover both industries and geographic regions. You can also contact your local chamber of commerce. These organizations often compile a great deal of data about local business conditions and companies operating within their sphere of influence. *Sales and Marketing Management* magazine annually publishes the "Survey of Buying Power," which analyzes sales by geographic region, and the "Survey of U.S. Industrial and Commercial Buying Power." The Department of

Commerce publishes the *Statistical Abstract*. If you determine the sales potential in an area, you can then establish the number of potential customers by matching the demographics against actual customers. This will then provide you with a good outline concerning the territorial structure of your firm. For instance, when using geographic territories, if an area has more potential sales and customers than one salesperson can handle, you will have to decide how the company can best deal with the situation. Based on your research, you may have to organize that geographic market differently—by account, by product, or unrestricted.

- **Transportation.** Another important factor is transportation. How easily can a territory be serviced? Say you've structured your sales force by account and a salesperson has three clients: one in Los Angeles, another in New York, and still another in Dallas. All the accounts are major customers and this particular salesperson has a great deal of expertise with the company's product, yet the transportation costs to provide sufficient customer service are tremendous. If these costs prove too burdensome, you are going to have to reorganize that particular salesperson's territory so that travel is not such an issue. That doesn't just go for air travel. Check the highways and roadways within territories to determine ease of access within a given market. For instance, if you were organizing territories in Los Angeles County, you might choose to divide it into two regions: North and South because the freeway system in Los Angeles is so congested that travel from the northern part of Los Angeles to the southern portion could take hours out of the salesperson's day. Keeping the salespeople concentrated in specific areas of Los Angeles County would decrease their time on the road.

MAKING THE SALE

In addition to planning and structuring your business to create sales, the goal of your management and research efforts is to make sure that your sales force has the necessary tools to meet projections. But while you want to plan, set goals, and implement control systems to make sure your goals are being met, the strategies of your sales force not only should conform to *accepted company guidelines* but should also be uniquely personal.

Sales is as much a creative process as developing a new idea. Sure, all your salespeople will have the benefit of the company resources you provide to make the sale and service the customer, but each individual salesperson should define *how* he or she will accomplish that sale. Every customer is different. While their needs may be similar, their goals and plans will most likely be very different. How salespeople approach, interact, and service their customers will very often spell the difference between making a sale and keeping a sale. And that strategy is the product of the individual salesperson. The rest of this chapter presents information that will be useful both to you and to your sales force.

Prospecting

Before you can begin to understand your customers, you have to determine just who your prospective customers are. If you have done your market analysis, you should already have gathered information regarding both current customers and prospects—a snapshot of their key characteristics. In fact, you may even have developed prospect lists for the territories of your sales force. This is a good example of the company providing valuable tools for their salespeople.

Since the first step in any successful personal sales strategy is effective prospecting, a list of prospects provided by the sales manager is a good starting point, but that is all it is—a starting point. *Your salespeople have to learn to prospect as well.* The more efficient they are at prospecting, the more effective they will be at closing the sale. In their prospecting, your salespeople must first define your target market according to the general demographic characteristics identified from your research. Next, they must start building a list of possible customers based on those demographics. Keep in mind, however, that the universe of possible customers is not equal to the universe of prospective customers.

Although possible customers may meet all the demographic requirements set forth in your research, not all of them will need your product, nor will all of them have the financial means to purchase it. The trick in good prospecting is to qualify possible customers quickly to determine if they will be good, solid prospects.

In some companies, qualifying possible customers is done by insider salespeople who determine the interest level and ordering requirements prior to setting up an appointment for the outside salesperson. With a small business, you may not have the luxury of hiring inside salespeople. In that case, prospecting can be accomplished through other avenues such as direct mail, flyers, cold calling, and so on. The idea behind qualifying is to screen the list of possible customers to avoid wasting time with individuals and organizations that really have no desire or lack the financial means to buy your product. This time can then be invested in prospects with more sales potential. Reference sources such as Dun & Bradstreet, the *Advertiser Red Book* published by National Register Publishing, and the *Thomas Register of American Manufacturers* published by the Thomas Publishing Company are good places to begin looking for leads.

You can often find good prospects through networking by making yourself visible in local community activities as well as industry activities. You don't have to pitch your products at the events you participate in, but you should keep your eyes and ears open to any opportunities that may arise.

Another important point is simply to listen. Too often, people fail to listen to what the other person is saying and miss valuable opportunities. Don't make that mistake. You may obtain important referrals or an actual prospect through your networking, but you need to focus your attention and listen to the people that you meet through your networking efforts.

Also, be sure to read through the local newspaper(s) each day. You may come across a good prospect in an article or an ad. The point is to be as observant as possible when prospecting because the more avenues you pursue when it comes to this important task, the more successful your sales will be.

Understanding Your Customers

Once possible customers have been qualified as good prospects, you need to start collecting as much information about them as possible so you can develop an understanding of their needs and goals. We can't stress this point enough. The more you know about a good, qualified prospect, the better chance you have of closing a sale and servicing that customer after the sale.

Part of the process of analyzing your customers' needs and goals is to conduct a *needs analysis* of each prospect. To conduct a needs analysis, you first have to understand the psychology of how people arrive at purchasing decisions. Most people, both as individuals or as buyers for an organization, are motivated by economic reasons. They consider all the economic factors involved in the purchasing decision, such as price, quality, service, performance, and convenience. Each of these economic factors has a different value for different people. Discovering the value that a particular prospect places on the various factors is one of the goals of a needs analysis.

For example, the Hyundai is one of the most economically priced cars on the market; yet when it was introduced, the Yugo was priced $1,000 less. However, the Hyundai became an overwhelming success while the Yugo struggled. While price was a significant economic factor in the sales of these two cars, consumers also considered other elements such as service, performance, and convenience. Hyundai had set up an aggressive dealership network and supported it sufficiently. The Yugo, on the other hand, suffered from an inadequate dealership network and a general lack of support from the manufacturer.

Although price is not the only determinant in the purchasing decision, many salespeople make the mistake of believing that myth. If, in fact, price was all that mattered, then any company would need only to make sure its price was always lower than every other company's; a needs analysis wouldn't be necessary. The reality, though, is that price points higher than the competition can be justified if they are offset by other economic factors.

Aside from economic factors, other motivational elements include individual needs such as basic living requirements, ego, lifestyle, personal goals, and safety-related necessities. Many times, these needs play a large part in the buyer's final purchasing decision. For instance, ego and lifestyle strongly influence some people when they purchase a car, home, or clothing. Someone in the market for a Mercedes isn't necessarily concerned about price as the primary motivating factor, but will consider safety, quality, and social impact.

Since many factors can affect the purchasing decision, the salesperson must identify the needs and goals of each prospect and then develop a strategy that closely parallels those concerns. The two most critical elements in a needs analysis are the ability to listen and to observe. By listening, you'll be able to pick up on remarks a prospect might make over the phone or at a meeting or in response to a question. For instance, a prospect might say "If I had a personal computer, it would improve my productivity!" Or, "My current car is much too slow!" In both statements, the prospects have identified their needs. The first individual is concerned about productivity and thinks a personal computer would be helpful. The second individual wants a car with more power.

Observation is another key because a good salesperson can learn a lot about a prospect from the person's clothes, car, and office furnishings. A prospect who is wearing a Rolex, an Armani suit, a silk tie, and Gucci shoes is likely to respond to primary motivating factors that focus on social needs such as ego and lifestyle.

You should also observe mannerisms and the way that a prospect answers questions. Body language can reveal a great deal. Is there excitement in the person's voice? What is his or her physical reaction when you mention price? These are all items you should observe when conducting your needs analysis.

Listening and observing are also important when talking to others about the prospect's needs. Don't rely totally on the information you gather from the prospect. To do a thorough needs analysis, talk to other individuals who are familiar with the prospect—administrative assistants, other managers in an organization, spouses, and so on. Ask questions that deal with the needs of the company or the individual, then listen closely and observe how people answer.

Finally, every person has his or her own point of view when it comes to the purchasing decision. Try looking at the situation from the customer's viewpoint. What would be your primary needs if you were in the same situation as the buyer? Try to empathize with the needs of the buyer so you can better understand where the person is coming from.

As you ask the prospect, and individuals close to the prospect, questions, be sure to write down their responses and any of your observations in a log book where you record the results of your sales meetings (or use a standardized sales follow-up report as shown in Figure 24.4). By logging your conversations and observations, you can go back and analyze them to determine the prospect's needs and goals when forming a strategy to meet those objectives. Also, prospects are impressed if you can reference details from past conversations. This shows that you are keenly interested in them and their business and will work hard to satisfy their needs.

Handling Objections

Defining the needs of a prospect and clearly detailing the features or functions of your product or service that parallel those needs are crucial to making the sale. Still, when making your sales pitch, you will most likely encounter a number of objections that you will have to deal with before closing.

Figure 24.4 Sales Follow-Up Form

CLIENT INFORMATION

Company Name:	Type of Business:
Company Address:	
City: State: Zip:	Phone No.: FAX No.:
Contact:	Title:
Proposal:	

SALES TRACKING SHEET

DATE	NOTES	DATE TO FOLLOW-UP	INITIAL

When handling objections, the first thing you should do is listen carefully to the prospect and let the person finish what he or she has to say. Don't get too excited and respond to an objection before you hear the entire concern. Interrupting the prospect is rude and can cause hard feelings. It indicates you have no real concern for what the prospect has to say. Furthermore, it shows that you aren't really listening to the needs of the prospect. Let the prospect finish the sales objection before you attempt a response.

There are several ways to handle an objection—the easiest way is to ignore it. That may seem a little extreme, but if the objection is trivial, then don't be afraid to let it go. For instance, a prospect may say he likes the product but wishes it had a specific feature. Depending on the feature, this may be an immaterial objection, and you can ignore it. But if the prospect raises the objection again, then he does consider it of some importance, and you will have to address it.

Before responding to any objection, though, you should make sure you thoroughly understand the objection. If necessary, you should ask the prospect questions to clear up any confusion. Using a clarification question, you can turn the objection into a positive situation. For instance, if the prospect objects to the product or service because the competition has a better price, you might respond by acknowledging that the competition does indeed have a better price and then follow up the statement with the clarification question: "So what you are really interested is in purchasing the best product for your money?" This is a direct question that clarifies the prospect's need. Almost invariably, the prospect will say yes. At that point, you can once again explain the benefits of the product or service and how they relate to the customer's needs. This will build value for the product in the prospect's eyes.

Another method of handling an objection is to postpone it. For instance, suppose the prospect objects to the price and payment terms before you ever mention them. You could postpone the objection by politely recognizing the concern of the prospect and asking if payment terms could be discussed in depth after you have covered the benefits of the product.

It's not a good idea to postpone an objection unless it is strategically necessary. In the preceding example, discussion of the benefits of the product or service, which is crucial before talking about price, hadn't been completed when the objection arose about price. If the prospect pushes the issue, you should address the objection at once; but if you are allowed to postpone the price objection until the prospect understands benefits of the product, you will then have a much better chance of overcoming the objection and closing the sale. When dealing with objections, the trick is to recognize the concerns behind the statement so that you can take the best action to overcome that particular hurdle. Prospects make objections over any number of things. Some of the more common objections include:

- **The delay.** Probably the most common form of objection, delaying or stalling allows the prospect to postpone the purchasing decision to a later date. When dealing with the delay, the first thing that needs to be determined is whether the stall is real or merely a way to get rid of the salesperson. Between the customer research and the needs analysis, you should be able to determine whether the stall is real. To overcome a stall, you must be polite, positive, and turn the objection around so you are addressing the needs and benefits of the prospect.

- **Don't need it.** This is another common objection. A prospect who claims not to need a product or service may be reacting to a poor presentation or truly feel no need for the particular product. Again, be polite and positive when responding to this objection and try to redirect the discussion toward the needs of and benefits to the prospect.

- **Don't have the money.** A prospect who really needs something will find the money to buy it. Usually, the prospect is concerned about price when making this objection. Generally, if price is the major obstacle, the prospect may be trying to determine what the best price is before making a decision. If the prospect is genuinely concerned about the cost of the product, responding with an affordable way to buy the product may overcome the objection. The main concern when facing this objection is to determine whether the prospect is negotiating for a lower price or better terms, or will respond to your turning around the presentation by justifying the price with superior quality.

- **The product.** Sometimes, a prospect will object to the product itself. He or she may like a competitor's product, or a competitor may have said bad things about your product. Whatever the reason, when responding, don't downgrade the competition. Try selling the product on its benefits. If necessary, point out warranties and guarantees, or provide a product demonstration.

- **The company.** The prospect may already be very loyal to a particular company or product brand, or he may have had a bad experience with your company in the past. Usually, when dealing with this objection, you will have to continually call on the prospect or send relevant information over time to break down the barriers. Eventually, you may convince the prospect that your product is superior to the competition's or that your company is working hard to develop solutions to the problems the prospect has experienced.

The Trial Close

Developing two-way communication is essential during a sales presentation. As previously mentioned, making sure the prospect understands the message that you are communicating is critical to success. We've covered several ways to obtain and interpret signals from the prospect that will establish two-way communication. One of the best methods, however, is called the "trial close." As the name implies, a trial close checks the readiness of the prospect to actually close the sale and indicates his or her receptiveness to the product or service being presented. You can attempt a trial close after a major selling point, after finishing the presentation, after responding to an objection, or just prior to an attempt to close the sale.

The best thing about trial closes is that they are good gauges for determining the readiness of a prospect, but they don't commit salespeople to attempting the actual close before they have earned that right by satisfying all the prospect's concerns. When there are no more hurdles, the prospect is either willing to buy or is determined not to buy. Trial closes don't ask for a decision to buy, they ask for the prospect's opinion. Based on that opinion, the salesperson can then form a strategy to close the deal if a positive response is received or proceed to address other concerns the prospect may have raised.

A trial close should be very simple and casual and is usually presented as a question. For instance, "Do you think the product fulfills your needs?" or "Based on the benefits of the product, do you think we can do business?" A positive response indicates that the prospect is almost ready to close. If the response is negative, the salesperson may need to ask more questions to pinpoint other objections.

Keep in mind that you can perform a trial close several times during a sales presentation. The idea behind the trial close is to make sure the prospect is in a positive frame of mind and that effective two-way communication is occurring.

Closing Techniques

Closing a sale is not a right! You have to earn the opportunity to close, and even then you may not be able to do so successfully. Earning a close can sometimes take a great deal of work. It means being patient enough to determine the prospect's needs and answer any objections. It also means being assertive when the occasion warrants.

To close a sale, the timing has to be right. Trying to close the sale before the customer is ready will result in no sale at all. Wait too long to close a sale and the prospect could lose enthusiasm. The right time to close a sale is when the prospect starts showing signs of being ready to buy. You have to be able to recognize these buying signals and attempt the close when you see them. Again, the two most effective ways to recognize buying signals are to listen carefully and observe the prospect. One buying signal you should be alert for is when the prospect begins to ask more and more questions about the product. That means the interest level is high and the person may only need prompting to close the sale. A second signal is the prospect may ask a trusted associate what he or she thinks of the product. Depending on the other person's answer, the prospect may be ready to close. A third sign is that the prospect shows a lot of enthusiasm and deep interest in the product and begins to examine it closely, indicating high buying interest. As the person examines the product, answer any questions, but generally give him or her enough time to look over all the features of the product before asking for an opinion. A positive and enthusiastic answer means you may need to give only a little push to close the sale.

In addition to the preceding top three signals, another sign to watch for is when the prospect becomes less guarded and more relaxed. Usually, when the sale is still up in the air, prospects are very guarded. They watch what they say, the way they sit, and so on. Once they reach a decision about purchasing a product, they will usually try to wrap up the meeting either by announcing they don't need the product or by relaxing their guard and becoming more friendly. If that happens, all they need is for you to pop the question.

Of course, sales are seldom that simple. You must gauge the prospect to determine how assertive you can be when attempting to close the sale. Different prospects will have different pressure thresholds. If you are too assertive, when attempting to close the sale, you can blow it altogether. The goal is to apply just enough pressure to close the deal, which will take a certain amount of judgment on your part. Based on your interaction with the prospect, you will have to decide just how much pressure the person will be able to take and adjust your selling style accordingly.

From the moment you start the selling process with your needs analysis, you must listen to what the prospect is saying, note how it is being said, and observe the person's body language. Keep in mind that people with a low threshold for pressure don't respond well to a high level of assertiveness. It builds resentment during the presentation, so much so that the prospect will probably tune out altogether. Be smart! If someone is laid back and doesn't seem assertive, use a low-pressure sales presentation and close. For someone who is forceful, a more direct and assertive presentation and close can be very effective.

The point is that you should adapt your level of intensity to match that of the prospect. Make the prospect feel comfortable so that when you attempt the close, the level of pressure does not come as a shock.

Depending on the type of prospect you are dealing with, you can choose one of several popular methods to close the sale:

- **The response close.** This technique is useful when the prospect still has small objections to the close. The primary tactic is to offer an inducement to close the sale. It doesn't have to deal with the terms and conditions of the sale (e.g., offering a discount or FOB terms) but it can amount to merely notifying the prospect of price increases or some other event that will affect the product in the future. The whole intent behind this technique is to offer the prospect something that demands a response or call for action.
- **The competition close.** This close works well for companies that service numerous competitors in a specific market. Letting the prospect know competitors utilize your product or service and explaining how it has benefited them can be an inducement to close the sale. Many companies research what their competitors are doing and, in certain situations, will try

to emulate their strategies. This is an excellent close for prospects who seem very concerned about the competition.

- **The alternate option close.** This close involves asking prospects to choose between two conditions of the sale instead of inquiring directly whether they want to buy the product. For instance, "Would you like 20 units in order to obtain the price break, or 10 units?" The choice of not buying is not even mentioned in the close. This technique is appropriate when trying to close a prospect who has signaled strong buying interest.

- **The summary close.** Using this closing technique, you will recap all the major benefits associated with the product that specifically meet the needs of the prospect. This is a good technique for prospects who have participated in the presentation by constantly relating their needs and desires.

- **The indirect close.** This casual, low-pressure close asks the prospect to decide whether to buy in an indirect manner. For instance, "Are you comfortable with the terms?" or "What do you think?" This is a good closing technique for passive prospects, who really don't like a great deal of pressure.

- **The direct close.** This assertive technique asks for the order with a direct question; for instance, "Would you like to buy the product?" Be careful with this close. It isn't the best for every prospect but usually works well on prospects who are assertive themselves.

- **The "carpe diem" close.** Seize the moment. That's what this type of close is all about. It relies on spotting opportunities that can be turned directly into a close. For instance, if the prospect is interested in the product and asks, "Do you have this product in black?" you would then answer with your own question to elicit a positive response from the prospect: "So you prefer black?" If the prospect answers yes, you have just closed the sale (if you have black). All you have to do is ask how many!

- **The assumption close.** This is not as assertive as a direct close but relies on the assumption that the prospect will buy; all the person needs is a little encouragement. Using this technique, you would bypass asking for the close and move directly into asking for the quantity of the order, delivery time, and so on.

- **The continual close.** This is an effective technique for some salespeople; it works by asking for the close after overcoming each objection. The close should be presented in an open-ended manner so that a negative answer won't jeopardize the success of the sale.

- **The customer close.** This approach relies on your ability to involve the prospect in a routine of making positive responses to relatively painless decisions. For instance, "Do you like the color of the product?" "Is the price generally what you were looking for?" The idea is to get him saying yes to little decisions so that when the big question is asked, he is ready to say "Yes!"

Whatever closing technique you choose, you should wait quietly for an answer after asking for the order. Don't say a thing while the prospect is deliberating whether to buy. Usually, anything you say will take the pressure off the prospect to make a decision. Remaining quiet can be nerve-racking, but while the prospect is deciding what to do, be positive and think of appropriate responses to use once the prospect states a decision.

Usually, a prospect won't wait long to reply. Most will provide an answer within a minute. If the reply is positive and the sale has been closed, you should get the written order, thank the prospect, now customer, for the business, then leave. Keep it simple when wrapping up the sale. Don't say too much. If you are overly enthusiastic and keep talking about the sale, you may say something that will change the buyer's mind.

Finally, when you don't make a sale, ask for a referral. If you've done your job correctly and have made a professional presentation, even buyers with no use for your product may know someone else who does.

RESOURCES

Associations

Association of Sales Administration Managers, P.O. Box 735, Harrson, NJ 07029, 201-481-4800

Dun & Bradstreet Corp Credit Services, 1 Diamond Hill Road, Murray Hill, NJ 07974-0000, 908-665-5000

National Register Publishing, A Reed Reference Publishing Company, 121 Chanlon Road, New Providence, NJ 07974, 800-323-3288

Sales and Marketing Executives International, Statler Office Tower, Suite 458, Cleveland, OH 44115, 216-771-6650

Thomas Publishing Company, Five Penn Plaza, New York, NY 10001, 212-695-0500

Magazines

Dartnell Sales and Marketing Executive Report, 4660 North Ravenswood Avenue, Chicago, IL 60640, 312-561-4000

Dartnell Sales and Marketing Newsletter, 4660 North Ravenswood Avenue, Chicago, IL 60640, 312-561-4000

The Sales Executive, 13 East 37th Street, 8th Floor, New York, NY 10016-5543, 212-683-9755

25

Advertising

Advertising is one facet of a comprehensive marketing campaign. This marketing tool provides a direct line of communication to your customers and prospective customers regarding your product or service.

There is little doubt that people are affected by advertising almost as soon as they are born. In fact, according to William Cohen in the book, *The Entrepreneur and Small Business Problem Solver,* people are exposed to about two million advertising messages from birth up to the age of 21.[1]

Within the context of the marketing or business plan, advertising does the following:

- Makes customers aware of your product or service.
- Convinces customers that your company's product or service is the best.
- Enhances the image of your company.
- Points out the need and creates a desire for your product or service.
- Announces new products or services.
- Reinforces salespeople's messages.
- Draws customers to your business.

While these are the general objectives behind every advertising plan, you should develop specific goals in conjunction with the objectives in your business plan. You may want to obtain a percentage growth in sales, more inquiries for sales to follow up, or more in-store traffic. The desired end result can simply be name awareness or a modification of the image you're projecting. Objectives will vary depending on the industry you're in. Nevertheless, within an overall marketing plan, you need to determine what role advertising can realistically play. This depends in part on where you are in the marketplace.

---

[1] William Cohen, *The Entrepreneur and Small Business Problem Solver,* 2nd ed. (New York: John Wiley & Sons, 1990).

All products and businesses go through three stages, but the order of these stages will vary:

1. **The start-up/pioneering stage.** You're new in the marketplace and you need to build your identity. Your company needs high levels of advertising to command the consumer's attention. Your grand opening requires an extra piece of the start-up budget.

2. **The competitive stage.** This stage of advertising takes place if you have built your identity and grabbed the consumer's attention, or if you have jumped into a marketplace already crowded with competitors. In this stage, you need to stress the differences between yourself and the others, as well as the benefits you provide. You must convince the consumers that yours is the company or product to try.

3. **The sustaining stage.** Remind consumers that you're still in business, either with lighter levels of continuous advertising, or by "flighting" your campaign—offering frequent intervals of advertising throughout the year. For example, if you've been running a radio campaign of 24 spots per week in six-week flights, along with a half-page ad in your local newspaper every week as a secondary medium, now is the time you can cut back your advertising expenditures to something like 18 radio spots per week for two weeks once a month, along with your half-page ad in the newspaper, which will run only during the weeks that your radio campaign is in progress. You can also run a smaller-sized newspaper ad to decrease your space costs, but keep in mind that this will incur additional one-time production charges.

No matter which stage you're involved in, good advertising causes action and persuades the prospective customer to try your product or service. It is important to create a desire or need in your target audience for your product or service. This is why new ideas and companies require extensive pioneering advertising, and it explains in part why advertising expenses are higher during the first few years. According to Lee Mulder in the book, *Handbook of Management for the Growing Business,* by Carl Heyel and Belden Menkus, "Each promotional dollar should return a minimum of $10 to $20 in new business by the end of a year's effort . . . this is in terms of a promotional plan."[2]

When developing your advertising campaign, you need to follow four steps:

1. **Market definition.** Determining who your most productive audience will be in order to target your advertising more effectively.

2. **Budgeting.** Setting up a budget based on what you can afford to spend, in the most effective media for your target audience.

3. **Media planning.** Gathering facts on the advertising media under consideration and determining the best way to reach your prospective customers.

4. **Creative strategy.** Choosing the most effective message and visuals for your advertising campaign.

---

[2] Carl Heyel and Belden Menkus, *Handbook of Management for the Growing Business* (New York: Van Nostrand Reinhold Company, Inc., 1986).

DEFINING YOUR MARKET

Your first step in advertising is to learn as much as possible about the market that you'll be targeting. Some questions you'll want to consider while doing this are:

1. Who are my potential customers? For example, for a retail business like a paint store or a donut shop, the market is normally going to be within a five-mile radius of your doorstep.
2. How many potential customers are there?
3. Where are they located?
4. Where do they now buy the products or services I want to sell them?
5. Can I offer them anything they are not getting now?
6. How can I persuade them to do business with me?

Taking a single message and aiming it at as many buyers as possible is not the way to reach your target audience. You need a clear, well-defined understanding of your market. Accurate demographic information is needed, including sex, income, and occupation (see the Demographic Comparison worksheet in Chapter 6). Even characteristics like hobbies and driving habits can be helpful. You need to determine who your prime users are, where they're located, and what media will reach them most effectively. For example, if your company sells car stereos, and your market research shows that your target audience is mainly men, 18 to 34 years old, and the optimum place for them to notice your ad would be while they're in their cars wishing they had a car stereo to listen to! You can conduct your own market research to generate demographic information, or you can hire a professional marketing firm to do it for you.

There are certain issues to consider, says Joseph Shetzen in the book, *Maximum Performance*. They are called the *Five M's of Advertising,* and how well you research this topic may determine success or failure in your advertising campaign. According to Shetzen, you should consider the following M's:

1. **Money.** How much should be spent for a complete advertising program?
2. **Message.** What should the advertiser say?
3. **Media.** What advertising medium should be used?
4. **Motion.** How should the advertising be introduced?
5. **Measurement.** What results should be expected from the advertisement and how should they be measured?[3]

CREATING THE AD BUDGET

How much should your business devote to an effective advertising campaign? This question weighs heavily on the small business owner's mind. The amount

---

[3] Joseph Shetzen, *Maximum Performance* (Homewood, IL: Dow Jones-Irwin, 1990).

varies from one business and/or industry to another. According to Lee Mulder, "Amounts are expressed as a percentage of gross revenue. Percentages range from some 40 percent of gross for direct mail merchandisers to 1 percent for small captive manufacturers."[4]

Most companies base their advertising budgets on a percentage of projected gross sales, usually anywhere from 2 to 5 percent. This is generally referred to as the "cost method," which theorizes that an advertiser can't afford to spend more money than is available. For example, if projected gross sales for the first year are $250,000 based on your business plan, then, using the cost method to determine the advertising budget (figuring 5 percent), you would have $12,500, or $1,042 per month, with which to work. For a grand opening, you would want to use twice your monthly amount, or $2,084 in this case, to plan advertising that announces your opening.

Although $12,500 might seem like a small amount for a year, and a drop in the bucket compared with the outlay of the competition down the street, here's how to plan an effective, cost-efficient advertising campaign using that amount. If your target audience can be effectively reached using print and outdoor media, you can run an ad in a community weekly paper every other week all year (26 weeks). Say a two-column-by-five inch ad will cost a total of $1,560 for the space for the entire year. You can then buy transit advertising on the two buses that pass by your front doorstep for a year for, let's say, $960. Place those ads on the back of the bus where they get the highest possible exposure. Inside ads on bus cards above passenger seating for 52 weeks will cost $480 for the year using the 20 buses that cover your neighborhood. You can do 10,000 pieces of direct mail for, let's say, 20 cents apiece, four times a year for about $8,000, including production. Budgeting $1,500 to cover freelance advertising and layout time by a qualified professional brings the total expenditure up to $12,500. You have put together a dynamite campaign for a small business owner.

Figures used to develop this advertising campaign are based on national averages for community weekly newspapers, transit advertising, direct mail, radio, and television. There are going to be variations from market to market, and you will need to adjust the overall campaign to take this into account from the cost standpoint. Large markets such as New York and Los Angeles will be much more expensive than smaller markets. Or, if you're planning on spending 3 or 4 percent of your gross sales on advertising instead of the 5 percent used as an example here, you'll need to adjust your figures to take that into account, and you'll have to pull out of some of the media space used in our example. Remember, if you don't have the budget to use all media effectively, it's best to dominate one or two media at a time rather than to spread yourself too thin.

For some companies, using the "cost method" to determine their advertising budgets won't work because it won't provide enough monthly funds to get the job done. These companies base their advertising budgets on the amount of money needed to move the product. This is called the "task method." There are

[4] Heyel and Menkus, *Handbook of Management for the Growing Business*.

many different ways to determine the amount of money needed using the task method; the most common way is through experience. Companies just starting out, however, won't have past records to guide them. In this case, companies will need to refer to their business plans and market surveys to set up their advertising budgets. It is also helpful to find out what the competition is spending and in what media.

Where can you cut corners effectively with advertising? To begin with, make sure you use freelancers as much as possible. Use the smallest advertising agency that you can find so that you're an important client to them, if you use an advertising agency at all. It's cheapest, if you have the time, to deal directly with the media yourself. The advantage is that you won't have to pay the advertising agency its standard commission, which can turn out to be substantial—traditionally 15 percent of the total media time and space cost and 17 percent of the production costs.

Trading or bartering your products or services in exchange for media time or space (called "trade-outs") is another advantage to working directly with the media. This is particularly common with small radio stations, smaller television stations and community weeklies. For example, a complete campaign for an automobile dealership can be financed by the trade of automobiles for the media time needed.

After you determine your advertising budget, you will want to consider what media will be appropriate for your product, and what the cost will be to effectively advertise with those media.

MEDIA PLANNING

Choosing the medium or type of advertising is especially difficult for small firms. Large market television and newspapers are often too expensive for a firm that services only a small area (although local newspapers can be used). Magazines, unless local, usually cover too much territory to be cost-efficient for a small firm although some national publications offer regional or city editions. Metropolitan radio stations present the same problems as TV and metro newspapers; however, in smaller markets the local radio station and newspaper may sufficiently cover a small firm's audience.

That is why it is important to put together a media plan for your advertising campaign. There are three basic components in a media plan:

1. **Define the marketing problem.** Do you know where your business is coming from and where the potential for increased business lies? Do you know the markets of greatest importance and greatest opportunity? Do you need to reach everybody or only a select group of consumers? How often is the product used? How much product loyalty exists?
2. **Translate marketing requirements into attainable media objectives.** If the marketing objective is to stimulate trial among all potential consumers,

then reaching many people is more important than reaching fewer people more frequently. If the product is purchased often, then reaching people more frequently might be a more appropriate tactic.

3. **Define a media solution by formulating media strategies.** If reaching people is a primary objective, you should select affordable vehicles that will generate more reach than other media forms. If you are trying to reach a specific demographic group, base your media selection on reaching that group effectively and efficiently.

The advertising media generally used include:

- Television.
- Cable television.
- Radio.
- Newspapers.
- Magazines (Consumer and Trade).
- Outdoor billboards.
- Public transportation.
- Yellow pages.
- Direct mail.
- Specialty advertising (on items such as matchbooks, pencils, calendars, telephone pads, shopping bags).
- Other media (catalogs, samples, handouts, brochures, etc.).

In appraising prospective advertising media and comparing them in cost-efficiency, you should consider the following factors:

1. **Reach.** Expressed as a percentage, reach is the number of individuals (or homes) you want to expose your product to through specific media scheduled over a given time span.
2. **Frequency.** In using specific media, how many times, on average, should the individuals in your target audience be exposed to your advertising message? It takes an average of three or more exposures to an advertising message before consumers take action, that is, buy your product.
3. **Cost per thousand.** How much will it cost to reach one thousand of your prospective customers? This method is used in comparing the print media. To determine a publication's cost per thousand, also known as CPM, divide the cost of the advertising by the publication's circulation in thousands.
4. **Cost per point.** How much will it cost to buy one rating point against your target audience? One rating point equals 1 percent of your target audience. This method is used in comparing the broadcast media. To determine a broadcast medium's CPP, divide the cost of the schedule being considered by the number of rating points it delivers.
5. **Impact.** Does the medium in question offer full opportunities for appealing to the appropriate senses, such as sight and hearing, in presenting design, color, or sound?

6. Selectivity. To what degree can the message be restricted to those people who are known to be the most logical prospects?

Reach versus Frequency

Perhaps one of the most important but least understood elements when scheduling your media is reach and frequency. Reach and frequency are important aspects of the advertising plan, and are used to analyze alternative advertising schedules to determine which produces the best results relative to the media plan's objectives.

By calculating reach and frequency you can compare the two on the basis of how many people you will reach with each schedule and the number of times you will reach the average person. For example, let's assume we aired one commercial in each of four television programs (A, B, C, D), and each program has a 20 rating. These four programs combined deliver 80 gross rating points (20 × 4). It is probable that many viewers will see more than one announcement; some of the viewers of Program A might also view program B, C, or D, or any combination of these.

For example, in a population of 100 TV homes, some homes view only one of a choice of four possible programs, some two, some three, and some all four. To calculate reach, viewers are counted only once. In this example, a total of 40 different TV homes are exposed to one or more television programs. The reach of the four programs combined is therefore 40 percent (40 homes reached divided by the 100 TV-home population).

Many researchers have charted the reach achieved with different media schedules. These tabulations are put into formulas from which you can estimate the level of delivery (reach) for any given schedule. A reach curve is the technical term describing how reach changes with increasing use of a medium. The media salespeople you work with or your advertising agency can supply you with these reach curves and numbers.

Now let's use the same schedule of one commercial in each of four television programs (A, B, C, D) to determine reach versus frequency. In our example, 17 homes viewed only one program, 11 homes viewed two programs, seven homes viewed three programs, and five homes viewed all four programs. If we add the number of programs each home viewed, the 40 homes in total viewed the equivalent of 80 programs and therefore were exposed to the equivalent of 80 commercials. By division (80 divided by 40), we establish that any one home was exposed to an average of two commercials. If reach were the only criterion, you would select Plan 1; if frequency was more important to the achievement of your media plan's objectives, Plan 2 has the advantage.

To increase reach, you would include additional media to your plan, or expand the dayparts you are using. For example, if you're only buying "drive time" on the radio, you might also include some daytime and evening spots to increase your audience. To increase frequency, you would add spots or insertions to your existing schedule. For example, if you're running three insertions in a local magazine, you could increase that to six insertions so that your audience would be exposed to your ad more often.

Gross rating points (GRPs) are used to estimate broadcast reach and frequency from tabulations and formulas. Once your schedule's delivery (reach) has been determined from your reach curves, you can obtain your average frequency by dividing the GRPs by the reach. For example, 200 GRPs divided by an 80% reach equals a 2.5 average frequency.

Frequency is important because it takes a while to build up awareness and break through the consumer's selection process. People are always screening out messages that aren't personally relevant, picking up on only those things that are important to them. Repetition is the key word here. For frequency, it is much better to advertise regularly in small spaces or in short flights than it is to have a brief, one-time, expensive advertising splurge.

Personal Contact or Word-of-Mouth Advertising

Word-of-mouth is always important to business growth. Each happy customer can steer dozens of new ones to you. Make sure that business cards and/or flyers are always available for customers or clients to pass on to others. Frequently, successful business owners are well-known in their communities. Smart businesspeople know the importance of making contacts. They become active in their communities—joining and leading civic organizations, attending charity events, speaking at seminars, getting involved in politics, and attending openings of other businesses and events at local institutions. Of course, running your business comes first, but time spent developing contacts will pay off.

Print Media

Once you know what your goals are, you can analyze them in terms of your budget to determine the best print media for reaching your target markets. Effective print advertising may include an overlap between the various forms of print advertising vehicles, such as regional magazines, newspapers, and the yellow pages. Study your competition to find out what they're doing, and look for alternative avenues as well.

You can find publications that are appropriate for your advertising campaign by looking through reference sources such as the directories put out by the Standard Rate and Data Service (SRDS), 3004 Glenview Road, Wilmette, IL 60091, 312-256-6067. The SRDS directories list all the relevant information about consumer and trade publications. You'll find a short description of each publication, its editorial content, who the publication goes out to, and a breakdown of circulation figures. Using this information, you can compile a list of suitable publications. To obtain more in-depth information, contact an ad representative at each publication you've chosen and request a media kit. These contain sample copies of the publication, and detailed information about the editorial content, a breakdown of readership demographics, the publication's ad rates, and an audited circulation statement from the publisher.

There are two primary audits: the Audit Bureau of Circulation (ABC), and the Business Publications Audit (BPA). Audited circulations are sworn statements by the publisher, verified by an outside source, that the publication is distributed to the number of people claimed in the circulation figures.

With this information in hand, you can determine the cost-effectiveness of advertising in a publication by determining an "efficiency ratio" between the circulation and the ad rates. This ratio is your CPM, or cost per thousand. The CPM is the cost of advertising divided by the circulation in thousands. So if the circulation is 30,000 and the rate for a full-page ad is $600, divide the cost by 30. In this case, you would have a $20 cost per thousand or CPM. This is the common denominator used to evaluate the cost-effectiveness of advertising in a publication.

As well as the CPM, you also want to consider what kind of "deals" you can work out with the ad rep from each publication. This can contribute to the cost-effectiveness of each magazine. For example, you can bargain for special "positioning" in the publication; inside the front cover, on the back cover, or within the first few pages of the book. Often publications will charge anywhere from 10 to 20 percent of the cost of the ad for special positioning, but if you're a good negotiator you can sometimes get it for free. Always ask for the first third of the book, right-hand page positioning for your ad if you're not going to negotiate for special positioning—this will not be considered a preferential position so it will be free, since readers are more interested in both the articles and the ads in the front of the magazine, your ad is more likely to get attention there.

You can also negotiate with the ad rep on a frequency discount. If you run your ad 3 times, 6 times, or 12 times instead of just once, you will get a discount on each insertion. The more times you run, the cheaper each insertion. Publications have standard frequency discounts that you will find in the SRDS or on the rate card the ad rep gives you, but often you can get the rep to go below rate-card cost on frequency discounts if you run a regular schedule in the magazine and if the rep is anxious for your business.

If your business draws its customers/clients primarily from the local community, you'll find newspaper advertising valuable. A display or classified ad is not expensive compared with the broadcast media and will expose your product or service to the attention of potential customers/clients. In large metropolitan areas, some papers have created special small-firm advertising sections and service directories where a dozen or more small-firm ads may appear on a single page.

Certain sections of the paper are more effective depending on the reader you want to reach. Over the years, certain facts about newspaper readership have evolved. The sports pages are better for men; feature sections are generally better for women; and the business pages are better for businesspeople. Certain days of the week are better than others for specific targeted groups. Moviegoers read the Saturday paper more than any other day. To reach your target audience effectively, you may want to request a certain section or day of the week as you see fit.

Whenever you're buying newspaper space, you will get a discount based on the total lineage that you run. Ask about special monthly runs or business edition specials within a certain industry sector. The rates for advertising in these sections are lower, making them more accessible to small businesses. By the same token, classified display ads, as they are called, cost much less than typical display ads in many magazines; however, not all magazines allow advertisers to take display ads in their classified sections. Certain advertisers may also be able to take advantage of specific industry rates. Retail (department stores), travel (airlines, etc.), and financial (banks) advertisers, for example, are all able to use industry-related below-rate-card rates.

Consider some major classifications of magazines: consumer-oriented, women's, farm, food, travel, business, men's, automotive, and sports. Though *Reader's Digest* thrives, the era of the general interest magazine is dead. Most magazines on the market are targeted toward a specialized sector of readers. You will be able to narrowly target your audience by using specific publications.

Newsletters are great print vehicles for reaching specialized markets. Because circulations are typically small, rates for advertising in newsletters are very reasonable. Their circulations are also very narrowly targeted because of their specialized editorial content. In terms of cost-effectiveness, this is one of the best types of print media to purchase. But you have to be careful. Many newsletters aren't audited publications. They operate on a controlled-circulation basis, so you basically have to take the word of the publisher that the newsletter is distributed to the number of people claimed.

Penny for penny, trade journals may be the most effectively targeted medium. The readers are narrowly grouped around a collective industry. For instance, just two trade journals serve the thousands of ministorage facilities throughout the nation. Sometimes your advertising can be effective in a different, but related, industry publication. For example, when a small firm that originally made miniaturized homes, buildings, and villages for architects advertised in a railroad hobby magazine, sales zoomed. The tiny structures were perfect for setting up around train sets. A manufacturer of a mobile car-washing compressor with an adjustable wand advertised in a window-care trade journal after finding that the compressor was ideal for washing miniblinds. Though generally more oriented toward products, trade journals will cost-effectively spread the word if you have an economical service that their readers can use.

Most local businesses advertise their goods and services in the yellow pages. Such advertisements may be illustrated and vary in size from simple one-line listings to half-page spreads. The phone company has specific categories according to which they classify businesses. Be careful to choose the most appropriate one(s). Sometimes it may be worthwhile to advertise in more than one category, that is, to cross-reference your listing. Be careful about making the deadlines the yellow pages companies give you for sending in your ad(s). Missing them can mean going a whole year without advertising in this important medium. Call your local phone company for details and costs.

To make your print media ads cost-efficient, buy space at the best rates. Advertising costs less if more space is purchased. In newspapers, for example, if your campaign calls for 45 column inches of space at $4.50 per inch, the cost will be $202.50. The publication's rate card may reveal that 50 inches can be purchased at a rate of $4 per inch, for a total of $200.

Don't scatter your ads. Skipping from one publication to another seldom gets results. It destroys the effectiveness of consistent advertising and, most important, you lose the handling and consideration privileges received by consistent advertisers. This can make a great deal of difference when you want to secure a favorable position for your ad in the publication.

Electronic Media

The most important goal in radio or television commercials is to get the listener's attention so he or she can imaginatively participate in the commercials. Good radio and television writing is simple in its sentence construction, clear and fresh. Strive for these four elements:

1. You need meaningful content—the listener has to believe the product provides some sort of reward.
2. You want to be able to arouse thoughts and feelings in the listener that relate to the commercial's central message. A commercial for a spaghetti sauce misses the boat, for example, if the listener starts thinking about the size of tomatoes in the garden instead of the possibility of having spaghetti for dinner.
3. Build identification in the mind of the listener by using dialogue that discusses the product—a straightforward presentation of the product or business, and why it is beneficial to the listener.

The best commercials in terms of recall are those that reinforce the attitudes or feelings the viewers already had about the product or company.

It's important to avoid several things with radio or television commercials. You don't want to offend or alienate the listener. You don't want to create suspicion, disbelief, or a fear of phoniness. Also, make sure that there is no confusion about what the message is in your radio or television commercial. When the message is unclear, the listener will quickly lose interest.

Creativity in today's marketplace is essential for a radio or television commercial, especially when you don't have a big enough budget to flood the marketplace for an extended period. You must achieve high impact and create an advertising campaign that repeats the same message over and over. Because of that repetition you want to make sure that what you are telling people isn't boring or dull; otherwise, they'll turn off in a big hurry. You can obtain samples of effective radio campaigns from local radio station salespeople, or from your local office of the Radio Advertising Bureau, which has headquarters in New York City (see Resources).

Advertising on major radio stations presents the same problems for small-business owners as advertising in metro newspapers. Such advertising may reach an audience far beyond the limits of a small business's trading area, and the cost may be prohibitive.

But radio advertising on small, local stations can be an effective and affordable medium. These stations, most with power of less than 1,000 watts, are limited to small geographic areas, and their programs are specifically designed to appeal to the people in this limited market. When you buy time on such a station, you're not paying for wasted circulation.

To get the complete story on a radio station's advertising costs, visit with one of the station's salespeople and examine the rate card. The Standard Rate and Data Service catalog will also furnish cost information.

Radio ads can work for small-business owners, especially if they supplement it with other advertising. Radio is great if your product has mass appeal and especially if you have exclusivity of the product in the marketplace, or if your competition isn't using the radio medium.

Radio advertising can be fairly inexpensive, and it will reach a different market segment than metropolitan newspapers. You can also add more "bang to your buck" by working out merchandising packages or sponsorships with your salesperson. An example of a merchandising program might be enlisting one of the station's disc jockeys to give away samples of, or coupons for, your product on the air. Or, you could "sponsor" the station's weather or traffic reports—anything that might relate to your product. The disc jockey would say something like, "Today's weather report has been brought to you by (name of your business)." These on-air mentions are separate from your scheduled radio campaign and give you additional exposure at no extra cost.

Always negotiate the cost per radio spot with your salesperson; you should never have to pay rate card rates. Put together a "package" of spots that you would like to use as your schedule. A good one might be something like this:

Weekday	Spots per Week	Daypart, Listening Time
Monday–Friday	5X, 6 A.M.–10 A.M.	A.M. Drive time
Monday–Friday	4X, 10 A.M.–3 P.M.	Daytime
Monday–Friday	5X, 3 P.M.–7 P.M.	P.M. Drive time
Saturday	2X, 6 A.M.–10 A.M.	A.M. Drive time
Saturday	2X, 10 A.M.–3 P.M.	Daytime
Total, 18X		

Morning commuter time has the highest listenership in radio; afternoon and evening "drive time" also has high listenership and may be cheaper than morning rates. Use your ideal schedule as a reference when negotiating with your salesperson, who may throw in some "overnight" spots (midnight–6 A.M.), which have low listenership but give you a lower cost in morning drive time if you take them. Your package will give you a point from which to negotiate. Tell your salesperson what you can afford to spend, put together your package, have your salesperson put together what he wants as an offer, and go from there.

Television advertising has a reputation for being expensive. Far too many small-business people are intimidated by stories of the high cost of television time. Major corporations spend millions on their advertising campaigns, but they plan to reach millions of viewers. On a smaller scale, TV costs can be surprisingly low. The price of television time depends on several factors: the size of the market area, the length of the ad, the time of day the ad appears, the rating of the program, the quantity of advertising purchased, and a handful of other factors. It's up to the advertiser to decide just how much money is available for television advertising, then to shop around for the best deal.

At many stations, a "grid" system is used to price TV time. This means that there may be several prices possible for the same commercial at the same time of day. The higher the price, the higher the priority of the spot. A high-priority commercial will preempt one of lower priority.

One additional cost is the production of a commercial. This can range from a low of $50 for a simple, station-produced announcement to a figure well into four digits for an ad produced with professional studio techniques.

Local stations often package deals designed to give small businesses an opportunity to use TV effectively while keeping costs low. There are programs to fit any advertising budget. The small-business owner's best friend can often be a local station's ad salesperson; a call to these people will usually answer all your questions. They can tell you what options and opportunities are available for low-budget advertisers.

As with radio, put together a schedule of programs you would like to advertise in. If your target audience is children, your best bet might be advertising during the Saturday morning cartoons. If sports fans are your target, try Monday Night Football or weekend sports. Your salesperson will offer other suggestions, and together you can come up with a schedule that fits your budgetary and advertising needs.

Standard Rate and Data Service also offers an information sourcebook for television, listing stations in the market, some rate information, and so on. This can be helpful in choosing the stations to contact.

Perhaps best attuned to small businesses is your local cable television station. The cable stations are very flexible, sometimes with anything from 10- to 120-second spots available. The prices depend on the number of subscribers to the channel, so you should check local rates.

The disadvantage is that there is no accurate method of determining just who is watching. Unlike network television, which has Nielsen and Arbitron ratings to statistically determine how many viewers are tuned to a specific show or station, no such system has been developed for cable thus far, although the ratings services are working on it. The cable salespeople themselves can supply some data on the numbers and demographics of their viewers, and the Nielsen ratings service can tell you the percentage of the market that subscribes to cable

TV. Usually the number of cable subscribers guarantees an adequate viewership that will provide substantial return for your advertising dollars.

Rates are usually quite reasonable. In fact, some local cable stations offer 60-second spots for as little as $5. Though rates can go much higher, an average figure cannot be readily determined because the number of subscribers in each community differs so radically.

As with standard television, put together your package of programming from which to negotiate. Keep in mind that you can buy local spots on national channels such as ESPN, MTV, and CNN—quality air time at a fraction of the cost of regular television advertising.

Flyers, Mailers, and Brochures

Flyers, mailers, and brochures are an affordable and selective means of getting information to a selected audience. They offer you more flexibility in budgeting and greater selectivity in choosing prospects than other kinds of advertising.

To generate an effective flyer, mailer, or brochure, start with straightforward, no-nonsense copy. You could write about the facts within the context of a human-interest story. Any number of different slants are possible: using simple words; developing imaginative, factual, forthright copy; using superlatives and teaser headlines, as in the newspaper approach; making competitive comparisons; incorporating humor or the believe-it-or-not approach.

Be specific and accurate. A clever, catchy phrase can help customers remember your firm, but a clumsy slogan will just as quickly deter them.

Layout is critical. Knowing that the reader's eye follows the page from top to bottom, left to right, you can plan to catch the reader's attention with pictures, charts, graphs, or any number of visual grabbers. Subtle placement of subheads and captions can highlight the best features and benefits of your product or service.

If you cannot afford to hire a professional copywriter, be prepared for a few rewrites. The box "Eighty Sales Letter Openings" provides a number of effective suggestions for capturing readers' interest. The pamphlet you finished at midnight last night may not be quite as crisp and clean when you wake up the next day and look at it in the morning light. When you are satisfied with your presentation, you'll need to get mailing lists to send your promotional literature to your selected market segment.

Flyers and handbills can be an inexpensive and highly effective form of advertising for small-business owners. They are especially useful for your grand opening announcement, for periodic reminders of the merchandise or services you offer, and for advertising special sales. Plan handbills carefully with attention to layout, message, appeal, headlines, and appearance. A good printer can advise you on the quality of paper to use, overall appearance, size, cost, and similar factors; however, do not depend on your printer to help with the sales message or the advertising copy.

Eighty Sales Letter Openings*

1. *If you're like me...*
2. *Ask a provocative question.*
3. *What if...*
4. *Suggest a cataclysmic decision.*
5. *I(we) need help.*
6. *Congratulations!*
7. *I invite you...*
8. *I have a free gift for you.*
9. *As you know...*
10. *I have something good for you.*
11. *A specific episode narrative.*
12. *Private invitation.*
13. *We don't know each other, but I think it's time we did.*
14. *The cry of "fire!"*
15. *What I want you to do is...*
16. *Because you did that, we're going to do this.*
17. *Because you are who you are, you'll get special attention.*
18. *Stroke, stroke, you're a rare bird.*
19. *Here's what the experts say...*
20. *Why are we doing this?*
21. *This is disgusting, and you're the one to fix it.*
22. *We've got bad news . . . and we've got good news.*
23. *Good news!*
24. *Are you paying too much?*
25. *Did you know... or did you know...*
26. *Have you ever wished...*
27. *You're in trouble (or you and I are in trouble), and this is what you'd better do.*
28. *Why do they... or why don't they...*
29. *I've enclosed...*
30. *Here's the sermon for the day.*
31. *We've missed you.*
32. *We're solving your tough problem.*
33. *This is short and sweet.*
34. *Believe it or not.*
35. *I know who you are.*
36. *Because you're "A," and you're also "B"*
37. *Historical buildup*
38. *You just might be (and probably are)...*
39. *I'll get right to the point.*
40. *These are critical times.*
41. *Visualize this scenario...*
42. *If you like that, you'll love this.*
43. *Whether you do this... or do that...*
44. *The classic question.*
45. *I have to tell you the truth.*
46. *You're important to us.*
47. *Now you can... or At last!*
48. *They think I'm nuts!*
49. *Before you do that, do this.*
50. *Wouldn't it be lovely if...*
51. *The best just got better.*
52. *If I can show you how to... will you?*
53. *Let's face it.*
54. *It's late and I'm tired, but I have to tell you this.*
55. *We've chosen you...or... You have been chosen.*
56. *I'm surprised I haven't heard from you.*
57. *How would you like to...*
58. *It gives me great pleasure to...*
59. *I used to think that, but now I think this...*
60. *Does this sound (seem) familiar?*
61. *I'll tell you what pleases me.*
62. *This is what happens when they (you) do it wrong.*
63. *Looking for...?*
64. *The cry of "Wolf!"*
65. *Here's the deal.*
66. *We can do it where others can't.*
67. *Remember when...*
68. *Isn't it sad?*
69. *Ouch!*
70. *Chances are...*
71. *Take just two minutes.*
72. *Things were going great. Then all hell broke loose.*
73. *I'm going to make your day.*
74. *Am I right about you?*
75. *When was the last time you...*
76. *Quick: What if...*
77. *Isn't it nice to know?*
78. *Today I found out that you...*
79. *You want it. We have it.*
80. *In the time it took you to open this envelope...*

* From *Sales Letters That Sizzle*, by Herschell Gordon Lewis, National Textbook Company. A complete exposition of this material can be found in that book.

Since handbills are likely to be used partly because of low cost, there is a real danger that efficient distribution may be neglected. Select reliable distributors and pay adequately for the work. Either you or some other competent person should supervise distribution. Organized handbill distributors who guarantee effective circulation can be found in many cities.

As a method of explaining the services you offer, a brochure conveys professionalism (see Figure 25.1). A brochure can give the impression of a serious, established, high-quality business—even if you just opened up yesterday, with your college diploma in one hand and a $5,000 check (your graduation present) in the other.

Your company brochure does not have to be a four-color job, if you want to keep expenses down. Rather, go for a light-color card stock measuring 7 to 8 inches. With one lengthwise fold down the center, the brochure fits easily into a No. 10 envelope. This makes it an ideal companion for your direct-mail marketing efforts as well as an excellent handout. We stress the size and stock because ordinary letter-size stationery will tend to blend in with other stacks of paper, and an oversized brochure can sometimes look pretentious.

Use the brochure to describe your services or products in a soft yet nononsense fashion. You are selling your contacts on using your products or services, and how your well-trained, qualified employees can save them trouble, time, effort, and money. If you know that you write well and persuasively, then write the brochure yourself. If you have any doubt about your ability to do a top-notch job, trust the writing and the design to professionals.

Be careful about the typeface, which should be easy to read and no smaller than 10-point. While it should take not much more than a minute for someone to scan your brochure, those 60-odd seconds should be packed with memorable information.

Your direct-mail advertising should be personal, informal, and selectively directed. Careful study of items such as zip codes, delivery records, and subscription lists, as well as your personal knowledge of your customers or clients, will enable you to classify most of the clientele into groups based on common buying interests. If you thoughtfully word your direct-mail pieces, you can create the impression of individualized attention to each recipient.

Mailing lists can be rented from list brokers. You can find them in your yellow pages under "Advertising—Direct Mail." Mailing lists today are ultrasophisticated, and you can get them in just about any category you want. There is a one-time rental fee that ranges in cost depending on your market and the number of names on the list.

How do you pick a list? Use the RFM formula: R stands for recency, F for frequency, and M for money. Because people and businesses move, and their economic status changes, recency is vital to the success of a list. Frequency refers to how many times the people on the list purchased your product or service. And money refers to how much they spent.

Because good mailing lists are essential for the success of a direct-marketing campaign, check out the list as thoroughly as possible. Buy only from

Figure 25.1 Brochure

JanetLynn House
390 East 200 South
PO Box 331
Parowan, Utah 84761

JanetLynn House

A Bed and Breakfast

Est. 1994

Open year round
Reservations suggested
801-477-1133

390 East 200 South
Parowan, Utah 84761

Welcome...

To the JanetLynn House, a spacious log and Tudor style Bed and Breakfast nestled at the mouth of Parowan Canyon off Highway 143.

Parowan is surrounded by Southern Utah's most spectacular scenery and is the year-round gateway to Brian Head Ski Resort and Cedar Breaks National Monument. Excellent stream and lake fishing is only minutes away.

Just a short drive away is the spectacular Bryce Canyon and Zion National Parks as well as Utah's Shakespearean Festival in Cedar City.

Enjoy the comforts of spacious bedrooms and bathrooms, delicious breakfasts, and amenities including exercise equipment, spa and recreation room.

Room Rates

<u>Main Floor</u>
"Parowan Trails"
Aspen log Queen size bed,
Western decor,
Shared bath.
$50.00

"Hundred Acre Wood"
Lodgepole pine log
Queen size bed,
Winnie the Pooh decor,
Shared bath.
$50.00

<u>Upstairs</u>
"Mary Catherine"
Classic brass and maple furnishings.
Queen size bed,
Private bath
$60.00

<u>Downstairs</u>
"Diamond Run"
Black wrought-iron Queen-size bed and double/twin bunk bed, ski decor.
Perfect for family.
Detached private bath.
$45.00

Our Policies

•Check in time after 2:00 p.m.
•Check out time 11:00 a.m.
•Visa and Mastercard accepted
(No personal checks, please.)
•All rates include breakfast.
•All rates are double occupancy-1 bed.
•$10.00 added for double occupancy-2 beds.
•$10.00 for each additional person per room, plus tax.
•One night deposit in advance.
•10 day cancellation required.
•For the safety and consideration.
of others, all rooms are nonsmoking.
•No alcoholic beverages or pets, please.

For Your Information...

Approximate mileage from these major
cities to Parowan

Las Vegas	190 miles
Salt Lake City	250 miles
Los Angeles	480 miles
Provo	205 miles

established services. Ask how many times the list has been sold in the previous six months and get the names and telephone numbers of some of the buyers. Call them and ask what their response rate was with the list, how many pieces were returned because of bad addresses, and whether they thought the list was worth the cost.

Established businesses are often able to trade their lists with other such businesses. This activity is something for entrepreneurs to aspire to because it is basically a no-cost way of building a list.

There are two ways to go as far as postage is concerned. Bulk rate requires filing an application with the U.S. Postal Service and involves a one-time application fee (remaining in force as long as you use the service at least once a year). There's also an annual fee, good from January through December. This means that if you pay your fee on December 10 and want to do a mailing after January 1, you will have to pay another annual fee when the new year begins. At this writing, cost per letter runs at a discount of about 45 percent from the current first-class rate. Minimum mailing is 200 pieces or 50 pounds.

Sending by bulk requires bundling the mail according to zip codes, and any nondeliverable pieces are tossed unless you state on the face, "Return postage guaranteed." Bulk is slow; local delivery can take five to seven days, and to get from one coast to the other may take two weeks or more. Postal workers deliver bulk mail only when they have room, after taking all other classes of mail.

Bulk mail has the advantage of being relatively cheap; a 45 percent discount is nothing to dismiss. But it has some important shortcomings—typically slowness and unpredictability. Also, bulk is generally perceived as junk mail. If image is important in your business, it makes sense to use first-class mail because you need to make a strong and favorable impression on customer or client prospects. The Postal Service also has first-class bulk rates at a discount for those mailers who bundle their mail. Investigate this in the same manner as described for bulk rate.

An alternative to the "directness" of direct mail is the coupon mailer (see Figure 25.2). Retail businesses within a community will be grouped together in a coupon mailer: Miniadvertisements, usually offering a discount or introductory special, are bound together in a small book. Each business represented in the mailer pays a fee to the company producing and distributing it. Several

Figure 25.2 Coupon

such companies should be listed in your yellow pages. These coupon books are mailed randomly to all homes within a zip-code area. They aren't as narrowly targeted as direct mail, but they still have great pull.

Outdoor Advertising

To advertise your product in specific geographic zones, billboards, bus benches, and transit advertising can be very effective for the small-business owner, but any good outdoor campaign begins with your own sign.

The sign is the most important contact between your business and much of the outside world. Usually it is the first thing a potential customer sees. Your sign should be sufficiently bright and conspicuous to attract attention (without being garish) and sufficiently informative to let prospective customers know what is sold there.

Ride around town and observe which signs catch your eye. Note which ones don't. Then think of the impression each sign leaves you with. Remember that first impressions last longest, and install a large, professional-looking sign that can be seen easily from all directions. Don't try to save money on this important advertising device. If your sign looks professional, potential customers are likely to assume that your business is a professional operation.

If you are involved in a business that has a fleet of vehicles conducting deliveries or providing a service, your company's name, logo, and phone number should be advertised on the vehicle. By doing this, you will increase your exposure into your local geographic markets, making your presence known to potential customers.

Billboards are most effective when located close to the business advertised. Because of their high cost, they are usually used to reach a very large audience, as in political campaigns. They are likely to be too expensive for most small firms, unless you are lucky enough to have access to a friend's vacant lot or to the building of another nearby business. Many communities have strict ordinances governing the placement of billboards. They are prohibited altogether in some areas.

Next time you're in your car waiting at a traffic light, look around you. Chances are you'll see a bus-stop bench with an advertisement painted on it, and you'll probably read all or part of it before the light turns green. So will thousands of others, day after day.

Bus-bench advertising is an excellent medium for any product or service. It's highly visible, like a billboard, because it is seen by vehicular traffic. Essentially, you have a huge captive audience, stuck at red lights or in slow-moving traffic. An account executive of a Los Angeles-based bus bench manufacturing company said that an advertisement on one bus bench at a busy Los Angeles intersection will be seen by 35,000 to 50,000 people per day.

Usually, the advertising consists of simple two-color artwork with your company's name, brief copy describing the service, address, and the telephone number. Think of it as a huge business card, conveying the same information in basically the same format.

Rates and terms will vary depending on the city you're in. In Los Angeles, you can rent bench space for a minimum of 12 months and a maximum of 36 months. If you rent two benches for 12 months, the cost averages $40 per bench, per month; if you rent five benches, the cost averages $29 per bench, per month; 10 benches are $27 each per month, and so on. For a 24- or 36-month rental, you'd take $1 and $2 off the cost of each bench per month, respectively. You will also pay a flat fee of anywhere from $175 to $300 for the artwork depending on whether you want your logo or a more complicated design. You only pay this fee once, whether you're renting one bench or 1,000.

Call your city's mass transit department or local bus company to find out who manufactures and/or rents advertising space on their bus-stop benches. Some outdoor advertising companies also handle this type of advertising.

Transit advertising (e.g., buses and taxicabs) is very underrated. It reaches a vast number of people and is cheaper for mass appeal than newspapers. It's excellent for reaching commuters. It gives your ad high visibility and the market research done on this type of advertising shows that it is very effective.

You don't need to spend a fortune to use transit or outdoor advertising. You can obtain boards in your neighborhood only, or negotiate with nearby retailers for space on the sides of their buildings.

Specialty Items

Ad specialties are primarily products that feature your company's name and/or logo. If used correctly, they can offer more diverse and long-lasting results than print or electronic ads. They work best for companies that are known for their service and attention to the customer. So when a customer buys a T-shirt with your company logo on it and wears it all over town, you are essentially getting an endorsement of satisfaction from that person. This kind of exposure can enhance the effects of other advertising and beef up your credibility.

You can inscribe your company's name and/or logo on visors, T-shirts, sunglasses, matchbooks, calendars, pens, and so on. The list of potential products is practically endless. Many pricey items can be sold, while the inexpensive specialties can be handed out free to customers for patronizing your business.

The purpose of ad specialties is to help your customers enjoy an identification with your company. Therefore, it helps if your company has a positive image. Without a solid reputation, you can put your company logo on everything in sight and it won't mean a thing. In addition to having a good reputation, you also have to know your market thoroughly and have a strong idea of the image you want to project. You can then go out and get the appropriate ad-specialty products.

Cooperative Advertising

Advertising is a big expense, but that cost can be cut down substantially by using co-op advertising. Each year, manufacturers budget millions of dollars for the specific purpose of cooperative advertising with their distributors and retailers. Unfortunately, the majority of this money is never used by distributors and retailers of the manufacturers' products.

Cooperative advertising is a cost-efficient and effective way for both the manufacturer and retailer or distributor to reach their target markets. Although co-op advertising policies differ from manufacturer to manufacturer, most will pay a portion of the advertising costs and supply the retailer with material to include in the ad, whether it is print, radio, or television. The backing of a manufacturer's cooperative advertising can range from immense financial outlays to promotional gimmicks and point-of-purchase displays like the sample for Diamond Tap beer shown in Figure 25.3. The norm lies somewhere in between.

Using co-op advertising cuts down not only on the media cost, but on the production and creative expenses as well. A smart advertiser will factor co-op advertising into the budget. The major drawback to co-op advertising is that some manufacturers have more restrictive programs than others. The retailer, of course, would like to tailor a message to the needs of his or her own individual service while mentioning the manufacturer's product; the manufacturer would prefer to run an ad featuring just the product.

The most striking benefit of any affiliated advertising is the increase in foot traffic. Though the gross profit may not be substantial for the item being offered, add-on items with high markup can increase your overall profitability. The best advice is to test the waters. Retail outlets have subtle marketing differences depending on whether they are in urban, mall, or strip center settings. The nature of the purchaser will differ, and buyers in various locales respond accordingly.

Another form of cooperative advertising is sponsored by strip centers, which will coordinate an advertisement from each merchant in the shopping center. These promotional presentations are seen in your local newspaper for back-to-school specials, St. Valentine's Day, Fourth of July, or Mother's Day and Father's Day.

Be careful to coordinate the cooperative advertising within your overall marketing scheme. If you have chosen a subtle approach to advertising, don't switch in midstream just to take advantage of some free advertising dollars. Steady and constant communications with your manufacturer and distributor will ensure a meeting of the minds.

THE CREATIVE CAMPAIGN

Advertising is used for three main reasons:

1. To promote awareness of your business.
2. To directly stimulate sales.
3. To create your firm's market niche.

Figure 25.3   Point of Purchase

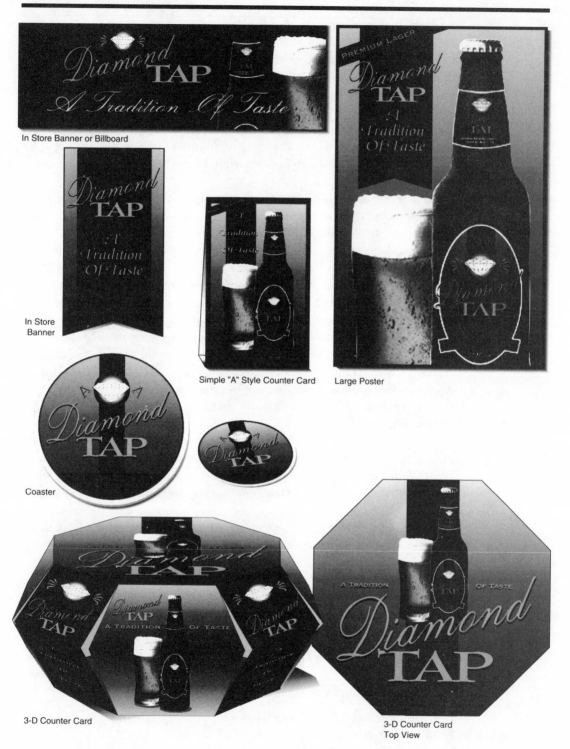

In Store Banner or Billboard

In Store Banner

Simple "A" Style Counter Card

Large Poster

Coaster

3-D Counter Card

3-D Counter Card
Top View

Word-of-Mouth Advertising

Why would Tracy Hosac print 600 or more business cards a month? As owner of an antique restoration mall, "Someplace in Time," she actually hands out that many—every month.

Word-of-mouth is Hosac's best form of advertising. Hosac opened her doors five years ago and since then has successfully built a steady clientele and a mailing list of thousands of names. While Hosac had to run quite a bit of print advertising in the beginning, she now coasts steadily on word-of-mouth and scattered promotions throughout the year. With each promotion, she will run an ad in a trade magazine and send a mailer out to her extensive list of names.

Still, by far, most of her business comes from word-of-mouth. her antique mall is unique in that 45 separate dealers or buyers work out of her one building. Those dealers are able to individually pass out her cards while selling and at trade shows. She also goes to some antique and garden shows herself, but she has been seeing show clientele slow down in recent years and so has tapered down on these advertising avenues.

How does Hosac make word-of-mouth work so well for "Someplace in Time"?

1. *She makes it a habit to tell people about her antiques business whenever she introduces herself.*
2. *She teaches all her salespeople to use friendliness. "We try to say 'Hello' to everyone who walks in the door," says Hosac. "Just a 'Hi, if you need anything let me know . . .' because I really think friendliness sells. If you ignore people and don't let them know you're there to help them, then they're not going to be as responsive." Just talking to customers helps them to trust and like her store and service.*
3. *Her prices are very reasonable, which allows resellers to shop at her store. In fact, about 25% of her business is to resellers and she collects a lot of cards and gives out a lot of cards to resellers.*
4. *When she buys antiques herself, Hosac always asks people if they know anyone interested in selling antiques and if they can send her information on other friends who may be interested in doing business. This is how she keeps the network growing.*
5. *Hosac also believes heavily in service. She keeps a "want/wish" book for items customers are looking for and if she's able to find them, she calls them right away to let them know. Her most recent bit of service is a tearoom she just opened. It adds a nice homey feeling and gives her a chance to show off china sets, with food catered every weekend. So far, the tearoom has been running successfully on word-of-mouth alone.*

As you can see, word-of-mouth advertising can be very cost-effective when combined with a touch of ingenuity.

Regardless of which advertising medium you select, the words you use to deliver the message are critical to these objectives. The advertising message must play an integral part in the overall marketing plan and must have as its primary goal—its ultimate purpose—grabbing the public's attention. A creative message can turn around a company's image, attracting purchasers who might otherwise have barely been considering buying your product.

Any creative message needs to have six basic characteristics:

1. It is simple and easily understood.
2. It is truthful.
3. It is informative.
4. It is sincere.
5. It is customer-oriented.
6. It tells who, what, where, when, why, and how.

When developing your creative campaign, you should plan on budgeting at least 5 percent of the total advertising budget. If your budget is sufficiently large, you can hire an advertising agency to put together your entire advertising campaign, including its creative elements. If you can't attract an advertising agency or don't feel the need for one, you can hire freelance copywriters and graphic artists to help you develop a solid creative campaign.

A large part of your creative campaign will be developing a theme line or memorable jingle. Ads in a campaign should tie together so that each time they're seen or heard, you remind consumers of your product. You want to design ads that work effectively in a variety of formats. In your copy, stress your company's strong points. You need a strong headline or opening, and the body copy should expand on the premise in the headline. End the ad with a "call for action"—encourage your audience to try your product.

Designing the Advertisement

No matter what communication vehicle(s) you select to advertise your product or service, good advertising usually follows established rules for form and content. It is a truism that rules are made to be changed and broken, and innovators are often successful when they do so; as a novice, however, learn to imitate the styles and techniques of successful advertisers before you try to become a maverick.

Most big-name advertisers spend millions of dollars analyzing their markets. They learn what their customers' deepest needs and anxieties are by studying psychographic data and using focus groups. The ads these companies come up with appeal to the basic emotions of consumers.

To put together an effective advertisement, you first have to analyze your company, the products or services you want to advertise, and the type of customers you want to attract. Next, you have to design an appeal—something that will benefit the target audience—and incorporate it into ad copy (see Figure 25.4). Here are some guidelines to help you create strong ads that will get a good response:

- **Create a sense of immediacy.** Because response diminishes over time, advertising relies on urging people to act immediately. Most people like to be led—particularly when in unfamiliar territory; tell your audience what response you want. At different points throughout the ad, and especially at

Figure 25.4 Ad Elements

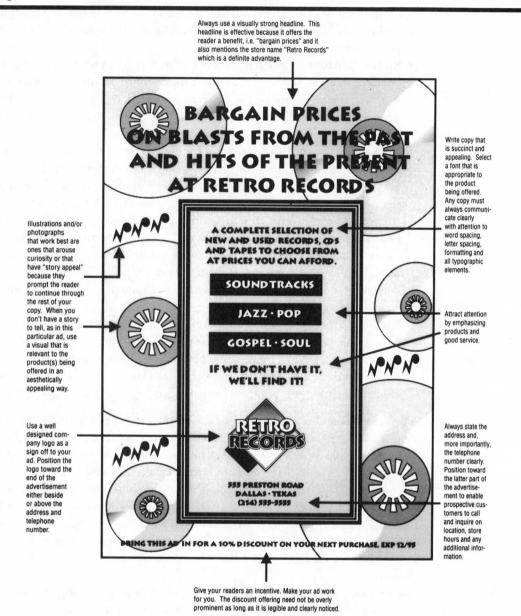

the conclusion, ask for a response: "Act quickly," "Limited-time offer," "Call now."

- **Repetition sells.** Keep weaving and reweaving the same sales pitch throughout the ad, each time adding a slightly new slant to the significant features and benefits of your product or service. Repetition sells because the more times someone hears or reads something, the more believable it becomes. Repetition is particularly important in advertising because you normally don't have the full attention of your audience. For a lot of people, writing repetitiously is difficult because they were taught in school to avoid redundancy. When writing ad copy, forget this training and repeat, repeat, repeat.

- **Hit the "buttons."** Different people will be turned on by different things about product or service. One person may admire quality, while another likes easy maintenance or the newness or simplicity of an item. Decide what is different and exciting about your product or service; then tell your audience how and why they need what you have to sell.
- **"Sell the sizzle, not the steak."** This old advertising axiom means sell the action, not the product or service. There's nothing wrong with talking about the features of your product or service, but unless you spell out how the customers will directly benefit, your ad won't have maximum effectiveness. To excite your audience, you must display and/or describe your product or service in a captivating way. This does not mean fancy words or constructions that might confuse the reader, listener, or viewer. Use plain, simple English and be straightforward. Keep your ad copy at an understandable level or you'll lose much of your audience. Figure 25.5 shows an effective action ad.
- **Evaluate other ads.** Collect all kinds of ads and study them. This is a habit of all good ad-makers. Use their ideas if they're worthwhile. Don't be a martyr, trying to create something new because you want to be different. While it is essential to put your own imagination to use, learn to emulate the strengths of others who are successful with their advertising.

For print ads and television, the next element you'll need to include is the visual art. Your visual element should create human interest, emotion, and realism. The visuals for television advertising will consist of a series of images that tell a story. A good television commercial should be able to convey your advertising message without ad copy. It should be entertaining and memorable. Use people, colors, animals, or anything that will create images with emotional appeal and sell your product or service at the same time. If you can afford photography in print ads, use it. Photographs are generally more believable than illustrations, as well as being more professional looking and easier to remember.

Another way to get attention for small-space advertising involves the layout. Because of the natural tendency of most small businesses to say everything that can possibly fit in an advertisement, typical small-space advertising is very crowded and busy. Instead, make your ad as simple as possible so readers can easily understand the one message you want them to remember. They can't do that when they have to fight through four different typefaces, screaming banner headlines, or tiny photographs. You're better off sticking with one typeface throughout the ad and staying away from a variety of type sizes. The headline should be in one type size and the body copy in another. Forcing readers to look at a variety of typefaces may annoy them.

Figure 25.5   Yellow Pages Ad

VIP LIMOUSINE

limo service
for
all occasions:

*weddings *anniversaries *birthdays
*a night out *any special event!

"CELEBRATE IN STYLE"

555-1212
3372 n. doheny st., greenville

One effective way to increase readership of small-space advertising is to use a reverse. That's when the type appears in white and the background is in black. You'd be amazed at the amount of reader interest that this generates. Or try using a color when the surrounding advertising is black and white; this makes your ad stand out.

Another effective way to draw attention to your ad in the newspaper or the magazine is to use a border. It will set off your ad from the others quite dramatically, but make sure that the border is not the most dominant thing in the ad.

In advertising layout terminology, white space is the blank area surrounding the headline or framing the advertisement to separate it from other advertisements on the page. Small-business owners seldom use white space creatively in their advertising, but it can dramatically set off your advertisement from the others, especially when it sets off a bold dramatic headline. To add visual impact to a print ad, include a lot of white space if you're advertising in the newspapers, "yellow space" if you're advertising in the yellow pages. These types of ad work well because of the dense columns of type used in such publications. Anything that breaks up the pattern stands out.

This is true not only for the design of the print ad, but also for its size. Ads that are different in size from standard formats will stand out in a publication. For instance, a diagonal ad will break up standard media formats, as will running three ads in rapid succession. Placing an ad that runs across two pages is another widely used method.

MEASURING ADVERTISING EFFECTIVENESS

As a business owner, you should never stop surveying and studying your customers. Neighborhoods and customers' habits change. If a customer drifts away, try at once to determine why.

Check the effectiveness of your advertising programs regularly using tests like the following:

1. Advertise one item in one ad only. Have no references to the item on the business premises. Then count the calls and requests for the advertised item.
2. Run the same ad in two different publications with an identifying mark on each. The reader is asked to bring in the ad to receive a special price or discount. See how many ads come in from each source.
3. Omit a regular advertising project for intermittent periods and watch any change in sales.
4. Check sales results when you place a new advertisement.
5. If you're using an advertising agency, they can perform a "postanalysis" on your broadcast buys, which compares the number of rating points you bought with the number of rating points actually achieved after your schedule ran. They can also obtain for you coupon redemption figures or card insert responses from your print schedules.

These checks can give you an idea of how your program is performing. Timing, items advertised, weather, season, economic conditions, and other such factors will affect any advertising program. If results are not significant, the program may still have served an institutional purpose by telling people your firm is there. Some consumers who saw the ads may give you future business.

It's more difficult to measure the effectiveness of your television advertising than it is when you use the newspaper. There are no coupons to be clipped, for instance, and you may not have an immediate, dramatic response to your ad. But your advertising agency can supply you with some figures on response. Another method is to ask your customers what brought them into your business. You can even advertise a special television sale, offering a discount to customers who mention your commercial. To make television work best, you need to advertise continually. Whether you buy a few spots a month or advertise heavily all year, you must advertise regularly to reach the customers.

Remember, your campaign is effective only if sales increase. That's the true test of any advertising program. All the major corporations as well as smaller businesses prove it every day. Keep in mind, however, that a good commercial can bring the customers into your store, but only you can make the sale.

ADVERTISING PROFESSIONALS

Professional advertising agency personnel and media representatives can help you plan your advertising efforts. Ad agencies earn a large portion of their profits in commissions from advertising media placed on behalf of their clients. The ads cost the client the same whether placed through an agency or directly with the media. However, the agencies usually bill their clients for other services performed, such as consultation, copywriting, and artwork. A thorough knowledge of advertising is essential to any businessperson.

Don't Buy the Rate Card

As already discussed, sharp media buyers for the big advertising agencies have a standard motto: "Never buy the rate card." Many people will accept the rate card from a magazine, radio, or television station as fact—unnegotiable and unshakable. Most of the time, this is not the case. Although the print media are more set in their rates, you can always negotiate in broadcast advertising.

Your biggest bargaining chip when negotiating off the rate card is cash. For example, most TV stations operate on a 90-day float. An advertising agency that buys 12 minutes of time for a client will bill that client for the time before it runs on the air and then wait up to 90 days to pay the station. So most stations are cash-hungry. They will sell more time on a cash basis than they will on a contract basis. Call the sales manager of the station, tell him what your maximum spending amount is and that you want to strike a deal. Let the manager know that you never buy the rate card and have no intention of doing so. Be persistent if necessary.

Selecting an Advertising Agency

As in any business endeavor, your primary goal is to reduce the consequences of risk. Perusing an advertising trade journal will enlighten you on the numerous reports of clients changing agencies and constant rumors of the same nature. It is to your advantage to choose an agency in a calm, systematic, methodical manner.

Think about what you want. Some advertising agencies specialize in various sectors emphasizing local or national campaigns. Some will coordinate an entire marketing campaign; others will only handle advertising. The needs of a retailer will be entirely different than those of a service-related organization or manufacturing firm.

Prepare a rough outline of your marketing and advertising objectives. Have these guidelines handy when you start your inquiries into ad agencies. Narrow down a half dozen that fit your selective criteria. Thoroughly screen at least three of these.

If you request it, some agencies will produce a sample of their work or speculative advertising to help you make a decision. Yet others will refuse to lay out such campaigns unless they are appropriately paid for the time. Charging a nominal fee is the compromise solution often worked out. Even then, results can be misleading. How the agency works, thinks, operates, and makes its presentation under stressful, pressurized situations is the real test.

Another criterion is to establish your minimum, maximum, and ideal advertising budget. See which agency is most willing to work within your parameters. This may be below the minimum account for a large national agency. How much cash you are willing to spend has some direct bearing on the size of the agency you may want to choose.

Discuss a payment plan. The so-called standard commission for advertising agencies is 15 percent of the amount a client spends on media billings—print media space and electronic media time. By all means be forthright and honest about the method of payment, and discuss the different options for a payment schedule with the agency you choose.

Not Ready for a Prime Time Agency?

An alternate route in putting an advertising campaign together without doing it all yourself is to use suppliers of print ad space. They can design an ad for you using guidelines that you provide in the way of a rough layout. Unfortunately, often they're not going to have a feel for your campaign unless you provide a rough layout or guidelines. If you just give an advertising idea to the yellow pages ad sale rep or the newspaper ad sales rep, you're going to get back what the rep thinks you should be saying. Try not to get yourself in that position.

The best alternative is to recruit help from freelance artists, designers, students, or professionals who moonlight. The advantage of working out your advertising campaign with broadcasting school students or art school students is they want to build a portfolio so that they can get a full-time advertising job later on. They're going to be excited about the challenge of working with your company. From your perspective, you could get some dynamic advertising ideas at an inexpensive price.

SUMMARY

It's not difficult to put together a winning, dynamic, and productive advertising campaign if you plan beforehand. You must take advertising into account as part of an overall marketing strategy for your business or product, and then develop advertising that drives home one major point to the listener or reader.

Remember to focus that message on those who are going to be buying most of your products or services. Concentrate on the 20 percent who will purchase 80 percent of your goods. Put together a well-thought-out, professional campaign using as much freelance and moonlighting talent as you can, which is available at inexpensive prices.

If you do all these things and pay attention to details, advertising will work for you. It will return its investment many times over.

RESOURCES

Associations

America Advertising Federation, 1101 Vermont Avenue, Suite 500, Washington, DC 20005, 202-898-0090

Association of National Advertisers, 155 East 44th Street, New York, NY 10017, 212-697-5950

Cable T.V. Advertising Bureau, 757 Third Avenue, 5th floor, New York, NY 10017, 212-751-7770

Newspaper Association of America, 711 Third Avenue, New York, NY 10017, 212-856-6300

Outdoor Advertising Association of America, 12 East 49th Street, 22nd Floor, New York, NY 10017, 212-688-3667

Point-of-Purchase Advertising Institute, 66 North Van Brunt Street, Englewood, NJ 07631, 201-894-8899

Radio Advertising Bureau, 304 Park Avenue South, New York, NY 10010, 212-254-4800

Magazines

Ad/Mag, 305 North Broadway, St. Louis, MO 63102, 314-231-4185

Advertising Age, 220 East 42nd Street, New York, NY 10017, 212-210-0100

Advertising Communications Times, 121 Chestnut Street, Philadelphia, PA 19106, 215-629-1666

Adweek, 1515 Broadway, New York, NY 10036, 212-536-5336

American Advertising, America Advertising Federation, 1101 Vermont Avenue, Suite 500, Washington, DC 20005, 202-898-0090

American Demographics, 127 West State Street, Ithaca, NY 14850, P.O. Box 68, Ithaca, NY 14851, 607-273-6343

Business Marketing, 740 North Rush Street, Chicago, IL 60611, 312-649-5200

Inside Media, Cowles Business Media, 911 Hope Street, Building 6, P.O. Box 4949, Stamford, CT 06907-0949, 203-358-9900

26

Telemarketing

In the past 20 years, marketing over the telephone has gained increasing acceptance as an effective and efficient way of selling a company's products or services. Some companies operate exclusively by telephone. For instance, it has been reported that some telemarketing firms, selling only office supplies, gross $10 to $15 million annually. Obviously, telephone solicitations can generate considerable business.

Telemarketing has become a compelling tool for several reasons:

- It is as easy to hit a desired market with the telephone as with a targeted mailing list.
- You can prequalify prospects for personal follow-up.
- The telephone works as a personal selling tool that allows you to talk directly with the sales prospect.
- It enables you to influence the prospect's decision because you are initiating contact and eliciting a response.

According to Eugene Kordahl in the book, *Handbook of Management for the Growing Business* by Carl Heyel and Belden Menkus, telemarketing is also used to tie together personal selling and advertising campaigns, and is often very effective at that task. It works so well because of its very nature as a planned activity. Since other promotional programs and advertisements are also planned, the combined effort is a hard-hitting package that rarely misses its mark.[1]

This chapter provides you with information concerning available telecommunications equipment, services, and sales techniques that can be useful in a telemarketing campaign. Keep in mind, however, that while most of this

---

[1] Carl Heyel and Belden Menkus, *Handbook of Management for the Growing Business* (New York: Van Nostrand Reinhold Company, Inc., 1986).

chapter is geared toward the telemarketer, much of the information can also be used to improve your day-to-day operations.

PHONE SYSTEMS

Today, the telephone is much more than just an instrument for social conversation; it is now part of a complex communications system for businesses and consumers. By utilizing new telephone technologies, you can open up new markets and generate revenue opportunities that spell the difference between making a profit and just breaking even. Innovations in telecommunications technology help business owners and consumers establish close, direct contacts, regardless of time and distance. By integrating telecommunications techniques and technologies with marketing, the telephone has proven to be the most cost-effective marketing tool available.

Installing a telephone system for your new business isn't simply a matter of deciding how many phones and phone lines to get. Telephone systems can now be set up to accommodate computer equipment add-ons in the future. The following will explain some of the various phone systems available to business owners and how they can enhance your sales effort.

Multiline Systems

For a small business with room to grow, it's important to invest in a telephone system that will grow along with the business. When choosing a system, consider the flexibility and economy the system can bring to your office. With the extensive advances made in the telecommunications industry over the past 50 years, you can find phone systems to meet the needs of businesses with anywhere from 1 employee to 5,000.

Because of the numerous systems available and the vast array of add-on features you can purchase, you should do a lot of investigating before you make a choice. Remember, the biggest system is not necessarily the best for your particular business. If you invest in a highly advanced system that provides a myriad of add-on features you never use, you have only wasted your money.

Entrepreneurs who run single-person operations won't need a technically advanced phone system. In fact, many single operators use a one-line phone system and simply buy an answering machine and/or have the added feature of call waiting installed. An answering machine can take the place of a receptionist, while call waiting informs you that another call is coming in and lets you answer that call. If you do not use the phone extensively in your business, this can be an ideal system for you. For one thing, it's very inexpensive. Since businesses that are just starting up need to keep expenses to a minimum, you may want to look into this simple telephone system. In addition to a minimal installation fee, your monthly charges will be moderate.

Another simple and economical phone system available to small business owners is the rotary system. This system features a main number with other numbers lined up behind it in rotation. To illustrate how this works, let's say your phone number is 555-1000. When callers phone your business and that number is busy, the calls will automatically go to 555-1001, 555-1002, and so on. With this system, you can put calls on hold and pick them up from any station. Installation costs and fees for a rotary telephone system are low compared with more sophisticated multiline systems.

Many small businesses start out with this type of phone system, then upgrade to a multiline system. A rotary phone system can be especially effective for entrepreneurs who run their business from their home or who have very few employees on the premises and only a couple of phones to answer.

If your business is more complicated, however, you'll probably need a multiline (pushbutton) phone system. A multiline system allows you to switch back and forth between lines on the same phone. These systems have a unit that controls the switching of those lines. The basic system also allows you a number of convenient features, such as transferring calls, placing calls on hold, and picking up lines at other stations.

While a variety of features are available on multiline systems, most work in one of two different ways:

1. **The key multiline system.** An older version that works on a purely mechanical basis.
2. **Electrical current.** The most modern multiline system, it works off of an electrical current that increases speed and accuracy.

Experts in the telecommunications industry recommend a multiline system for businesses that anticipate rapid growth. When looking for a multiline system, try to choose a system that can be upgraded without replacing the entire system. This can save you a lot of money and will avoid the added problem of learning a new phone system.

Since the telecommunications industry is developing at such an accelerated pace, you should contact your telecommunications company for information concerning the latest multiline systems available.

Computer Switching Systems

As your business grows, you may need a computerized switchboard and a receptionist to operate it. Although it is more costly than a simple multiline system, a computer switching system can speed up calls and increase the overall efficiency of your office. Computer switching systems are known as PBX (private branch exchange) systems. This covers any type of system that has a central answering port where all incoming lines (including lines in rotary) arrive and appear on the phone. In addition to transferring calls, the PBX switchboard is computer programmed to return calls to the PBX board when a station is busy or unanswered. A main switching console allows you to do that.

Since PBX systems vary greatly in terms of price and capabilities, you should shop around before you buy. Your local phone company's business-sales rep should have the answers to your specific needs.

Add-On Features

By simply adding on new features to your existing telephone system, you can upgrade your current system without incurring a great expense. The following list describes some of the add-on features that are currently available:

- **Least call routing.** Automatically directs all outgoing calls by the least expensive route.
- **Cordless phone.** Allows more mobility. Uses FM frequency for transmission.
- **Music-on-hold.** Lets the caller listen to preselected music while on hold.
- **Paging.** Gives you the capability to page the person being called.
- **Call sequencer.** Answers calls in order of their arrival with a taped message or music, and holds them until the attendant can process them.
- **Call diverter.** Diverts calls from one number to another prearranged number.
- **Automatic dialer.** Allows user to store numbers in memory and dial them by pushing only one button.
- **Call restriction.** Allows your employees to make only certain kinds of predetermined calls, limiting long-distance or internal calls.
- **Automatic answering machine.** A common device that allows you to play and record messages from incoming phone calls.
- **Call parking.** Lets you retrieve a call placed on hold from any phone in the system.
- **Automatic computer record dialing machine.** Dials a prearranged number, then plays an automatic recording.
- **Telephone record control.** Can record both sides of a phone conversation.
- **Station message detail recording.** Can be very helpful to the small business owner in eliminating phone abuse by issuing printouts that show who called whom, at what time, for how long, how often, and at what cost.
- **Direct-in-line.** Allows callers to reach the party they're calling without going through a central receptionist or console.
- **Automatic call distributor.** Announces that all operators are busy and requests the caller to remain on the line until an operator is available. This also directs calls to the operator who has been idle the longest.
- **Speakerphone.** Allows you to talk without picking up the handset.
- **Call waiting.** Notifies the user that another call is waiting and gives the user the option of answering the second call.
- **Do not disturb.** Allows you to restrict incoming calls.
- **Hands-free dialing.** Lets you dial without picking up the handset.
- **Transfer.** Lets you transfer calls from one station to another.

- **Automatic redial.** Lets you store numbers and redial them with the push of a single button.
- **Camp-on.** Allows attendant to camp a call onto a busy line and lets the party know another call is waiting.
- **Alphanumeric liquid crystal display (LCD).** Usually shows the date and time when the phone is not in use. When dialing, the number called appears on the display, which will time the length of the call.
- **Direct inward system access.** Allows you to access your main office line from a remote location using any pushbutton phone.

Peripheral Phone Products

In addition to features that you can add directly to your phone system, modern technology allows you to utilize other products in conjunction with your telephone. The following is just a sample of the services your telephone can provide:

- **Direct electronic mail.** Enables you to send messages to other electronic mail stations. This requires a microcomputer, a modem, and some communications software.
- **Facsimile mail.** The most popular form of electronic mail today. The fax machine produces hard-copy duplicates of documents, photographs, drawings, and graphs. You will need a fax machine and a modem in addition to your phone system.
- **Voice mail.** Computer systems that communicate with more than one telephone line, giving users the ability to record, retrieve, and forward messages recorded with the caller's voice. A microcomputer is necessary for this capability, or you can contract with voice mail service companies that will provide you with the service for a small monthly fee.

Once your company has become established, chances are you will need one or more of these peripheral phone products. When first starting up a business, however, be sure not to go overboard with products you don't really need.

800-NUMBERS

The 800-number exploded in the early 1970s as a national and regional marketing tool. If your customers are scattered across the country, they have to invest in a long-distance call to get in touch with you. This is a strong deterrent, and many potential customers won't spend the money to find out what you have to offer. An 800-number allows them to contact you without spending a cent, and without obligation.

These days, 800-numbers are so common that they are virtually a competitive necessity for any business that markets and sells to a wide territory. The opposing argument is that an 800-number, if handled incorrectly, encourages a certain number of "shoppers"—aka unqualified leads—on whom you waste time and money.

The main reason for the increased use of 800-numbers as a telemarketing tool is the cost factor. Closing a sale through telemarketing usually costs less than one-fifth of what it would cost to send a salesperson on-site to make the same sale. For a small company, this can mean the difference between making a profit and losing your shirt on excessive travel and entertainment expenses.

In addition to their cost-effectiveness, 800-numbers can increase the small business owner's sale in a variety of ways. Improving customer relations and tracking the effectiveness of advertising are just two ways that toll-free numbers can increase sales. Allowing customers to call your company toll-free for information or orders lets them know that you value their patronage. Knowing that your company is available to them at all times free of charge can keep existing customers satisfied with your performance and coming back for more.

Very few businesses can survive without some kind of advertising. By placing ads that give your 800-number more information or orders, you can see which ads are effective and which are not. You can also determine which media work best for your product or service. If you receive 100 calls from a flyer you mailed out, but only 20 from a radio spot, you'll know that you should concentrate your advertising on handbills and flyers. Naturally, using the proper advertising media is essential to increasing your sales.

In addition to tracking advertising, an 800-number can act as an actual ad for your company. With an alpha translation—a phone number that spells out the name of your company—you can increase awareness of your business just by giving out your toll-free number. For example, a balloon shop might want to use a number like 1-800-BALLOON to help potential customers remember the number.

To benefit from an alpha translation for your 800-number, you should find a word that uses either part or all of the seven digits. Once you have settled on a number, dial it to see if it is already in use. If it isn't, check with the phone company to see if it's available for use. If so, place your order. Remember that if your company's number is easier to recall than your competitor's number, you'll get the extra sales.

Installation

When setting up an 800-number, there are several practical matters to consider. If you are thinking of installing an 800-number, you should first analyze the costs versus the potential benefits of such a system. You can derive a cost-per-minute figure based on the service by dividing the minutes into the costs. This will help you decide which service is most economical for your company.

When analyzing the various carriers, you should also look at the service levels and trunk group size. If you add circuits, you can reduce the possibility of incomplete calls. Also, remember to look at the economy-of-circuit scale. By purchasing in bulk, you may be able to get reduced prices that will, in turn, reduce your cost-per-minute figure.

Vendors of toll-free numbers vary, which can make it difficult to find one that offers you the ideal system. To ensure you receive the best possible service for your company's needs, have the carriers do traffic studies, estimate costs, and make suggestions for your system. Make sure the carrier you choose can meet the demands of the calling patterns of your business.

The installation, monthly service charges, and usage rates for a toll-free number can add up to a substantial sum. (Your phone company will give you the current fees.) Before you get a toll-free number, make sure that the benefits outweigh the costs.

Fees

Many small and medium-size businesses can't afford the expense of their own 800-numbers. Because the cost of an 800-number can amount to several thousand dollars per month, plus an additional installation fee, smaller companies may want to look into toll-free answering services.

There are toll-free answering services that will take orders for your product over the phone. Usually, customers can dial an 800-number 24 hours a day. For a per-order fee of about 25 cents to one dollar, the service's operator will take the name and address, credit-card number, and whatever other information is needed from each caller.

This cuts into your profit, but if you wanted to install your own inbound WATS (Wide-Area Telecommunications Service) line, hire operators, and do the paperwork, it could cost you several thousand dollars each month. These companies will give you access to comparable service for no money directly out of your pocket.

Before installing an 800-number, compare expected profit increases with installation and maintenance fees to see if this service will be worthwhile for your business. Once again, prices for an 800-number vary from company to company, so shop around for the best deal.

TELEPHONE SALES

To ensure a telemarketing campaign's success, you must first set your goals. Once you are sure of your objectives, you must define employee responsibilities with job descriptions and reporting structures. You should let all employees know exactly what you expect of them. Tell them how many calls they should make during their shift and what percentage of those calls should result in qualified leads.

If you have prospects calling in on a WATS line, sales representatives who answer the calls should determine the extent of interest and whether or not a salesperson should return the call. They can do this easily by asking a series of prepared questions.

Since telemarketers face rejection throughout the day, there is often a very high turnover rate in this field. If your company does heavy telemarketing, you may want to have your sales staff work only four-hour shifts to avoid burnout and increase productivity. Most telemarketers agree that shorter shifts generally translate into increased productivity.

The Sales Force

Telemarketing programs are gaining in popularity due to their profitability and cost-effectiveness. One conventional sale can take as many as four face-to-face calls. With the costs of salaries, commissions, travel and entertainment expenses, your profits are severely decreased with in-person sales.

By using the telephone as a sales tool, you can cut down on the number of face-to-face visits your sales force has to make, thereby increasing your profits. Because they spend less time on the road, your sales staff can be in the office calling other prospective customers. You'll also need fewer employees to accomplish the same amount of work. This way, you can reduce your overhead while increasing productivity.

Prospecting

Prospecting is the search for potential customers or buyers. Salespeople are constantly seeking new methods to present traditional products and services to the marketplace. The telephone is one of the most effective devices for locating new customers. The telephone is such an effective marketing tool, in fact, that many "traveling salespeople" have given up traveling to recruit customers over the phone.

Not only is prospecting by telephone less expensive than keeping a salesperson on the road, the equipment is decreasing in price and many innovative techniques are being discovered. These advantages have made telephone prospecting the most reliable and cost-effective method for business-to-business prospecting.

For a telephone prospecting program to be successful, you must first analyze what role prospecting is going to play in your overall marketing strategy. The major goals of any prospecting program are determining which prospects require your product or service, showing the prospect why they should buy, and closing the sale.

To identify which prospects need your goods, you should start with a pre-screened list of prospects (see Figure 26.1). Callers will ask them a series of questions to further determine if they are qualified. Depending on their answers, you will either delete them from your list or keep them.

For calls to be successful, each telemarketer should have a checklist for determining a prospect's interest and should be responsible for obtaining responses

Figure 26.1 Prospecting Sheet

CLIENT INFORMATION   Send Media Kit ☐

Company Name:		Type of Business:	
Company Address:			
City: State: Zip:		Phone No.:	FAX No.:
Contact:		Title:	
Decision Maker:		Title:	

GOALS OF THE CALL

GOALS OF THE CUSTOMER

WAYS TO HELP CUSTOMER FULFILL GOALS

OBJECTIONS OF CUSTOMER

RESPONSES TO OBJECTIONS

WAYS TO ENSURE CUSTOMER SATISFACTION

to each of the questions on that list. Here are some of the items you should include on the list:

- What is the goal of this phone call?
- What are the customer's goals?
- Who is the customer's decision maker and what are the decision criteria?
- How can your company help the customer's company reach its goals?
- Do you have a media kit to send to the customer after the call?
- What objections does the customer make?
- How can you respond to those objections?
- How will you follow up to ensure customer satisfaction once an agreement has been made?

Telecomputers

A new device that is gaining popularity in the telephone prospecting field is the telecomputer. Computer dialers can generate a great number of leads on a daily basis, whether your sales force is in the office or not. Here's how this simple and effective system works.

The computer dials a number, introduces itself, then presents your service or product. Depending on responses to programmed questions, the computer weeds out unqualified prospects. One of the greatest advantages of telecomputers is that prospects who hang up early don't bother the computer in the least. Unlike salespeople, computers are oblivious to phone abuse and don't need any time to "regroup" after a rejection.

Therefore, telecomputers can usually complete a much greater percentage of calls in a day. Telecomputers have the ability to call hundreds of prospects each day to determine qualification. Most are able to complete an average of more than one call a minute. Telecomputers range in price from $3,000 to $10,000.

Telecomputers can also save money in the sense that they reduce sales staff turnover. A sales staff whose job requires cold calling generally experiences a high turnover rate due to the salespeople's inability to withstand repeated rejection.

Sales Techniques

A sales pitch, delivered over the telephone, is definitely different from face-to-face negotiations. But it is not necessarily less effective. In fact, there are many advantages to making a sales pitch by phone. Often, in face-to-face meetings, a potential client will become sidetracked by the salesperson's personality and forget the facts. On the telephone, it's easier to remain focused on the matter at hand. For this reason, you should know how to use telephone-sales techniques that get the prospect to listen and increase your chances of making a sale:

1. **Create a selling mood.** You'll want to come across as knowledgeable, friendly, helpful, and trustworthy. Speak firmly and clearly, and amplify your voice so you don't lose the person.

2. **Be specific.** Tell the person the advantages of dealing with you. Being vague is a good way to make your listener lose interest or become distrustful: If you're not clear, you must have something to hide.

3. **Control the time.** Don't tell a bunch of chatty stories. Also, don't try to top a story that the listener tells. This is not a contest.

4. **Control the pace.** Slow down when making important comments so that you can emphasize these points. This will get the listener's attention at just the right moments.

5. **Don't use a lot of "ums" or "ahs."** If you can't think of anything to say, say nothing. Moments of silence can be used to your advantage; filling them up with meaningless sounds eliminates this advantage and is annoying to the listener.

6. **Ask questions.** This can be very effective. These should be phrased so that they cannot be readily answered in the negative: "Do you like to see results?" "Do you want this year to be your best ever?" By getting prospects to keep saying yes, you make them think positively about you and your product or service. Such questions force prospects to listen and to agree with you continually. The questions should focus on what, why, and where. The prospect is tied down by questions starting with "Wasn't it . . . ?" "Hasn't it . . . ?" "Don't you agree . . . ?" "What would you say to . . . ?" This accomplishes a series of closes that, in telephone sales, are points where the prospective customer has to make a decision, however small or seemingly insignificant. The closes build to the most important one—that of the sale, when the final agreement is pinned down. Once the deal has been struck, compliment the prospect on a good decision. Make the person feel positive about him- or herself and about you.

7. **Don't monopolize the conversation.** Most of us like to talk, particularly if we are salespeople. One of the worst things to do when selling over the telephone is to monopolize the conversation. If you don't let the prospect get a word in, it will convince that person you're not really listening. If that's the case, the prospect will decide not to listen to you. And if the prospect is not listening, it's very unlikely that there will be any sale. You are not the center of attention, your prospect is; so steer the conversation in that person's direction.

8. **Don't use unnecessary humor.** You can use humor, but be smart about it. Jokes that fall flat or make you sound silly will not project the image you want. The best way of avoiding the problem is not to crack jokes in the first place. Just as you like to feel important, so do your prospective customers. Because you are trying to sell something to them, don't build yourself up, particularly at the expense of your listener. Make the listener the center of attention.

It is not enough that the prospect listens to you—you must listen to your prospect. A conspicuous weakness of modern Americans is the inability to listen. Many, if not most, people really don't understand the techniques necessary for effective listening. For the telemarketer, knowing how to listen is essential if the marketing is to succeed.

Here are some additional hints:

- **Don't interrupt.** It's not only rude, but interrupting says you are not listening. Once the prospect comes to that conclusion, you can kiss your sale good-bye.
- **Don't rush the person.** If the prospect is a slow speaker, be patient. This will payoff, especially if the lead is a good sales prospect. Speeding the prospect along will likely cause antagonism.
- **Meet objections.** Really listen to what the prospect says, and read between the lines. You want to address the real problems that confront you, not surface problems. The prospect may come up with several surface problems that really don't have anything to do with the main objection. However, by listening carefully, you'll be able to decipher the real problem and confront it.
- **Decide on a sales pitch.** A prepared script is essential when starting out. Prepare answers to questions you think will be asked and to objections that will be raised. Turn objections and questions into positives. Get the prospect to agree to something. When you become familiar with your pitch, throw the script away. Let's face it: Reading sounds like reading.
- **Don't take rejection too hard.** At no time are you more likely to be rejected than when you try to sell something—especially if you're making cold calls. All the guy has to do to get rid of you is hang up. This is just what many of them will do. If telemarketing is going to be a successful sales tool for you, you will have to resign yourself to being dumped on. It's a numbers game; when a prospect turns you down, shrug it off and dial the next telephone number.

In addition, salespeople must take careful notes during negotiations to make sure they know what the client wants and is willing to pay. While this practice can be annoying to a client sitting across from the salesperson, it can be accomplished easily over the phone without making the salesperson seem rude.

Another common pitfall associated with the traditional face-to-face sales pitch is that negotiations between principals often turn into meetings with employees who aren't involved with the decision. Basically, this means that decisions are delayed, thereby creating extra expenses for your company. With the telephone, you can reach the decision maker and keep your conversation to the point. This means that you can concentrate on the other person, instead of having to win over an entire group. Even if several people are involved in the phone conversation through teleconferencing, each party acts individually, providing more productive discussion and much less showmanship than in a meeting situation.

On the telephone, sales negotiations are considerably briefer than in traditional sales meetings. Much of the small talk is avoided and business is conducted efficiently. And if an impasse is reached, it is much easier to hang up the phone and call back in a few hours when you have a new approach than to leave a meeting and come back later.

Whenever you make a call, you must eliminate all distractions from your work area. If you lose your concentration because you start looking at other work on your desk, you will not be able to focus on your potential client, who may realize that you are not giving your undivided attention to the call. Remember that nothing makes a client feel less important and less inclined to buy something from you.

Moreover, you should keep an open mind when calling. Don't assume that you know what a client will say before the person says it. When making sales calls, be patient. Let the potential client complete sentences, and whatever you do, don't interrupt clients. Letting the speaker talk without interruption can be the best way to get information. However, if the speaker starts to wander, you can keep the person on track by asking for clarifications and leading the conversation in the direction you want it to go. Try to do this tactfully without offending the caller.

Encourage your caller to continue talking by interjecting short comments that let the person know that you are listening. If you don't say anything at all while the caller talks, they may think you aren't listening and become annoyed. Saying "I see" or "Tell me more" may be all that's needed to show you're really interested in what the person has to say.

Everyone knows that body language is important in face-to-face meetings, but it can also aid in telephone negotiations. Adopting an upright posture as opposed to a slouching one can help you remain alert and attentive to the caller. While this is more of a psychological boost than anything else, salespeople claim it really does work.

One of the best ways to improve communications on the phone is to take notes during the conversation. In addition to helping you remember what was said after you hang up, it also keeps you attentive during the call. When taking notes during a conversation, include a column of facts and statements, as well as a column for your impressions of what was said. Be sure to maintain these notes for your records so that you will have formal, written records of any conversations in case you need proof someday in court.

Probably the most effective way to avoid misunderstandings is to repeat and verify all key facts. You should take responsibility for getting the message right. Don't make it sound as if the potential client is unable to get a clear message across. Don't say something like "What you just said, Mr. Rice, was very confusing. You didn't explain yourself well. Could you repeat that for me?" Instead, say something like this: "Before we move on, Mrs. Rice, I want to make sure that what I've understood is perfectly accurate. Let me verify the information I have . . ."

By taking these simple precautions, you can save a tremendous amount of time and money on follow-up calls to verify unclear information. Not only do calls of this sort take up your employees' time, they can also delay the delivery of products or services, and bother clients who have to repeat what they thought was understood. By following these guidelines, you should improve your phone negotiating power and ultimately increase sales.

While listening carefully will definitely help you conduct productive phone negotiations, you will also have to make an effort to speak clearly. This does not mean speaking to win the other person over with eloquence, but simply speaking to be understood. If the two parties involved truly understand each other's viewpoint, the agreement you reach will accurately reflect your mutual interests. However, don't confuse understanding with agreement. Agreement can only come after mutual understanding has been reached.

Although speaking clearly will ensure understanding, experienced telemarketers agree that it's not always what you say that sells the client, but how you say it. The tone, volume, and inflection you use are often more important than the words you choose. When making your sales pitch, you should pay attention to volume, diction, and speaking rate. Speaking too loudly, too quickly, or too slowly can irritate a potential customer and distract the person from the purpose of your call.

Even though the way you say something is often more important than what you say, your choice of words is also critical in shaping your phone image. Speech experts claim that positive, active words are the best choice for creating a good phone personality. You will appear more authoritative and responsible if you use active verbs and stay away from negatives.

Closing Sales

Once you have made your sales pitch and have determined your potential client's interest, you will usually need to make at least one more call to close the deal. In addition to listening and speaking skills, preparation for closing the sale is essential to successful phone negotiations. Experienced salespeople agree that preparation for closing is usually what gives you the edge in the session. This preparation period can be more time-consuming than the phone session itself.

Before you make a call, you should make a list of the viewpoints, goals, concerns, and needs of both your company and the other party's company. In addition, you should add any concessions you will be willing to make, as well as those the other party may make. If you consider these aspects from both standpoints carefully before you call the other party, you will be in a much better position to negotiate a mutually beneficial agreement.

When making the call, you can increase effectiveness by focusing on the long run. Remember that a repeat customer is much more profitable to you than a one-time buyer. For this reason, you may want to make some concessions regarding price or delivery dates to ensure that the customer will come back to you. Thinking in short-term dollars may get you more money right now but it can also discourage the buyer from becoming a repeat customer or entering a long-term relationship with your company.

Other tips to make your phone sales calls successful include assessing the call after it has been made and following up once an agreement has been reached.

Calling your clients simply to say that it is a pleasure to do business with them is a nice touch that doesn't go unnoticed. Let clients know that they can always reach you by phone when they have a question or problem. This telephone technique ensures customer satisfaction and increases repeat sales.

The telephone is changing the way people conduct business. New technology has enabled the telephone to take over traditional marketing purposes with great success. You can use the telephone to enhance your promotional, sales, and advertising activities, and to maintain a high degree of customer satisfaction.

Using the telephone to perform tasks traditionally done in person can reduce costs and increase productivity. To tap the full marketing potential of your telephone, you should make sure that the phone system you choose is adequate for your use, and that your salespeople know how to use the phone effectively.

RESOURCES

Associations

American Marketing Association, 250 South Wacker Drive, Suite 200, Chicago, IL 60606, 312-648-0536

American Telemarketing Association, 444 North Larchmont Boulevard, Suite 200, Los Angeles, CA 90004, 213-463-2330

Magazines

JATA: Journal of the American Telemarketing Association, 444 North Larchmont Boulevard, Suite 200, Los Angeles, CA 90004, 213-463-2330

Telemarketing, 1 Technology Plaza, Norwalk, CT 06854-1924, 203-852-6800

Teleprofessional, 209 West Fifth Street, Suite N, Waterloo, IA 50701-5420, 319-235-4473

27 Expansion Capital

I t's a common dilemma among small and large businesses alike. They reach a point in their growth where they need additional capital to continue to expand, yet they haven't made provisions to do so. They wait until the exact point in time when they need it, and by then desperation becomes a factor: Expansion capital comes at a very high price such as an abnormally high interest rate or equity within the company, both of which can retard the return on investment made in the business.

When financing the future expansion of your company, plan ahead. Revise your business plan on a yearly basis, and generate marketing plans to complement your business plan. These strategic planning tools not only help you define goals and objectives, they also provide you with a time frame on which to build your financial projections.

Armed with this knowledge, you'll be able to determine the amount of expansion capital necessary and the general time period when you'll need it. Combined with proper financial control techniques, that awareness will allow you to be prepared when you need to go knocking on doors for additional capital.

It will also allow you to shop for a loan before you need it, instead of when you need it. By giving yourself the luxury to shop, the type of financing available, and the terms being offered, you will be able to arrange a better deal for yourself—you won't have to take whatever is available.

WHEN DO YOU NEED EXPANSION CAPITAL?

There's a big misconception among entrepreneurs that expansion capital is *only* required when the firm reaches a level of profitability and production that requires additional personnel, equipment, or facility expansion. Certainly, increases in the volume of production indicate a growth in sales volume, a rise in costs associated with production, and a need to expand capacity if necessary. All these factors require additional capital to fuel the continued growth, but that still doesn't really address the question of when you need expansion capital.

Why? Profitability is a measure of the company's performance in relation to sales, cost of sales, and overhead, all of which are included in a monthly income statement that charts the business's performance. However, while the income statement portrays the performance of the company, it doesn't denote the timing differences in cash flow.

Why is cash flow important? Cash flow is an endless cycle that companies experience over their existence. It is the actual investment in additional material to continue production (usually referred to as *cost of sales*), the outlay of capital to meet all payables and overhead, and the collection of receivables, all of which occur at different times during the cash flow cycle.

To meet customer demand, production materials have to be purchased at a predetermined time based on your inventory control system so that you can replenish your existing inventory of finished goods. Usually, within 30 days after ordering your goods, you must make payment. Depending on your production cycle, your inventory of finished goods may or may not have been replenished at that point. In any case, you still have to sell the product, which could take some time, and then you have to collect if the purchase was not made in cash. If you invoice someone, you will have placed an account on your books as a receivable (average collection period–30 days).

Based on the preceding scenario, you will have paid for the production of the product long before you collect any cash for it from a sale. In the meantime, you still have to meet overhead. If you're not careful, that could lead to the dreaded "cash flow crunch."

As you can see, the need for expansion capital originates long before you start experiencing increased sales. To make a sale, first and foremost your operations must have the resources to create the product. Without enough product in inventory to sell, it is very unlikely that you'll experience any increase in sales. The only way to make sure you have enough product present is to plan and evaluate your financial position in relation to projected growth, both in sales and operations requirements.

Expansion Plans

Many times, entrepreneurs get so wrapped up with the actual operations of the business—producing a product and selling it—that they fail to plan adequately for the future. Ideally, the owner, president, or CEO, should allot 80 percent of his or her time for planning. Small-business owners rarely achieve that ratio, but it suggests how important planning is to a company, and who ultimately bears the responsibility for forming strategy.

Planning the overall strategy and goals of the company should be done on an annual basis and is a combined effort of the executive management team. It is not uncommon for large companies to hold off-site meetings where the entire executive group can gather and chart the company's strategy for the upcoming year and beyond. For smaller companies where the executive management team may consist of the owner and a few key people, the principle is still the same, just on a smaller scale.

The main goals of an annual meeting are to do the following:

1. **Set goals.** Both long-term and short-term goals should be defined. These goals can center around any number of business factors such as market share, sales, profit, geographic expansion, or product expansion. One objective can be set or several depending on an analysis of external as well as internal forces.
2. **Review company performance.** Year-ending financial statements should be generated to provide a snapshot of the company's profitability, cash position, liquidity, and net worth. These figures can easily be retrieved from an income statement, cash flow statement, and balance sheet, all of which are discussed in Chapter 16.
3. **Evaluate operation requirements.** Meeting the goals of the company requires an accurate appraisal of operations requirements. This includes all phases of the business: marketing, production, administration, and research and development. To plan, you need to know the requirements for advertising, sales, equipment investment, factory expansion, administrative support, and so on. Without this information, attaining your goals will be impossible.
4. **Create a budget.** Goals, performance of the company, and operational requirements have to be translated into budgets for planning purposes. These budgets are produced in the form of the familiar income statement, balance sheet, and cash-flow statement.

As a result of this annual meeting, the various strategic plans will be updated including the business plan and marketing plan. It is essential that the company strategy be formalized into some type of written plan. It not only organizes your strategy and projections into a presentation that can be presented to your managers and any investors, but it also illustrates projected growth, cash requirements, and capital investment needs. It tells you when you'll need money and how much. That is measured against profit and revenues. With this type of information, you will know whether you can finance expansion from within or through outside sources.

As already discussed in Chapter 8, the business plan is developed from a thorough market analysis and internal analysis. It is structured in the following manner:

- **Business description.** Defines the purpose of the business.
- **Marketing strategies.** Defines the scope of the market and stipulates pricing, distribution, and sales strategies in addition to sales potential.
- **Competitive analysis.** Defines the impact of the competition, their key assets and skills, their competitive advantages, their strategies, and any entry barriers that may be present.

- **Design and development plans.** Outlines the requirements to bring a product to market. This is crucial if you are expanding your product line or introducing a new version of an old product.
- **Operations and management plans.** Defines the management team and describes the resources required to operate the company in terms of personnel, materials, and equipment.
- **Financial components.** Defines budgets through financial projections from the income statement, cash-flow statement, and balance sheet.

Using your business plan or marketing plan as a foundation, you can refine your budget; determine time frames where additional capital, personnel, and equipment is required; and form strategies to account for increased working capital and capital expansion. This is important to your expansion plans because costs are identified, time frames stipulated, financial strength defined, and borrowing capacity illustrated. Refer to Chapter 8 for a sample cash flow projection, balance sheet, and income statement.

Aside from their value as a strategic tools, the business and marketing plans also provide you with the type of information lenders and investors look for when evaluating whether or not to extend a loan or invest in a company, which is important when you approach outside financing sources to secure expansion capital.

Cash Flow Reality

We mentioned the importance of cash flow already, but within the scope of planning, it becomes a crucial barometer that measures not only when you will need additional capital, but the amount at that given time.

When forming a cash flow budget you have to use several tables as a reference:

- The sales/revenue table.
- Development expense table.
- Cost of goods table.
- Capital requirements table.
- Operating expense table.

From these tables, you'll be able to form your various financial statements, including your cash-flow projection. However, while the other tables you'll draw information from quantify the amounts you'll need for expansion to meet the revenue projections, the cash flow projection places that information in conjunction with the revenue and cost cycles associated with the business.

For instance, if the revenue table projects a 60 percent growth in sales over the coming year, that will necessitate investment into new equipment to handle the additional volume as well as the obsolescence of current equipment, the hiring of additional personnel to manage the workload, and the financing of increased working capital to operate the company. The cost of goods table, capital requirement table, and operating expense table formed in the business plan will provide a breakdown of costs to meet the 60 percent growth projected in the revenue table. The next thing you need to do is infuse that information into the cash flow cycle.

Based on past performance, first break down projected sales over the next year according to the percentage of business volume generated each month. Divide each month's sales according to cash sales and credit sales. Cash sales can be logged into the cash flow statement in the same month they are generated. Credit sales are a different matter. These sales don't refer to credit card sales, which we'll treat as cash; they refer to invoiced sales that are tied to agreed-on terms. Refer to your accounts receivable records and determine your average collection period. If it is 30 days, then sales made by credit can't be logged into cash until 35 to 40 days after they are made. (Although the collection period is 30 days, you still have to deposit the money and draw on another bank to receive payment.)

The next line item on a cash-flow statement is other income. Other income refers to any revenue derived from investments, interest on loans that have been extended, and the liquidation of any assets. Total income is the sum of cash sales, receivables, and other income. In the first month of your cash budget, it will usually consist of cash sales, other income, plus any receivables from the previous budget that have aged to a point of collection during the first month of the current budget.

Also tied to the breakdown of sales is cost of goods and direct labor. To sell the product, you must first produce it. Since you already have broken down sales by months, you need to determine the cost in material and labor to produce those sales. Refer to your cost of goods table in your business plan. Determine what direct labor will be for the year to produce your product. Divide that number by the percentage breakdown of sales. Direct labor can be logged into cash flow during the same month in which it is accrued.

Material costs, on the other hand, are a little different. You need to include the material cost in cash flow using a time frame that allows you to convert raw material into finished goods for fulfilling the sale. Therefore, if it requires 60 days to convert raw material to finished goods, and your payable period is 30 days after delivery, then insert the cost of goods under material in cash flow 30 days before sales are logged.

Working capital can be derived from the operating expense table. All personnel and overhead costs are tied to sales, as depicted in Chapter 8. You can determine your working capital and payroll requirements by dividing marketing and sales, general and administrative, and overhead expenses by the total projected operating expenses by the percentage breakdown of sales for each month and applying that amount to the appropriate line items in the cash flow statement.

As for capital equipment, there are two realms of thought. The first is to purchase and install the needed equipment at a point during the year where additional volume will warrant the expenditure, thereby assuring sufficient cash flow to handle the additional debt service or the outright purchase of the equipment. The second method is to have the equipment purchased and installed at the beginning of the business year or quarter closest to the time when you will require the equipment, allowing for training time and a debugging period where any problems the equipment has can be worked out before placing it into full production. Which avenue you choose depends on the strength of your cash flow. If you can handle the additional drain of servicing more debt or purchasing the equipment entirely without the benefit of increased sales, then the latter method would be beneficial. If your cash flow is extremely tight, then choose the former method. Either way, the infusion of capital equipment costs will be logged into cash flow under capital.

In addition to the preceding costs, you need to include your tax obligations and any long-term debts currently being serviced in the cash flow budget under loans. These items should be readily obtainable from loan schedules and tax charts used to project these costs.

Once all these costs have been logged into the cash flow budget, add them together to produce your total expenses. Total expenses are subtracted from total income. The result is your cash flow, which will either be a surplus or deficit. If it is a deficit, you need to determine the minimum cash balance that you wish to maintain. Calculate the difference between the minimum cash balance and the cash flow deficit. This will result in the total amount required for financing purposes. This will also equal the ending cash balance that needs to be added to cumulative cash flow, which is the total of current cash flow and cash flow from the previous period.

When forming a cash flow budget, any amounts financed within a given month need to be included in the cash flow under a projected repayment schedule. You should consult your accountant or financial officer when developing this repayment schedule.

Evaluating Your Financial Position

Not everything is subject to the cash flow statement. It is an important tool when charting the approximate period when infusion of capital will need to be made and the amounts required to maintain a comfortable cash flow situation. One thing it doesn't tell you, though, is your capacity to borrow money. This is often determined by the profitability of the company and its net worth.

By analyzing your income statement and balance sheet you'll be able to determine your borrowing capacity. This involves the use of financial ratios, specifically, measure of liquidity.

The first measure of liquidity you can perform is the *current ratio*. The current ratio measures your ratio of assets to liabilities. This ratio provides lenders with a quick look at the business's ability to meet its obligation within a short-term period. If you have strong assets compared with your liabilities, your capacity for additional financing is fairly good. To calculate a current ratio, divide your current assets by your current liabilities, both of which can be found on your balance sheet. Current assets are cash and other assets such as receivables and inventory that will be converted into cash within the upcoming year, whereas current liabilities are those obligations that need to be paid within a year. Generally, a two-to-one current ratio is more than appropriate.

As mentioned in Chapter 13, another measure of liquidity is the *quick ratio*. Like the current ratio, this measure of liquidity gauges all your liquid assets against current liabilities. Liquid assets refer not only to current assets but all those assets that can be easily converted into current assets. For most businesses, a quick ratio of two or more to one is sufficient for borrowing needs.

Another common measure to determine borrowing capacity is *net profit on sales*. This measure determines the percentage of profit the firm experiences compared to sales. To find out what your net profit is on sales, divide net profit before taxes, which can be found in your income statement, by net sales. The result is the profitability of your company. Compare this against industry averages and current interest rates to determine your strength.

The preceding measures of liquidity are indicators of any short-term financing needs you might have. If you already have low current and quick ratios, taking on additional short-term loans will further weaken your ability to meet your obligations within the upcoming year because the loan would be a current liability. On the other hand, by taking out a long-term loan, you would improve your liquidity because only the portion of the loan that is due and payable during the first year would be applied to current liabilities and the remaining portion would be a current asset.

Generally, a business should be as profitable as the amount of money that can be earned from interest or dividends in securities. If your profitability is strong, the amount of money investors will be willing to place within your business will be equally strong.

The last measure we'll discuss is the *debt-to-equity ratio*. This ratio measures the total liabilities against the total equity within the company. This is done by dividing total liabilities by total equity. Most businesses try to stay at a ratio of one-to-one or below. It is not a good idea to leverage your business so much that it cannot maneuver when the unexpected hits.

Also, if you are already loaded with debt, you may not be able to get the long-term financing you want, at least not at a favorable rate. Then you'll have to look at equity financing as an option. The difference between equity financing and a regular loan is, of course, that you're giving up a piece of your business, profits, and possibly some control. And you may find it more difficult to find someone to buy part of your business, either as a partner, limited partner, or perhaps as a shareholder of your corporation.

SOURCES OF EXPANSION CAPITAL

Once you've established the need for additional capital, you need to determine which source or sources of financing would be the most appropriate for your needs. In Coopers & Lybrand's July/August 1994 issue of *Growing Your*

Business, 66 percent of fast-growth companies reported that at the initial growth stage, they had been funded predominantly by external sources: bank loans, investors, and alliances.[1] Owner funding accounted for less than 1 percent, down from 17 percent at the critical break-even or "survival" stage and 73 percent at their start-up. External sources are a primary source of financing, and they do not invest carelessly. That's why charting your goals is so vital, both in the short term and the long run, as well as performing the proper market analyses, and drawing up your business and marketing plans. By doing this, you will not only know how much you need and when, but have a good idea of the type of financing that would be most appropriate. Also, by being thoroughly prepared, you will have a lot more flexibility and credibility when you go shopping for additional capital.

From the viewpoint of investors, nothing could be more important than the strength and credibility of the business they intend to support with financing. They will want every bit of financial, operational, and development information available so they can make an informed decision. It doesn't matter whether you are applying for a short-term working capital loan or offering stock to the public, you'll need to present that information.

So be prepared. The sources for expansion capital are numerous and can be utilized very productively by entrepreneurs who understand their impact and relationship to the overall needs of the company. The upcoming sections highlight several sources of expansion capital, all of which can be grouped into the following categories:

1. **Bootstrap financing.** Relies on the creative use and control of internal resources to meet short-term operational and growth requirements.
2. **Debt financing.** Offers the widest choice of financing possibilities. Under this type of financing, loans are extended by an outside agency at prescribed terms and interest rates.
3. **Equity financing.** Under this type of arrangement, a percentage of the business is forfeited to the investor for infusion of capital.

Bootstrap Financing

When thinking of capital for expansion or short-term operational needs, consider bootstrap financing. As discussed in Chapter 21, this method is probably one of the best and most inexpensive routes an entrepreneur can explore when raising capital. Bootstrap financing utilizes unused opportunities within your own company through wise financial management. It is a way to pull yourself up without the help of others. You are the one financing your growth by your current earnings and assets.

A lot of different methods are involved in bootstrap financing, and this is going to be very advantageous to you. You will not only be able to finance

[1] Coopers & Lybrand, "Growing Your Business" (July/August 1994).

your expansion or working capital internally, you will also have a business that will be worth more because less money has been borrowed and no equity positions had to be relinquished. It's also going to help you because you're not going to have to pay the high cost of borrowed money. This will make you look more desirable to external lenders and investors when the time does come to raise money through these routes. Bootstrap financing allows you to reduce the amount of money that you're going to have to borrow and increase your profits.

The first source is *trade credit.* As explained in Chapter 13, a supplier will normally extend credit for 30 to 90 days without charging interest if you are a regular customer. For instance, suppose that a supplier ships something to you, and that bill is due in 30 days. In most industries, it would typically be paid in 45 to 60 days.

Essentially what you are doing through the use of trade credit is artificially extending the payable portion of your business cycle to more accurately correspond with actual sales of finished goods. It means more cash on hand for your business and less money tied up in inventories.

This is a powerful tool if your suppliers will allow it to continue. Most, however, will allow you to extend the terms of your credit agreement a few times, but if it continues on a regular basis, they will start to rein in their receivables, which means a more active involvement in the collection of their credit sales.

Customers are another source of bootstrap financing. One of the better ways to use your customers to obtain financing is by having them write you a letter of credit. For example, suppose you're manufacturing industrial bags and a large corporation has placed an order with your firm to supply it with a steady flow of cloth bags. In this scenario, you obtain a letter of credit from your customer when the order is placed, and purchase the material for the bags using the letter of credit as security. You don't have to put up a penny to buy the material.

Factoring is a financing method whereby you actually sell your accounts receivable to a buyer, such as a commercial finance company, to raise capital. A factor usually buys accounts receivable at a discount rate that ranges between 1 and 15 percent. The factor then becomes the creditor and assumes the task of collecting the receivables as well as doing what would have been your paperwork chores. Factoring can be performed on a nonnotification basis, which means that your customers are not aware that their accounts have been sold.

Factoring has many advantages. Consider the costs associated with maintaining accounts receivable such as bookkeeping, collections, and credit verifications, and compare those expenses against the discount rate you'll be selling them for; sometimes it even pays to utilize this financing method. Even if the factor only takes on part of the paperwork chores involved in maintaining accounts receivables, your internal costs will shrink significantly. The factor will often assume full responsibility for the paperwork.

In addition to reducing internal costs, factoring also frees up money that would otherwise be tied to receivables. This money can then be used to generate profit through other avenues of the company. In the long run, factoring is an excellent method of raising capital. To locate a factor, contact commercial finance companies in your area.

Another bootstrap financing source is *real estate*. There are several options for taking advantage of real estate. The first is simply to lease your facility. This reduces your working capital requirements because your lease payments are usually not as high as the outright purchase of the property. You also gain important tax benefits such as property tax deductions. Most leases can be modified to include responsibility of all executor-related costs associated with the property. When negotiating a lease, you may be able to arrange payments that correspond to seasonal peaks or growth patterns.

The drawback to leasing, however, is that it is not considered an asset on your balance sheet. Since the lease is a cash disbursement, it is included in the balance sheet under current liabilities.

If you enter a business in which buying the facility is a necessity, your initial cost will be high, but the purchase price can be financed over a period of 15 to 30 years. Again, the loan on the facility can be structured to make optimum use of your planned growth or seasonal peaks. For instance, you can arrange a graduated payment mortgage that initially has small monthly payments with the cost increasing over the lifetime of the loan. The logic here is that you have low monthly payments that give your business time to grow. You can eventually refinance the loan when time and interest rates permit.

Another advantage of purchasing the facility outright is the continuing appreciation of the property and the decrease of your principal amount to create a valuable asset called equity. You can borrow against this equity; lenders will often loan up to 75 or 80 percent of the property's value.

Equipment suppliers can be a source of financing. If you spend a lot of money on equipment, you may find yourself draining working capital to continue purchasing equipment. Instead of paying out cash for your equipment, the manufacturers can loan you the money through extension of credit; that is, they sell the equipment over a period of time.

This reduces the amount of money that you need up front. Some lenders will finance 60 to 80 percent of the equipment value. The balance represents the borrower's down payment on a new purchase. The loan is repaid in monthly installments, usually over one to five years or the usable life of that piece of equipment.

Consider also leasing instead of purchasing equipment. Generally, if you are able to shop around and get the best kind of leasing arrangement, it's much better to lease. While the installment purchase of equipment may require you to put 20 percent down, an equipment lease often requires no down payment or one lower than 10 percent. You might be able to lease equipment from a factory that would include the maintenance. If you must assign employees or someone else to do maintenance on equipment you purchase, it will cost you more than if you had leased. Generally speaking, it might be better to lease equipment to improve your cash flow.

Debt Financing

Chances are, if your company has built a good track record, has a solid customer foundation, and a strong financial position, banks and other traditional debt financing institutions will want to talk to you about your additional capital requirements. After all, you're their perfect customer. You already have a solid business, you will generally have good assets with which to secure loans, and you will have the capacity to incur additional debt.

For growth and expansion purposes, debt financing is a strong consideration from your point of view as well. It infuses capital based on your needs, provides a time frame suitable for repayment of the loan, and doesn't require any surrender of equity within the company. It is a straightforward business transaction in which money is loaned to the business at a prescribed user's fee, or interest rate, over a designated period of time. It is usually secured by some form of collateral that is forfeited unless the loan is repaid when it matures.

Several forms of collateral are used to secure loans and the type you'll need depends on the kind of loan you'll procure. Three types of loans are generally available through debt-financing sources for growth and expansion purposes:

1. **Working capital loans.** Usually short-term loans tied to the business cycle of a company. They can be secured or unsecured loans and are used to increase working capital to fund the purchase of inventory, meet overhead, and increase the number of sales made on credit. Collateral used for working capital loans includes receivables and inventory.
2. **Term loans.** These are generally intermediate- to long-term loans used to finance the purchase of capital equipment, expand the facility, increase working capital, or acquire another business. Term loans aren't tied to the cyclical nature of a business, but to projections of higher earnings and larger profit margins by the business. A specialized type of term loan is the capital loan. This long-term loan is used for fixed asset acquisitions, and which is secured by the equipment purchased.
3. **Interim loans.** On rare occasions, you may be able to finance a short-term interim loan. These are loans made as a bridge until repayment by either the borrower or from another creditor.

When seeking any of the preceding loans, you'll need to offer security that the loan will be repaid. Security is posted in the form of collateral, which can take a variety of forms. (See Chapter 13 for a complete list of possible forms of collateral.)

A loan can also be unsecured, in which case your credit reputation is the only security the lender has. You may either receive a signature or personal loan for several thousand dollars or more if you are on good terms with the bank. These loans usually have short terms and high interest rates.

Unsecured loans are typically arranged with the bank to provide a revolving line of credit to the business for meeting short-term needs usually tied to the business cycle of the company. Generally a few stipulations are associated with this type of debt financing. They require that the principal amount be paid off periodically and that a compensating balance, usually 10 percent of the outstanding balance, be held by the bank in a non-interest-bearing account.

Now that you know a little about debt financing, what sources are available to you when tapping these external funds?

Banks are the largest source of external funds and are known for being conservative. They are usually the best source for debt financing once your business has established a good track record. Banks require a complete loan proposal or a revised business plan consisting of:

- Cover sheet
- Cover letter
- Table of contents
- The purpose and amount of the loan
- Business description
- Market analysis
- Operations/management outline
- Financial components
- Possible collateral
- Personal financials
- Notes

You want to be as up front as possible with the banker. You want the banker to receive any information about you and your company from you personally, not from somebody else. This will improve your chances of gaining a loan considerably. A small business loan usually costs a little more than a loan at the prime rate, which is the rate that banks charge their most favored customers (see "Start-Up Financing").

For most small business owners, *commercial lenders* are the key financing source. Banks want to lend to small companies experiencing rapid sales growth. Business lenders will often lend when banks won't because they are designed to handle business loans and because they know they can recoup most or all of their money by selling the borrowing business's collateral.

Lenders are generally reluctant to fund high-tech companies or services operating in a volatile field which obviously don't have collateral.

The Small Business Administration (SBA), an agency of the Department of Commerce, aids small businesses in obtaining loans and also offers management assistance. There are two types of SBA loans:

1. **Guaranteed loans.** These are loans made through private lending institutions and guaranteed by the SBA for up to 75 percent of the principal loan amount, up to a limit of $500,000. SBA-guaranteed loans are by far the most prominent form of financial help representing over 90 percent of all SBA loans of the guaranteed type.
2. **Direct loan.** Under this program, the SBA lends the funds appropriated to it by Congress to applicants up to a maximum of $150,000. Direct loans are

made only to the handicapped or nonprofit sheltered workshops employing the handicapped, disabled veterans or Vietnam-era veterans, businesses located in high unemployment areas or owned by low-income persons, local development companies (LDCs) designed to help small businesses acquire plant and facilities, and Small Business Investment Companies (SBICs). Other direct loans funded through the SBA are for disaster relief to businesses experiencing natural catastrophes, and for businesses unable to obtain private financing or an SBA-guaranteed loan.

Even those who qualify for either a direct or guaranteed loan cannot solicit a loan from the SBA if they can legitimately obtain a loan from a bank or private source. Therefore, you must first apply to a bank or alternate lending source; if you live in a city with a population over 200,000 you must have been turned down by two financial institutions before seeking funds.

Keep in mind that under a loan guarantee, the SBA is not making the loan. It is simply protecting the lending institution against default of the loan. In essence, the SBA is a form of security in a guaranteed loan that reduces the risks perceived by lending sources when dealing with small-business loans.

As stated in Chapter 14, the interest rate charged on SBA-guaranteed loans is based on the prime rate. The SBA does not set interest rates, but it does regulate the amount of interest a lender may charge an SBA borrower. If the loan has a term of seven years or more, the SBA-approved lenders may charge as much as 2¾ percent above the current prime rate. If the loan has a term of less than seven years, the rate is as much as 2¼ percent above prime.

The SBA loan-processing period varies depending on the circumstances involved. It can take at least 12 to 18 months before you are approved. It should be noted, however, that a properly prepared application for an SBA loan might be processed in as little as two months, with the applicant receiving the money within one week after a bank willing to participate in a guarantee is found. These time periods can fluctuate, depending on economic climate, business concept, a tight money market, the loan application volume, and finding a bank willing to participate in a loan program.

To find out how to apply for an SBA loan, refer to Chapter 14.

Equity Financing and Venture Capital

Equity financing is the selling off of a portion of your business to investors who may or may not actively participate in the management of the company (see Chapter 13). Depending on how you raise equity capital, you may relinquish anywhere from 25 to 75 percent of the business.

Through equity financing, you can raise money through private, public, or professional venture capitalists that specialize in the industry in which you are involved. A relatively minor segment of business financing prior to the 1980s, the rise of high technology and the increasing sophistication of individuals starting their own companies fueled the growth of venture capital funding.

Today, there are an estimated 720,000 private, public, and professional venture capital investors in the United States accounting for over $58 billion in risk capital.

That doesn't take into account selling equity in the business through private and public placement of securities, an activity that records another $2.3 billion each year.

As you can see, equity financing is not a minor factor in the business financing world any longer. There are a lot of players and options from which to choose. The idea is to find the right type of equity financing for your needs; the legal form of your business will have a direct impact on raising equity capital.

Another form of equity financing is *venture capital*. As the name implies, venture capital is used to finance relatively new, unproven ideas that are high-risk, high-return businesses. Venture capitalists typically expect high returns and a method of exit from businesses they invest in. They must go into each deal with the possibility of a 500 to 1000% return within three to five years because the companies they finance often do not survive. The amount of equity a venture capitalist holds is a factor of the company's stage of development when the investment occurs, the perceived risk, the amount invested, and the relationship between the entrepreneur and the venture capitalist.

Venture capitalists usually invest in businesses of every kind. Many individual private venture capitalists, also known as angels, prefer to invest in industries that are familiar to them. The reason for this is simple: even though angels will not actively participate in the day-to-day management of the company, they do want a voice within the strategic planning phase of the business to reduce the risk faced by the business and optimize the profits.

On the other hand, private venture capital partnerships and industrial venture capitalists like to invest primarily in technology-related industries, especially applications of existing technology such as computer-related communications, electronics, genetic engineering, and medical/health-related fields. There are also a number of investments in service and distribution businesses, and even a few in consumer-related companies, that attract venture capitalists.

In addition to the type of business they invest in, venture capitalists often define their investments by life cycle: seed, start-up, second-stage, bridge, and leveraged buyout. Some venture capitalists prefer to invest in firms only during the early stages of seed and start-up where the risk is highest and the potential for a high return is also the best. Other venture capital firms will deal only with second-stage financing for expansion purposes or bridge financing where they supply capital for growth until the company goes public. Finally, there are those venture capital companies that concentrate solely on supplying funds for management-led buyouts.

Generally, venture capitalists like to finance firms during the early and second stages where growth is very rapid, cashing-out of the venture once it is established. As the owner of the business, that is one thing of which you must be aware. At some point down the line, the venture capitalist will want out. This is usually when the risk-reward quotient moderates and the possibility for a high return on investment is no longer present. This exit will have been discussed in some depth at the time you negotiated the original deal. You will either take your company public, repurchase the investor's stock, merge with another firm, or, in some circumstances, liquidate your business.

The primary attraction for venture capitalists is the potential for rapid growth. Some venture capitalists tie this to earning power. If a company cannot become a $50 million company in seven years, raising money through venture capitalists is unlikely. If, however, investors have an opportunity to earn five to ten times their investment in three to five years, they will look very closely at the business.

There are several sources you can turn to for venture capital:

1. **Private venture capital partnerships.** Perhaps the largest source of risk capital, private venture capital partnerships generally look for businesses that have the capability of generating a 30 percent return on investment annually. They like to actively participate in the planning and management phases of the businesses they finance, and have very large capital bases, up to $500 million, to invest in all stages.

2. **Industrial venture capital pools.** Financing from this arena is very limited. Only about 75 large industrial companies have formed their own investment pools of risk capital. Their strategies usually center around funding promising firms that might succeed and make a good acquisition later. They usually prefer high-tech firms or companies that are utilizing current technology in a unique manner.

3. **Investment banking firms.** These are firms that traditionally provide expansion capital by selling stock within a company to public and private equity investors. Some also have formed their own venture capital divisions to provide risk capital for expansion and early-stage financing.

4. **Individual private investors.** Also known as angels, these investors range from friends and family who have only a few thousand dollars to invest to financially secure individuals who have built their own successful businesses and are willing to invest some of their money, sometimes up to a million dollars in a venture, as well as their experience with businesses of all sizes and at different stages of growth.

5. **Small Business Investment Corporation (SBICs).** Licensed and regulated by the SBA, SBICs are private investors that receive three to four dollars in SBA-guaranteed loans for every dollar they invest. Under the law, SBICs must invest exclusively in small firms with net worth less than $6 million and averaged after-tax earnings (over the past two years) of less than $2 million. They are also restricted in the amount of private equity capital for each funding with a minimum of $500,000 and a maximum of $10 million. Being licensed and regulated by a government agency distinguishes SBICs from other "private" venture capital firms, but other than that, they are not significantly different from those firms.

6. **Minority Enterprise Small Business Investment Company (MESBICs).** Like SBICs, MESBICs are privately capitalized investment agencies licensed and regulated by the SBA. They are designed to aid minority-owned and

minority-managed firms by providing equity funds from private and public capital. As with the SBIC, MESBICs are restricted in the amount of their private funding—currently a minimum of $1 million. If your business has already gotten started but needs more capital, then check into these investors. They will want a company that looks as if it will become very profitable. When they sell in three or four years, they want three to five times return on their money.

7. **Small Business Development Companies (SBDCs).** Similar to SBICs, SBDCs are capitalized entirely by private sources such as banks, corporations, utility companies, and transportation firms. Like SBICs and MES-BICs, SBDCs make investment commitments on a long-term basis.

Before approaching any of the preceding venture capital firms, do your homework and find out if your interests match their preferred investment strategy, and the strengths the venture capitalists possess that may help you in building your company. There are a number of directories that list the investment preferences of venture capitalists.

The best way to contact venture capitalists is through an introduction from another entrepreneur or business professional who knows you and the venture capitalist well enough to approach them with the proposition.

If you cannot secure capital through other equity financing options, you may want to give some thought to going public. On the plus side is the infusion of massive amounts of new capital into the company. Because a successful public offering increases a company's net worth and standing in the business community, it enables the corporation to borrow additional funds on more favorable terms. Having publicly traded shares can also make acquisition of other firms considerably easier (those firms might prefer stock to a cash payment for tax reasons) and improve the position of previous shareholders, both in terms of liquidity and in the dollar value of their holdings.

There are drawbacks, however. For starters, it is expensive: industry insiders estimate that it costs a firm about 15 percent of its total offering to make the move. For small offerings (between $1 million and $3 million), that means the client would spend at least $250,000.

There are also reporting requirements—always a factor in any securities issue but multiplied in a public offering. All companies that want to sell stock to the public must supply those potential investors with detailed information about the corporation on a continuing basis. Those reports include audited financial statements, discussions of the company's plans and transactions, and even information concerning the fiscal relationships between directors, managers, shareholders, and the firm. This is an expensive and time-consuming process, not to mention the feeling it creates of living in a fishbowl. If you're the kind of person who likes to keep your business dealings private, this might not be a viable option.

Finally, there is the potential for losing control of the company to large shareholders, particularly if the firm keeps diluting the value of the original holdings with additional stock offerings.

There are still other consequences of going public. Perhaps the most important is that corporate insiders can't take personal advantage of information they have access to but the public doesn't. For example, management can't use its advance knowledge of an impending deal to make a killing in the company's stock. The law also requires that all transactions between a firm and its fiduciaries—its officers, directors, shareholders—be fair and reasonable to the corporation. That means, for instance, that a director cannot buy land he or she knows the corporation needs and wants for its business. (Public stock offerings are covered in the Chapter 28.)

RESOURCES

Government Agencies

Export-Import Bank of the United States, 811 Vermont Avenue NW, Washington, DC 20571, 202-566-2117

U.S. Department of Agriculture, 14th and Independence Avenue SW, Washington, DC 20250, 202-477-2791

U.S. Department of Energy, 1000 Independence Avenue SW, Washington, DC 20585, 202-586-8021

U.S. Department of Interior, 18th and C Streets NW, Room 2747, Washington, DC 20240, 202-208-3100

U.S. Securities and Exchange Commission, 450 Fifth Street NW, Stop 7–10, Washington, DC 20549, 202-272-2644

U.S. Small Business Administration, 1441 L Street NW, Washington, DC 20416, 800-368-5855

Associations

National Association of Investment Companies, 1111 14th Street NW, Suite 700, Washington, DC 20005, 202-289-4336

National Corporate Cash Management Association, 7315 Wisconsin Avenue, Suite 1250 West, Bethesda, MD 20814, 301-907-2862

28

Public Offerings

A s your business grows, you will need money to fuel and maintain its growth. One way to raise money is to "go public" and sell stock in your company. Although going public can be an excellent way to obtain a large sum of capital, it is a long, complex, and expensive process. This chapter will give you an introduction to the costs and benefits of going public.

THE ADVANTAGES AND DISADVANTAGES

Raising expansion capital is the main reason why companies go public. Selling shares of stock can bring in quite a large sum of money. Companies that go public usually expect to sell shares worth about $1 million to $10 million. They can use this money to pay off debt, to buy new facilities, materials, or equipment, and so on. They also raise their net worth, which is not only good in itself, but also helps the business to obtain loans. Publicly traded stock also allows the business owners to "cash in" their equity in the business. Owners of businesses generally hold a large number of shares in their companies. They can sell part of their stock either during the initial public offering (IPO) of stock, or at a later time.

In addition to providing these direct financial advantages, trading company stock publicly brings other, less obvious advantages as well. If you sell stock, you can offer stock options as benefits to your employees, or even give them shares of stock outright. You not only make your benefits package more attractive by offering stock, but also give employees an added reason to work for the company's success. The more profitable the company is, the more their stock will be worth. Operating as a publicly traded company can also give your business and your employees added prestige. The operations of publicly traded businesses are highly visible to the media and the public, and news of good performance can travel fast. Favorable news regarding your business both enhances its reputation and inspires investors to buy more of your stock.

Going public, however, also has a number of disadvantages, and they are major considerations. First of all, when your company goes public, your operations really do become *public*. Most businesspeople value their privacy and attempt to keep information regarding their operations as confidential as possible. If you go public, however, you will need to reveal quite a bit of information regarding your operations. The Securities and Exchange Commission (SEC), a government agency that regulates the offering and sale of public stocks, requires all public firms to disclose certain bits of information to potential investors, so that they can make intelligent investment decisions. You will need to disclose your company's sales and profits, as well as the salaries and perquisites paid to top executives, among other items. If any of your customers account for very large percentages of your gross sales, you may need to reveal the names of those customers. Not only will you need to reveal this information when you submit your IPO, you will need to continue reporting it in quarterly or annual reports after you go public.

You will also need to spend a great deal of money in bringing your IPO to market. You will require the services of a number of professionals, including lawyers and accountants, to start trading stock in your business. You will also need to work with clerical staff to produce various documents, such as your prospectus, which will most likely go through several drafts, and which we will discuss in more detail later in this chapter. Once you have produced a final, approved prospectus, you will need to have this document printed by a financial printer, who should be experienced in printing prospectuses in the appropriate format. You will then need to mail prospectuses to thousands of potential investors. You will also need to have stock certificates printed. In addition to these costs, you will have to pay various filing fees to the SEC, to the National Association of Securities Dealers (NASD), and to the states in which you plan to offer securities. These fees can run in the tens of thousands of dollars. You will also need to hire and pay underwriters, who will bring your stock to market. Their fees will typically eat up a percentage of the selling price of your stock. Altogether, expect an IPO to cost a few hundred thousand dollars. In addition to these one-time expenses, you will have to prepare and print new quarterly or annual reports updating stockholders on the condition of your business. You might also need to hire new permanent employees, such as chief financial officers or other executives when you decide to go public, if your current executives do not have sufficient experience running public businesses. You might also decide to hire an employee to maintain public or stockholder relations. Although going public can bring a great deal of money into your business, it can also take a significant sum out of it.

Another disadvantage of going public is that you risk being sued by your stockholders. People buy stock expecting that the value of the stock will rise. Of course, it does not always do so. A number of factors affect the value of a given stock on any given day. In some cases, businesses make fraudulent claims about their financial health and future prospects when they go public, deceiving investors into believing that they are sound investments. When investors discover that the business is poorly managed, or is financially unhealthy, they generally begin selling stocks, causing the value of the stock to fall. In such cases, investors will sue the company issuing the stock, hoping to recoup the money they have lost. Not all such lawsuits, however, are well founded. In many cases, investors will attempt to bring suit against companies that operate honestly and competently, but whose sales or profits are decreasing. Be aware that, by going public, you increase the risks of having a lawsuit brought against you.

Another disadvantage in going public is that you run the risk of losing control of your business. A public business not only needs to run efficiently and profitably for its own good; it also needs to satisfy its stockholders. If stockholders feel that a company is not profitable or if they are otherwise unhappy with it, they will sell their stock. As more stockholders sell a given company's stock, that stock tends to lose its value. Because companies need to retain existing stockholders to attract new ones, and to preserve their reputation, public companies are generally quite concerned with keeping their stockholders happy. This renders them vulnerable to the demands of their stockholders, who may want changes made in company operations; if management doesn't comply, they can threaten the business with selling off their shares. In some cases, you might find yourself not running the business the way you want to, but the way the stockholders want you to.

You can also lose control of the company in a more dramatic manner. Each share of stock represents a share in the ownership (or equity) of the business. As you start out, you will maintain ownership of the majority of the stock in your company. The remainder will be spread among a number of individual and institutional stockholders. In some cases, however, you may come to sell off a majority of the company's stock. A large piece of this outstanding stock (or stock that the company does not own) could fall into the hands of a single individual or institution, which could then become the new owner of the business. Such a majority stockholder could take over the business, changing it drastically. This situation rarely occurs in small businesses, however; when such hostile takeovers do occur, they usually strike large, multimillion-dollar businesses. You can also defend yourself against such takeovers by writing defensive clauses into your IPO charter.

PREPARING TO GO PUBLIC

Going public is a very big step, but the process will be easier for you if you prepare for it properly. Good preparation will also make your company more attractive to investors.

It will be easier to go public if you simply follow good business practices. By collecting timely and thorough financial data on your company and filing it properly, you will have this information handy when you need to supply it to the government in the process of going public. If you require accountants to search for years' worth of poorly maintained or even nonexistent records, you will have to spend thousands of dollars you might have saved.

You also need to take a good, objective look at your employees, especially your top executives. Do they have experience managing a public company? Although they may be excellent at what they do, will they be able to maintain their current workloads and handle the new tasks associated with public firms? Will they be able to attract investors and cultivate relationships with them? If not, you may need to replace your current officers.

You also need to look at your sales and your growth pattern. Investors want to buy stock in businesses with a high potential for growth. One of the best indicators of this potential is current growth. If your company's sales have remained stagnant or have declined, investors will not be too keen to buy shares in your firm. If you can show a history of growth, however, and demonstrate how added funds from a public offering can help your business continue to grow, you will have a better chance of attracting investors.

THE PROCESS OF GOING PUBLIC

Finding an Underwriter

Once you have decided to go public, you will need to attract an investment banking firm that will act as an underwriter, selling your stock to a variety of institutions (mutual funds, retirement funds, etc.) and individuals. In many cases, one firm acts as the managing underwriter, and forms a syndicate of similar firms that will also market the offering. In some cases, an IPO might have two managing underwriters, one of whom will be the lead managing underwriter. Because you and your current personnel may be inexperienced in approaching underwriters, you should probably hire a consultant to help you attract an underwriter.

You might choose to work with a national, regional, or local underwriter; your syndicate may consist of underwriters of all three types. Large, national underwriters tend to be better known and more prestigious than the other types. If you can attract such an underwriter, potential investors are more likely to view your stock as a sound investment.

Look for an underwriter that has experience in handling offerings of the same size as yours and that has worked with other firms in your field. You will need to contact underwriters and explain your offering to them. Tell them what your business does, how long it has been in operation, what your sales and profits are, how much money you intend to raise by going public, and so on. If the underwriter is interested in handling your offering, you will need to provide a detailed information package. From there, you may proceed to a meeting with the underwriter. You might need to meet with several underwriters before you find one that is interested in handling your offering, and with which you also want to work.

Underwriters generally sell stock under one of two types of arrangements. If they sell it on a "firm commitment" basis, they agree to buy all the shares offered, at a set price, and resell them. If they cannot sell all the shares, they keep unsold shares until they can sell them. Underwriters also sell stocks on a "best efforts" basis. In this case, the underwriter does not take any responsibility for any unsold stock. There are several best efforts arrangements, but none of them obligate the underwriter to buy any unsold stock. Try to find an underwriter who will sell your stock on a firm commitment basis.

When you settle on an underwriter, you will have to decide the underwriter's commission, which usually ranges from 7 to 10 percent of the stock sold. Although this will be the underwriter's main source of compensation, you may have to pay certain other fees. The underwriter may also ask (or require) you to give it a certain number of shares before you make the public offering, or to give it the option to buy shares at a certain fixed price in the future. You and the underwriter will also have to decide the selling price of the stock before you go public.

Plan the Registration

Once you have finalized all agreements with your underwriter and the lawyers and accountants with whom you will work to bring your offering to market, you should call a meeting bringing all these parties together. You need to decide exactly what tasks need to be accomplished, and who will accomplish them, to bring the offering to market on time and in compliance with all applicable regulations. It is important to bring your entire IPO team together, because their work will be interrelated. You need to set schedules for all the different tasks that need to be finished. After this meeting, you will need to check regularly on everyone's progress. Try to keep everything moving as smoothly as possible.

The Registration Statement

The registration statement consists of two parts: the prospectus and supplemental information. You need to file both parts with the SEC. You will distribute the prospectus to the public and to other potential investors. The SEC will keep the supplemental information on file, where members of the public will have access to it; companies registering IPOs generally do not need to distribute this information to the public.

The prospectus contains detailed information about your business and your offering. It will tell potential investors what kind of business you run, what your market is, who your competitors are, what your sales and profits are, and what experience your officers have. You need to indicate how many shares of stock you are selling and what you plan to do with the money you raise by selling them. If your business represents an unusually high risk, you need to inform potential investors of that fact. You also need to describe how you plan to pay dividends. If the company is involved in legal proceedings that have a bearing on the offering, you must let investors know. You also need to include a number of financial statements in the prospectus.

The supplemental information includes certain other financial documents, a copy of the underwriting agreement pertaining to your offering, and a listing of expenses related to the offering.

Your prospectus is a sales tool, in that the information it contains ideally will spur investors to buy shares in your business. At the same time, it must contain enough information to give them a complete picture of the activities, financial status, and projected growth of your company, allowing them to make a sound decision. The prospectus is not a simple document to assemble. You, your accountants, your lawyers, your underwriter, and their lawyers will probably need to meet several times before you can all produce a satisfactory prospectus.

In addition to the preceding information, you will need to fill out the appropriate SEC form(s) for your offering. Depending on the size of the offering and on what type of business you operate, this might be a Form S-1, S-18, SB-1, or SB-2.

Waiting Period

Once you have filed all your documents with the SEC, it will take them a few weeks to review them. The SEC will most likely have a few questions regarding your offering, and you should do your best to answer them quickly. The faster you can address the SEC's comments, the faster the SEC can approve your offering.

While the SEC reviews your prospectus, you can make copies of it and distribute it to potential investors, through your underwriter and marketing syndicate. You must, however, print a notice in red ink on the cover, indicating that you have filed the offering with the SEC, but it has not yet been approved. You also need to write that you will not sell any shares until the offering has been approved, nor will you take any orders for shares. This preliminary version of the prospectus is known as the "red herring." You can also present your company to potential investors at formal meetings and presentations during the waiting period.

In addition to applying for federal authorization to sell your stocks, you need to meet state regulations. Most states have their own laws affecting the sales of securities, and you need to abide by any applicable laws in those states in which you plan to offer shares. If you or your underwriter have not already filed the appropriate forms for meeting these various state regulations, you should do so during the waiting period.

Revising the Prospectus and Selling Stock

After you have received and responded to the SEC's comments, you might need to revise your prospectus to comply with the SEC's requests. In fact, you will probably go through more than one draft even when you are producing the first version of the prospectus. When you produce the final prospectus, you need to agree on the selling price of the stock with your underwriter. Although the underwriter will have been working with you up to this point, this is when the underwriter finally and formally agrees to sell your securities. Once you and the underwriter have executed the underwriting agreement, the underwriter will begin selling your stocks. After you have done so, you will be ready to go public.

Closing

The underwriter will generally sell shares in your firm for about five business days after the offering becomes effective. After that period, the sales are "closed," and the underwriter will give you a check for the income produced by the sale of the stocks, after deducting their percentage or discount. In exchange for the check, you will provide the underwriter with stock certificates for all the stock sold.

OPERATING AS A PUBLIC COMPANY

Once you become public, you have to meet a number of requirements that apply specifically to public companies. You will need to file a number of forms with the SEC:

- **Form S-R.** Lists what funds you have received in exchange for stock, and describes how you have used them.
- **Form 10-Q.** Summarizes the performance of the company on a quarterly basis.
- **Form 10-K.** Summarizes the company's performance on an annual basis.
- **Form 8-K.** Used to report certain significant events in the life of the company.

In addition to filing these forms, you also need to maintain good relations with your current shareholders, and with the public at large. You want to remain attractive to investors, both to keep your current shareholders and to attract new ones in case you ever decide to sell more stock.

ADDITIONAL METHODS OF GOING PUBLIC

In addition to the traditional IPO, you may choose to go public in a number of fairly new ways. You may, for instance, choose to underwrite your own offering. Although you will act as the underwriter for the offering, you will need to work with a local or regional underwriter who will help you market your stock. Underwriting your own offering is in some ways riskier than entering a traditional relationship with an underwriter. Large underwriters are highly experienced in taking companies public, and are familiar with all of the applicable federal and state regulations. Because you probably will not have this knowledge, however, and because the smaller underwriters with whom you will work may also be somewhat unfamiliar with these legalities, you run a greater risk of failing to meet all the requirements.

In about 38 states, you can use the Form U-7 to raise funds. This form is also known as the SCOR or *small corporate offering registration* form and the ULOR or *uniform limited offering registration* form. Businesses can use this form to raise about $1 million. It reduces the documentation companies need to file, and it cuts legal and accounting costs as well.

We have provided an introduction to the traditional process of going public, and outlined two additional methods for raising capital in this chapter. Because going public is such a complex procedure, however, you should certainly consult the SEC and a professional consultant or underwriter before you decide to go public and before you decide which method of going public would be best for your company.

RESOURCES

Government Agencies

U.S. Securities and Exchange Commission, Office of Small Business Policy, 450 Fifth Street NW, Washington, DC 20549, 202-942-8945; 800-732-4711

SEC Regional and District Offices

Atlanta (District Office): 3475 Lennox Road Northeast, Suite 1000, Atlanta, GA 30326-1232, 404-842-7600

Boston: 73 Tremont Street, 6th Floor, Boston, MA 02114, 617-424-5900

Chicago: 500 West Madison Street, Suite 1400, Chicago, IL 60661-2511, 312-353-7390

Fort Worth: 801 Cherry Street, 19th Floor, Fort Worth, TX 76102, 817-334-3821

Los Angeles (Pacific Regional Office): 5670 Wilshire Boulevard, 11th Floor, Los Angeles, CA 90036, 213-965-3998

New York: 7 World Trade Center, 13th Floor, New York, NY 10048, 212-748-8000

Philadelphia (District Office): 601 Walnut Street, Suite 1005 East, The Curtis Center, Philadelphia, PA 19106, 215-597-3100

29

Selling Your Business

Suppose you want to retire or would like to raise capital for another venture you are planning. Perhaps there are health problems or other extenuating circumstances (one being that you are not making quite enough money at what you're doing now). Whatever the reason, you have been thinking about the possibility of selling your business. The purpose of this chapter is to put you on the right track and help you make the best deal possible.

We start, though, by asking two questions:

1. Should you sell the business at all?
2. Is this the right time to sell?

In deciding whether to sell, consider all your alternatives:

- If health or time is a factor, could you profitably hire a manager to run the business (a management whiz who might increase profits substantially, over and above his or her salary)?
- Could you keep the business in the family by selling to a son or daughter?

If these are not options, ask yourself whether this is the right time to sell. If the economy is on a downturn, you might wind up selling at a loss, or for an amount substantially less than what you might obtain a year or two down the road.

Other considerations include:

- Where is your business in your industry cycle?
- Is your industry healthy right now?
- Is your business keeping pace with or outpacing your industry as a whole?

An ideal time to sell your business would be during a strong economic cycle, with your industry cycling upward, and your business either keeping pace with or outperforming your industry. You might also consider selling if your industry is doing well during a recession, and your business is matching or surpassing industry performance.

SHOULD YOU USE A BROKER?

If at all possible, it makes sense to use an agent to sell your operation. A good agent will cost you nothing. He or she will more than make up the commission you pay by getting a higher price for your business and effecting a smooth and legal transaction.

The main role of an agent is to act as a buffer between the personal emotions of the buyer and those of the seller. The agent is someone who can be believed because he or she has no vested interest in the business being sold. For example, the agent can make flattering statements and reflect enthusiasm about the business that, coming from you directly, would be disregarded or viewed with suspicion. The buyer can also ask the broker pointed, pertinent, private questions that would be extremely difficult if not downright insulting, to put to you directly. The agent can take the unique position of advocate of both parties, agreeing with seller and buyer alike while helping to iron out and resolve any problems that develop in the course of the sale. They can point out or agree with the buyer's assessment of your shortcomings, enhancing his or her opinion of the business's potential. Never forget that all buyers think they can do better than the seller at running the business.

The business broker can greatly assist you by determining whether your buyer has sufficient equity for financing, or whether the buyer's background is suitable for your type of business (if this consideration applies). Most important, the broker can attract and screen potential buyers, qualifying them in a way an individual seller usually cannot because the agent knows what to look for. This saves you time and concern. For it is quite true that there are as many "tire kickers" in business sales as on the used car lots.

The broker can say effortlessly, "If you're interested, Mr. Buyer, sign this offer and give me a deposit on the basis of the business picture presented to us. Then we will ask to inspect the facility and see Mr. Seller's books." You can readily see how awkward this kind of statement would be if it came directly from you as the seller.

Of utmost importance, the broker can carry out a legal sale for you. A broker has the proper forms, both written and unwritten, that can keep you out of trouble. He or she has covered the business-sale ground before and knows the kinds of things that must be disclosed or need not be disclosed to conclude a mutually satisfactory deal. Trouble over any alleged misrepresentations, that could result in buyer litigation after the sale, can be avoided.

Selecting an Agent

If you are convinced you need a broker to help you with your business sale, you should do the following:

- **Check local newspaper ads under "Business Opportunities."** Why is this important? You will frequently see businesses for sale under this heading, and just as the prospective buyer is invited to call to take a look at various individual businesses, the prospective seller, not yet listed in the column, is being tacitly urged to take a look at who in the community is facilitating these sales. Choose several ads that appeal to you and call those agents in for a possible listing.

- **Look in the yellow pages under "Real Estate" or "Business Brokers."** You can also find brokers listed in your area's yellow pages. Check with more than one, and don't make a decision too fast. It's best to find a broker who specializes in businesses and does not simply handle real estate.
- **Don't let the broker list your business on a realtors' multiple listing service.** Any broker who wants to do this is not willing to devote the time and work necessary to sell your business and hopes someone else will sell it and split the commission.
- **Make sure to get in writing that the broker will advertise.** But be sure that the advertisement is not by business name. This can cause all kinds of problems—with your personnel, with your vendors, and with customers. Once the word gets out locally, particularly in a smaller community, you can be branded with negative press.
- **Develop a good relationship with the agent you select.** The need for ease of communications between seller and broker cannot be overestimated.

Should You Sell

If you're considering selling your business, the following questionnaire will help you determine whether or not it is the appropriate time to do so.

1. *How long have you been actively involved in the business?*
2. *Are you still as excited about the business as the day you started?*
3. *Do you want to start another venture?*
4. *Do you want to retire?*
5. *Is your company growing too fast for you to handle it?*
6. *Does the business make sufficient profit for your standard of living?*
7. *Are you satisfied with the type of work you're involved in?*
8. *What are future industry prospects like?*
9. *Is the location of your business attractive?*
10. *Is the industry your business is in currently on an upswing or a recession?*
11. *What is the performance of your business like compared with the industry?*
12. *Is your business profitable compared with your competitors?*
13. *Is damaging competition moving in?*
14. *Will it be profitable for you to sell?*
15. *If you have developed a strong business, can you pass it along to a sibling or another family member?*

Agent commission rates vary slightly with geographic area but tend to run around 10 percent of the selling price of the business opportunity. If real estate is involved, another 6 percent goes for that portion of the sale. Where the selling price of the business opportunity exceeds $100,000, an agreed-on fee, in writing, should be determined, which typically comes in at around 5 percent of the balance.

PRICING YOUR BUSINESS

How much is your business worth? The old adage warns, "Only what someone is willing to pay for it." This is true to the extent you are eager to sell your business. Just as critical a factor, however, is the way the business is presented to the potential buyer.

Experienced business brokers report that proper presentation of image is the single most difficult task facing a typical seller. Left to their own devices in approaching the problem, the seller usually sets an initial price that is unrealistic and outrageous. Sellers who take the opposite approach are almost worse; in some instances they depreciate the value of their own business so much in their minds that they are ready to give it away. The result on one hand is that the business itself either stays on the market for an inordinate period or is picked up inexpensively by buyers with quick minds and good negotiating skill.

According to C. D. Peterson, author and publisher of *How to Sell Your Business* (as quoted in a recent *Entrepreneur* article), "A business's value comes from three factors: what the business owns, what it earns, and what makes it unique and different." He continues to explain that what a business *owns* is obviously its assets, but not as shown on the balance sheet; rather, it owns the market value of the assets. Similarly, what the business *earns* is not what you would necessarily see on a profit and loss statement. Instead of profit, you need to work with what's called an "adjusted owner's cash flow." This means adjusting the profit to reflect real numbers (excluding depreciation and interest) while making sure there's an appropriate salary for the owner. Finally, what makes the business *unique,* says Peterson, is risk and desirability. No matter what formulas you use, this will always involve some subjectivity; somebody has to decide how risky the business is. Still, the risk a buyer sees in a business can be expressed as the percentage rate of return the buyer would demand from the business.[1] You will see Peterson's philosophies implemented as we cover business pricing methods.

Basically, there are two ways to price a business:

1. Price Building. Evaluates the tangible assets and includes a value for goodwill, lease value, trade names, and other intangibles.

[1] *"Business Hotline—Experts Answer Your Questions," Entrepreneur* (July 1993).

2. **Return on Investment.** Measures the value of a business based on its return on the initial investment.

Before you begin pricing your operation, realize that one of these methods will be most favorable to you—the "best" strategy and the "only one" right for your type of business. This is why it makes sense for you to work the figures out each way and decide which method appeals to you most strongly before you become heavily involved with a broker.

Price Building

The price-building process is a simple one. The first thing to do is to list on a sheet of paper what are known as *hard dollars*—those tangible, touchable assets you have. These are referred to as *long-term assets* on a balance sheet:

- Real estate.
- Leasehold Improvements.
- Equipment.
- Fixtures.
- Inventory.
- Supplies.

When appraising real estate, you actually need to consider two factors: the land and improvements. Land value can be appraised by your agent and is determined by a review of the tax-assessed value compared with the selling prices of like-sized parcels in similar locations in the current market.

Evaluating improvements is another matter entirely. One way is to take current construction costs for your type of building and multiply that price per square feet times the number of square feet you have. The more realistic approach, which would appeal to a banker, is to calculate everything as a function of cash flow. For instance, if the normal rental rate for your building is $1,000 per month ($850 net to you after expenses), and $850 will discharge an amortized loan balance of $100,000 for 25 years at the going rate of interest in your area, then this balance, plus the down payment, will equal the maximum market value of both your land and improvements. This kind of analysis can be adapted to the needs of your own business. A good broker will be familiar with the kinds of factors being considered here. This is the kind of analysis, indeed, that you are paying for.

Now estimate the value of your leasehold improvements, fixtures, and equipment. Leasehold refers to those things attached to the building that are not easily removed, such as partitions, toilet facilities, special electrical wiring, and the like. Fixtures are carpeting, shelving, special lighting, counters, and so on. Equipment refers to any other freestanding objects necessary to conduct your business. Make an inventory of these items and estimate their replacement value (not the depreciated value on your books).

Next come your product inventory and supplies. Because these are a day-to-day variable, you need to take inventory at this time. Inventory will be what it is on the last day of escrow. The buyer along with the seller will physically take this count and agree on cost. If the original estimate of inventory value was included in the sale price, this will have to be adjusted accordingly. Another way to handle the matter would be to quote the price of the business as sales price plus inventory.

We have now figured out the hard dollars of equity (real estate, leasehold, fixtures, equipment, inventory, and supplies). The balance of the sale price is what is known in the trade as "blue sky." This is divided into specific categories of goodwill, lease value, covenant not to compete, trade name and other patent rights, and so on. Brokers have observed that these divisions are made mainly for buyer palatability.

Generally speaking, unless you have something very special to sell, the combined net total of these should not be much in excess of one year's probable net. Many formulas are used in arriving at a figure, but on the bottom line, few people are willing to work more than a year for nothing. Add this figure to your hard dollars, place agent's commission on top of that, throw in a few thousand more to leave you some negotiating/barter room, and you have arrived at your asking price. The price you finally accept for your business will be entirely up to you and the circumstances that prevail.

Return on Investment

You begin this method of pricing by asking once again what the business is worth. How do you determine the price and justify it? Whatever method you use, there are no easy answers. Every business sale develops a life of its own, and no two resolutions of the pricing problem have ever been the same.

Starting with the books will give you some idea, with the numbers there in black and white. An income statement and capital equipment schedule will do for starters. The capital equipment records will provide an accurate accounting of all fixtures, equipment, real estate (if any) or leasehold, and all other assets owned by the business. An income statement will provide either a monthly, quarterly, or annual barometer of how the business is performing.

Still, keep in mind that the numbers on these documents won't provide a complete solution to your pricing problem. As you will see, there can be variations between book values and real-world values.

Since the real-world purpose of a capital equipment schedule is usually to address favorable tax income through the depreciation of assets, often capital items are written off in three to five years as worthless or of negligible value on the schedule. But most business operators know that equipment may have a serviceable life of 10 years. Also, since depreciation does not allow for inflation, some items can have a value that equals or exceeds the original cost of the equipment. So, as long as these differences are kept in mind, a capitalization schedule can prove a useful tool in helping to determine a business's worth.

Similarly, the values found on an income statement may not be completely accurate in reflecting all the operating expenses of a business over time. Often,

Documentation

"Let's see the books" is the ever-present buyer demand echoes and reechoed in every deal. The more unfamiliar John Q. Buyer is with a business, the more importance he places on these "tell-all" documents. They are salve to the wound of inexperience and suspicion. These books include your profit and loss statements, sales tax records, and probably the business portion of your income tax submissions for the past one to three years.

Your accountant-prepared P&L will probably be detrimental to a sale where this inexperienced buyer is involved because it is tax oriented. In other words, it will reflect your attempts to minimize tax obligations on a minimum net profit through write-offs, both real and imaginary, and will not present the best possible picture to the buyer. Additionally, whatever the picture, it will not be the buyer's picture. His debt discharge is not yours, nor is his telephone bill, ad budget, family labor supply, and so on.

At this point he isn't interested in your clever method of equipment depreciation. In fact, he may question what you're asking for your equipment now. He may also question the charging of your leased car and insurance against the business. You can readily see that if you have tried to put one over on the tax man in this area, the buyer may think that you have done so in other areas of business as well. The buyer is interested in one thing: What is the maximum profit that can be made from this business right now?

Preparing a simplified P&L will go a long way toward quickly giving the buyer the answers. The new computerized spreadsheet software programs on the market can vastly streamline the creation of such financials. The important thing is that key questions can be answered with a minimum of fuss on a simplified statement: Provable sales for 1991–1992 were . . . ? Provable sales for 1993 were . . . ? Projected sales this year . . . ? Cost of goods is . . . ? Rent is . . . ? Utilities and telephone cost . . . ? Salaries excluding manager's are . . . ? Number of full-time/part-time employees is . . . ? Average per hour wage . . . ? Benefits and FICA costs are . . . ? Business insurance is . . . in the amount of . . . ?

These are the tangible, nonvariable dollar amounts the buyer will want to see. Of course, there will be other expenses, but he can elect to control these. There may be some exceptions to the preceding simplifications, and if they are important to your particular business, you should list them. The buyer wants to see the numbers that will affect the potential profit he can earn.

Though this is not a total picture and the buyer realizes there will be other expenses, this is definitely a major decision point. If he likes what he sees, he will buy in spite of other conditions not totally to his liking.

an income statement may reflect unfavorable expenses such as personal phone calls, exaggerated travel expenses, cash labor, depletion of consumables, spoilage, shrinkage, loss, theft, and miscellaneous items that occurred in the time period the income statement reflects. A prospective buyer, then, would have to view performance as a brand-new ball game—with new capitalization, debt discharge, and return on investment, together with any such special factors as absentee ownership, personal management, family-run operations, and the like.

The value of a business is generally viewed from opposite perspectives by buyer and seller. As an owner-seller, you want the price that your fixtures, equipment, and leasehold/real estate will bring *today* in their present condition. Then there is the matter of your inventory; that is the same as cash. If you have a long-term lease with favorable conditions or your rent is low, or your location is considered prime, that should be worth something extra. And your established name? What about a promise not to compete with the new owner in the same business for a certain length of time, and within a certain radius? You are not going to forget the time, sweat, and tears that went into this place to build it up to what it is today; that's got to be worth money. And if it is not, then the flourishing amount of business you have today most certainly is. You are practically offering a turnkey operation.

These conclusions sound perfectly all right. But they are meaningless if they do not add up to an attractive value to the buyer in terms of return on investment—the *buyer's* investment, not yours.

In most cases, however, the exercise of evaluating price or worth preoccupies both owner and potential buyer in haggling over fixed assets. They lose sight of

Attractive Value

Before looking at what attractive value is, let us look first at what it is not. It is certainly not 6 percent or even 9.2 percent, which has been typical of a number of large corporations. All too often, it is forgotten by small-business owners that the law of large numbers does not apply to the entrepreneurial venture. The principals and owners of large-volume companies are already making all the salary they can stand for tax purposes. An overflow return of 6 percent on an investment of $500 million is $30 million. This creates a problem only of what to do with the money. Small business cannot and does not operate this way. The overall profit is smaller, which is why the rate of return must be significantly higher than it is in big business.

From the viewpoint of investors or absentee owners, therefore, such return has to approximate 20 percent per annum for them to assume risk. Some analysts will settle for 15 percent, but we have found no one who will consider anything less. Working or managing owners must receive a salary equal to what they are getting now or can get elsewhere plus a 12 to 14 percent return on their investment. Otherwise, why take the risk in the first place?

Admittedly, you can't get this percentage in the bank without a large volume, but you can in vehicles of less risk such as real estate or second mortgages. What about future potential? This has value only if you can convince someone of it besides yourself. Experience tells us, however, that worth must be proven. The demand side of the picture, the buyer's side, is where worth will ultimately be established. For now, let us eliminate a common hangup and basis of negotiation argument, the tangible assets of a business, and concentrate on its real purpose, which is its ability to make money based on a proven or provable track record.

whether this is an equitable deal in the first place. This is a normal occurrence simply because we all feel more comfortable in dealing with tangibles—things we can touch and feel, and feel safe in asserting an opinion about.

The trick is for both parties to stay with the return-on-investment approach. If the deal is equitable and attractive, then everything else is incidental to achieving that goal. If Mr. X can take a salary or draw of $30,000 or $40,000 a year and still realize 12 percent on his investment, while controlling the risk, the importance of intangible assets—and even some of the tangible ones—can begin to fade. In establishing price, value, and worth, this makes much more sense than to become committed to the idea that Asset A or Asset B has to be adequately appreciated by a buyer.

There are many exciting ways of looking critically at numbers on a balance sheet, upping return while not lowering price, to the benefit of all parties concerned. To do this correctly, you need to understand what we mean by and how we arrive at the return on investment (ROI). Quite simply, ROI is bottom-line results after all expenses, including debt discharge and owner salary, are subtracted from gross sales and then divided by up-front cash investment used to buy the business. How do we arrive at it correctly? We get rid of the seemingly unnecessary, imaginative clutter on the P&L statement and settle down to actual—real-world—expense requirements:

1. **Cost of goods sold.** This has historically been observed as a common area for "skimming" from a business, which is here defined as stealing from one's own business to avoid income taxes. Reputable business owners realize that skimming has no place in its tax-accounting procedures, but it is a foolish as well as illegal enterprise where valuing a business for sales purposes is concerned. Unless value is questionable in terms of ROI and it becomes necessary to delve into this, ignore it and use stated costs.
2. **Rent.** Also use the equivalent in real-estate costs.
3. **Utilities.** This figure includes payments for gas, electricity, water, and garbage.
4. **Insurance.** Make certain only fire, legal, and liability premiums applying to the business are used.
5. **Expenses.** There may be specific expense items peculiar to a business. They must be mandatory and completely justifiable.
6. **Payroll.** There will be at least the owner's salary. If there are several salaries, do not state them as a percentage of gross sales or even a gross cost unless the situation involves purely investment or absentee ownership.

New ownership will tend to change the structure. It may alter the owner's participation, moving from a working owner to the lesser salary of a hired manager. If a husband and wife comanage the business, this will change the financial structure, as will participation by immediate family members. Accordingly, state salary in terms of worker hours required to run the business; no one person should be stated as working more than 40 hours per week.

Next, eliminate exaggerated and personal expenses: phone calls, auto expense, insurance, supplies, professional services, miscellaneous/casual labor, repairs, spoilage, bad checks, unrecoverable debt, and so on. All of those items are thrown in for quite another purpose, as we have seen. Once you have clean numbers, you can develop an acceptable ROI.

What ideal ROI should we shoot for? There is no "ideal" number. If an evaluation reveals an ROI in the 12- to 14-percent area, it represents an attractive price and a good buy for reasons already stipulated. Whatever figure is used to produce this result is the real worth of the business. Does this mean that businesses are not bought or sold at prices reflecting higher or lower ROIs? Of course not. A price producing ROI higher than 12 to 14 percent would be a tremendous buy. Conversely, a lower ROI means a poor buy. To achieve equitable marketability, the price-worth value of a business should be adjusted upward or downward to reflect the attractive price.

Despite the tools of analysis available to buyers and sellers of businesses, you would be surprised how many businesses change hands on the basis of "adequate net income" or "good price for fixtures and equipment," without much, if any, attention paid to ROI. Results? Fantastic to lousy buys—and for reasons that surprise everybody.

If in the downward adjustment of price to get the ROI into the 12- to 14-percent area, this number becomes less than the value of the hard, fixed assets of the business, then the business is worth no more than the demand value of its assets. In fact, it is not a business any longer but a potential garage sale of fixtures and equipment.

Naturally, there are exceptions to every rule as extenuating circumstances permit. A business without ROI still may command a premium above asset value if it has prime location, low rent, an excellent long-term lease or someone sees it ideal for another purpose. But be aware that these are exceptions that should not be counted on.

In determining the worth of a business, the seller can relieve a tight marketability (code for low ROI) situation without lowering the price by adjusting or introducing a debt contract.

Example A

Business net profit	$ 7,000
Business sale price	$100,000
ROI ($7,000/$100,000)	7%

This example is typical of a "poor buy." Further, it is doubtful such incentive would produce any marketability.

Example A-1

Business net profit	$ 7,000
29% down payment	$ 29,000
ROI ($7,000/$29,000)	24%

Look better? Of course it does. In addition to bringing us much closer to an actual sale by turning a poor buy into a great buy, the introduction of the debt contract, which is a contract of sale and an installment agreement, has accomplished other decided benefits for both buyer and seller. The seller can now defer capital gain taxation over the term of the contract. The buyer now has a hedge against risk ($29,000 versus $100,000). The balance money continues to work for the buyer, drawing interest and offsetting interest owed on contract. In the three to four years it will pay to retire the contract, even if the business nets no more than $7,000 per year, the ROI will decrease but will never fall below 15 percent.

Now look at some examples of "tight" ROI, where the business must pay for the debt discharge to produce an attractive sale and a good buy.

Example B

Business price	$67,000
Down payment	$22,000
Business net before debt discharge	$18,000

Example B-1

Business net	$18,000
Debt discharge ($45,000 @ 9%/3yrs fully amortized).	−17,200
Difference	$ 800
ROI (($800/$22,000)/down payment)	3.6%

Nothing to get excited about here. In fact, it has all the earmarks of a poor to so-so buy up front (we will discuss prorate later). But this situation can be fixed easily, extending the contract term for five years, fully amortized, instead of three:

Example B-2

Business net	$18,000
Debt discharge (5 yrs)	−11,200
Difference	$ 6,800
ROI (($6,800/$22,000)/down payment)	31%

Example B-2 is more like it. Now there is an attractive price, though it is unchanged, and the result is a fantastic buy. Now, however, let us create what appears on the surface to be a near impossible situation. The same business, the same price, and the same down payment, but let's drop the business net income to $10,000 from $18,000 used earlier. Thus:

Example C

Business net	$10,000
Debt discharge	−11,200
Difference	$ 1,200
ROI (($1,200/$22,000)/down payment)	00.6%

Suddenly there is not only no ROI but also a deficit position. There is neither a good buy nor a sale. But do we fold up our business and sell off the assets at 50 cents on the dollar? No. Simply revise the figures to reflect the new situation:

Example C-1

Business net	$10,000
Debt discharge (9% interest only w/balloon payment)	−4,050
Difference	$ 5,950
ROI (($5,950/$22,000)/down payment)	27%

Using the interest-only approach, which is quite common, such a good result is produced that we could increase payback to $7,000 per year ($583.33 per month), including interest and principal, balance due and payable in three years, five years, or whatever the seller wants. This would keep the ROI at 13.6 percent, which is in the good-buy ballpark. One final point. How can the buyer make a balloon payment in five years when the net income shown ($5,950×5 years=$29,750) is less than $30,000? If the buyer banked wisely under the best compounding conditions, it might come closer to the $45,000 that is owed. But that is not the whole story.

In all the examples used, the net business income is allowed to stay at the current figure without projecting normal, expected increases in the future. Even if we did nothing with the proposed business other than its current operation, increase in demand would result in greater volume and subsequently more net profit. Nobody buys a business visualizing it in a stagnant mode in the future. The buyer brings new ideas, energy, and enthusiasm. And frequently even if the ideas don't work, energy and enthusiasm will. This enthusiasm may be naive, but its presence can cause excitement in customers. The result will be more business, hence higher net.

Also, when we have quoted ROIs, we did so only through the debt-discharge periods. What happens when the debt has been repaid? The ROI zooms up. Therefore, another way a seller can attempt to show an attractive price, or a buyer who wants to convince themselves of a good buy, would be to project an average ROI over a longer period, perhaps 10 years. A realistic, averaged net profit increase might be cranked in to present a better picture of what to expect as the business develops. Thus, an immediate ROI of 15 percent may average out to 30, 40, or 50 percent over an extended period. This looks quite attractive to a prospective buyer.

People want to get into business for themselves for other, very strong emotional reasons—so strong, in fact, that they may overshadow negative numbers or conditions. Pride of ownership is one of these. Freedom from supervision by others is a strong second. The feeling or belief that their personal efforts will be directly rewarded without chance interference of people or circumstances is another. Subconsciously, they will make allowances in other areas to achieve these goals. A husband and wife will replace two hired people in a business who get $30,000 in salary, and take $20,000 as a joint income, increasing the ROI of the business to a positive figure. In short, there are a number of personal and psychological tradeoffs people are willing to make even if numbers are not quite right, and sometimes even in preference to sound financial judgment.

From a buyer's standpoint, it is not poor business judgment to view a potential business opportunity with ideas of innovation and projected goals. Necessity is the mother of invention, and this is what fortunes are made of. In partnership with this thinking, you too must take a good, hard look at return on investment, making sure that the terms and agreements provide you with sufficient cash flow to meet your commitments. For you, the longer the terms the better. It will provide you with a secure feeling to know that the present owner is securing the balance you owe by the business you are taking over, though their terms may be the only way you can avail yourself of the opportunity.

The use of the ROI approach as a major point of discussion in price-terms negotiations will prove itself as the most valuable tool available. The facts are numbers, cut and dried, without the emotionalism attached to fixtures or equipment the owner has lived with and used. No one can argue for profit that's just not there. If the right numbers are there, we have a deal. If they're not, we don't—or at least won't until we massage those numbers a bit as strong investment analysis requires.

FINANCIAL CONSIDERATIONS

Financing of the purchase price may be the only way you can make the sale or get a top price. True, the buyer might be able to go to the bank or the Small Business Administration and get a business loan, but this sometimes endangers a sale. Bankers are traditionally negative about business loans; they are certainly very cautious and exacting, requiring much more backup data than you would normally have to furnish to a buyer.

If you do decide to accept carryback financing, you will want to make absolutely certain that the risk you assume is well secured and of short duration. This makes the paper negotiable should you wish to use it for equity prematurely. The cash down payment should be at least equal to the cost of inventory and supplies. Put the balance owed in the form of a note or chattel mortgage, secured by the business in its entirety. The interest rate charged is normally 10 percent and can be fully or partially amortized, or be interest only, or any combination thereof. You know your business. Don't kill the buyer with debt discharge by setting up payments that will hurt their cash flow.

The term of the note should be from three to five years maximum, with the balance due and payable on or before this time. Buyer default, however, is not as bad an experience as you might imagine. It is a relatively simple, expedient, and inexpensive legal procedure to reacquire the business intact, retaining the buyer's down payment and all loan payments to date. Such provisions, of course, would have to be written into the contract.

Tax concerns come into play as well. It's not how much you get, but what you get to keep that counts. If you've never heard that before, when the federal government gets a look at your capital gain, you will. This is another reason that some owner financing may be desirable. If you take less than 30 percent down (29 percent is the magic number according to the experts), this constitutes a contract of sale and defers taxation obligation until the end of the note. IRS rules also allow for an exchange of your business for a "like" income-producing business, with lengthy deferment of taxes.

The Lease

If you own the real estate involved in the sale of the business and are selling it along with the business opportunity, there is no particular problem. However, you are more than likely leasing the property for your business purposes from a third-party landlord. The terms of your rental agreements are therefore of vital interest to the buyer who needs a satisfactory long-term arrangement to protect his or her investment.

If your lease has less than four years to go, talk to the lessor in advance of the sale. Explain that you are thinking of selling and suggest that it would be advantageous to renegotiate a new lease with the new owner. Impart the lessor's willingness to do so, along with anything you've learned about the probable terms to your agent, who can then field the buyer's questions or objections up front.

Legal Escrow

By all means, use a formal escrow to close a business sale. This will assure a clean transfer of the business's assets and clarify debt responsibility for the business. If, for example, any monies are still owed to creditors for inventory, a "bulk sales transfer" should be used. Millie Cork, president of Opportunity Escrow of Orange, CA (and a fifteen-year veteran in bulk sales and liquor license transfer escrows), describes "a bulk sales transfer" as "the transfer of the assets of a business including tangible and intangible personal property used, held for use, or arising from, the seller's business together with inventory and equipment." Cork explains that bulk sales requirements are specified in the Uniform Commercial Code as adopted by each individual state, with only a few exceptions. For example, she says, "when combined with the transfer of an alcoholic beverage license, other codes and provisions may apply." She recommends hiring an experienced attorney or escrow company who is familiar with the rapidly changing provisions of the Uniform Commercial Code. Your banker of CPA may be able to recommend someone in your area, or you can look in the Business-to-Business Yellow Pages under "Escrow Services." Whomever you select, this qualified third party can see to it that all moneys are paid to the correct parties, protect you legally from claims, and save you a world of grief over last-minute disagreements on inventory or supply costs.

THE PSYCHOLOGY OF SELLING YOUR BUSINESS

Something happens to you from the time you make the decision to sell, through the mechanics of preparation of sale, through the ups and downs of buyers, until the time you actually consummate the deal. This is a dangerous time for the seller psychologically. Virtually any psychological transformation can come over a seller. Business brokers report spending hours with sellers without ever feeling sure how they will react to a situation. Sellers who declare that X amount is positively the bottom dollar they will take for their business—end up taking less. Other sellers say, "It's all cash or no deal!" Yet they finance the sale.

The message is this: Prepare yourself for some disappointments. The sale may not come immediately. Or you may think you have the business sold and the deal will fall through. If you have priced your business fairly and have presented major factors in a straightforward manner, you will get your price. Be patient.

Logistics of a Sale

The business broker can be used as liaison between you and the buyer. Until the sale is actually set, avoid direct contact with the buyer and let your agent do the public relations work. Be available to answer only technical questions, in the presence of the agent, and then provide information in a modest way. The reason behind this strategy is the very real danger of saying something that can be interpreted as misrepresentation in a later lawsuit. You must be judicious about what you say and when you say it.

Although you should keep communication with the buyer at a minimum, one thing that the buyer will want to know, and that will help overcome any initial suspicion, is why you are selling. If you do not answer this question satisfactorily up front, the question of *why* will rear its ugly head time and again in the course of a sale. Satisfactory answers are personal problems, ill health, retirement. If one of these is not the real reason, do not confide otherwise in your agent. A sincere answer to the buyer is vital, and you don't need to create the kind of tension that can destroy a sale.

Be aware that at some point along the way a negotiation is going to have to take place. This is why it is good business to set up little roadblocks of your position in your agent's mind—points on which you appear to be firm but that will be challenged and on which you will concede. These are known as straw issues, and they are of great use in helping you win on the big issues. Straw issues get everyone's attention diverted from the major issues such as price or other conditions important to you.

Keep in mind that the buyer will also have straw issues and big issues. When negotiating, therefore, it is important to understand that straw issues will be present when an offer is placed on the table. Never flatly reject an offer, no matter how outrageous it seems. This closes the door, burns the bridge. Rather, always be prepared to counteroffer and sift through some of those straw issues while giving up some of your own. If the buyer counteroffers again and you still don't like it, don't get indignant about countering a counteroffer if you have to do so. It's all a matter of playing the game.

Along these same lines, stalling for time in answering offers or counteroffers doesn't necessarily show that you are uninterested. It's usually interpreted to mean you are seriously, carefully considering the offer—though this may not be your intention at all. Always respond promptly, however, before the ardor of the moment cools.

Seller Concerns

No prudent prospective buyer would consummate a deal without performing a detailed and complex investigation of the selling firm. An acquiring firm will investigate the seller's history, review financial statements, and ask probing questions to determine the reasons for past performance. For sophisticated business buyers, however, this is only the starting point. Present and future markets for the seller's product line are evaluated based on market-research studies. The product's ability to effectively compete in these markets is studied, and other major factors affecting the company's future are considered and their impact projected.

These are some of the factors a business buyer will use in deciding whether to pursue the acquisition and, if applicable, to determine an appropriate offering price. Failure to perform this type of examination would be considered negligent by many business veterans.

Even though buyers research the seller thoroughly, very few sellers investigate prospective buyers with the same diligence. If a seller wants successful results, the same painstaking thoroughness should be employed in the evaluation of the buyer. The seller should investigate the following items:

1. Can the acquisition be financed? The seller must be certain that the buyer can adequately finance the transaction. Many "completed" deals have fallen through due to the buyer's inability to obtain the appropriate financing. The seller's time and consulting fees spent on negotiating these deals have been foolishly wasted.
2. Can the buyer satisfy the future payments in an installment deal, and in a situation where the buyer's stock represents the proceeds, will the stock hold its value in the future?
3. If the seller and the company's current employees are going to remain as a part of the new company structure, are their needs adequately addressed in the deal? This is quite common when a small business is bought by a big corporation, which makes the former independent business owner an executive vice president in the umbrella organization.
4. Will the seller's existing staff and procedures fit into the buyer's plans? If they can't, the future prosperity of the seller's firm and everyone employed

by it will be in jeopardy. This is often of utmost concern to owners of closely held corporations who have strong personal ties and feelings for their employees and obviously for sellers who agree to an installment deal.

5. Can the seller's firm be administered effectively by the buyer? This shouldn't be assumed automatically. The buyer's desire to make the acquisition happen only indicates the belief in its own ability. Most failures do not result from companies attempting to accomplish what they don't think they can do. The seller has to do an independent evaluation.

6. The seller needs to find out what kinds of policies and procedures will be put into effect after the sale is made. This becomes especially important if the selling owner is going to stay on after the acquisition. Many disenchanted sellers who accepted hollow promises have rued the day they sold their firms.

An acquisition that is to provide a beneficial, profitable deal requires the seller to obtain information in a sound and independent manner. Two basic approaches should be taken. The first will be a review of historical data and records. The second will include professionally conducted interviews with and observations of the buyer's management team, suppliers, customers, and so on.

The probable starting point would be the buyer's financial statements for the past five years. The seller should verify the buyer's capability to finance the transaction. The balance sheet should be reviewed to define the business's liquidity; the buyer's capacity to handle additional debt can be determined by how leveraged it is. Also, the buyer's present debt instruments should be reviewed for any restrictive covenants that might prevent the incurring of additional debt to finance an acquisition.

The buyer's current liquidity and cash flow should indicate whether the required funds are available for expansion. This should be considered in light of the seller's cash needs based on their own financial condition and cash-flow projections.

The buyer's performance should also be compared with firms in the same industry. This can be done by evaluating the following financial ratios:

- Profit on sales.
- Profit on net worth.
- Current ratio.
- Inventory turnover.
- Debt to worth.
- Fixed assets to worth.
- Sales to fixed assets.
- Sales to working capital.

Industry performance figures can be obtained from the Robert Morris Associates' Annual Statement Studies or the Dun & Bradstreet Business Ratios. This comparison will indicate the buyer's strength within its own industry, though there may be valid reasons for a variation from what is considered "average." It should also provide a guide as to the buyer's ability to sustain future growth once the sale of the business is final. Most important, it indicates the competence of the buyer's management.

The buyer's inventory levels and inventory turns should be analyzed. This can indicate many things, including its philosophy on sales and service. The buyer will probably expect the seller to adopt similar inventory-control policies after the acquisition. This may have an impact on any of the seller's employees who remain on board, as well as on the successful operation of what the buyer is supposedly interested in; consequently, the seller has to determine the implications of these inventory levels on future growth and profitability.

Personnel policies of the buyer and the seller come into play when a business is sold. The buyer's benefit package might provide a guide as to the future direction of the seller's benefits program. Any prudent buyer will probably not reduce the level of benefits provided to the seller's employees, but not all buyers are prudent. Meetings with officers of the buyer's previously obtained companies, if any, should indicate how management has behaved in the past.

If you're selling your business and this is a concern of yours, look at the average length of service of the buyer's employees—both hourly and on salary. This will give a clue as to the buyer's true personnel philosophy. And if there's evidence of an excessive turnover rate, find out why. It might indicate a problem with the buyer's promotion policies, pay adjustment practices, or just the way employees are treated.

An extremely critical clue, which could indicate how satisfied the seller is going to be after the sale is finalized, might be in the buyer's organizational chart. Most sophisticated companies that routinely make acquisitions of smaller firms have a formal chart, but even if there is not a formal chart, the seller should request that one be drawn up for review. This will reflect how good the buyer's staffing practices are. Are there adequate human resources to operate a firm profitably? Is there enough staff to provide the required technical skills in the areas where they're needed? Is there satisfactory delegation of duties to help along the decision-making process? Is there a normal flow of information, or is there an excessive amount of reporting to the chief executive officer? These questions are particularly important if the seller is going to remain on board as one of those executive vice presidents. And the level of access and responsibility to the CEO may be the most significant measure of how much autonomy the seller can expect after the closing.

So far, we've been talking about what you as a seller can learn from a review of "hard" data. But the most critical information about the buyer is more subjective. This can be obtained through personal contacts, interviews, and observations of people working for or with the buyer. The most effective methods of obtaining this information and the pitfalls to avoid can be determined from the following:

- Plant visits.
- Interviews with the buyer's management staff.

- Interviews with officers or sellers of companies previously purchased by the buyer.

Suppose the buyer is a manufacturer. A tour of the company plant or plants can provide the seller with a wealth of information. The caliber of the machinery should indicate management's awareness of the benefits arising from a modern, efficient plant. It should signify the value that they place on manufacturing a quality product at a competitive cost. An extremely close look should be taken at the condition of the equipment. This shows the buyer's commitment to an effective maintenance program.

If you are the seller in this situation, make a careful observation of the employees on your tour of the plant. If nobody seems dedicated to the work, try to get a sense of the factors causing this. An evaluation of the cooperativeness and friendliness of the employees should be made to determine how they relate to management. A negative employee attitude is usually symptomatic of a much deeper organizational problem.

The seller should try to arrange meetings with key personnel, such as certain vice presidents and the sales and manufacturing managers, and find out how they relate to their employer. Extreme caution should be taken to ascertain that they are not just playing to their audience. In this light, consider what is *not* said along with what is. Evaluate their facial expressions, tone of voice, and other mannerisms that might be signs of anxiety, reflecting on the authenticity of their answers or indicating possible major problem areas.

Make a judgment as to the buyer's management competence. A firm that doesn't hire talented people for key management positions is often a firm the seller would prefer not to associate with. For one thing, look at the autonomy provided to management. How much decision-making responsibility do they have? That level should be compared with their position in defining the degree of autonomy. Another key factor is whether the personnel are granted authority along with responsibility.

How long have management personnel been working for the buyer? High management turnover and limited service time for a significant portion of the key management employees have serious implications. If the buyer has made previous acquisitions, the seller should arrange meetings with top management of the acquired firms or preferably the selling owner, if that person is still active in management. The seller should determine the changes that were instituted after the acquisition, along with the necessity and reasons for these change, as far as possible.

What had been promised by the buyer versus what actually happened after the previous sales should be compared. The track record should be of great benefit when it comes time to evaluate all the "unwritten promises" that go into so many business negotiations. The relationship to the parent organization and the level of control exerted over policy and operations of the newly acquired firm should be determined because it is likely the seller will be in the same situation when the deal goes through. Many acquisition veterans believe that the buyer's relationship with previously acquired firms is the most meaningful indicator of the buyer's future intentions. In all but the rarest cases, this is what the seller has to look forward to. This is reality, while the words uttered by the buyer prior to the acquisition may be fact or fantasy.

The seller should obtain the buyer's permission to talk to current customers. Preferably, the customers would be selected independently by the seller from the buyer's customer list. The seller in contacting these customers, should not reveal the reason for the call. In fact, the buyer might insist on this before giving permission for this contact.

Information obtained from these calls should contribute to the seller's evaluation of the capabilities of the buyer's distribution network, the impact of the company's sales-service policies, and the competence of the sales force. Where there is a similarity between the product line of buyer and seller, this investigation is even more important because there will probably be some consolidation of the two firms' sales or distribution networks after the buy. If the newly acquired company is going to be an independently operating division of the buyer's company, the effectiveness of the buyer's marketing programs might substantially affect the seller's future profitability. The long-range impact on the seller's operation should be determined as far as possible.

In evaluating the feasibility of the acquisition, the seller and any advisors should absorb all the information they can, and make a decision based on informed judgment. This is complex and has to be undertaken with care. Some sellers decide to retain a consultant to help in this process. However, if the seller performs a detailed evaluation and solicits the necessary guidance in analyzing the results, it increases the chances for entering a corporate marriage made in heaven.

RESOURCES

Associations

Association of Small Business Development Centers, 1050 17th Street NW, Suite 810, 202-887-5599

Center for Entrepreneurial Management, Inc., 180 Varick Street, New York, NY 10014, 212-633-0060

National Small Business United, 1155 15th Street NW, Suite 710, Washington, DC 20005, 202-293-8830

Small Business Service Bureau, 554 Main Street, Worcester, MA 01601, 508-756-3513

Magazines

Business and Acquisition Newsletter, 2600 South Gessner Road, Houston, TX 77063-3214, 713-783-0100

The Business Owner, Thomas Publishing, Inc., 383 South Broadway, Hicksville, NY 11801, 516-681-2111

Entrepreneurial Manager's Newsletter, 180 Varick Street, Penthouse Suite, New York, NY 10014-4692, 212-633-0060

Journal of Small Business Management, West Virginia University, College of Business Economics, Bureau of Business Research, P.O. Box 6025, Morgantown, WV 26506-6025, 304-293-5837

Statistical Reviews

Annual Statement Studies, Robert Morris Associates, 1616 Philadelphia National Bank Building, Philadelphia, PA 19107

Key Business Ratios, Dun & Bradstreet, Inc., Corporation Credit Services, 1 Diamond Hill Road, Murray Hill, NJ 07974-0000, 908-665-5000

GLOSSARY

Accounts receivable: A record of the total number of sales made through the extension of credit.

Accrual basis: An accounting method that charges all income and expenses to the period to which they apply, regardless of whether money has been received.

Acid-test ratio: An analysis method that measures the liquidity of a business by dividing total liquid assets by current liabilities.

Asset earning power: A common profitability measure that determines the profitability of a business by taking its total earning before taxes and dividing that by total assets.

Audit Bureau of Circulation (ABC): A third-party organization that verifies the circulation of print media through periodical audits.

Balance sheet: A financial statement for reporting a business's total assets, liabilities, and equity.

Bonding: A guarantee by a service company to its clients that it has the necessary ability and financial backing to meet its obligations.

Break-even analysis: An analysis method for determining the number of jobs or products that need to be sold to reach a break-even point in a business.

Business plan: A plan charting a new or ongoing business's strategies, sales projections, and key personnel. It is used to obtain financing and provide a strategic foundation for growth.

Business Publications Audit (BPA): Similar to the Audit Bureau of Circulation, a third-party organization that verifies the circulation of print media through periodical audits.

Capitalization: The long-term financing of a company—in the form of money, common stock, long-term debt, or in some combination of all three. It is possible to have too much capital (in which case the firm is overcapitalized) or too little capital (in which case the firm is undercapitalized).

Cash basis: An accounting method in which income is logged when received and expenses are charged when they occur.

Chattel mortgage contract: A credit contract for the purchase of equipment where the purchaser receives title of the equipment on delivery but the creditor holds a mortgage claim against it.

Collateral: Assets used as security for the extension of a loan.

Commercial loans: A short-term loan usually issued for a term of six months.

Conditional sales contract: A credit contract for the purchase of equipment where the purchaser does not receive title of the equipment until the amount specified in the contract has been paid in full.

Cooperative advertising: Joint advertising strategy used by a manufacturer and another firm that distributes its products.

Copyright: A form of protection to safeguard original literary works, performing arts, sound recordings, visual arts, and renewals.

Corporation: A legal form of operation that declares the business as a separate legal entity guided by a group of officers known as the board of directors.

Cost per thousand (CPM): Terminology used in buying media. CPM refers to the cost it takes to reach a thousand people within a target market.

Cost-of-living lease: A lease that ties yearly increases to the cost-of-living index.

Current ratio: A ratio to determine the difference between total current assets and total current liabilities.

Demographic characteristics: Attributes such as income, age, and occupation that best describe a target market.

Depreciation: The lessening in value of fixed assets that provides the foundation for a tax deduction based on either the declining-balance or straight-line method.

Disability insurance: A payroll tax required in some states that is deducted from employees' paychecks to ensure income during periods when an employee is unable to work due to an injury or illness.

Disclosure document program: A form of protection that safeguards an idea during its developmental stage.

Dollar control systems: A system used in inventory management that reveals the cost and gross profit margin on individual inventory items.

Dun & Bradstreet Inc.: An agency that furnishes subscribers with market statistics and the financial standings and credit ratings of businesses.

Equipment loan: A loan for the purchase of capital equipment.

Equity capital: A form of financing in which equity in a business is sold to private investors.

Equity financing: A financing method in which the owner of a business exchanges a portion of the business to investors for new capital.

Exploratory research: A method of gathering primary information for a market survey in which targeted consumers are asked very general questions geared toward eliciting a lengthy answer.

Factoring: A financing method in which the owner of a business sells accounts receivable to raise capital.

Fair Labor Standards Act: A federal law that enforces minimum standards that employers must abide by when hiring employees.

Federal Insurance Contributions Act (FICA): A law that requires employers to match the amount of Social Security tax deducted from an employee's paycheck.

Fictitious name: Often referred to as a DBA (doing business as), a fictitious name is frequently used by sole proprietors or partnerships to provide a name, other than those of the owners or partners, under which the business will operate.

First in, first out (FIFO): An accounting system used to value inventory for tax purposes. Under FIFO, inventory is valued at its most recent cost.

Fixed expenses: Expenses that must be paid each month and do not fluctuate with the sales volume.

Flat lease: A lease where the cost is fixed for a specific period of time.

401(k) plan: A retirement plan for employees that allows them to deduct money from their paychecks and place it in a tax-sheltered account.

Frequency: The number of times an advertiser hopes to reach a target audience through an advertising campaign.

Income statement: Also called a profit and loss statement; a statement that charts the sales and operating costs of a business over a specific period of time, usually a month.

Inventory loan: A loan that is extended based on the value of a business's inventory.

Inventory turnover: An analysis method to determine the amount of capital invested in inventory and the total number of times per year that investment will revolve.

Investment tax credit: A credit that allows businesses to write off the first $10,000 of equipment purchased for business use.

Investment turnover: A profitability measure to evaluate the number of times per year that total investment or assets revolve.

Keogh: A pension plan that lets business owners contribute a defined portion of their profits toward a tax-sheltered account. There are several Keoghs to choose from such as profit sharing and defined contribution.

Last in, first out (LIFO): An accounting system for valuing inventory. Under LIFO, inventory is valued according to the remaining stock in inventory.

Leasehold improvements: The repairs and improvements made to a facility before occupation by the lessee.

Liability: In the analysis of insurance risks, possible areas of exposure. While there are numerous comprehensive and special coverages that blanket almost every known exposure a business may be liable for, insurers usually underwrite three forms of liability coverage: (1) *general liability,* which covers any kind of bodily injury to nonemployees except that caused by automobiles and professional malpractice; (2) *product liability,* which covers injury to customers arising as a direct result of goods purchased from a business; (3) *public liability,* which covers injury to the public when they are on the business's premises.

Manual tag system: An inventory management system that tracks inventory using tags removed at the point of purchase.

Market survey: A research method for defining the market parameters of a business.

Markup: The amount added to the cost of goods to produce the desired profit.

Measure of liquidity: An analysis method that measures the amount of available liquid assets to meet accounts payable.

Media plan: A plan that details the usage of media in an advertising campaign including costs, running dates, markets, reach, frequency, rationales, and strategies.

Modified accelerated cost recovery system (MACRS): In accounting, a defined rate and method by which a fixed asset is depreciated for tax purposes.

Net leases: A lease specifying a base rent plus an additional charge for taxes. Typically, there are three net leases: net lease, double-net lease, and triple-net lease. A double-net lease is a base rent plus an additional charge for taxes and insurance. A triple-net lease is base rent plus an additional charge for taxes, insurance, and common area expenses.

Net profit on sales: A profitability measure that determines the difference between net profit and operating costs.

Occupational Safety and Health Act (OSHA): A federal law requiring employers to provide employees with a workplace free of hazardous conditions.

Open to buy: The dollar amount budgeted by a business for inventory purchases for a specific time period.

Overhead: All nonlabor expenses needed to operate a business.

Partnership: A legal form of business operation between two or more individuals. The federal government recognizes several types of partnerships. The two most common are general and limited partnerships.

Patent: A form of protection that provides a person or legal entity with exclusive rights by forbidding others from making, using, or selling a concept or invention for the duration of the patent. Three types of patents are available: design, plant, and utility.

Percentage lease: A lease specifying a base rent plus an additional percentage of any profits produced by the business tenant.

Personal loan: A short-term loan that is extended based on the personal integrity of the borrower.

Point-of-sale (POS) system: A computerized network operated by a miniframe computer and linked to several checkout terminals.

Profit: The excess of selling price over cost. Businesses generally consider two kinds of profits: gross profit and net profit. Gross profit is the difference between gross sales and cost of sales, while net profit is the difference between gross profit and all costs associated with operating a business.

Quick ratio: The ratio of liquid assets to current liabilities.

Reach: The total number of people in a target market that an owner contacts through an advertising campaign.

Return on investment (ROI): A profitability measure that evaluates the performance of a business by dividing net profit by total assets.

Return on owner's equity: A profitability measure to gauge the earning power of the owner's total equity in the business by dividing the average equity investment of the owner by the net profit.

Signature loan: *See* **Personal loans.**

Sole proprietor: A legal form of operation under which only one owner can exist.

Specific research: A method of gathering primary information for a market survey in which targeted consumers are asked very specific, in-depth questions geared toward resolving problems found through exploratory research.

Standard Rate and Data Service (SRDS): A company that produces a group of directories for each different type of media listing rates, circulation, contacts, markets serviced, and so on.

Step lease: A lease outlining annual increases in the tenant's base rent based on an approximation of what the lessor thinks expenses may be.

Subchapter S: A federal law allowing small corporations to pay out all income proportionately to their shareholders, who then claim the income on their personal income taxes.

Sublet: The lease of space in a rented facility by the original lessee.

Uniform Franchise Offering Circular (UFOC): A disclosure document that franchisors send to potential franchisees.

Unit-control system: A system used in inventory management that tracks inventory using bin tickets and physical inventory checks.

Variable expenses: Business costs that fluctuate from each payment period according to the sales volume.

Venture capital: A source of financing for either start-up or expansion capital based on providing private investors with equity positions within the business.

Worker's Compensation: A state or privately managed insurance fund that reimburses employees for injuries suffered on the job.

Working capital: Net current assets required for the company to carry on its work; the surplus of a firm's current assets over its current liabilities.

Index

1995 Expo Schedule

CHICAGO
April 8-9, 1995
Rosemont Convention Center

ATLANTA
May 20-21, 1995
Cobb County Galleria

DALLAS
Sept. 30-Oct. 1
Dallas Market Hall

SAN FRANCISCO
October 28-29, 1995
Moscone Center

PHILADELPHIA
November 18-19, 1995
South Jersey Expo Center

MJWE

Entrepreneur Magazine's
SMALL BUSINESS
EXPO

Save $5.00 when you bring this ad to any Expo.

For more information, call (800) 864-6864.

Get your FREE Small Business Development Catalog today!

Name: _____

Address: _____

City: _____

State/Zip: _____

MJWC

SMALL BUSINESS
DEVELOPMENT CATALOG

Get the book. **FREE!**

To receive your free catalog, return this coupon to:
ENTREPRENEUR MAGAZINE,
P.O. Box 50370, Boulder, CO 80321-0370.
OR CALL (800) 421-2300, Dept. MJWC
Step-by-step guidance to help you succeed.